CRITICAL SURVEY
OF
POETRY

CRITICAL SURVEY
OF
POETRY

English Language Series

REVISED EDITION

A-Cae

1

Edited by
FRANK N. MAGILL

SALEM PRESS
Pasadena, California   Englewood Cliffs, New Jersey

Library of Congress Cataloging-in-Publication Data
Critical survey of poetry. English language series/edited
    by Frank N. Magill. — Rev. ed.
        p.   cm.
    Includes bibliographical references and index.
    1. English poetry—Dictionaries. 2. American
poetry—Dictionaries. 3. English poetry—
Bio-bibliography. 4. American poetry—Bio-
bibliography. 5. Poets, English—Biography—
Dictionaries. 6. Poets, American—Biography—
Dictionaries.
I. Magill, Frank Northen, 1907-   .
PR502.C85   1992   92-3727
821.009′03—dc20   CIP
ISBN 0-89356-834-1 (set)
ISBN 0-89356-835-X (volume 1)

PUBLISHER'S NOTE

Magill's *Critical Survey of Poetry: English Language Series, Revised Edition*, updates and expands, in eight volumes, the original edition of 1982. This major revision of the original set contains a total of 390 articles: 368 on individual poets, plus 22 comprehensive "overview" essays. A one-volume *Supplement* to the *Critical Survey*, published in 1987, contained articles on new poets in all languages; English-language poets from this volume have been incorporated into the *Revised Edition*.

Of the 390 articles in the current edition, 27 are completely new, never-before-published entries on poets who have come to be regarded as important figures. Included in this group are Frank Bidart, Kenneth Fearing, and Stevie Smith. Some poets were added because their significance has now extended beyond a particular genre or other appeal: from Carolyn Forché and Sharon Olds to Gary Soto and Jay Wright. An additional 44 articles were commissioned to be rewritten entirely; these replace earlier entries (on poets such as Robert Duncan, Denise Levertov, or Gary Snyder) that had fallen substantially out of date in the decade separating the original publication from the *Revised Edition*.

Fully 91 (nearly one-quarter) of the articles have been substantially revised to reflect the current status of the poets' development and opus, in terms of both life events and literary career. In most of these cases, especially where still-living poets are concerned, new publications, new biographies and critical studies, new honors and awards, and new biographical events necessitated careful scrutiny of all sections of these articles. The reader will also find many of these articles to contain one or more pages of additional "Analysis," updating the critical interpretation of these poets' works in the light of their recent production. Another group among the revised articles constitutes poets who have died in the past decade. These articles underwent similar revision; in cases where little had changed in the poet's literary career, the essential facts of death were added and appropriate alterations were made in the text.

The remaining articles were re-read to make standard corrections. All articles, however—whether revised, new, or essentially the same—were updated in one substantial respect: In place of the original secondary bibliographies which appeared at the ends of these articles, new, updated, and annotated bibliographies appear. These bibliographies provide the interested reader with possibilities for further reading about the author and his or her works, up to the time of publication of the *Revised Edition*.

In the final volume, those interested in obtaining an overview of the development and subgenres of poetry will find fifteen essays that appeared in the original edition. These cover poetry in chronological periods (the essay on the twentieth century has been revised), as well as critical and cultural areas.

An additional five essays were newly commissioned for the *Revised Edition*; they address areas that have come into their own in the past decade: Asian-American poetry, Chicano poetry, Native American poetry, Commonwealth poetry, and feminist criticism. Finally, two articles that close the essay section—"An Explanation of Poetical Terms" and "Index for Stanza Poems"— elucidate the terminology of poetry and the technicalities of scansion.

The comprehensive subject index, listing names of literary personages, titles of works receiving substantial discussion, and literary terms and concepts, has, of course, been revised to cite new material.

An updated list of contributors of articles, as well as those who contributed updated bibliographies and text, appears in the front matter to the first volume. The expertise and efforts of these individuals are gratefully acknowledged.

CONTRIBUTORS

Paul Acker

James Lovic Allen

John Alspaugh

Andrew J. Angyal

Stanley Archer

Rosemary Ascherl

James R. Aubrey

Jane Augustine

Linda C. Badley

Angela Ball

David Barratt

Larry David Barton

Sharon Bassett

Robert Bateman

Walton Beacham

Kirk H. Beetz

Kate Begnal

Elizabeth J. Bellamy

Todd K. Bender

Robert Bensen

Eleanor von Auw Berry

Nicholas Birns

Richard Bizot

Patrick Bizzaro

Robert G. Blake

Lynn Z. Bloom

Robert E. Boenig

Allyson Booth

Neal Bowers

Kevin Boyle

Harold Branam

Gerhard Brand

Anne Kelsch Breznau

Jeanie R. Brink

David Bromige

Mary Barnes Bruce

Mitzi M. Brunsdale

Edward Butscher

Richard J. Calhoun

David Cappella

David A. Carpenter

Peter Carravetta

Michael Case

Leonard R. Casper

G. A. Cevasco

Allan Chavkin

Balance Chow

Paul Christensen

John R. Clark

Kevin Clark

Patricia Clark

Richard Collins

John J. Conlon

Joseph Coulson

John W. Crawford

Galbraith M. Crump

Diane D'Amico

Reed Way Dasenbrock

William V. Davis

Dennis R. Dean

Paul J. deGategno

Mary De Jong

Bill Delaney

Lloyd N. Dendinger

K. Z. Derounian

Robert DiYanni

David C. Dougherty

John Drury

Doris Earnshaw

Richard A. Eichwald

Robert P. Ellis

Richard Kenneth Emmerson

Ann Willardson Engar

Bernard F. Engel

David L. Erben

Thomas L. Erskine

Welch D. Everman

Nettie Farris

Howard Faulkner

Sandra K. Fischer

John Miles Foley

Thomas C. Foster

Walter B. Freed, Jr.

Kenneth Friedenreich

Lawrence S. Friedman

Jean C. Fulton

Kenneth E. Gadomski

Elaine Gardiner

Edward V. Geist

Donna Gerstenberger

Jay A. Gertzman

Scott Giantvalley

Kenneth Gibbs

Morgan Gibson

Richard F. Giles

Ronald K. Giles

C. Herbert Gilliland

Dennis Goldsberry

Lois Gordon

Sidney Gottlieb

Robert Edward Graalman, Jr.

William H. Green

John R. Griffin

Daniel L. Guillory

Jeff Gundy

Stephen I. Gurney

R. S. Gwynn

Steven L. Hale

Katherine Hanley

Maryhelen Cleverly Harmon

John Harty III

Nelson Hathcock

David M. Heaton

William J. Heim

Michael Heller

Michael Hennessy

Jeffrey D. Hoeper

Hilary Holladay

Wm. Dennis Horn

Helen Jaskoski

Philip K. Jason

Ed Jewinski

Judith L. Johnston

Robert C. Jones

Paul Kane

James M. Kempf

Karen A. Kildahl

Sue L. Kimball

Arthur Kincaid

Frederick Kirchhoff

B. G. Knepper

Philip Krummrich

Vera M. Kutzinski

Patricia Ondek Laurence

Michael M. Levy

Leon Lewis

James Livingston

Archie K. Loss

Rick Lott

Michael Loudon

Perry D. Luckett

Sara MacAulay

Janet MacCann

John F. MacDiarmid

CONTRIBUTORS

Fred R. MacFadden

Ron MacFarland

Richard D. MacGhee

Arthur E. MacGuinness

Joseph Maltby

Bruce K. Martin

Richard P. Martin

Linda K. Martinez

Richard E. Matlak

Laurence W. Mazzeno

Richard E. Meyer

Edmund Miller

Jim Wayne Miller

Mark Minor

Thomas Moisan

Gene M. Moore

Michael D. Moore

Ronald Moran

Bernard E. Morris

Claire Clements Morton

Gerald W. Morton

Carole Moses

C. Lynn Munro

Russell Elliott Murphy

Joseph Natoli

Cynthia Nichols

Edward A. Nickerson

Emma Coburn Norris

Leslie Norris

Michael Paul Novak

George O'Brien

Elizabeth Spalding Otten

Robert M. Otten

Coílín Owens

Richard J. Panofsky

Michael P. Parker

Ward Parks

Jay Paul

Alice Hall Petry

Chapel Louise Petty

Janet Polansky

Francis Poole

Charles H. Pullen

Honora Rankine-Galloway

Jed Rasula

David Rigsbee

Nancy Weigel Rodman

Samuel J. Rogal

Jill Rollins

Joseph Rosenblum

Diane M. Ross

Robert L. Ross

Kathy Rugoff

Jay Ruud

Gregory M. Sadlek

Ruth Salvaggio

Mark Sanders

John F. Schell

Paul Schlueter

Richard J. Schneider

Steven P. Schultz

Mary de Shazer

John C. Shields

Anne Shifrer

Linda Simon

Carl Singleton

William Skaff

Katherine Snipes

Robert Lance Snyder

Sherry G. Southard

Charlotte Spivack

Vivien Stableford

Virginia Starrett

Karen F. Stein

Shelby Stephenson

L. Robert Stevens

Eve Walsh Stoddard

Michael L. Storey

Ann Struthers

Ernest Suarez

James Sullivan

Betty Taylor-Thompson

Christopher J. Thaiss

John Thomson

Jonathan L. Thorndike

Shelley Thrasher

John Clendenin Townsend

Nance Van Winckel

Edward E. Waldron

Sue Walker

Gary F. Waller

Marie Michelle Walsh

John Chapman Ward

Craig Werner

Bruce Wiebe

Barbara Wiedemann

Edwin W. Williams

Patricia A. R. Williams

Donald E. Winters, Jr.

Chester L. Wolford

Cynthia Wong

Philip Woodard

Eugene P. Wright

New Editorial Provided by

Robert Bensen
David Bromige
David A. Carpenter
Patricia Clark
Mary K. DeShazer
Richard A. Eichwald
Thomas C. Foster
Jeffrey D. Hoeper
Helen Jaskoski
Philip K. Jason
Paul Kane

Kevin McNeilly
C. Lynn Munro
Michael Paul Novak
George O'Brien
Charles Pullen
Shelby Stephenson
Ruth Goring Stewart
Edwin W. Williams
John Wilson
Donald E. Winters

New Bibliographies Provided by

Bryan Aubrey
Jim Baird
JoAnn Balingit
David Barratt
William W. Betts, Jr.
Cynthia A. Bily
Jean R. Brink
C. L. Brooke
Edmund J. Campion
Pamela Canal
Richard Collins
Stephen H. Crane
Thomas M. Curley
Bill Delaney
Doris Earnshaw
Bruce L. Edwards
David Lawrence Erben
Thomas L. Erskine
Samuel B. Garren
Ron Giles
Sidney Gottlieb
Glenn Grever
Jeffrey D. Groves

L. M. Grow
Bettina L. Hanlon
Caroline Hunt
Heidi Kelchner
F. L. Kersnowski
Robert T. Lambdin
James Livingston
Richard D. McGhee
Jim Martin
Laurence W. Mazzeno
Emma Coburn Norris
Peter Persic
Francis Poole
Carl Rollyson
Robert L. Ross
D. Dean Shackelford
Genevieve Slomski
Ruth Goring Stewart
Gerald H. Strauss
Michael Stuprich
James Sullivan
Catherine Swanson
Binah Taylor

LIST OF AUTHORS IN VOLUME 1

CRITICAL SURVEY
OF
POETRY

DANNIE ABSE

Born: Cardiff, Wales; September 22, 1923

Principal poetry

After Every Green Thing, 1949; *Walking Under Water*, 1952; *Tenants of the House*, 1957; *Poems, Golders Green*, 1962; *A Small Desperation*, 1968; *Demo*, 1969; *Selected Poems*, 1970; *Funland and Other Poems*, 1973; *Collected Poems 1948-1976*, 1977; *Way Out in the Centre*, 1981; *Ask the Bloody Horse*, 1986; *White Coat, Purple Coat: Collected Poems 1948-1988*, 1989; *Remembrances of Crimes Past: Poems 1986-1989*, 1990.

Other literary forms

Dannie Abse has always been a prolific writer, not only contributing poems to many journals, including *The American Review, The Times Literary Supplement, Encounter,* and *The Jewish Chronicle Literary Supplement,* but also producing a volume of semiautobiographical prose, *Ash on a Young Man's Sleeve* (1954), and two novels, *Some Corner of an English Field* (1956) and *O. Jones, O. Jones* (1970). In 1974 he published his autobiography, *A Poet in the Family. A Strong Dose of Myself* (1983), another collection of autobiographical pieces and reflections on the writing of poetry and autobiography, was followed in 1986 by *Journals from the Ant-Heap*, a set of musings on various public and personal events.

He has also written four plays: *House of Cowards*, which was first produced in 1960; *The Dogs of Pavlov* (1969); *Pythagoras* (1976); and *Gone in January* (1978). In the late 1940's and early 1950's, he and some friends edited a poetry magazine called *Poetry and Poverty*, which led to the anthology *Mavericks*, edited by Abse and Howard Sergeant. This was intended to rival the fashionable *New Lines* anthology, which featured the work of such poets as Philip Larkin, John Wain, and Kingsley Amis. In his autobiography, Abse explains his editorial policy in producing *Mavericks*, comparing it to A. Alvarez's *The New Poetry* (1962). He concedes that *Mavericks* was not a success, attributing its failure to the fact that not enough of the poems lived up to his editorial ideal "of being written out of the heat of personal predicament and therefore imbued with a strong current of feeling."

Achievements

Abse's literary achievement is all the more remarkable considering that he is a practicing physician having been the specialist in charge of the chest clinic at the Central Medical Establishment in London since 1954. His literary interests extend even into the field of medicine, as may be seen in his book *Medicine on Trial* (1967). Poetically, he owes allegiance to no particular school. A humanist, his tendency is to explore complex philosophical themes through things visible and comprehensible in daily existence.

At the beginning of his career, he was strongly influenced by the work of Dylan Thomas. He has, however, long since moved away from the mode of adjectival and rhetorical excess that was Thomas' hallmark, to a quieter, more questioning style of writing. Drawing on his professional life for incident and metaphor, he has acquired his own poetic style, easily recognized by the student of modern poetry. His voice is gentle, never strident; the personality which emerges from the writing is endearing, not irritating. He expresses ideas which occur to all but which not everyone has the ability to voice.

In the "Introductory Note" to his *Collected Poems 1948-1976*, he outlines briefly some of the impulses which motivate his writing and makes it clear that one of his strongest motivations is his desire to share the wealth of his experiences with the reader. There is a strand of humanism in his work reinforced by his obvious belief that in communication lies humankind's hope of salvation. Over and over again, his poetry stresses man's common humanity and the vulnerability of each person without the support and understanding of his fellows. Paradoxically, however, he also states that one of his ambitions is "to write poems which appear translucent but are in fact deceptions. I would have the reader enter them, be deceived he could see through them like sea-water, and be puzzled when he cannot quite touch the bottom." Here, he seems to be balancing a wish to communicate with an artist's prerogative to retain some of his work for himself.

Biography

Dannie Abse was born in 1923 in South Wales, the youngest of four children. Two of his brothers were influential in his education. Wilfred (the oldest) introduced him to Sigmund Freud and guided him toward medicine as a profession. His other brother, Leo, was instrumental in his becoming interested in politics. (Leo Abse has been Member of Parliament for Pontypoll—a Welsh Labor constituency—for many years and is a vocal and dynamic Labor figure.) Both of these interests have remained with Dannie Abse throughout his life and have had a pronounced effect upon his writing.

Abse had become interested in poetry during the Spanish Civil War and began writing during his last year at school. His first book of poems was accepted for publication in 1946, and in 1947, as he relates in his essay "My Medical School," he returned to Cardiff, having virtually decided that he no longer wished to be a physician. Strongly urged by his family, however, he returned to London, where he was qualified in 1950. Since that time, he has continued to pursue simultaneously his professional and artistic careers, with considerable success in both.

He was married in 1951, and his wife and family are obviously an important stimulus to his writing. In fact, it might be said that Abse is essentially a family man, for parents, brothers, wife, and children frequently appear in his writing; he is no isolated artist, intent upon solving the world's problems in the abstract without reference to the everyday concerns of his fellow human beings.

His reputation has grown over the years, and in 1973 through 1974, he held a Visiting Fellowship of the Humanities at Princeton University. Some of his experiences there are recounted in "Pages from a Princeton Journal," first published in *The Jewish Quarterly*, but also available in *Miscellany One*, published by Poetry Wales Press in 1981.

Analysis

The essence of Dannie Abse's poetry is to be found in his longest and perhaps most impressive poem, "Funland." The poem itself was read on BBC Radio 3 in 1971, and in his introductory remarks, Abse made this observation about the poem's origin: "Many years ago in conversation, the novelist, Elias Canetti, said to me, 'The man suffering from paranoia is correct. Someone *is* standing behind that door pumping invisible gas through the keyhole. For we are dying, right now, a little every minute.'" Abse believes that a kind of paranoia is natural to man. (Perhaps this stems from the fact that he is himself a member of three minority groups, two ethnic and one professional.)

Abse is Jewish, and he is Welsh; and these two factors are significant in his work. He is also a practicing physician, and of "Funland" he says that "the earth is no ordinary 'hospital' but a lunatic asylum whose inmates live out suffering lives of black comedy." In "Funland" he combines elements of the surreal with images of deception and illusion, utilizing his knowledge of psychoanalysis as well as a more elementary overview of human motivations to produce what is the cornerstone of his poetic achievement to date.

In his early work (perhaps surprisingly, considering the fact that many of his most impressionable early years were overshadowed by World War II), his Jewishness is not a particularly noticeable factor. The scientific (if not always specifically medical) cast of his mind is ever-present in his analytical, questioning style; he is capable of seeing at least two sides to every question. Apparently he believes that nothing is as it seems; all is deception and ambiguity, and when he speaks of attempting to achieve a "translucence" in his writing, what he seems to mean is poetry of infinite possibility, an effect produced by infinite ambiguity.

His ability to see two sides of every question is particularly noticeable in his early work and is clearly illustrated by such poems as "Duality" and "Odd." Now he writes less fancifully and rhetorically, having taken very much to heart the aphorisms which he quotes at the beginning of his *Collected Poems 1948-1976*: William Carlos Williams' "No ideas but in things," and Alfred North Whitehead's "Truth adds to interest."

In his early writing, Abse is concerned with religion in an abstract rather than a personal sense, as though his emotions only become engaged in the question after he has first thought the matter out. His feelings of paranoia are much more noticeable in the early work, combined with an uncertainty of identity and expressions of anger and alarm, directed against those impersonal forces which may shape the ultimate destiny of modern man. Questions of faith come to interest him only later in his writing. For example, in "Verses at Night" and "New Babylons," he expresses his anxiety, both about the possibility of the holocaust and the intolerable social pressures which men exert upon one another.

These themes appear repeatedly in his work, sometimes expressed rather enigmatically. For example, in "The Uninvited," Abse reflects on the effect upon the person of the unforeseen and unexpected events in his life, those occasional moments when he may feel that one of life's overwhelming questions may be about to be answered. In this poem, the moment of revelation passes, leaving the speaker changed by disappointment, and very much aware of his own isolation. There is often an almost mystical strain in Abse's early work which seems to have diminished as he has matured.

A related question which preoccupies him is the person's reaction to the unexpected and to change. In his autobiography, Abse relates that even moving from one street to another nearby in the same city would distress him considerably as a child, and this awareness of and sensitivity to change has remained with him throughout his life.

The related questions of change and man's search for identity appear in "Duality," "The Trial," "The Magician," and, in modified form, in "The Second Coming," among other poems. Magicians, illusion, and the difficulties which man creates for himself in society are major themes in Abse's most ambitious poem-sequence, "Funland." In the Introduction to "Funland," he refers to the contrast between the modern white "disguise" of today's medicine and the purple cloak of an old-style charismatic magician, as though recognizing the important part played by faith and illusion in the work of the modern healer, just as faith and illusion were of paramount importance in more primitive times. Here again, a half-expressed tendency toward mysticism is found, which provides continual tension in Abse's writing. Hand in hand with his apparent belief that mankind as a whole is involved in a collective crisis of identity, Abse also seems to believe that if man is foolish enough to take life at its face value, he deserves to be deceived by it. This is all a part of his attempt to imbue his work with "translucence."

Less elusive than some of his other themes, Abse's sense of nationality permeates his writing, especially in such poems as "Leaving Cardiff," "The Game," and "Return to Cardiff," as well as in his more colloquial poems relating to childhood figures and incidents. Especially in these latter poems, which are worlds away from his usual abstract, questioning style, the influence of Dylan Thomas is apparent. It must be pointed out that the influence of

Dylan Thomas upon most writers of this generation, and especially on Welsh writers, was virtually unavoidable. In Abse's case, it is possible to see an awareness of Thomas' work in "Epithalamion," "The Meeting," "The Mountaineers," and, more appropriately, in "Elegy for Dylan Thomas." He then seems to shake himself free of Thomas' ghost until much later in his poetic career, when his character sketches begin to emerge.

Abse's allegiance, however, seems stronger to his family and to the ties of memory than to Wales. In his poetry, there is no equivalent to Swansea and Cwmdonkin Park to nurture his imagination, however necessary they were to Thomas. Abse has shaped his own voice. In his autobiography, Abse relates the tale of his visit to America under the aegis of John Malcolm Brinnin, where he followed in Thomas' footsteps, watched hopefully but apprehensively by an audience which seemed constantly to be waiting for him to give evidence of being a wild Welsh bard. "I, at once," says Abse, "became nicer than myself, more polite, better behaved." Perhaps this ever-present reminder of a very different artistic persona serves to underline Abse's preoccupation with crises of identity.

Vivien Stableford

Other major works

LONG FICTION: *Some Corner of an English Field*, 1956; *O. Jones, O. Jones*, 1970.

PLAYS: *House of Cowards*, 1960; *The Dogs of Pavlov*, 1969; *Pythagoras*, 1976; *Gone in January*, 1978.

NONFICTION: "My Medical School," 1947; *Ash on a Young Man's Sleeve*, 1954; *Medicine on Trial*, 1967; *A Poet in the Family*, 1974; *Miscellany One*, 1981; *A Strong Dose of Myself*, 1983; *Journals from the Ant-Heap*, 1986; *The Music Lover's Literary Companion*, 1988 (with Joan Abse).

Bibliography

Abse, Dannie. "Interview: Dannie Abse." Interview by J. P. Ward. *The New Welsh Review* 2 (Autumn, 1989): 8-12. Abse reveals his poetic goal: to illuminate allegory with human experience. He describes how his work as a medical doctor informs his poetry. An interesting article for both undergraduates and advanced students.

Cohen, Joseph, ed. *The Poetry of Dannie Abse: Critical Essays and Reminiscences*. London: Robson Books, 1983. Authors of the appreciations collected here are mostly fellow poets; they include Donald Davie, D. J. Enright, Theodore Weiss, Vernon Scannell, and Daniel Hoffman. John Ormond contributes "An ABC of Dannie Abse," cataloging numerous recurring images in the poetry. Abse's musicality, his treatment of Jewish identity, and other important themes in the poetry and plays are examined as well.

Includes an interview with Abse and a selected bibliography. Not indexed.

Curtis, Tony. *Dannie Abse.* Cardiff: University of Wales Press/Welsh Arts Council, 1985. An artfully made book that reviews Abse's life and works chronologically. Curtis examines influences on the poet; his study is more thematic than technical, calling attention to Abse's views of religion, the practice of medicine, and love. Provides a bibliography.

Hoffman, Daniel. "Doctor and Magus in the Work of Dannie Abse." *Literature and Medicine* 3 (1984): 21-31. In our modern culture, scientists have replaced priests in the role of wise men. Dannie Abse is like a sorcerer, or a magus, for he blends his real-life role as a man of science into his poetry, thus melding art and science.

Walters, Michael. Review of *Remembrances of Crimes Past: Poems 1986-1989. The Times Literary Supplement,* November 2-8, 1990, p. 1184. A rather uncomplimentary review of Abse's 1990 collection. Walters faults "hackneyed writing" that at times is "too comfortably nonchalant," at other times manifests "over-exertion." Yet, "two or three poems . . . recall how fine a craftsman Abse can be," says Walters.

JOSEPH ADDISON

Born: Milston, England; May 1, 1672
Died: London, England; June 17, 1719

Principal poetry

"To Mr. Dryden," 1693; *A Poem to His Majesty*, 1695; *Praelum Inter Pygmaeos et Grues Commisum*, 1699; "A Letter from Italy," 1704; *The Campaign*, 1705; *The Spectator* Hymns, 1712; "To Her Royal Highness," 1716; "To Sir Godfrey Kneller on His Portrait of the King," 1716.

Other literary forms

Joseph Addison wrote in almost every genre frequent in British literature during the reigns of William III and Queen Anne. Besides poetry in Latin and English, Addison composed an opera, a tragedy, a comedy, a travel book, a scholarly account of ancient Roman coins, political pamphlets, and hundreds of essays contributed to *The Tatler* (1709-1711), *The Spectator* (1711-1712, 1714), and other periodicals. The variety of works he attempted is a reflection of the active literary culture of the time, an index of Addison's wide learning, and the story of a writer in search of his proper niche. The numbers show that he found it in periodical journalism.

Because of Addison's varied canon, there has yet to be a satisfactory complete edition. The first collection, edited by Thomas Tickell in 1721, omitted some embarrassing early works and many of the periodical essays. A new collected edition a century later restored some early works and offered a fuller selection of essays. Two good modern critical editions cover most of Addison's corpus: *The Miscellaneous Works* (1914) includes everything but the essays, and Donald Bond's *The Spectator* (1965) covers the most famous periodical to which Addison contributed. The other papers for which he wrote await modern editions. Addison's *Letters*, an unrevealing collection, were published in 1941.

Achievements

Addison's literary reputation has risen and fallen periodically, for reasons which have had little to do with his artistic achievement. His contemporaries and the next generation praised Addison highly for expressing not only Whig political principles but also classical qualities which gave English literature a dignity it had previously lacked. Readers and writers in the Romantic Age, however, found Addison unoriginal and conventional. The Victorians restored Addison to the pedestal because he spoke well of virtue and painted the picture of the Christian gentleman. Twentieth century critics often assail his work as only a historical reflection of growing bourgeois society; many personally dislike the man for accommodating himself to the class structure of eighteenth century England.

While such judgments affect how often Addison is reprinted and how much he is read, his place in literary history rests firmly on two achievements: his role in the development of the periodical essay, and his prose style. Through his collaboration with Richard Steele on *The Tatler* (1709-1711), *The Spectator* (1711-1712, 1714), and *The Guardian* (1713), Addison helped establish the periodical essay as a permanent part of literature. These periodicals made the twin activities of reading and thinking about literary topics part of an educated person's daily life. Although ostensibly essays, Addison's and Steele's works really constitute a fascinating variety of stories, sketches, sermons, and lectures. What won readers to the periodical essay was its resourcefulness and flexibility in both form and content.

Addison's second lasting achievement was his prose style, seemingly informal and natural, yet rhetorical and artistic, capable of handling a wide range of topics. Addison was one of several writers (including John Dryden and Jonathan Swift) whose innovations enabled prose to rival poetry as a fit medium for literary expression. For the next two centuries, writers literally went to school with Addison; stylists as diverse as Benjamin Franklin and Thomas Hardy began by imitating Addison. Samuel Johnson defined Addison's achievement in an immortal assessment: "Whoever wishes to attain an English style, familiar but not coarse, and elegant but not ostentatious, must give his days and nights to the volumes of Addison."

Biography

Joseph Addison might easily have followed in his father's footsteps: attending Oxford University, becoming a minister of the Anglican Church, pursuing a series of increasingly important ecclesiastical posts, and supporting the divine right of the Stuart kings. Like many other sons, however, Addison took a different path.

Two revolutionary currents swept up Addison while he was at Oxford. The first was an enthusiasm for the "New Philosophy," the scientific method that was challenging the supremacy of classical learning. The second was the Glorious Revolution of 1688 which brought William III to the throne in place of James II and established the principle that Parliament's choice for a king weighed equally with God's anointing of His earthly representative. Addison followed the traditional classical curriculum at Oxford (so well that he achieved repute for his Latin poetry), but with the idea of supporting a new English culture and political order. Modeled on the Roman concept of an educated citizenry, this new order would be the greatest civilization England had ever known: a literate and cultivated populace would sensibly cooperate in their own governance with an eye toward developing a thriving commercial economy at home and leadership among European nations.

While at Oxford, Addison expressed his enthusiasm for this new concept of civilization in poems that brought him to the attention of leading Whig politicians. In 1699, Lord Somers and Lord Halifax secured for Addison a grant from William III allowing him to travel throughout the Continent and to prepare for government service. Addison remained abroad until late 1703, when the death of William ended his pension. He did little for a year until, at the request of two of Queen Anne's ministers, Halifax and Sidney Godolphin, he wrote "The Campaign" to celebrate the military victories of the Duke of Marlborough against the French. This successful poem won for him a position as a Commissioner of Appeals.

Addison now moved in a circle of Whig politicians and writers called the Kit-Kat Club. The politicians, when in power, supported the writers by patronage; the writers helped the politicians gain or keep power by writing public relations puffs and pamphlets. Addison's new position and circle of contacts paved the way for a series of increasingly important appointments within the government. His contacts with other writers introduced him to new literary endeavors, some of which were taken up to support the government and some for their own sake.

In the next decade, from 1707 to 1717, Addison worked his way to prestigious positions in both the political and the literary worlds. His governmental progress was not even, for ministers came and went rapidly under Queen Anne, and Addison's party was sometimes out of favor. Addison was elected to Parliament in 1708, served as secretary to the council that oversaw the accession of George I in 1714, and became Secretary of State in 1717. His literary progress was likewise by fits and starts. His first try at the theater, an opera, *Rosamond* (1707), was a failure. His joint ventures into periodical journalism with Richard Steele (1709-1712) were spectacularly successful. His writing for *The Tatler* and *The Spectator*, along with his dramatic success *Cato* (1713), enabled Addison to create his own literary circle, "The Little Senate," which met at Button's Coffeehouse and continued the traditions of the Kit-Kat Club.

His pen was at his party's call. When George I's accession in 1714 brought a military challenge from the Stuart "Pretender," Addison's literary skills came to the Hanovers' support. In poems such as "To Sir Godfrey Kneller on His Portrait of the King" and in the periodical *The Freeholder: Or, Political Essays* (1715-1716) Addison argued that the nation was better off with a king who supported the reforms of 1688 than one who promised a return to Stuart absolutism.

Political and literary success had substantial rewards. Addison bought the pleasant estate of Bilton Hall, married the widowed Countess of Warwick, and fathered a daughter, Charlotte. In 1718, however, illness forced him to resign the post of Secretary of State, and the last months of his life were marred by a public fight with his former partner Steele over the Peerage Bill.

On his deathbed, legend holds, Addison summoned his dissolute stepson to witness "how a Christian can die." Addison never lacked confidence in his religious, political, or literary convictions.

Analysis

Joseph Addison wished to incorporate the style and qualities of classical Greek and Roman poetry, with appropriate adjustments, into English. The adaptation met with some success: his poetry brought him literary recognition and political favor, but—unlike his prose—it has not endured. The reasons are clear: his ideas about poetry were limited, his comic talent found better expression in other genres, and popular taste turned away from classicizing when it grew sated. Addison's ideas about poetry were simple ones and commonplace in his time. He defined poetry as ornamented thought; as a truth, which the poet wished to teach, made pleasant to the mind by the images created through elegant language. He judged the most important kind of poetry to be public poetry which treated moral and heroic topics.

These criteria were derived from classical Roman poetry, which Addison praised highly in his youthful essays for its power to raise "in our minds a pleasing variety of scenes and landscapes, whilst it teaches us." Addison especially admired the concept of the poet as a teacher who expressed to his society its highest ideals and principles. He wished England to have its Vergils and Horaces who would be the familiar acquaintances of the nation's leaders and would sing the glory of their country. Finally, Addison found in the classical Roman poets an urbane and cultured tone that stressed simplicity and civility. To a nation that had undergone a political revolution in 1688 and would experience two decades of intense Whig and Tory rivalry for office, such virtues seemed appropriate for the whole society as well as for individuals.

Addison first published in Latin and first achieved note among his contemporaries for a series of Latin poems written in the 1690's and issued collectively in *Musae Anglicanarum Analecta* (1699). Two are complimentary odes to Oxford professors, two are descriptions (of an altar and a barometer), three are comic verses (on a puppet show, on a bowling match, and on an imaginary war), and one is a celebration of peace with France. They are, for the most part, elegant pieces designed to show off the author's stylistic ability to ornament mundane as well as special topics.

The best of these Latin poems is the *Praelum Inter Pygmaeos et Grues Commisum* (the war between the pygmies and the cranes), a mock-heroic poem whose humor derives from applying the conventions of epic poetry to the strife between foot-and-a-half tall men and a flock of birds. Filled with descriptions of the combatants, landscapes, and fighting, the poem nevertheless hinges on the reader's appreciation of the incongruity between epic conventions and unheroic matter, and Addison wisely does not prolong the narration; the tale comprises one hundred and fifty-nine lines.

Latin verse, however, could please only an academic audience. If Addison wished to reach a wider audience, he would have to try his hand at English verse. His success in Latin verse won for him a chance to translate passages of Vergil and Ovid for an anthology. While keeping the original stories intact, Addison did not hesitate to add running explanations to his translations or to substitute familiar allusions for unfamiliar ones. In these poems and in subsequent translations, Addison strove to make classical literature accessible to an audience whose knowledge of the originals was often perfunctory and polite.

One classical poetic form that Addison imitated in English was the poem of personal compliment to an important person. Most of his major poems are in this mode: "To Mr. Dryden," "To the King," "A Letter from Italy," "To Her Royal Highness," and "To Sir Godfrey Kneller on His Portrait of the King." Each addresses some personage at a crucial moment in that personage's or the nation's life. Each expresses the writer's admiration for the subject with the implication that the writer speaks on behalf of the larger public. Since the occasion is noteworthy, the writer achieves dignity by finding an appropriate classical parallel.

Holding these works together as dignified statements is the poetic line. Addison's consistent verse form is the iambic (a pair of ten-syllable, rhyming lines), which he writes almost prosaically. His couplets have been called "correct" or "polite" because they are obviously arranged and proceed logically. They are not difficult to follow, either alone or in groups; single couplets seldom invert word order, and pairs or triplets tend to restate central themes or images. Addison's poetry requires little effort from reader or listener; rather, it suggests authoritative and declarative statements that are already within the reader awaiting expression.

Addison's use of ornamental but subdued poetic structures reflects his belief that on important public occasions, "Poetry in higher thoughts is lost." Clear expression of important ideas outweighs virtuoso technique. In each of his compliment-poems Addison mixes personal admiration, classical ornament, and public sentiment. The best of them is "A Letter from Italy," which Addison addresses, while on his European tour, to his patron Charles Montagu, who helped secure the pension that allowed him to travel. The poem was highly regarded in the eighteenth century because of its easy mixing of personal experience and political themes.

The first forty lines report the pleasure of the Latin scholar looking for the first time at the actual landscape depicted in the poems he knows so well: "I seem to tread on Classic ground." The poet realizes that the landscape, while attractive, does not possess in reality the greatness which the ancient poets attributed to it in their verse. Their words have worked upon the reader's imagination, revealing an importance or meaning in the landscape undetected by the senses.

The next section applies this insight to Charles Montagu, who himself had written a poem praising King William's victory over James II in the Battle of the Boyne. Montagu's verse brings out the significance of a clash that in numbers appears minor, but in meaning is crucial. The battle reminds all Englishmen that they are the maintainers of European liberty against the French and their Stuart lackeys.

The rest of the poem contrasts the warm climate and natural fertility of Italy with the cool climate and rocky soil of England. The former appears more fortunate but suffers under the oppression of French occupation, while the latter is happily free under a brave king and wise statesmen. The most vigorous lines in the poem are those describing the political liberty that Englishmen enjoy. When Addison wrote the poem, his patron had just been removed from the ministry, and the traveler must have wondered whether his tour of the Continent would ever lead to a government position. "A Letter from Italy" offers the consolation that both poet and patron, exiles of different sorts, are suffering for a good cause.

Addison tried his hand once at an epic poem, *The Campaign*, written to celebrate the Duke of Marlborough's victories over the French army in the summer of 1704. The poem was popular upon publication, gained Addison a government post, and remained in circulation for most of the century, but a growing sense that it was little more than "a gazette in rhyme," to use Joseph Warton's famous phrase, gradually eliminated it from the ranks of great English poems. It is not, however, a mean performance; it demonstrates how Addison applied classical poetic conventions and values to English material. Of many poems written about Marlborough's victory, only *The Campaign* comes close to being remembered. While modern readers seldom appreciate poems that make warfare seem gallant—especially if that gallantry is expressed in polite couplets—this poem is an accurate and just celebration of one of England's most extraordinary generals, John Churchill.

Addison might have written a great poem because the situation boasted "a theme so new" that it could have revolutionized heroic poetry. Churchill was not a typical epic hero; he was a commoner whose father's loyalty to Charles II and whose own military prowess had brought him into aristocratic rank. Addison intends to praise a man who achieves princely honors more on "the firm basis of desert" than by bloodline of birth.

Unfortunately, despite this new theme, Addison had difficult material with which to work. Churchill had indeed won two crucial and bloody battles over the French in that summer of 1704, but important to his success was the skillful way he had marched his troops into enemy territory and seized tactical advantages in the field. Marching and maneuvering are not the stuff of great epic poetry, yet Addison could hardly omit them, because his readers knew all the details from newspaper accounts.

Addison is therefore restricted to obvious sequences of march, fight, march, fight, march. Classical conventions help elevate this mundane structure: the marches rise in dramatic intensity by epic similes of the hunt as Marlborough's army stalks the French. The battles are similarly pictured in heroic metaphors that describe them as clashes of elemental powers in Nature. Around and in between these sections, Addison recounts the context of the battles of Blenheim and Schellenberg: England's struggle against France for European leadership. As does any epic hero, Marlborough fights (as England does) with divine sanction. In the style of his complimentary poems Addison finds a classical parallel for the new kind of hero: the Roman general Flavius Stilicho who, although not a patrician, won honor by marching from frontier to frontier to protect the empire against barbarian invasion.

The Campaign may be likened to a series of *tableaux* which verbally depict the crucial episodes of that summer; to make sure that no observer misses the importance of the occasion, Addison arrays all the mighty personages there, and the hero is dressed resplendently. Such dignified and static description is not to modern taste, but in his time Addison's adaptation of classical trappings to English materials was fresh and novel.

Ironically, Addison's most lasting poems are those least concerned with public statements. In the late summer and early fall of 1712, Addison published, as part of five *Spectator* essays, five original hymns. Each hymn appeared as an illustration of the essay's thesis. For example, the topic of *Spectator* 444 is the vulnerability of human beings to unexpected catastrophes which can only be countered by man's reliance upon God's supporting grace. As a model of reliance, Addison offers a rendering of the twenty-third Psalm, in which David trusts the Lord, his Shepherd.

Addison's hymns have none of the drama of the religious poetry of John Milton or John Donne, but they offer common Christian attitudes in beautifully simple language. They were frequently anthologized in hymnals after their publication. The hymn of *Spectator* 465, "The Spacious Firmament on High," expresses what might be called Addison's "classical Christianity," that rational piety which found its motive for faith in the magnificence of the world instead of in the preachings of churchmen:

> The spacious firmament on high
> With all the blue ethereal sky,
> And spangled heavens, a shining frame,
> Their great original proclaim. . . .

Such hymns have neither the insight nor the form to capture the drama of spiritual struggle, but there are many occasions on which a community prefers to celebrate its faith rather than express its doubts or review its struggles. For those occasions Addison's hymns are just right.

Robert M. Otten

Other major works

PLAYS: *Rosamond*, 1707 (libretto; music by Thomas Clayton); *Cato*, 1713; *The Drummer: Or, The Haunted House*, 1716.

NONFICTION: *Remarks upon Italy*, 1705; *The Tatler*, 1709-1711 (with Richard Steele); *The Spectator*, 1711-1712, 1714 (with Richard Steele); *The Guardian*, 1713 (with Richard Steele); *The Freeholder: Or, Political Essays*, 1715-1716; *Dialogues upon the Usefulness of Ancient Medals*, 1721; *Letters*, 1941 (Walter Graham, editor); *The Spectator*, 1965 (Donald Bond, editor).

TRANSLATION: *Fourth Georgic*, 1694 (of Vergil's *Georgics*).

MISCELLANEOUS: *The Miscellaneous Works*, 1914 (A. C. Guthkelch, editor).

Bibliography

Bloom, Edward R., and Lillian D. Bloom. *Joseph Addison's Sociable Animal: In the Market-Place, on the Hustings, in the Pulpit.* Providence, R.I.: Brown University Press, 1971. This study of Addison as a social critic focuses on the range of his intellectual curiosity and on his combination of the study of human nature, in various contexts, with moral judgment.

Carritt, E. F. "Addison, Kant, and Wordsworth." *Essays and Studies* 22 (1937): 26-36. This landmark study reveals Addison's anticipation of the succeeding era of poets. Shows how Immanuel Kant, often connected with the first Romantic generation in England, was influenced by Addison and how Samuel Taylor Coleridge is the catalyst between Kant and William Wordsworth.

Damrosch, Leopold, Jr. "The Significance of Addison's Criticism." *Studies in English Literature* 19 (1979): 421-430. Shows Addison's humanistic viewpoint and concentrates on Addison's own view of the critic as aid to the reader for purposes of clarification, rather than the deviser of meaning for a text.

Gay, Peter. "The Spectator as Actor: Addison in Perspective." *Encounter* 29 (1967): 27-32. Although the article is a review of Donald F. Bond's edition of *The Spectator*, it is useful in a broader sense because Gay discusses traditional assessments of Addison. Samuel Johnson saw Addison as a moralist in the classical tradition, while twentieth century critics, led by Bonamy Dobrée, have considered him more like the Victorians.

Smithers, Peter. *The Life of Joseph Addison.* 2d ed. Oxford, England: Clarendon Press, 1968. The standard biography, this comprehensive study covers the private and public life of the visible and influential poet, essayist, and critic. A comprehensive portrait is developed of the statesman and administrator, as well as the man of letters. Smithers explains how Addison patterned his life in the English Augustan Age after the Roman ideal of citizenship.

Æ
George William Russell

Born: Lurgan, Ireland; April 10, 1867
Died: Bournemouth, England; July 17, 1935

Principal poetry

Homeward: Songs by the Way, 1894; *The Earth Breath and Other Poems*, 1897; *The Divine Vision and Other Poems*, 1903; *The Nuts of Knowledge: Lyrical Poems Old and New*, 1903; *By Still Waters: Lyrical Poems Old and New*, 1906; *Collected Poems*, 1913, 1919, 1926, 1935; *Gods of War with Other Poems*, 1915; *Voices of the Stones*, 1925; *Midsummer Eve*, 1928; *Dark Weeping*, 1929; *Enchantment and Other Poems*, 1930; *Vale and Other Poems*, 1931; *The House of the Titans and Other Poems*, 1934; *Selected Poems*, 1935.

Other literary forms

In addition to his enormous amount of poetry, Æ wrote pungent essays in almost every imaginable field, from literary criticism to politics, economics, and agriculture. These essays are collected in such volumes as *Some Irish Essays* (1906) and *The Living Torch* (1937). His interest in that department of letters would eventually lead him to become editor of *The Irish Homestead*, and later *The Irish Statesman*. He also tried his hand at fiction with *The Mask of Apollo and Other Stories* (1904), ranging from the Orientalism of "The Cave of Lillith" and "The Meditation of Ananda" to the Celticism of "A Dream of Angus Oge," in which Æ characteristically blends East and West. He also attempted drama with *Deirdre* (1902), the first important play to be performed by the company that was later to become the Irish National Theatre. Æ compiled his own spiritual autobiography, *The Candle of Vision* (1918), and in both it and *Song and Its Fountains* (1932) he attempted to explain his mysticism and poetic theory, which for him were one and the same. In *The National Being* (1916) Æ combines history with prophecy. *The Interpreters* (1922) consists of a dialogue between several characters typifying various positions in the Irish revolutionary movement—the heretic, the poet, the socialist, the historian, the aesthete, and the industrialist. In *The Avatars* (1933) Æ created a "futurist fantasy" in which mythical heroes, Avatars, appear and spread joy wherever they go. They are removed by the authorities but their cult grows through legends and artistic records. In addition to his literary and journalistic work, Æ still managed to keep up an extensive correspondence, a part of which has been published in *Some Passages from the Letters of Æ to W. B. Yeats* (1936), *Æ's Letters to Mínánlabáin* (1937), and *Letters from Æ* (1961).

Achievements

Æ's greatest contribution to Irish literature came from neither his artistic endeavors nor his journalistic and political involvement but rather from his unceasing kindness to younger writers. Frank O'Connor has said that Æ was the father of three generations of Irish poets. Among his discoveries were James Joyce, Padraic Colum, James Stephens, Frank O'Connor, Austin Clarke, and Patrick Kavanagh. As a poet, Æ is less known today for his own work, most of which is now out of print, than for his enormous influence on the younger generation, including William Butler Yeats. Although earlier critics grouped Æ with Yeats and John Millington Synge as one of the three major figures in the Irish literary revival, later criticism, such as Richard Finneran's *Anglo-Irish Literature* (1976), generally considers Æ among the lesser revival figures such as Lady Gregory, Oliver St. John Gogarty, and James Stephens.

It is difficult to select one artistic achievement for which Æ is remembered today, so much of his work being indirect, involving support of other artists, ideas, revivals, friendship, political expression, agriculture, economics, nationalism, mysticism, the Abbey Theatre, and art in general. Yeats's wife may have best summarized Æ's achievements when she told her husband that he was a better poet, but that Æ was a saint.

Biography

The events of Æ's early years are somewhat obscure. He was born George William Russell into the Northern Irish Protestant family of Thomas Elias Russell and Mary Anne (Armstrong) Russell. When he was eleven his family moved to Dublin and Æ was educated at the Rathmines School. From 1880 to 1900 he attended the Dublin School of Art for a few months every year, where he met Yeats, a fellow student. Their long friendship was a troubled one, since Yeats felt that Æ never fulfilled his artistic potential.

Æ's first employment may have been as a clerk in a Guinness brewery, a job he soon quit. Painting was Æ's natural activity but this was sacrificed because his family could not afford such luxuries, and he turned to literature. From 1890 to 1897 he worked in a warehouse twelve hours a day; in the evenings he served as librarian of the Dublin Lodge of the Theosophical Society, where he lived. In the midst of all this, he still found time to publish his first two volumes of poetry, *Homeward: Songs by the Way* and *The Earth Breath and Other Poems*.

The most important event in Æ's life occurred in 1887 when he discovered Theosophy. He had been a mystic from childhood, and, becoming an ardent adherent, he utilized the principles of Theosophy. It was only after the death of Madame Blavatsky, the founder of the Theosophical Society, that he severed his official connection with Theosophy.

The mystic Æ later evolved into a philosopher and a political sage respected on both sides of the Atlantic. For his entire adult life he was active in the cooperative agricultural movement of Sir Horace Plunkett's Irish Agricultural

Organization Society and in the Home Rule movement.

Having achieved a certain security through his position as organizer in the Irish villages for Horace Plunkett, the agrarian reformer, Æ married Violet North. They had two sons, one of whom became an American citizen. Æ was never a domestic man since his variety of interests kept him busy and often away from home. When his health showed signs of deteriorating, Plunkett made him editor of the cooperative journal *The Irish Homestead*. In 1923 it merged with *The Irish Statesman*, with Æ again as editor; in 1930, however, the paper failed because of enormous legal expenses. Æ remained in Ireland until late in his life, when he toured the United States, and after the death of his wife, he spent most of his time abroad.

Æ was nearly six feet tall and became corpulent in old age. He had a russet beard, "mousecolored" hair, and blue-gray eyes covered by spectacles; he wore shabby clothes and was a perpetual pipe smoker. Æ looked like what he was—a thinker somewhere between a farmer and a mystical poet. In accord with Irish tradition, he was a great talker and an inspired speaker. His voice was mellow, with a strong north Irish accent. He painted all his life but never exhibited or sold his paintings, preferring instead to give them to his friends. Æ was intensely involved in the arts but he always felt that man was more important, and he worked throughout his life for the welfare of humankind.

His pen name Æ (or A. E.) grew out of this tradition. It was originally "AEon" but a proofreader let it appear as "Æ." Russell accepted the change and used it from that point on. Why AEon? John Eglinton recounted that once Æ made a drawing of the apparition in the Divine Mind of the idea of Heavenly Man. Unable to sleep one night, a voice gave him a title for his work, "Call it the Birth of Aeon." His eye was caught by a passage in Johann Neander's *General History of the Christian Religion* (1858), on the doctrine of the Aeons. In a letter, he described the following elements of the word— *A*, the sound for God; *AE*, the first divergence from *A*; *Au* sound—continuity for a time; and *N*, change. Thus Aeon represents revolt from God, the soul's passage through its successive incarnations in man homeward to God, and finally God's amplification.

In 1935 Æ died from cancer at Bournemouth, England, his home after the death of his wife. Some years earlier he had written that the dead are happier than the living and that he did not fear death for himself or for others.

Analysis

In his excellent introduction to *The Living Torch*, Monk Gibbon remarks that Æ's poetry began as that of a mystic and remained so to the end. Æ saw the poet not as an artisan of beauty but rather as a seer and prophet who derived a special authority from communion with the esoteric wisdom of the past. As Gibbon points out, Æ's poetry contains a beauty of thought and a sincerity of utterance, but in some poems the form seems inadequate and the imagery vague.

Like other poets in the Irish Renaissance, Æ attempted to define Irishness in terms of the mysticism, reverie, and wavering rhythms of the Celtic Twilight; but his poetic voice remained a faint one. Some of Æ's best poetry is contained in his first two books: *Homeward: Songs by the Way* and *The Earth Breath and Other Poems*. Some of his late work is also very good, but it is marred by a tendency to philosophize.

Æ's philosophy includes a pantheistic adoration of nature, and he argues that the important thing about Ireland is the primitiveness of the country and its people. The very title of *Homeward: Songs by the Way* indicates the author's attitude toward life. Ernest Boyd in his *Appreciations and Depreciations: Irish Literary Studies* (1918) has stated that "home" for Æ signifies the return of the soul to the Oversoul, the spirit's absorption into the Universal Spirit—a doctrine which reflects his interest in Ralph Waldo Emerson, Henry David Thoreau, and Walt Whitman.

Homeward: Songs by the Way is a narrative of Æ's spiritual adventures, a record of the soul's search for the Infinite. Æ's poems are songs with sensuous, unearthly notes, records of the inner music of his life. They do not speak of man's mundane experiences but rather those moments of divine vision and intuition when man's being dissolves into communion with the Eternal. In that moment when the seer has come to his spiritual vision, he is truly at home.

Alone with Nature, Æ beholds in his poetry the beauties of the phenomenal world and through this experience the poet is lifted toward participation in the Eternal. The conditions which usually produce an exalted mood are those associated with morning or evening twilight, the quietude of the hills, and the silent, lonely countryside; such scenes are typical of his paintings as well as of his poetry. On innumerable occasions the poet seeks the soft dusk of the mountains for meditation. Often his verses suggest the coming of daylight and the initial glories of sunlight as the seer pays homage to the light after a night of rapture on the mountainside.

Yet solitude is not the *sine qua non* for Æ's visions. In "The City" one finds his mood unaltered by the change of setting. The poet's immortal eyes transfigure the mortal things of the city. One is reminded of another Metaphysical poet, T. S. Eliot, as Æ paints the gloom of the metropolis while managing to retain bright glimmers of hope.

Wayne Hall in his *Shadowy Heroes* (1980) has pointed out that in recording his most intense experiences (his ecstatic visions), Æ produced his most notable work. The most successful poems in *Homeward: Songs by the Way* are "By the Margin of the Great Deep," "The Great Breath," and the sequence "Dusk," "Night," "Dawn," and "Day." "Dusk" begins at sunset, that special moment for poetic visions. At this early point in the volume the vision of the speaker draws him away from domestic life and human contact toward "primeval being." Sunset also introduces "The Great Breath." The fading sky of this poem seems to suggest both a cosmic flower and an awareness that the death of beauty occasions its most complete fulfillment. This unstable insight, Hall points out, as with the paradox of spiritual union through physical separation in "By the Margin of the Great Deep," becomes more nearly resolved in the four-poem sequence. In "By the Margin of the Great Deep," rather than a sunset, chimney fires of the village mingle in the sky, signifying the merging of humanity within the vastness of God.

For Æ, night usually brings despair and the loss of vision, as in "The Dawn of Darkness." In "Waiting" the speaker can only hope that dawn will reawaken humanity to its former joy. In the poem "Night," however, Æ changes directions as night brings on a rebirth of spirit and beauty, a complete union of souls, while "Dawn" initiates a fragmentation of unity. In the light of common day vision is lost but not entirely forgotten.

The sequence of poems from "Dusk" to "Day" succeeds far better than Æ's other attempts to link mortal pain with immortal vision. For Æ, in order for one to have a human spirit one must know sorrow. The path to wisdom is a road paved with the burdens of the world. Too often, however, he fails to integrate one world into the other, beyond the level of unconvincing abstraction.

Æ will continue to have a place in literary history, but his prose and poetry are comparable only to the best imaginative work of the secondary figures of his day. Æ survives not as a painter or poet but as an exemplar of his age.

John Harty III

Other major works
LONG FICTION: *The Avatars*, 1933.
SHORT FICTION: *The Mask of Apollo and Other Stories*, 1904.
PLAY: *Deirdre*, 1902.
NONFICTION: *Some Irish Essays*, 1906; *The National Being*, 1916; *The Candle of Vision*, 1918; *The Interpreters*, 1922; *Song and Its Fountains*, 1932; *Some Passages from the Letters of Æ to W. B. Yeats*, 1936; *The Living Torch*, 1937; *Æ's Letters to Mínánlabáin*, 1937; *Letters from Æ*, 1961.

Bibliography
Davis, Robert Bernard. *George William Russell ("Æ")*. Boston: Twayne, 1977. The first chapter sketches the external events of Æ. His varied interests are elaborated in six succeeding chapters, with focuses on the mystic, the poet, his drama and fiction, the economist, the statesman, and the critic. A brief conclusion assesses Æ's contributions. Provides a chronology, notes, an index, and an annotated, select bibliography.
Kain, Richard M., and James H. O'Brien. *George Russell* (A. E.) Lewisburg,

Pa.: Bucknell University Press, 1976. The first three chapters, by Kain, present a biography of Æ by examining his personality, his early success, and his decline. The last two chapters, by O'Brien, examine Æ's interests in theosophy and his work as a poet. Contains a chronology and a select bibliography.

Loftus, Richard J. *Nationalism in Modern Anglo-Irish Poetry.* Madison: University of Wisconsin Press, 1964. Chapter 5, "The Land of Promise," is a substantial examination of Æ's attitudes toward Irish nationalism. His optimism turned to anger, then to disillusionment. Rarely did he include his private political feelings in his public verse. *The House of the Titans* is analyzed for nationalistic implications. Supplemented by notes, a bibliography, and an index.

Mercier, Vivian. "Victorian Evangelicalism and the Anglo-Irish Literary Revival." In *Literature and the Changing Ireland*, edited by Peter Connolly. Irish Literary Studies 9. Gerrards Cross, Bucks, Ireland: Colin Smythe, 1982. Evangelicalism is examined as the background to Æ's career. His father made Æ aware of the power of conversion, which occurred away from Evangelicalism to Theosophy for him. He helped to establish Theosophy as a sect similar in status to that of a Protestant Evangelical group. Includes notes and an index.

Summerfield, Henry. *That Myriad-Minded Man: A Biography of George William Russell "A.E.," 1867-1935.* Gerrards Cross, Bucks, Ireland: Colin Smythe, 1975. Chapter 1 explains Russell's mysticism. His nationalism is then examined. Chapter 4 focuses on farm interests and the next one describes his journalism from 1905 to 1914. Russell's pacifism is then posed against the violence of war in two chapters, and a final chapter covers his last years. Complemented by illustrations, notes, and an index.

CONRAD AIKEN

Born: Savannah, Georgia; August 5, 1889
Died: Savannah, Georgia; August 17, 1973

Principal poetry

Earth Triumphant and Other Tales in Verse, 1914; *Turns and Movies and Other Tales in Verse*, 1916; *The Jig of Forslin*, 1916; *Nocturne of Remembered Spring and Other Poems*, 1917; *The Charnel Rose*, 1918; *Senlin: A Biography and Other Poems*, 1918; *The House of Dust*, 1920; *Punch: The Immortal Liar*, 1921; *Priapus and the Pool*, 1922; *The Pilgrimage of Festus*, 1923; *Changing Mind*, 1925; *Priapus and the Pool and Other Poems*, 1925; *Prelude*, 1929; *Selected Poems*, 1929; *John Deth: A Metaphysical Legend, and Other Poems*, 1930; *Gehenna*, 1930; *The Coming Forth by Day of Osiris Jones*, 1931; *Preludes for Memnon*, 1931; *And in the Hanging Gardens*, 1933; *Landscape West of Eden*, 1934; *Time in the Rock: Preludes to Definition*, 1936; *And in the Human Heart*, 1940; *Brownstone Eclogues and Other Poems*, 1942; *The Soldier: A Poem by Conrad Aiken*, 1944; *The Kid*, 1947; *Skylight One: Fifteen Poems*, 1949; *The Divine Pilgrim*, 1949; *Wake II*, 1952; *Collected Poems*, 1953, 1970; *A Letter from Li Po and Other Poems*, 1955; *The Fluteplayer*, 1956; *Sheepfold Hill: Fifteen Poems*, 1958; *Selected Poems*, 1961; *The Morning Song of Lord Zero*, 1963; *A Seizure of Limericks*, 1964; *Cats and Bats and Things with Wings: Poems*, 1965; *The Clerk's Journal*, 1971; *A Little Who's Zoo of Mild Animals*, 1977.

Other literary forms

Although best-known as a poet, Conrad Aiken also published five novels, six short-story collections, two plays, a poetic autobiographical essay, two collections of criticism, four books for children (including one of limericks), and two anthologies of poetry.

Achievements

A poet and artist of the Second American Renaissance, Aiken pursues the theme of the poet alone, whose only true friends appear to be the characters of his writings. Technically, his poetry extends from the rhymes and measures of couplet and quatrain and blank and free verse to the more richly concentrated forms of the commemorative ode and "symphony," sonnet ("little song") and its sequence such as "And in the Human Heart," and aubade ("morning song"), among a variety of experimental forms.

Aiken's experiments constantly remind readers of the tradition of meter, and especially of rhyme. Even his free verse uses enough rhyme to let one know that Aiken's sense of poetic tradition is important. Aiken is perhaps most admired for his exploration of music within poetic forms as he mixes iambs with polysyllables, ranging from five- to three-stress meters.

From his mature years onward, Aiken was much honored. In 1930, he received the Pulitzer Prize for *Selected Poems*, as well as the Shelley Memorial Award. He was chosen to edit *A Comprehensive Anthology of American Poetry* for The Modern Library (1929) and published a revision in 1944. He continued to receive honors: a Guggenheim Fellowship (1934); editor, *Twentieth Century American Poetry*, for The Modern Library (1944); Poetry Consultant, Library of Congress (1950-1952); National Book Award for Poetry for *Collected Poems* (1954); Bollingen Prize (1956); and Gold Medal for Poetry of the National Institute of Arts and Letters (1958). An Aiken issue of *Wake* magazine (1952), in which there appeared new and reprinted writing by Aiken and others, signaled a step forward in the critical reappraisal of Aiken's contributions.

Biography

Conrad Aiken, born in Savannah, Georgia, in 1889, was the oldest of three sons and one daughter. His father was a surgeon, and the Aikens were well off, but the family was fractured by strife. In "Obiturary in Bitcherel," the last of his *Collected Poems* (1970), and in *Ushant: An Essay* (1952), Aiken records the crescendo of violence that tore his family apart. In "Obituary in Bitcherel," Aiken gives himself a very good beginning, with a distinguished father who was not only a physician and surgeon but a writer and painter as well, and with a mother, a New England beauty, whose father, William James Potter, the Congregational minister, was a friend of Ralph Waldo Emerson. Two Mayflower passengers and six generations of the Delanos ran in Aiken's veins. His parents reared him to appreciate literature and writing, and he had happy hours of play besides. Then the parents seemed to turn against each other. The atmosphere of the house became strained. Aiken was beaten, barebacked, for reasons unknown. In his autobiography, *Ushant*, he tells of the argument flaring up between his parents early one morning, of his mother's half-smothered cry, of his father's voice counting to three, of the handgun exploding twice, and of the two still bodies lying separately in the dim daylight of the room. Aiken was about eleven and a half, and ever after the murder and suicide he was to be in search of a literary consciousness that would do them credit.

Sent to live with a great-great aunt in New Bedford, Massachusetts, Aiken entered Harvard University in 1907, but in protest at being placed on probation for irregular class attendance, he went on a six-month tour of Europe; he did receive his Harvard degree in 1912. His marriage, the first of three, took place a few days later. After a year of honeymooning in Europe (to which he was to return many times), he settled in Cambridge, Massachusetts, devoting his full time to writing on a small but independent income.

In 1914, with the publication of *Earth Triumphant and Other Tales in Verse*,

Aiken began a search for poetic monuments to his parents' memory. Although he argued that there was no other possible judge of a poet's excellence than the consciousness of the poet himself, he did reach out to people. There were, for example, his onetime mentor, John Gould Fletcher; his Harvard classmate, T. S. Eliot; and his three children by his first wife. Wherever he took up residence, however, it was the "evolution" of his artistic consciousness, the legacy of his parents, that held first place in his thoughts. Living in England from 1922 to 1925, in Massachusetts, New York City, and again in Georgia, and living as a traveler, Aiken sang with a unique and solitary voice.

His single-minded purpose gained him early recognition. From 1910 to 1911, he published many pieces in the Harvard *Monthly* and the Harvard *Advocate*, of which he served as president. From 1916 to 1922, he was a critic, mainly of contemporary poets, for *The Poetry Journal*, *The New Republic*, and *The Dial*, to which he was one of the contributing editors from 1917 to 1918. He also contributed to *Poetry* and the Chicago *Daily News*, among other periodicals. In the London *Mercury* and the London *Atheneum*, he published "Letters from America." He also published several volumes of poems during these years, and nearly thirty more thereafter.

There were interesting side excursions from Aiken's main road of poetry and criticism. He spent a year as an English tutor at Harvard (1927-1928) and wrote his play, *Fear No More*, based on his short story "Mr. Arcularis," which was performed in London in 1946, and in Washington, D.C., in 1951. In the 1930's, he conducted a summer school in painting and writing. In spite of his interludes, Aiken spent the last two decades of his life almost exclusively writing and revising his poems.

Analysis

Conrad Aiken is part of a Romantic humanist tradition which seeks to heal the hurt of human bereavement and the failure of social revolution by substituting the idea of the creator God for the godly creator. The poet-hero shows that it is possible to achieve solitary pleasure in the "resurrected" imagination, and in spite of social failures and inadequacies, there is a type of poetry, a wry music of spiritual revolution, in which lyric narrative and dialogue resist social distress. Aiken creates the enduring mock- or anti-hero, seen best in Punch in his early writings and in the later figures of the Kid and of Lord Zero.

Aiken's monistic, dream view of life and art is expressed in his protagonists, who range from ironic middle-class types—Forslin and Senlin—to mock- and anti-hero types—Punch, John Deth, the Kid, and Lord Zero. In Aiken's mythology, death is a regulation, a point of genesis, perhaps because of the traumatic context of the deaths of Aiken's parents. Aiken's ironic rejoinder to death, the binding regulation on life, is the apotheosis of mankind through unity with godhead and nature in an endless cycle of death and rebirth, a pantheistic form of resurrection, as seen, for example, in Aiken's use of the phoenix in *The Morning Song of Lord Zero* and in another late poem, "Thee."

Aiken is a personal Romanticist. In his vaudeville poems, for example, which he wrote off and on well into his seventies, he tells of the sordid lives of the performers whose passions and violence catch the tonal quality of his own terrified childhood recollections. To what purpose the passion and the violence? the sad, wry music of Aiken's poetry seems to ask. Natural death is enough to contend with, without the horror of passion and murder.

Over the stratum of the reality of death, Aiken builds a dreamworld of resurrection in many forms, ranging from the would-be type of Christ, through middle-class "monarchs of all they survey," a Faustian puppet, a master demon and a vampire of the cyclic dance of death, various reincarnations of the American culture hero, to, finally, the apotheosis of man in the form of Lord Zero.

The Divine Pilgrim is a collection of six "symphonies"—*The Charnel Rose*, *The Jig of Forslin*, *The House of Dust*, *Senlin: A Biography*, *The Pilgrimage of Festus*, all collected from earlier publications, and *Changing Mind*, which was added in 1925. Aiken spelled out his musical principle in "Counterpoint and Implication" (*Collected Poems*, "Notes"), reprinted as "Aiken, Conrad (1919)," in *A Reviewer's ABC* (1958). His principle was to build each poem out of its key to emotional masses arranged so that each massing would set an elusively particular musical tone or subtheme to the words, and each mass-tone, or "sub-key," would dominate a brief movement and its contrapuntal fellows until a "movement," or main section or part, had been stated, developed, and restated to give a general tonality out of the units and subunits of poetic composition.

The Charnel Rose, in the traditional four-part division of the sonata and symphony, treats carnal love, idealistic or Romantic love, erotically mystical love, and, finally, purely mystical love in the crucifixion of Christ and His resurrection, which for Aiken is the symbol of flesh crucifying itself through its own lusts. At the end of the "symphony," the cycle of humanity is ready to begin again with carnal love. Throughout, the third-person narrator views women, phantoms, and the crucifying crowd as projections of his own frustrated dreams. The entire poem may be considered as having the standard sonata form, with the second main "movement" holding well to the andante tempo while weaving some andante texture into the last two "movements." The whole poem may be viewed as a musical theme with variations, as Aiken's tempos range from allegro quatrains to *allegro manon troppo*.

In *The Jig of Forslin*, Forslin is all men, an organic compound of the Latin *forsan* and *fors*, meaning "chanceling" *or* "weakling." Through all his dreams, ranging from the urge of his body to control his mind, and his mind's struggle to control his body, he *is* a man of will, however misdirected. In the aquarium light of his imagination, his adopted personae—the suicidal juggler; the killer of both priest and inebriated sailor, as well as of children, wife, and her lover; the alluring lamia; the bodiless voice of Jesus; and the harlot's lover and the harlot herself—all can, by choice, be resurrected in mankind's dreams. This five-part poem employs both blank verse and free verse, rhymed and rhymeless. The poem is of an earlier, less sophisticated music than *The Charnel Rose* but is placed after it because, apparently, the imagery of *The Jig of Forslin* corresponds more closely to the imagery in *The House of Dust*, which comes next in *The Divine Pilgrim*.

The House of Dust, is another four-part poem which Aiken has compared to a symphonic poem. This poem, however, emphasizes more programmatic detail, and sets forth man's innate ability to become divine by becoming divinely conscious of the individual lives of urban residents. The poem points ahead to the Metaphysical period in Aiken's work when, in *Preludes for Memnon* and *Time in the Rock: Preludes to Definition*, the poetic self examines traditional, polarizing, concepts of divinity, apparently dispenses with them, and then attempts to set up a new polarity, the self unto itself, in the continuing search for man's divine potential.

Senlin: A Biography, is a three-part poem, which contains Aiken's most famous composition, the "Morning Song from Senlin" (section two of Part II). Senlin, whose name means "little old man," is an ironic or slightly comical middle-class imperturbable figure, who is potentially explosive and who shines like the sun as he rises from sleep in the morning. "Morning Song from Senlin" is a display of musical prosody, consisting of a variety of adapted ballad stanzas, refrains, and heroic quatrains. An evening ode of Senlin's (section three of Part I), in ternary order, inverts the usual Pindaric or even Cowleyan sequence, and finds its musical echoes in the refrains. Senlin, himself, is both a dreamer and everybody's dream.

The Pilgrimage of Festus, in five parts and in rhymed free verse, is another step along the road to Lord Zero. Possessed of a Faustian thirst for the ultimate knowledge, Festus searches out the world of temporal conquest and then that of spiritual power as he converses to no avail with Buddha, Mephistopheles, Confucius, and Christ. Finally, Festus hears a music that is so lovely that it must be the sign of eternal womanhood, the ultimate symbol of Romantic humanism. Old Man of the Rain, however, Festus' alter ego soon disillusions him. The music comes from the instruments of a group of butchers on holiday who are still dressed in their spotted aprons. Festus emerges as a wry figure of paternalism in blithe search for truth, to be found only in his private self.

Changing Mind is a poet's poem, in traditional four-part "music." Aiken's stated intention is to enunciate his newfound goal to help mankind "evolve" a higher consciousness pointing toward the divine, but he admits that, as such a helper, he must "die daily" to self. A mixture of farce and brutality, this poem, which moves from free verse narrative and dialogue to prose and "prayer," advances Aiken from mere hedonism to a kind of creativity that recognizes its source in dust, which is the "true father."

"John Deth: A Metaphysical Legend" is a rollicking, five-part Hudibrastic literary ballad about John Deth, the master of the death dance, and his two doxies, Millicent Piggistaile and Juliana Goatibed, demons, all three. These death demons sleep and dream forever now in the mind of the poet, but not until they have led many in the dance to death and have crucified the "god" of beauty itself, Venus Anadyomene. To Aiken, himself never sure of the total meaning of this poem, Deth seems to represent the negative, Piggistaile the positive pole of Aiken's being, while Goatibed stands for the conjoined consciousness of the two poles. Deth is Father Death, capable of using the power of unholy resurrection by word-magic, even as he can do to death by the word of his mouth, always assisted by his magic wand and by the walking dead who serve as heralds of his deadly work. John Deth is also a grieving anti-hero, a Comus who, to lust, has added the dimension of death.

"The Room," a marvelous blank verse ode in three stanzas, celebrates memory. An isolated single leaf is able to construct a great tree out of chaos through a reverse creation reflected in the reverse order of the stanzas. The mystic tree of the poem is a cycle in which both life and death, joined by their intermediary, chaos, deserve praise for perpetuating the cycle. The same theme occurs in *Preludes for Memnon*, composed of sixty-three preludes, in which Aiken attempts to bring order out of chaos and death.

In expanding and contracting lines of mainly free verse, rhymed and unrhymed, the fourteen poems of *The Morning Song of Lord Zero*, much of the time in dialogue, explore the image of the incarnate word of Romantic humanism as the "I" who has become Lord Zero. Lord Zero, however, is "The Island," Death, into which the soul or self takes only a memory of love that has no perfect community. The blessed isle of Romantic humanism here presents death as the ultimate identity. Finally, *A Little Who's Zoo of Mild Animals* mocks its own analysis of an evolved, portmanteau creation and consciousness. In the leaf there is already the seed, the branch, the trunk and the root. In the heart of the child is the true beginning of heaven.

Fred R. McFadden

Other major works

LONG FICTION: *Blue Voyage*, 1927; *Great Circle*, 1933; *King Coffin*, 1935; *A Heart for the Gods of Mexico*, 1939; *Conversation: Or, Pilgrim's Progress*, 1940; *The Collected Novels of Conrad Aiken*, 1964.

SHORT FICTION: *Bring! Bring! and Other Stories*, 1925; *Costumes by Eros*, 1928; *Among the Lost People*, 1934; *Short Stories*, 1950; *Collected Short Stories*, 1960; *Collected Short Stories of Conrad Aiken*, 1966.

PLAYS: *Fear No More*, 1946; *Mr Arcularis: A Play*, 1957.

NONFICTION: *Skepticisms: Notes on Contemporary Poetry*, 1919; *Ushant: An Essay*, 1952; *A Reviewer's ABC: Collected Criticism of Conrad Aiken from 1916 to the Present*, 1958; *Selected Letters of Conrad Aiken*, 1978.

ANTHOLOGIES: *A Comprehensive Anthology of American Poetry*, 1929, 1944; *Twentieth Century American Poetry*, 1944.

Bibliography

Butscher, Edward. *Conrad Aiken, Poet of White Horse Vale*. Athens: University of Georgia Press, 1988. This 518-page biography is equipped with portraits, indexes, and a seven-page bibliography. Butscher attempts to examine both Aiken's flaws and achievements without exaggerating either. He covers Aiken's life through 1925 and traces the poet's relationships with other important literary figures of modernism.

Hoffman, Frederick John. *Conrad Aiken*. New York: Twayne, 1962. Hoffman's introduction to Aiken treats him as a representative American mind, one who explored and acutely expressed the problems of modern consciousness. Of the six chapters, the final four deal with the poetry. Hoffman holds that Aiken should be judged primarily as a poet. Contains notes, bibliographies, and an index.

Marten, Harry. *The Art of Knowing: The Poetry and Prose of Conrad Aiken*. Columbia: University of Missouri Press, 1988. Marten's book is a treatment of selected novels and significant narrative poems. He analyzes, for example, *Senlin: A Biography*, *Punch: The Immortal Liar*, *Preludes for Memnon*, and *Changing Mind*. Marten intends to illuminate Aiken's quest to understand the capabilities of the human mind. Includes an index and a five-page bibliography.

Martin, Jay. *Conrad Aiken: A Life of His Art*. Princeton, N.J.: Princeton University Press, 1962. Focuses on Aiken's growth and development as evidenced in his poetry and prose. The poetry is emphasized in this investigation, which uses his work in part to study how literary reputations in the twentieth century have been achieved. A thorough index and notes.

Peterson, Houston. *The Melody of Chaos*. New York: Longmans, Green, 1931. The earliest written on Aiken. When it was published, Aiken became the first poet of his generation to be the subject of a full-length study. Peterson used Aiken's poetry as a vehicle for a study of literary complexity and chaos. He also sought to defend and enhance Aiken's literary reputation.

Spivey, Ted R., and Arthur Waterman, eds. *Conrad Aiken: A Priest of Consciousness*. Georgia State Literary Studies 6. New York: AMS Press, 1989. The editors have selected essays that provide a variety of critical views on Aiken. Some of the articles discuss overall themes in the work, others interpret specific poems, such as "Mayflower" and "Hallowe'en." A special bibliographic section discusses works on Aiken. Contains a chronology, full notes, and an index.

WILLIAM ALLINGHAM

Born: Ballyshannon, Ireland; March 19, 1824
Died: London, England; November 18, 1889

Principal poetry

Poems, 1850; *Day and Night Songs*, 1854; *The Music Master, a Love Story, and Two Series of Day and Night Songs*, 1855; *Laurence Bloomfield in Ireland*, 1864; *Fifty Modern Poems*, 1865; *Songs, Ballads and Stories*, 1877; *Evil May-Day*, 1882; *Blackberries*, 1884; uniform collected edition, variously titled, 1887-1890 (6 volumes); *By the Way*, 1912.

Other literary forms

Although known primarily as a poet of light lyrics, William Allingham also wrote prose pieces and a diary. Few would deny that *A Diary* (1907) is one of the best literary diaries of the Victorian period. Primarily a product of his English years, it records conversations and encounters with an impressive array of eminent Victorian personalities. Alfred, Lord Tennyson, and Thomas Carlyle were intimates, and there is much about Robert Browning and Dante Gabriel Rossetti. Allingham's formal prose turns out to be surprisingly substantial. Starting in 1867, he wrote more than twenty travelogues for *Fraser's Magazine*. Narrated under the paronymatic pseudonym Patricius Walker, the travelogues are notable for their expository emphasis. The traveler will sometimes pass opinion on what he has seen in his wanderings (Wales, Scotland, provincial England, parts of the Continent), but for the most part he concentrates on describing scenery and reporting local customs and historical tidbits about the area. A selection of these pieces was later issued as *Rambles* (1873), while most of them were collected in the first two volumes of a posthumously published edition of his prose. The third volume of this work, *Varieties in Prose* (1893), contains Irish sketches and literary criticism.

Achievements

Allingham deserves the elusive label "Anglo-Irish." His reputation as a minor Victorian poet is largely the result of the popularity of a few frequently anthologized poems of Irish inspiration, subject matter, and sentiment. Like so many other "minor" literary figures, however, his historical significance goes beyond his accomplishment in any single genre. His foremost achievement is in lyric poetry. He had a knack for spinning songs and ballads. The most famous of these is "The Fairies," a delightful children's rhyme about the elvish world, which inevitably appears in anthologies of Irish verse. Also frequently anthologized is "The Winding Banks of Erne," a tender farewell to Ireland from an emigrant as he sets sail for the New World. Over the years, these two favorites have been included in most of the standard collections of

Irish verse: Brooke and Rolleston's (1900), Padraic Colum's (1922), Robinson and MacDonagh's (1958), and Devin Garrity's (1965), among others. To complete their selection from Allingham's work, editors often include lyrics such as "A Dream" and "Four Ducks on a Pond," and ballads such as "Abbey Asaroe" and "The Maids of Elfin Mere."

A dozen or so preservable short poems from a canon of several hundred does not seem to be a very significant achievement. The quality of these poems is sufficiently high, however, to secure at least a minor position in Irish poetry, and, when considered in the light of Irish literary history, Allingham's stature grows substantially. As Ernest Boyd points out in *Ireland's Literary Renaissance* (1916), the third quarter of the nineteenth century was a transitional period in Irish literature, sandwiched between an earlier period of predominantly political verse and the later full renaissance led by W. B. Yeats and his circle. During this transitional period, there appeared a few poets who, though not of the first rank, were nevertheless serious, competent artists who celebrated Irish themes without lapsing into propaganda. Allingham was one of these, ranking alongside Aubry de Vere and just below Samuel Ferguson in importance. A country seeking to establish its cultural identity cannot afford to overlook the literary accomplishments of any of its native sons. Allingham helped to set the stage for the later flowering of Irish verse, and his historical importance was recognized by poets of the Irish Renaissance, particularly Katherine Tynan, William Butler Yeats, Lionel Johnson, and Padraic Colum.

Yeats above all is responsible for securing Allingham's modest niche in literary history. In an article entitled "A Poet We Have Neglected," Yeats gave an appreciation of Allingham's Irish songs and ballads, noting the poet's facility at capturing ephemeral moods and moments. "It is time," he declared, "for us over here to claim him as our own, and give him his due place among our sacred poets; to range his books beside Davis, Mangum, and Ferguson." Four years later he was writing to Katherine Tynan that "you, Ferguson and Allingham are, I think, the Irish poets who have done the largest quantity of fine work." In 1905, he put together and published a small selection of Allingham's best poems (*Sixteen Poems by William Allingham*). More important than Yeats's service to Allingham's reputation, however, is Allingham's influence on Yeats's own poetry. In 1904 Yeats wrote to Mrs. Allingham, "I am sometimes inclined to believe that he was my own master in verse, starting me in the way I have gone whether for good or evil." Allingham's success with ballads and songs encouraged Yeats to explore those genres during the early part of his career, and specific borrowings have been noticed by critics.

Allingham's short verse deserves wider recognition than its slight representation in anthologies seems to warrant. It is true that an enormous amount of inferior work must be waded through, but a reading of his entire canon reveals several dozen poems worth keeping in addition to the well-known ones. There is, for example, an interesting series of poems all entitled "Aeolian Harp." Although these poems are inspired more by English poetic convention than by "Irish scenes and Irish faces" (Yeats's phrase), they are nevertheless fairly successful imitations of the type of reflective poem for which Samuel Taylor Coleridge is known. Some of the sonnets, such as "Autumnal Sonnet" and "Winter Cloud," are very expressive, and there is even a sparkling translation of "The Cicada" from the Greek Anthology. The most judicious twentieth century selection of Allingham's poetry is found in Geoffrey Taylor's anthology *Irish Poets of the Nineteenth Century* (1951), which contains about fifty pages of his shorter poetry. A selection that appeared in 1967 (*The Poems of William Allingham*, edited by John Hewitt) contains about twenty shorter poems, plus excerpts from longer ones.

Allingham's second major achievement was *Laurence Bloomfield in Ireland*, a long narrative in verse about Irish tenant-landlord relations in the mid-nineteenth century. Many twentieth century critics, including Taylor and Alan Warner, place *Laurence Bloomfield in Ireland* first on the list of Allingham's achievements. Yeats castigated it, as he did all of Allingham's longer poetry, but William Gladstone praised it and even quoted from it in the House of Commons. After reading it, Ivan Turgenev told a mutual friend, "I never understood Ireland before!" Allingham himself considered *Laurence Bloomfield in Ireland* his best work. The poem's modest popularity was partly owing to its contemporary subject matter, partly to its artistic strengths. It ran through several editions during Allingham's lifetime.

His third major area of achievement is his prose, including travelogues, occasional pieces, and a diary. Critic Sean McMahon labels Allingham's posthumously published *A Diary* his "greatest" work, ranking it above *Laurence Bloomfield in Ireland* and the lyrics.

Biography

William Allingham can be considered more quintessentially Anglo-Irish than other representative of that breed because he was truly poised between the two spheres. In his first thirty-nine years Ireland was his home; the last twenty-six were spent almost exclusively in England. Allingham's final visit to Ireland occurred as early as 1866, on the occasion of his father's funeral. The demarcation between the two lives, however, is not as clear as the mere circumstance of residence would seem to indicate. During the Irish years (1824-1863), he often visited England, where most of his friends and correspondents were. During the English years (1863-1889), his mind constantly returned to Ireland, as is evidenced in his writing and conversation.

Allingham was born in the western Ireland port town of Ballyshannon, County Donegal, situated at the mouth of the River Erne. Ballyshannon and vicinity would provide the setting for most of his well-known ballads and lyrics. His family was Protestant, having migrated from Hampshire more than two hundred years earlier. *A Diary* reports that the parents, William and Elizabeth, were both "undemonstrative," and the mother's early death in 1833 probably contributed to a curious personality trait observable in Allingham throughout his life—a simultaneous love of solitude and desire for companionship. "Has anyone walked alone as much as I?" he asked in his diary in 1865, and then immediately gave the counterpoint: "And who fonder of congenial company?"

The father, formerly a merchant, removed his son from a local boarding school at the age of thirteen and installed him as a clerk in the branch bank which he had managed for several years. Thenceforth Allingham educated himself at home during his spare time, no mean feat in the light of his later scholarship. When he was twenty-two, he secured a position in the Customs Service at eighty pounds a year, serving in Ballyshannon and other Ulster towns, and even for a short time on the Isle of Man. He assayed cargoes, visited shipwrecks, audited crew payrolls, no doubt did reams of paperwork, and, significantly, inspected fittings and provisions on immigrant ships heading for the United States. During those years he produced his first three volumes of poetry—*Poems, Day and Night Songs,* and *The Music Master, a Love Story, and Two Series of Day and Night Songs*—which, together, contain the core of his best ballads and lyrics.

Allingham's Irish period ended in 1863 when he transferred to the English port of Lymington, on the southern coast opposite the Isle of Wight. Long before this, however, he had become acquainted with England. Starting in 1847 he had made annual visits to London, eventually breaking into several different circles of artists. Through Leigh Hunt, Allingham met Carlyle; Coventry Patmore introduced him to Rossetti and the Pre-Raphaelites, as well as to Tennyson. During the early 1850's he was especially intimate with Rossetti, "whose friendship," he wrote in a dedication to one volume of his collected works, "brightened many years of my life, and whom I never can forget." Rossetti's letters to Allingham are numerous, interesting, and accessible (*The Letters of Rossetti to Allingham,* 1897, G. B. Hill, editor). The intimacy with Tennyson and with Carlyle deepened after the transfer. In 1864, he published *Laurence Bloomfield in Ireland,* much revised from its original form in *Fraser's Magazine*; and in 1865, *Fifty Modern Poems.* The latter must be considered more a product of his Irish period.

In 1870, acting upon Carlyle's advice, Allingham retired from the civil service to become subeditor of *Fraser's Magazine,* under J. A. Froude, whom he succeeded as editor in 1874. The same year he married Helen Paterson, an established watercolorist only half his age. They had three children. In 1879, Allingham retired permanently, moving to Witley, Surrey, in 1881, then to Hampstead in 1888, his final home. He had been awarded an annual civil pension of sixty pounds in 1864; it was increased to one hundred pounds in

1870. The last twenty years witnessed a decline in poetic output. *Songs, Ballads and Stories* contains mostly work from previous volumes, though as a collection it may be the best single repository of Allingham's poetry. *Evil May-Day* will remain his least successful volume, mainly because of the heavy didactic nature of the title piece, which whines and frets in blank verse for some eight hundred lines. Ironically, the book also contains his most succinct lyric, the gem-like "Four Ducks on a Pond." His last major original production was *Blackberries*, composed entirely of short aphoristic verse.

Analysis

The chief strengths of William Allingham's best lyrics and songs are their simplicity and musicality. His themes are the universal ones: the joys and frustrations of romantic love, the many faces of nature, the quality of country life, man's ultimate relation to an indecipherable universe, memories of happier times, the supernatural, and death. His simplicity of style is typified by the following stanza from "The Lighthouse":

> The plunging storm flies fierce against the pane,
> And thrills our cottage with redoubled shocks:
> The chimney mutters and the rafters strain;
> Without, the breakers roar along the rocks.

As he does here, Allingham commonly uses familiar rhyme schemes, keeps syntax straight, and restrains metaphor to an unusual degree. His syntactical purity is such that the only departures from normal word order permitted are entirely conventional poetic inversions ("Many fine things had I glimpse of"). Even then he manages to avoid the grosser sort of inversion, as when the main verb is delayed until the end of the line for mere rhyme's sake ("Loud larks in ether sing"). Implicitly in several poems, explicitly in personal conversations, Allingham criticized the convoluted style of Robert Browning's poetry, friend though he was. Instead, in poetry (see "The Lyric Muse") and prose (*Rambles*, "To Dean Prior") he holds up Robert Herrick as a model of lyricism. Not too much should be made of that, however, since the serious Allingham would never imitate the cavalier element in Herrick's verse, although he did approve of its "elegant naivete." One might discern an elegance, certainly a gracefulness, in the naïve treatment of idyllic love in the following lines:

> Oh! were my Love a country lass,
> That I might see her every day,
> And sit with her on hedgerow grass
> Beneath a bough of may.

Here as elsewhere in his most successful lyrics, Allingham keeps diction simple. Surely the freshness of lines such as these has some value today.

The musical element is so omnipresent in Allingham's poetry that the distinction between song, lyric, and ballad is sometimes obscured. Many of his enduring poems tend toward song. To the simplicity of his poetry the musical element adds sweetness, or in some instances liveliness. *A Diary* records a conversation with William Makepeace Thackeray, in which Allingham wholeheartedly agrees with the novelist's dictum, "I want poetry to be musical, to run sweetly." It is not always easy, however, to determine whether the musical charm of a particular song derives from meter, rhyme, phonetic effects, or from a combination of the three. From *A Diary* and other prose writings it is apparent that Allingham considered meter to be the very soul of poetry. In fact, some of the most significant entries in *A Diary* include those in which Tennyson and his Irish devotee discuss the technicalities of metrical effects. Lines such as "The pulse in his pillowed ear beat thick" (from "The Goblin Child of Ballyshannon") echo Tennyson both metrically and phonetically. Repetition of the haunting place-name "Asaroe" in "Abbey Asaroe" shows that Allingham could choose a word for its rhythm and sound; its precise placement in each stanza shows a talent for emphasis. On the other hand, rhyme is a prominent feature of Allingham's verse. Triplets, internal rhyme, and refrains are not uncommon.

Sprightly music, such as that which makes children laugh and sing, contributes in part to the popularity of Allingham's beloved fairy poems. Justly most famous of these is "The Fairies," with its traditional opening:

> Up the airy mountain,
> Down the rushy glen,
> We daren't go a-hunting
> For fear of little men.

Others, however, are almost as highly cherished. "Prince Brightkin," a rather long narrative, has some brilliant touches of whimsicality. In "The Lepruchan," the wee shoemaker escapes his captors by blowing snuff in their faces. In "The Fairy Dialogue," mischievous sprites confound housewives attempting to do their daily chores. It should be noted, however, that much of Allingham's verse contains an opposite charm, that of sweet sadness. Many of his descriptive poems, as well as many of the romantic lyrics, are tinged with a sense of regret, of longing for something unattainable. Allingham could sing in a minor key. This tendency derives partly from personal temperament, partly from the fashion of the times, partly from literary imitation of the Graveyard School or even the Spasmodic School of poetry. He might be said to have anticipated the tone of voice adopted by writers of the Celtic Twilight. For example, one, "Aeolian Harp," opens and closes with the question, "O what is gone from us, we fancied ours?" William Butler Yeats so appreciated the way the poem enshrouds its *sic transit* theme with a meditative plaintiveness that he included it in his selection of Allingham's verse.

Allingham wrote only a handful of ballads, but his work was sufficiently crucial to establish him as a modern pioneer in this form. During his Irish period, study of the local folk ballad became a sort of hobby. He listened to balladeers at country market fairs, transcribed lyrics and melodies, and collected anonymous broadsheet ballads sold by hawkers. Next, he produced his own ballads, printed and circulated them as anonymous ha'penny broadsheets (a few of which have survived), and had the pleasure of hearing them sung in the streets and cottages of Ireland. Later, Yeats, Padraic Colum, and other poets of the Irish Renaissance took up the genre. Five of Allingham's broadsheet ballads were collected in the volume of 1855, which also has a preface describing the difficulties of adapting peasant Anglo-Irish idiom to verse. The best of these are "Lovely Mary Donnelly" and "The Girl's Lamentation." There is in the former poem a blind fiddler who, although sad because he could not see the pretty lass, "blessed himself he wasn't deaf" upon hearing her winsome voice. The girl's lament is for the perfidy of her lover, but also for her own loss of chastity, since "a maid again I can never be/ Till the red rose blooms on the willow tree." A third broadside ballad, "Kate O' Ballyshanny," belongs with these two in quality. Allingham also wrote a few literary ballads, perhaps imitating Rossetti or the Romantic poets. The best of these are "The Maids of Elfinmere," "The Abbot of Innisfallen," "Squire Curtis," and "St. Margaret's Eve."

Allingham liked Herrick's lyrics for their simplicity "without flatness." The problem with his own verse is that most of it is both simple and flat. His failings as a poet, which, in Sean McMahon's phrase, keep him entrenched "on the foothills of Parnassus," are largely ones common to his period. Victorian oppressive seriousness, mediocrity of thought, and gushy sentimentality too often invade his poetry. At times the effusion of emotion becomes embarrassingly urgent:

> Mine—Mine
> O Heart, it is thine—
> A look, a look of love!
> O wonder! O magical charm!
> Thou summer-night, silent and warm!

One is reminded of Percy Bysshe Shelley's "Indian Serenade." This tendency toward triteness extends past content into the realm of technique. For instance, eighteenth century poetic diction is resurrected and put to facile uses, so that one finds the earth to be "the whirling sphere," the night sky "the starry dome," and a field of wildflowers "the daisied lea."

Allingham's typical faults are magnified in his longer poems. "Evil May-Day" suffers especially from high seriousness. It is a philosophical discussion about the impact of science on traditional morality. The crisis of doubt, of the disorientation caused by a widespread questioning of creeds outworn, was a legitimate concern to Victorians, but Allingham's handling of it becomes painfully didactic. He treated the same issues more palatably in prose (see *Rambles*, "At Exeter," and "At Torquay"). "The Music Master," a tale about the tragic effects of prematurely severed love, suffers somewhat from sentimentality, but more so from lack of dramatic incident. Dante Gabriel Rossetti, who often asked Allingham for advice about his own poetry, wrote that " 'The Music Master' is full of beauty and nobility, but I'm not sure it is not TOO noble or too resolutely healthy."

The exception to this general awkwardness in the longer forms is *Laurence Bloomfield in Ireland*, which runs to nearly five thousand lines. Its fictionalized account of tenant-landlord relations provides a valuable sketch of economic and class struggles in rural Ireland a decade before the Land League and just prior to the first heated period of Fenian activity. The extreme right and extreme left are staked out by the reactionary landlords and the incendiary Ribbonmen respectively; the sensible, humane middle is occupied by Bloomfield (the ideal landlord) and the Dorans (the ideal peasant family). In outline form the plot seems unpromisingly thin. Bloomfield, who has recently assumed control of his estate, is feeling his way cautiously into landlordism. He objects to the bigoted, self-servicing attitudes of the other landlords in the district, but as yet lacks the confidence to challenge the *status quo*. In addition, the secret societies are active in the district. Their activities, usually directed against the ruling class, range from the merely disruptive to the criminally violent. Neal Doran, a good lad, son of an aging tenant farmer, is drawn into the fringes of the insurgent movements. When he is arrested for fighting at a market fair, Pigot, the hardhearted agent for Bloomfield and other landlords, moves to evict the Dorans from the farm they had worked so hard to establish. It is then that Bloomfield acts decisively. Moved by the sight of the old man's grief, he dismisses Pigot, who is assassinated on his way home, and releases Doran. Time is telescoped in the latter section of the narrative: in the years to come Bloomfield works hard at being the ideal landlord. He institutes revolutionary reforms, such as allowing tenants to buy their farms, and in general plays the enlightened, paternal ruler.

The poem's flaws are readily apparent. The lengthy coda, consisting of two whole books, seems tacked on, and occasionally a digression unnecessarily interrupts the flow of narrative. The poem was originally written under the pressure of monthly serial publication, which probably accounts for some of the structural flaws. After receiving proofs of Book 12 from *Fraser's Magazine*, Allingham confided in *A Diary*, "It's not properly compacted to plan, and never will be now." Another flaw is that Bloomfield, the central figure, is weakly drawn. The same might be said for the Dorans. Both are too pure to be believable. Nevertheless, a more pervasive and damaging problem is inconsistency in the quality of the verse.

The poem's strengths, however, far outweigh its weaknesses. In fact, virtually every modern critic writing on Allingham has given it high praise, particularly for its portraiture of Irish types, its many fine character sketches. The satiric portraits of the landlords in Book 2 are worthy of Alexander Pope. A wide spectrum of types is surveyed, from the haughty aristocrat to the licentious absentee to the clever usurer who hides his exploitation behind a surface of unctuous piety. Less barbed but equally effective are the portraits of clergymen, especially Father John Adair. The poem is also strong in its close observation of Irish life. Depicting "every-day Irish affairs" was a "ticklish literary experiment" (Preface, edition of 1864), but Allingham seems to have captured the essential fabric of life in his native Ballyshannon. To John Drinkwater, the poem is "second to none in the language as a description of peasant life and peasant nature" ("The poetry of William Allingham," *The New Ireland Review*, February, 1909). In this regard *Laurence Bloomfield in Ireland* is often compared to Oliver Goldsmith's "Deserted Village" and George Crabbe's "Borough." Allingham goes among the people, even into the most wretched hovel, showing their virtues and their vices. The description of the harvest fair in Book 9 is alive with sights and sounds—the throngs of people, traders' disputes, beggars' blessings, the flourish of Her Majesty's recruiting party—a sort of poetic Irish version of William Powell Frith's *Derby Day* (1858).

Dealing with potentially flammable political material, Allingham strives for a precarious neutrality. Actually, however, this noncommittal position is a fusion of conservative and liberal elements. Allingham was not an advocate of Home Rule. He felt that Ireland did not yet have the political experience or the administrative skills to assume such responsibility. On the other hand, his advocacy of peasant proprietorship of land (or at least increased security of tenancy) puts him firmly in the liberal camp.

After *Laurence Bloomfield in Ireland* and *Fifty Modern Poems* the quality and quantity of Allingham's verse fall off sharply. Yeats and others have seen this atrophy as evidence that his Muse was essentially Irish. Undeniably, the only substantial, entirely new poetic work of the English period was *Blackberries*. Many of its aphorisms and short satiric rhymes are very good, but as a whole they lack brilliance, and one suspects that reliance upon abbreviated modes indicates a faltering confidence in the ability to create more ambitious poetry. As a poet, Allingham will remain known primarily for his lyrics and for *Laurence Bloomfield in Ireland*. He had a lyric voice of unusual charm. He had an eye alert to local beauty. He had a heart sensitive to those passing emotions and thoughts, which, in the aggregate, form the very fabric of human experience. The voices that moved his voice to sing were principally Irish, though not exclusively so. He chose to live the latter third of his life in England; his temperament was largely English; he derived his sense of literary community and artistic purpose from English sources. What poetic strengths he did have are a product of his love for England and Ireland. Those strengths should not be underrated. "I am genuine though not great," he once wrote to a friend, adding "and my time will come."

Michael Case

Other major works
PLAY: *Ashby Manor*, 1883.
NONFICTION: *Rambles*, 1873; *Varieties in Prose*, 1893 (3 volumes); *A Diary*, 1907.

Bibliography

Cronin, Anthony. *Heritage Now: Irish Literature in the English Language.* New York: St. Martin's Press, 1983. An excellent, concise review of Allingham's life, work, and importance in the poetic canon. The significance of Allingham's Irish heritage and his love of London are well explained and vividly rendered. Cronin also includes assessments of Allingham's poetry by his contemporaries.

Howe, M. L. "Notes on the Allingham Canon." *Philological Quarterly* 12 (July, 1933): 290-297. Howe offers a distinctly personal critique of Allingham's work. He defends "The Fairies" from critics who labeled it hastily written, reveals the history behind "The Maids of Elfen-Mere," and untangles the relationships between Allingham, Dante Gabriel Rossetti, and William Morris. Howe also effectively argues the importance and grace of Allingham's overlooked dramas, essays, and short poems.

Husni, Samira Aghacy. "Incorrect References to William Allingham." *Notes and Queries* 30 (August, 1983): 296-298. An essential document for all Allingham scholars and students. Husni sets the record straight regarding common mistakes related to Allingham. These errors range from incorrect dates and titles of poems and books to generalizations about his poetry and relationships with contemporaries. Among those found guilty of libel are critics Katherine Tynan, Ifor Evans, and M. L. Howe.

Warner, Allan. *William Allingham.* Lewisburg, Pa.: Bucknell University Press, 1975. Warner devotes his study to three aspects of Allingham: first, his narrative poem "Laurence Bloomfield in Ireland," second, his achievements as a lyric poet and writer of ballads and songs, and third, his prose as exemplified in "Diary." In each of these areas, Warner illustrates Allingham's real powers of observation, imagination, and reflection.

Welch, Robert. *Irish Poetry from Moore to Yeats.* Potowa, N.J.: Barnes & Noble Books, 1980. Welch examines Allingham in the context of his contemporaries—such as Thomas Moore, Jeremiah Joseph Callanan, and James Clarence Mangan—and the Irish poetic tradition. He skillfully guides the reader toward an appreciation of Allingham's objectivity, love of common life, political common sense, appreciation of nature, and, most important to Welch, his warmth and humanity.

A. R. AMMONS

Born: Near Whiteville, North Carolina; February 18, 1926

Principal poetry
Ommateum, with Doxology, 1955; *Expressions of Sea Level,* 1964; *Corsons Inlet,* 1965; *Tape for the Turn of the Year,* 1965; *Northfield Poems,* 1966; *Selected Poems,* 1968; *Uplands,* 1970; *Briefings: Poems Small and Easy,* 1971; *Collected Poems, 1951-1971,* 1972; *Sphere: The Form of a Motion,* 1974; *Diversifications,* 1975; *The Snow Poems,* 1977; *The Selected Poems 1951-1977,* 1977; *Highgate Road,* 1977; *Six-Piece Suite,* 1979; *Selected Longer Poems,* 1980; *A Coast of Trees,* 1981; *Worldly Hopes,* 1982; *Lake Effect Country,* 1983; *The Selected Poems: Expanded Edition,* 1987; *Sumerian Vistas,* 1987; *The Really Short Poems of A. R. Ammons,* 1990.

Other literary forms
Although A. R. Ammons is known primarily for his poetry, he has also published reviews and essays. Central to an understanding of his work are "A Poem Is a Walk" and his short autobiographical reflection "I Couldn't Wait to Say the Word." Ammons' several published interviews give additional insight into his poetics, especially that by Cynthia Haythe.

Achievements
Through a distinguished and prolific career, Ammons has always succeeded in seeing the particulars of the world within a longing for a sense of unity. He immerses himself in the flow of things, celebrating the world and the self that sees and probes it.

Ammons' work can be seen within the Emersonian tradition: he writes out of his life without any set poetic form. Yet more than any other poet since Ralph Waldo Emerson, he has developed a transcendentalism rooted in science and in a poetic which includes himself in the work. His epigrams, his short to moderate-length nature lyrics, and his long verse-essays are popular reading among poets.

His many awards include the Bread Loaf Writers' Conference Scholarship (1961), a Guggenheim Fellowship (1966), an American Academy of Arts and Letters Traveling Fellowship (1967), a National Endowment for the Arts grant (1969-1970), a Levinson Prize (1970), a National Book Award for *Collected Poems, 1951-1971* (1973), an honorary Litt.D. from Wake Forest University (1973), a Bollingen Prize for *Sphere: The Form of a Motion* (1974-1975), a National Book Critics Circle Award for *A Coast of Trees* (1981), a John D. and Catherine T. MacArthur Foundation Award (1981), and the North Carolina Award for Literature (1986). In 1990, he was inducted into the National

Academy and Institute of Arts and Letters. Ammons' place in the poetry of the twentieth century is, clearly, recognized as one of major significance.

Biography

Archie Randolph Ammons was born on February 18, 1926, near White-ville, North Carolina, in a house bought by his grandfather and situated on the family farm. The main book in the house was the Bible. Ammons' early experiences on the farm, working the land, helped shape his imagination. The self in his poems appears most frequently in relation to the natural world he knew as a child.

He was his parents' fourth child. Three sisters were born before him and two brothers after; one sister lived for only two weeks, and both brothers died, one in infancy and the other stillborn. Ammons remembers the deaths of his brothers, saying that they account in part for the undercurrent of loss and loneliness in his work.

Upon graduation from high school in 1943, Ammons took a job in the shipyard in Wilmington, North Carolina. In 1944, he joined the navy, spend-ing nineteen months in service, including time in the South Pacific, where he began writing poems. Returning home after the war, Ammons attended Wake Forest College (his tuition paid for by the government under the terms of the G.I. Bill) and was graduated with a B.S. in 1949. That year he married Phyl-lis Plumbo and took a job as principal of an elementary school in the remote coastal community of Hatteras, North Carolina. From 1950 to 1952, he stud-ied English at the University of California at Berkeley. In 1952, he took a position with a New Jersey medical glassware firm, a job he held for twelve years. He began to send poems to literary magazines, and in 1953 *The Hud-son Review* took two of his poems. His first book of poetry, *Ommateum, with Doxology*, appeared in 1955. Nine years later, *Expressions of Sea Level* ap-peared. That same year, 1964, he began teaching at Cornell University. Other books of poems followed, and in 1972 most of his poems were published as *Collected Poems, 1951-1971. Sphere: The Form of a Motion*, his poem of more than two thousand lines, published in 1974, gained for him the Bollingen Prize for Poetry for 1974-1975. Whitmanesque in its tendency toward a demo-cratic feeling, *Sphere* presents Ammons' aesthetic of continual motion and the musical affirmation of the interworking of relationships in the energy of all life.

Ammons is Goldwin Smith Professor of Poetry at Cornell University. He lives in Ithaca, New York, with his wife and son, John. Ammons makes fre-quent trips to eastern North Carolina, a place which figures prominently in his poems.

Analysis

In one of A. R. Ammons' early poems, "So I Said I Am Ezra," from *Om-*

mateum, with Doxology, the speaker is whipped over the landscape, driven, moved by the natural elements. He is at once ordered and disordered, close and far, balanced and unbalanced, and he exclaims: "So I Ezra went out into the night/ like a drift of sand." The line is representative of Ammons' entire body of work, for its searches through language for an attempt to mean and to be clear, and failing to succeed completely in such clarity, ends by affirming a presence of radiance.

Ammons' poems have a tendency, like most contemporary poems, to take their own process, their own making, as a theme. Wanting to express something changeless and eternal, he is constrained by his own intricate mortality. So in the title poem of *Expressions of Sea Level,* he presents the ocean as permanent and impermanent, as form and formlessness. He is interested in what man can and cannot know, giving full sway and expression to the ocean's activity: "see the dry casting of the beach worm/ dissolve at the delicate rising touch."

Ammons attempts always to render visual details accurately. Some of the most moving poems in this regard are the poems inspired by his background in Columbus County, North Carolina. "Nelly Meyers" praises and celebrates a woman who lived on the farm where Ammons grew up; "Silver" records Ammons' love for and rapport with a mule he used to work. "Hardweed Path Going" tells of his life as a boy, doing chores on the farm, his playtime with a pet bird (a jo-reet) and a hog named Sparkle. Almost all memory, these poems represent Ammons' past, particularly his boyhood, which he renders in astonishingly realistic details.

Ammons infuses the natural world with his own attuned sensibilities, acknowledging in the title poem of *Corsons Inlet* that "Overall is beyond me." The form of the poem is a walk over the dunes. What lives beyond his perception reassures, although he knows "that there is no finality of vision." Bafflement is a feeling in the poem which may be studied for what it says about the relationship between logic and reason, imposed order and discovered order, art and life, reality and illusion, being and becoming. "Corsons Inlet" concludes the walk/quest on the note that "tomorrow a new walk is a new walk." Ammons' desire to say something clearly, therefore, is not so much a search for the Word as it is an attempt to find original ways to make and shape poetry.

With *Tape for the Turn of the Year,* Ammons writes a long, narrow poem on adding-machine paper. The poet improvises and spontaneously records his thoughts and moods in what resembles a poetic diary. In one place, he praises how writing gets done, suggesting that doing it is almost its own practical reward, as the speaker acknowledges in another poem, "Identity," "it is wonderful how things work."

By the mid-1960's, Ammons' major themes had emerged, his sensibility oscillating between extremes: formlessness-form, center-periphery, high-low, motion-stasis, order-disorder, one-many. One of his most constant themes has been the self in the work and in the world. He is concerned not only with the form of natural fact but also with form in the abstract sense, that is, with physical laws that govern the way individual entities act and behave. Ammons reaffirms the resonance of his subject, as in "The Eternal City," in which destruction must "accept into itself piece by piece all the old/ perfect human visions, all the old perfect loves."

Motion within diversity is perhaps Ammons' major theme. In "Saliences," from *Northfield Poems*, he discovers continuity in change. In "Snow Log," from *Uplands*, recognizing that nature's intentions cannot be known, he responds simply as an individual to what he sees in the winter scene: "I take it on myself:/ especially the fallen tree/ the snow picks/ out in the woods to show." In "The City Limits," from *Briefings*, a poem whose urban subject removes the speaker from nature, Ammons celebrates the "gold-skeined wings of flies swarming the dumped/ guts of a natural slaughter or the coil of shit."

Awarded the National Book Award for Poetry in 1973, *Collected Poems, 1951-1971* comprises most of Ammons' first six volumes, except for *Tape for the Turn of the Year* and three long verse-essays—"Extremes and Moderations," "Hibernaculum," and "Essay on Poetics." In these poems, Ammons is a seer, lamenting man's abuse of the earth and appreciating the immediacy of a world that takes care of itself. "Essay on Poetics" considers the structural advantages and disadvantages of poetry. One reads this essay to appreciate more fully Ammons' views on writing.

In perhaps his major work, the book-length poem *Sphere: The Form of a Motion*, Ammons explores motion and shape in a set form: sentences with no full stops, 155 sections of four tercets each. He relies on colons, perhaps suggesting a democratization and a flow. Shifting freely, sometimes abruptly, within a given stanza, phrase, or word, Ammons says, "I do not smooth into groups." Thus the book explores the nature of its own poetics, the poet searching everywhere for a language of clarity. In one place, he says that he is "sick of good poems." Wanting the smooth and raw together, Ammons reminds the reader that his prejudice against neat, traditional structures in poetry relates to the natural world where "the shapes nearest shapelessness awe us most, suggest the god." He regards a log, "rigid with shape," as "trivial."

Ammons, therefore, makes his case for the poem of the open form as opposed to strong, traditional verses.

Ammons demythologizes poetics and language, while testifying to an Emersonian faith in the universe as flowing freely and spontaneously. At the same time, there is a counter feeling always working. He refers often to clarity and wants his poems to arrive and move forward "by a controlling motion, design, symmetry."

While he is writing the poem, commenting on it, writing himself into it, he shows his instinct for playfulness, for spoofing. This aspect of his work—

the clowning humor—adds an inherent drama to his work, as Jerald Bullis has written:

> The tone of the poem or, I should say, of the voices of its "parts," ranges and range from that of the high and hard lyric, the crystalline and *as if* final saying, through a talky and often latinate professorial stance, to permutations of low tone: "bad" puns, catalogues that seem to have been lifted from a catalogue, and, in the example below, the high-pressure pitch-man tone of How-To scams: "Now, first of all, the way to write poems is just to start: it's like learning to walk or swim or ride the bicycle, you just go after it."

The poem goes on, praising the ability of man to write and to appreciate being alive.

Reverence for creation runs throughout *Sphere*, investing the work with a vision beyond and through the details of the poet's aesthetic. This religious strain has its source in Ammons' absolute reverence for the natural world. A religious vocabulary, then, is no surprise in his work and connects with his childhood, when church services and hymn-sings were dominant parts of his life. As in *Sphere*, he questions what is "true service," saying "it must be a service that is celebration, for we would celebrate even if we do not know what or how, and for He is bountiful if/ slow to protect and recalcitrant to keep." Ammons goes on to say: "What we can celebrate is the condition we are in, or we can renounce the condition/ we are in and celebrate a condition we might be in or ought/ to be in." Ammons fuses and plays on the relationship between creation and imagination, hoping and trying to discover "joy's surviving radiance." In the presence of this radiance—the hues and bends of Ammons' music—exist the crux of his aesthetic, his art and his being: the solitary man never surrendering as he is being imposed on and whipped about, as he writes in one of his earliest poems, "So I Said I am Ezra/ and the wind whipped my throat/ gaming for the sounds of my voice." Yet the self is not dwarfed by the world. Ammons understands his moral and aesthetic convictions and will not cease to assert them. Such desire allows the visionary in Ammons to discover constantly new ways to see and understand his life. In this regard, key words crop up often: "salience," "recalcitrant," "suasion," "periphery," "possibility," tentative words that tend to illuminate or seek the proper blend in experience. So *Sphere* ends as it began, clear and free of all encumbrances except the spoken voice: "we're ourselves: we're sailing." The ending is right for the "form of a motion," the sense of wonder and uncertainty going on beyond the finality of the poem. Past, present, and future are one, and the poem and its end recall Walt Whitman's absorption into the dirt in "Song of Myself."

In *The Snow Poems*, Ammons continues his experimental attempt to arrange a poetic journal, recounting in lyrical splendor the concerns of daily life, including details about weather, sex, and the poet's attempt to write and to experience a dialogue between the specific and the general.

Ammons' work since the mid-1970's marks a return to his more visionary tendencies contained in his earlier terse, fierce lyrics of short or moderate length. "Progress Report" is an epigram from *Worldly Hopes*:

> Now I'm
> into things
>
> so small
> when I
>
> say boo
> I disappear

The words flow in natural motion.

Lake Effect Country continues Ammons' love of form and motion. The whole book represents one body, a place of water, a bed of lively recreation. In "Meeting Place," for example, "The water nearing the ledge leans down with/ grooved speed at the spill then,/ quickly groundless in air." His vision comes from the coming together of the natural elements in the poem, rising and falling, moving and forming the disembodied voices that are the real characters in his poems: "When I call out to them/ as to the flowing bones in my naked self, is my/ address attribution's burden and abuse." "Meeting Place" goes out "to summon/ the deep-lying fathers from myself,/ the spirits, feelings howling, appearing there."

A major contemporary poem is "Easter Morning," from *A Coast of Trees*. Based on the death in infancy of the poet's younger brother, the poem is filled with reverence for the natural world, Ammons' memory ever enlarging with religious and natural resonances. "I have a life that did not become,/ that turned aside and stopped,/ astonished." The poem carries the contradictory mysteries of the human condition—death, hope, and memory—working together in a concrete and specific aesthetic. Presented in the form of a walk, "Easter Morning" reveals the speaker caught in the motion, as two birds "from the South" fly around, circle, change their ways, and go on. The poem affirms, with the speaker in another poem called "Working with Tools," "I understand/ and won't give assertion up." Like Ezra going out "into the night/ like a drift of sand," the poet celebrates "a dance sacred as the sap in/ the trees . . . fresh as this particular/ flood of burn breaking across us now/ from the sun." Though the dance is completed in a moment, it can never be destroyed, because it has been re-created as the imagination's grand dance.

Another major contemporary poem is "The Ridge Farm" from *Sumerian Vistas*. In fifty-one parts, the poem renders the Farm itself on a ridge, on the edge of everything and nothing. Ammons' speaker joyfully resigns himself to the "highways" and the dammed-up brooks. The implication is that poetry— like Nature—breaks through and flows, exploring the motion and shape of the Farm's form. The Farm itself it a concrete place wherein Ammons explores the nature of poetics and other realities.

In *The Really Short Poems of A. R. Ammons*, the poet continues his necessity to really *see* the natural world. That seeing becomes the poem; its motion, the story moving through the images. The form and subject move in a terse, fierce way as the poem discovers itself. In "Winter Scene," for example, the natural world changes radiantly when the jay takes over the leafless cherry tree. The landscape transformed, the poet notes what he sees: "then every branch// quivers and/ breaks out in blue leaves." Motion formerly void of color brightens with vision and sway.

The range and flow in Ammons' poetry, his search for balance, move him to create his philosophical music, using a vocabulary drawn largely from everyday speech. He celebrates the need in every human being to discover a common experience in the least particular thing.

Shelby Stephenson

Bibliography

Bloom, Harold, ed. *A. R. Ammons.* New York: Chelsea House, 1986. This volume contains eighteen essays on Ammons' work, plus an introductory essay by Bloom. Among the contributors are contemporary poets John Ashbery, Richard Howard, and John Hollander. Ammons himself offers an essay. Perhaps the central theme of all the essays is that Ammons, like Walt Whitman, is a solitary self in the world. The text is supplemented by a chronology, notes, a bibliography, acknowledgments, and an index.

Elder, John. *Imagining the Earth: Poetry and the Vision of Nature.* Urbana: University of Illinois Press, 1985. Elder writes about poets who remember and re-create the earth. His chapter on Ammons is called "Poetry and the Mind's Terrain." Elder's prose is clear and uncluttered; he presents Ammons from the fresh perspective of contemporary poets. Includes chapter notes and index.

Hans, James S. *The Value(s) of Literature.* Albany: State University of New York Press, 1990. This book addresses the ethical aspects of literature by discussing three major American poets: Walt Whitman, Wallace Stevens, and A. R. Ammons. The chapter on Ammons is called "Ammons and the One:Many Mechanism." In a concluding chapter, "The Aesthetic of Worldly Hopes," Hans speculates that one of the reasons poetry is not read widely in the United States is that it is "perceived to have nothing of ethical value inherent in it." What Hans calls "patterns of choice" exist in poems such as *Corsons Inlet* and "Essay on Poetics." Contains chapter notes.

Haythe, Cynthia. "An Interview with A. R. Ammons." *Contemporary Literature* 21 (Spring, 1980): 173-190. Ammons responds to questions about his Southernness and his "exile" in the North. He discusses *Sphere* and other poems, as well as his affinity with other contemporary poets.

Holder, Alan. *A. R. Ammons.* Boston: Twayne, 1978. This rare book-length study of Ammons introduces Ammons and his life and works up through *Sphere.* The text is supplemented by a chronology, notes, a select bibliography (with annotated secondary sources), and an index.

Spiegelman, Willard. *The Didactic Muse.* Princeton, N.J.: Princeton University Press, 1989. A study of W. H. Auden, Howard Nemerov, Anthony Hecht, Allen Ginsberg, Robert Pinsky, Adrienne Rich, James Merrill, and Ammons, the book's chapter on Ammons is called "Myths of Concretion, Myths of Abstraction: The Case of A. R. Ammons." Spiegelman ranges over Ammons' work, particularly the longer poems through *Sumerian Vistas.* Spiegelman's concern is the relation between poetry and philosophy. His "case" for Ammons concludes that Ammons' dominant conceit is motion: his attempt to find that place where the conscious and unconscious move, yet stay. The book is important to any student who wishes to see Ammons' work within the larger context of contemporary poetry.

Vendler, Helen, ed. *Voices and Visions: The Poet in America.* New York: Random House, 1987. A companion to *Voices and Visions*, a PBS television series. See Calvin Bedient's essay on Walt Whitman. Bedient discusses Ammons' *Sphere* within Whitman's energetic thrust out—toward a desire to create a motion within the American attraction for space, for going on, for expanding one's self in a larger world. The book contains pictures of poets, illustrations, notes on chapters, suggestions for further reading, notes on contributors, a list of illustrations, and an index.

MATTHEW ARNOLD

Born: Laleham, England; December 24, 1822
Died: Liverpool, England; April 15, 1888

Principal poetry

The Strayed Reveller and Other Poems, 1849; *Empedocles on Etna and Other Poems*, 1852; *Poems*, 1853; *Poems, Second Series*, 1855; *Merope*, 1858; *New Poems*, 1867; *Poems, Collected Edition*, 1869; *Poetical Works of Matthew Arnold*, 1890.

Other literary forms

Throughout his life Matthew Arnold wrote critical works on literature, culture, religion, and education which made him the foremost man of letters in Victorian England. This large body of prose is available in a standard edition: *The Complete Prose Works of Matthew Arnold* (1960-1976, R. H. Super, editor), with textual notes and commentary. Essays important to an understanding of Arnold's contribution to the discipline of literary criticism include *Preface to Poems* (1853), "Wordsworth," "The Study of Poetry," and "Literature and Science." "Culture and Anarchy" explains the philosophical positions, and biases, from which Arnold criticized literature and society. Also available are editions containing his letters and notebooks.

Achievements

In 1840, while he was a student at Rugby, Arnold won the Poetry Prize for "Alaric at Rome," and three years later, then at Oxford, he won the Newdigate Poetry Prize for "Cromwell." From this official recognition of his poetic gift, Arnold began a career which produced what T. S. Eliot calls in *The Use of Poetry and the Use of Criticism* (1933), "academic poetry in the best sense; the best fruit which can issue from the promise shown by the prize-poem." Yet Arnold wrote many poems which rise far above the merely academic, though popular interest in his poetry never approached the following of his more technically and expressively gifted contemporaries, Alfred, Lord Tennyson and Robert Browning. Admittedly, Arnold's poems lack the polished texture that characterizes the great Victorian poetry; critics often complain about Arnold's lack of "ear." The novelist George Eliot, however, early recognized, in the *Westminster Review* (July, 1855), what has been increasingly the opinion: "But when . . . we linger over a poem which contains some deep and fresh thought, we begin to perceive poetic beauties—felicities of expression and description, which are too quiet and subdued to be seized at the first glance." Whatever his prosodic deficiencies, Arnold still composed several lyric and narrative poems which take their place with the best that the age produced.

In a century notable for elegies, "Thyrsis," for Arnold's friend Arthur Hugh Clough, ranks with *Adonais* (1821), "When Lilacs Last in the Dooryard Bloom'd" (1865), and *In Memoriam* (1850) as distinguished additions to the genre. "The Scholar-Gipsy" and "Dover Beach" contain the lyric energy and power which justify both their numerous anthology appearances and a body of criticism that places them among the most frequently explicated poems in the language.

In 1857, Arnold won election as Professor of Poetry at Oxford and, in 1862, was reelected to another five-year term. Receiving permission to abandon the customary Latin, Arnold delivered his lectures in English and invigorated the professorship with lectures ranging from the individual (Homer, Dante) to the topical ("The Literary Influence of Academies") to the broadly critical (*On the Study of Celtic Literature*, 1867). Though his critical writings on English culture, literature, and religion made him a controversial figure, Arnold gained respect in his post as Inspector of Schools, serving twice as Assistant Commissioner on official committees dispatched to study European schools, and eventually becoming a Senior Inspector in 1870, the same year in which Oxford conferred on him an honorary D.C.L. degree. In 1883, he visited the United States on a lecture tour which, though not triumphal, was at least a measure of his commanding stature as a critic and poet.

Biography

Matthew Arnold, born on Christmas Eve, 1822, at Laleham, England, was the second child and eldest son of five boys and four girls in the family of Dr. Thomas Arnold and his wife, Mary Penrose Arnold. At the time of the poet's birth, Dr. Arnold, a graduate of Oxford, was performing his duties as master at the school in Laleham, preparing himself intellectually and professionally for his appointment in 1828 as Headmaster of Rugby, where he set about reforming the narrowly classical curriculum to include emphasis on language, history, and mathematics and to reflect his "broad church" liberalism, while insisting that his students maintain his own high standards of discipline and moral conduct. Though his reformist views on both church and school invited attack from traditional quarters, Dr. Arnold exerted over his students, family, and English education a lingering influence after his premature death at the age of forty-seven.

Although there was an undoubtedly tense relationship between headmaster father and poetically inclined son (who, at times, neglected his studies and sported the dress and talk of a dandy), Arnold's elegiac tribute to his father in "Rugby Chapel" confirms his mature appreciation for Dr. Arnold's magisterial qualities of mind and conduct. Likewise, Arnold took a distinct pride in the Cornish ancestry of his mother, whose father was a clergyman named John Penrose and whose mother's maiden name was Trevenen. Arnold's interest in Celtic literature derived from this ancestral connection, received further stimulation from a trip to Brittany in 1859 to visit the schools, and finally resulted in the lectures *On the Study of Celtic Literature*. Whatever the exact influence of his parents, Matthew Arnold certainly felt the familial strains which, on the one side, tended toward the moral and intellectual honesty and practicality of the headmaster and, on the other, toward the imaginative and expressive charm of the Celtic mother.

Arnold married Frances Lucy Wightman in 1851 after his celebrated infatuation, rendered in the "Switzerland" poems, for the beautiful "Marguerite," a woman now identified by Park Honan in *Matthew Arnold: A Life* (1981) as Mary Claude, "a descendant of French Protestant exiles" who came to live near the Arnold family home at Fox How. Matthew and Frances Lucy had six children, two daughters and four sons, in a happy marriage three times saddened by the early deaths of Basil at two, Thomas at sixteen, and William at eighteen.

Two years after his retirement from the travel-wearying post of school inspector, Arnold entered in his diary, under the date of April 15, 1888, "Weep bitterly over the dead." That day, at Liverpool awaiting the arrival of his daughter and granddaughter from the United States, he collapsed from a heart attack and died.

Analysis

A commonplace beginning for criticism of Matthew Arnold's poetry is one or another of his many well-known critical statements which provide a basis for showing how well or how poorly the critic's precept corresponds with the poet's practice. One must remember, however, that most of Arnold's best work as a poet preceded his finest work as a critic and that his letters reveal dissatisfaction with his poetic "fragments," as he called them. He did believe that his poems would have their "turn," just as Tennyson's and Browning's had, because they followed closely the trend of modern thinking. Indeed, Arnold's modernity—his sense of alienation, moral complexity, and humanistic values—makes his work, both critical and creative, a continuing presence in the literary world.

The sense of alienation which carries so much thematic weight in Arnold's poetry reaches back into his childhood. As a child, he wore a brace for a slightly bent leg. This had an isolating, restricting effect on a boy who enjoyed running and climbing. Also, he early realized the irony of numbers, because, as the second born, he found that his parents' time and attention did not easily spread over nine children, and, at fourteen, he spent what surely seemed like a year in exile at Winchester School. The need for attention influenced his pose as a dandy, and he probably enjoyed his reputation as an idler, especially in his circle of family and friends who upheld and practiced the Victorian principles of work and duty.

Of course, the religious and social atmosphere in which Arnold approached manhood conditioned his perception of the alienating forces at work in England: he entered Oxford during the Tractarian controversy that divided conservative and liberal elements in the Church of England, and he knew about the general economic and social discontent that separated the working class from the wealthy. With such factious elements at work—including the dispute between religion and science on the origin of earth and man—Arnold, facing his own lover's estrangement in "To Marguerite—Continued," could write with justifiable irony that "We mortal millions live alone." With good reason, then, Arnold formed his ideas on the wholesome effect of order and authority, of education and culture recommended in his prose—evident alike in that quest for unity, wholeness, and joy which, in the poems, his lyric and narrative speakers find so elusive.

In the early sonnet "To a Friend," Arnold praises Sophocles, in one of his memorable lines, because he "saw life steadily, and saw it whole." "Wholeness" was the controlling thought behind the poet's vision: "an Idea of the world in order not be prevailed over by the world's multitudinousness," he tells Clough in a letter critical of the "episodes and ornamental work" that distract both poet and reader from a sense of unity. This unity of idea, in perception and execution, is necessary for poetry "to utter the truth," as Arnold says in his essay on William Wordsworth, because "poetry is at bottom a criticism of life . . . the greatness of a poet lies in his powerful and beautiful application of ideas to life,—to the question: How to live." For Arnold, this question is itself "a moral idea."

If Sophocles saw life "whole," he also, according to Arnold, saw it "steadily." For Arnold, Sophoclean steadiness implies two distinct but complementary processes. First, as physical steadiness, *seeing* is the broad sensory reaction to the range of stimuli associated with the poet's "Idea of the world." One may note, for example, the last six lines of "Mycerinus" with their heavy emphasis on auditory imagery—"mirth waxed loudest," "echoes came," "dull sound"—which perfectly conclude the preceding philosophical implications of six long years of reveling by King Mycerinus. These implications appear in a series of "it may be" possibilities, and the imagery underscores the essential uncertainty of the auditors ("wondering people") because the sounds are really once-removed "echoes," partly "Mix'd with the murmur of the moving Nile." There is an attempt to match appropriately the sensations with the subject.

The second point, related to physical steadiness, implies a type of mental fixity on the part of the observer, a disciplined exercise of consciousness operating throughout the temporal context of creative urge and eventual artistic fulfillment. Explaining the difficulty of this exercise for his own poetic practice, Arnold writes to Clough that "I can go thro: the imaginary process of mastering myself and the whole affair as it would then stand, but at the critical point I am too apt to hoist up the mainsail to the wind and let her drive." In short, Arnold recognizes a lack of mental fixity to accompany the poetic inspiration; he can, imaginatively, see the "whole," but, at the critical point of artistic execution, he lets go, becoming, at the expense of the whole, too insistent or expansive in one thematic or descriptive part. The lyric "Despondency" addresses this problem in the typically elegiac tone of Arnold's poetic voice. The lyric speaker says that "The thoughts that rain their steady glow/ Like stars on life's cold sea" have "never shone" for him. He has seen the thoughts which "light, like gleams, my spirit's sky," but they appear "once . . . hurry by/ And never come again." He laments the absence of that conscious persistence which preserves the "steady glow" of thought bearing directly on the moral vastness of "life's cold sea."

In a more general way, seeing life steadily allies itself to the "spontaneity of consciousness" for which Arnold praises Hellenism in *Culture and Anarchy* (1869). This spontaneity suggests a physical and mental alertness which instantly responds to "life as it is," a consciousness prone to thinking but unencumbered by the predisposition to action which describes the force of "conduct and obedience" behind Hebraism, the other major tradition in Western civilization. Sophocles, the model Hellenist, possesses the "even-balanced soul" which holds in steady counterpoise the old dichotomy of thought and feeling, a pre-Christian possibility coming before the "triumph of Hebraism and man's moral impulses." Thus, as a letter to Clough shows, Arnold appreciates the burden of seeing steadily and whole for the modern poet whose subject matter is perforce a criticism of life, a burden compounded because "the poet's matter being the hitherto experience of the world, and his own, increases with every century." This "hitherto experience," both Hellenic and Hebraic, overlaying Arnold's own, accounts for his interest in remote, historical subjects such as "Mycerinus," "Empedocles on Etna," "Tristram and Iseult," "Sohrab and Rustum," and "Balder Dead"—which nevertheless contain critical implications for living morally, even joyfully, in the incipiently modern world of Victorian England.

This "then and now" conception of the human experience has its analogues in the dualities which, as critics often note, Arnold's poems constantly explore: the moral and the amoral, the mind and the body, thought and feeling, the contemplative life and the active life, or, as Professor Douglas Bush labels them in *Matthew Arnold* (1971), the "Apollonian-Dionysian antinomy" of Arnold's ideas. Here again the dynamics for seeing steadily emerge because the poet must look simultaneously in polar directions, resisting all the while the temptation to "hoist up the mainsail to the wind and let her drive."

In his best poems, Arnold seeks the vantage point—call it a poetic situation—from which he can see steadily the dualities that, in the poem's thematic reconciliation, coalesce in the wholeness of the "Idea." Arnold warns, however, in the "Preface to Poems" against the poetic situations "from the representation of which, though accurate, no poetical enjoyment can be derived . . . those in which the suffering finds no vent in action . . . in which there is everything to be endured, nothing to be done." For Arnold, the problem of poetic situation means finding "a vent in action" which does not overwhelm the speculative nature of the idea, and the solution often comes in the form of the "quest," the symbolically active.

"The Scholar-Gipsy" is on a quest, "waiting for the spark from heaven to fall." When the spark falls, he can share with the world the secret art, learned from the "gipsy-crew," of ruling "the workings of men's brains." Until then, he wanders mysteriously from Berkshire Moors to Cumner Hills, pensively cast in an ageless "solitude," exempt from the "repeated shocks" and "strange disease of modern life." The shepherd who lyrically tells the scholar-gipsy's story speaks for the Victorians who also "await" the spark from heaven, but, with "heads o'ertax'd" and "palsied hearts," cannot acquire the immortalizing agency of a quest with "one aim, one business, one desire." The antithesis is clear: "Arnold's Gipsy," as Honan says, "represents stability in a world of flux and change, creative inwardness in a world of lassitude, stagnation, frustration, and dividedness." The shepherd, a part of the modern world but temporarily secluded in the imaginative distance of "this high field's dark corner," discovers the physical and mental steadiness to tell the story, to see concurrently the past and present, and to indict his society through the quest of the mythic wanderer.

"Thyrsis," a monody for Clough, follows the same stanza form and rhyme scheme of "The Scholar-Gipsy," continuing too the unifying strategy of the quest, this time for the "signal elm-tree" which has itself become a symbol for the perpetual existence of "our friend, the Gipsy-Scholar." In this way, Arnold aligns Clough with the legendary rover; Clough, however, unlike the Gipsy, "could not wait" the passing of the "storms that rage" in their fragmented society. With night descending, Corydon (Arnold's persona) sees, but does not achieve, the object of his quest; but he cries "Hear it, O Thyrsis, still our tree is there!" So lives the Gipsy-Scholar, so remains, in the symbolic activity of the quest, the idea of hope: Corydon will "not despair." As in "The Scholar-Gipsy," Arnold turns the old genre of pastoral elegy to topical account, and the poem achieves a balanced steadiness, as much about Corydon as about Thyrsis, as much about hope as about despair, as much about life as about death.

The idea of the quest—or the hunt, or the journey—recurs again and again in Arnold's poetry, providing the "vent in action" required by the expanding idea. The journey may be inward, as in "The Buried Life," where Arnold says that man's impulse to know the "mystery" of his heart sends him delving into "his own breast." Here the poet tries to reconcile the dualities of outward "strife" (in "the world's most crowded streets") and inner "striving" (toward "the unregarded river of our life"). This self-questing journey, however, ironically needs the impetus of "a beloved hand laid in ours," "another's eyes read clear," and then, in the respite of love, one "becomes aware of his life's flow." There is, though faint, an optimistic strain rising through the modern sense of isolation, even permitting the poet, in "Resignation," to make a virtue of necessity by accepting "His sad lucidity of soul."

For Arnold, though, isolation and solitude are not similar; they represent yet another set of opposites: isolation, a state of rejection and loneliness, is to be shunned, while solitude, a state of reflection and inspiration, is to be sought. Away from the "sick hurry" of modern life, the poet in solitude achieves the steadiness of feeling and perception required for the aesthetic fulfillment of his idea. Arnold's lyric speakers enjoy solitude: the shepherd in "The Scholar-Gipsy" and "Thyrsis," or the lounger in Kensington gardens who finds "peace for ever new" in the "lone, open glade," is analogous, in the "Austerity of Poetry," to the "hidden ground/ Of thought" within the muse herself. Yet there is always the ironic danger: Empedocles, on the verge of suicide, drops his laurel bough because he is "weary of the solitude/ Where he who bears thee must abide." Arnold needs the creative succor of a solitude that carries over, as he says in "Quiet Work," into a life "Of toil unsever'd from tranquillity," a life that, even as Empedocles admits, still "Leaves human effort scope." This "human effort" becomes the dynamics behind Arnold's own quest to focus and balance the idea with the action, to elevate and juxtapose the moral propositions of antagonistic extremes: life and death, love and hate, alliance and alienation.

"Stanzas from the Grande Chartreuse" follows the typically Arnoldian pattern. The first sixty-five lines witness the sensory perception and steadiness of the speaker, his spontaneity of consciousness comprising a mixture of imagery—visual ("spectral vapours white"), auditory ("strangled sound"), tactile ("forms brush by"). There is the anticipatory journey or quest: "The bridge is cross'd, and slow we ride/ Through forest up the mountainside." Then, at line sixty-six, there is the idea, framed in the rhetorical question: "And what am I, that I am here?" The speaker admits that the object of his ultimate quest is really elsewhere, for the "rigorous teachers" of his youth "Show'd me the high, white star of Truth,/ There bade me gaze, and there aspire." That abstract quest, though, must temporarily defer to this cold physical journey to the Grande Chartreuse, a monastery in the French Alps, where the troubled speaker can shed his melancholy tears in the presence of a profound religious faith. No longer young, and feeling caught in the forlorn void between the faiths of a past and future time, he is "Wandering between two worlds, one dead,/ The other powerless to be born." The past age of faith, still ascetically practiced in the Carthusian monastery, and a desirable future age "Which without hardness will be sage,/ And gay without frivolity" bracket a divisively inert time in which the sciolists talk, but, with their fathers' history of pain and grief as justification, "The Kings of modern thought are dumb."

Fraser Neiman, in *Matthew Arnold* (1968), summarizes the common emotional ground of the anchorite and Arnold: they both "turn to a quest for inward peace," but Arnold must find his in solitude, in the buried life, in quiet work, in, as Neiman says, "a profound inwardness . . . not incompatible with the world of activity." The poem concludes with images of "action and pleasure"—the "troops," the "hunters," the "gay dames" passing below the monastery—representing a life again rejected by the Carthusians but, as the reader infers, accepted by the speaker, who has had, at least, the catharsis of his tears. The emphasis, though, is on the idea, an idea which Arnold tries to see steadily and whole through the confrontation of opposites: the ascetic, contemplative life of anchorite, "Obermann," and the past at the top of the Etna-like mountain (where, one gathers, the "suffering finds no vent in action"), versus the secular, restless life of "Laughter and cries" at the bottom of the mountain where "Years hence, perhaps, may dawn an age,/ More fortunate." "Stanzas from the Grande Chartreuse" renders in setting, mood, and idea the predicament of the poet, expressed in Arnold's earlier poem, "Stanza in Memory of the Author of 'Obermann'":

> Ah! two desires toss about
> The poet's feverish blood.
> One drives him to the world without,
> And one to solitude.

"Dover Beach" fits into the same structural pattern of imagery, idea, and resolution. The opening of the poem establishes the physical and mental awareness of the speaker, a person attuned to the sensory stimuli of the scene before him. The counterpointed imagery of sight and sound in the first verse paragraph divides as naturally as a Petrarchan sonnet: the visual imagery of the first eight lines suggests peace and serenity ("the moon lies fair," "the tranquil bay"), but the auditory imagery of the next six lines, signaled by the turn of the imperative "Listen!," introduces the "grating roar/ Of pebbles" which, in the climax of the paragraph, "Begin, and cease, and then again begin,/ With tremulous cadence slow, and bring/ The eternal note of sadness in." The Imagistic division, the modulated caesura, and the irregular pattern of end and internal rhymes provide the lyric energy leading up to the emotional dimension of sadness which the second verse paragraph quickly converts to the mental dimension of thought. In a transitional effect, the auditory imagery surrounding the "note of sadness" connects with the image of Sophocles who "long ago/ Heard it on the Aegaean," bringing "Into his mind the turbid ebb and flow/ Of human misery." Critics sometimes object to the shift in imagery from full to ebb tide, but the crucial thematic point lies not so much in the maintenance of parallel imagery as in the formulation of idea: "we/ Find also in the sound a thought/ Hearing it by this distant northern sea." Thus, the perception of dualities—full and ebb tide, present and past time, physical and metaphorical seas—prepares for the "then and now" structure of the third verse paragraph: the "Sea of Faith" was once full, like the tide at Dover, but the lyric speaker can "only hear/ Its melancholy, long, withdrawing roar."

The sociological interpretation, to select just one critical approach, maintains that the disillusioned speaker refers to the debate between religion and science then dominating the intellectual effort of so many Victorians. If the "Sea of Faith" came to full tide with the "triumph of Hebraism and man's moral impulses," the preceding image of Sophocles adds poignance to the speaker's resignation in the face of the constant factor of "human misery." Whereas Sophocles could, in an ancient world, see life steadily and see it whole in its tragic but nevertheless human consequences, the speaker enjoys no such certainty. The retreating Sea of Faith takes with it the moral and spiritual basis for "joy" and "love" and "peace." The speaker's own attempt to see modern life steadily and to see it whole, successful or not as the individual critic may determine for himself, leads to the resolution of the lyric cry: "Ah, love, let us be true/ To one another!" The world may no longer offer the comfort of "joy" and "certitude" and "help for pain," but the lovers may create their own interpersonal world where such pleasures presumably exist.

Some critics fault the ending of "Dover Beach," which imaginatively transports the couple to "a darkling plain," leaving behind the sea imagery which guides the speaker's emotional and mental state throughout the poem. The ending, however, maintains the consistency of auditory imagery ("confused alarms," "armies clash") which concludes each of the preceding verse paragraphs, and the "struggle and flight" of the "ignorant armies" echo, in appropriately harsher terms, the "retreating" roar of the Sea of Faith. Furthermore, the principle of duality, carefully set up in the poem, works at the end: physically, the lovers are still by the quiet, beautiful cliffs of Dover, but, figuratively, at an opposite extreme, they find themselves "as on a darkling plain."

In addition to the ones already mentioned or discussed, the following poems are considered among Arnold's best work: "The Forsaken Merman," "The Strayed Reveller," "Palladium," "The Future," "A Dream," and "A Summer Night." Although Arnold's work has been very influential, even at its best it contains elements which can bother the modern reader, such as the over-reliance on interrogative and exclamatory sentences, giving to his ideas in the former case a weighty, rhetorical cast and, in the latter, an artificial rather than a natural emphasis. There is, however, a consistency in the melancholy, elegiac tone and in the modern concern with man's moral condition in a world where living a meaningful life has become increasingly difficult that makes Arnold's poetry rewarding reading.

Ronald K. Giles

Other major works

PLAY: *Merope: A Tragedy*, 1858.

NONFICTION: *Preface to Poems*, 1853; *On Translating Homer*, 1861; *Essays in Criticism*, 1865; *On the Study of Celtic Literature*, 1867; *Culture and Anarchy*, 1869; *Friendship's Garland*, 1871; *Literature and Dogma*, 1873; *God and the Bible*, 1875; *Last Essays on Church and Religion*, 1877; *Discourses in America*, 1885; *Civilization in the United States*, 1888; *Essays in Criticism, Second Series*, 1888; *The Complete Prose Works of Matthew Arnold*, 1960-1976 (R. H. Super, editor).

MISCELLANEOUS: *The Works of Matthew Arnold*, 1903-1904 (15 volumes).

Bibliography

Bloom, Harold. *Matthew Arnold: Modern Critical Views*. New York: Chelsea House, 1987. Gathers together ten critical articles written between 1940 and 1986, representing a variety of critical approaches and analyzing the poetry and prose works of Matthew Arnold. Contains a chronology, a bibliography, and an index.

Dawson, Carl, ed. *Matthew Arnold, the Poetry: The Critical Heritage*. London: Routledge & Kegan Paul, 1973. Collects more than sixty reviews and essays written between 1849 and 1898. Gives a fascinating view of how Arnold was received and understood by his contemporaries. Presents some of the contexts to which his writing was responding. Contains an extensive bibliography and an index.

Honan, Park. *Matthew Arnold: A Life*. New York: McGraw-Hill, 1981. The definitive biography of Arnold, accessible to the general reader and illuminating to the scholar. Most of this biographical information had never before appeared in print. The biography is lively, as well as thoroughly researched and documented. Includes a generous index.

Neiman, Fraser. *Matthew Arnold*. New York: Twayne, 1968. This fine introduction to Arnold's wide-ranging work presents only enough biographical information to give shape and meaning to the analysis of Arnold's writing. Presents the study of Arnold's thought as a way into the study of mid-Victorian thought. Includes a chronology and a brief annotated bibliography.

Trilling, Lionel. *Matthew Arnold*. New York: W. W. Norton, 1939. Rev. ed. New York: Columbia University Press, 1949. This "intellectual biography" is an early but still unsurpassed study of Arnold's thought. Clear and insightful, it is the standard critical work on Arnold. Includes an extensive bibliography of early studies.

JOHN ASHBERY

Born: Rochester, New York; July 28, 1927

Principal poetry

Turandot and Other Poems, 1953; *Some Trees*, 1956; *The Tennis Court Oath*, 1962; *Rivers and Mountains*, 1966; *Selected Poems*, 1967; *The Double Dream of Spring*, 1970; *Three Poems*, 1972; *Self-Portrait in a Convex Mirror*, 1975; *Houseboat Days*, 1977; *As We Know*, 1979; *Shadow Train*, 1981; *A Wave*, 1984; *Selected Poems*, 1985; *April Galleons*, 1987; *Flow Chart*, 1991.

Other literary forms

A Nest of Ninnies (1969) is a humorous novel about middle-class American life written by John Ashbery in collaboration with James Schuyler. Ashbery has also produced a volume of art criticism, *Reported Sightings* (1989).

Achievements

John Ashbery won three major literary awards for *Self-Portrait in a Convex Mirror*: the National Book Award, the Pulitzer Prize, and the National Book Critics Circle Award. Ashbery has served as a member of two prestigious organizations, the American Academy and Institute of Arts and Letters and the National Academy of Arts and Sciences. Twice he has been honored with a Guggenheim Fellowship. In 1982 John Ashbery was awarded the Annual Fellowship of the Academy of American Poets, and in 1984 he received the important Bollingen Prize, awarded by Yale University. In 1985 he was named a winner of both a MacArthur Prize Fellowship and a Lenore Marshall/ Nation Poetry Prize.

Biography

Born in Rochester, New York, in 1927, John Lawrence Ashbery grew up in rural Sodus, New York. He attended Deerfield Academy and Harvard University, where he became friends with poet Kenneth Koch. Ashbery received his B.A. from Harvard in 1949 and his M.A. from Columbia University in 1951. After leaving university life, Ashbery worked for various publishers in New York City until he moved to Paris in 1955. He remained in Paris until 1965, writing for the *New York Herald Tribune*, *Art International*, and *Art News*. From 1965 until 1972 Ashbery worked as executive editor for *Art News* in New York, before becoming a distinguished professor of writing at the Brooklyn College campus of the City University of New York.

Analysis

As a brief review of his biography would suggest, John Ashbery has had a considerable amount of exposure to the world of art and to the language of art criticism. Ashbery spent a full decade of his life in Paris, the art capital of Europe, where he read deeply in French poetry and immersed himself in the day-to-day life of French culture. Readers of Ashbery's poetry, then, should not be surprised to encounter references to art and occasional snatches of the French language as part of the poetic texts. For example, one of his poems is entitled "Le Livre est sur la table." There are other titles in German, Latin, and Russian, and the poetry as a whole bristles with references from every department of highbrow, middlebrow, and lowbrow culture, including cartoons ("Daffy Duck in Hollywood"), silent movies ("The Lonedale Operator"), literature ("Sonnet," "A Long Novel," and "37 Haiku"), history ("The Tennis Court Oath"), and linguistics ("The Plural of 'Jack-in-the-Box'").

Because of its unpredictable style and subject matter, Ashbery's poetry has managed to infuriate, befuddle, amuse, delight, and instruct its readers. His work remains some of the most difficult verse produced at any time during the twentieth century, for he refuses to provide the reader with a poetic "reality" that is any less complex than the "reality" of the world outside of poetry. Ashbery cannot be simplified or paraphrased, because his work has no "content" in the ordinary sense. His poetry is "about" the act of knowing, the process of imagining, the curious associational leaps made by the human mind as it experiences any given moment in time. To read Ashbery is to be teased into a whole range of possible meanings without finally settling on a single one. Although this openness might confuse the reader at the outset, the process of reading Ashbery becomes more pleasurable on each encounter. New meanings appear, and Ashbery's voice comes to seem strangely present, as if he were intoning directly into the reader's ear. These poems are filled with little verbal cues and signals aimed directly at the reader; many of the poems depend upon a complicated dialogue or interplay between the author and the reader (a technique he exploits masterfully in *Three Poems*). Thus his work is a kind of half-poetry, always requiring an active reader to make it whole. Ashbery achieves his trademark effect of apparent intimacy while simulating the very process of thought itself.

How Ashbery came to create this new kind of poetry is actually a subchapter in the general history of art and culture in the twentieth century. Certainly he benefited mightily from his study of other artists and thinkers. During his formative years in Paris, he absorbed the French language and the famous paintings of the Louvre while immersing himself in all kinds of printed matter: cheap pamphlets and paperback novels bought from the bookstalls, as well as journalistic prose (in French and English) and the rarefied language of art criticism (which he himself was producing).

In addition, it is clear that a strong line of influence connects Ashbery with writers such as Gertrude Stein, who used disjointed syntax and unorthodox grammar as part of her surrealistic poetry. He owes a clear debt also to Wallace Stevens, who taught him how to philosophize in poetry and also how to approach subjects obliquely. Stevens, also, was a great lover of French Impressionist painting and Symbolist poetry. From W. H. Auden, who chose Ashbery's *Some Trees* for the Yale Series of Younger Poets, Ashbery learned a conversational naturalness and a lyrical or musical way of phrasing. It might be argued that Ashbery, as a literate artist, was influenced by all the great thinkers of the century, but these poetic debts seem particularly obvious, especially in the early books. He probably learned something from Ludwig Wittgenstein's idea of language as a game, just as he must have responded to Jackson Pollock's expressionist paintings, which use paint in much the same way that Ashbery uses words. Something of the sheer shock value and unpredictability of musicians such as Igor Stravinsky, John Cage, and Anton Webern must have touched him also, since Ashbery is clearly fond of similar effects in his own poems.

These debts to the artistic pioneers of the twentieth century are most obvious in Ashbery's earlier books—that is, those preceding the publication of *Three Poems* (1972): *Some Trees* (1956), *The Tennis Court Oath* (1962), and *Rivers and Mountains* (1966). All these books are relatively short and compact, typically containing one long or major poem, often positioned near the end of the volume.

In *The Tennis Court Oath*, the reader encounters the long quasi-epical poem entitled "Europe," a work related in overall form to T. S. Eliot's *The Waste Land* (1922) and to similar efforts by Ezra Pound, Hart Crane, and William Carlos Williams. In the most general terms, "Europe" here means the accumulated cultural wealth of European history and its ability—or inability—to help the creative artist in the twentieth century. The decay, or "wasteland," of Europe is juxtaposed to or "intercut" (in filmic terms) with a trivial story of two travelers, Pryor and Collins, whose unheroic status stands in sharp contrast to the old order. As the poem begins, the poet registers all these complex feelings, while focusing on the shocking blueness of the morning sky, here presented surrealistically:

> To employ her
> construction ball
> Morning fed on the
> light blue wood
> of the mouth

The wrecking-ball of construction crews is one of the most visible symbols of the typical cityscape, suggesting simultaneously the twin processes of de-creation and re-creation. The sudden, destructive impact of the steel ball approximates the elemental power of the morning light as it, too, rearranges and alters the city and all of its facets. The bystander is left open-mouthed and speechless, like the sky itself. This analysis does not fully explicate Ashbery's lines, because, like all dream imagery, they resist final explication. One can describe their suggestiveness and allusiveness, but the dream itself remains a mystery, as does this purely perceived moment of an ordinary morning in the city.

More typical of Ashbery's later poems are "The Instruction Manual" (from *Some Trees*) and the title poem from *Rivers and Mountains,* each of which forces the reader to perform another kind of imaginative leaping, one that is different from the mere shock of the surreal. In "The Instruction Manual," the speaker is bored with his job of writing an instruction manual on the uses of a new metal and, instead, falls into a prolonged aesthetic daydream on the city of Guadalajara, Mexico, which he has never visited. He invents this city in magical detail for the rest of the poem. In like manner, the places described on a map and the map itself become utterly indistinguishable in "Rivers and Mountains," as if Ashbery were suggesting that one's most vivid moments are those that have been rescued or resurrected by the fertile powers of the poetic imagination. Ashbery always emphasizes the primacy of the imagination. In his view, the most vivid reality occurs in the poem itself, because that is the precise point where the inner and outer (spiritual and sensory) experiences of life actually intersect.

Two more of the early poems bear analysis here, because they also illustrate the poetic techniques favored in many of Ashbery's later poems. "Le Livre est sur la table" and "The Picture of Little J. A. in a Prospect of Flowers" (both found in *Some Trees*) are magnificent feats of imaginative power, and each operates on the same principle of aesthetic meditation. In each poem, the poet looks at reality through a work of art, or as if it were a work of art (in "The Picture of Little J. A." a photograph is the medium). The effect is largely the same, because the world is always transformed and made into a work of art by the conclusion of the poem. Wallace Stevens is probably the model for this kind of poem, in such works as "Thirteen Ways of Looking at a Blackbird" and "A Study of Two Pears." Other poets, particularly William Carlos Williams, Marianne Moore, and Elizabeth Bishop, were to involve themselves passionately in the writing of aesthetically oriented poems, and one can look to some of their pioneering work to explain the sureness and control of Ashbery's similar efforts.

In "Le Livre est sur la table," Ashbery offers the reader a number of aesthetic propositions to contemplate, the most important of which is the notion that beauty results from a certain emptiness, or from the placement of an object in an unusual or unaccustomed position. In both instances, the viewer is forced to see the object in a new way. Ashbery again underlines the power of the imagination, giving the example of an imaginary woman who comes alive in her stride, her hair, and her breasts as she is imagined. Most important of all is the artist who creates small artistic catalysts, new and strange relationships that haunt the perceiver with their beauty. Neither the sea nor a simple birdhouse can make for innovative art, but placing them together in a fundamental relationship changes them forever:

> The young man places a bird-house
> Against the blue sea. He walks away
> And it remains. Now other
> Men appear, but they live in boxes.

The men in the boxes are the nonartists, who do not realize that the newly created sea is a highlighted thing. All along, the sea has been "writing" a message (with its waves and lines), but only the "young man" (the artist) can read it.

The other "young man," or artist figure, in *Some Trees* is Ashbery himself, described in the snapshot that serves as the aesthetic focal point for the autobiographical poem "The Picture of Little J. A. in a Prospect of Flowers." He has a head like a mushroom and stands comically before a bed of phlox, but this little fellow has the makings of a poet precisely because he appreciates the value of words—especially lost words, those tip-of-the-tongue utterances, and slips of the tongue, where the speaker strains to specify clear meaning. "The Picture of Little J. A. in a Prospect of Flowers" is a typical Ashbery performance, not merely because of its high aesthetic theme but also because of its inclusion of low comedy, irony, and parody. The epigraph (taken from Boris Pasternak's *A Safe-Conduct*, 1931) seemingly contradicts the rest of the poem in what is the first of many jokes (Dick and Jane of childhood books become Dick and Genevieve, conversing in complicated Elizabethan sentences). Childhood is full of jokes and embarrassments, like standing in front of the clicking shutter of a camera, but childhood can also be the beginning of the artist's journey: The poem ends by praising the imagination and its ability to rescue this early phase of life through the power of words. "The Picture of Little J. A. in a Prospect of Flowers" is a bittersweet portrait of the self-conscious and precocious young man who was destined to become a great artist.

Some of that greatness is evident on nearly every page of the book that many critics cite as Ashbery's masterpiece: *Three Poems*, a long, meditative work composed of three interlocking prose poems, "The New Spirit," "The System," and "The Recital," totaling 118 densely packed pages of text. Most of that text is written in prose, a highly interactive prose that constantly urges the reader forward, raises questions, voices doubts and suspicions, and generally plunges the reader headlong into a highly meditative process of thinking and reflecting. *Three Poems* is Ashbery at his most difficult and most satisfying, even though there is virtually no story or tidy paraphrase that can be made of the reading experience itself. Nevertheless, a few elusive details do emerge, and one dimly begins to realize that *Three Poems* is an oblique narrative that in general terms charts a deep relationship between two lovers, one that somehow flounders, so that the narrator grows more and more self-possessed. The narrator becomes less and less likely to address the familiar "you" who is called upon again and again in the opening pages of the book. By the end the "you" has virtually disappeared, as if the loss of love might be charted by the absence of the "you" from pages where only the "I" can finally dominate.

The form of *Three Poems* deserves some attention, because the poems are cast in the form of prose, though their imagery, tonal shifts, and complicated rhythms all suggest poetic (not prosaic) form. To complicate matters even further, Ashbery originally published the second section of the work, "The System," in the *Paris Review* in 1971, the year before the whole work appeared in the form of a book. Ashbery specifically allowed "The System" to be published as a prose work, so by titling the whole three-part composition *Three Poems*, he seems to be teasing the reader again on the simplest level and at the same time calling attention to the arbitrariness of literary labels and taxonomy. As if all those complications were not enough, Ashbery carries the joke further by inserting several poems (or at least texts that look like poems) into the texture of the longer work. What counts in the end is the sustained act of meditation and empathy with the narrator which these manipulations of typeface and marginal format will induce in the reader.

The reader, facing *Three Poems*, has a Herculean task to perform: absorbing a long, oblique narrative that requires constant reflection, analysis, and thoughtful meditation. The difficulty is an intentional by-product of Ashbery's stated goal on the first page of the book: to leave out as much as possible in order to create a newer and truer form of communication. Any love story the reader could have encountered would have finally become banal; what Ashbery gives, however, cannot grow stale. To read *Three Poems* is to invent on every page the pain and exaltation that make up the essence of a love story. In that way, the "private" person of the book remains mysterious, as all lovers essentially must remain. Thus, one cannot summarize Ashbery's love story, but one can experience it vicariously.

In "The System," the second and most difficult part of the poem, the narrator becomes utterly preoccupied with himself. In "The New Spirit" even small details of urban life were associated with something the beloved had said or done; here, however, the details and the lover have disappeared. Instead, the narrator is trapped in a kind of mental rat-maze, or "system." In one memorable passage, he imagines the members of the human race boarding a train, which is, of course, their whole life. No one has any idea where the train is going or how fast it is moving. The passengers are ignorant of their journey and—the narrator insists—ignorant of their fundamental situation. The very core of their being is ignorance, yet they fail to recognize this crucial fact. Hence, the narrator views them with contempt.

Three Poems concludes on a lighter note, literal notes of music, which offer a kind of deliverance for the narrator, who has been trapped in the labyrinth of his doleful thoughts. "The Recital" is important because Ashbery often sees music as an analogue to poetry. Indeed, at one point he had planned to become a musician, and music has remained a rich source of inspiration throughout his career. The power of music and its essential abstractness make a powerful appeal to the narrator, who at this juncture is exhausted by his Hamlet-like speculations. The poem ends, and with it the whole book, with a description of the power of music (and of art)—the power to inspire new beginnings and new possibilities. In a final jest, Ashbery offers the reader an ending that is actually a beginning: "There were new people watching and waiting, conjugating in this way the distance and emptiness, transforming the scarcely noticeable bleakness into something both intimate and noble." With this brilliant virtuoso effect, Ashbery concludes a poem that is at once a continuance of the great Western tradition of meditative writing (one that includes Saint John of the Cross and Sir Thomas Browne)—and a dramatically arresting rendition of how it feels to be alive in the last decades of the twentieth century. The old and the new come together in a synthesis that is as disturbing, fascinating, and elusive as the century that produced it.

Having reached a kind of artistic plateau with *Three Poems*, Ashbery's career took a new direction. In many ways, *Three Poems* occupies the kind of position in his life that *The Waste Land* did for Eliot. Both works explore psychological traumas and deeply sustained anguish; both plumb the depths of despair until a kind of spiritual nadir is reached. After Eliot completed *The Waste Land*, his work took on a new, spiritual dimension, culminating in the complex Christian poem he called *Four Quartets* (1943). Ashbery's work also changed after the publication of *Three Poems*, but he has not embraced Christian or even theistic belief; he has always insisted on a kind of agnostic or even atheistic vision of life, in which art supplants all conventional notions of divinity. Nevertheless, like Eliot, he has passed through the proverbial dark night of the soul, and his work after *Three Poems* is somehow more confident, less self-consciously experimental, and less opaque. The newer poetry is still impossible to paraphrase, but it is much more accessible and more readable (at least on first sight) than the most extravagant of the early poems, and its subject matter generally seems more central to human experience.

All these tendencies culminate in a book that won the National Book Award, the Pulitzer Prize, and the National Book Critics Circle Award, *Self-Portrait in a Convex Mirror* (1975). Those prizes and the book itself helped to put Ashbery on the literary map, so that he could no longer be summarily dismissed as an eccentric aesthete turning out brilliant but inaccessible work. Readers began to look more closely at what Ashbery was saying and to embrace his message (however complex) as never before.

"Self-Portrait in a Convex Mirror," the title poem, is a brilliant piece of autobiographical writing that does not reveal gritty details of Ashbery's personal life so much as his opinions about art and its power to transform the artist. Self-portraits are as old as art itself, but Ashbery as an art critic and former expatriate had encountered some especially powerful examples of the genre. He must have encountered the great self-portraits of Rembrandt van Rijn and Vincent Van Gogh, but the particular work that inspired this poem is a famous masterpiece of the High Renaissance, *Self-Portrait in a Convex Mirror* (1524) by Parmigianino (Girolamo Francesco Maria Mazzola), which now hangs in the Kunsthistorisches Museum in Vienna. Ashbery tells the reader that he encountered Parmigianino's famous painting in the summer of 1959, during a visit to Vienna. Parmigianino's self-portrait is uniquely circular in overall form and, as the title suggests, resulted from the artist's close inspection of his visage in a convex mirror, an optical device that creates interesting distortions of scale and distance. Parmigianino's hand, for example, is grossly exaggerated and dominates the foreground of the painting, while his head seems undersized and nearly childlike. It is possible that the Italian artist's childlike appearance appealed to Ashbery because it reminded him of the snapshot of little John Ashbery that had inspired his earlier, much shorter autobiographical lyric, "The Picture of Little J. A. in a Prospect of Flowers."

It is in the nature of self-portraits, then, to conceal and reveal simultaneously—hence the appropriateness of the convex mirror, whose powers of transformation and distortion apply equally to Parmigianino and Ashbery. The poet begins the poem by quoting and paying homage to Vasari, the first great art critic (Ashbery, too, had been an art critic at the time he saw the painting in Venice). Vasari explains the complicated arrangements that preceded Parmigianino's actual painting: the use of a barber's convex mirror and the necessity of having a carpenter prepare the circular wooden substratum of the painting. These operations are mere preliminaries, however, to the much more important work of the eyes themselves once the painting has been set up. The eyes cannot penetrate the artificial depth created by this strange mirroring device; therefore, everything that results is a kind of speculation—a word that derives from the Latin word for mirror, *speculum*, as Ashbery points out. Thus in the self-portrait one kind of "mirroring" leads to another; what one sees is not precisely what is there. To hold the paradox in the mind is to enter the world of the artist.

The argument that Ashbery then goes on to develop may perhaps be summarized by the adagelike statement that stability (or order) can be maintained in the presence of instability (or chaos). The movements of time, weather, Ping-Pong balls, and tree branches are all potentially elements for the synthesizing and harmonizing power of art, no matter if it distorts something in the process. Perhaps the greatest distortion is that of stability; the stable simply cannot be found in nature, as Isaac Newton showed through his laws of thermodynamics. It is only in the mirror of art (a symbol also favored by William Shakespeare) that stability, order, and form may thrive. Since all art is by definition artificial, then, stability is an artifice, too.

Nevertheless, artistic stability is all the artist and the race of human beings can rely upon to reveal meaning in an otherwise meaningless space. So Parmigianino's Renaissance painting, like all art, is applicable to all future generations, and Ashbery borrows Parmigianino's technique of mirroring until the world seems to spin around him in a merry-go-round of papers, books, windows, trees, photographs, and a desk, and "real life" itself becomes a kind of trick painting. Addressing the Italian master, Ashbery admits that the "uniform substance" or order in his life derives from the Italian genius: "My guide in these matters is your self."

He goes on to quote a contemporary art critic, Sydney Freedberg, who finds the idealized beauty and formal feeling of Parmigianino's self-portrait to depend on the very chaos Ashbery had earlier described. For Freedberg this instability is a collection of bizarre, unsettling aspects of reality which somehow the painting enfolds and harmonizes.

Readers might at this point recall similar discussions—though in radically different language—by John Keats, especially in his great meditation on art, "Ode on a Grecian Urn," which asks the reader to accept art precisely because it transforms the chaos and changeability of human life. Ultimately, this process results in a complete fusion of truth (or reality) and beauty (or art), in Keats's formulation. Ashbery is not Keats, but one has to note the similar posture of the two poets, both contemplating the power of art, both commencing with an art object (the Grecian urn and the Italian self-portrait) and concluding on a note of affirmation. For Ashbery the power of art is not only magnificent but terrifying, like a pistol primed for Russian roulette with only one bullet in the chamber. The art has the potential to "kill" our old perceptions. Some people might consider this power to be only a dream, but for Ashbery the power remains, and art becomes a kind of "waking dream" in the same unhappy world of human beings that Keats evokes in "Ode on a Grecian Urn." Even in the city, which Ashbery imagines as an insect with multifaceted eyes, art somehow survives. He envisions each person as a potential artist holding a symbolic piece of chalk, ready to begin a new self-portrait.

Ashbery continues with this more accessible (and essentially more affirmative) kind of poetry in the volume *Houseboat Days*, the title poem of which likens the mind and its vast storehouse of memory to a boardinghouse that is open to everyone, taking in boarders of every possible type and description. This metaphorical way of describing the sensory, intellectual, and imaginative powers of human beings is a valuable clue for understanding another poem in the volume, one of Ashbery's wittiest and most polished performances, "Daffy Duck in Hollywood"—a poem that manages to be tender, lyrical, comic, outrageous, and serious without losing its sense of direction. An obscure opera serves as a kind of grid or structural framework for this rather freewheeling poem. The poem begins with a stupefyingly absurd collection of mental odds and ends, the flotsam and jetsam of a highly cultured and sophisticated mind that also appreciates the artifacts of popular culture: an Italian opera, Rumford's Baking Powder, Speedy Gonzales, Daffy Duck, Elmer Fudd, the Gadsden Purchase, Anaheim (California), pornographic photographs, and the comic-strip character Skeezix. All these apparent irrelevancies are entirely relevant, because they illustrate the random nature of the mind, its identity as a stream of consciousness. Yet these items are also a kind of dodge or subterfuge to block out images of a significant other, possibly a lover. Because of the odd way the mind works through the principle of association, however, these same cartoonlike images also remind the narrator of that other person.

As in so many of his other poems, Ashbery is again insisting that the only reality is the one we make, and he concludes by wisely noting that no one knows all the dimensions of this mental life or where the parts fit in. The goal, in Ashbery's opinion, is to keep "ambling" on; thus, each person might remain "intrigued" and open to all the extravagant invitations of life. The mind, with its interminable image-making, is strangely cut off from life, but when used properly (that is, aesthetically) it can lay hold of the abundant and unanticipated gifts that always surround and endow impoverished human beings.

This optimistic vein is apparent in most of *A Wave*, but especially in the title poem, which seems to contrast crests of positive feelings with troughs of despair. The poem is a long discursive work in which Ashbery plays variations on one essential theme: that a fundamental feeling of security (not to be confused with superficial happiness), a deep and abiding sense of the goodness of life, can, in fact, sustain the person through the pain that life will inevitably bring. In this poem human beings do have final control of their destiny, because they are supported by something powerfully akin to older notions of grace or faith. Having this power or "balm," as Ashbery terms it, no one is ever really stripped of autonomy: "we cannot be really naked/ Having this explanation."

This mood of sustained hope continues in the exquisitely lyrical *April Galleons* (1987), a book that, like *Houseboat Days*, relies on the metaphor of a boat as a vehicle for psychological as well as physical travel. Included is "Ice Storm," a poem that is highly original yet somehow manages to echo Robert Frost (especially "Birches" and "Design"). As Frost did in "Birches," Ashbery describes winter ice in glittering detail. As Frost did in "Design," Ashbery questions the fate of small things that are out of their accustomed places, such as the rose he stumbles upon, growing beside a path entirely out of season. Yet none of these matters disturbs him fundamentally, because he is beginning to get his "bearings in this gloom and see how [he] could improve on the distraught situation all around me, in the darkness and tarnished earth."

In one fashion or another John Ashbery's poetry has, indeed, improved the distraught situation of everyday life. A clear pattern of spiritual and artistic growth unifies Ashbery's work from the earliest books, such as *Some Trees* and *Rivers and Mountains*, to later ones such as *Three Poems* and *Self-Portrait in a Convex Mirror*. In all these books Ashbery has been the tireless experimenter, the poetic innovator who writes without any true peer. His voice is unique, and readers respond to that unpredictable, playful, moody, meditative voice because it speaks a kind of truth that one hears rarely, if at all—the truth of a mind that still lives in a world of wonder. With Ashbery there is no limit to the possibilities inherent in human life. Regular readers of Ashbery will begin to inhabit a world that is larger, more unpredictable, and infinitely more interesting than anything they have known before.

Daniel L. Guillory

Other major works

LONG FICTION: *A Nest of Ninnies*, 1969 (with James Schuyler).

PLAYS: *Everyman*, 1951; *The Heroes*, 1953; *The Compromise: Or, Queen of the Carabou*, 1956; *The Philosopher*, 1964; *Three Plays*, 1978.

NONFICTION: *Reported Sightings*, 1989.

TRANSLATIONS: *Murder in Montarte*, 1960; *Melville*, 1960; *The Deadlier Sex*, 1961; *Alberto Giocometti*, 1971.

Bibliography

Carroll, Paul. *The Poem in Its Skin*. Chicago: Follett, 1968. One of the very first books of poetry criticism to include a chapter on the poetry of Ashbery, Carroll's study contains a brilliant chapter entitled "If Only He Had Left the Finland Station," which explores one of the poet's early surrealist poems, "Leaving the Atocha Station." Carroll guides the reader through many possible responses to Ashbery.

Howard, Richard. *Alone with America: Essays on the Art of Poetry in the United States Since 1950*. Enl. ed. New York: Atheneum, 1980. Richard Howard's essay on Ashbery in this landmark study of contemporary poetry, "You May Never Know How Much Is Pushed Back into the Night, Nor What May Return," has two important virtues: it shows sensitivity to Ashbery's French and European sources, and, since Howard is a fellow poet, there is a genuine appreciation of Ashbery's phrasing, rhythm, and craftsmanship.

Keller, Lynn. *Re-making It New: Contemporary Poetry and the Modernist Tradition*. New York: Cambridge University Press, 1987. "'We Must, We Must Be Moving On': Ashbery's Divergence from Stevens and Modernism" is the title of the very clearly written and cogently argued chapter in which Keller shows both Ashbery's debt to and divergence from Stevens, as well as his use of surrealism.

Kermani, David K. *John Ashbery: A Comprehensive Bibliography, Including His Art Criticism, and with Selected Notes from Unpublished Materials.* New York: Garland, 1976. Ashbery actually wrote the foreword to this book, an indispensable reference tool for beginning or advanced students of Ashbery's work. This book makes an excellent companion to his *Reported Sightings* (a collection of the poet's art criticism).

Ross, Andrew. *The Failure of Modernism: Symptoms of American Poetry.* New York: Columbia University Press, 1986. An excellent analysis of doubt and self-reflection in Ashbery's poetry, Ross's long chapter "Doubting John Thomas" also shows interesting connections between Ashbery and such diverse writers as John Ruskin, Lawrence Sterne, and Henry James. Ross's comments on "Self-Portrait in a Convex Mirror" are particularly astute.

Shapiro, David. *John Ashbery: An Introduction to the Poetry.* New York: Columbia University Press, 1979. If students could read only one book on the poetry of Ashbery, then Shapiro's study would be an excellent choice: it is clearly written, intelligently organized, and generously documented. The book covers most of the early books and dwells considerably on *Some Trees, Three Poems,* and *Self-Portrait in a Convex Mirror.* This book has an excellent index and a short biography and bibliography.

Vendler, Helen H. *The Music of What Happens: Poems, Poets, and Critics.* Cambridge, Mass.: Harvard University Press, 1988. Vendler writes persuasively about Ashbery's subject matter, which she sees as similar to that of the great poet Keats. In her chapter on Ashbery and Louise Glück, she provides an especially detailed analysis of *Shadow Train* and *A Wave.*

MARGARET ATWOOD

Born: Ottawa, Ontario, Canada; November 18, 1939

Principal poetry

Double Persephone, 1961; *The Circle Game*, 1966; *The Animals in That Country*, 1968; *Procedures for Underground*, 1970; *The Journals of Susanna Moodie*, 1970; *Power Politics*, 1971; *You Are Happy*, 1974; *Selected Poems*, 1976; *Two Headed Poems*, 1978; *True Stories*, 1981; *Interlunar*, 1984; *Selected Poems II: Poems Selected and New, 1976-1986*, 1986; *Margaret Atwood: Selected Poems 1966-1984*, 1990.

Other literary forms

Margaret Atwood's publishing history is a testimonial to her remarkable productivity and versatility as a writer. As well as poet, she is novelist, short-fiction writer, children's author, editor, and essayist. *The Edible Woman* (1969), Atwood's first novel, defined the focus of her fiction: mainly satirical explorations of sexual politics, where self-deprecating female protagonists defend themselves against males, chiefly with the weapon of language. Other novels are *Surfacing* (1972), *Lady Oracle* (1976), *Life Before Man* (1979), *Bodily Harm* (1981), and *Cat's Eye* (1988). *The Handmaid's Tale* (1985), a dystopian novel set in a postnuclear, monotheocratic Boston where life is restricted by censorship and state control of reproduction, is the best known of Atwood's seven novels and was made into a commercial film of the same title, directed by Volker Schlondorff. *Dancing Girls and Other Stories* (1977) and *Bluebeard's Egg* (1983) are books of short fiction. Atwood has written three children's books: *Up in the Tree* (1978), which she also illustrated, *Anna's Pet* (1980), and *For the Birds* (1990).

Atwood's contributions to literary theory and criticism have also been significant. Her idiosyncratic, controversial, but well-researched *Survival: A Thematic Guide to Canadian Literature* (1972) is essential for the student interested in Atwood's version of the themes that have shaped Canadian creative writing over a century. Her *Second Words* (1982) is one of the first works of the feminist criticism that has since flourished in Canada.

Achievements

Critical success and national and international acclaim have greeted Margaret Atwood's work since her first major publication, the poetry collection *The Circle Game* (1966). Poems from that collection were awarded the 1965 President's Medal for Poetry by the University of Western Ontario in 1966, and after commercial publication the collection won for Atwood the prestigious Governor-General's Award for poetry in 1967. In that same year,

Atwood's *The Animals in That Country*, her second poetry collection, was awarded first prize in Canada's Centennial Commission Poetry Competition. The Chicago periodical *Poetry* awarded Atwood the Union Prize in 1969 and the Bess Hoskins Prize in 1974. Since that time Atwood's numerous awards and distinctions have been more for her work in fiction, nonfiction, and humanitarian affairs. She has received several honorary doctorates and many prestigious prizes, among them the Toronto Arts Award (1986), *Ms.* magazine's Woman of the Year for 1986, the Ida Nudel Humanitarian Award from the Canadian Jewish Congress, and the American Humanist of the Year Award for 1987.

Biography

Margaret Atwood was born into a family that encouraged inquiry and discovery. An important stimulus to her intellectual curiosity was certainly the family's yearly sojourns in the remote bush of northern Ontario and Quebec, where Atwood's father, an entomologist, carried out much of his study and research. It is likely in this environment that Atwood's ironic vision and her imagery were shaped. Atwood's writing, especially her poetry and her second novel, *Surfacing*, are permeated with her intimate knowledge of natural history and with her perception of the casual brutality with which the weak are sacrificed for the survival of the strong.

Studying between 1957 and 1961 for her undergraduate degree in English at Victoria College, University of Toronto, Atwood came under the influence of Canadian poet Jay MacPherson and especially of Northrop Frye, one of the twentieth century's preeminent critical theorists. They encouraged Atwood's early poetry and directed her toward biblical and mythological symbol and archetype, still strong shaping forces in her writing.

Between 1961 and 1963, Atwood did postgraduate studies in English at Harvard University, receiving her M.A. in 1962. In 1963, she met fellow graduate student James Polk, whom she married in 1967, when, after a period of working, writing, and teaching, Atwood returned to Harvard to pursue a Ph.D. (beginning thesis work on the English metaphysical romance). In Canada, however, her burgeoning success as a writer and her involvement as a university teacher of creative writing soon superseded her formal studies.

In the early 1970's, Atwood traveled in Europe and then returned to Canada to continue writing and teaching. She became an editor at House of Anansi Press, one of the many Canadian publishing houses that sprang up in the fertile late 1960's to encourage young, often-experimental writers. She also met novelist Graeme Gibson, who may have influenced her own foray into experimental fiction, *Surfacing*. After her divorce from James Polk in 1973, Atwood moved with Gibson to rural Alliston, Ontario, where their daughter Jess was born in 1976.

Throughout the 1980's, Atwood's output was steady, though not in new poetry, from which she seems to have evolved away. In the latter 1980's, Atwood made successful forays into the field of scriptwriting for film and the musical theater. Her increased involvement with world social and political issues is evident in her vice-chairmanship of the Writers' Union of Canada and her presidency of P.E.N. International, where she has done vigorous battle against literary censorship. Her association with Amnesty International has prompted an increasingly strong expression of her moral vision. She has continued to publish regularly in Canadian, American, and European media and has received worldwide recognition as a major contemporary writer.

Analysis

Margaret Atwood's poetry deals essentially with paradox and struggle in both art and life. Her first (and now generally inaccessible) chapbook of poetry, *Double Persephone*, contains the components of her vision, which she elucidates in her next nine poetry collections with more depth, conviction, and stylistic maturity, but whose elements she changes little. An overview of Atwood's poetry reveals patterns expressed through mythological and biblical allusion and recurring imagery relating to mutability, metamorphosis, near-annihilation, and, ultimately, adaptation and definition. References to eyes, water, mirrors, glass, photographs, maps, and charts abound. The archetypal journey/quest motif is a vital component of Atwood's vision. It is worked out metaphorically in the historical context of European exploration and settlement of the Canadian wilderness, the pioneer's battle with alienation, loneliness, and the struggle to articulate a new self in a new world. If he masters the new "language," he will survive; his divided self will become whole. This life-and-death struggle is also carried out in the psychological arena of sexual politics. Much of Atwood's poetry (especially *Procedures for Underground* and *Power Politics*) explores—at first with anger, later with resignation, always with irony—the damage that men and women inflict on one another despite their interdependence. In Atwood's poetry, chaos is perceived as the center of things; it is the individual's quest, as both artist and natural being, to define order, meaning, and purpose—to survive.

The Circle Game, Atwood's first major poetry collection, represents the outset of an artistic and personal journey. The artist-poet (whose voice is personal, ironic, and female) struggles to shape chaos into order through language, whose enigmatic symbols she must master and control. Language is a set of tools, the key component of the poet's bag of tricks, packed for the (metaphoric) journey undertaken, for example, in *The Circle Game's* "Evening Trainstation Before Departure":

> Here I am in
> a pause in space
> hunched on the edge
> of a tense suitcase.

Yet language is duplicitous; it is a weapon that can rebound against the poet herself. She is engaged in a constant struggle to interpret and communicate without being subsumed, as suggested in "The Sybil": "she calls to me with the many/ voices of the children/ not I want to die/ but You must die."

In life, chaos comprises process, flux, the temporal; the struggle for the individual is both to understand her own nature and to reconcile herself to the processes of nature, history, and culture. The external, natural world mirrors the self; it speaks the siren language of the primitive and lies in wait to ambush with casual cruelty human beings' fragile civility. Through recognition, struggle, and reconciliation, the individual can transcend his destructive self, mirrored in the natural world. Throughout *The Circle Game*, the self, both artistic and psychological, struggles to be born. The creative impulse is strong, the instinct for survival great, but *The Circle Game*'s "Journey to the Interior" says that the individual does not yet understand the ambiguous messages of either art or life and is in danger: "and words here are as pointless/ as calling in a vacant/wilderness."

The opening poem, "This Is a Photograph of Me," presents a paradox. In the photograph, the speaker's image is barely discernible, suspended as if in a watery grave, yet awaiting redefinition, new birth: "I am in the lake, in the center/ of the picture, just under the surface." In "Camera," the artist is reviled for the impulse to capture life in a static form when the impulse to the kinesis, the process of life, is so compelling: "Camera man/ how can I love your glass eye? . . . that small black speck/ travelling towards the horizon/ at almost the speed of life/ is me." Who is "me"? It is the androgynous, divided self, defined metaphorically in the powerful poem "After the Flood, We." "We" are Deucalion and Phyrra, in Greek mythology the sole male and female survivors of the mythic flood, suspended over the misty shapelessness of the drowned old world, designated by Zeus as the only humans deserving of survival. The female speaker differentiates between "I" and "you," "you" being an intimate who is here (as elsewhere throughout Atwood's poetry) the male. These two are charged with creating a new world. The self-absorbed male is a casual progenitor, "tossing small pebbles/ at random over your shoulder," but the female persona perceives horror, a Frankenstein's monster rising up to overwhelm "the beauty of the morning." The threat to process and growth, both artistic and personal, is the strongest of perceived evils. A sense that the artist-speaker is not yet equal to the task, has not yet found the appropriate language, is particularly strong in "The Messenger," where "a random face/ revolving outside the window" fades into oblivion because, the poem's ironic tone implies, the message is brought to the inappropriate recipient; the messenger shouts "desperate messages with his/ obliterated mouth/ in a silent language."

In *The Circle Game*, a game motif is evident in the titles and metaphoric significance of several poems ("Playing Cards," "An Attempted Solution for

Chess Problems," and the collection's title poem). Intelligence, even cunning, is required. Knowing the divided self is the key to becoming the artist fit to pass on the message vital for survival. The collection's final poem, "The Settlers," suggests that perhaps success will come in laying the foundation for future understanding. The poet-narrator optimistically envisions their transformation through natural evolution into messages for the future, though understanding is still in doubt: "children run, with green/ smiles (not knowing/ where)." As yet the tools, the language, are lacking. The simple innocence of a children's circle game becomes weighted with foreboding; critic Rosemary Sullivan observes, "The narcissism of the circle game claims the narrator, and confines Atwood herself in its prisoning rhythms. We have yet to see the circle effectively broken."

The journey of discovery continues in *The Animals in That Country* and is undertaken in several metaphorical arenas: the natural, the historical, the cultural, and, above all, the arena of the self. Again, the artist-self is found wanting. Several poems such as "Provisions" and "The Surveyors" suggest that the pioneer brings the wrong equipment to the new world because he or she has a faulty concept of the terrain and its natural inhabitants. Later generations distance themselves as soon as possible from the natural interrelationship of human and animals, the hunt being transformed into a ritualized game and then an irrelevance, as the collection's title poem points out.

Self-definition in a modern cultural setting also eludes the speaker in this collection's poems. At its writing, Atwood was on the second of her two sojourns at Harvard. Her own dislocation in American society and her distaste (expressed in letters to friends and colleagues in Canada) for American materialism and the accelerating Vietnam War are expressed in poems such as "The Landlady" and "It Is Dangerous to Read Newspapers." Her sense of alienation, from both place and people, is sadly noted in "Roominghouse, Winter": "Tomorrow, when you come to dinner/ They will tell you I never lived here." An ironic view emerges in an encounter with a relief map of Canada in the poem "At the Tourist Centre in Boston." An increasingly irate narrator asks first herself and then the receptionist, "Do you see nothing/ watching you from under the water?// Was the sky ever that blue?// Who really lives there?" That series of ominous questions signals a return journey to the interior of both Canada and the still unmapped and undefined self.

The definitive exploration of humankind's relationship with the natural world, with history, and with their own warring selves takes place in two of the collection's most powerful poems, "A Night in the Royal Ontario Museum" and "Progressive Insanities of a Pioneer." In the former, the speaker is inadvertently locked in the museum, "this crazed man-made/ stone brain," and is compelled to undergo a metaphoric journey to the beginnings of natural and human history. The worst horror to contemplate is preexistence, nondefinition: "I am dragged to the mind's/ deadend, . . . lost/ among the mastodons." In "Progressive Insanities of a Pioneer" this struggle to redefine the self out of chaos is explored in a metaphorical battle between a pioneer and the wilderness. In seven sections, or chapters, the story of the pioneer's failure unfolds relentlessly, the poem's flat and terse diction underscoring the horror of his descent into insanity and death. Seeking to impose order on the perceived chaos of his surroundings, the pioneer fails to acknowledge the necessity of adapting to the wilderness rather than subjugating it. He does not learn the language; instead, he makes a futile effort to structure, to classify. He is doomed to failure and annihilated, drowning in a metaphorical flux of Leviathan proportions.

Success in these parallel journeys both into the physical wilderness and into the self is achieved, however, by the persona who informs and narrates Atwood's next collection of poems, *The Journals of Susanna Moodie.* J. W. Dunbar Moodie and his wife Susanna were impoverished English gentry who emigrated to Canada in 1832 and took up a land grant in the bush near what is now Peterborough, Ontario. Their seven-year sojourn in the bush before they settled in the town of Belleville was a searing experience for Susanna. Steeped in nineteenth century Romanticism and possessing to no small degree the arrogance of her class, Susanna arrived in Canada with the rosy expectations of vulnerable people unscrupulously lured from home by the promise of bountiful land, a temperate climate, congenial neighbors, and best of all, freedom from taxation. The harsh reality of life in the wilderness destroyed many; Susanna, though, was able to draw on a previously untapped toughness of spirit that eventually turned her from a homesick gentlewoman into a selfsufficent, grudgingly loyal Canadian who contributed much to a fledgling Canadian culture. She recorded her experiences in a pair of accounts entitled *Roughing It in the Bush: Or, Forest Life in Canada* (1852) and *Life in the Clearings Versus the Bush* (1853). In them, readers detect a duality of her attitude and personality that Atwood exploits to advantage in *The Journals of Susanna Moodie.* In her contemplation of the physical and spiritual wildernesses that confront her, Susanna's fear and despair is evident, but so, increasingly, is a testy strength and a reluctant love for her new country.

The collection is divided into three sections that treat respectively Susanna's immigration, her sojourn in the bush, and her later years in Belleville and Toronto. Metaphorically, the "journals" chronicle the passages of Susanna's life: the rebirth and redefinition of the self that beginning in a new land requires; the trial by fire (in Susanna's case, literal) of life in the hostile wilderness; finally, reconciliation and death, where physical burial marks a spiritual intermingling with the new land, ironically becoming alien again through twentieth century urbanization.

In "Journal 1," Susanna repeatedly expresses the realization of her need for a new identity; familiar psychological landmarks are now irrelevant. In "Further Arrivals" she observes, "We left behind . . . our civilized/ distinctions// and entered a large darkness." At first she is threatened at every level, perceiving her husband as "the wereman," her "first neighbours" as "speaking a twisted dialect," and the wilderness as consciously malicious. Despite the familiar human instinct to order, catalog, and impose, Susanna recognizes the need for compromise: "Resolve: to be both tentative and hard to startle/ . . . in this area where my damaged knowing of the language means/ prediction is forever impossible." Susanna survives seven years of loneliness and physical hardship that transform her. She departs for Belleville with a sense that she does not yet fully understand her relationship with the wilderness. In "Departure from the Bush," she observes, "In time the animals/ arrived to inhabit me./ . . . There was something they almost taught me/ I came away not having learned." From the relatively civilized perspective of Belleville, Susanna contemplates the relationship between pioneer and wilderness with a mixture of bitterness and resignation. In the three "dream" poems of the "journal 2" section, she recognizes in the natural cycle the inexorable interrelationship of life and death (often violent) of which humankind is an integral part. Her own ambivalence is expressed in "The Double Voice": "Two voices/ took turns using my eyes"; while one saw "the rituals of seasons and rivers," the other pointed out "a dead dog/ jubilant with maggots." In "Journal 3," Susanna's reconciliation with her new self and with her harsh new land is completed; after her death, her defiant voice can still be heard over the roar of the twentieth century Toronto built over her bones. As Atwood says in the afterword to this collection, "Susanna Moodie has finally turned herself inside out, and has become the spirit of the land she once hated."

Having left Susanna Moodie speaking prophetically from her underground grave, Atwood made the underground the shaping metaphor of her next poetry collection, *Procedures for Underground*. She returns to a theme that dominated *The Circle Game*: the power of the artist to shape and articulate both internal and external experience. Critic Jerome Rosenberg reminds readers of Atwood's observation that artists who experience the creative process make "a descent to the underworld"; the artist's role is a mystical and powerful one (and perhaps subversive, the collection's title suggests). The artist persona is set apart from ordinary human relationships, as a seer is, by the ability to interpret experience outside the literal. In the title poem, the expectations of the artist blessed (or cursed) with second sight are grimly described: "Few will seek your help/ with love, none without fear."

The artist's compulsion to define, shape, interpret, and preserve permeates the collection's imagery. In "Three Desk Objects," the writer's tools are transformed by this purpose: "My cool machines/ . . . I am afraid to touch you/ I think you will cry out in pain// I think you will be warm, like skin." Many of the poems describe the capturing of images, meanings, and moments through a variety of artistic media. "Woman Skating" ends with "Over all I place/ a glass bell"; "Younger Sister, Going Swimming" has her dive recorded on the poet's paper; "Girl and Horse, 1928" and "Projected Slide of an Unknown Soldier" explore time and history through the "freeze-frame" of photography. Yet the artist fails to capture or interpret the "underground" aspect of the person. Human nature remains impenetrable, a language unlearned, a primeval mystery unsolved, as the poem "A Soul, Geologically" says. "Where do the words go/ when we have said them?" is the plaintive question in "A Small Cabin."

The most ominous note in the collection is struck by a poem that returns to the game motif of *The Circle Game* and makes a sad commentary on the passage from innocence to experience. In "Game After Supper," a memory of a happy children's game of twilight hide-and-seek turns macabre when the reader understands that the small child plays with spectral cousins long dead of diphtheria, and that the seeker is a threatening, anonymous male figure. "He will be an uncle,/ if we are lucky," comments the speaker wryly, but the sexual threat is clear, and the stage is set for the largely sexual struggle that provides the primary focus in Atwood's next collection. From here onward, her concern is more with external relationships; it is probably fair to say as well that this shift in focus marks the end of her most powerful work as a poet.

Power Politics, written when Atwood's first marriage was breaking up, focuses primarily on human relationships, though Atwood's parallel concerns with humans in natural and social history and with interpreting the dual self are also strongly present. Specifically, *Power Politics* chronicles the destructive love-hate relationship that can exist between incompatible men and women. In this pessimistic collection, signals are missed, messages are misinterpreted, the battle is mutually lost. The menacing, shadowy "tall man" of "Game After Supper" resolves into an aggrieved male partner; the anguished female speaker explores their inability to fulfill each other sexually, intellectually, or spiritually. The inevitable failure of the relationship is evident from the collection's terse, vicious (and gratuitous) opening epigram: "you fit into me/ like a hook into an eye// a fish hook/ an open eye." The poems' titles provide an inexorable chronology of descent from love through suspicion, mutual betrayal, and accusation to sad resignation and parting. Much of the imagery is of battle; in the central, seven-section poem "They Are Hostile Nations," battle lines are drawn despite a perceived mutual need: "Instead we are opposite, we/ touch as though attacking" Ultimately, the speaker blames herself for bringing to bear the weight of her expectations, emotional and artistic, on a partner unable to carry them. In "Hesitation Outside the Door," she addresses him sadly: "Get out while it is/ open, while you still can." Yet in the final poem, "He Is Last Seen," the speaker mourns her partner's seeming escape "towards firm ground and safety" and away from the still-unresolved conflict underlying all Atwood's poetry thus far: that of the divided, unreconciled self.

In *You Are Happy*, progress is made toward the resolution of this conflict. The ironic, pessimistic tone of *Power Politics* continues in the opening section. Human relationships fail once again for both emotional and artistic reasons; they cannot withstand the double assault of misunderstanding and misinterpretation. Imagery of water, ice, mirrors, eyes, and particularly cameras still prevails, as "Newsreel: Man and Firing Squad" shows: "No more of these closeups, this agony/ taken just for the record anyway." Yet in the collection's middle sections, "Songs of the Transformed" and "Circe/ Mud Poems," the limitations of art in controlling and interpreting human nature and behavior are confronted. Through the voice of the sorceress Circe, a compelling character in Homer's *Odyssey* (c. 800 B.C.) who transformed men into swine, Atwood acknowledges the limitations of mythmaking and the attraction of accepting life as it is, with its ambivalence and vitality: "I search instead for the others,/ the ones left over,/ the ones who have escaped from these/ mythologies with barely their lives." This positive realization is reiterated in the collection's last section. In "Late August," a new mood of voluptuous acceptance and fruitfulness is evident: "The air is still/ warm, flesh moves over/ flesh, there is no// hurry."

In this collection, too, Atwood's poetic skills show new direction. She intersperses her familiar spare, short poetic forms with more fluid prose poems. Indeed, the early 1970's marked the beginning of Atwood's shift away from poetry toward prose writing; the themes and imagery in many poems are explored more fully in novels from the same periods. There was a hiatus of four years until *Two-Headed Poems* appeared.

Interestingly, much of *Two-Headed Poems* relates closely in tone, theme, and imagery to *The Journals of Susanna Moodie*, but where the voice in the latter was objectified and dramatized as Moodie's, the voice in *Two-Headed Poems* is subjective and intimate. This relationship can perhaps be partly explained by the fact that Atwood gave birth to her daughter Jess in 1976, and her experience of motherhood is strongly reflected in this first collection of poems since her daughter's birth. There is a subtle softening of the irony of tone and vision and of terse diction, a perceptible turn toward acceptance rather than rejection. Now Atwood seems to have experienced personally, not only artistically, Moodie's sense of purpose and place in human history; Atwood too belongs to "the procession/ of old leathery mothers// passing the work from hand to hand,/ mother to daughter,// a long thread of red blood, not yet broken" ("A Red Shirt"). Poems such as "You Begin" reflect a renewed emotional and artistic purpose; "All Bread," with its motifs of sacrifice, sacrament, and Communion, expresses on one level acknowledgement of the rhythms of life and death inherent in nature, and on a parallel level the interdependence of the sexes, which marriage sanctifies. The poet has reconciled herself to the sometimes violent paradoxes that define life:

natural, human, and artistic.

That emerging attitude of acceptance is put to the test in *True Stories*. This collection is Atwood's poetic response to her increasing political commitment; its focus is even more external and marks a renewed emphasis on social themes less markedly evident in earlier collections such as *The Animals in That Country*. The generalized setting of many of the poems is the dusty, brutal and brutalized countries of the Caribbean and Central America. The central group of poems in *True Stories* deals with political torture: the description of actual tortures is graphic, horrifying, emphasized rather than undercut by the spare, brutal, direct diction and imagery of Atwood's poetic style. Whether the original accounts themselves are true is a question with which Atwood grapples. In the three groups of poems in the collection (including a group of prose poems, "True Romances") she examines the role of artist as witness-bearer, and the ironies inherent in the examination of truth and reality through art. As in *Two-Headed Poems*, there is a final expression of a tentative faith in and acceptance of life, for all its paradoxes. "Last Day" declares, "This egg/ in my hand is our last meal,/ you break it open and the sky/ turns orange again and the sun rises/ again and this is the last day again." The collection's final allusion, then, is to the egg, universal symbol of immortality and hope.

After *Interlunar* (1984), two books of selected poems have appeared, the first including twenty poems written in 1985-1986 and the second containing no new poems. Atwood's career has seen her turn almost exclusively to prose, perhaps best suited to the very public nature of her position as social arbiter and artistic guru of cultural life in Canada. Interestingly, *Interlunar* returns to the strongly mythological themes, characters, and imagery of her first collections of poems. From the first, the components of Atwood's complex vision have been clear; reading her poetry in chronological order is an odyssey through the maturing and honing of her artistic skills rather than through a definition and articulation of vision.

The mysticism suggested in *Interlunar*'s title is confirmed in the poems themselves. They are arranged in subtitled groups, a favorite device of Atwood; the most fascinating is "Snake Poems," which explores the symbolism of snakes throughout human cultural and religious history. This includes their association with darkness, evil, destructiveness, and the male principle, as well as with wisdom, knowledge, creativity, and the female principle. Above all, their association with resurrection (for their ability to shed their skins) is explored and viewed (especially in "Metempsychosis") with Atwood's customary ambivalence. Resurrection is also a central theme of the title group of poems, "Interlunar." Intimations of mortality are seen to be on the poet's mind in such poems as "Bedside," "Anchorage," and "Heart Test with an Echo Chamber"; the doubtful comfort of resurrection is ironically considered in a set of poems titled for and concerned with the mythological figures of Orpheus, Eurydice, and Persephone. So Atwood's poems and vision come full circle to her earliest poetic works, *Double Persephone* and *The Circle Game.*

The tone of the collection's title poem, "Interlunar," is uncharacteristically comforting and serene, the statement of a mature artist who recognizes that her odyssey toward understanding in art and life must be without end, but need not be frightening: "Trust me. This darkness/ is a place you can enter and be/ as safe in as you are anywhere."

Jill Rollins

Other major works

LONG FICTION: *The Edible Woman,* 1969; *Surfacing,* 1972; *Lady Oracle,* 1976; *Life Before Man,* 1979; *Bodily Harm,* 1981; *The Handmaid's Tale,* 1985; *Cat's Eye,* 1988.

SHORT FICTION: *Dancing Girls and Other Stories,* 1977; *Bluebeard's Egg,* 1983.

NONFICTION: *Survival: A Thematic Guide to Canadian Literature,* 1972; *Days of the Rebels,* 1977; *Second Words,* 1982; *The CanLit Foodbook: From Pen to Palate, a Collection of Tasty Literary Fare,* 1987.

CHILDREN'S LITERATURE: *Up in a Tree,* 1978; *Anna's Pet,* 1980; *For the Birds,* 1990.

MISCELLANEOUS: *Murder in the Dark: Short Fictions and Prose Poems,* 1983.

Bibliography

Davey, Frank. *Margaret Atwood: A Feminist Poetics.* Vancouver: Talonbooks, 1984. Presented from a feminist perspective, this book is a nine-chapter examination of Atwood's language, patterns of thought, and imagery in her poetry and prose. The accompanying bibliography and index are thorough and useful.

Grace, Sherrill E., and Lorraine Weir, eds. *Margaret Atwood: Language, Text, and System.* Vancouver: University of British Columbia Press, 1983. These essays by nine different critics treat Atwood's poetry and prose, examining the "Atwood system," her themes, and her style from a variety of perspectives, including the feminist and the syntactical.

McCombs, Judith, ed. *Critical Essays on Margaret Atwood.* Boston: G. K. Hall, 1988. This indispensable volume comprises thirty-two articles and essays, including reviews of all Atwood's poetry collections and assessments of patterns and themes in her poetry and prose. The entries are arranged in the chronological order of Atwood's primary works, beginning with *The Circle Game* and ending with *The Handmaid's Tale.* It includes a primary bibliography to 1986, and a thorough index. Judith McCombs' introduction provides an illuminating overview of Atwood's writing career and is a satisfying rationale for her choices of the critical pieces in the book.

Mallinson, Jean. "Margaret Atwood." In *Canadian Writers and Their Works: Poetry Series.* Vol. 9, edited by Robert Lecker, Jack David, and Ellen Quigley. Downsview, Ontario: ECW Press, 1985. This study is divided into the four parts dictated by series format, with "Atwood's Works" the longest and most analytical. In her clear prose, Mallinson provides insight into Atwood's poetry, considering as well the literary and critical influences on it. The concluding selected bibliography is useful.

Rosenberg, Jerome H. *Margaret Atwood.* Boston: Twayne, 1984. This highly satisfying book consists of six chapters examining Atwood's works, poetry and prose, up to the early 1980's. Chapters 2 and 3 deal exclusively with her poetry. The chapters are preceded by a useful chronology and succeeded by thorough notes, references, a selected bibliography, and an index. Rosenberg's writing is lucid and readable; his rationale for this study is presented in his preface. This is an indispensable study.

W. H. AUDEN

Born: York, England; February 21, 1907
Died: Vienna, Austria; September 29, 1973

Principal poetry

Poems, 1930; *The Orators*, 1932; *Look, Stranger!*, 1936 (also known as *On This Island*, 1937); *Letters from Iceland*, 1937 (poetry and prose, with Louis MacNeice); *Spain*, 1937; *Journey to a War*, 1939 (poetry and prose, with Christopher Isherwood); *Another Time*, 1940; *The Double Man*, 1941 (also known as *New Year Letter*); *For the Time Being*, 1944; *The Collected Poetry*, 1945; *The Age of Anxiety*, 1947; *Collected Shorter Poems, 1930-1944*, 1950; *Nones*, 1951; *The Shield of Achilles*, 1955; *Homage to Clio*, 1960; *About the House*, 1965; *Collected Shorter Poems, 1927-1957*, 1966; *Collected Longer Poems*, 1968; *City Without Walls and Other Poems*, 1969; *Epistle to a Godson and Other Poems*, 1972; *Thank You, Fog*, 1974; *Collected Poems*, 1976 (Edward Mendelson, editor); *The English Auden: Poems, Essays and Dramatic Writings, 1927-1939*, 1977 (Edward Mendelson, editor); *Selected Poems*, 1979 (Edward Mendelson, editor).

Other literary forms

Though known primarily as a poet, W. H. Auden worked in a number of other forms, making him one of the most prolific and versatile poets of his generation. During the 1930's he wrote one play on his own—*The Dance of Death* (1933)—and collaborated on three others with his friend Christopher Isherwood. These retain their interest today both as period pieces and, to a lesser degree, as experimental stage dramas. The best of the plays, *The Dog Beneath the Skin: Or, Where Is Francis?* (1935), is an exuberant, wide-ranging work containing some of Auden's finest stage verse and illustrating many of his early intellectual preoccupations, including his interest in post-Freudian psychology. The other plays, *The Ascent of F6* (1936) and *On the Frontier* (1938), are of less interest, especially the latter, which is largely an anti-Fascist propaganda piece. After the 1930's, Auden turned his dramatic interests toward the opera, writing his first libretto, *Paul Bunyan*, in 1941 for Benjamin Britten. (The work was not published until 1976, three years after Auden's death.) His better-known librettos, written in collaboration with Chester Kallman, are *The Rake's Progress* (1951), *Elegy for Young Lovers* (1961), *The Bassarids* (1966), and *Love's Labour's Lost* (1972). The assessment of the librettos and their relationship to the poetry has scarcely begun. Auden's prose writing, by contrast, has been quickly and widely recognized for its range, liveliness, and intelligence. His work includes dozens of essays, reviews, introductions, and lectures written over the span of his career. Many of his best pieces are gathered in *The Dyer's Hand and Other Essays* (1962) and

Forewords and Afterwords (1973); other prose includes *The Enchafèd Flood* (1950) and *Secondary Worlds* (1969). In addition to his plays, librettos, and prose, Auden wrote for films and radio and worked extensively as an editor and translator. *Plays and Other Dramatic Writings by W. H. Auden, 1928-1938*, edited by Edward Mendelson, was published by Princeton University Press in 1988. It includes Auden's collaborations with Christopher Isherwood and works by Auden alone; it is the first volume of a projected eight-volume series, *The Complete Works of W. H. Auden.*

Achievements

At a time when poets no longer enjoyed the wide readership they once did, Auden achieved a considerable popular success, his books selling well throughout his lifetime. He was also fortunate in having several sympathetic, intelligent critics to analyze and assess his work. It is true that Auden had his share of detractors, beginning, for example, in the 1930's with the negative response to his work in the influential journal *Scrutiny*, and, later, in two essays by Randall Jarrell taking him to task for his various ideological changes. Even today some argue that Auden's work is uneven or that his later poetry represents a serious decline from the brilliance he demonstrated in the 1930's. In a sense, his reputation has been granted grudgingly and, by some, with reservations. Despite all this, however, Auden is generally regarded today as one of the major poets of the twentieth century. Several of his lyrics are well-established as standard anthology pieces—"Lullaby," "As I Walked Out One Evening," "In Memory of W. B. Yeats," "Musée des Beaux Arts,"— but his larger reputation may well rest not on the strength of individual poems, but on the impressive range of thought and technical virtuosity found in his work as a whole.

Auden's poetry is quintessentially the work of a restless, probing intelligence committed to the idea that poise and clear-headedness are possible, indeed necessary, in a world beset by economic, social, and political chaos. Auden possessed, in the words of Chad Walsh, an "analytic power," an "ability to break a question down into its elements, to find new ways of putting familiar things together." "There is hardly an Auden poem," Walsh concludes, "that does not bespeak, and speak to, the brain at work." Auden's intelligence, however, is rarely ponderous or pedantic, and part of his lasting achievement may be the blending of playfulness and seriousness that he managed to sustain in much of his best work.

While some may doubt the profundity of Auden's thinking, few question his technical virtuosity. No poet in recent times can match the range of traditional forms he used and often revitalized in his work—oratorio, eclogue, sestina, sonnet, villanelle, closet drama, verse epistle, and ode. Auden often boasted, perhaps with justification, that he had written successfully in every known meter. Perhaps even more than for his use of traditional literary forms, however, Auden is admired for his songs, which Monroe Spears sees as "his most distinctive accomplishment and his most popular." Auden borrowed from an array of musical forms, using irony and parody to transcend the limits of the genre in which he was working. His ballads are especially well regarded, as are many of the lyrics he wrote for the stage.

Over the course of his career Auden received numerous literary honors, beginning in 1937 with the King's Gold Medal for poetry. His other awards include Guggenheim fellowships in 1942 and 1945; the Pulitzer Prize in 1948; the Bollingen Prize in 1954; the National Book Award in 1956; and the Austrian State Prize for European literature in 1966. From 1956 to 1960, Auden held the honorary position of Professor of Poetry at Oxford.

Biography

Wystan Hugh Auden was born in York, England, in 1907, the third and youngest son of George and Constance Auden. Before his youngest son was two years old, George Auden gave up a private medical practice in York and moved his family south to Birmingham, where Dr. Auden worked as the city's School Medical Officer. Auden's devout, middle-class family (both his parents were the children of clergymen) gave him a strong sense of traditional religious values and encouraged his early intellectual bent. His mother, Auden frequently said, was the strongest presence in his early years. He was particularly close to her and believed throughout his life that her influence was largely responsible for shaping his adult character. His father, a widely educated man in both the humanities and sciences, acquainted his son at an early age with classical literature and Nordic myths, and encouraged his reading in poetry and fiction as well as scientific subjects, including medicine, geology, and mining. This early reading was supported by a close familiarity with nature, and Auden as a child developed a fascination for the landscape of limestone caves and abandoned mines that is recalled in several of his poems. Auden's first inclinations were, in fact, toward the scientific and natural rather than literary, and as a young boy he fancied himself a mining engineer. His interest in science continued throughout his life and is reflected in the frequent use of scientific ideas and images in his poetry, and accounts, perhaps, for the stance of clinical detachment found in his early work.

In 1915, Auden was sent as a boarder to St. Edmund's school in Surrey, and, after completing his studies there in 1920, attended Gresham's school, an institution known for its excellence in the sciences. While at Gresham's, Auden gradually came to acknowledge his homosexuality and to question many of his middle-class values and religious beliefs; by the time he left Gresham's, he had abandoned his faith. It was also during this period that Auden, at the suggestion of Robert Medley, began to write his first poems.

In 1925, Auden enrolled at Christ Church, Oxford, where he discovered a congenial social atmosphere far different from the repressive climate at

Gresham's. He found in the young don Nevill Coghill a sympathetic, stimulating tutor who was soon informed of Auden's intentions to become a "great poet." After a year of reading in the sciences, Auden turned his interests to English studies and soon developed an enthusiasm for the then unfashionable poetry of the Anglo-Saxon period. This confirmed his preference for the Nordic-Germanic rather than Romance Continental literary tradition, a bias evident in much of his early poetry and, later, in *The Age of Anxiety*, with its close imitation of Old English metric and alliterative patterns.

During the Oxford years and in the decade that followed, Auden was the central figure of a group of writers, including Cecil Day Lewis and Stephen Spender, who shared his liberal political leanings. The 1930's became a sort of golden decade for Auden, a time of intellectual excitement and artistic vitality. With various friends he traveled widely—to Iceland with Louis MacNeice, and to China with Christopher Isherwood. Both visits resulted in collaborative books containing poetry by Auden. In 1937 Auden went to Spain where he worked for the Loyalist cause in the Civil War, which had become a rallying cause for intellectuals of the time. His experience led to the writing of *Spain* (1937), the celebrated political poem which Auden later rejected because of the "wicked doctrine" of its concluding lines; he purged the poem from most subsequent collections of his work. During the 1930's Auden was also active in his home country: He taught school from 1930 to 1935; helped found the Group Theatre in 1932; and published two volumes of poetry that secured for him a reputation as one of the most promising young poets of his generation. In 1935 he married Erika Mann, daughter of the German novelist Thomas Mann, in order to provide her with a British passport.

Auden's writing during the 1930's—both his poetry and the plays written in collaboration with Isherwood—largely constitutes a diagnosis of industrial English society in the midst of economic and moral decay. The diagnosis is made from the perspective of various ideologies that Auden adopted or toyed with during the late 1920's and 1930's—Freudian and post-Freudian psychology, Marxism, and liberal socialism.

In 1939, at the end of a full and brilliant decade, Auden and Isherwood decided to leave England permanently and move to the United States, which they had visited in the preceding year on their return trip from China. Auden's move to New York marked a major turning point in his life and career, for during this period he was gradually shifting away from many of his earlier intellectual convictions and moving toward a reaffirmation of his childhood faith; in October, 1940 he returned to the Anglican communion. Many of his poems in the 1940's record the gradual move toward Christianity, including, most explicitly, his Christmas Oratorio, *For the Time Being*. Auden's concern for the ills of modern society did not end, however, with his affirmation of faith, for he pursued this concern in various ways in his poetry, most notably in *The Age of Anxiety*, whose title became a catch phrase for the war-torn decade in which it was written. During the 1940's Auden held teaching posts at several American colleges but continued to write prolifically, working chiefly on his ambitious longer poems.

Auden's life after the 1940's fell into a somewhat more staid routine. In the 1950's he began writing libretti with Chester Kallman, whom he had met shortly after his arrival in America; he and Kallman remained companions and collaborators until the end of Auden's life. From 1948 to 1957 Auden spent each spring and summer on the island of Ischia, prompting some to suggest that he had entered a post-American phase in his career. Then, beginning in 1957, and for the remainder of his life, he stayed half of each year in New York and half in a converted farmhouse that he and Kallman purchased in the village of Kirchstetten, Austria. In a poem written at the time, Auden saw his departure from Ischia as a reaffirmation of his essential northernness. In Kirchstetten he settled into the happy domesticity celebrated in his *About the House* volume.

In 1972, his health failing, Auden decided to leave New York permanently and spend his winter season each year in a "grace and favour" cottage offered to him by the governing board of his old college, Christ Church, Oxford. As usual, he stayed the following spring and summer in Kirchstetten, and, on his way back to Oxford that fall, died of a heart attack in Vienna. He was buried, as he had wished, in Kirchstetten.

Analysis

Read chronologically, W. H. Auden's poetry moves from alienation to integration; his work is a quest for wholeness, an escape from the isolated self, "where dwell/ Our howling appetites," into a community where the essential goodness of life is acknowledged despite the presence of sin. Over the course of his career, Auden's quest takes many forms, but his goal never varies; from beginning to end, he seeks to discover how love, in all its manifestations, can fulfill man's social and personal needs.

Auden began in the 1930's as a critic of his society, an outsider looking in and finding little to admire in what he saw. His early work is essentially a record of social ills; love is sought, but rarely found. As he matures, however, Auden gradually becomes less of a diagnostician and more of a healer; he arrives eventually at a vision of love informed by human sympathy and, later, by religious belief. Once this vision is affirmed in his poetry, Auden again shifts direction, becoming more fully than before a comic poet, intent on celebrating the redemptive power of love and acknowledging the essential blessedness of life. These shifts in Auden's work are, of course, gradual and subtle rather than abrupt, but the division of his career into three phases provides a way to bring some sense of order to a body of work remarkable, above all else, for its diversity.

The early Auden is very much a poet of the 1930's—a time of economic depression and Fascism, war and rumors of war. Faced with such a world, he adopts the pose of a clinical diagnostician anatomizing a troubled society. He sees the social and spiritual malaise of his time as a failure of communication; individuals are trapped inside themselves, unable to escape the forces of psychological and social repression that block the possibility of love.

The poems which record Auden's diagnosis of his society are still considered by some to be his best. Although they are often bewildering to readers, they are admired for their energy and intensity, their brilliant, elusive surfaces. One of the most highly regarded of these early poems is "Consider," which illustrates Auden's early technical skill as well as his characteristic themes. The poem is divided into three verse paragraphs, each addressed to a different auditor by a speaker whose heightened theatrical language gives him an aloofness of tone that matches his arrogant message. Auden's voice in "Consider" typifies the detachment and impersonality of the early poems.

The first verse paragraph addresses the reader directly, asking that he "consider" a symbolic modern landscape "As the hawk sees it or the helmeted airman." From this great height, with the objective eye of the hawk, the speaker observes images of society on the verge of collapse: a cigarette end smoldering at the edge of a garden party; decadent vacationers at a winter resort, surrounded by signs of an impending war; and farmers "Sitting in kitchens in the stormy fens." The vacationers, incapable of emotion, are "Supplied with feelings by an efficient band," while the farmers, separated from them by physical distance and class barriers, yet equally lonely, listen to the same music on the wireless. Though explicitly social and political, the poem is also developed in personal and psychological terms; like the landscape, the individuals in the poem are "diseased," unable to establish genuine personal contacts.

Having drawn this grim picture of "our time," the speaker turns in the second verse paragraph to elucidate the psychological foundation of social ills, addressing, in the process, a "supreme Antagonist," who, according to Edward Mendelson, is the "*inner* enemy" that "personifies the fears and repressions that oppose love." The Antagonist finds an ample number of victims in the decadent society and spreads its evil, "Scattering the people" and seizing them with "immeasurable neurotic dread." In this section, the poem's intense language and deliberate rhetorical excess are beautifully modulated, making the speaker aloof and detached, yet with an edge of hysteria in his voice.

The final verse paragraph is addressed to the banker, the don, and the clergyman (representatives of the social elite), along with all others who seek happiness by following the "convolutions" of the distorted ego. The poem ends by warning the selfish and the elite of the inescapable psychological diseases that the Antagonist holds in store for them, diseases that will further destroy the possibility for love.

Auden's adaptation of various psychological theories in "Consider" is typical of his method in the 1930's, as is the detached clinical posture of the speaker and the explicit social and political concern voiced in the poem. Auden characteristically offers little hope and, given the extent of the ills he describes, his doing so might well have seemed facile. Auden's earliest poetry sometimes offers an idealized, vague notion of Love as a healing force capable of breaking down repression and restoring social and personal relationships to their proper order. Usually, though, this message is faint and clearly secondary to the diagnostic aim of the poems.

In two love poems written somewhat later than "Consider," Auden approaches more explicitly the view of love hinted at in the earliest poems. "Lullaby," his best-known lyric, ends with the speaker's hope that his beloved may be "Watched by every human love." The poem's emphasis, however, rests on the transience of "human love": the arm upon which the sleeping lover rests is "faithless"; love is at best a temporary stay against loneliness. Likewise, in "As I Walked Out One Evening," Auden stresses the limitations of romantic and erotic love. "Time" lurks in the shadows and coughs when the lovers "would kiss," deflating the romantic delusions satirized at the beginning of the poem. Later, though, near the end, the chiming clocks of the city offer an injunction that suggests a new direction: "You shall love your crooked neighbor/ With your crooked heart." Though undercut by a number of ironies, the love described here moves tentatively toward the vision of the 1940's. Even so, the "human love" that Auden evokes in the 1930's seems insufficient to resolve the social and personal ills diagnosed by his poetry.

During the 1930's, Auden gradually left behind the various ideologies he had seriously (and, perhaps, half-seriously) adopted during the decade. Humphrey Carpenter, Auden's biographer, suggests that these ideologies—Marxism, post-Freudianism, liberal humanism—all had in common a fundamental belief in the natural goodness of man. Near the end of the decade, Auden began to question his liberal humanism, partly because of its inability to offer, as he put it, "some reason why [Hitler] was utterly wrong." The reason he sought turned out to be in Christianity, particularly the doctrine of man's sinful nature and his need, because of that nature, for forgiveness and redemption. The quest for love that began in the early poetry thus grows in the 1940's into a quest for Christian love. There is, of course, no sudden shift in Auden's poetry as a result of the new direction in his thinking. Rather, at the end of the 1930's, he begins *gradually* to formulate this vision of *agape*; in a sense, he was already doing so in the two love poems examined above.

The poem "Herman Melville," though written a year before Auden "officially" rejoined the Church in 1940, demonstrates his thinking at this crucial period, a time which coincided with his arrival in the United States. The poem also suggests something of Auden's more relaxed, lucid style, a shift which began in the mid-1930's away from the verbal glitter and rhetorical intensity of poems such as "Consider." "Herman Melville" is thus a good example of Auden's thematic and stylistic direction in the shorter poems published during the 1940's.

In the poem Auden describes Melville's life and literary career as a metaphorical "gale" that had blown the novelist "Past the Cape Horn of sensible success" and "deafened him with thunder." Near the end of his life, after Melville had exorcised his demons, he "sailed into an extraordinary mildness," entering a domestic contentment where he discovered "new knowledge"— that "Evil is unspectacular and always human" (Auden develops a similar idea in "Musée des Beaux Arts") and "that we are introduced to Goodness every day." What Melville found, in essence, is what Auden himself was in the process of accepting—the universality of man's sinfulness and the possibility that goodness (that is, grace and redemption) can, in an unspectacular fashion, transform the corrupt present, enabling man to transcend his sinfulness.

At the end of the poem Auden describes Melville's exultation and surrender at his discovery of the transforming power of *agape*. The poem, while not autobiographical, certainly seems to be Auden's testing ground, his rehearsal of an idea that had been forming in his mind. Melville's discovery that his love had been "selfish" suggests perhaps that Auden has come full circle from his early poems, now denying completely the efficacy of eros, sexual-romantic love. Auden himself suggests, however, that this is not the case; writing for *Theology* in 1950, he argues that "Agape is the fulfillment of eros, not its contradiction." Perhaps "Herman Melville" contains an early formulation of a position whose full complexity Auden had not yet resolved.

If "Herman Melville" records Auden's initial approach to Christianity, then *The Age of Anxiety* shows his response to a modern society at odds with the directives of *agape*. The poem is the longest of the four extended works Auden wrote in the 1940's. The bulk of his energy during the decade went into these poems, which were ambitious undertakings in an age when the long poem had all but died out. *The Age of Anxiety* is a "baroque eclogue," a pastoral form entirely incongruous with the poem's urban setting (New York) and its subject matter (four modern-day city dwellers during World War II). Auden also achieves irony with his imitation of Old English metric patterns. The contrast between an epic measure and the pettiness of modern life creates a mock-heroic tone.

The poem begins in a Third Avenue bar where four customers—Quant, Malin, Emble, and Rosetta—drink and discuss their lives. The conversation of these four representatives of modern man becomes an effort to find order in an age of chaos and disbelief. At the outset the characters drink in private corners of the bar, each dreaming (as Monroe Spears puts it) "of his own way of escape, but aware . . . of no recourse beyond the human level."

Rosetta, for example, has "a favourite day-dream" of "lovely innocent coun-trysides," while the youthful Emble dreams of success achieved only in a hollow "succession of sexual triumphs." The four dreamers eventually move out of their private corners and begin to discuss the war. As they grow more and more drunk their discussion turns, in the second part of the poem ("The Seven Ages"), to man, "the traveller through time . . . As he bumbles by from birth to death." Their analysis constitutes a psychological study of the maturation process of the individual and leads them to recognize their own failure in coming to terms with life. Their recognition is, however, only momentary, for in the poem's third section ("The Seven Stages") the four figures lapse into a drunken state of unconsciousness and travel over an allegorical dream landscape searching again for a solution of their own, and hence man's, dilemma.

Their journey, however, is doomed to fail, for they seek not spiritual enlightenment, but a way of escaping it. The first six stages of their vision carry them through (and they believe away from) the anxiety and suffering of the world; but they are merely led deeper into themselves. The truth revealed in the dream is that the world and its anxieties—which they can only see in distortion—are unbearable for modern man. The egotism of the dreamer will not allow them salvation.

The first six stages of the dream explore every possible path of escape. In the seventh stage, however, all hope is lost. They are now, as Emble says, "miles" from any "Workable world." The quest has taken them into a land-scape of "Ravenous unreals." As the chaos closes in on them they turn away from it, refusing to attempt the only true quest—the seeking of spiritual knowledge not in their own illusions but in the redemption of the present moment through a religious commitment. At the end of the poem Malin recognizes the failure of their journey. The moment is not redeemed, but the resolution of the poem defines their failure in Christian terms. In his final speech Malin describes modern man's unwillingness "to say Yes" to "That-Always-Opposite" who "Condescended to exist and to suffer death/ And, scorned on a scaffold, ensconced in His life/ The human household."

Thus the poem ends with man's refusal of *agape*, his resignation to lone-liness, and his unwillingness to forgo egotism and accept the world as redeemed through the Incarnation. *The Age of Anxiety* takes up two main strands in Auden's work—the diagnosis of social and personal ills and the possibility of *agape* as a release from isolation. The four characters in this poem fail to achieve that release.

The Age of Anxiety brings to an end what some have called Auden's American period. From 1948 to the end of his life he spent half of each year abroad, and many of the poems of this time reflect the change of landscape. There is also a change in perspective, certainly not as radical as some of the earlier changes, but a change nevertheless. Justin Replogle suggests that after

1950 Auden becomes an essentially comic poet whose emphasis shifts away from poetry as a repository for ideas. His work, says Replogle, "begins less to proclaim a belief than to celebrate one." The later poetry, then, is generally lighter in tone and technique than his earlier work, and Replogle's word "celebrate" is especially apt, for there are a variety of celebrations going on in the later work: of the natural world ("Bucolics"); of the five senses ("Precious Five"); of friends ("For Friends Only"); of the ordinary and domestic ("Thanksgiving for a Habitat"); and the earthly happiness ("In Praise of Limestone"). All these celebrations are enacted in *About the House*, a collection which typifies Auden's later style. The book celebrates the rooms of his converted farmhouse in Kirchstetten, Austria, becoming a sort of homage to domesticity.

"Tonight at Seven-Thirty," the dining-room poem, discusses with wit and charm the place where man enacts a ritual of celebration (the dinner party) that is nearly religious or mythical in its implications—the breaking of bread with friends. If many of Auden's poems call on man to love (often with didactic urgency), then the dining-room poem, like all of *About the House*, is informed by a gentle spirit of love. In one sense, the volume is a celebration of friendship; all the poems are dedicated to close friends, and several of them are addressed to people Auden loved. The *agape* proclaimed earlier now unobtrusively informs every poem as each room of the house becomes a celebration of some ordinary human activity—eating, sleeping, conversing, working.

"Tonight at Seven-Thirty" opens with a clever comparison of the eating habits of several species: plants ("one solitary continuous meal"), predators ("none of them play host") and man (who alone can "do the honors of a feast"). This definition is designed, first of all to amuse; it nevertheless makes a serious point in asserting that only man—"Dame Kind's thoroughbred lunatic"—can invite a stranger to the table and serve him first. Auden celebrates man's capacity for kindness, ritual, and even good manners—another recurrent motif in the later poems.

About the House is the work of a poet who, in a sense, has arrived. Auden's quest for love as a cure for man's ills took him in the 1930's to a landscape of desperation, isolation, and decay. Gradually he discovered a basis upon which, in the 1940's, he could build a vision of *agape*, a knowledge that, despite his sinfulness and guilt, man could be forgiven through grace; love was possible. In *About the House*, nearly forty years after his first poems appeared, the "cure" of love is still at the center of Auden's work; in his later work, however, the possibility of love is not so much proclaimed as celebrated.

Michael Hennessy

Other major works

PLAYS: *Paid on Both Sides: A Charade*, 1930; *The Dance of Death*, 1933; *The Dog Beneath the Skin: Or, Where Is Francis?*, 1935 (with Christopher Isherwood); *The Ascent of F6*, 1936 (with Christopher Isherwood); *On the Frontier*, 1938 (with Christopher Isherwood); *Paul Bunyan*, 1941 (printed in 1976, libretto); *The Rake's Progress*, 1951 (libretto, with Chester Kallman); *Delia: Or, A Masque of Night*, 1953; *For the Time Being*, 1959; *Elegy for Young Lovers*, 1961 (libretto, with Chester Kallman); *The Bassarids*, 1966 (libretto, with Chester Kallman); *Love's Labour's Lost*, 1972 (libretto, with Chester Kallman); *The Entertainment of the Senses*, 1974; *Plays and Other Dramatic Writings by W. H. Auden, 1928-1938*, 1988.

NONFICTION: *Letters from Iceland*, 1937 (poetry and prose, with Louis MacNeice); *Journey to a War*, 1939 (poetry and prose, with Christopher Isherwood); *The Enchafèd Flood*, 1950; *The Dyer's Hand and Other Essays*, 1962; *Selected Essays*, 1964; *Secondary Worlds*, 1969; *A Certain World*, 1970; *Forewords and Afterwords*, 1973; *The English Auden: Poems, Essays and Dramatic Writings, 1927-1939*, 1977 (Edward Mendelson, editor).

ANTHOLOGIES: *The Oxford Book of Light Verse*, 1938; *The Portable Greek Reader*, 1948; *Poets of the English Language*, 1950 (with Norman Holmes Pearson, 5 volumes); *The Faber Book of Modern American Verse*, 1956; *Selected Poems of Louis MacNeice*, 1964; *Nineteenth Century British Minor Poets*, 1966; *A Choice of Dryden's Verse*, 1973.

Bibliography

Bloom, Harold, ed. *W. H. Auden: Modern Critical Views.* New York: Chelsea House, 1989. Arguably the most valuable anthology of Auden's criticism in print because of its comprehensive look at the life, times, and work of the poet, sometimes mistakenly considered a glib or arch-modern poet. Bloom has assembled essays that elucidate the biographical undercurrents of Auden's aesthetic vision with frank consideration of his homosexual relationships and conversion to Christianity. Included here is Edward Mendelson's seminal essay, "Auden's Revision of Modernism."

Callen, Edward. *Auden: A Carnival of Intellect.* New York: Oxford University Press, 1982. A skillful explication of Auden's main poetic themes, chronologically ordered from his 1930's interest in Romanticism to his later embracing of neoclassic aesthetics in the 1960's. Callen stresses Auden's misgivings about Romanticism's weakness in combatting Fascism and violations of human individuality that he witnessed in writers such as William Butler Yeats and D. H. Lawrence.

Carpenter, Humphrey. *W. H. Auden: A Biography.* Boston: Houghton Mifflin, 1981. Carpenter had access to private and unpublished material in crafting this comprehensive and compelling critical biography of the poet. It is the key source to biographical detail that an Auden researcher should begin with to situate Auden's poetry within his world and worldview.

Fuller, John. *A Reader's Guide to W. H. Auden*. New York: Farrar, Straus & Giroux, 1970. Fuller has created a sensitive and invaluable guide to Auden's early and later works, offering clear and precise readings of difficult passages. Especially useful is Fuller's careful attention to many of the poet's allusions and influences.

Gingerich, Martin E. *W. H. Auden: A Reference Guide*. Boston: G. K. Hall, 1977. An immensely useful and annotated compendium of criticism of Auden's major poems through 1974. Auden's students will find this work indispensable in tracing the reception and appreciation of Auden through his early years as a poet to his posthumous reputation.

Spears, Monroe K., ed. *Auden: A Collection of Critical Essays*. Englewood Cliffs, N.J.: Prentice-Hall, 1964. This early compendium of Auden's criticism contains excellent exposition of well-known Auden poems and stands out for its inclusion of appreciations and contextualizations by Auden's fellow poets, including Cleanth Brooks and Marianne Moore. Also included are seminal articles by American critics Edmund Wilson ("Auden in America") and G. S. Fraser ("The Career of W. H. Auden") that provide essential biographical backgrounds to Auden's most productive periods of work.

AMIRI BARAKA
LeRoi Jones

Born: Newark, New Jersey; October 7, 1934

Principal poetry

Preface to a Twenty Volume Suicide Note, 1961; *The Dead Lecturer*, 1964; *Black Magic: Sabotage—Target Study—Black Art: Collected Poetry, 1961-1967*, 1969; *It's Nation Time*, 1970; *In Our Terribleness: Some Elements and Meaning in Black Style*, 1970; *Spirit Reach*, 1972; *Hard Facts*, 1975; *Selected Poetry of Amiri Baraka/LeRoi Jones*, 1979; *Reggae or Not!*, 1981.

Other literary forms

Amiri Baraka is a protean literary figure, equally well-known for his poetry, drama, and essays. In addition, he has written short stories, collected in *Tales* (1967), and an experimental novel, *The System of Dante's Hell* (1964), which include numerous poetic and dramatic passages. Baraka's early plays, most notably *Dutchman* (1964), *The Slave* (1964), and *The Toilet* (1964), were produced under his given name of LeRoi Jones and derive from his period of involvement with the New York City avant-garde. Later plays, such as *Slave Ship* (1967), reflect his experiments with ritual drama during his involvement with black nationalist politics. More recent plays, such as *The Motion of History* (1977) and *The Sidney Poet Heroical* (1979), have been produced much less frequently than his earlier work and have generally failed to appeal to either Baraka's avant-garde or his black nationalist audiences. Baraka's critical and political prose has been collected in *Blues People: Negro Music in White America* (1963), *Home: Social Essays* (1966), *Raise Race Rays Raze: Essays Since 1965* (1971), *Selected Plays and Prose* (1979), and *Daggers and Javelins: Essays* (1984). Throughout his career Baraka has been active as an anthologist, editing significant volumes such as the avant-garde anthology *The Moderns: New Fiction in America* (1963) and the Black Arts movement anthology *Black Fire: An Anthology of Afro-American Writing* (1968). *The Autobiography of LeRoi Jones/Amiri Baraka* appeared in 1984.

Achievements

Amiri Baraka's importance as a poet rests both on the diversity of his work and the singular intensity of his black nationalist period. In fact, Baraka's diversity helps give the nationalist poetry a symbolic significance with personal, political, and aesthetic dimensions. Perhaps his most substantial achievement is his ability to force reconsideration of the relationship between the artist, his work, its audience, and the encompassing social context. Reconstructing his own vision of this relationship both at the beginning and the end of the nationalist period, Baraka has increasingly stressed the necessity for an art which will alter the context and increase the real freedom of both artist and community.

During his black nationalist period, Baraka concentrated on exposing the unstated racist premises of Euro-American art, and developing an alternative "Black Aesthetic." In part because he had demonstrated mastery of Euro-American poetic modes, Baraka's black nationalist philosophy commanded an unusual degree of white attention. Coming from an unknown poet, his militant poetry might well have been dismissed as a naïve kind of propaganda. It did, in fact, alienate many of his earlier admirers who came to see him as a literal embodiment of the civil disorders of the mid-1960's. On a more profound level, however, he spurred many to ponder the complex logic of his transformation and to reassess the political implications of their own aesthetic stances. Even as his relationship with the "mainstream" audience underwent this metamorphosis, his call for a militant—and if necessary violent—response to American racism received an affirmative answer from many younger Afro-American writers. Challenging them to speak directly to and for the Afro-American community, Baraka pursued the implications of his demand and employed his poetry as a direct political force. His subsequent turn to a socialist position, reflecting his growing conviction that simple nationalism unintentionally contributed to capitalist oppression, forced many black nationalists to reassess their own positions. Though Baraka again alienated much of his audience, he continued to generate serious debate on central issues. Throughout his career, but especially in the 1960's and early 1970's, Baraka has exerted a combined political and aesthetic influence matched by few other figures in American literary history.

Biography

Amiri Baraka, as he has been known since 1967, was born Everett LeRoi Jones into a black middle-class family in Newark, New Jersey. An excellent student whose parents encouraged his intellectual interests, Jones was graduated from Howard University of Washington, D.C., in 1954 at the age of nineteen. After spending two years in the United States Air Force, primarily in Puerto Rico, he moved to Greenwich Village where he embarked on his literary career in 1957. During the early stage of his career, Jones associated closely with numerous white avant-garde poets, including Robert Creeley, Allen Ginsberg, Robert Duncan, and Dianne DiPrima, with whom he founded the American Theatre for Poets in 1961. Marrying Hettie Cohen, a white woman with whom he edited the magazine *Yugen* from 1958 to 1963, Jones established himself as an important young poet, critic, and editor. Among the many magazines to which he contributed was *Downbeat*, the jazz journal where he first developed many of the musical interests which were to have such a large impact on his later poetry. The political interests which were to dominate Jones's later work were unmistakably present as early as

1960 when he toured Cuba with a group of black intellectuals. This event sparked his perception of the United States as a corrupt bourgeois society and seems particularly significant in relation to his later socialist emphasis. Jones's growing political interest conditioned his first produced plays, including the Obie Award-winning *Dutchman* (1964), which anticipated the first major transformation of Jones's life.

Separating from Hettie Cohen and severing ties with his white associates, Jones moved from the Village to Harlem in 1965. Turning his attention to direct action within the black community, he founded the Black Arts Theatre and School in Harlem and, following his return to his native city in 1966, the Spirit House in Newark. After marrying a black woman, Sylvia Robinson (Amina Baraka) in 1966, Jones adopted his new name, which means "Prince" (Ameer) "the blessed one" (Baraka), along with the honorary title of "Imamu." Over the next half dozen years, Baraka helped found and develop the Black Community Development and Defense Organization, the Congress of African Peoples (convened in Atlanta in 1970), and the National Black Political Convention (convened in Gary, Indiana, in 1972). As a leading spokesman of the Black Arts movement, Baraka provided support for young black poets and playwrights, including Larry Neal, Ed Bullins, Marvin X, and Ron Milner. During the Newark uprising/riot of 1967, Baraka was arrested for unlawful possession of firearms. Although he was convicted and given the maximum sentence after the judge read his poem "Black People!" as an example of incitement to riot, Baraka was later cleared on appeal.

Baraka supported Kenneth A. Gibson's campaign to become the first black mayor of Newark in 1970, but later broke with Gibson over what he perceived as the bourgeois values of the administration. This disillusionment with black politics within the American system, combined with Baraka's attendance at the Sixth Pan-African Conference at Dar es Salaam in 1974, precipitated the subsequent stage of his political evolution. While not abandoning his commitment to confronting the special problems of Afro-Americans in the United States, Baraka came to interpret these problems within the framework of an overarching "Marxist-Leninist-Mao Tse-Tung" philosophy. In conjunction with this second transformation, Baraka dropped the title "Imamu" and changed the name of his Newark publishing firm from "Jihad" to "People's War." In recent years, he has taught at Yale and the State University of New York at Stony Brook while performing with an experimental jazz/poetry group. Although he has had some difficulty finding publishers for his socialist writing, he has continued to speak in public both inside and outside the Afro-American community. He is the editor of *Black Nation*, the organ of the League of Revolutionary Struggle, a Marxist organization.

Analysis
Amiri Baraka's poetry falls into three distinctive periods, each reflecting

an attempt to find a philosophy capable of responding adequately to a corrupt culture. The voice of each period is shaped in accord with a different set of assumptions concerning the nature of the cultural corruption, the proper orientation toward political action, and the poet's relationship with his audience. During his early period, Baraka built an essentially aesthetic response on premises shared primarily with white poets and intellectuals. Although Baraka always recognized the importance of his racial and economic heritage, the intricate philosophical voice of the early period sounds highly individualistic in comparison with his later work. During his middle black nationalist period, Baraka shifted his emphasis to the racial dimension of American culture. The associated voice—much more accessible, though not nearly so simple as it first appears—reflects Baraka's desire to relate primarily to the Afro-American community. During his third "Marxist-Leninist-Mao-Tse-Tung-Thought" period, Baraka adapts a less emotionally charged voice in accord with his stance as a scientific analyst of capitalist corruption.

Differing from the voices of the earlier periods, which assumed an equality between Baraka and his audience, whether based on aesthetic awareness or racial experience, this socialist voice frequently takes on the didactic tones of a teacher lecturing an audience unaware of its potential identity as a revolutionary proletariat. The diversity of Baraka's work makes it extremely difficult to find a vocabulary equally relevant to the complex postmodernism of *Preface to a Twenty Volume Suicide Note*, the militant nationalism of *Black Magic*, and the uncompromising economic analysis of *Hard Facts*. Nevertheless, Baraka is not three different people. Anticipations and echoes of each voice occur during each period. Throughout his career several constants emerge, most notably a philosophical refusal to conform to the demands of a corrupt culture and an emphasis on the oral/musical nature of the poetic experience.

Baraka's early work emphasizes the relationship between psychological experience, vocal rhythm, and the poetic line. This aesthetic adapts and develops those of Euro-American poets such as Robert Duncan, Robert Creeley, and Charles Olsen, whose essay "Projective Verse" states many of the general premises of the group with which Baraka associated. Olsen insists on "the possibilities of breath" as the central element of "Open" verse and develops the idea that "FORM IS NEVER MORE THAN THE EXTENSION OF CONTENT." Given this aesthetic, the poetic voice should embody the precise rhythm and emphasis of the poet's immediate experience and perception. The poem "Duncan spoke of a process" both explicitly recognizes Baraka's aesthetic affinities (he also inscribed poems to Gary Snyder, Allen Ginsberg, and Michael McClure during this period) and analyzes the experience and premises shaping his voice. The poem typifies Baraka's early work in that it is philosophical, abstract, and nonracial. While it may obliquely relate to Baraka's experience as a black man, it is equally accessible to a reader whose emotional state derives from different specific circumstances. In addition, it typifies the early work in its intimation of the deep dissatisfaction with Euro-American culture which led to Baraka's later political development.

Assuming an audience familiar with Duncan, Baraka meditates on the emotional and intellectual implications of his work and revises its aesthetic in accord with his own perceptions. Although he repeats the word "repeat" three times in the first stanza, he is not simply repeating Duncan's words. The poem most closely resembles Duncan in its syntax, which mirrors the hesitations of a consciousness struggling to embody a natural process, to find words which repeat experience "as a day repeats/ its color." Frequently "sentences" consist of a string of perceptual units with ambiguous syntactic relationships. Many sentences contain no concrete images ("Before that, what came easiest"); the images which do occur are in relation to poetic consciousness rather than external "reality." Like Duncan's, Baraka's landscape is part psychological, part mythic or archetypal. The image of unidentified people traveling across the "greenest earth" represents his struggle to unite these landscapes, to bring the nurturing archetypal world to life in the persona's mind.

The remainder of the poem, however, emphasizes the persona's inability to achieve this rejuvenating unity. He insists that all abstract ideas and assumptions be validated in relation to memory (of psychological states rather than of external experiences). His memory, however, confronts him with an internal wasteland, "a heap of broken feeling." Starting with this consuming feeling of loss—whether of lover, childhood innocence, affinity with Duncan, or spiritual resiliency remains purposefully ambiguous—the persona's process leads him increasingly toward solipsism. No longer able to distinguish between "love" and "opinion," he feels no sense of the reality of past connections; even the archetypal Eden seems to be an illusion. Existing "where there/ is nothing, save myself," he is unable to "fill" that suffering self. The isolation of the word "myself" in its own line emphasizes the isolation which momentarily overwhelms the persona. Paradoxically, the line expressing the moment of existential terror intimates the pure merging of voice and consciousness associated with the processes of nature in the first stanza.

Perhaps because of this resemblance, the moment generates in the persona a resolve to reestablish contact with the external world. His determination, however, collapses in a way which, at least in retrospect, seems to anticipate Baraka's later political development. His first reaction to the existential terror is a perception of what he "love[s] most." Rather than reassuring him, however, this engenders a cynical determination—perhaps reflecting the continuing sense of loss—that he will "not/ leave what futile lies/ I have." In a context where "love" is a "futile lie," the persona's subsequent decision to "go out to/ what is most beautiful" demands ironic revaluation. The irony increases when the persona derives his conception of the "beautiful" from the platitudinous appeal to nobility of "some noncombatant Greek/ or soft Italian prince," the originators of the Machiavellian slavocracy of Euro-American culture. The persona's concluding questions anticipate the insistence on social and political processes which characterizes Baraka's later works: "And which one/ is truly/ to rule here? And/ what country is this?" Duncan spoke of a process which was essentially mythic, natural, and psychological. While mirroring this process, Baraka's internal processes are clearly carrying him toward the political arena where questions concerning control and possession are central rather than subordinate.

Throughout his early work, Baraka tries on a variety of personae, indicating a fascination with masks which provides the center for some of his most interesting early work. The "Crow Jane" sequence, echoing both William Butler Yeats's "Crazy Jane" poems and a blues by Mississippi Joe Williams, focuses on the limits of social masking. "Crow Jane," a white woman unconsciously adopting the old Jim Crow racial patterns, attempts to escape her role in "straight" America only to find herself a "wet lady of no image." Even more uncompromising in its dissatisfaction with masks which take their meaning from Euro-American cultural patterns, "An Agony. As New." develops the image of a persona being burned within a mask of "white hot metal." Tormented by the constrictions of a corrupt, mechanical white role, the persona feels himself "inside someone/ who hates me." Although that someone can easily be seen as a white self tormenting a black soul, the poem is not developed in explicitly racial terms. It could apply, for example, to a homosexual living a "straight" life or a businessman on the verge of a breakdown. Its implications are clear, however; inexorably, the agony leads to the final line consisting only of the word "screams." Again, the "projective" merging of voice and experience is pure, but the echoes of the scream sound in a voice which is no longer intended for the ears of the white avant-garde.

Baraka's nationalist voice, collective where the earlier voice was individualistic, aspires to a specifically "black" purity. Even while assuming the role of teacher, Baraka claims authority for his voice only to the extent that it reflects the strength and values of his Afro-American heritage. In "Leroy" he offers up his old voice to the black community, urging it to "pick me apart and take the/ useful parts, the sweet meat of my feelings. And leave/ the bitter bullshit rotten white parts/ alone." The alienation associated with Euro-American culture, expressed in the word "alone" as a line by itself, contrasts with the expansive sense of connection felt by the Amiri who rejects the masks of his predecessor "Leroy."

It would be misleading, however, to suggest that Baraka simply rejects all masks imposed by white society in order to reveal his "true" black face. Even while rebelling against the masks associated with his avant-garde personae, Baraka continues to explore the potential of masking in relation to his new orientation. This exploration takes two distinct forms, both designed to bring Baraka closer to the black community. First, he realizes that his own family background distances him from the "black angels" and "strong nigger feeling" described in "Leroy." Even while envisioning Leroy's mother "getting into/ new blues, from the old ones," he sees her "hypnotizing" him as she stares into "the future of the soul." In relation to Afro-American culture, the future of the black bourgeois appears increasingly white and alienated. To become "purely black," Baraka must to some extent mask the influence of his class origins. Second, the mask itself is a central image in both African and Afro-American culture. Invoking both the ritual knowledge of Africa and the survival strategy of the black South, the mask has been exploited in Afro-American literature from Charles Waddell Chesnutt and Langston Hughes through Ralph Ellison and William Melvin Kelley. To speak with a black voice, Baraka must, like Brer Rabbit, present a variety of shifting surfaces, both to defend against and to attack the predatory forces of his environment.

These surfaces are extremely elusive, deriving their meaning as much from audience as from speaker. Using musical forms and images as primary points of reference, Baraka explores this relationship between group and individual voices. His music criticism frequently refers to the primacy in Afro-American culture of the "call and response" mode of work songs and spirituals. Playing off this dynamic, many of Baraka's nationalist poems identify his individual voice with that of a group leader calling for an affirmative response from his community. "Three Movements and a Coda," for example, concludes: "These are songs if you have the/ music." Baraka can provide lyrics, but if they are to come alive as songs, the music must be provided by the participation of a responsive community. The conclusion of "Black Art" makes it clear that this music is more than a purely aesthetic response: "Let the world be a Black Poem/ And Let All Black People Speak This Poem/ Silently/ or LOUD." If the world is to be a poem for the black community, a political response must accompany the aesthetic one.

Determining the precise nature of the desired response demands an awareness of the differing implications of Baraka's poetry when interpreted in relation to white and black cultural traditions. Euro-American reactions to Baraka's nationalist voice tend to attribute even its most extreme statements to the poet himself, dismissing the possibility that he is wearing a mask for political purposes. This is particularly significant in relation to the poems in which Baraka appears to suggest random violence against whites. "Three Movements and a Coda" presents the image of looting a drugstore as a guerrilla attack on the "Vampire Nazis." "Black People!" includes the exhortation: "you can't steal nothin' from a white man, he's already stole it he owes/ you anything you want, even his life." The same poem identifies "Up against the wall mother/ fucker this is a stick up" as "magic words," and pictures looting as a "magic dance in the street." Frequently, Baraka pictures violence in graphic images of "smashing at jelly-white faces" or "cracking steel knuckles in a jewlady's mouth." Given the unqualified intensity of these images, it hardly seems surprising that many white and less militant black readers dismiss the Baraka of this period as a reverse racist forwarding the very modes of thought he ostensibly rejects. In essence, they take the call which concludes "A Poem Some People Will Have To Understand" on a literal level. When Baraka asks "Will the machinegunners please step forward," they respond that a military race war can end only in catastrophe for both races.

As the title of the poem suggests, however, the call should not be interpreted simplistically. To be understood, it must be seen in the context of Baraka's view of the historical response of Afro-Americans to racist oppression. Describing a society in which "the wheel, and the wheels, wont let us alone," he points out that blacks have "awaited the coming of a natural/ phenomenon" to effect a release. Only after repeating "But none has come" three times does Baraka summon the "machinegunners." The call sounds Baraka's response to what he sees as the traditional passivity of the Afro-American community. Recognizing that practically all black experience involves direct contact with psychological racism tied to economic exploitation, Baraka treats these shared experiences hyperbolically in order to shake his community into political action. Placed in a social context where violent group rebellion has been the exception, there is much less chance than most white readers believe that his words will be acted on literally. The use of this aesthetic of calculated overstatement demonstrates Baraka's willingness to use the tradition of masking for a new set of political purposes. Where the form of most Afro-American masks has been dictated by their relationship to white psychology, however, Baraka shapes his new masks to elicit response from blacks. Far from oversimplifying his awareness in the nationalist period, Baraka demonstrates his developing sense of the complexity of poetry designed to function in a real social and political context.

The contextual complexity, however, adds a new dimension of seriousness to attacks on Baraka's use of anti-Semitism and racism as rhetorical strategies. Baraka negotiates extremely treacherous territory when and if he expects readers to concentrate on his desire to "Clean out the world for virtue and love" in the same poem ("Black Art") which endorses "poems that kill . . . Setting fire and death to/ whities ass." A similar apparent paradox occurs in "Black People!" which says both "Take their lives if need be" and "let's make a world we want black children to grow and learn in." Baraka's aesthetic approach, which vests ultimate authority in the authenticating response, raises the problematic possibility that the audience's real social actions will authenticate the destructive rhetoric rather than the constructive vision.

Baraka attempts to diminish this possibility by developing his constructive vision in celebratory nationalist poems such as "It's Nation Time" and "Africa

Africa Africa," which introduce a new musical/chant mode to his work. Exhortations such as "Black Art," which, like Baraka's earlier work, manipulate punctuation and syntax to express fully the urgency of an emotional experience, also anticipate the chant poems by introducing oratorical elements reflecting participation in communal ritual. "A Poem for Black Hearts," for example, varies the opening phrase "For Malcolm's eyes" to establish a focal point for audience response. "For Malcolm's words," "For Malcolm's heart," and similar phrases provide a kind of drum beat for Baraka's meditation on the fallen leader. In "It's Nation Time" and "Africa Africa Africa" this drumbeat, clearly the constitutive structural element, often sounds explicitly: "Boom/ Boom/ BOOOM/ Boom." Writing primarily in short lines echoing these single drumbeats, Baraka uses reiteration and rhythmical variation to stress his vision of Pan-African unity. The first thirteen lines of "Africa Africa Africa" include no words other than "Africa" and "Africans." Anticipating Baraka's developing interest in reggae music, these poems call for the transformation of the old forms of Afro-American culture into those of a new Pan-African sensibility. "It's Nation Time" phrases this call: "get up rastus for real to be rasta fari." Baraka rejects those "rastus" figures content to wear the passive masks imposed on Africans unaware of their heritage, and celebrates the rastafarians, a Caribbean sect associated strongly with reggae.

The most effective poems of Baraka's socialist period redirect the music of these nationalist chants in an attempt to lead the proletariat, black and white, to a new awareness of the implications of its own experience. "Am/ Trak," Baraka's celebration of John Coltrane, attempts to chart this new social and aesthetic awareness by relating Baraka's poetic processes to those of the great jazz saxophonist. Beginning with a section which, like "Trane's" piercing high notes, merges "History Love Scream," Baraka explores the origins of Coltrane's art, which combines individual intensity and the communal response of the bars and churches of Coltrane's Philadelphia. At once purely black and more highly aware than any single voice from the community, Coltrane's voice combines "The vectors from all sources—slavery, renaissance/ bop Charlie Parker/ nigger absolute super-sane screams against reality." Just as Coltrane's voice incorporates and surpasses that of Charlie "Yardbird" Parker, Baraka's incorporates Coltrane's and places it in a wider socialist perspective. Meditating on the aesthetic "difficulty" of both Coltrane's experimental sounds and his own philosophical works, Baraka considers the threat of losing the communal response: "'Trane you blows too long.'/ Screaming niggers drop out yr solos." Of course, the phrase "drop out" is ambiguous: even as the audience refuses to make the effort to comprehend the call, the call perfectly expresses the implications of the audience's experience. Such a call, Baraka insists, can never simply fade into silence. Rather, it will receive a response from artists such as Thelonius Monk, the jazz pianist who played "Street gospel intellectual mystic survival codes."

Coltrane's audience, according to Baraka, consists largely of fellow artists able to perceive the depths of his involvement with black reality.

By associating his own voice with Coltrane's, Baraka points to the developing distance between himself and his wider audience, a distance reflecting his shift to a socialist stance. The poem's final section, especially, is much more politically explicit than either the previous sections or Coltrane's music. As he does in numerous poems of the period, including "Dictatorship of the Proletariat" and "Class Struggle in Music," Baraka insists that the capitalist economic system bears full responsibility for the aesthetic and political corruption of American life. Seeing that "the money lord hovers oer us," he concludes that "only socialism brought by revolution/ can win." Meditating on Coltrane's death in relation to the Newark disorders, Baraka responds to his music as an implicit call for the socialist revolution which will "Be reality alive in motion in flame to change." The intensity of the call for change is unmistakable, in both Coltrane's music and Baraka's poetry. Baraka's identification of the change with "socialism brought by revolution," however, seems abstract and unconvincing in contrast, perhaps because of the relative flatness of diction.

As in many of the poems of the socialist period, Baraka's rhetorical strategy seems unclear. "Am/Trak" contains few indications that the last section should be seen as some type of intricate mask. In fact, American socialist writing both lacks a dominant tradition of masking and tends to reject philosophically anything other than direct confrontation. Still, Baraka certainly retains his knowledge of the Afro-American tradition of masking and has the ability to adjust his voice in accord with shifting social contexts. His extreme didactic stance may be intended as much to spark debate as to enforce agreement. The direct attacks on Don L. Lee (Haki R. Madhubuti) and Nikki Giovanni that occur in Baraka's works, however, suggest that such an interpretation may be overly ingenuous and that Baraka does in fact seek total agreement.

No simple aesthetic analysis suffices to explain either Baraka's new poetic voice or his difficulty in calling forth an affirmative response from either the artistic or the working-class community. Lines such as "This is the dictatorship of the proletariat/ the total domination of society by the working class" can easily be dismissed as lacking either the intellectual complexity or the emotional power of Baraka's earlier work. Such a dismissal, however, risks avoiding the issue of cultural conditioning, which Baraka now sees as central. Arguing that capitalist control of the media deforms both the proletariat's image of itself as a revolutionary force and its response to a "pure" socialist art, Baraka attempts to shatter the psychological barriers through techniques of reiteration similar to those used in the nationalist poetry. His relationship with the proletariat audience, however, generates a new set of political and aesthetic problems. While the nationalist voice assumed authority only insofar as it was validated by the experience of the Afro-American community, the socialist voice must take on the additional burden of convincing the proletarian audience that its interpretation of its own experience had been "incorrect." If the community does not respond to Baraka's voice as its own, the problem lies with a brainwashed response rather than with a tainted call (the source of the problem in "Leroy"). As a result, Baraka frequently adopts a "lecturer's" voice to provide the "hard facts" which will overcome resistance to political action by proving that capitalism deceives the proletariat into accepting a "dictatorship of the minority."

The lack of response to his poems based on this aesthetic may simply reflect the accuracy of his analysis of the problem. What is certain is that Baraka remains determined to resist corruption in whatever form he perceives it, and that he continues to search for a voice like the one described in "Class Struggle in Music (2)," a voice which "even reached you."

Craig Werner

Other major works

LONG FICTION: *The System of Dante's Hell*, 1965.

SHORT FICTION: *Tales*, 1967.

PLAYS: *The Baptism*, 1964; *Dutchman*, 1964; *The Slave*, 1964; *The Toilet*, 1964; *Experimental Death Unit #1*, 1965; *Jello*, 1965; *A Black Mass*, 1966; *Arm Yourself or Harm Yourself*, 1967; *Great Goodness of Life (A Coon Show)*, 1967; *Madheart*, 1967; *Slave Ship: A Historical Pageant*, 1967; *The Death of Malcolm X*, 1969; *Bloodrites*, 1970; *Junkies Are Full of (SHHH . . .)*, 1970; *A Recent Killing*, 1973; *S-1*, 1976; *The Motion of History*, 1977; *The Sidney Poet Heroical*, 1979 (originally as *Sidnee Poet Heroical*, 1975); *What Was the Relationship of the Lone Ranger to the Means of Production?*, 1979, *Money: A Jazz Opera*, 1982; *Primitive World*, 1984.

NONFICTION: *Blues People: Negro Music in White America*, 1963; *Home: Social Essays*, 1966; *Raise Race Rays Raze: Essays Since 1965*, 1971; *The Creation of the New Ark*, 1975; *Daggers and Javelins: Essays*, 1984; *The Autobiography of LeRoi Jones/Amiri Baraka*, 1984; *The Artist and Social Responsibility*, 1986; *Reflections on Jazz and Blues*, 1987.

ANTHOLOGIES: *The Moderns: New Fiction in America*, 1963; *Black Fire: An Anthology of Afro-American Writing*, 1968.

MISCELLANEOUS: *Selected Plays and Prose*, 1979.

Bibliography

Baker, Houston A., Jr. *The Journey Back: Issues in Black Literature and Criticism*. Chicago: University of Chicago Press, 1980. Traces the evolution from the "elegant despair" of Baraka's early poems to his later black nationalism. Baker sees Baraka's transformation as groundbreaking, pivotal in the development of a "Black Aesthetic" that would define itself apart from the Western white canon. The reader must use the index to find references to Baraka, as the chapters are organized historically rather than by authors considered.

Benston, Kimberly W., ed. *Imamu Amiri Baraka (LeRoi Jones): A Collection of Critical Essays.* Englewood Cliffs, N.J.: Prentice-Hall, 1978. Benston, who has written a full-length work on Baraka (*Baraka: The Renegade and the Mask*, 1976), here brings together essays that shed light on various aspect of his poetry and drama. Includes a bibliography.

Brown, Lloyd Wellesley. *Amiri Baraka.* Boston: Twayne, 1980. By a scholar who specializes in African, Afro-American, and Western Indian literary studies, this is the standard critical piece on Baraka's poetic achievement. Provides a bibliography and a index.

Gibson, Donald B., ed. *Five Black Writers: Essays on Wright, Ellison, Baldwin, Hughes, and LeRoi Jones.* New York: New York University Press, 1970. Particularly valuable for setting Baraka in context of other major Afro-American writers of the twentieth century. The assessment of him in the introduction, moreover, places him firmly within the wider literary culture and argues that as of 1970 he had not yet become a "social activist" in his poems and plays. In one chapter Stephen Schneck takes an unflattering look at Baraka's contradictory political statements and maneuverings, while in another, "Black Man as Victim," Donald P. Costello explores Baraka's early plays.

Hudson, Theodore. *From LeRoi Jones to Amiri Baraka: The Literary Works.* Durham, N.C.: Duke University Press, 1973. This sympathetic work provides a biographical chapter based on interviews with Baraka and his parents. Other chapters examine his nonfiction, fiction, poetry, and drama; his philosophical stance is surveyed in one chapter, his forms and styles in another. Notes and an index are provided, along with a bibliography that lists primary and secondary works through the early 1970's.

Johnson, Charles. *Being and Race: Black Writing Since 1970.* Bloomington: Indiana University Press, 1988. Places Baraka in the tradition of Negritude and credits him as having "for the most part established the style of Cultural Nationalist poetics in the period between 1960 and 1970—for an entire generation of writers." Examines his "art-as-weapon" philosophy and his influence on Ntozake Shange. There is no chapter devoted to Baraka, so the reader must consult the index.

Jones, LeRoi. "Philistinism and the Negro Writer." In *Anger, and Beyond: The Negro Writer in the United States*, edited with an introduction by Herbert Hill. New York: Harper & Row, 1966. This essay is useful to the student of Baraka as an articulation in prose of the commitments that were being made simultaneously in the poetry. The tone is rather quiet and reasoned, relative to Baraka's later rhetoric, but the radical central theme is clear: "The Negro writer can only survive by refusing to become a white man."

Lacey, Henry C. *To Raise, Destroy, and Create: The Poetry, Drama, and Fiction of Imamu Amiri Baraka (LeRoi Jones)*. Troy, N.Y.: Whitston, 1981. As the subtitle indicates, this is a wide-ranging study that attempts to do justice to Baraka's work in several genres. Bibliographical references are included as well as an index.

MARY BARNARD

Born: Vancouver, Washington; December 6, 1909

Principal poetry

Cool Country in *Five Young American Poets*, 1940; *A Few Poems*, 1952; *Collected Poems*, 1979; *Time and the White Tigress*, 1986; *Nantucket Genesis*, 1988.

Other literary forms

While Mary Barnard's principal genre is poetry, she has also worked with translations from the Greek, most notably in her well-known *Sappho: A New Translation* (1958). The bulk of her fiction, published in widely read periodicals in the 1950's, is as yet uncollected, though *Three Fables* appeared in 1983. Her essays from her research into Sappho, *The Mythmakers* (1966), also inform her poetry collection *Time and the White Tigress*. Perhaps her best-known work, aside from the poetry, is the autobiography *Assault on Mount Helicon* (1984), which features portraits of many of the chief figures in modern American literature but especially of Ezra Pound and William Carlos Williams.

Achievements

Barnard's work shows the influence of the modernists transposed to a minor key. While it lacks the cosmopolitan effusiveness of Ezra Pound, or the cultural skeet-shooting of T. S. Eliot, or the secret ambition of William Carlos Williams, it nevertheless sets forth a legitimate agenda and succeeds in convincing its readers that while it is small as an oeuvre, it is by no means slight. Moreover, the scope belies the small size. If one believes with Samuel Taylor Coleridge that one of the distinguishing characteristics of high art is its ability to pack maximum content into minimum space, then the miniatures of Mary Barnard offer more aesthetic satisfaction than their collective heft would suggest. By invoking the mythical within the ordinary and the everyday within the mythical, she has created a resonant parallel device for treating the subjects of her choice: childhood, the meaning of change, the pervasiveness of limits, man's relation to nature and to his past, and the fate of women.

While she has written essays and fiction as well as translating from the Greek, these endeavors provide—to use one of her favorite images—a spring from which to enlarge and refresh her poetry. In its classical approach to hidden truths about human nature, it bears resemblance to such earlier writers as Leonie Adams and Louise Bogan. Her translations of Sappho show what can be done to breathe life into revered but seldom-read classics, and the autobiographical *Assault on Mount Helicon* is an important and engaging document of literary history and literary survival from one who wrote from "the far shore" but was nevertheless in the midst of one of the great cultural revolutions of modern times.

Biography

Born of parents who moved west from Indiana, a move inspired in part by the Lewis and Clark Exposition of 1905, Mary Barnard was born on December 6, 1909, in Vancouver, Washington. Her father ran a lumber mill, and Barnard was able to grow up happily in congenial surroundings. Her parents encouraged her early interest in poetry, and Barnard—unusual for her time— attended Reed College, where she took creative writing courses and was graduated in 1932.

Twice during the 1930's, Barnard took up summer residencies at Yaddo in upstate New York and met a number of writers, including Muriel Rukeyser, Kenneth Fearing, Eleanor Clark, and Delmore Schwartz. It was during this decade that she also began corresponding with Ezra Pound and William Carlos Williams, who further encouraged her. In 1935, she won the Levinson Prize from *Poetry* magazine, and her poems were first collected in New Directions' *Five Young American Poets* in 1940. From 1939 to 1943, she worked as curator of the poetry collection at the University of Buffalo, and from 1943 to 1950, she worked as a research assistant to Carl Van Doren and wrote fiction that appeared in such periodicals as *The Saturday Review of Literature*, *The Kenyon Review*, and *Harper's Bazaar*. *A Few Poems* appeared from Reed College in 1952, and in the mid-1950's she worked on her translations of Sappho. In 1957, simultaneously with their acceptance, she moved back to the West Coast and settled in Portland, Oregon. Her collection of essays, *The Mythmakers*, appeared in 1966. The 1979 publication of her *Collected Poems* brought Barnard's poetry to the attention of a new generation of readers. Both this book and her memoir, *Assault on Mount Helicon*, were widely reviewed and warmly received. *Time and the White Tigress* won the 1986 Western States Book Award for Poetry and prompted the jury to cite it as "an impressive achievement from a distinguished writer, and an admirable new American poem."

Analysis

Mary Barnard's poetic output, while quite slim, nevertheless spans and reflects more than half a century of involvement in the art. Her brief, solicitous early lyrics delineate the natural world of the Pacific Northwest with quiet precision, while her later poems reveal her increasing interest in mythological models. Devoid of gimmick and rhetoric, they are as unassuming and well-made as Shaker furniture. The world described in the earlier poems is a world in transition—mostly gone, a remote place of springs and rivers, of meadows and deer, where railroads provide the transfusions of people and goods necessary for a human population to flourish. The later poems cease to reflect a period aspect and, with increasing awareness and confidence in her powers, rely more heavily on invention than recollection. The dominant elements throughout are water and earth rather than air or fire.

Collected Poems opens in childhood, not a childhood toggled to personal memory, but a childhood that any adult might imagine as belonging to a young girl. In "Playroom," there is

> mournfulness of muddy playgrounds,
> raw smell of rubbers and wrapped lunches
> when little girls stand in a circle singing
> of windows and of lovers.

The lives within the playground sing of the life beyond their experience and place, just as the mature poet sings of her "beyond," the past:

> Hearing them, no one could tell
> why they sing sadly, but there is in their voices
> the pathos of all handed-down garments
> hanging loosely on small bodies.

The poem suggests that life itself is a process of outgrowing "garments," that the provisional is the domain of the living. Thus, the girls "sing sadly," not because they understand this condition but because, literally, they embody it.

If the girls have to content themselves with hand-me-downs, a young girl in "The Fitting" must contend with a "trio of hags . . . with cold hands" who roam over her young body and "compress withered lips upon pins" in order to produce a dress for her. They are the three Fates, who determine the quality and duration of life. As they fit the girl, "The knocking of hammers comes/ from beyond the still window curtain. . . ." Some portion of the future, pertinent to others, is being constructed, but her hands will make nothing: "Her life is confined here, in this depth/ in the well of the mirrors." The poem ends with the soft snipping of scissors and pulled threads—also not to be hers—lying on the carpet. The tiny separations imparted by the scissors suggest many more consequential leavetakings to come.

The understanding of limitations of which the young may only have vague intimations, and their delineation, drawn from images in the natural world, are the subjects of many of Barnard's poems. To define a limit, to put a form to what is already form, is to pay it authentic homage. One of the most elemental limits and the source of centuries of solemn meditation from Homer to Wallace Stevens is the seashore. The sea, as a self-sufficient, obverse universe, confronts people both with their otherness, with respect to their mutually incompatible biologies, and with their own "shores," beyond which begins the vast Not-me, a country about which they are impelled to educate themselves, education being the development of commerce between the two realms. Yet their bodies feel a distant affinity to that otherness not easily accessible to language. As the Metaphysical poet Thomas Traherne noted, humanity is "both with moons and tides."

In "Shoreline," one of Barnard's longer poems (and her first published poem), the poet states flatly, "Sand is the beginning and the end/ of our dominion." Yet "The way to the dunes is easy," as children, who have not yet transformed the sea and land, water and earth, into concepts, instinctively know: "their bodies glow/ in the cold wash of the beach." When they return from the beach, "They are unmoved by fears/ that breed in darkening kitchens at sundown/ following storm. . . ." Barnard asserts of the shoreline: "This, then, is the country of our choice." The operative word here is "choice," for one would have thought that limitation was, on the contrary, merely the country of necessity. By choice, however, one stands by the shore "and long[s] for islands"; thus, in some measure, one equally and consciously partakes of one's limitations as well. As one gets older, on the other hand, and one's choices dwindle in the face of increased experience, "We lose the childish avarice of horizons." The poem ends with the refrain, "sand/ is the beginning and the end/ of our dominion," though with a different line break, as if to suggest its shifting against "our dominion." One hears a gentle corrective here both to the infinitude of William Blake's sand and, prophetically, to the sonorous "dominion" of which death shall have none in Dylan Thomas. Barnard's poem seems more thoughtfully located in the actual experiences of people, less in the seductive undertow of language.

Those childhoods, suspended in the ancestral and the domestic, however unique they may seem to the individual and web-spun consciousness of children, carry with them the evidence of their lineages. This evidence, which bespeaks generations of labor needed to produce the child into its time, is present everywhere but especially in those objects that address the body, as in "Beds": "The carved oak headboards of ancestral beds tilt/ like foundered decks from fog at the mouth of the river." The lovely image of care and protection is addressed specifically to the body, whose vulnerability reaches its apex at night. Fear—of being abducted (into the night, into the future, into death)—alternates with remembered or implied assurances of protection:

> Lulla, lulla, will there be, will there
> always be a place to sleep when smoke gathers in the rafters?
> . . . .
> Lulla, lulla. Flood after flood. When the beds float
> downstream, will there be a place to sleep, Matthew, Mark?

Unlike the children's playground, the sanctuary of the bed is permanent, even obligingly providing, although somewhat transformed, humanity's last "resting place." Consequently, the bones' sanctuary posture is the horizontal, and it is through this "angle" that one can see that the eternal nature of the forms links people from biology to biography to history, from their bodies to those of their ancestors and of all humankind:

> The feathers of my grandmothers' beds melted into earlier darkness
> as, bone to earth, I lay down. A trail that leads out, leads back.
> Leads back, anyway, one night or another, bone to earth.

Limits, which provide Barnard with so much of her subject matter, are not inert barriers but, because they are "our choice," are rather actively engaged in transformations. In "The Rapids," the poet focuses on the distinction between the boundary as limit and as transformer: "No country is so gracious to us/ as that which kept its contours while we forgot them. . . ." The precisely placed "gracious" suggests how accommodating a contour a boundary can manage to be to satisfy one's need for orientation and security. At the same time, it is an agency of change: "The water we saw broken upon the rapids/ has dragged silt through marshland/ and mingled with the embittered streams of the sea." In the last stanza of this three-stanza poem, Barnard telescopes the stationary and the moving into a single image of "ungatherable blossoms floating by the . . . rock." These "have flung light in my face, have made promises/ in unceasing undertone." The promises are guarantees made subliminally that one will be at home in the world, or at least that one can recover his home. "Alienation"—one of the most self-incriminating buzzwords of the twentieth century—and all the philosophical ramifications tangled up with it, are, after all, of human manufacture, and while the mind can surely suffer from alienation, it can also break out of it in an instant. Such an instant constitutes the poetic moment of this and other of Barnard's poems.

Being at home in the world means also adjusting to its cyclic nature, which involves death. Usually, human beings do all they can to insulate themselves from its blows, and when the time comes when they can no longer do that, they remember, if they still can, the traditional loophole, lamentation, channeling their sorrow, paying homage, and letting off the steam of outrage and fear all at once. The ability and courage to confront death (of others and one's own) is inversely proportional to the amount of insulation one has accumulated (in the twentieth century, quite a lot). In "Winter Evening," Barnard examines the mythical place of death, for mythological treatment tends to "naturalize" death and so render it less psychically damaging by treating it as an equal partner in the scheme of things. On the other hand, modern middle-class living has tried, in countless ways and to its detriment, to dust its hands of the unflattering fact of terminal being:

> In the mountains, it is said,
> the deer are dying by hundreds.
> We know nothing of that
> in the suburbs.

Doubtless, suburban life has what passes for myths, too, but these are not "ancestral myth," the myth of origins. Rather, "our century/ clings to the novel./ Coffee and novels." Only the train whistles "howl against death/ . . . like Lear in his heartbreak,/ savage as a new myth." Lear, in his vanity, also upset a primoridal set of precedents and suffered madness and death for his trouble. The odd juxtaposition of Lear (though, appropriately, Lear is a winter king) and the suburbans clearly boosts the latter into a mythical realm of danger, for the forces involved are huge and indifferent to human willfulness. The leveling snow that is the immediate cause of the animals' deaths goes on quietly covering all the houses in the town.

While Barnard has clearly absorbed the image-based tenets of Pound and Williams, she most clearly follows the homegrown variety of Williams. In the slyly self-referential "The Spring," Barnard follows the course—one is tempted to say "career"—of a spring, "a mere trickle," as it "whispers" out from under a boulder and fills, first, a pond, then travels (somehow keeping its integrity as a separate spring as it does so) over a spillway, fills another pond, and then falls between trees "to find its fate in the river." The poet concludes,

> Nameless, it has two little ponds
> to its credit, like a poet
> with two small collections of verse.

> For this I celebrate it.

Executed in Williams-style tercets, the poem concerns the question of poetic identity, as the simile makes clear. It is also a self-celebration, for the spring is a decidedly naturalistic image and so in Barnard's canon gets a de facto seal of approval. From the boulder of obscurity to the river of judgment, the stream has avoided dilution, just as a poet with two small collections will, one hopes, have avoided assimilation. To the untrained eye, however, the spring's continuity, its purposefulness, will be invisible: At the point that it is a pond, it *is* a pond; at the river, the river. Guiding her own stream between the "tall cottonwoods" of Pound and Williams (as one would imagine) becomes a matter of integrity that she does not need to spell out, just as it is an act of homage in form and feeling.

Barnard's revival ("arrival" might more accurately indicate the tone of her reception) in the late 1970's was to a considerable degree enhanced by her feminist principles. "Inheritance" addresses the theme of the woman's largely uncommemorated contribution to the settling of America:

Spoon clink fell to axe-chink
falling along the Ohio. These women
made their beds, God bless them,
in the wandering, dreamed, hoped-for
Hesperides, their graves
in permanent places.

The poet admits that, indeed, she was left no tangible inheritance, only pride, and not even pride, but the memory of it, which she identifies as "armor/ . . . against time and men and women." The final placement of women in the list of the enemies of women is a fine idea, and the poem, armored, ends on that note. Barnard obviously believes that one of the chief battles of feminism must be fought on the field of memory, and indeed much of feminist work has been in rectifying the obscured and mystified history of the sex and in transferring future custodianship to women.

Barnard's reading of the classics, from which emerged her translations of Sappho, shows up in poems such as "Persephone." Here, the poet disposes of the hierarchical view of the surface as implicitly preferable to the underworld:

I loved like a mole. There were
subterranean flat stone stairways
to columns supporting the earth and its
daffodils. Or shall we say, to the façade
of the hiding place of earth's treasure?

Nostalgia has no place in the erection of hell: "Homesickness here/ is for the raw working and scars of the surface. . . ." Persephone will make do with what is at hand and will not be enticed into living by "hunger—to which/ . . . surrender is death." She will return to the surface, but not by giving in to her hunger for it. Rather, she will have her pride, and presumably the memory of it, to strengthen her for her return:

How many times it is said to the living,
Conquer hunger! If you
want to go back, up, up where the sun falls
warm on flowering rock and make garlands again.

Barnard puts an effective feminist spin on Persephone's self-denial: Neither the hunger for the world nor the conquering of it is tinged with the desire to return to men (they are conspicuously absent from the poem); rather, Persephone's desire is "to make garlands again."

The image of another "buried" woman appears in "Ondine." Here, the speaker has invited the mermaid into her house to eat, but instead of eating, she sits weeping and blames the speaker for stealing driftwood to burn, a charge the speaker denies. At this, the mermaid stands up and wrings her hair "so that the water made a sudden splash/ on the round rug by the door" and leaves to return to the sea. The speaker throws the knot of wood where the mermaid had sat into the fire ("I beat it out with a poker/ in the soft ash"). At length, she comes to regret her fit of anger:

> Now I am frightened on the shore at night,
> and all the phosphorescent swells that rise
> come towards me with the threat of her dark eyes
> with a cold firelight in them . . .

Her sense of self-reproach at her inability to establish any but the most cursory of relationships with the strange creature gives way to anxiety and guilt. The poem ends with an apocalyptic image that hints at the psychological forces involved in her failure:

> Should she return and bring her sisters with her,
> the withdrawing tide
> would leave a long pool in my bed.
> There would be nothing more of me this side
>
> the melting foamline of the latest wave.

It is in her mythological voice that Barnard most comfortably addresses the larger themes. In one of these, "Fable from the Cayoosh Country," the subject is the power and influence of language. The poet and an unnamed companion lie beside a lake in a pastoral setting. Aware of the nature surrounding them, their thought "pushed forward into the margins of silence/ . . . the boundaries of an inarticulate world." Falling asleep, she dreams of being a missionary of language to the beasts:

> I preached the blessing of the noun and verb,
> but all was lost in the furred ear of the bear,
> in the expressive ear of the young doe.
> What the doe said with her ear, I understood.
> What I said, she obviously did not.

Exasperated, she hurls her grammar books into a pool that immediately begins to address her. It relates the story of a time when all nature could speak with the eloquence that human beings have, but found it was a curse, not a blessing:

> . . . The blade of this tool, useless for digging, chopping,
> shearing, they used against each other with such zeal
> they all but accomplished their own extermination.

The creatures of nature therefore "abandoned speech" yet "retained cries expressive of emotion,/ as rage,/ or love." The pool adds, "They have never seen any cause to repent their decision." The speaker then dreams that the lake his risen over them and confesses, "My consternation was that of a poet, whose love/ if not his living was gravely endangered." She wakes and, finding the lake in place as before, wonders whether it is not a pity that it had not, in fact, flooded over them. As a visionary poem, "Fable from the Cayoosh Country" locates in language not the tool that binds human beings together in a mutually satisfying quest for articulation, but a tempting means to allow oneself to become separate from nature and from one's self. Unfortunately, language cannot police its abuses. In fact, it is not usually aware of them until the harm has been done. Obviously, the poem is a retelling of the Fall, and the striving after language (not in the sense of naming but in the proud rise to eloquence) becomes an activity inappropriate to either Paradise or redemption, the beasts having already fallen and redeemed their natures through a return to the inarticulate. The triumph and burden of language being the human lot, however, the wish to do as the beasts do becomes moot, as language is, for humankind, an irreversible phenomenon.

Another fine poem that speculates on erasure (and mentioned approvingly by Ezra Pound) considers the return to the tabula rasa of the soul recycled and made ready for reincarnation by the waters of Lethe. The soul in "Lethe" pauses over the waters and ponders the enormous human loss necessary to prepare the soul for return to earth:

> Will a few drops on the tongue
> like a whirling flood submerge cities,
> like a sea, grind pillars to sand?
> Will it wash the color from the lips and the eyes
> beloved? It were a thousand pities
> thus to dissolve
> the delicate sculpture of a lifted hand. . . .

The cost of such forgetting, is, for a poet, unbearable, even as it is inevitable. Oblivion is the exact enemy of art, just as Satan is the enemy of virtue, and the poet, "hesitant, unwilling to drink," is ennobled by her resistance.

Time and the White Tigress is a series of verse essays (Barnard refers to it as a single long poem) about the celestial and natural cycles and their impact on humanity's understanding of its place in the cosmos. Harking back to her classical studies and the archaeological arcana of *The Mythmakers*, the poems present, complete with contextual notes, a rationale for the capture and implementation of time as a series of demarcations suitable to the use of custom, since there is "no society without customs. . . ." Hence, the possession of knowledge about time is power inasmuch as it gives its possessor(s) knowledge of the cycles through which one conducts one's life:

A rhythm established by moon after moon,
tide after tide, and year after year
has formed the framework for all our cultures,
a pattern of custom that echoes the pattern
woven by time in the heavens.

Principally, it is to the ancient astronomers, whose priestly function it was to observe and mime the activities of the sky, that beginnings of mythology can be traced: the Twins (dark and light), the signs of the Zodiac, the gods and goddesses of the ancient religions. Yet far from pushing mythology deeper into the mists, Barnard shows that the sky watchers were pragmatic sages who interpreted the heavens in ingenious and economic ways and set the stage for the growth of civilization, from the role of priests and kings to the use and democratization of time to the techniques of mythologizing as a form of advancing out of the darkness. Miming her own subjects, she writes,

We are following here the spoor
of a White Tigress who prowled
Time's hinterlands. . . .
. . . .
Her teats, dripping a moon-milk,
suckled the Twins. The savor,
still on our tongues, is fading.

Here, a pug-mark in the path.
There, bent grass where she crouched.
From this I construct a tigress?

A mythical one?
Perhaps. Why
should we cease to make myths?

One of Barnard's achievements will be seen to be a conscious invention and perpetuation of myths, which are the "necessary fictions" by which human beings try to invoke principles of memory and harmony in their otherwise partial and painful existence through time's indifferent hallways.

David Rigsbee

Other major works
SHORT FICTION: *Three Fables*, 1983.
NONFICTION: *The Mythmakers*, 1966; *Assault on Mount Helicon*, 1984 (autobiography).
TRANSLATION: *Sappho: A New Translation*, 1958.

Bibliography
Fantazzi, Charles E. Review of *The Myth of Apollo and Daphne from Ovid*

to Quevedo, by Mary Barnard. *Choice* 25 (September, 1987): 112. Fantazzi comments on Barnard's highly learned book of comparative literature, which traces the story of Apollo and Daphne from Ovid to the Spanish Golden Age. Barnard's facility with myth is apparent here, as it is in her poetry. Gives an idea of the breadth of Barnard's accomplishment as a writer.

Helle, Anita. "Dialogue with Mary Barnard." *Northwest Review* 20, nos. 2-3 (1982): 188-198. Few biographical sources on Mary Barnard exist, therefore this interview is very important. Barnard explains that she uses myth to reveal lost history, especially the history of women in Western society. Interesting for all students.

Swift, John. "Separations." *Northwest Review* 18, no. 3 (1980): 114-119. Swift explains Barnard's attempt to separate the idea of boundaries as limits and the notion of limits as powers that enable transformation. This is related to Barnard's connection with the land of the Pacific Northwest.

Van Cleve, Jane. "A Personal View of Mary Barnard." *Northwest Review* 18, no. 3 (1980): 105-113. Barnard's work did not find a large audience until the late 1970's, when feminist writing came into vogue. Van Cleve discusses how Barnard's poetry affects Van Cleve as a woman.

Whitman, Ruth. Review of *Time and the White Tigress*, by Mary Barnard. *Choice* 24 (December, 1986): 620. Whitman calls Barnard's book of poetry "extraordinary." She describes how it weaves comparative mythology with comparative science in a beautiful, simple way. Provides students with a helpful overview and understanding of Barnard's book. Informative for all students.

SAMUEL BECKETT

Born: Foxrock, Ireland; April 13, 1906
Died: Paris, France; December 22, 1989

Principal poetry

Whoroscope, 1930; *Echo's Bones and Other Precipitates,* 1935; *Poems in English,* 1961; "Zone," 1972 (translation of Guillaume Apollinaire's poem); *Collected Poems in English and French,* 1977.

Other literary forms

Samuel Beckett is far better known for his fiction and plays than for his poetry, even though it was as a poet that he began his writing career. In fact, Beckett explored almost every literary form, writing in English and in French. His early fiction, the collection of stories *More Pricks than Kicks* (1934) and the novels *Murphy* (1938) and *Watt* (1953), was written orginally in English, but his best-known fictions, including the trilogy of *Molloy* (1951), *Malone meurt* (1951, *Malone Dies*), and *L'Innomable* (1953, *The Unnamable*), and *Comment c'est* (1961, *How It Is*) and *Le Dépeupleur* (1971, *The Lost Ones*) were written and published originally in French. From the beginning, Beckett's greatest strength was as an innovator, writing prose works which do not seem to fit easily into traditional categories but which extend the possibilities of contemporary fiction and which have had a profound influence on the writers who have followed him.

Beckett was also a writer of plays, and, when his name is mentioned, most people think of *En Attendant Godot* (1952, *Waiting for Godot*). This difficult theatrical work met with astounding success on stages throughout the world, and it is still Beckett's best-known and most-discussed piece. Other works for the stage, *Fin de partie* (1957, *Endgame*), *Krapp's Last Tape* (1958), *Happy Days* (1961), and *Rockaby* (1981), to name only a few, have extended the possibilities of live theater. His *Collected Shorter Plays* was published in 1984.

Never content to restrict himself to a single medium, Beckett demonstrated that radio and television can serve as vehicles for serious drama with radio plays such as *All That Fall* (1957), *Cascando* (1963), and *Words and Music* (1962), and television scripts such as *Eh Joe* (1966). Beckett also wrote the filmscript for the short movie *Film* (1965), produced and directed by Alan Schneider and starring Buster Keaton. Like the novels and the plays, these works for the mass media tapped new possibilities and pointed out new directions which other younger writers are only now beginning to explore.

Early in his career, Beckett also showed that he was a brilliant critic of the arts, writing on the fiction of James Joyce and Marcel Proust and on the paintings of his longtime friend Bram van Velde. In addition to translating his own works, he has translated other writers, including Robert Pinget, Paul Eluard, Alain Bosquet, and Sebastien Chamfort from the French and *An Anthology of Mexican Poetry* (1958) from the Spanish. His English version of Arthur Rimbaud's *Le bateau ivre* (*The Drunken Boat*), done in the 1930's but lost for many years and rediscovered and published for the first time only in the 1977 *Collected Poems in English and French*, is masterful, but his best-known translation is of Guillaume Apollinaire's "Zone" (1972), a long poem that addresses many of Beckett's own themes and which opens with a line that could well characterize Beckett's efforts in all forms: "In the end you are weary of this ancient world."

Achievements

When the Swedish Academy selected Beckett to receive the Nobel Prize in Literature in 1969, the award only confirmed what critics and readers had known for some time: that he is one of the most important literary figures of the late twentieth century. Few authors in the history of literature have attracted as much critical attention as Beckett, and with good reason; he is both an important figure in his own right and a transitional thinker whose writings mark the end of modernism and the beginning of a new sensibility, postmodernism. The modernists of the early twentieth century—James Joyce, W. H. Auden, Virginia Woolf, Marcel Proust, and others—were stunned by the absurdity of their world. Previous generations had filled that world with philosophical, religious, and political meanings, but their orderly visions of reality no longer seemed to apply to life in the early 1900's. The modernists lacked the faith of their forebears; they had experienced the chaos of the modern world with its potential for global war and the destruction of civilization, and they believed that the order of reality was a fiction, that life was unknowable. In response to their doubts, they turned literature in upon itself, separating it from life, creating an art for its own sake. These writers trusted in language to create new meanings, new knowledge, and a separate, artistic human universe.

As a young man, Beckett also experienced this sense of absurdity and meaninglessness in the modern world, but, unlike his modernist predecessors, he could not even muster faith in his art or in language. Thus, while Joyce could revel in the possibilities and textures of the written word, Beckett could not. Instead, he reduced his fictions, his plays, and his poems to the barest elements, and, throughout his career, he tried to rejoin art and life in his own way. For the pre-modernists, art imitated the world beyond the human mind. The modernists rejected this idea of imitation, and so did Beckett. Instead, his art reflects the inner world, the world of the human voice, the only world human beings can ever really experience. In the pre-modern era, art was successful if it depicted some truth about the world. For the modernists, art succeeded only on its own terms, regardless of the world beyond the scope of the arts. For Beckett, art never succeeds. It is a necessary failure which never manages to link the inner mind to outer reality. As such, art is an exercise in courage, foredoomed to failure, like human life itself. Man is man not because he can give meaning to the world or because he can retreat into aesthetics but because he can recognize that his world is meaningless and that his life is leading him only toward death; yet he must continue to live and strive. As a philosopher of failure, Beckett was the first thinker of our own age.

Biography

Samuel Barclay Beckett grew up in a suburb of Dublin, Ireland, a Protestant in a Catholic country and therefore something of an exile in his own land. He attended Trinity College in Dublin, where he discovered his talent for languages and studied English, French, and Italian. He taught for two terms at Campbell College in Belfast and then, in 1928, traveled to Paris, where he lectured in English at the École Normale Supérieure. It was during this tenure that he met his countryman James Joyce. Beckett returned to Ireland to teach four terms at Trinity College, but, in 1932, after much consideration and anguish, he left the teaching profession for good, convinced that he could not survive as a writer in academe. For the next five years, he wandered through Europe, and, in 1937, he settled in Paris permanently. It was in Paris that Beckett died in 1989, at the age of eighty-three.

There were probably many reasons for Beckett's self-imposed exile and for his decision to write in a language not his by birth, but surely one reason was the influence of Joyce, who recommended exile for artists. It would be difficult to overestimate the effect that Joyce had on Beckett's life and work. In the late 1930's, the younger Irishman was an intimate member of Joyce's inner circle. He worked on a translation of Joyce's "Anna Livia Plurabelle" into French, took dictation for his friend, wrote a critical study of Joyce's writings, ran errands for the Irish master, and even attracted the romantic interest of Joyce's daughter, Lucia. Apparently, Joyce thought a great deal of Beckett, and Beckett looked upon Joyce as a consummate master, so that it is possible he decided to write in French in order to avoid the language which, in his own mind, Joyce had all but exhausted.

As Beckett grew older and developed as a writer, Joyce's influence began to weaken, and, in many ways, Beckett's later style—spare, flat, reduced to the barest elements—is the antithesis of Joyce's rich, punning, heavily textured prose. Beckett also rejected Joyce's "Irishness" in favor of characters and settings without specific nationality or history. In the early poetry, however, the influence of Joyce and Ireland is still strong, and, in fact, it was in his poems that Beckett first began to work through Joyce's voice and to discover his own.

Analysis

Whoroscope was Samuel Beckett's first major publication. It is a long poem, written originally in English, and published in book form by the Hours Press after winning a prize offered by the publisher for the best poem on the subject of time. The first-person narrator of the work is René Descartes, the seventeenth century French philosopher, mathematician, and scientist, and the poem is so full of obscure allusions to his life and times that, at the publisher's request, Beckett added a page and a half of notes to the ninety-eight-line piece. In fact, the notes are almost as interesting as the poem itself, and, without them, it is unlikely that the average reader would even recognize Descartes as the speaker.

Whoroscope is an important poem not only because it marked Beckett's official entry into the literary world but also because it introduced the basic themes that continued to occupy him as a writer and thinker. Clearly, Beckett himself recognized this fact, because he chose to keep this early work intact in the subsequent collections of his poetry, *Poems in English* and *Collected Poems in English and French*, which include all the works discussed here. In many ways, *Whoroscope* is quite unlike the author's later writings. The structure of the piece is open, without rhyme or regular meter. The poem shows the influence of the French surrealists in its associative juxtaposition of images, but the influence of Joyce is also apparent in the punning title and in the body of the text.

On first reading, it is not at all obvious that this is a poem about time. From the opening line, Descartes rambles on, apparently at random, about various events in his life, without respect for chronology or even historical accuracy. In the closing section, it becomes clear that the philosopher is on his deathbed and that his ramblings are the result of illness and fever. In a sense, his life is flashing before his eyes. He is trying to grasp the fullness of time at the moment of his death, and a closer reading shows that the sequence of memories is not random at all but associative, each a memory leading to the next—not in chronological order but in the order dictated by Descartes' subjective thought process.

In fact, the poem is very much about time—the time of a man's life and the attempt to recapture lost time in the instant before time runs out. The Joycean influence in Descartes' stream-of-consciousness narrative is evident, but it is also obvious that Beckett has learned a great deal from Marcel Proust's *A la recherche du temps perdu* (1913-1927, *Remembrance of Things Past*), which the young Beckett knew well—so well, in fact, that in 1931 he published *Proust*, a book-length study of this French masterwork.

Whoroscope, then, is about time as the great destroyer, time that eats up a man's life and leads only to death. It is important to remember, however, that this poem is about the lifetime of a particular man, Descartes, and there is good reason for Beckett's choice of this philosopher as his narrator. Like

Beckett himself, Descartes was a transitional figure, the father of modern philosophy and the opponent of Aristotelian scholasticism. He and his contemporaries initiated a new age in Western civilization, an age that is only now passing away, and, in his poem, Beckett pays tribute to other great thinkers such as Galileo and Francis Bacon, who directed Western thought into the era of science and rationalism.

Descartes was a great builder, but he was also a great destroyer of the philosophies of the past, and, in the poem, he speaks with pride of "throwing/ Jesuits out of the skylight." He devoted his life to the development of a new system of thought, but, in so doing, he also undermined the Aristotelian metaphysics that had served as the basis of European philosophy for centuries. Ironically, while Descartes was destroying his predecessors, the time of his own life was destroying him.

This is one of the key themes of Beckett's work: the fact that death comes to all living things, without reason, without justice, regardless of whether one is innocent or guilty. As Beckett writes in a later, untitled poem, man lives "the space of a door/ that opens and shuts." He is born to die; he is dying even in the womb, losing time from the moment of conception, and there is nothing that can stop or even delay this process. Each man's life cancels itself, moment by moment.

The historical Descartes died while in the service of Queen Christina of Sweden, a harsh woman who forced the aging philosopher to call upon her at five o'clock each morning although he had been in the habit of staying in bed until midday all his life. This change in his routine, coupled with the northern weather, led to his final illness. In the poem, the fictional Descartes refers to Queen Christina as "Rahab of the snows." Rahab was a biblical harlot mentioned in *The Divine Comedy* (c. 1320) of Dante (whom Beckett has called "the only poet"), and so it would seem that the Queen is the whore of the title. In his notes to the poem, Beckett points out that Descartes kept his birthday secret so that no astrologer could cast his horoscope. The philosopher was opposed to such mysticism, not only because it was unscientific but because he felt that many people let their entire lives be dictated by astrology; he even knew of two young men who had allowed themselves to die simply because their horoscopes had predicted death for them. With this knowledge, the Joycean pun of the title becomes clear. Queen Christina, the harlot, has cast Descartes' death, which was present from the moment of his birth. His "whoroscope" is her prediction of his inevitable end.

This theme of the inevitability of death, of death as a necessary function of birth, runs through the poem in the form of a recurring motif. Again in the notes, Beckett explains that Descartes liked his morning omelette to be made from eggs that had been hatched from eight to ten days—that is, eggs in which the embryo was partially developed. Time and again in the poem he asks about his morning eggs: "How long did she womb it, the feathery one? . . . How rich she smells,/ this abortion of a fledgling!"

For Beckett, the egg is the symbol of the fetus conceived only to die, its brief span of life lived out in the instant between nonexistence and nonexistence. The time of the egg is the time of the philosopher as well. As with all human beings, Descartes is dying before he has even really lived, and, like the fledgling in the egg, he is dying for no purpose, simply because that is the way things are.

Beckett explored the themes of the inevitability of death and the meaninglessness of life time and again in his works, but he has always coupled these themes with another: the necessity of going on, of raging against the inevitable, of refusing to accept man's fate. In the poem "Serena III," he insists that human beings must "keep on the move/ keep on the move," and, in *Whoroscope*, he depicts Descartes first as angry, cursing his fate, then as begging for another chance at a life he has never managed to understand, a "second/ starless inscrutable hour." There is no reason for him to go on, and yet, as a human being, he must.

For Beckett, man must die, but he must also live and think and speak, as Descartes does, even to the last possible instant. He must live in his own inner world which is always dying, and he must also live in the outer world which will live on after him and which, therefore, is not his. This theme of the conflict between the inner and the outer worlds which runs through Beckett's later work is present in *Whoroscope* as well. The very structure of the poem, which follows the philosopher's associative thinking, places the narrative within Descartes' inner mind, though in the end it moves to the outer world, to "Christina the ripper" and to her court physician, Weulles, who is attending to Descartes in his last moments. In his inner world, Descartes is alive and reliving his past, but it is the outer world which is leading him to inevitable death. Descartes devoted his life to trying to understand the outer world, but the very foundation of his thought, the dictum "cogito, ergo sum" ("I think, therefore I am") trapped him within his own subjectivity, and generations of later philosophers have tried to understand how one can move from the certainty of the "cogito" to the world beyond which is not oneself. The "cogito," the single point of certainty in the Cartesian philosophy of doubt, is the fulcrum of modern Western philosophy, and yet it restricts the thinker to his own inner world, to what Beckett calls, in his poem "The Vulture," "the sky/ of my skull."

For Beckett, it is impossible for man to come to know the world beyond his skull, that very world in which he must live and die. In the play *Endgame*, the characters Hamm and Clov live within a skull-like structure; Hamm is blind, and Clov can see the world only through two eyelike windows which restrict his vision. In the short novel *The Lost Ones* an entire society lives and passes away within a huge white dome, a skull. In *Whoroscope*, Descartes can know his inner world, but the outer world remains "inscrutable."

He knows that he thinks and, therefore, that he is, but he does not know why. He wants to know the truth and to speak it, but the "cogito" cannot lead him to knowledge of the outer world. In the poem, he mentions St. Augustine, who also sought a single point of certainty in a world in which everything was open to question, and found that the only thing he could be sure of was that he could be deceived. The Descartes of the poem states the Augustinian dictum as "Fallor, ergo sum!" ("I am deceived, therefore I am"). At the moment of death, this certainty seems truer to the philosopher than his own "cogito." To be a man is to be deceived, to fail, and, for a human being, courage is the courage to fail. Man is man only insofar as he knows that failure is inevitable and yet keeps going in spite of that knowledge.

There is another important Beckett theme which surfaces only briefly in *Whoroscope* but which becomes the main focus of the author's second collection of poems, *Echo's Bones and Other Precipitates*: the theme of the impossibility of love in the face of absurdity and death. For Beckett, love is another of man's basic needs, as important as the quest for meaning, and as futile. The Descartes poem touched on the theme only briefly, in the philosopher's memory of a little cross-eyed girl who was his childhood playmate and who reminds him of his only daughter, Francine, who died of scarlet fever at the age of six. The implication is that love always ends, if not now, then later; and, like the rest of life, love is both essential and hopeless, necessary and frightening. Knowing that love is impossible, pretending that it is not, man loves, and that love is the source of his pain but also of his life.

The poems of *Echo's Bones and Other Precipitates* differ from *Whoroscope* not only because they focus on love but also because the narrator is not a fictional version of a historical character but the author himself. The title of the collection comes from Ovid's *Metamorphosis* (before A.D. 8), from the story of Echo, who, after being spurned by Narcissus, lets herself wither away until only her bones and voice remain. The connection between Ovid's tale and Beckett's theme of love is clear, but the story of Echo also provides the poet with two of his favorite images: the inevitability of death and the survival of the voice.

Most of the titles and forms of the poems in this collection are based on the songs of the troubadours which Beckett knew well and which attracted him no doubt because they were songs of love and, often, of loss, and also because the troubadours were usually wanderers and exiles, like Beckett himself and like the narrators of most of these poems. The work "Enueg I" draws its title from the traditional Provençal lament or complaint, and, as might be expected, it is a complaint of love. In the poem, the narrator leaves the nursing home where his beloved is dying of tuberculosis ("Exeo in a spasm/ tired of my darling's red sputum") and wanders through Dublin, traveling in a wide circle. He finds that the world is full of images of death ("a dying barge," "the stillborn evening," "the tattered sky like an ink of pestilence") and that he cannot forget his beloved or the fate of their love. Of course, these signs of death are not really present in the outer world; they reflect the narrator's inner life, the only life he can know, and, like Descartes, he rages against what he knows to be true as his own blood forms a "clot of anger."

There is no romance in Beckett's lament, only the all-encompassing awareness of mortality. Love and romance are like "the silk of the seas and the arctic flowers/ that do not exist," figments of the imagination that lose all sense of reality in the face of "the banner of meat bleeding."

The narrator keeps moving, however, and throughout the poem he has contact with others, with a small boy and "a wearish old man," an archetypal Beckett character, "scuttling along between a crutch and a stick,/ his stump caught up horribly, like a claw, under his breech, smoking." These meetings show the continuing possibility of human contact, even in a dying world; they also make clear the need for going on even in the face of futility. Perhaps the others, like the narrator, are also moving in circles, but circular movement is still movement, and even the old man, crippled and in pain, does not remain motionless, does not give up.

"Sanies I" is also modeled on a Provençal form; the title is derived from a Latin term meaning "morbid discharge." For Beckett, writing is such a discharge, a residue, a "precipitate." It is a by-product of living and dying, but it is also that which remains, like Echo's voice.

Like the narrator of "Enueg I," the narrator of "Sanies I" is a wanderer in the process of completing a circle; in this case, he is returning home to Ireland after traveling in Europe, apparently in Germany, for his speech is full of Germanic terms. Like later Beckett protagonists, he rides a bicycle, and he describes himself as "a Ritter," a German knight, and, therefore, a somewhat ironic hero, though perhaps the only kind of hero who remains in the postmodern age: the hero who keeps moving. He has been wandering for a long time, and he says that he is "müüüüüüüüde now." The German "müde" means "tired," but the extended "ü" sound also gives a sense of boredom, an essential element in most of Beckett's work. Clearly, the narrator is both tired and bored, and, as a result, he is "bound for home like a good boy." Thinking about home and his parents, he recalls his birth and longs for that sweet oblivion of the womb: "Ah to be back in the caul now with no trusts/ no fingers no spoilt love."

This is a key passage. "The caul" to which the narrator would like to return is a fetal membrane covering the head, and, according to folklore, the child who is born with a caul is born to good luck. The implication here, however, is that the best of luck is never to have been born at all and, therefore, to have avoided "trusts" and "spoilt loves," those exercises in futility. The unborn child also has "no fingers," and one without fingers cannot, and therefore need not, travel on a bicycle as the narrator does. Even better, one without fingers cannot write, no matter how strongly he might feel the need to do so.

Of course, the narrator no longer has the option of not being born. He is "tired now hair ebbing gums ebbing ebbing home," and yet he approaches his hometown like a "Stürmer," German slang for "lady-killer." It would seem that, despite his "spoilt loves," he is prepared for love again, and, indeed, he sees his beloved waiting for him. "I see main verb at last/ her whom alone in the accusative/ I have dismounted to love." In German, the "main verb" comes at the end of the sentence, and in this sentence that word is "love." At the last moment, however, the narrator sends the girl away ("get along with you now"), refusing to make the mistake his parents made by bringing another being into the world. Although one cannot return to the peace of the womb, one can at least refuse to pass on the curse of life to another.

If "Sanies I" is about nonexistence in the womb (the Cartesian egg), and if "Enueg I" is about nonexistence in the tomb, the title poem of the collection brings these two notions together. "Echo's Bones" is a short lyric that restates Beckett's key themes in capsule form. The first word of the poem is "asylum," a reference to the womb, but this is an "asylum under my tread," a shelter underground, a tomb. Like those in the womb, those in the tomb are beyond the confusions and pains of living now that they have run the gauntlet of life, "the gantelope of sense and nonsense." Only now, in death, are they free to be themselves, "taken by the maggots for what they are," and what they are is fleshless bone, without love or dreams and without the need to keep striving. The title of the poem, however, is a reminder that something more than bone remains: the voice. The words may be only a "morbid discharge," but, like Echo's voice, they survive.

Leaping ahead four decades to "Something There," a poem composed in 1974, the reader finds that the author's voice has changed, although his key themes remain. Here the lines are short and direct, flat and prosaic. There are no obscure allusions, no Joycean puns. The "something there" of the title is "something outside/ the head," and this contrast of inner and outer worlds returns the reader to *Whoroscope* and to the Cartesian dilemma of subjectivity which cannot reach beyond itself. The poem tries to reach that "something" in the only way it can, through words, but "at the faint sound so brief/ it is gone." The reality beyond the inner mind disappears as soon as the words of the mind try to grasp it, and so language, in the end, describes only the inner world which becomes something like a womb and a tomb in the midst of life. The inner world is not life, and yet, despite the fact that man cannot reach beyond his inner self to comprehend the "something outside/ the head," still he must try to do so, and the sign of his failure is language, the voice which always remains.

One can argue that Beckett's view of existence is largely negative. On the other hand, however, it is important to remember that he was influenced greatly by the medieval theologians who argued that truth, in the person of God, is beyond positive statement and that man can know the truth only in the negative, by describing what it is not. Beckett seems to have taken the same approach. It is true that he wrote about the curse of life, but he did so beautifully, raging against the inevitability of silence. The beauty of his work is the beauty of the human will to live in the face of death. Beckett sings the praises of those who say, with the nameless, formless, faceless narrator of *The Unnamable*: "I can't go on, I'll go on."

Welch D. Everman

Other major works

LONG FICTION: *Murphy*, 1938; *Molloy*, 1951 (English translation, 1955); *Malone meurt*, 1951 (*Malone Dies*, 1956); *L'Innomable*, 1953 (*The Unnamable*, 1958); *Watt*, 1953; *Comment c'est*, 1961 (*How Is It*, 1964); *Mercier et Camier*, 1970 (*Mercier and Camier*, 1974); *Le Dépeupleur*, 1971 (*The Lost Ones*, 1972); *Company*, 1980; *Mal vu mal dit*, 1981 (*Ill Seen Ill Said*, 1981); *Worstward Ho*, 1983.

SHORT FICTION: *More Pricks Than Kicks*, 1934; *Nouvelles et textes pour rien*, 1955 (*Stories and Texts for Nothing*, 1967); *No's Knife: Collected Shorter Prose 1947-1966*, 1967; *First Love and Other Shorts*, 1974; *Pour finir encore et autres foirades*, 1976 (*Fizzles*).

PLAYS: *En attendant Godot*, 1952 (*Waiting for Godot*, 1954); *Fin de partie: Suivi de Acte sans paroles*, 1957 (*Endgame: A Play in One Act; followed by Act Without Words: A Mime for One Player*, 1958); *All That Fall*, 1957 (radio play); *Krapp's Last Tape*, 1958; *Embers*, 1959 (radio play); *Act Without Words II*, 1960 (one-act mime); *Happy Days*, 1961; *Words and Music*, 1962 (radio play); *Cascando*, 1963 (radio play); *Play*, 1963 (English translation, 1964); *Come and Go: Dramaticule*, 1965 (English translation, 1967); *Film*, 1965 (screenplay); *Eh Joe*, 1966 (teleplay; *Dis Joe*, 1967); *Not I*, 1972 (teleplay); *Tryst*, 1976 (teleplay); *That Time*, 1976; *Footfalls*, 1976; *Shades*, 1977 (teleplay); *A Piece of Monologue*, 1979; *Rockaby and Other Short Pieces*, 1981; *Quad*, 1981 (teleplay); *Rockaby*, 1981; *Ohio Impromptu*, 1981; *Catastrophe*, 1982; *Company*, 1983; *What Where*, 1983; *Collected Shorter Plays*, 1984.

MISCELLANEOUS: *I Can't Go On, I'll Go On: A Selection from Samuel Beckett's Work*, 1976 (Richard Seaver, editor).

Bibliography

Alvarez, Alfred. *Samuel Beckett*. New York: Viking Press, 1973. Alvarez discusses Beckett's literary output and argues that he is creative for the originality with which he restates the same case in unexpected ways. This good introduction to a difficult writer identifies Beckett's themes as expressing "a message of undifferentiated gloom . . . and a spirit of pure desolation." Really a praise of Beckett, not a criticism.

Bair, Deirdre. *Beckett: A Biography.* New York: Harcourt Brace Jovanovich, 1978. This unauthorized biographical account follows Beckett from his childhood in Ireland through his years in Paris. It covers his relationships with James Joyce, his family, and others, and it examines the autobiographical influences on his work. This interpretive biography tends to trivialize the mysterious universality of Beckett's life and work. Bair interviewed Beckett, his friends, and his colleagues and was given access to correspondences hitherto unpublished. Not without its detractors, this is the only full biography of the writer.

Esslin, Martin, ed. *Samuel Beckett: A Collection of Critical Essays.* Englewood Cliffs, N.J.: Prentice-Hall, 1965. This collection includes a survey of Beckett's verse by John Gould Fletcher and is an excellent reference book on Beckett with material from Beckett's leading critics and observers. These essays are definitely mid-twentieth century opinions and reflect Esslin's own philosophical bent toward existentialism.

Harvey, Lawrence E. *Samuel Beckett: Poet and Critic.* Princeton, N.J.: Princeton University Press, 1970. This study, devoted almost entirely to Beckett's poetry, looks at the early writing from 1929 to 1949. It combines analyses of the poems with comments on the young Beckett based on conversations with the author and unpublished manuscripts. A thoughtful examination of Beckett's poetry, it analyzes Beckett's first poem, *Whoroscope*, and points out the early incarnation of Beckett's philosophical disposition and the roots of his future characters.

Kaelin, Eugene F. *The Unhappy Consciousness: The Poetic Plight of Samuel Beckett.* Boston: D. Reidel, 1981. Characterizing Beckett as a philosophical writer, Kaelin analyzes his creative work from a phenomenological, structuralist point of view attempting to show the degree to which the philosophical structures of Beckett's works have changed. Comparisons and references to Georg Wilhelm Friedrich Hegel, Martin Heidegger, Jean-Paul Sartre and Maurice Merleau-Ponty are discussed.

Kenner, Hugh. *Samuel Beckett: A Critical Study.* New York: Grove Press, 1968. This new edition of a 1961 study contains a supplementary chapter and explores Beckett's themes with careful readings of all the existing material up to the date of publication. Beckett's relationships to Marcel Proust and James Joyce as well as Homer, Vergil, Dante, philology, René Descartes and phenomenology are examined. This "classical" study of Beckett also notes what he has done with the forms of drama and the novel.

Mercier, Vivian. *Beckett/Beckett.* New York: Oxford University Press, 1977. Each chapter sets up a dialectic to explore the dualistic elements found in Beckett's work, including Ireland/The World, Gentleman/Tramp, Classicism/Absurdism, Painting/Music, and Woman/Man, ending with an epilogue on Intellect and Emotion. This study of polarities looks at Beckett on the basis of his own dichotomies as a guide to his methods and meanings.

THOMAS LOVELL BEDDOES

Born: Clifton, England; June 30, 1803
Died: Basel, Switzerland; January 26, 1849

Principal poetry
The Improvisatore, 1821; *The Poems, Posthumous and Collected, of Thomas Lovell Beddoes*, 1851; *The Poetical Works of Thomas Lovell Beddoes*, 1890; *The Poems of Thomas Lovell Beddoes*, 1907; *Selected Poems*, 1976.

Other literary forms
During his lifetime, Thomas Lovell Beddoes published only one volume of poetry, one play, scattered incidental poems, and a few newspaper articles written in German. His most substantial publications, *The Improvisatore* and the play *The Bride's Tragedy* (1822), appeared when he was very young. The poems were published at Oxford; the play appeared on the London stage.

Achievements
Beddoes was recognized during his lifetime as a promising young lyrical dramatist who never fulfilled the early expectations he raised. The one volume of poems and the single play—virtually all of his work to be published during his lifetime—appeared while he was an undergraduate. They attracted sufficient attention to earn him the acquaintance and support of a small circle of London literary figures including Mary Shelley and William Godwin. Throughout the remainder of his life, however, Beddoes became increasingly aloof from literary "insiders." He gained a modest notoriety on the Continent for the fiery radicalism which caused him repeated conflicts with the authorities.

In the twentieth century, a number of scholars have returned to Beddoes' work (most of it unpublished before his death, much of it never finished) with a new seriousness which has given him a firm though not exalted reputation among late Romantic (or early Victorian) writers. Beddoes is no longer seen as a mere anachronism, writing Elizabethan plays out of their time. Rather, he is seen as a man of deeply romantic temperament who tried to ground his commitment to the imagination in a rigorously scientific account of the human faculties. His failure to integrate these opposing tendencies resulted in strong tensions which generated a few powerful poetic characters and a poignant imagery in his work. The same tensions perhaps also contributed to the mood of despair which ended in his suicide.

Biography
Born at Clifton, England, Thomas Lovell Beddoes grew up under the shadow of a distinguished father (usually referred to as "Dr. Beddoes" to

avoid confusion with the poet). Dr. Beddoes had been the friend of Erasmus Darwin, Samuel Taylor Coleridge, and other celebrated figures. The poet also grew up in the reflected fame of his aunt—the novelist Maria Edgeworth.

As a schoolboy at Charterhouse, Beddoes was a precocious student of the classics. There he wrote a juvenile short story, "Scaroni: Or, The Mysterious Cave" and also, apparently, some plays no longer extant. At Pembroke College, Oxford, Beddoes distinguished himself both as a student and as a writer. The success of *The Improvisatore* and *The Bride's Tragedy* led him to believe that he might expect a future in letters. He did not then know that he had already published the last significant work he would ever see in print. In 1825, after taking his degree in classics, Beddoes went abroad to improve his German and to scoop the cream of German learning at a time when both letters and the sciences were enjoying a burst of brilliance in Germany. In fact, however, Beddoes was never to return to England except for short interludes.

At Göttingen University he polished the manuscripts of *Torrismond* (1851) and *The Second Brother* (1851) and tried to complete the project which was to occupy him for the rest of his life—*Death's Jest-Book* (1850). Failing in his attempt to complete these projects, Beddoes attempted suicide in 1829. In the same year, he was expelled by the university court on charges of drunken and disorderly behavior. His fortunes grew still more turbulent after he had transferred to the University of Würzburg: desultory composition, occasional political articles for the *Volksblatt*, a revolutionary speech at Gaibach, deportation from Munich, imprisonment for debt at Würzburg, a move to Zurich. In Switzerland he found a temporarily safe haven and entered the University at Zurich in 1833, remaining there until 1837.

During the period of his German studies, Beddoes had become increasingly absorbed by a scientific interest which finally led to a degree in physiology. Thus, he can be seen as an interesting case of the nineteenth century polymath, trying fiercely to hold the humane and scientific cultures together in his own mind, on the eve of Matthew Arnold's and T. H. Huxley's open acknowledgment that classical and scientific education had become adversarial. Beddoes himself seems to have practiced his dissections in the futile hope of finding some undiscovered organ which could authenticate the arguments for human immortality, thus grounding metaphysics in physics.

Beddoes continued to create social difficulties for himself through both his political radicalism and his casual disregard for bourgeois conventions. In 1839, he experienced a continuing conflict with the Zurich police over his lack of a residence permit. In 1840, he moved to Berlin and attended the university. Back in Zurich in 1845, he was fined for disturbing the peace. He traveled to Frankfurt, where he suffered a long illness brought on by an infection he incurred while dissecting. After a brief trip to England, he went to Basel, Switzerland. On the morning following his arrival there, Thomas Beddoes deliberately opened an artery in his left leg. Six months later, after recuperating from the second attempt on his own life, Beddoes died—most likely a suicide—on January 26, 1849—too early in the year to enjoy the fall of Metternich and the broad victory of radicals throughout Europe. He was forty-five years old.

The fate of Beddoes' manuscripts is one of the most curious in literary history. Hours before his death he bequeathed all of his papers to his English friend T. F. Kelsall. Kelsall, in turn, left the extensive collection of largely unpublished Beddoes manuscripts to Robert Browning; Browning showed them to Edmund Gosse and Dykes Campbell, both of whom laid the foundation for modern critical studies by transcribing extensively from what they saw. At his own death, Browning left the black box containing the Beddoes materials to his son, Robert Waring "Pen" Browning. At the subsequent sale of Pen Browning's estate, the "Browning Box" of Beddoes papers did not appear. Its fate is still a mystery.

Analysis

Thomas Lovell Beddoes' poetry (including his verse drama) focuses on three subjects: love, death, and madness. There is a constant theme: love offers an entrance to the charmed world where spirit and nature are one; yet, just when love asserts its claims and some ideal of joy seems realizable, either madness or death intrudes with an ironic laugh to snatch away that love—the best hope that human beings have for something approximating transcendence. The reader is left with an ironic ambivalence toward the expectations of the spirit. Those expectations are linked ever more tightly, as Beddoes' poetry unfolds, with the mocking ironies (death and madness) which give the lie to dreams of love, immortality, and transcendence. Beddoes' ambivalence toward his own dream of immortality is partly a result of his progressively deeper commitment to scientific inquiry, with its rigorous rules of evidence. It is also in part a reflection of the ambivalence of the whole age. John Herschel, William Whewell, and Augustus De Morgan were all Victorian scientists, for example, who wrote highly romantic poetry. Charles Darwin enjoyed a wide reading in imaginative literature. Yet, it was becoming progressively clear that the specializations of scientific thought would soon put an end to the ideal fusion of science and the humanities which Beddoes sought.

Such ambivalence appears as early as *The Improvisatore* and grows progressively more profound and ironic all the way through his work, culminating in *Death's Jest-Book*. *The Improvisatore* is a series of three ballad-like tales which suffer from a trite and overheated romanticism. These tales were published when Beddoes was eighteen, and they reflect his early quest for a lyrical style which would give voice to his yearnings for a mythopoeic, spiritual world. His images, however, are often clichés: "'Twas as though Flora had been sporting there,/ And dropped some jewels from her loosened hair." Sometimes the images are absurd conceits, similar to those of the metaphysical poets two centuries earlier: "Her mouth!—Oh pardon me, thou coral cave,/ Prison of fluttering sighs . . . if I fail to tell/ The Beauty and the grace, that in thee dwell."

These early tales share in common the themes listed above: love, madness, and death. In each ballad, youthful or infant love loses its object—a sweetheart, a parent. This loss starkly transforms the protagonist. The youthful sense of a charmed and summertime reality gives way to a madness expressed in images of a horrific supernaturalism. The only escape from that madness is into death.

The Bride's Tragedy and *The Second Brother* are more accomplished than *The Improvisatore*. There are fewer clichés. Still, these plays too might be thought melodramatic except that the romanticism is less feverish, and Beddoes' ability to control his lyricism, his characterizations, and his plot construction have clearly matured. In *The Bride's Tragedy*, Hesperus is secretly married to Floribel. Orlando, son of the Duke, also loves Floribel but knows nothing of the marriage. He imprisons Hesperus' father and offers Hesperus his (Orlando's) sister in order to have Floribel for himself. Trapped (and jealous), Hesperus murders his secret wife. What enables this play to transcend such a melodramatic plot is a more mature lyricism, as in the song "Poor Old Pilgrim Misery" where the strong feelings of Hesperus are not merely enunciated (as Beddoes had enunciated emotions in *The Improvisatore*) but suggested through controlled images: "Beneath the silent moon he sits,/ a listening to the screech owl's cry,/ and the cold wind's goblin prate."

In 1825, Beddoes published his translation of some of J. C. F. Schiller's philosophic letters (their first translation into English) in *The Oxford Quarterly Magazine*. His Preface reveals the depth of the bifurcation of his own mind. "We seldom attain truth otherwise than by extremes; we must first exhaust error, and often madness before we end our toil at the far goal of calm wisdom." By this time his enthusiasms—poetry and science—have been polarized into a rigorous dialectic. His effort to integrate them is failing. His extremes are tending toward madness. He further claims that "scepticism and free-thinking are the feverish paroxysm of the human spirit, and must, by the very . . . concussion which they cause . . . help to confirm the health [of the soul]." His assurance on this point seems a romantic's whistling in the dark of rationalist doubt. Consider, for example, his translation of Schiller's first letter, Julius to Raphael: "There is nothing holy but truth. What reason acknowledges is truth . . . I have sacrificed all my opinions. . . . My reason is now my all; my only security for diversity, virtue, immortality." Beddoes has set himself on an irreversible track. During the whole course of his writing he will find, like Julius, no earnest for love, wholeness, nor peace.

Beddoes' lyrical poems may be grouped under the headings Juvenilia (1818-

1821), Outidana (1821-1825), The Ivory Gate (1830-1839), German Poems (1837-1845), and Lost Poems (1843-1848). These headings are used in H. W. Donner's definitive one-volume edition of Beddoes' complete works. Although the topics are various, a selected list of titles suggests how closely the lyrical poems are tied to the major themes already identified: "Threnody," "Fragments of a Dirge," "Epitaph," "The Tree of Life," "Dirge and Hymeneal," "Lament of Thanatos," "Thanatos to Kenelm," "The Last Judgment," "The Phantom-Wooer," and others of the same sort.

The poem "Dream Pedlary," written for use in *Death's Jest-Book*, is typical of the mature Beddoes. It consists of five stanzas, the first of ten lines, rhyming ababccaaab, and the remaining four of nine lines each, rhyming ababccaab. Because some of the rhyming words are carried from one stanza to the next, a spare economy of form emerges which is well-suited to the stark theme of the poem. The poem begins with a question: "If there were dreams to sell,/ What would you buy?" Beddoes then offers images of various dreams for sale. In the first stanza, these dreams are described as "merry and sad," but in the second stanza the image chosen is a sad one, "a cottage lone and still." In the next stanza, the dream for sale is a "spell to call the buried," which gives way in the fourth stanza to the dream that "there are no ghosts to raise./ Out of death lead no ways." The last stanza expresses a death wish ("lie as I will do/ And breathe thy last") because the fear that death is a void at least validates the claim that "all dreams are made true"; that is, all dreams are only dreams and therefore truly dreams. The images have progressed from merry and sad dreams, through solitude (the lone cottage), to the dream of ghosts, to the dream of a nihilistic void where there are no ghosts. This terrible finality is so unthinkable to Beddoes that it draws and fascinates him.

No other work of Beddoes has achieved as high a standing with critics as *Death's Jest-Book*. He worked on this poetic drama for more than twenty years, and it was still unpublished at his death. This macabre play provides a historical link between the revenge tragedy of the Renaissance and the tale of terror in modern times. It strings together a powerful series of images: the court jester (Isbrand) in cap and bells who is driven by the wish for revenge to try to usurp the throne of Münsterberg; a conjuration scene in which the Duke opens the tomb of his wife only to find there the ghost of a man he has murdered; and a dance of death consisting of painted figures who actually descend from the wall to act out a grotesque masque.

The play has the eloquence, the ghosts, and the strong-willed characters of an Elizabethan swashbuckler, but it also hints at the nihilism of a modern tale of terror. It is this latter fact which sets it apart from contemporaneous Gothic tales such as those of Ann Radcliffe. The macabre events of *Death's Jest-Book*, such as the conjuration scene in a derelict Gothic cathedral, suggest the possibility that behind the terrors there lies no supernatural law of justice or piety, but rather a lawless abyss just a finger-reach beyond everyday normalcies. The critic John Agar believes that Isbrand's tragedy is that he aspires to be a hero, not a villain (his motive, after all was to avenge his father's and his brother's deaths), but—lacking an adequate sense of his own limits—he becomes as evil as he had hoped to be good. Good intentions, it might be observed, do not save us in a naturalistic world where there is no omnipotent judge to weigh them.

Although the images of horror in the play are fairly conventional—a ghost (Wolfram, Isbrand's murdered brother), the skeletal *danse macabre*—nevertheless Beddoes' keenly spiritual sensibility, faced with the persuasions of a rigorous skepticism, suffers much as Franz Kafka suffered from a tormenting recognition that life, love, kingdoms, even efforts at revenge, may be nothing but a macabre joke—Death's Jest. The characters in Beddoes' play sustain the conventional hope that death is only a mask for immortality: "Death is old and half worn out: Are there no chinks in it?" Yet death keeps its mocking secret as these stage directions show: "The Deaths . . . come out of the walls, and dance fantastically to a rattling music. . . ; some seat themselves at the table and drink with mocking gestures." Later, as Isbrand dies, having briefly occupied the usurped throne, the ghost of his brother places the cap and bells upon his head again. All are absurd fools in *Death's Jest-Book*.

The main body of Beddoes' work shows the ambivalence which he felt about all of the great themes of literature: love, the meaning of suffering, the significance of everyday life, the possibilities for some sort of redemptive experience, the hope for immortality. The fragmentation of his work, his desultory efforts to polish and finish it, his inability to commit himself to a dramatic poem with sufficient force to work it through, all suggest Beddoes' dilemma. He was a man whose learning and instincts were grounded in the classical past, a man who loved the great sureties of the great poets. In his own age, however, and in his own mind, those sureties were being eroded by a secular skepticism which denied him the assurance and joy of the old world, yet revealed no credible options for a man of the spirit living in an empirical and pragmatic age. Before Matthew Arnold, Beddoes was "caught between two worlds,/ One dead, the other powerless to be born." Before Kafka, he sensed the abyss which underlies everyday experience. Biographies can never, of course, reconstruct all of the sorrows, the intense impressions, of a private man who lived long ago. It is clear enough from his work itself, however, that Beddoes believed that the illusions of a sacred and mythopoeic world were breaking up, that the losses to be suffered would throw enormous stress on the devices of sanity, and that in the end, Death would mock the illusions, the losses, and even the madness itself by keeping its eternal secret.

L. Robert Stevens

Other major works

PLAYS: *The Bride's Tragedy*, 1822; *Death's Jest-Book*, 1850; *Torrismond*, 1851; *The Second Brother*, 1851.

NONFICTION: *The Letters of Thomas Lovell Beddoes*, 1894.

MISCELLANEOUS: *The Complete Works of Thomas Lovell Beddoes*, 1928; *The Works of Thomas Lovell Beddoes*, 1935 (H. W. Donner, editor).

Bibliography

Donner, H. W. *The Browning Box: Or, The Life and Works of Thomas Lovell Beddoes.* London: Oxford University Press, 1935. A collection of letters about Beddoes' life and poetry, by friends and admirers. The odd title refers to the box of materials given to Robert Browning after Beddoes' death. The box has disappeared, but "probably all the letters of real importance" survived through transcriptions.

_____. *Thomas Lovell Beddoes: The Making of a Poet.* Oxford: Basil Blackwell, 1935. This comprehensive study of Beddoes' life and times balances biography with literary interpretation. Contains an informative introduction on nineteenth century theater and the influence of Elizabethan drama on Romantic poetry. A conclusion summarizes Beddoes' aesthetics. Illustrated.

Snow, Royall H. *Thomas Lovell Beddoes: Eccentric and Poet.* New York: Covici-Friede, 1928. This early biographical study concentrates on the poet's morbidity as his defining characteristic. Somewhat dated, especially in the ways it deals with the literature. Contains an annotated bibliography of Beddoes' books and periodical publications.

Thompson, James R. *Thomas Lovell Beddoes.* Boston: Twayne, 1985. The most useful critical introduction to Beddoes. Includes a brief biography, a chronology, and a selected bibliography. Follows Beddoes' career from the early poems of Shelleyan and Gothic derivation, through his growing interest in Jacobean drama and his satiric verse dramas, to his mature work obsessed with death.

Watkins, Daniel P. "Thomas Lovell Beddoes' *The Bride's Tragedy* and the Situation of Romantic Drama." *Studies in English Literature, 1500-1900* 29 (Autumn, 1989): 699-712. Considers Beddoes' poetic drama as a work of Gothic horror on the order of Mary Wollstonecraft Shelley's *Frankenstein.* Watkins utilizes historical analysis to show that Beddoes' concerns are less a throwback to Jacobean drama than an essentially Romantic "desire for a return to an aristocratic feudal" order.

PATRICIA BEER

Born: Exmouth, Devon, England; November 4, 1924

Principal poetry
Loss of the Magyar and Other Poems, 1959; *The Survivors,* 1963; *Just Like the Resurrection,* 1967; *The Estuary,* 1971; *Driving West,* 1975; *Selected Poems,* 1979; *The Lie of the Land,* 1983; *Collected Poems,* 1988.

Other literary forms
Aside from her poetry, Patricia Beer has published two books of criticism, *An Introduction to the Metaphysical Poets* (1972) and *Reader, I Married Him* (1974), the latter being a study of the women characters in the works of Jane Austen, Charlotte Brontë, Elizabeth Gaskell, and George Eliot. She has also published a book of fiction, *Moon's Ottery* (1978), and a nonfictional account of her childhood, *Mrs. Beer's House* (1968). The latter provides insights into the poet's development and serves as a gloss for much of her poetry, particularly that which is rooted in her childhood experiences. Although her publications reveal a variety of interests and a willingness to work in various literary forms, Beer's most significant writing and the principal focus of her energies is her poetry.

Achievements
Beer is not as widely known in the United States as some of her British contemporaries, but she has achieved a solid reputation in her native England as a deft craftsperson and a poet of genuine perception. Her accomplishments become even more significant when one considers how few of her fellow poets in the British Isles are women. Certainly, the poets with the widest reputations—Philip Larkin, Ted Hughes, and Danny Abse, to name only a few—are all men. In this context, Beer occupies a position of considerable importance, and although she considers herself a feminist, she writes without rancor, and her poems never become polemical. Hers is a calm voice, and the views she expresses in her poems are, more often than not, understated. Moreover, she is not a single-issue poet and so does not feel bound to champion the cause in every line of every poem, thereby avoiding the trap into which politically aroused poets have frequently fallen. Beer has commented that she wants equality, not superiority, and that such a position precludes any kind of attack on the male establishment.

It would be a mistake, however, to view Beer only in the role of feminist poet; she transcends any such narrow category in both her aspirations and her accomplishments. Her voice is as unique and genuine as that of Hughes or Larkin, and her carefully crafted poems are an important contribution to contemporary British poetry. At her best, she invites comparison with Elizabeth Bishop, for she has the same perceptive eye, the same gift for the exact image. A poem such as "Spanish Balcony," with its moon suspended "uselessly, in the smooth sky/ White and rumpled like a vaccination mark," is as precise and evocative as Bishop's celebrated description of the rainbow trout in "The Fish." The controlling mind behind the poem is sure and accurate.

Biography

Patricia Beer is a member of the first generation in England to have ready access to higher education through the state school system. Coming from a working-class background, she made her way through the state schools by excelling at her studies and eventually took a B.Litt. degree at St. Hugh's College, Oxford. As a native of Devon with a pronounced Devonian accent, she remembers being drilled by elocutionists who were determined to teach her "proper" speech. She resisted the instruction and retained the accent that no doubt exerts an influence, however, subtle, on her poetry. She would eventually divide her time between homes in Hampstead Heath (London) and Devon, considering her continued connection with the place of her birth an element essential to her creativity.

As a child, Beer was strongly influenced by the Plymouth Brethren Church, a loosely structured, fundamentalist sect that flourished amid the working and lower-middle classes. Its principal theology was a strict moral code and a dependence on literal interpretation of the Bible. Beer recalls vividly the extemporaneous hell-fire sermons and the hymns offering salvation, and these bits of childhood have found their way into her poetry. In a larger context, the pervasive sense of death that she experienced regularly at the church services may well have afforded the main impetus for her poetry. In much of her work, she is preoccupied with death, and she has frequently commented that she writes poems against death. The relationship between her religious upbringing and her craft is a complex one, but there is little doubt that Beer's fundamentalist training helped to form her as a poet.

Beer's childhood in Devon and her experiences in the Plymouth Brethren Church afforded her abundant material for poetry and a unique point of view. Just as her semirural Devonian background accounts for the rustic quality of much of her work, her childhood among the Plymouth Brethren helps to explain her ambivalent attitude toward death, a mixture of fascination and fear. It is this subtle but fundamental tension that underlies some of her most successful poems.

Analysis

The publication of *Selected Poems* in 1979 marked an important milestone in Patricia Beer's career. In addition to winning for her the kind of recognition she had long deserved, it provided her with the opportunity to assess her own development and to select from twenty years of writing the poetry that she most wanted to preserve. Significantly, she included only eight poems from her first two books, *Loss of the Magyar and Other Poems* and *The Survivors*. Although she was in her thirties when those books were published, she now regards them as juvenilia. Those early books, in Beer's assessment, lack conviction, an authentic voice. Beer's major development as a writer has involved a movement toward the more personal and autobiographical. Along the way, she has abandoned her reliance on mythology and has consciously tried to pare down her style, seeking simplicity and directness.

Ironically, Beer grew distrustful of the spareness that characterized her writing and turned to a language that she regards as more heightened. She did not, however, regard this as a return to her earlier style but rather as a progression into a kind of language that would have a more immediate impact on the reader. It seems that, during the middle part of her career, Beer was trying to find some point of balance between her initial work and her subsequent reaction to it. She later began to seek a marriage of technique and inspiration, and the fifteen "New Poems" that constitute the final section of *Selected Poems* suggest that she found it.

It has often been remarked that the two most common themes in poetry are the possibility of love and the inevitability of death, so it is perhaps unremarkable to find a poet dealing with either of these matters. Even so, Beer's preoccupation with death is noteworthy because she succeeds in capturing so much of the ambivalence that most people have toward it—the attraction and repulsion of the unknown. This viewpoint is effectively communicated in a short poem entitled "Dilemma," in which Beer projects two possible role models for herself. The first is a Buddhist monk who screams so loudly when seven brigands approach to murder him that businessmen in Peking can hear him twenty miles away. The second is "the Queen in corny historical plays," who fixes her hair, forgives everybody, and moves to the executioner's block "With only a sidelong glance/ At the man with the axe." The monk and the queen represent two attitudes toward death—resistance and acquiescence—and Beer is free to choose the one she wishes to adopt. Thus, the poem's final line is a question: "Which ought I to be?" On the surface, this poem appears to be very simple, but it compresses a great deal of thought and attempts to bridge a gap as wide as the one between William Cullen Bryant's advice in "Thanatopsis" to embrace death gently like a sleeper and Dylan Thomas' exhortation to his father not to go "gentle into that good night."

A variation on this theme is found in "The Clock," an excellent example of Beer's mastery of syllabics and her skillful employment of sounds, particularly assonance. She is most adept at using and then defusing the irresistible iambic trimeter in her six-syllable lines, as in the following pair: "Where once a pendulum/ Thudded like a cart-horse." The regularity of meter is effectively broken by an abundance of stresses, as though the thudding horse himself had broken in, and the entire poem is carried forward by the subtle suggestion of rhyme as exemplified by the four end-words in the fourth stanza: "this," "is," "death," "stairs." It is no accident that "death" stands out so starkly among the off-rhymes, because that is where Beer wishes to put the stress, on obtrusive death itself. In this fashion, she makes form and content work together in a most remarkable way. The focus of the poem is an old clock that stops every few days when its weights catch on the case. The old saying that "A stopped clock foretells death" leads Beer to speculate about the symbolic meaning of the event and she finds a lesson of her own in such folklore: "Obviously/ Death cannot come each time/ The clock stops. It may be/ Good practice to think so." The malfunctioning clock, then, becomes an important element in a rehearsal for death. As in "Dilemma," where Beer tries to decide how she will face death when it finally arrives, she is preparing herself for the inevitable, for the moment when time will truly stop for her. In a very real sense, Beer's poetry in general is a kind of rehearsal for death. She herself has acknowledged that the impetus behind her decision to write poetry was a fear of dying.

Initially, Beer's horror of death was somewhat mitigated by a fantasy of becoming famous and having thousands of people mourn her passing. The vehicle for her fame, decided upon when she was only eight years old, was to be poetry. She "Turned poet for a lying-in-state/ As though comfort came from cut flowers," a decision that she examines at length in "The Eyes of the World." Somehow, to her child's mind, having the world take note of her death would make the event less terrifying: "Something like this I felt might make it/ Tolerable: if everyone would stare/ At my last breaths and speak about them." She envies the fame of kings, of men on the moon, of Leda and Mary and the martyrs Latimer and Ridley, all seared into the consciousness of millions and thus given a kind of immortality. The fantasy passes, however, when she matures and begins to view the world more cynically, suspecting that the watchers are more likely to notice flaws and weaknesses than accomplishments. Further, she suspects that "The audience shut their eyes before we/ Shut ours," insensitive to another person's death or unable to see the process through to completion. The poem ends with the following reflection on the eyes of the world: "I cannot imagine now/ Why I believed they were the answer." As Beer discovered, the true answer to her fear of death was not to become famous but to learn to write about her fears. She found that she could not chase them away in the glare of public recognition but could embrace them privately and learn to live with them. Poems such as "Concert at Long Melford Church" and "After Death" show her bravely coming to terms with what she most fears. If the truce is shaky and the question of how to face death when it arrives remains unresolved, Beer has nevertheless expanded her personal and poetic boundaries by confronting head-on what she would most like to run away from.

Related to the poems about death are Beer's poems about religion, particularly so since the religious group on which she focuses is the death-obsessed Plymouth Brethren of her childhood. In "Called Home," the title recalls something that "the Plymouth Brethren used to say/ When someone died." The phrase creates a picture of "eternal domesticity," which was intended to be comforting, assuring the congregation that families would be reunited after death, as in the hymns "Shall We Gather at the River?" and "In the Sweet By-and-By." Having lost her ability to accept this simple picture of life after death, Beer claims that "Loving an atheist is my hope currently." She wants an "Ally who will keep non-company/ With me in a non-life, a fellow tombstone." The rejection of her previous belief and the adoption of a nihilistic view of life and death are integral to Beer's struggle. In order to come to terms with death she must imagine it at its most horrible, and this necessitates relinquishing the convenient crutches offered by the church and courageously confronting nothingness in its plainest form, not draped in domestic imagery.

The loss of faith is also treated in "Arms," but without the cynical, intellectual toughness that characterizes "Called Home." Indeed, "Arms" is poignant precisely because Beer gives in somewhat to her emotions and looks back on the lost faith of her childhood with sorrow and regret. She recalls that her innocent reliance on the "Everlasting Arms" gradually gave way to nightmare visions of drowned animals "Holding each other like bars" and then remembers her grandfather sinking with his brig in the North Sea, his arms around his son, "Protector, up to his knees/ In death, and that was the last/ That anyone saw of him." The poem progresses from a child's concern with the mortality of animals to an understanding that humans, even her grandfather, share in that mortality, and the immortal arms of her childhood belief become the ineffectual arms of her grandfather, disappearing forever beneath the waves.

Beer's poems of death have immediacy because of their autobiographical nature, because the poet is willing to expose herself. The details of poems such as "The Clock," "The Eyes of the World," and "Arms" are factually accurate. The clock that stops every few days did exist; Beer did decide to become a poet when she was eight because she thought fame would help her accept death; and her grandfather went down with his brig, the *Magyar*, and was last seen by the only survivor with his arms around his son and the water rising. Getting the facts down, however, is not Beer's final objective. She is after the truth behind the facts, and it is that truth that produces a response in the reader. Beer is, in the best sense of the term, a confessional poet, because her view always penetrates through the self to the larger background. It may be that she will come to rely even more on the confessional approach as she continues to write. Her movement as a poet has been steadily away from the detached, manufactured poem toward the autobiographical, and as the poetry becomes more sharply focused on the immediate self rather than on the self's past, Beer is likely to draw nearer to the confessional vein. Instinctively wary of the confessional poem, Beer's progress toward it has been slow. There are, after all, the dangers of becoming too self-involved, too obscure, and Beer resists the mode because of these potential hazards. Nevertheless, she seems irresistibly led to write more and more about her immediate life. She has thoroughly explored and exploited the material of her childhood, and so it is only natural that she turn her attention to her present self. Her best poems have been those that risk an intense look at the self.

In the title poem of her fourth book, *The Estuary*, Beer looks intensely at herself and effectively brings together past and present as she reflects on the body of water that separated the two towns of her childhood—Exmouth, her father's home, and Torquay, her mother's place of origin. She finds in the division a symbol not only of the distance between her mother and father in terms of their personalities but also of her own character, which must be a combination of attributes inherited from both parents. On one side "stiff fields of corn grow/ To the hilltop, are draped over/ It surrealistically." On the other side, small white boats lean sideways twice a day as the tide goes out and comes in and "the sea pulls away their prop." One side is covered with lush and vigorous growth, while the other is represented by fragile boats that seem as susceptible to the intermittent tides as people are to fate or chance.

A reader does not need to know a great deal about Beer's background to appreciate the geographical metaphor, though some knowledge of her childhood may enhance one's understanding of the poem. It is clear from the poem itself that Beer was forced by circumstances to move from a normal life on one side of the river to "a house where all was not well" on the other. The poem does not indicate, however, just what the circumstances were nor why things were not well on the other side, focusing on effect and leaving the cause unspecified. There is no exposition to reveal that the move was precipitated by the death of Beer's mother when Beer was fourteen and that she crossed the river to live with relatives because her father seemed unable to manage his children alone. With this information in hand, a reader may better understand the source of the poem, but the significant details of the poem itself operate independent of any such biographical footnotes. By dealing with the effects of the move rather than its causes, Beer is able to take a highly personal experience and give it a more general significance. The estuary, rather than remaining a simple fact of Beer's childhood, becomes a symbolic boundary that everyone must cross, and the move is not simply from Exmouth to Torquay but from childhood to adulthood, from the dreamlike growth on one side to a more conscious life on the tides of the other. The opposing banks are innocence and experience, and the move from one to the other is archetypal. Underscoring this symbolism is the estuary itself, the meeting place of fresh and salt water. The flow of the individual river into the sea parallels the movement of the child from her small, self-involved world into the larger community of responsibility.

Beer uses essentially the same technique in "Self-Help," employing her personal experiences as a telescope through which the larger world can be viewed. Meditating on the fact that she "was brought up on notions of self-help," she realizes that she got where she is because she believed "that if/ You didn't help yourself in worldly matters/ Nobody else was at all likely to." She struggled alone and now enjoys her success alone, sitting on her sofa in Hampstead Village listening to the threatening noises of all those on the streets outside who want desperately to help themselves as well. She has separated herself from the "Cockney accents" and "bathless flats," virtually becoming a living example of the model described in books on self-help, "Practising lawful self-advancement, preaching/ It, enjoying its rewards." Yet behind her smugness and her sense of separation, she feels a bond with all those who have not succeeded in helping themselves. She sees that "through/ The white comfortable mist a wind blows holes/ Lays bare the quagmire reaching for us all./ Whispers how soon we could be shouting 'Help.'" What she senses is the common link of death, and she realizes that despite her accomplishments she can never raise herself beyond the quagmire that reaches out for everyone. If there is truth in this perception, there is also humility, for Beer puts her successes into context and implicitly understands how small they look in terms of the ultimate struggle. In the final sense, she is alone, and yet, paradoxically, she is united with everyone. Death is the great separator, but it is also the great leveler, mindless of class distinctions and accomplishments.

Although Beer herself rejects the confessional label, poems such as "The Estuary" and "Self-Help" work as the best confessional poems have always worked, by using the personal details of the poet's life to discover larger meanings. Beer prefers to call her poems in this vein "autobiographical," perhaps because the term "confessional" has come to connote obscurity and tedious self-involvement. Whatever label the poems are given, they unquestionably transcend the limitations of the purely personal, for Beer masterfully uses her experiences and emotions as a bridge to the common ground shared by her and the reader. The personal is always a means to an end and never an end in itself. In fact, Beer's strengths as a poet seem to have increased in direct proportion to her willingness to exploit her personal life for poetic material.

Beer knows, too, how to approach sensitive topics, not by taking a position and arguing directly but by presenting a point of view obliquely, subtly. Her skills in this area are clearly on display in "Female, Extinct." The female of the title is never identified by species, and her wired-together ribcage and "bony gloves" with no marrow in them could belong to any vertebrate animal. The reference to "her sons, little dragons" suggests something reptilian, but the term "little dragons" is appositional and may be meant figuratively rather than literally. Now on display in the museum, the female once "Stood up with hundreds/ As if to bellow/ The Hallelujah Chorus." As a reconstructed arti- fact she seems to be saying something else: "Her passionate jaws/ Shout 'Give me time.'" This may well be a poem about the primordial struggle to survive, but it may just as well be about the more contemporary efforts of women to overcome their symbolic extinction. Beer creates the possibility of the latter reading by leaving the type of female unspecified. Quite probably, she intends the poem to function on both levels of meaning, for the real point of the poem is the implied connection between the two kinds of females.

Equally subtle and effective is a short poem entitled "Home." Here, the speaker, presumably a woman, looks out from her house, "as warm/ And secure as bathwater." Curiously, her sense of responsibility begins with a rejection of that responsibility. She discovers that she cannot remove herself from the world of human suffering, and she is beginning to understand that home has a larger significance than the safe house in which she would prefer to seal herself.

Both "Female, Extinct" and "Home" may be regarded as feminist poems because both address issues of great concern to women. The first may be taken as an implied warning of a present danger and the second as a charge to move beyond the walls of home into the surrounding world. Because she does not argue a position, she avoids the didactic and the abrasive, and her point of view seeps slowly into the reader's receptive consciousness.

Indeed, perhaps the best word to describe Beer's poetry in general is "understated." Whether writing about death, her childhood, or topics of a political nature, Beer's characteristic voice is one of composure. This is not to say that her poems are lacking in vitality; quite the opposite, for she has learned that the disparity between her calm perceptions and the themes derived from them creates a great deal of energy. One often has the sense that in Beer's poetry things have been defused, only to find upon reflection that a small explosion has occurred in the mind.

Neal Bowers

Other major works

FICTION: *Moon's Ottery*, 1978.

NONFICTION: *Mrs. Beer's House*, 1968; *An Introduction to the Metaphysical Poets*, 1972; *Reader, I Married Him*, 1974.

Bibliography

Beer, Patricia. *Mrs. Beer's House*. London: Macmillan, 1968. This is Beer's autobiography, the main source of public information about her life. No other books have been written about her. Easy to read and an essential source for any student of the poet.

Cherry, Caroline. "Patricia Beer." In *Dictionary of Literary Biography.* Vol. 40, *Poets of Great Britain and Ireland Since 1960*, edited by Vincent B. Sherry, Jr. Detroit: Gale Research, 1985. Few articles have been written on Beer, so this seven-page entry is important. Cherry provides a short biography, mixed with some critical analysis of beer's poetry. A good introduction to Beer and suitable for all students.

Magee, Wes. "Beer, Patricia." In *Contemporary Poets*, edited by James Vinson and D. L. Kirkpatrick. 6th ed. New York: St. Martin's Press, 1985. In this short article, Magee provides critical commentary on Beer's poetry, as well as biographical information and a primary bibliography. Beer herself provides several paragraphs explaining her philosophy as a writer. Appropriate for students who need a good, quick rundown on the poet.

Metzger, Linda, ed. *Contemporary Authors.* Vol. 13. Detroit: Gale Research, 1984. Contains a short entry on Beer, listing her biographical statistics, and a primary bibliography. The chronology of her works demonstrates Beer's scope as a writer. This is a good, quick reference source for those seeking a complete list of her works.

Skelton, Robin. "Leaders and Others: Some New British Poetry." *Kenyon Review* 30, no. 5 (1968): 689-696. Skelton reviews Beer's volume, *Just Like the Resurrection*, and discusses it in comparison with the work of Ted Hughes and Thom Gunn, two other British poets who also published collections at that time. Interesting in that it offers a rare look at how Beer's contemporaries perceived her at that point in her career.

APHRA BEHN

Born: Wye, England; July(?), 1640
Died: London, England; April 16, 1689

Principal poetry

Poems upon Several Occasions, with A Voyage to the Island of Love, 1684 (adaptation of Abbé Paul Tallemant's *Le Voyage de l'isle d'amour*); *Miscellany: Being a Collection of Poems by Several Hands,* 1685 (includes works by others); *La Montre: Or, The Lover's Watch,* 1686 (prose and verse); *The Case for the Watch,* 1686 (prose and verse); *Lycidus: Or, The Lover in Fashion,* 1688 (prose and verse; includes works by others); *The Lady's Looking-Glass, to Dress Herself By: Or, The Art of Charming,* 1697 (prose and verse).

Other literary forms

Although Aphra Behn wrote more than a dozen separate pieces of fiction that critics of her day called *novels,* only a portion may legitimately be labeled as such. Principal among these is her most noted work of fiction, *Oroonoko: Or, The History of the Royal Slave* (1688); others worthy of consideration are *Agnes de Castro* (1688), *The Fair Jilt* (1688), *The History of the Nun* (1689), and *The Nun* (1697). During her lifetime, Behn established her literary reputation by writing for the London stage, creating more than fifteen plays.

Achievements

Critics may defend Behn's talent for drama and prose fiction as worthy of recognition beside that of her male contemporaries. As a writer of verse, however, she cannot claim a place among the poets of the first rank. This does not mean that her poetry has no value for the critic, the literary historian, or the general reader; on the contrary, her occasional verse is no worse than the political pieces of her colleagues (with the exception of John Dryden), while the songs and poems from her plays reflect her ability to manipulate verse as reinforcement for dramatic theme and setting.

In the nineteenth century, such poet-essayists as Leigh Hunt, Edmund Gosse, and Algernon Swinburne recoiled initially from what they saw in Behn's occasional verse as indelicate and indecent language. They recovered sufficiently to find some merit in her songs. Hunt bemoaned her association with the rakes of the age, yet praised the songs as "natural and cordial, written in a masculine style, yet womanly withal." Gosse dubbed her "the George Sand of the Restoration"—an obvious reference that had nothing whatsoever to do with her literary abilities—although "she possessed an indisputable touch of lyric genius." Swinburne looked hard at a single poem, "Love in fantastic triumph sate," and concluded that "the virtuous Aphra towers above her sex in the passionate grace and splendid elegance of that melodious and magnificent song. . . ." The most attractive quality of her lyrical pieces is their spontaneity, demonstrating to the reader (or the theatergoer) that the best poetry need not be anchored to learning, but can succeed because the lines are memorable, singable, and direct.

In her public verse, Behn had to compete with a large number of poets who tended to be more skilled mechanics and versifiers than she, and all of whom sought the same limited patronage and political favors as she. She found herself at a disadvantage because of her sex, which meant, simply, that her occasional verse did not always reach the widest possible audience. For example, such pieces as "A Pindarick on the Death of Charles II" (1685) and "A Congratulatory Poem to Her Most Sacred Majesty" (1688) may appear stiff and lacking in sincerity, but certainly no more so than the verses on the same subjects written by her contemporaries. Her elegy on the death of Edmund Waller and her other contributions to a volume in memory of the departed poet in 1688, do, however, reflect a deep feeling of sorrow because of the occasion; these poems serve as a transition to her private verse, representing perhaps the highest level of Behn's poetic achievement. In "The Disappointment," for example, she reveals herself as a woman whose real desires have been obscured by frivolity and professionalism and who realizes that her laborious life is drawing to a close. The importance of such poems is that they provide the deepest insight into Behn; they draw a picture of the poet far more honestly and realistically than do the rumors, allusions, and innuendos set forth in countless biographical sketches and critical commentaries.

Biography

Although the details surrounding the life of Aphra Behn have at least become stabilized, they have not always been clear. Her earliest biographer, the poet Charles Gildon (1665-1724), maintained that she was born at Canterbury, in Kent, the daughter of a man named Johnson. In 1884, however, Edmund Gosse discovered a marginal note in a manuscript belonging to the poet Anne Finch, Countess of Winchelsea (1661-1720), revealing that Behn had actually been born at Wye, near Canterbury, the daughter of a barber—which John Johnson certainly was not. The Countess' note receives support from an entry in the parish register of the Sts. Gregory and Martin Church, Wye, to the effect that Ayfara Amis, daughter of John and Amy Amis, was baptized there on July 10, 1640. Apparently Johnson, related to Lord Francis Willoughby of Parham, adopted the girl, although no one seems certain of the exact year. Nevertheless, Ayfara Amis accompanied her stepparents on a journey to Surinam (later Dutch Guiana) in 1658, Lord Willoughby having appointed Johnson to serve as deputy governor of his extensive holdings there. Unfortunately, the new deputy died on the voyage; his widow and children proceeded to Surinam and took up residence at St. John's, one of Willoughby's plantations. The exact length of their stay has yet to be determined; more recent biographers, though, have settled upon the summer of 1663 as the most probable date of return. The family's tenure at St. John's forms the background of Behn's most celebrated production, her novel *Oroonoko*.

By 1665, the young woman was established in London, married to a wealthy Dutch merchant (or at least a merchant of Dutch ancestry) who may well have had connections in or around the court of Charles II. In 1665 came the Great Plague and the death of Behn's husband; his death proved disastrous for his widow. For unknown reasons, the Dutch merchant left her nothing of substance—with the possible exception of his connections at court. Charles II, in the midst of his first war against the Dutch, hired Behn as a secret agent to spy against Holland; for that purpose, she proceeded to Antwerp. There she contacted another agent, William Scott, from whom she received various pieces of military information for forwarding to London. Although her work earned her little acknowledgment and even less money, Behn did conceive of the pseudonym "Astrea," the name under which she published most of her poetry. Essentially, the venture into foreign intrigue proved a dismal failure for her; she had to borrow money and pawn her few valuables to pay her debts and provide passage back to England.

Once home, early in 1667, Behn found no relief from her desperate financial situation. Her creditors threatened prison, and the government ministers who had employed her refused any payment for espionage service rendered. Prison followed, most probably at Caronne House, South Lambeth, although again the specifics of time and length of term are lacking. Behn's most recent biographers speculate that she may have been aided in her release by John Hoyle (d. 1692)—a lawyer of Gray's Inn, a wit and an intellectual, at times an active homosexual, the principal subject and reason for Behn's sonnets, and the man with whom the writer carried on a long romance. In fact, Hoyle, to whom she refers often in her poems, is the only one of Behn's supposed lovers who can be identified with any certainty. When she finally gained her release from prison, she determined to dedicate the rest of her life to pleasure and to letters, to trust her own devices rather than to rely upon others whom she could not trust.

Behn launched her career as a dramatist in late December, 1670, at the New Duke's Theatre in Little Lincoln's Inn Fields, London. Her tragicomedy, *The Forced Marriage: Or, The Jealous Bridegroom* (1670), ran for six nights and included in the cast nineteen-year-old Thomas Otway, the playwright-to-be only recently down from Christ Church, Oxford. The neophyte bungled his lines, and with that his acting career came to a quick halt. Because of the length of the run, however, Behn, as was the practice, received the entire profit from the third performance; she could now begin to function as an independent artist. She followed her first effort in the spring of 1671 with a comedy, *The Amorous Prince*, again at the New Duke's; another comedy, *The Dutch Lover*, came to

Drury Lane in February, 1673, and by the time of her anonymous comedy, *The Rover: Or, The Banished Cavaliers*, I, in 1677, she had secured her reputation. Now she mixed easily with the likes of Thomas Killigrew, Edward Ravenscroft, the Earl of Rochester, Edmund Waller, and the poet laureate, John Dryden— who would publish her rough translations from Ovid in 1683. With the reputation came offers for witty prologues and epilogues for others' plays, as well as what she desired more than anything—money. A confrontation, however, with the Earl of Shaftesbury and the newly formed Whigs during the religiopolitical controversies of 1678, when she offended the opponents of Charles II in a satirical prologue to an anonymous play, *Romulus and Hersilia*, brought her once again to the brink of economic hardship; for the next five years, she was forced to abandon writing for the stage.

Fortunately, Behn could find other outlets for her art in popular fiction and occasional verse, although neither proved as profitable as the stage. Her series of *Love Letters Between a Nobleman and His Sister* (1683-1687) and *Poems upon Several Occasions* were well received, but the meager financial returns could not keep pace with her social expenses. When she did return to the stage in 1686 with a comedy, *The Lucky Chance*, she met with only moderate success and much public abuse. *The Emperor of the Moon*, produced the following season, fared somewhat better, although the London audience had seemingly lost its stomach for a woman playwright with Tory sympathies. She continued to write fiction and verse, but sickness and the death of her one true artistic friend, Edmund Waller, both occurring in October, 1688, did little to inspire confidence in her attitudes toward life or art. Five days following the coronation of William III and Mary, on April 16, 1689, Aphra Behn died, the result, according to Gildon, of incompetent surgery. Nevertheless, she had risen high enough to merit burial in Westminster Abbey; in fact, her memorial, interestingly enough, lies near that of the famous actress Anne Bracegirdle (d. 1748), whose acting skills prolonged Behn's popularity well after the playwright's death. The fitting epitaph to Behn was provided by her lover, John Hoyle, who declared: "Here lies proof that wit can never be/ Defense against mortality."

Analysis

The history of English poetry during the Restoration of Charles II and the reign of James II seems to have no room for Aphra Behn. The reasons, all having little or nothing to do with her true poetic abilities, are fairly obvious. To form a composite of the Restoration poet, one must begin with an outline of a gentle*man* who wrote verse for other gentle*men* and a few literate ladies, who directed his efforts to a select group of coffeehouse and drawing-room wits, who wrote about politics, religion, scientific achievement, or war. He wrote poetry to amuse and to entertain, and even, on occasion, to instruct. He also wrote verse to attack or to appease his audience, those very persons who served as his readers *and* his critics. Thus, the Restoration poet vied with his colleagues for recognition and patronage—even for political position, favor, and prestige. He hurled epithets and obscenities at his rivals, and they quickly retorted. Of course, that was all done in public view, upon the pages of broadsheets and miscellanies.

Reflect, for a moment, upon the career of John Dryden (1631-1700), who dominated the London literary scene during the last quarter of the seventeenth century. He stood far above his contemporaries and fulfilled the practical function of the Restoration man of letters: the poet, dramatist, and essayist who focused upon whatever subject or form which happened to be current at a particular moment. Dryden succeeded because he understood his art, the demands of the times upon that art, and the arena in which he (as artist and man) had to compete. Around 1662 to 1663 he married Lady Elizabeth Howard, daughter of the Earl of Berkshire and sister of Sir Robert Howard. Sir Robert introduced the poet to the reestablished nobility, soon to become his readers and his patrons. In 1662, Dryden joined the Royal Society, mainly to study philosophy, mathematics, and reason, in order "to be a complete and excellent poet." One result, in 1663, was a poem in honor of Dr. Walter Charleton (1619-1707), physician to Charles II; the poet praised the new scientific spirit brought on by the new age and lauded the efforts of the Royal Society and its support of such geniuses as Robert Boyle and Sir Isaac Newton. In February, 1663, *The Wild Gallant*, the first of Dryden's twenty-eight plays, appeared on the stage; although the comedy was essentially a failure, it marked the beginning of an extremely successful career, for Dryden quickly recognized the Restoration theater as the most immediate outlet for his art.

Certainly Dryden became involved in the major religious and political controversies of his day, both personally and poetically, and his fortunes fluctuated as a result. His reputation, however—as critic, dramatist, and poet laureate of England—had been secured, and he remained England's most outstanding, most complete writer. As a poet, he headed a diverse group of artists who, although not consistently his equals, could compete with him in limited areas: the classicists of the Restoration, carryovers from an earlier age—Edmund Waller and Abraham Cowley; the satirists—Samuel Butler, John Oldham, Sir Charles Sedley, the Earls of Rochester and Dorset; the dramatists—William Wycherley, Sir George Etherege, Nathaniel Lee, Thomas Otway, William Congreve, George Farquhar, and Aphra Behn.

The point to be made is that unlike Dryden and his male counterparts, Behn had little time and even less opportunity to develop as a poet. Her sex prevented her from fitting the prototype of the Restoration poet; she lacked access to the spheres of social and political influence, mastery of classical languages and their related disciplines, and the luxury of writing when and what she pleased. The need for money loomed large as her primary motive, and, as had Dryden, she looked to the London stage for revenue and reputation. She certainly viewed herself as a poet, but her best poetry seems to exist within the context of her plays.

At the head of the list are two songs from *Abdelazar* (1676), the first a sixteen-line lyric known by its opening, "Love in fantastic triumph sate." Despite the trite (even by Restoration standards) dramatic setting—the usurper who murders his trusting sovereign and puts to death all who block his path to the throne—the poem reflects pure, personal feeling, as the poet laments over the misery of unrequited love. Behn depicts Love as a "strange tyrannic power" that dominates the amorous world; there is nothing terribly complicated, either in the sound or the sense of the language, for she relies upon simple sighs, tears, pride, cruelty, and fear. In the end, the poem succeeds because it goes directly to the central issue of the poet's personal unhappiness. "But my poor heart alone is harmed,/ Whilst thine the victor is, and free." The other song from *Abdelazar* is a dialogue between a nymph and her swain. The young lady, cognizant of the brevity of "a lover's day," begs her lover to make haste; the swain, in company with shepherds, shepherdesses, and pipes, quickly responds. He bears a stray lamb of hers, which he has caught so that she may chastise the creature ("with one angry look from thy fair eyes") for having wandered from the flock. The analogy between man and beast is obvious and nothing more need be said; the swain begs her to hurry, for "how very short a lover's day!"

There are other songs of equal or slightly less merit, and they all seem to contain variations on the same themes. In one, "'Tis not your saying that you love," the speaker urges her lover to cease his *talk* of love and, simply, love her; otherwise, she will no longer be able to live. Another, a song from *Lycidus* beginning "A thousand martyrs I have made," mocks "the fools that whine for love" and unmasks the fashion of those who, on the surface, appear deeply wounded by the torments of love when they actually seek nothing from love but its shallow pleasures. In a third song, "When Jemmy first began to love," Behn returns to the shepherd and his flock motif. On this occasion, the nymph, overpowered by Jemmy's songs, kisses, and general air of happiness, gives herself completely to him. Then the call to arms beckons; Jemmy exchanges his sheephooks for a sword, his pipes for warlike sounds, and, perhaps, his bracelets for wounds. At the end, the poor nymph must mourn, but for whom it is not certain: for the departed Jemmy or for herself, who must endure without him? Finally, in one of the longest of her so-called songs, a 140-line narrative entitled "The Disappointment," Behn introduces some of the indelicacies and indiscretions of which Victorian critics and biographers accused her. By late seventeenth century standards, the piece is indeed graphic (although certainly not vulgar or even indecent); but it nevertheless succeeds in demonstrating how excessive pleasure can easily turn to pain.

Although Behn, whether by choice or situation, kept outside the arena of poetic competition of the sort engaged in by Dryden and his rivals, she managed to establish personal relationships with the major figures of her age. Dryden always treated her with civility and even kindness, and there are those who maintain that a piece often attributed to Behn—"On Mr. Dryden, Renegade," and beginning "Scorning religion all thy lifetime past,/ And now embracing popery at last"—was not of her making. In addition, she remained on friendly terms with Thomas Otway, Edward Ravenscroft, Edmund Waller, and the Earl of Rochester. Behn wrote elegies for Waller and Rochester, and both poems are well suited to their occasion; yet they are two distinctly different poems. "On the Death of the Late Earl of Rochester" (written in 1680, published in 1685) is an appeal to the world to mourn the loss of a great and multifaceted personality: the muses must mourn the passing of a wit, youths must mourn the end of a "dear instructing rage" against foolishness, maidens the loss of a Heaven-sent lover, the little gods of love the loss of a divine lover, and the unhappy world the passage of a great man. Draped in its pastoral and classical mantles, the poem glorifies a subject not entirely worthy of glorification; yet, if the reader can momentarily forget about Rochester, the piece is not entirely without merit. After all, the poet did demonstrate that she knew how to write a competent elegy.

More than seven years later, on October 21, 1687, the aged poet Edmund Waller died, and again Behn penned an elegiac response entitled "On the Death of Edmund Waller." Her circumstances, however, had changed considerably since the passing of Rochester in July, 1680. Her health was poor, her finances low, her literary reputation not very secure. Apparently she had to write the piece in some haste, specifically for a collection of poems dedicated to Waller and written by his friends. Finally, Behn was deeply affected by Waller's death and chose the opportunity to associate that event with her own situation—that of the struggling, ailing, and aging (although she was then only forty-seven) artist. Thus, she sets the melancholy tone at the outset by identifying herself as "I, who by toils of sickness, am become/ Almost as near as thou art to a tomb." Throughout, she inserts references to an untuned and ignorant world, the muses' dark land, the low ebb of sense, the scanty gratitude and fickle love of the unthinking crowd—all of which seem more appropriate to her private and professional life than to Waller's. Still, the poem is a not unusual example of the elegy; Behn was not the first poet to announce her own personal problems while calling upon the world to mourn the loss of a notable person.

Midway through the elegy to Waller, Behn provides a clue that may well reveal her purpose as a poet and, further, may help to establish her legitimacy within the genre. She writes of a pre-Wallerian world of meaningless learning, wherein dull and obscure declamations prevented the blossoming of sensitive poets and true poetry and produced nothing that was "great and gay." During those barren years, she laments, there existed only thoughtless labor, devoid of instruction, pleasure, and (most important) passion. In a word, "the poets knew not Love." Such expressions and sentiments may appear, on the surface, as attempts to elevate the memory of her subject; in reality, they serve well to underline her own concerns for poetry as a means of bringing harmony to disorder, comfort to discord, love to insensitivity. As a woman, she looked upon a poetic field dominated by masculine activity and masculine expression, by masculine attitudes and masculine ideals. Where, she must certainly have asked herself, could one find the appropriate context in which to convey to an audience composed of both males *and* females those passions peculiar to her sex and to her person?

Whether she actually found the form in which to house that passion—or whether she even possessed the craft and the intellect to express it—is difficult to determine. One problem, of course, is that Behn did not write a sufficient quantity of poetry outside of her plays and novels to allow for a reasonable judgment. Nevertheless, she never ceased trying to pour forth the pain and the love that dominated her emotions. She wrote (as in "'Tis not your saying that you love") that actions, not words, must reinforce declarations of love, for only love itself can sustain life. Without love, there is no life! Throughout her poems, that conclusion reverberates from line to line: love is a triumph, a lover's day is short, the death of one partner means the spiritual (and automatic) death of the one remaining; a lover's soul is made of love, while the completion of an empty (and thus meaningless) *act* of love leaves a lover "half dead and breathless."

Perhaps the most interesting aspect of Behn's poetry is her taste for exotic settings. These backdrops appear to contradict her very way of life. Behn was a woman of the city, of the urban social and intellectual center of a nation that had only recently undergone political trauma and change. She belonged to the theater, the drawing room, the coffeehouse, the palace—even to the boudoir. Not many of those settings, however, found their way into her poetry. Instead, she selected for her poetic environments a composite that she called the "amorous world" ("Love in fantastic triumph sate"), complete with listening birds, feeding flocks, the aromatic boughs and fruit of a juniper tree, trembling limbs, yielding grass, crystal dew, a lone thicket made for love, and flowers bathed in the morning dew. Even the obviously human subjects, both alive and dead, rarely walk the streets of the town or meditate in the quiet of their own earthly gardens. Thus, Dryden, in the midst of religious disorientation, wanders about upon the wings of his own shame, in search of "Moses' God"; Rochester flies, quick as departing light, upon the fragrance of softly falling roses; and Waller, a heaven-born genius, is described as having rescued the chosen tribe of poetry from the Egyptian night. Of course, in the last two instances, Behn wrote elegies, which naturally allowed her departed subjects greater room for celestial meanderings. Love, however, had to be relieved from its earthly, banal confines. Love was very much Behn's *real* subject as a poet, but she was never prepared to discuss it within the context of the harsh and often ugly realities of her own time and place.

One problem in discussing Behn's poetry is that one cannot always catalog with confidence those pieces attributed to her and written by others. Also, there is confusion regarding those pieces actually written by her but attributed to others. For example, as late as 1926, and again in 1933, two different editors of quite distinct editions of the Earl of Rochester's poetry erroneously assigned three of Behn's poems to Rochester, and that error remained uncorrected until 1939. Textual matters aside, however, Behn's poetry still provides substantive issues for critical discussion. Commentators have traditionally favored the songs from her plays, maintaining that the grace and spontaneity of these pieces rise above the artificiality of the longer verses—the latter weighed down by convention and lack of inspiration. True, her major poem (at least in terms of its length) of two thousand lines, *A Voyage to the Island of Love*, while carrying the romantic allegory to extremes, does succeed in its purpose: a poetic paraphrase of the French original, and nothing more. Indeed, Behn, as a playwright, no doubt viewed poetry as a diversion and exercise; she considered both activities useful and important, and both provided added dimensions to her art. She was certainly not a great poet; but few during her time were. Her poetic success, then, must be measured in terms of her competence, for which she may, in all honesty, receive high marks and be entitled to a permanent place on the roster of poets.

Samuel J. Rogal

Other major works

LONG FICTION: *Love Letters Between a Nobleman and His Sister*, 1683-1687 (3 volumes); *Oroonoko: Or, The History of the Royal Slave*, 1688; *Agnes de Castro*, 1688; *The Fair Jilt: Or, The History of Prince Tarquin and Miranda*, 1688; *The History of the Nun: Or, The Fair Vow-Breaker*, 1689; *The Lucky Mistake*, 1689; *The Nun: Or, The Perjured Beauty*, 1697; *The Adventure of the Black Lady*, 1698; *The Wandering Beauty*, 1698.

PLAYS: *The Forced Marriage: Or, The Jealous Bridegroom*, 1670; *The Amorous Prince*, 1671; *The Dutch Lover*, 1673; *Abdelazar*, 1676; *The Town-Fopp*, 1676; *The Debauchee*, 1677; *The Rover: Or, The Banished Cavaliers*, 1677 (I), 1681 (II); *Sir Patient Fancy*, 1678; *The Young King*, 1679; *The Roundheads: Or, The Good Old Cause*, 1681; *The False Count*, 1681; *The City Heiress: Or, Sir Timothy Treat-All*, 1682; *The Lucky Chance*, 1686; *The Emperor of the Moon*, 1687; *The Widow Ranter*, 1689; *The Younger Brother*, 1696.

TRANSLATIONS: *Aesop's Fables*, 1687; *Of Trees*, 1689.

MISCELLANEOUS: *The Works of Aphra Behn*, 1915, 1967 (6 volumes).

Bibliography

Duffy, Maureen. *The Passionate Shepherdess: Aphra Behn, 1640-1689.* London: Jonathan Cape, 1977. This reliable, scholarly examination of Aphra Behn and the Restoration period in which she wrote informs readers about the social and political life that governed Behn's style. Duffy treats Behn as a serious artist, not as the superficial, almost unknown figure that earlier biographers painted. Generously illustrated with portraits, maps, and drawings of theaters.

Gardiner, Judith Kegan. "Aphra Behn: Sexuality and Self-Respect." *Women's Studies Quarterly* 7 (1980): 67-78. Gardiner's useful study contrasts Behn's attitudes toward sex, as shown in her poetry and plays, with those of male writers of her time. She finds in Behn, who was as much a Restoration character as the men, a more wholesome attitude toward sexual power games, impotence, and erotic wit. Behn seeks "a cavalier balance in independent sexuality capable of mutual pleasure and mutual response."

Goreau, Angeline. *Reconstructing Aphra: A Social Biography of Aphra Behn.* New York: Dial Press, 1980. Goreau attempts to recover a heroic life in the story of the first woman to earn her living by her pen. The contradictions of a woman trying to be both independent and competitive in the theater world and at the same time trying to live the feminine roles of lover and wife occupy Goreau's attention throughout the study. Presents the political background and the social scene of fashionable London in the 1660's and 1670's. Includes sixteen pages of portraits and theater scenes.

Link, Frederick M. *Aphra Behn.* New York: Twayne, 1968. A thorough account of the sum of Behn's work: plays, poetry, stories, novels, and translations from the French. Behn's criticism of social conditions, forced marriage and economic dependency of women, colonial oppression, and slavery are all treated in the analysis of her writings. Augmented by a chronology, notes, a bibliography, and an index.

Sackville-West, Victoria. *Aphra Behn: The Incomparable Astrea.* New York: Russell & Russell, 1927. Written in a sprightly, somewhat superficial style, this ninety-three-page study nevertheless defends Behn and treats her work and life with admiration for the courage required. The economic and social obstacles for a seventeenth century woman writer receive full attention. Supplemented by a list of works and a short bibliography.

Woodcock, George. *Aphra Behn: The English Sappho.* 1948. Reprint. Montreal: Black Rose, 1989. First published in 1948 in England, this book is now reprinted in its entirety with a short introduction by the author. Woodcock reflects that since writing the original version, he has come to see Behn less as a revolutionary and more as a participant in her times. Reviews the history of the debate about her childhood in Central America, her life as a spy, her prison experience, her career as a playwright, and her years of success.

BEN BELITT

Born: New York, New York; May 2, 1911

Principal poetry

The Five-Fold Mesh, 1938; *Wilderness Stair*, 1955; *The Enemy Joy: New and Selected Poems*, 1964; *Nowhere but Light: Poems 1964-1969*, 1970; *The Double Witness: Poems 1970-1976*, 1977; *Possessions: New and Selected Poems*, 1985.

Other literary forms

Ben Belitt is a major translator of verse into English in this century. He has translated works by Arthur Rimbaud, Jorge Luis Borges, Federico García Lorca, Rafael Alberti, and, preeminently, Pablo Neruda. Among a host of notable collections that he has translated, his Grove Press texts of Neruda are best known: *New Poems 1968-1970* (1972) and *Five Decades: Poems, 1925-1970* (1974). He has also written a book on the subject, *Adam's Dream: A Preface to Translation* (1978).

Achievements

Belitt's poetry is, by common assent, difficult, owing to its casual erudition, allusiveness, exacting vocabulary, and compact figuration. He has so assiduously avoided being a public poet that his reserve seems an explanation of why his work is not more anthologized. Belitt has received the Shelley Memorial Award (1937), the Oscar Blumenthal Award (1957), the National Institute of Arts and Letters Award (1965), and the Russell Loines Award (1981).

Biography

Ben Belitt joined the faculty of Bennington College (Vermont) in 1938; he has remained on Bennington's faculty since and continues to teach on an occasional basis. He has preferred a provincial to an urban setting for what he has called his "obsessional" writing habits. His poems and translations, however, reveal the least provincial of men. In 1936 and 1937, while still working on a doctoral degree (which he never finished) at the University of Virginia, he served as an assistant literary editor of *The Nation*, and late in World War II he served with the U.S. Army Department of Historical Films.

Belitt was orphaned early in life after the death of his father and subsequent abandonment by his mother. He and his sisters returned to their mother after her remarriage, but Belitt felt permanently isolated where family was concerned. He is an unconfessional sort of poet, but this experience and its consequences are presented in his poem "Orphaning" and elsewhere.

Analysis

From the outset, Ben Belitt's poetry has been aurally remarkable. Though his first volume was excessively alliterative and was spoken in a too-mannered voice, it revealed a poet whose first priority was control of traditional forms, metrically and stanzaically. He managed this with a fluent prosody driven equally by the line and the sentence. Since then, Belitt has written a freer verse in accommodating his times and the dictates of his own sensibility. His genius for linking the sounds of words abides, however, and he would rather risk verbal excess than speak flatly.

Belitt's imagination is demanding. Images and the terms of his similes and metaphors are brought together rapidly in his work. The reader may feel that some unimaginable step by which the poet mediated the associations has been left out. Moreover, Belitt requires intellectual rigor from his reader. Often, he brings an immediately realized object or event into relation with historical figures and their ideas. His practice assumes that these unions are self-evident.

Perhaps more than anything else, Belitt's poems strive to realize and throw light upon the nature of place and his response to place, which originates in alienation and need, moves on to solace and immersion and thence to a mature acceptance of rootlessness. (The reader who interprets this as the displacement of childhood anxieties overlooks the philosophical richness of Belitt's mind.) This enterprise is only roughly chronological in his work, as Belitt works by perpetually reconnoitering the old ground of his thought. As he goes, place is always complex, sometimes consoling, sometimes inscrutable, sometimes antagonistic; it can be all of these at once. The reader sees then that place, though sharply focused and delineated by Belitt, is rendered in an essentially impressionistic manner and stands more for the poet's metaphysical and aesthetic probings than for its own pictorial value. Thus his common practice of envisioning place through contrasting entities like stone and tree, gem and flower, desert and water, is deeply related to his existential struggle to achieve, without self-delusion or the consolations of defunct mythologies, stable and abiding worldview. It is not surprising that such a poet would eventually write a book entitled *Nowhere but Light*, having touched with clarity the innumerable dark places of his outer and inner landscapes.

In a prefatory note to *The Five-Fold Mesh*, Belitt speaks of two of its sequences, "Many Cradles" and "In Time of Armament," as dealing, respectively, with a "problem in orientation" and an "expanding record of change." The whole collection he sees as moving from "simple responses to the natural world" to "usable relationships between the personal and the contemporary world." This is the case. The poet is lost in the face of absolute flux. His "contemporary world" is not rife with technological paraphernalia; it is the psychological state of incertitude in the province of metaphysics and value. Thus he says in "The Unregenerate": "Cherish this disbelief/ For final truth, although the end be grief." The "heart," he argues, should confront and "accept this thing" (disbelief); the mind has been long aware of it. This collection then is largely about the heart and mind's taking up the "problem in orientation" to utter mutability.

Many of the poems, to test the poet's integrity, confront suffering and death. In these provinces mutability is most vexing and makes disbelief small consolation. "John Keats, Surgeon" is preeminent in this category. It goes beneath the ceaselessly kindling fever of that poet's tubercular dying to discover first his broken heart and then his great integrity. He sees every impulse of Keats as rejecting the balm of easy, traditional consolation (the "kindly unguent") and, equally, any kind of nepenthe. Better to treasure the merciless truth, a poet's duty, and be left with the "ruined heartbeat ailing still." This is the archetypal spirit of the poet, who must be surgeon to himself. Yet if darkness and this tragic unconsolability mark much of the collection, it is noteworthy that Belitt closes with the more hopeful touches of "Battery Park: High Noon." Here the controlled and behatted individual of workaday lower Manhattan is pulled irresistibly toward the allurements of nature's ancient condition by a concert of spring's forces.

The Wilderness Stair continues in a dark vein, its concluding sequence of war poems contributing largely to that effect. There is, however, much balance of joy and despondency here, an "equilibrium" in Belitt's lexicon.

Four sequences make up the volume. The first, "Departures," dominates by length. Its main body is a tour of places, each a blend of antithetical features that usually astound by their grace on the one hand and their starkness on the other. A maple in a Vermont quarry constitutes the wholeness of fragile fruitfulness and hard duration. A dead bull in a Mexican bull ring testifies to the commingling of dark and light: the "hilt . . . in a column of gristle" but also "Dionysus drowsing in a meadow." The second section, "The Habit of Angels," suggests transcendence and entails a struggle with the inner conflict created by the world's wildness. Belitt is moved by the call of moral rectitude, sent to one sensually engaged upon the "wilderness stair." (Stairwells and ladders, venues of psychological and spiritual ascent and descent, make up much of Belitt's terrain.) Yet his testament is, finally, an affirmation of the worldly stance, there being a "void at the sheer of the stair" and a fading godhead at the "place of the rock and the ladder."

The third section, "Karamazov," gets at the wish to murder the father. It is a tribute to Dostoevski, like Keats esteemed by Belitt, and an exploration of the oedipal urge. Certainly, the section has biographical overtones but is very distanced in accepting a mother's peaceful counsel, which leads to the poet's generic blessing of the father.

Four grim war poems make up "In Agamemnon's Color." A paratrooper's "Descent in a Parachute" renders his fall a traumatic birth. Fumbling the cord ("on his broken navel"), what he had expected to be easeful becomes only a terrifying "question" in "his brute and downward waste." "The Spool" is a cinematic account of a day at war. The most rhetorically straightforward poem in Belitt's whole corpus, it is a narrative of filmed action, beginning with the routine of the morning march and ending with the field surgeon's rubber-gloved hands poised above a "nerveless and saline wound." The surgeon's "mouth rejects contemplation" as Belitt mines a dark vein.

Belitt's title for his third collection, *The Enemy Joy*, comes from a poem published in *The Five-Fold Mesh* that is reprinted there, though not among the new poems. It is significantly positioned, however, as the book's final piece. The paradoxical title refers to Belitt's sense that joy is always accompanied by its antagonist. In the poem, which is basic to understanding the continued balancing of the contrarieties of place in the new work, a bird "in jackal country" sings "for pure delight." The bird suggests Thomas Hardy's darkling thrush, but Hardy's bird seemed to announce some hope of which Hardy remained unaware. Belitt's bird sings "the enemy joy as it were grief"; its utterance is powerful, manifold, and paradoxically evident to Belitt. Simply put, this bird is the spirit of Keats, of the "Ode on Melancholy."

Thus, a quite productive orientation to the new poems may be to approach them in terms of aesthetics or of art understood as worldview, though life per se is nowhere shunned by Belitt. "Battle-Piece," a poem in five parts, is not simply an extension of the interest in war that was the finale to *The Wilderness Stair*. It is an envisioning of Paolo Uccello's painting *Battaglia di San Romano* (1456-1460). Belitt regards the "champion" of the field as awaiting some interpretation of the deadly event. The poet concludes simply with "Nothing responded." This is not just colloquial; this is the veritable "nada" of a nihilistic insight. It is the artistic representation, ostensibly by Uccello but really by Belitt, of that "nerveless wound" speaking in the face of the surgeon's stilled mouth. In the penultimate line of this brilliant sequence, Belitt uses the word "placeless" with a cunning ambiguity. In one of its principal designations, it states the irreducible position of the artist. He is the poem's "Begetter," whose vision goes beyond the "landscape." He is the one to "fight that battle after the battle,/ Inward and naked." A commensurate realization caps "Memorial Hospital: Outpatient," dedicated to a physician. It is conveyed by the utterance "There is nowhere but light."

That line, of course, prefigures the title of Belitt's fourth volume. It derives, as mentioned, from his steady effort to illuminate the darkness of the world and of his experience. *Nowhere but Light* also points, however, to the acceptance of a placeless condition, to some vanquishing of an old desire. The zone of his concern shifts here to being itself. Indeed, the first line of the first poem is merely "To be." Yet place, especially contrastive place, though differently regarded, remains important.

Thus the sequence entitled "Antipodal Man" comes to a head in "Siesta: Mexico/Vermont." (The term "antipodal man" appears here.) Like many of

Belitt's poems, this one suggests the Hartford/Florida and Nova Scotia/Brazil frames of reference of Wallace Stevens and Elizabeth Bishop. All have required antitheses of climate and topography for their work. Yet here it is the light of a dual setting, glimpsed in siesta, that dominates and grants the "antipodal man" his bearing. He enters simultaneously "the tropic/ and the polar fires." There is a mystic, albeit humanistic, dimension to this; the poem is about the rarefield human experience in which the poet enters fire and circles "the precision/ of a moment." Specific place yields to archetypal place, which yields to light, which yields to an enlightened moment.

The volume's first poem, one of Belitt's finest, "The Orange Tree," sets the stage for such experience. Belitt meditates on the idea that if one can "live in the spirit" perhaps it is a state analogous to "the orange's scent/ in the orange tree." It is the marriage of the palpable tree and the ephemeral scent that excites the poet's imagination. In tying that union to conceivable spirituality, he arrives at a synesthetic figure in which the tree's branch, then twig, then leafage lead irrepressibly to the "sunburst of white in the leaves," which he calls "the odor's epiphany." Scent inhabits color. This natural epiphany dictates a paring of excess to Belitt, a search for the "minimal." The epiphany and its lesson stand as emblems of the questing and goal particular to this collection that, with *The Enemy Joy*, considerably broadens Belitt's use of his materials and his idea of his art.

Belitt continues to explore his isolation in *The Double Witness*, though he employs "we" more than before. The title comes from the opening poem, "Xerox," wherein an "original" man lies down upon a copy machine's glass to double all that was "lonely, essential, unique." In witty prayerfulness, he calls from the machine's inky pit, "Forgive our duplicity." Belitt uses the volume to track the individual into the species, locating a range of doubles. The poems are worlds of mirroring.

The volume's key piece is the sequence "This Scribe My Hand," about Belitt's relation to Keats, which is represented by the contact of their pens' nibs as Keats writes on the underside of Belitt's page. Its exquisite realization of psychological pain does not check its despair and nihilistic feeling. These become the dominant tones of the volume's final section, where "chaos" rules and the mundane lament that "nothing will happen today" is a refrain. Belitt's despair is attributable to his continuing appraisal of his art, which—especially in "This Scribe My Hand"—grows utterly pessimistic in this volume. He feels his own work as posthumous and envisions Keats writing his own solitude "in water" on his side of the page. He sees that "something murderous flows/ from that page," a silence that stills their language and is the fate of which they are the double witness. He calls the silence "mortal."

These are the poems of a poet's most extreme crisis, come inexorably to haunt his sixties. They give us suicides, exiles, and deep anxiety about the poet's own enterprise. Belitt's skill in connecting detail within and between them, his management of paradox and the forthrightness of his self-questioning, all preserve integrity in a volume menaced by disintegration. Belitt has always considered poetry his talisman. That these poems so thoroughly doubt themselves philosophically yet remain so exquisitely executed suggests that for Belitt the true poem of the chaotic, even one written against itself, retains its talismanic power.

There are only twelve new poems in *Possessions.* They are not easily characterized, as each picks up on some dominant strain long at work. "Graffiti" is a "vandal's dream" in which Belitt writes himself large and pervasively, in his "double initials," on a subway's every surface. It is, first, an absurd fantasy of a literary status denied and, second, a dealing with the commensurate sense that his work has only posthumous prospects. "Walker" is an old woman's revery of dancing as she stands, shut in and stalled, before her doorframe, which holds the image of Candlewood Mountain at an impossible distance. Belitt does not let her drift into a nostalgic past; rather, he makes up the fantastic satisfaction of her longing from her present condition. "Walker" belongs to a group that takes the difficult lives of elderly women as subject. It originates with the excellent "Charwoman" (*The Five-Fold Mesh*) and comes to full development both here and in "A Suicide: Paran Creek" (*The Double Witness*).

The poem entitled "Possessions" glimpses King Tutankhamen's realization that grave robbers have done him out of the wherewithal of his immortality. Belitt takes the point to heart, seeing his own desire through the boy king's. Each of the volume's poems ties in with "Possessions" in some way. The quite dissimilar "Sumac" ends with a remark about how the "marauders move in," and the subterranean setting of "Graffiti" is characterized as "the tomb-robber's darkness."

"Thoreau on Paran Creek" and "Voyage of the *Beagle*" get finely at Thoreau's and Darwin's probing to discover precisely why certain particulars and not others constitute the world. The poems relate to "Possessions" and its spiritual search to locate and possess what can bestow some abiding meaning on human existence. Belitt knows that nothing can be so possessed except in illusion, and that everyone is robbed even of that, one way or another. Though *Possessions* is a small volume, it is not skimpy. It is a plenitude from the lively mind of a poet in his seventies.

David M. Heaton

Other major works

NONFICTION: *Four Poems by Rimbaud: The Problem of Translation,* 1947; *Adam's Dream: A Preface to Translation,* 1978.

TRANSLATIONS: *Poet in New York,* 1955, by Federico García Lorca; *Selected*

Poems of Pablo Neruda, 1961; *Juan de Mairena*, 1963, by Antonio Machado; *Selected Poems of Rafael Alberti*, 1965; *Poems from the Canto General*, 1968, by Neruda (with Alastair Reid); *A New Decade: Poems, 1958-1967*, by Neruda; *New Poems, 1968-1970*, 1972, by Neruda; *Splendor and Death of Joaquin Murieta*, 1972, by Neruda; *A la pintura*, 1972, by Alberti; *Jorge Luis Borges: Selected Poems, 1972*; *Five Decades: Poems, 1925-1970*, 1974, by Neruda; *Skystones*, 1981, by Neruda; *The New York Poems: Poet in New York/Earth and Moon*, 1982, by Federico García Lorca; *Late and Posthumous Poems, 1968-1974*, 1988, by Neruda.

Bibliography

Goldensohn, Lorrie. "Witnessing Belitt." *Salmagundi* 44 (1979): 182-196. Analyzes Belitt's habit of "cannibalizing" prior books so as to enrich his current aproach to a theme, a habit that goes beyond the borrowing of a line or image; it entails whole poems, which when newly placed revisit, enlarge, and reshape a concern. Also offers insight into Belitt's "gloominess" and spirituality.

Landis, Joan Hutton. "A Wild 'Severity': Toward a Reading of Ben Belitt." In *Contemporary Poetry in America*, edited by Robert Boyers. New York: Schocken, 1974. Excellent overview of Belitt's work (excepting the new poems in *Possessions*) links the poet's dominant attitude to Keats's "melancholy." Treats also the recurrent balancing of opposites in the poems, whether the rock and flower of the world or the joy and despair of humanity.

Nemerov, Howard. "The Fascination of What's Difficult." In *Reflexions on Poetry and Poetics*. New Brunswick, N.J.: Rutgers University Press, 1972. Nemerov argues the efficacy of Belitt's difficultly grasped verbal associations and demanding vocabulary. He sees Belitt's typical manner as a blending of "great elaboration" and "great intensity" (conciseness) and contends that one must read "around" rather than "through" his lyrics and see them in combination.

Salmagundi 87 (1990): 3-231. Indispensable issue devoted to readings of Belitt's poems. Mary Kinzie's "A Servant's Cenotaph" is broadest in scope, taking up the whole of *The Double Witness* and noting that there as elsewhere Belitt's "vision of human experience is fateful and symbolic." Hugh Kenner's "Meditations On 'Possessions'" deals with Belitt's predilections for lists and the "rite" of naming. He sees these characteristics as the poet's means for manifesting both the intense particularity of things and the dilemma of valuing what one is attached to but cannot possess. Terence Diggory's "On Ben Belitt's 'The Bathers: A Triptych'" discusses the poet's work as frequently conscious of itself as art. It characterizes Belitt's particularly rich way of revealing the division between the work and the object it contemplates.

HILAIRE BELLOC

Born: La Celle-Saint-Cloud, France; July 27, 1870
Died: Guildford, England; July 16, 1953

Principal poetry

Verses and Sonnets, 1896; *The Bad Child's Book of Beasts*, 1896; *More Beasts for Worse Children*, 1897; *The Modern Traveller*, 1898; *A Moral Alphabet*, 1899; *Cautionary Tales for Children*, 1907; *Verses*, 1910; *More Peers*, 1911; *Sonnets and Verse*, 1923, 1938; *New Cautionary Tales*, 1930; *Sonnets and Verse*, 1954 (Reginald Jebb, editor); *The Verse*, 1954 (W. N. Roughead, editor).

Other literary forms

Hilaire Belloc was a prolific and popular writer of prose. He is identified primarily as a historian and defender of the Roman Catholic religion, but he wrote history, biography, travel, literary criticism, church history and religious doctrine, political theory, and translation, as well as some autobiographical travel books which are difficult to categorize. In all, he wrote more than 150 books, as well as many book reviews and magazine articles. His prose and poetry both show a wide range of themes and forms.

Belloc was one of a number of Catholic writers of the period, including Francis Thompson, Gerard Manley Hopkins, Alice Meynell, and G. K. Chesterton. He wrote rebuttals to views of his Church held by the historians Edward Gibbon, H. G. Wells, and George Coulton, but he could also see its imperfections, remarking to a friend that such an institution could not have lasted a fortnight if it had not been divine.

Achievements

Although he was a man of letters in many genres, Belloc often said in later years that he hoped to be remembered for his poetry. He wrote more than 170 poems in all and was a writer of both light and serious verse. Much of the former was intended for children, but it appealed to adults as well. The first edition of *The Bad Child's Book of Beasts* (1896) sold out in four days, and four thousand copies were sold in three months. This was followed by other nonsense books which were much praised. *The Spectator* ranked his satirical and comic verse with Edward Lear's, and Sir Arthur Quiller-Couch commended it.

A volume of Belloc's serious poetry also appeared in 1896, and it increased in size in succeeding editions. Belloc was said by Desmond McCarthy to be the most underrated of poets. At a dinner in his honor on his sixtieth birthday, Chesterton said that such a ceremony "might have been fitting thousands of years ago at the festival of a great Greek poet," and that "Belloc's sonnets and strong verse would remain like the cups and carved epics of the Greeks."

In later years, his poetry has been generally neglected, although the serious poems include many beautiful works. This neglect is probably the result of three circumstances. First, his themes and forms were traditional and classical rather than avant-garde. Second, his reputation as a prose writer made his poems seem secondary. Third, some of his best poems were not published in his collections of poetry until 1938. This was true of many of his epigrams and of the Juliet poems, which had been privately printed. His "Heroic Poem in Praise of Wine" probably has been his most admired work.

Biography

Joseph Hilaire Pierre Belloc was born in 1870 in La Celle-Saint-Cloud, near Paris, of a French father and an English mother. He was called Hilaire after his grandfather, a celebrated painter. His father died when he was a baby, and, after his mother suffered financial reverses when he was eight years old, they moved to England, his home in Sussex becoming a major influence in his life. He wrote his first poem when he was eight years old. In 1882, he was sent to the Oratory School at Edgbaston, a boarding school that had been established by Cardinal Newman. While he did not like school, he nevertheless learned the classics, took parts in Latin plays, and won a prize in his last year. After leaving school, he considered joining the French Navy, since he loved sailing, but he studied for only a term at the Collège Stanislas at Paris before finding it too restrictive. He was then apprenticed to a farmer to learn to be a land agent, but that did not work out either. He then turned to journalism and edited a weekly paper called *The Lamp*, in which some of his early poems appeared. Other early poems appeared in *The Irish Monthly* and *Merrie England*.

In 1889, he fell in love with Elodie Hogan, an Irish-American visiting Europe with her family whom he met at his mother's house. Belloc wanted to marry her, but she returned to California. He followed her to the United States in 1890, and made his way westward laboriously, often on foot, selling sketches to pay his way. Elodie's mother did not favor the marriage, and Elodie considered becoming a nun. She persuaded Belloc to take the military training required of all French citizens. When he returned east, she sent him a letter refusing his proposal. He did join the Battery of the Eighth Regiment of Artillery at Toul, serving from November, 1891, to August, 1892, and very much enjoyed military life.

Although Catholics were not yet formally permitted to attend Oxford or Cambridge, Belloc became a student at Balloil College, Oxford, helped financially by his sister and her husband-to-be. In October, 1892, he received a history scholarship. During his three years at Oxford, he received the Brackenbury Prize for history, took a brilliant first, became President of the Union, and walked from Oxford to London in record time. He was deeply disappointed, however, that he did not receive a history fellowship, especially since it was awarded to another Catholic for the first time since the Reformation.

Elodie entered the convent, but soon left, suffering from physical and nervous disorders. In 1896, Belloc went again to California, where they were married on June 16 despite Elodie's mother's objections; Belloc also did some lecturing while he was in the United States. The couple then lived in Oxford, where Belloc published his first collection of poems. He earned money by tutoring, giving University Extension lectures, and writing books, including *The Bad Child's Book of Beasts* (1896). He wrote political articles and gave speeches for Liberal candidates. He wanted to apply for the Professorship of History at Glasgow University, but that university did not favor a Catholic and prevailed upon Elodie to discourage him from applying.

In 1902, Belloc became an English citizen, and in 1906, he entered Parliament as the Liberal member from South Salford. Although he saw the House of Commons as a place of corruption and hypocrisy, he was reelected as an Independent.

He founded a weekly review, *The Eye Witness*. He moved from Oxford to Cheyne Walk, and then in 1906 to King's Land, a house in Sussex near Horsham, where he enjoyed his four children and his many friends, including the Chesterton brothers. His wife, whose literary judgment he greatly respected, died at forty-three in 1914, and ever after he dressed in black and used black-bordered stationery. He traveled frequently to the continent to study the scenes of his historical works. Unable to get an active appointment in World War I, he spent some time writing articles concerning the war.

He became ill in 1941 after his youngest son died in military service and had a stroke at the beginning of the next year, from which he recovered slowly. He died on July 16, 1953, just short of his eighty-third year.

Analysis

What Hilaire Belloc praised in others' verse he tried to achieve in his own. He said, in a preface to Ruth Pitter's poetry, that the classical spirit, which involved "rhythmic effect without emphatic lilt," subtlety without obvious complexity, and artistry without artifice, was almost unknown in his time. In his preface to D. B. Wyndham Lewis' book on François Villon, he remarked that the clarity, relief, and vigor mentioned by Lewis were qualities of "hardness," explaining that the marks of hardness were inevitability, the sense that to change a line would be to destroy it; a sense of sequence, of smooth linking; and economy of speech. Belloc's most successful poems, particulary his epigrams, have this intensity.

Belloc was classical in his ideals but innovative in his practice. His classicism bore poetic fruit in his "Heroic Poem in Praise of Wine," probably his best-known poem. The work (which was influenced by the French writer Clément Marot's vineyard song) was finished in 1928, although fragments of it had appeared earlier. Although it is a poem of praise treating a subject in an exalted way, Belloc the classicist is careful to refer to it as a heroic poem rather than an ode, for it is written in neither the Pindaric nor the Horatian form. The poem changes direction several times and ranges from heroic to mock-heroic.

The first stanza begins in the classical convoluted manner with infinitives of purpose, followed by several lines giving appositives for wine, and finally, five lines below the infinitives, the material to which they refer, an admonition to the Ausonian Muse. The stanza thus incorporates the classical statement of theme with the invocation of the Muse. The invocation to the Ausonian Muse, however, is amusing, since there was no Muse of lower Italy, thus making the reader suspect a partly humorous purpose in the elaborate beginning. The poet personifies wine as a mysterious friend of humanity, begetter of the arts and avenger of wrongs, and he calls upon the Muse to praise and enthrone it.

In the second stanza, the poet requests the Muse to sing of how the Charioteer from Asia with his panthers and the thyrsus twirling came to Greece. The wine of the first stanza has become Dionysus the god. Belloc achieves a sense of anticipation in his description of the ill-at-ease sea, the sudden glory of the mountain, the luminous sky, and the wind with the wonderful word that goes before the pageantlike progress. The group becomes a "something" or a shining cloud as it passes over the land; but everywhere it goes there is the miracle of the creation of vines, exuberantly portrayed with a double exclamation. The god is not named here; he is only alluded to by his characteristics. The next stanza shows the vines spreading everywhere, even as far as Africa, but also covering human habitations, thus being both wide and deep, exotic and domestic. In the next section, the day ends with Dionysus completing his journey, going from Spain to Ocean, where Hercules adores him. The author alludes to Hercules, expecting that his readers will have read of the Pillars of Hercules. The next section consists of only a single line, set off for emphasis, stating that the wine is better than riches or power.

The poet then seems to see people who breathe foul air from a well that is oozing slime along the floor of Hell and asks a rhetorical question concerning their identification—rhetorical because he answers it himself. They are the brood of sin, the cursed water-drinkers, and he says with ironic humor that their mothers must have been gin-sodden. This section is mock-heroic and satirical; Belloc attempts to guess their genealogy in the classical manner, calling them white slugs, an apt use of insect imagery to indicate their lack of vitality and character. Those who drink water instead of wine must, by implication, disapprove of it. Thus he uses the explosive "What!" to show indignation that the human race that was exiled from Paradise should have to suffer an evil (these people) with every good (the wine). In the next stanza, he says that even these filthy creatures were permitted to exist in the shadow of the bright Lord, an ambiguous term probably meaning Christ or Dionysus. Like John Milton, Belloc blends classical motifs with such Christian ones as Paradise. Whoever is contaminated by these creatures is condemned to drink the beverage of beasts. In the next section, the poet declares that the grapes are raised in vain for such as these in the various wine-growing regions to which he refers and, again proceeding in the negative, says that it is not for them "the mighty task/ Of bottling God the Father in a flask." The imagery is once more ambiguous, ostensibly Christian but possibly classical. He compares the dull, lifeless behavior of the water-drinkers with the inspired creativity of the wine-drinkers, who have companions in their sleep, as Dionysus had Ariadne. He exhorts the reader to forget the water-drinkers, to form the Dionysian ring and let Io sing. The inclusion of Io in the poem is appropriate since her frenzied condition produced by the gadfly sent by Hera was akin to the divine frenzy of the followers of Dionysus; furthermore, Io was an ancestor of Semele, the mother of Dionysus.

In the next stanza, Belloc addresses Dionysus directly as "Father Linaean" and entreats him not to abandon ruined humanity, as the other gods have done, attributing both architectural elements and rhyme to the god. The following stanza praises the god in three lines stating his powers of enlightening seers, making statues live, and making the grapes swell. In a pastoral strain, he wishes a peaceful life for a farmer; but, knowing that this is not possible, he remembers that all must face their passion (a Christian concept) and gives examples of ironic unsung tragedies.

The last stanza dramatizes old age and death in a series of images. He, too, having wasted long labor, will leave the sun and walk with the shadows, will look at the plain, not at the mountain, and will be alone with nothingness before him. The image of God becomes a military one, understandable in Belloc, who loved the military life: his Comrade-Commander (Christ) will drink with him in His Father's Kingdom. When the hour of death comes, Belloc says, let his youth appear with a chalice bearing an engraved blessing for his dying lips. His youth is here personified to provide a contrast to his age, but the image of a youth with a chalice also suggests Dionysus, who was portrayed as a youth in later representations, one of whose attributes was the *kantharos*, a large two-handled goblet. Dionysus was associated with death and the afterlife through the story of his descent into the underworld to rescue his mother and, in Thrace and in Orphic mythology, his death and resurrection. The ending of the poem would seem to be Christian in its references to wine as sacramental, although the image of wine as his last companion and of wine as raising the divine is not necessarily so. Belloc skillfully blended Christian and classical references in this unusual poem. His sonnet XXXVI in praise of wine ascribed its creation to the Christian God, who made men vintners as well as bakers so that they could have the sacraments. Belloc, it may be added, also wrote several drinking songs.

166 Critical Survey of Poetry

The epigram is another classical form employed by Belloc, possessing that element of hardness that he so much admired. He achieved great economy in his use of comparisons. "On a Dead Hostess" begins with an explicit comparison of the subject to other people in this "bad" world by stating two superlatives. The hostess is lovelier than all others and better than everyone else; she has smilingly bid her guests goodnight and gone to her rest, a metaphor for her quiet death, mentioned only in the title. Belloc achieved delicacy here by implying rather than stating. In some of his epigrams suitable for inscriptions on sundials, the shadow represents death, as in one which says that "Loss and Possession, Death and Life are one,/ There falls no shadow where there falls no sun." In a few words, he conveys the idea of the positive inherent in the negative, the theme of John Keats's "Ode to Melancholy." In some of his humorous sundial epigrams, the sundials identify themselves as such and make some wry comment, such as that it makes a "botch/ Of what is done far better by a watch," and "I am a sundial/ Ordinary words/ Cannot express my thoughts on birds."

The Epigrams were generally published for the first time in the collected poems of 1938, while the epigrammatic Juliet poems were privately printed in 1920 and 1934. Thus, some of these poems have not been as accessible as some of his lesser efforts. Many of the Juliet poems are compliments, some of them making use of classical allusions. In "The little owl that Juliet loved is dead," he explains that Pallas Athene took him, since "Aphrodite should not keep her bird," thus identifying Juliet with Aphrodite. In "On a Sleeping Friend," he declares that when she awakens, Dawn shall break over Lethe, the river of forgetfulness.

Belloc experimented with French forms, particularly the ballade and triolet. The triolet, which rhymes abaaabab, lines 1, 4, and 7 being identical, is appropriate for playful praise, but Belloc used it for more serious themes. The triolet beginning "The young, the lovely and the wise" says that they are intent on their going and do not seem to notice him. This makes him wonder about "my losing and my owing," presumably the things he has lost and the things he intended. In addition to the repetition of line 1 in lines 4 and 7, line 2 is repeated as line 8, thus giving the poem a strong echoic quality. Delicacy is also achieved by ambiguity; the reader is not exactly sure what is meant by the young's "going." It may be their going out into the world, being on their own. The young people are certain that they know where they are going, paying no attention to others. On the other hand, their "going" may be their death, to which the young are indifferent but about which older people are very much concerned.

Belloc considered the sonnet to be the "prime test of a poet," as he said in his book *Milton* (1935). The sonnet "Your life is like a little winter's day" has a delicacy comparable to "The young, the lovely and the wise," and again an ambiguity contributes to the delicacy. It speaks directly to the reader, using "you" throughout, giving unusual immediacy to the subject of death. In the first line, the poet compares "your" life to a "little" day in winter, while the second line elaborates with a mention of a "sad" sun rising late and setting early; thus life seems sad and wintry. The third line questions your going away, since you have just come; and the fourth line elaborates, saying that your going makes evening instead of noon. The reader is thus likened to the winter sun, and the theme of departure is introduced. The next quatrain compares life to something else that is "little," a flute lamenting far away, beyond the willows. Willow trees are associated with sorrow and death. "A long way off" at the beginning of line 6 is repeated at the beginning of line 7, and because the music is far away, only its memory is left in the breeze. The poet implies that life is faintly heard, like the flute. The octave is Shakespearean in form, but the sestet reverses the usual rhyming couplet at the end, placing it at the beginning of the sestet. The sestet's rhyme scheme is eefggf, enabling another rhyming couplet, gg, to appear where it is hardly expected, before the last line. The sense of reversal and paradox of the rhyme scheme conveys the ironic nature of the subject matter. The third comparison here is that life is like a pitiful farewell that is wept in a dream, with only shadows present. Belloc's ending is couched in religious terms, calling the farewell a benediction that has no fruit except a consecrated silence. The benediction or farewell is whispered and comes too late, so that there is no response to it. The three comparisons, a little day in winter, a flute playing at a great distance, and a farewell made too late in a dream, all contribute to the sense of incompletion. Life is unfulfilled, fleeting, and inconsequential, and the reference is not only to life in general but to "your" life. This discrepancy between expectation and actuality is reinforced by the unexpected rhyme scheme.

Belloc also experimented by trying to make the rhythm of a poem simulate the action. "The End of the Road" is a poem about the successful completion of Belloc's difficult journey to Rome and is reminiscent of the Carmina Burana of the Middle Ages. He manages to portray a rollicking hike by using many variations of the word "walked," by inverting the subject, and by making trochaic lines with a tripping meter: "Walked I, went I, paced I, tripped I." He goes on in that way for eleven lines, changes to Latin, then back again to English, calling on the major, doubtful, and minor prophets, among others. Another poem in which he tries to imitate motion by meter is his "Tarantella," in which he simulates the beat of the dance with short lines and internal rhymes.

Belloc's inventiveness extended to his satirical poems. "To Dives," the name meaning "rich man" in Latin, was inspired by Belloc's indignation at instances of unjust social and financial influence; it was written a week after Sir Henry Colville, Commander of the Ninth Division in South Africa, was dismissed without court martial or public investigation. Unlike the fiery directness of some of his other satirical poems, including the sonnet "Almighty God, whose justice like a sun," which speaks indignantly of the plight of the poor, Belloc in "To Dives" adopts the manner of Horatian rather than Juvenalian satire. He satirizes himself as well as his subject, saying to Dives that when they both go to Hell, Dives will stagger under his pack. Charon the ferryman will tell Dives that his baggage must go overboard. There are many humorous touches here, including the formal address and the many possessions, including the fifteen kinds of boots for town, and the gifts for those already there, such as the working model of a burning farm to give to the little Belials, as well as the three biscuits for Cerberus. Dives assures Belloc that he will not burn with him, though he will have to leave his possessions behind and enter Hell as tattered and bare as his father was when he pushed a wheelbarrow (Belloc's smirk at the *nouveau riche*). When Charon sees how lightly the poet is provided with such things as honor, laughter, debts, and trust in God, he lets him pass, having tried to write poetry himself. The poem ends with the rhetorical question to Dives as to who will look foolish, Dives, Belloc, or Charon. The answer is uncertain because "They order things so damnably in hell." Here Belloc has placed a contemporary rich man in the classical underworld and contrasted him with a poet. Yet he represents himself as going there as well.

Belloc enjoyed playing with various forms of verse while adhering to the ideals of the classics. His range was unusual: he could write, with almost equal facility, a heroic poem or an epigram, a sonnet or a ballade, a satire or a piece of nonsense verse.

Rosemary Ascherl

Other major works

NONFICTION: *Paris*, 1900; *Robespierre*, 1901; *The Path to Rome*, 1902; *Avril*, 1904; *The Catholic Church and Historical Truth*, 1908; *Marie Antoinette*, 1909; *The Pyrenees*, 1909; *The French Revolution*, 1911; *The Four Men*, 1912; *The Servile State*, 1912; *The Cruise of the "Nona,"* 1925; *A History of England*, 1925-1941; *The Catholic Church and History*, 1926; *Milton*, 1935; *On the Place of Gilbert Chesterton in English Letters*, 1940.

Bibliography

Corrin, Jay P. *G. K. Chesterton and Hilaire Belloc: The Battle Against Modernity.* Athens: Ohio University Press, 1981. Two champions of "democratic anarchy" are juxtaposed as writers and polemicists in an exploration that illuminates both of their careers. Corrin ably demonstrates the near inseparability of intellect and theological commitment of the two allies, while offering good expositions of the histories, fiction, and poetry of the lesser known Belloc.

Kantra, Robert. "Irony in Belloc." *Renascence* 17 (Spring, 1965): 131-136. An excellent, though brief, treatment of the ironic elements in Belloc's prose, using Northrop Frye's definition of irony.

McCarthy, John Patrick. *Hilaire Belloc: Edwardian Radical*. Indianapolis: Liberty Press, 1978. McCarthy's concern is to elucidate Belloc's career as a political conservative who opposes statism and the growing intervention of government in the private lives of individuals. This resourceful volume explains the relationship between Belloc's politics and economics, and his poetics, while offering an apologia for reading Belloc in the present.

Markel, Michael H. *Hilaire Belloc*. Boston: Twayne, 1982. Markel provides a sympathetic overview of Belloc's life and a mostly thorough exposition of his major and minor works. This source is the best starting place for gaining a sense of the breadth of Belloc's writing career and political commitments. Markel's bibliography of primary and secondary sources is succinct, but valuable.

Speaight, Robert. *The Life of Hilaire Belloc*. New York: Farrar, Straus & Cudahy: 1957. Until A. N. Wilson's 1984 biography, this volume was the authoritative biography of Belloc, offering the facts of his life and the best available exposition and critique of his wide-ranging oeuvre. It remains a helpful starting place for Belloc's life and times even if its mid-century judgments about Belloc's work—as an "authorized biography"—have been superseded by later scholarly perspective.

Wilson, A. N. *Hilaire Belloc*. New York: Atheneum, 1984. A renowned novelist and biographer, Wilson provides researchers with an impeccable source of critical biographical material. Using Belloc's letters and manuscripts previously unavailable, Wilson places Belloc and his writing within his historical milieu with affection and candor, refusing to ignore the darker side of Belloc's sympathies with the anti-Semitism of the 1930's and 1940's.

STEPHEN VINCENT BENÉT

Born: Bethlehem, Pennsylvania; July 22, 1898
Died: New York, New York; March 13, 1943

Principal poetry

Five Men and Pompey, 1915; *Young Adventure*, 1918; *Heavens and Earth*, 1920; *King David*, 1923; *Tiger Joy*, 1925; *John Brown's Body*, 1928; *Ballads and Poems, 1915-1930*, 1931; *A Book of Americans*, 1933 (with Rosemary Carr Benét); *Burning City*, 1936; *The Ballad of the Duke's Mercy*, 1939; *Western Star*, 1943.

Other literary forms

Stephen Vincent Benét made his major contribution to literature as a poet and primarily as the author of the book-length poem *John Brown's Body*. Benét was a prolific writer in several genres, however, and his canon includes short stories, novels, radio scripts, and nonfiction.

His short stories are collected in *Thirteen O'Clock* (1937) and *Tales Before Midnight* (1939). The first collection contains the well-known "The Devil and Daniel Webster," which he adapted as a play, opera, and film script. He wrote several novels: *The Beginning of Wisdom* (1921), *Young People's Pride* (1922), *Jean Huguenot* (1923), *Spanish Bayonet* (1926), and *James Shore's Daughter* (1934). Benét chose to support himself and his family as a writer and, as a result, his short stories and novels often were hack work churned out for whoever would pay him the most money.

He also composed radio scripts, collected in *We Stand United, and Other Radio Scripts* (1945), plays, and a short history. These writings were propagandistic, wartime efforts that he felt he had to do no matter what the effect on his literary reputation.

The best collections of his works are the two-volume hardback edition, *Selected Works of Stephen Vincent Benét* (1942, Basil Davenport, editor), and the paperback edition, *Stephen Vincent Benét: Selected Poetry and Prose*, also edited by Davenport (1942).

Achievements

Benét's achievements began early in his life. In 1915, when he was only seventeen years old, he made his first professional sale of a poem—to *The New Republic*—and published his first book of poems (*Five Men and Pompey*). He published his second book of poems (*Young Adventure*) in 1918 just before he was twenty years old. Between 1916 and 1918, while at Yale, he was, first, on the editorial board of the *Yale Literary Magazine*, and then chairman. He received a traveling fellowship from Yale in 1920 that enabled him to go to Paris, where he completed his first novel, *The Beginning of Wisdom*.

Benét received many literary and academic awards throughout his life, and he was popular with the public. His collection of poems *King David* received *The Nation*'s poetry prize in 1923, when he was twenty-five years old. A Guggenheim Fellowship allowed him to return to Paris, where he worked on *John Brown's Body*. In 1929, a year after the publication of *John Brown's Body*, when he was thirty-one years old, he received the prestigious Pulitzer Prize for poetry and became famous overnight.

He accepted the editorship of the Yale Series of Younger Poets competition in 1933, and in 1935 he began regular reviewing for the New York *Herald Tribune* and the *Saturday Review of Literature*. He was elected to the National Institute of Arts and Letters in 1929 and to the American Academy of Arts and Letters in 1938, and he received the Theodore Roosevelt Medal for literary accomplishment in 1933.

In addition, Benét won the O. Henry Memorial Prize for the best American short story of the year several times; among his winning stories were "The Devil and Daniel Webster" and "Freedom's a Hard-Bought Thing."

Finally, he received posthumously the Gold Medal for Literature from the National Institute of Arts and Letters and the Pulitzer Prize a second time for the unfinished epic poem *Western Star*.

Biography

Stephen Vincent Benét was born July 22, 1898, in Bethlehem, Pennsylvania. His parents were Frances Neill Rose Benét and James Walker Benét, Captain of Ordnance, United States Army, a man with poetic and literary tastes. Stephen was their third child and second son; his sister and brother were Laura Benét and William Rose Benét, who were both active in the literary world. Well-read from his youth and thoroughly educated, Benét began writing early in his life.

During his childhood, his family moved throughout the United States because of his father's position in the Army. Benét and his family were at the Vatervliet, New York, Arsenal from 1899 until 1904; the Rock Island, Illinois, Arsenal during 1904; the Benicia, California, Arsenal from 1905 until 1911; and the Augusta, Georgia, Arsenal from 1911 until he was graduated from a coeducational academy and entered Yale College in 1915. There he was with such undergraduates as Archibald MacLeish, Thornton Wilder, Philip Barry, and John Farrar. He left Yale after completing his junior year in 1918 to enlist in the Army, but was honorably discharged because of his bad eyesight. After working briefly for the State Department in Washington, D.C., he reentered Yale. Benét received his B.A. degree in 1919 and his M.A. degree in 1920. At that time, he was given a traveling fellowship by Yale and went to Paris, where he completed his first novel.

Unlike other expatriates in Paris, Benét was not disillusioned or dissatisfied with America; he went to Paris because he could live there cheaply. He was very patriotic and loved his country deeply. While in Paris, he met Rosemary Carr; about a year later, in 1921, they were married in her hometown of Chicago. Their marriage was a happy one, producing three children: Stephanie Jane, born in 1924; Thomas Carr, born in 1925; and Rachel, born in 1931.

Benét earned his living by writing. In order to support his family, he was often forced to devote less time than he would have liked to his serious writing—rather than concentrating on his poetry, he sometimes had to spend time and energy writing short stories and novels that would bring in money. Although *John Brown's Body* generated substantial sales, he lost most of his capital in the crash of 1929 and never again enjoyed financial security.

When World War II broke out, fiercely loyal to democracy, he felt compelled to contribute to the war effort as much as he could. As a result, in the early 1940's he devoted much of his time and energy to writing propagandistic radio scripts and other needed pieces.

During Benét's most creative years, he was handicapped by poor health; from 1930 until his death in 1943, he suffered from arthritis of the spine and other illnesses. He was hospitalized for several weeks in 1939 for a nervous breakdown caused by overwork. On March 13, 1943, when he was forty-four years old, he died in his wife's arms following a heart attack.

Analysis

In the nineteenth century, Walt Whitman called for a national poet for America and sought to be that poet. While he envisioned himself as the poet working in his shirt sleeves among the people and read by the population at large, he was never really a poet of the people, absorbed by the people. Ironically, Stephen Vincent Benét became the poet that Whitman wanted to be. Although Benét's approach as a poet was a literary, academic one, his poetry was widely read and popular with the public.

Using American legends, tales, songs, and history, he was most effective writing in epic and narrative forms, especially the folk ballad. Benét's primary weakness is related to his strength. He lacks originality; he takes not only his subjects but also his techniques from other sources. In his first published poems, a series of dramatic monologues called *Five Men and Pompey*, the influence of Robert Browning and Edward Arlington Robinson is evident. As Donald Heiney indicates in *Recent American Literature* (1958), Benét never developed a single stylistic quality that was his own.

His poetry, particularly *John Brown's Body*, is nevertheless worth reading for its presentation of American folklore and history. As Benét himself indicated in a foreword to *John Brown's Body*, poetry, unlike prose, tells its story through rhyme and meter. By using such a method to tell stories and convey ideas, the poet can cause the reader to feel more deeply and to see more clearly; thus, the poet's work will remain in the reader's memory.

Benét's strengths are evident in the volume preceding *John Brown's Body*, *Tiger Joy*. The best poems in this collection include an octave of sonnets, "The Golden Corpse," and two very good ballads "The Mountain Whippoorwill" and "The Ballad of William Sycamore."

In "The Mountain Whippoorwill, or, How Hill-Billy Jim Won the Great Fiddlers' Prize," subtitled "A Georgia Romance," Benét uses the dialect of the inhabitants of the Georgia hills. The rhythm of the poem suggests the music that is produced as Big Tom Sargent, Little Jimmy Weezer, Old Dan Wheeling, and Hill-Billy Jim attempt to win the first prize at the Georgia Fiddlers' Show. The mountain whippoorwill serves as a unifying element; initially, the whippoorwill is supposedly the mother of Hill-Billy Jim, the narrator, but then becomes symbolic of him as fiddler and of his genius.

"The Ballad of William Sycamore," one of Benét's frequently anthologized poems, is the autobiography of William Sycamore, an archetype of the pioneer. The son of a Kentucky mountaineer, Sycamore was born outdoors near a stream and a tall green fir. Following a childhood during which he learned his woodsman's skills from his father, he and his wife were part of the westward movement; he lost his eldest son at the Alamo and his youngest at Custer's last stand, and died with his boots on. At the end of the poem he tells the builders of towns to go play with the towns where they had hoped to fence him in. He has escaped them and their towns, and now sleeps with the buffalo. According to Heiney, the poem differs from the traditional ballad primarily in that it is written in the first person and covers Sycamore's life from his birth to his death.

John Brown's Body, a book-length narrative poem, became immediately popular with the American public when it was published in 1928; it was the poem that established his position in American literature. Although many critics have complained that a major weakness of the poem is a lack of unity, Parry Stroud points out, in *Stephen Vincent Benét* (1962), several ways in which the epic is unified—through the characters, through the symbolism, and through the consistent and purposeful use of several meters.

First, John Brown himself and the imaginary characters representing the major regional areas of America serve to unify the poem. Jack Ellyat, a Connecticut boy who enlists in the Union Army, is the counterpart of Clay Wingate, a Southerner from Wingate Hall, Georgia. Ellyat eventually marries Melora Vilas, who, with her father, stands for the border states and the West. At the end of the war Wingate also marries the woman he loves, the Southern belle Sally Dupre. There are several other minor fictional characters typifying various regions and classes in America: Lucy Weatherby, a Southern coquette; Spade, a slave who runs away; Cudjo, a slave who remains loyal to the Wingates; Jake Diefer, a stolid Pennsylvania farmer for whom Spade works after the war; Luke Breckinridge, an illiterate Tennessee mountaineer who fights for the South; and Shippey, a spy for the North. The war resolves the fates of most of these fictional characters.

Parry Stroud disagrees with the many critics who believe that Benét's style disrupts the unity of the poem. Benét uses three basic meters: traditional blank verse, heroic couplets, and what Benét called his "long rough line." This versatile long line approximates the rhythm of everyday speech more than traditional meters do. Benét also uses rhythmic prose and lyrics. In the foreword that he wrote for the poem in 1941, he states that he intentionally used a variety of meters. For example, he used a light, swift meter for the episodes concerning Clay Wingate, the Southerner, to suggest dancing, riding, and other aspects of Southern culture.

In the foreword, Benét indicates that the poem deals with events associated with the Civil War, beginning just before John Brown's raid on Harpers Ferry and ending just after the close of the war and the assassination of Abraham Lincoln. Although he did not intend to write a formal history of the Civil War, he did want the poem to show how the events presented affected different Americans; he was concerned with the Americans of the North and South as well as those of the East and West.

By describing the American landscape and people, Benét gives American historical events a reality greater than mere names and dates can confer. He believed that the people living during the Civil War encountered problems similar to those of his time and that the decisions they made then had a great effect upon future generations of Americans.

Growing out of Benét's fondness for his country, *John Brown's Body* will have a permanent place in American literature because it is an epic having uniquely American themes and qualities. He researched the historical details of the war extensively, but he also understood the human complexities involved. Exhibiting a high level of narrative skill, Benét presented five of the most crucial years in American history, poetically interpreting part of the great heritage of America.

Western Star, a fragmentary work, which was to have been another epic like *John Brown's Body*, was published after Benét's death in 1943. He had begun writing it previous to World War II, but upon the entry of America in the war, he put it aside, planning to resume work on it when peace was achieved. *Western Star* was to have been Benét's interpretation of the settlement of the United States and of the westward movement of frontier life. He intended to present frontier life in a way similar to that he had used to present the Civil War in *John Brown's Body*—by using actual events and both actual and imaginary persons for his characters. Unfortunately, his early death prevented his completing this work.

Sherry G. Southard

Other major works

LONG FICTION: *The Beginning of Wisdom*, 1921; *Young People's Pride*, 1922;

Jean Huguenot, 1923; *Spanish Bayonet,* 1926; *James Shore's Daughter,* 1934.
SHORT FICTION: *Thirteen O'Clock,* 1937; *Tales Before Midnight,* 1939; *Twenty-five Short Stories,* 1943.
PLAYS: *Nerves,* 1924 (with John Farrar); *That Awful Mrs. Eaton,* 1924 (with John Farrar); *The Headless Horseman,* 1937; *The Devil and Daniel Webster,* 1939; *We Stand United, and Other Radio Scripts,* 1945.
NONFICTION: *America,* 1944; *Stephen Vincent Benét on Writing: A Great Writer's Letters of Advice to a Young Beginner,* 1946; *Selected Letters of Stephen Vincent Benét,* 1960.
MISCELLANEOUS: *Selected Works of Stephen Vincent Benét,* 1942 (Basil Davenport, editor); *Stephen Vincent Benét: Selected Poetry and Prose,* 1942 (Basil Davenport, editor); *The Last Circle,* 1946.

Bibliography

Davenport, Basil. Introduction to *Stephen Vincent Benét: Selected Poetry and Prose.* New York: Rinehart, 1960. Davenport's short essay is a good overview of Benét's life and literature for those unfamiliar with his writing. He stresses how unusual Benét's Americanism seemed during a time when Paris overflowed with expatriates cynical of American idealism. The poet is seen as essentially a romantic, able to show extraordinary feeling for his subjects.

Fenton, Charles A. *Stephen Vincent Benét: The Life and Times of an American Man of Letters, 1898-1943.* New Haven, Conn.: Yale University Press, 1958. Based chiefly on several interviews with friends and relatives and on Benét's own writings, this detailed biography paints an admirable and sympathetic portrait of a struggling writer striving to live according to his literary conscience. The few critical evaluations of Benét's writings show insight. The 440-page text includes an index and several illustrations.

LaFarge, Christopher. "The Narrative Poetry of Stephen Vincent Benét." *Saturday Review* 27 (1944): 106-108. LaFarge presents a glowing evaluation of Benét, seeing him as an enduring and timely writer who contributed much to the political writing of his day. Benét is lauded for his complex patterns of rhythm, meter, and form and for his rich characterization, but most of all for his clear style that makes his work accessible to the general reader.

Stroud, Parry. *Stephen Vincent Benét.* New York: Twayne, 1962. This work is an informative critical study of Benét, focusing on liberalism and patriotism as it appears in his best writings. Stroud's close and thorough readings help place Benét in historical and literary pespective, emphasizing his contemporary relevance. The 173-page book is arranged by genre and includes a chronology of Benét's life, a selected annotated bibliography, and an index.

Wells, Henry W. "Stephen Vincent Benét." *College English* 5 (1943): 8-13. Written soon after Benét's death, this critical survey of the author's major works, *John Brown's Body* and *Western Star*, strikes an elegiac tone, although a negative one. Wells mostly examines possible reasons for Benét's waning reputation as a poet, but also deals briefly with his achievements and skill.

WENDELL BERRY

Born: Henry County, Kentucky; August 5, 1934

Principal poetry

November Twenty-six, Nineteen Hundred Sixty-three, 1963; *The Broken Ground*, 1964; *Openings*, 1968; *Findings*, 1969; *Farming: A Hand Book*, 1970; *The Country of Marriage*, 1973; *An Eastward Look*, 1974; *To What Listens*, 1975; *Horses*, 1975; *Sayings and Doings*, 1975; *The Kentucky River: Two Poems*, 1976; *There Is Singing Around Me*, 1976; *Three Memorial Poems*, 1976; *Clearing*, 1977; *The Gift of Gravity*, 1979; *A Part*, 1980; *The Wheel*, 1982; *Collected Poems: 1957-1982*, 1985; *Sabbaths*, 1987; *Traveling at Home*, 1989.

Other literary forms

In addition to poetry, Berry has written nonfiction, fiction, essays, and a biography of Harland Hubbard.

Achievements

Wendell Berry has achieved regional prominence as a poet, essayist, and novelist who writes about the small tobacco farmers of his fictional Port William community in northern Kentucky. As a poet, Berry has published widely since 1957, in small magazines, poetry volumes, private printings, and a collected edition of his verse in 1985. His major topics are the land, the family, and the community, especially the way that each has been affected by greed and indifference. Berry is a deeply traditional poet in theme and form, celebrating a timeless agrarian cycle of planting and harvest. He affirms a strong sense of place and ancestral inheritance, stemming from local family ties stretching back almost two centuries. His values are a curious blend of conservative and radical, combining a strong commitment to marriage and family with a pacifist stance and criticism of corporate exploitation of rural Appalachia. His voice is that of the farmer-poet, husband, father, and lover.

Biography

Born in Henry County, Kentucky, on August 5, 1934, Wendell Berry grew up in a family of strong-willed, independent-minded readers and thinkers. His father, John M. Berry, was an attorney and a leader of the Burley Tobacco Growers Association. After attending the University of Kentucky for his bachelor's and master's degrees, Berry was married and taught for a year at Georgetown College in Kentucky. He then accepted a Wallace Stegner Fellowship in creative writing (1958-1959) at Stanford University. A Guggenheim Foundation award allowed him to travel to Europe in 1962 before he returned to teach English at New York University from 1962 to 1964. Berry wrote a moving elegy for President John F. Kennedy that won critical praise, and his first poetry volume, *The Broken Ground*, appeared in 1964.

Berry and his family returned to Kentucky in 1964, when he was appointed to the English Department at the University of Kentucky in Lexington. He purchased Lane's Landing Farm in Port Royal in 1965 and moved back to his native county, where he has continued to farm and write. Berry has also served as a contributing editor to Rodale Press. He and his wife, Tanya (Amyx) Berry, have two children, Mary and Pryor Clifford.

Analysis

Wendell Berry is a poet of deep conviction. Like Henry David Thoreau, he has felt a need to reestablish himself from the ground up by articulating the ecological and economic principles by which he would live, and by trying to live and write in accordance with those principles. He has striven to achieve a rigorous moral and aesthetic simplicity in his work by reworking the same basic themes and insights; the proper place of human life in the larger natural cycle of life, death, and renewal; the dignity of work, labor, and vocation; the central importance of marriage and family commitments; the articulation of the human and natural history of his native region; and precise, lyrical descriptions of the native flora and fauna of his region, especially of the birds, trees, and wildflowers. Expanding on these basic themes, he has included elegies to family members and friends, topical and occasional poems (especially antiwar poems expressing his strong pacifist convictions), didactic poems expressing his environmental beliefs, and a surprising number of religious poems expressing a deeply felt but nondenominational faith.

One finds in Berry's verse a continual effort to unify life, work, and art within a coherent philosophy or vision. Put simply, that vision includes a regional sensibility, a farming avocation, a poetic voice of the farmer-husband-lover-environmentalist, and a strong commitment to a localized environmental ethic. His most notable persona is the "Mad Farmer," though it is not clear why he is "mad"—does Berry mean passionate, exuberant, or merely eccentric? From childhood, Berry always hoped to become a farmer, and his verse celebrates the life of the land. His vision, however, is that of diminishment: of the land, of the community, and even of his art. In his literary works, Berry expresses nostalgia for the kind of small-scale, labor-intensive tobacco farming that was practiced in his region before World War II. His style of unmechanized organic farming is practiced today mainly by the Amish and the Mennonites. Berry has admitted that farming his hilly, eroded land has not been profitable, and while it may be ethically admirable to restore damaged land to production, it is generally not economically feasible without another source of income.

One senses in Berry's poetry a keen awareness of living in a fallen world, to be redeemed, if at all, through hard work, disciplined self-knowledge, and a gradual healing of the land. Yet though he is a lyric poet, too often his lyrics do not sing: His muse is Delphic rather than Orphic, prophetic instead of lyrical. His verse is carefully worked and thoughtful but burdened at times by didacticism. The Berry persona is often detached and impersonal, preoccupied with its own sensibility, or with an environmental theme. His lyrics are often descriptive meditations in which too little happens aside from the registration of impressions on the poet's sensibility. The simplicity of his verse becomes drab, colorless, even oppressive at times. It needs to be lightened by a sense of humor, a sense of proportion, and awareness of others. Sometimes his lyrics seem sanctimonious or self-righteous. His verse echoes the rhetorical question of Robert Frost's "The Oven Bird"—"What to make of a diminished thing?"—and the answer seems uncertain.

Berry first published many of his poems in literary journals or small magazines or specialty presses, so that original editions of his works are often hard to find. His individual poetry volumes were published first with Harcourt Brace (*The Broken Ground, Openings, Farming: A Hand Book, The Country of Marriage,* and *Clearing*) and later with North Point Press (*A Part, The Wheel, Collected Poems,* and *Sabbaths*). The pieces in *Collected Poems* are selected from each volume, but the collection is not entirely inclusive. Yet he has added some important poems, such as the contents of the volume *Findings* (1969), which was originally published by small specialty press and was out of print.

Though Berry had been publishing poems in literary magazines and journals since the mid-fifties, his first critical recognition came in 1964, with the appearance of *The Broken Ground*, his first poetry volume, and *November Twenty-six, Nineteen Sixty-three*, his elegy for John F. Kennedy, which first appeared in the December 21, 1963, issue of *The Nation*. Berry's elegy, which was accompanied by woodcuts by Ben Shahn, has been called the most successful commemoration of Kennedy's death. Though written in free-verse form, Berry's elegy makes use of a traditional stanzaic organization and refrain and incorporates the traditional elegiac cycle of grief, mourning, the funeral procession, the interment, and the apotheosis of the subject's memory. Berry's interest in the elegy was also apparent in "Elegy," the opening poem in *The Broken Ground*. Other elegiac works include "Three Elegiac Poems" (*Findings*), "In Memory: Stuart Engol" (*Openings*), and "Requiem" and "Elegy" (*The Wheel*). Death is always present in Berry's work, but it is presented naturalistically, without a compensating *carpe diem* theme or renewal except in the natural cycle of life.

The Broken Ground is a collection of thirty-one free-verse lyrics with a distinctly regional flavor, twenty of which were later included in his *Collected Poems*. Many of these poems first appeared in *Stylus, Poetry* magazine, *The Nation*, and *The Prairie Schooner*. This early collection introduces the Berry voice and some of his major themes: the cycle of life and death, a sensitivity to place, pastoral subject matter, and recurring images of water, the Kentucky River, and the hilly, pastoral landscape of north-central Kentucky. His language is terse, intense, and compressed, his style imagistic and at times almost epigrammatic. The stylistic influence of William Carlos Williams and the Orientalism of Kenneth Rexroth seem apparent in these early poems. Berry's sharp, sculpted images also recall those of his friend and fellow poet Gary Snyder. Some of the poems seem curiously detached and impersonal. They are animated by no great myths, legends, or events, aside from the figures of Daniel Boone and other early settlers. Instead, the poems are intensely private, detached, and descriptive. Although many of them are set in his native Kentucky, the Berry persona seems curiously detached from members of his local community beyond his family. One does not find the social engagement Williams shows in his Patterson poems, a warmth that came from his lifelong involvement as a local pediatrician. Instead, the Berry persona seems solitary and austere: too much the detached observer, quiet and understated, though perhaps not intending to project a sense of social isolation. The parallels with Williams are instructive: While Williams was a practicing local physician whose poetry often reflects his sympathetic understanding of his patients and their families, Berry presents himself as a working farmer whose poetry reflects his love of his work. What redeems Berry's poems is his love of farming and the rhythms of physical labor: its purposefulness, its physicality, and its tangible rewards.

There is a mythic vision in Berry's poems of a lost, primeval paradise, a fall from grace, and a guarded hope in work, discipline, and renewal. "Paradise might have appeared here," he announces in "The Aristocracy," but instead he finds a wealthy old dowager airing her cat. Like Robert Frost's pastoral world of a diminished New England landscape, Berry's Kentucky River Valley has suffered from neglect and abuse. The moments of grace are few— bird songs, the return of spring, the cycle of the seasons, glimpses of the natural order—and death is always present. Like Frost, Berry has chosen to make a "strategic retreat" to a pastoral world in which the poet-farmer can take stock of his resources, but his sensibility differs from Frost's. For Frost, the sense of diminishment came from the abandonment of farms in rural New England after the Civil War, while for Berry the sense of loss comes from environmental despoilation of the Cumberland plateau, first by careless farming practices and later by timber interests and the big coal companies.

Berry's version of the Paradise Lost myth centers on the massive environmental destruction visited upon the Cumberland region by absentee corporate owners. He has been radicalized by Kentucky's legacy of corrupt government and indifference to environmental concerns, which has left the region virtually a Third World economy, based upon cheap, large-scale mineral extraction with little regard for the human or environmental consequences of pit or surface mining. The practice of strip-mining has been particularly devastating to the land and water resources. Living downstream from the despoiled hills and polluted creeks of Appalachia, Berry has seen at first hand the flooding and water pollution that have occurred on the Kentucky River.

As Berry recounts in *The Kentucky River*, the first white settlers who entered the Kentucky territory were unable to respond to the richness and abundance of natural resources except by exploitation. Hence, in "July, 1773," the first of the "Three Kentucky River Poems," young Sam Adams fires heedlessly into a herd of peacefully grazing buffalo at a salt lick.

Not only did the publication of Berry's *Collected Poems* in 1985 permit the republishing of nearly two hundred poems from his previous eight volumes, many of which were by then out of print, but it allowed him to select which poems he could retain and which he would drop from those early volumes. Among Berry's best early work was the sequence of three long poems from *Findings*. "The Design of a House" is a poem about beginnings and intentions, the conscious fabrication of a dwelling and a marriage relationship that had previously existed merely as a vague dream or desire, and a wish to reestablish roots in one's native place. It becomes a nuptial poem, the speaker's dedication of his love to his wife, Tanya, and his daughter, Mary, and the continuation of their life together. The design of their house comes to signify the design of their family relationship.

The second poem in *Findings*, "The Handing Down," continues this theme of family and place, this time in terms of an old man's memories and reflections, his sense of satisfaction with the life he has led, as expressed through conversations with his grandson. The speaker in this poem recalls Jack Beecham, the protagonist of Berry's novel *The Memory of Old Jack* (1974). Both the poem and the novel have to do with an old man's preparations for death, his gradual letting go of life through the memories that run through his mind. The third part of *Findings*, "Three Elegiac Poems," commemorates the death of the old man, which the speaker hopes will occur quietly at home, away from the sterile coldness and isolation of hospital wards and the indifference of physicians.

Openings, Farming: A Hand Book, The Country of Marriage, and *Clearing* celebrate his return to Kentucky and the satisfaction he found in taking up farming. After living in California, Europe, and New York City, he came to appreciate the possibilities of writing about his native region. Berry was particularly impressed with the hill farms of Tuscany, around Florence, which showed him that such "marginal land" might remain productive for many centuries with the proper care and attention. The quality of these farms led him to rethink the possibilities of hill farming in his native Kentucky. As he indicates in the autographical title essay in *The Long-Legged House* (1969), he kept feeling himself drawn back home, particularly to the small cabin built on the Kentucky River by his uncle Curran Matthews. After it was flooded, Berry moved this house farther up the riverbank and rebuilt it to create his writer's study.

Berry's poems in these middle volumes show a new depth of craft and responsiveness to nature. They celebrate the values of land and nature, family and community, marital love and devotion. They are quietly attentive to the cycle of seasons, of the organic cycles of growth and decay, of the subtle beauty of the native flora and fauna. As philosopher, visionary, and political activist, his "Mad Farmer" persona speaks out against war, wastefulness, and environmental destruction. He dreams of a new, gentler orientation to the land that will encourage people to cherish and preserve their natural heritage. He finds deep spiritual sustenance as he reflects on the beauty and fitness of the natural order and the richness of the present moment.

Berry's poems are broadly pastoral in orientation, but they reflect the Kentucky frontier tradition of pioneer homesteading and yeoman farming rather than artificial literary tradition. Some pastoral themes evident in his work include an idealization of the simple life, an implied city-country contrast, a yearning for a past "golden age" of rural life, a celebration of the seasonal tasks of farming life, a strong affirmation of small-scale, organic farming, and an identification of the poet with his native region.

In *Openings*, the poem "The Thought of Something Else" announces the speaker's desire to leave the city for country life, but first he must make peace with the legacy of the past, which he does in "My Great-Grandfather's Slaves." The next three poems are autumnal in tone, establishing the speaker within a seasonal cycle. In "The Snake," he comes upon a small reptile preparing for winter hibernation. The "living cold" of the snake, replete with its engorged meal, parallels the contented winter solitude of the speaker in the next poem, "The Cold." The starkly descriptive "Winter Rain" leads to "March Snow" and "April Woods: Morning," which resemble haiku in their delicate imagery. In "The Porch over the River," the speaker establishes himself in his riverside writer's cabin, like the classical Chinese poet Tu Fu. In "The Dream," he imagines the surrounding countryside restored to its pristine beauty, unspoiled by greed or acquisitiveness. The tree celebrated in "The Sycamore," a venerable specimen whose gnarled trunk is scarred by lightning, becomes a symbol of natural resiliency. Like the tree, the poet wishes that he might be shaped and nurtured by his native place. The longest and most abstract piece, "Window Poems," is composed of twenty-seven sections that reflect the speaker's changing moods as he watches the shifting patterns of river scenery from his study window. "Grace" and "A Discipline" reflect the strength the speaker draws from nature, allowing him to withstand the destructiveness of his culture, in which people are at war with the environment, one another, and themselves.

Farming: A Hand Book and *The Country of Marriage* are less solitary in mood. They introduce the colorful persona of the "Mad Farmer," an exuberant, Bunyanesque figure who flaunts social conventions in "The Mad Farmer's Revolution" and "The Contrariness of the Mad Farmer," dances in the streets in "The Mad Farmer in the City," and—through his prayers, sayings, satisfactions, and manifestos—offers a wry and humorous commentary on Berry's own views as expressed in his books and essays. "The Birth," a dramatic dialogue, constitutes an interesting departure from Berry's customary lyrical verse. A group of farmers, up late with lambing on a cold winter night, unexpectedly come upon a couple and child who have taken sanctuary in their barn for their own nativity. Berry's poem captures the cadences and flavor of ordinary country talk, in which more is implied than said.

Berry's poems are noted for quiet attentiveness to surroundings, almost as if the speaker tried to make himself part of his habitat. His farmer persona is a keen naturalist, carefully observing the seasonal behavior of the birds and animals. His speaker is especially attuned to bird songs, and the variety of birds mentioned in his poems is notable—kingfishers, song sparrows, phoebes, herons, wild geese, finches, wrens, chickadees, cardinals, titmice, and warblers. Implicit in his poems is a sense of grace and renewal, a deep satisfaction and contentment.

Berry's relationship with his wife and children has been central to his task of renewal as a pastoral poet. An accomplished love poet, Berry has written many poems to his wife Tanya, on the anniversaries of their marriage or to express his gratitude for their common life. For his children, too, Berry has written poems on their births, comings of age, and marriages, and on the births of grandchildren. In "The Gathering," the speaker recalls that he now holds his son in his arms the way his father held him. In "The Country of Marriage," farming and marriage serve as complementary and inseparable extensions of each other. Husbandry and marriage are recurring tropes in Berry's poetry, illustrated in clearing fields, sowing crops, planting a garden, tending livestock, mowing hay, and taking in the harvest. He celebrates farming as a labor of love, the work of regeneration and fecundity that is at once vital and procreative.

The poems in *Clearing* articulate Berry's sense of region and place. "Where" is a long pastoral meditation on the history and ownership of the fifty-acre farm, Lane's Landing, which the Berrys purchased between 1965 and 1968. The history of the farm provides a case study in attitudes toward stewardship and land use, from the earliest settlers to the developer from whom Berry bought the farm. The transition from wilderness to settlement to worn-out land rehearses an ecological myth of the fall from primeval abundance to reckless waste and decay. Berry presents the history of his farm as a parable of the American frontier and an indictment of the reckless habits that quickly exhausted the land's natural richness and abundance. "Where" is both a personal credo and a contemporary ecological statement of what needs to be done, both in terms of land management and in changing cultural attitudes toward the land.

Berry's next two poetry volumes, *A Part* and *The Wheel*, reflect in their titles his deepening ecological awareness. *A Part* includes short pastoral lyrics; some religious verse; translations of two poems by the sixteenth century French poet Pierre de Ronsard; "Three Kentucky River Poems," a narrative triptych based in part on historical accounts of the McAfee brothers' 1773 expedition into Kentucky; and "Horses," a verse tribute to the skills of working draft horses, in which Berry excoriates tractors and internal combustion engines for destroying the quiet pleasures of farming.

The Wheel takes its title image from the mandela, or "wheel of life," of which Sir Albert Howard speaks in his classic study *An Agricultural Testament* (1943), which influenced Berry's thinking about organic farming. This collection is a book of elegies of remembrance and praise, celebrating the continuities of birth, growth, maturity, death, and decay. An increasing self-assurance is evident in Berry's voice, a relaxed, self-confident voice free of anxiety. His verse forms also become more formal, with an increased use of rhyme and regular stanzaic form, though he still seems to prefer a short line.

"Elegy," one of Berry's finest poems, appears in this collection. A pastoral elegy, it is one of a series of three poems dedicated to Owen Flood, whom Berry honors as a teacher and friend. The first poem, "Requiem," announces his passing, though his spirit remains in the fields he had tended. "Elegy" pays tribute to the quality of Flood's life in eight sections, invoking the spirits of the dead to reaffirm the traditional values that Flood embodied: duty, loyalty, perseverance, honesty, hard work, endurance, and self-reliance. It reaffirms the continuity of the generations within a permanent, stable agricultural order. There is a sense of recycling human life, as nature recycles organic materials back into the soil to create the fertile organic humus of the soil. The poem also celebrates human permanences: marriage, work, friendship, love, fidelity, and death. The dominant image is of life as a dance within the circle of life, implying closure, completeness, and inclusion. "Elegy" affirms farm labor as an honorable calling, true to the biblical injunction to live by the sweat of one's brow. The opening line of the poem reaffirms an implicit purpose in all Berry's work: "To be at home on its native ground." The poem honors the elders of the community who were the speaker's teachers, including Flood, and concludes with the affirmation that "the best teachers teach more/ than they know. By their deaths/ they teach most."

Another important poem in this collection, "The Gift of Gravity," reaffirms the life-sustaining cycles of sunlight, photosynthesis, growth, decay, and death. The poem announces its major theme, "Gravity is grace," with the dominant image of the river of life and the return of all life to its source. There is an almost mystical unity conveyed in the opening lines: "All that passes descends,/ and ascends again unseen/ into the light." Two other poems,

"The Wheel" and "The Dance," affirm the interlocking unities that knit the community together in festive celebrations of song and dance.

Dissatisfied with Harcourt Brace, Berry changed publishers in the early 1980's, moving to North Point Press, a small publisher in Berkeley, California. One immediate result was the issuing of his *Recollected Essays* (1981), and *Collected Poems.* Including the better part of his first eight volumes of poetry, the *Collected Poems* is certainly the definitive volume for the reader of Berry's verse.

Sabbaths marks something of a departure in tone and style from Berry's earlier works. It is at once more formal, more structured, and more overtly religious in its sensibility. The forty-six poems in this collection were written over a six-year period, from 1979 to 1985. The poems are untitled, arranged by year, and identified only by their first line. There are quiet, restrained, almost metaphysical meditations that incorporate a number of lines from Scripture. Here Berry makes use of traditional rhyme and meter. These poems show a deep, nonsectarian religious sensibility, akin to the personal faith of the New England Transcendentalist poets—especially Emily Dickinson. Like Dickinson, Berry applies Christian tropes to nature to imply a natural religion. The many allusions to Eden, Paradise, worship, hymns, song, grace, gift, Maker, heaven, resurrection, darkness, and light invoke a kind of prophetic vision of a new earth, healed and reborn—a paradise regained. Berry again describes the primal fertility and richness of the Kentucky landscape before it was ruined by the rapacious settlers. His poems combine a moral awareness of a deep wrong done to the earth by human greed and ignorance with an ecological awareness of the need for a change that can come only from within. His poems offer a dichotomized moral vision of nature as basically innocent and human nature as the source of evil.

The overall theme of *Sabbaths* is the need for rest and renewal—both within human hearts and in the natural world. People need to take time away from their heedless ravaging of the environment to try to understand and appreciate the earth's beauty and strength. Berry calls for the cultivatation of a different kind of sensibility—less inclined to impose human will on nature and more inclined to appreciate the natural world on its own terms, as a kind of heaven on earth. Berry weaves many scriptural allusions into his poems, quoting from the Psalms, the Old Testament prophets, and the New Testament. The poems manage to convey a deep meditative sensibility without making any formal religious affirmations except by implication. The speaker comes across as a deeply thoughtful but independent spirit, reverent but unchurched. One finds in *Sabbaths* a new blend of spiritual and ecological awareness, a sense of life, of the earth, of the land, as worthy of the deepest veneration.

Wendell Berry's poetry marks him as one of the most important contemporary American nature poets. His sense of the sacredness and interdependence of all life places him within the tradition of Ralph Waldo Emerson, Walt Whitman, and Henry David Thoreau. He is also one of the foremost American regional writers, insisting that his poetry be firmly rooted in a sense of place. His poetry reflects the same deep concern for the natural environment and for sound conservation and farming practices that is evident in his essays and fiction. His emphasis on marriage, family, and community allows him to affirm these necessary human bonds. His poems reflect his loyalty to his native region, his love of farming, his view of marriage as a sacrament, and his deep awareness of the beauty and wonder of the natural world.

Andrew J. Angyal

Other major works

LONG FICTION: *Nathan Coulter*, 1960, rev. 1985; *A Place on Earth*, 1967, rev. 1983; *The Memory of Old Jack*, 1974; *Remembering*, 1988.

SHORT FICTION: *The Wild Birds*, 1986.

NONFICTION: *The Long-Legged House*, 1969; *The Hidden Wound*, 1970; *The Unforeseen Wilderness*, 1971; *A Continuous Harmony*, 1972; *The Unsettling of America*, 1977; *Recollected Essays, 1965-1980*, 1981; *The Gift of Good Land*, 1981; *Standing by Words*, 1983; *Home Economics*, 1987; *What Are People For?*, 1990; *Harland Hubbard: Life and Work*, 1990.

Bibliography

Cornell, Daniel. "*The Country of Marriage:* Wendell Berry's Personal Political Vision." *Southern Literary Journal* 16 (Fall, 1983): 59-70. Through a close reading of the poems in *The Country of Marriage*, Cornell offers a thoughtful examination of the thematic implications of Berry's pastoral metaphors. Cornell locates Berry within a agrarian populist tradition that defies conventional conservative or liberal labels.

Hicks, Jack. "Wendell Berry's Husband to the World: *A Place on Earth.*" *American Literature* 51 (May, 1979): 238-254. In perhaps the best critical overview of Berry's work, Hicks examines the farmer-countryman vision in Berry's fiction, stressing the need of atonement for past neglect or abuse of the land and discussing the strengths and weaknesses of Berry's protagonists—especially Mat Feltner—as farmers, husbands, and parents. Hicks traces thematic connections between Berry's essays, poetry, and fiction.

Morgan, Speer. "Wendell Berry: A Fatal Singing." *The Southern Review* 10 (October, 1974): 865-877. Morgan attemps to place Berry's work within a broader Romantic/Transcendentalist tradition of nature writing. In particular, he discusses the centrality of death and decay in Berry's work as part of the great cycle of life. Morgan compares Berry and Thoreau as regional nature writers.

Nibbelink, Herman. "Thoreau and Wendell Berry: Bachelor and Husband of Nature." *The South Atlantic Quarterly* 84 (Spring, 1985): 127-140. Another study of the farmer-husbandry theme in Berry's work. Nibbelink, too, traces the influence of Thoreau in Berry's work and contrasts Thoreau's appreciation of wildness with Berry's perference for cultivated land as the difference between naturalist and farmer.

Weiland, Steven. "Wendell Berry: Culture and Fidelity." *Iowa Review* 10 (Winter, 1979): 99-104. Weiland points out that Berry's values, though seemingly personal and domestic, are nevertheless radical in their political implications.

JOHN BERRYMAN

Born: McAlester, Oklahoma; October 25, 1914
Died: Minneapolis, Minnesota; January 7, 1972

Principal poetry

Five Young American Poets, 1940 (with others); *Poems*, 1942; *The Dispossessed*, 1948; *Homage to Mistress Bradstreet*, 1956; *His Thought Made Pockets & the Plane Buckt*, 1958; *77 Dream Songs*, 1964; *Short Poems*, 1967; *Berryman's Sonnets*, 1967; *His Toy, His Dream, His Rest*, 1968; *The Dream Songs*, 1969; *Love & Fame*, 1970, 1972; *Delusions, Etc. of John Berryman*, 1972; *Henry's Fate & Other Poems*, 1977; *Collected Poems, 1937-1971*, 1989.

Other literary forms

In addition to his poetry, John Berryman produced a considerable number of reviews and critical pieces. A posthumous collection, *The Freedom of the Poet* (1976), gathers a representative sample of his criticism, published and unpublished. Berryman did not produce much prose fiction, preferring to use verse as a narrative vehicle. He did, however, write several short stories, and an unfinished novel, *Recovery* (1973), was published as he left it at his death. Other critical writing includes *Stephen Crane* (1950), a rather psychologized critical biography, and *The Arts of Reading* (1960), a collection of essays coauthored with Ralph Ross and Allen Tate. Berryman also edited a 1960 edition of Thomas Nashe's *The Unfortunate Traveller: Or, the Life of Jack Wilton*.

Berryman may be heard reading his poems on several recordings produced by the Library of Congress.

Achievements

In *Beyond All This Fiddle* (1968) A. Alvarez remarks that

> John Berryman is one of those poets whom you either love or loathe. Yet even the loathers have grudgingly to admit that the man is extraordinary . . . with a queer, distinct voice of his own.

No doubt, there are "loathers" who would apply "extraordinary" in no laudable sense, and who would use far cruder adjectives than "queer" and "distinct" in describing Berryman's voice. Still, decades after his death, Berryman's place in modern poetry seems as secure as that of any of his contemporaries, living or dead—Robert Lowell, Delmore Schwartz, Richard Wilbur, Adrienne Rich, or W. D. Snodgrass. Though he died a most unsatisfied man, his poetic career certainly brought him his share of recognition and praise: the Levinson and Guarantors Prizes from *Poetry* and the Shelley Memorial Award, 1948; the University of Chicago's Harriet Monroe Poetry Prize, 1957; the Brandeis Creative Arts Award, 1960; the National Institute of Arts and Letters' Loines Award for Poetry, 1964; the Pulitzer Prize in Poetry for *77*

Dream Songs, 1965; and both the National Book Award and the Bollingen Prize (shared with Karl Shapiro) for *His Toy, His Dream, His Rest*, 1969. In addition, he won grants and fellowships from such organizations as the Guggenheim Foundation (1952, 1966), the Rockefeller Foundation (1944), the National Institute of Arts and Letters (1950), and the Academy of American Poets (1966). He was much in demand for public readings, even though, especially toward the end of his career, his alcoholism and unpredictable personality made some of these appearances traumatic for both poet and audience.

In his poetry, Berryman moved from an ordered, restrained style, imitative of William Butler Yeats and W. H. Auden, to a passionate, energetic, deeply personal mode of expression, held in check—though just barely in places—by skilled attention to rhythm and sound. So decisive was this movement that comparing such early poems as "Winter Landscape" with a random sample from his later work, *The Dream Songs*, is almost like comparing two different poets. It is easy enough to look back at Berryman's early work and find it too poised, too urbane and academic. A number of critics, however, have objected to much of his later work, finding in it too little restraint and much too large a dose of the poet's raw experience. He is placed by some, with Anne Sexton and Lowell, in the "confessional school." The label does not quite apply, for Berryman's work at its best—and, unfortunately, he did frequently allow it to be published at its worst—remained for him a means of using personal experience to get at human experience. He retained too much formal control to be considered a "Beat," and was too inventive in his use of language to be classed with the vernacular mode of William Carlos Williams. Whatever else may be said about him, Berryman is one of the most individual voices in twentieth century American poetry.

In spite of his successes, however, it is difficult not to wonder whether Berryman has been overpraised. His *Homage to Mistress Bradstreet*, for example, was extolled by Robert Fitzgerald (*The American Review*, Autumn, 1960) as "the poem of his generation," while Edmund Wilson, solicited for a back-cover blurb for a 1968 paperback edition of the poem, responded with, "the most distinguished long poem by an American since *The Waste Land.*" There must certainly be a middle stance, somewhere between overpraise and Stanton Coblentz's view that "*77 Dream Songs* has all the imaginative fervor of a cash register." Such a moderate perspective would see Berryman as a major poet of his generation, and view *77 Dream Songs* as one of the major poetic events of the 1960's. His *Collected Poems, 1937-1971*, was published in 1989.

Biography

John Berryman was born John Allyn Smith, in McAlester, Oklahoma, the eldest son of a banker and a schoolteacher. His early childhood, spent in various small Oklahoma towns, was normal enough until his father's work took the family to live in Tampa, Florida; marital problems developed and the boy's father became increasingly troubled and unstable. In June, 1926, he shot himself in the chest at the family's vacation home across Tampa Bay. Young John heard the shot just outside his window—one sharp report that would echo through his consciousness for the rest of his life. When the boy's mother moved to New York and remarried, his name was changed to John Allyn McAlpin Berryman. Berryman wrote many letters to his mother as an adult, which were published as *We Dream of Honour: John Berryman's Letters to His Mother* in 1988.

Berryman attended a Connecticut prep school, South Kent; though he showed great intellectual promise, he was only intermittently moved to apply it. He was graduated in 1933 and went on to Columbia University in New York. There he felt much more at home academically and socially, and there he began a lifelong friendship with Mark Van Doren, who, by Berryman's account, was the first person to inspire and encourage him to be a poet. Not long after this association began, Berryman published his first poem, an elegy on Edwin Arlington Robinson, in the *Nation*. In 1936 he received his Bachelor's degree from Columbia, Phi Beta Kappa, and won the University's Kellett Fellowship, which he used to pursue further studies at Clare College, Cambridge University. Academically, his Cambridge experience was extremely rewarding. In 1937, he served as Oldham Shakespeare Scholar, and received a Bachelor of Arts degree in 1938. His social contacts were rewarding, to say the least, including as they did William Butler Yeats, W. H. Auden, and Dylan Thomas.

Back in New York, Berryman was a friend of another young poet, Delmore Schwartz, and became poetry editor of the *Nation*. His teaching career began in 1939 at Wayne State University in Detroit. After a year there, Berryman took a position at Harvard, where he remained until 1943. During this time, his first published collection of poems appeared in *Five Young American Poets* (1940). His work was well received, as were the poems of another promising young talent, Randall Jarrell. In 1942 Berryman published a self-contained selection, *Poems*. On October 24 of the same year, he married Eileen Patricia Mulligan. From 1943 to 1951, Berryman lectured in creative writing at Princeton, taking time out frequently, with the help of grants and fellowships, to write poetry and criticism, as well as a few short stories. In 1948 he published a new book of poems, *The Dispossessed*, which was received more politely than enthusiastically. His most significant work while at Princeton was his critical study, *Stephen Crane*. His psychoanalytic approach was not popular with most reviewers, but the book, on the whole, attracted a good deal of praise.

In 1951 Berryman accepted a one-year position as Elliston Lecturer in Poetry at the University of Cincinnati, and spent the next academic year in Eu-

rope with the help of a Guggenheim Fellowship. While in Europe he completed the poem that, upon its publication in 1956, would bring him his first
great critical success as a poet—*Homage to Mistress Bradstreet.* The price of
this success, however, was high. Berryman later cited his preoccupation with
the poem, coupled with an increasing dependence on alcohol, as the cause
of his separation in 1953 from his first wife. Certainly, the marriage had not
been helped by an intense, guilt-ridden love affair in which Berryman had
indulged during the summer of 1947, an affair portrayed in painful detail in
the sequence *Berryman's Sonnets.* In the meantime, however, Berryman's academic and literary careers proceeded without serious hindrance. In the fall
of 1954, having spent the preceding spring and summer semesters, respectively, at the University of Iowa and at Harvard, he began his long tenure
as a professor of humanities at the University of Minnesota in Minneapolis,
where he became a popular, if eccentric academic figure. In 1969 he received the University's most prestigious faculty award, a Regents' Professorship, and he remained on the faculty there until his death.

In 1956, Berryman divorced Eileen and married Ann Levine, who gave
birth to a son in 1957. The marriage lasted only until 1959. When he again
remarried, in 1961, it was to Kathleen Donahue, twenty-five years his junior.
In the same year he lectured at Indiana University, then moved on, in 1962,
to a visiting professorship at Boon University. During that year, Kate Berryman gave birth to a daughter, Martha. In 1965, Berryman won the Pulitzer
Prize for *77 Dream Songs*; his place as a major contemporary poet seemed
secure. He had begun work on these "songs" around 1955, and continued to
work in this form for nearly twenty years, publishing in 1968 *His Toy, His
Dream, His Rest,* a collection of 308 more poems that won the National
Book Award in 1969. The two volumes were combined in *The Dream Songs*
(1969).

The 1960's were a time of triumph for Berryman. The decade saw, along
with *The Dream Songs,* the long-delayed publication of *Berryman's Sonnets,*
and of *Short Poems,* a compilation of the earlier collections, *The Dispossessed* and *His Thought Made Pockets & the Plane Buckt,* with the addition
of "Formal Elegy," a poem on the death of John F. Kennedy. Yet, the kind
of success that most poets only dream of left Berryman dissatisfied and unfulfilled. His drinking problem became more serious than ever, interfering
not only with his family life but with his professional responsibilities as well,
disrupting classes and public readings, much to the dismay of students, admirers, and colleagues.

Berryman's next book of poems, *Love & Fame,* did not fare well with the
critics, and the poet took their disapproval hard. He had been, by this time,
in and out of alcoholic treatment programs, and, while he had found some
consolation in a renewal of his Roman Catholic faith, he could not overcome
the addiction to alcohol; drinking had for too long been, in Joel Conarroe's

words, "both stabilizer and destroyer, midwife and coroner, focuser and de-
pressant." He spent many weeks of 1971 in the alcohol treatment facility at
St. Mary's Hospital in Minneapolis, the hospital that provided the setting for
Recovery. He remained, however, busy. He prepared a new book of poems
for publication, and his plans for work included a translation of Sophocles
and a book or two on Shakespeare. Unfortunately, the prospect of hard work,
the comfort of family and friends, his affection for his daughters, Martha
and Sarah—these were not enough.

On January 7, 1972, readers of the *St. Paul Dispatch* were greeted with the
front page headline: "Poet Berryman Leaps to Death." That afternoon, Berryman had thrown himself some one hundred feet from the railing of a bridge
in Minneapolis; his body was recovered from among the rocks on the frozen
west bank of the Mississippi. In a circumstance worthy of the most bitterly
ironic of his poems, the only identification he carried was a blank check.

After a Requiem Mass, he was buried in Resurrection Cemetery in St. Paul.

Analysis

In his essay "Tradition and the Individual Talent," T. S. Eliot asserts that

> the more perfect the artist, the more completely separate in him will be the man who suffers
> and the mind which creates; the more perfectly will the mind digest and transmute the pas-
> sions which are its material.

Poetry, to Eliot, is "not a turning loose of emotion, but an escape from
emotion; it is not the expression of personality, but an escape from personality." Regardless of what Eliot's critical stock is worth these days, there is
an essential truth in what he says. Of course, poetry has brought to its readers the sweetest joys and the bitterest sorrows that human flesh is heir to,
from "sweet silent thought" to "barbaric yawp." To the extent, however, that
a poet presents his passions to the reader undigested, untransmuted, he dam-
ages the quality of his work *as poetry.* The more loudly personality speaks
in a poem, the more art is forced to falter, to stutter. The poem—and the
poet, and the reader—suffers.

To the extent to which "the man who suffers" and "the mind which creates" are not kept separate, to that extent will that poet's art be imperfect. A
case in point is John Berryman. There is much in his work that is brilliant;
since his death, perhaps, his stature has grown. There is no denying that he
suffered much in his life, and risked much, dared much, in his poetry. What
he was never really able to do was to find the voice and mode that would
allow him, not to banish personality from his poems but to keep personality
from getting in the way, from obstructing the proper work of the poem.

Berryman's Sonnets, though unpublished until 1967, was mostly written some
twenty years earlier. These poems are the poet's first sustained use of what
may be called his "mature style," much of his previous work being rather

derivative. The 115 sonnets form a sequence that recounts the guilty particulars of an adulterous love affair between a hard-drinking academic named Berryman and a harder-drinking woman named Lise, with the respectively wronged wife and husband in supporting roles. The affair, as the sonnets record it, is a curious mixture of sex, Scotch, and Bach (Lise's favorite, her lover preferring Mozart), punctuated by allusions right out of a graduate seminar, from the Old Testament to E. E. Cummings.

In form, the sonnets are Petrarchan, with here and there an additional fifteenth line. In his adherence, more or less, to the stanzaic and metric demands of the sonnet, Berryman pays a sort of homage to earlier practioners of the form. At the same time, he is attempting to forge a mode of expression that is anything but Petrarchan, in spite of the fact that, as Hayden Carruth pointed out in a review in *Poetry* (May, 1968), the poems "touch every outworn convention of the sonnet sequence—love, lust, jealousy, separation, time, death, the immortality of art, etc." Carruth points out in the same review that "the stylistic root of *The Dream Songs*" is present in the sonnets, with those attributes that came to be trademarks of Berryman's style— "archaic spelling, fantastically complex diction, tortuous syntax, formalism, a witty and ironic attitude toward prosody generally." A concentrated if somewhat mild example of how Berryman combines any number of these traits within a few lines is the octet of "Sonnet 49":

> One note, a daisy, and a photograph,
> To slake this siege of weeks without you, all.
> Your dawn-eyed envoy, welcome as Seconal,
> To call you faithful . . . now this cenotaph,
> A shabby mummy flower. Note I keep safe,
> Nothing, on a ration slip a social scrawl—
> Not that it didn't forth some pages call
> Of my analysis, one grim paragraph.

There are enjoyable juxtapositions here. Outdated words such as "slake" and "cenotaph," the over-sweetness of "dawn-eyed envoy," ranged about the all-too-contemporary simile, "welcome as Seconal," are no accident. There is an irreverent literary mind at work here, orchestrating intentionally a little out of tune. It is harder to appreciate or justify a phrase such as "not that it didn't forth some pages call/ Of my analysis." Such syntax is a high price to pay for a rhyme, and much more extreme examples could be cited.

On the whole, the sequence is successful, but the seeds of Berryman's eventual undoing are here. The confessional nature of the poems (Berryman did experience just such an affair in 1947, and required a good deal of psychoanalysis afterward) makes it plain enough why their publication was delayed so long, but it also leads the reader to wonder whether they should have been published at all. In his attempts to work within a fairly strict form, he shows a tendency to force rhyme and overburden meter. His literary name-dropping ("O if my syncrisis/ Teases you, briefer than Propertius' in/ This paraphrase by Pound—to whom I owe three letters"), private allusions, and inside jokes present a dangerous intrusion of the idiosyncratic, the personal. With more shaping, more revision, more distance generally, the sequence could have been much more artistically successful than it is. Perhaps part of Berryman's intention was to get the thing on paper "as it was," to share his raw feelings with the reader. The best of the sonnets, by their wit and craft, speak against such a supposition. They contain, as a group, too much undigested Berryman to be placed, as some have placed them, beside the sonnets of William Shakespeare. Lise is all too actual, "barefoot . . . on the bare floor riveted to Bach," no Dark Lady. Further, while Shakespeare's sonnets have much to say about love, loss, youth, age, success, and failure, they tell the reader little if anything about William Shakespeare, while Berryman's sonnets reveal more than one may care to know about Berryman.

Not long after the strenuous summer of the sonnets, Berryman began a poem on the seventeenth century American Puritan poet, Anne Bradstreet. Part of the initial task was to find the right stanza for the job; an eight-line stanza suggested itself, the pattern of feet running 5-5-3-4-5-5-3-6, with a rhyme scheme of abcbddba. Neither meter nor rhyme are adhered to inflexibly in the resulting poem, *Homage to Mistress Bradstreet*, but for the most part Berryman succeeded in his choice of a stanza "both flexible and grave, intense and quiet, able to deal with matter both high and low." He achieves beautiful effects in the fifty-seven stanzas of this poem. The birth of Bradstreet's first child after several years of barrenness is portrayed in images wonderfully right: "I press with horrible joy down/ my back cracks like a wrist." The words sweep forward, charged with the urgency of this experience, "and it passes the wretched trap whelming and I am me/ drencht & powerful, I did it with my body!/ One proud tug greens Heaven. . . . " In fact, some of the most touching moments in the poem focus on Bradstreet and her children, whether the occasion be death, as in stanza 41: "Moonrise, and frightening hoots. 'Mother,/ how *long* will I be dead?'," or nothing more than a loose tooth, as in stanza 42: "When by me in the dusk my child sits down/ I am myself. Simon, if it's that loose,/ let me wiggle it out./ You'll get a bigger one there, & bite." Moving outdoors, away from the hearth, there are lovely scenes of natural description: "Outside the New World winters in grand dark/ white air lashing high thro' the virgin stands/ foxes down foxholes sigh. . . . "

Berryman, however, has his problems with the poem. As in the sonnets, he sometimes tangles his syntax unnecessarily: "So were ill/ many as one day we could have no sermons." To write "so were ill many" instead of "so many were ill," without even the excuse of a stubbornly kept rhyme scheme, seems at best eccentric, at worst, sloppy. As in the sonnets, also, there is an unfinished quality about the poem. Tangled phrasing, the inconsistent use of a rather carefully established rhyme scheme—these in spite of the fact that Berryman spent years on the poem, even blamed the demise of his first marriage partly upon the intense effort that the work required. One may wonder, in spite of his long labors, whether he relinquished it to the public a bit unfinished.

The major flaw in *Homage to Mistress Bradstreet*, however, has not so much to do with details of diction or prosody. Anne Bradsteet was, by historical accounts, a happily married, deeply religious woman, devoted to her husband and children, who happened to write poetry. Berryman needed for his poem a passionately suffering artist, plagued by religious doubt, resentful of her husband and family, thwarted in her dream of artistic commitment, so he altered the historical Bradstreet to suit his purposes. This reshaping of history is necessary for the centerpiece of the poem—a seduction scene between a modern poet and a woman three hundred years buried. In an understandably surrealistic dialogue, the poet speaks his love for the poor, tormented Anne in a rather far-fetched variation of the designing rake's "Let-Me-Take-You-Away-From-All-This." Bradstreet (Berryman's, that is) is tempted to religious doubt, to extramarital dalliance (she *does* ask the poet for a kiss), to despair over her misunderstood lot. Her domestic commitments, however, overrule her temptations, and the poem ends with the modern poet standing before Bradstreet's grave and uttering words that are supposed to be touching and solemn, but which somehow fail to convince:

> I must pretend to leave you . . . O all your ages at the mercy of my loves
> together lie at once, forever or
> so long as I happen.
> In the rain of pain & departure, still
> Love has no body and presides the sun . . . Hover, utter, still
> a sourcing whom my lost candle like the firefly loves.

The rhyming of "still" with itself is a nice touch, and "the rain of pain & departure" rings true, but the passage has a disturbing, self-conscious quality that is not at all helped by a reference, in one of the closing stanzas, to contemporary (post-World War II) anxieties—"races murder, foxholes hold men,/ reactor piles wage slow upon the wet brain rime."

The above summary oversimplifies and leaves much unsaid. In all fairness, there are a good many brilliant moments in Berryman's poem, but, as a whole, *Homage to Mistress Bradstreet* is somewhat less than brilliant. John Frederick Nims, reviewing the poem in *The Prairie Schooner*, termed it a "gallant failure," finding it "magnificent and absurd, mature and adolescent, grave and hysterical, meticulous and slovenly." In the end, his major complaint is that the poem,

> purportedly concerned with Anne Bradstreet . . . is really about "the poet" himself, his romantic and exacerbated personality, his sense of loneliness, his need for a mis-

tress, confidante, confessor. One might think there would be more satisfactory candidates for the triple role among the living.

Nims's position is persuasively put and strikes at the heart of what is wrong with *Homage to Mistress Bradstreet*. Rather than conveying any true homage to this first American poet, Berryman lets his own personality, his own needs and concerns, dominate the stage, to the extent that the Bradstreet of his poem becomes a just version of himself. Far from "escaping personality," to recall Eliot's term, Berryman forces Bradstreet into the mold of his own personality.

From "Berryman" of the sonnets, to "the poet" of *Homage to Mistress Bradstreet*, Berryman moved on to "Henry," the narrator and protagonist of *The Dream Songs*, the sequence of 385 poems that is considered to be his major work. Berryman apparently began with the notion of writing another long poem, about as long as Hart Crane's *The Bridge* (1930). What resulted, however, was something closer to Ezra Pound's *Cantos* (1925-1972). At the center of the poems is a character known variously as Henry House, Henry Cat, Pussycat, and Mr. Bones. Within flexibly formal songs of three sestets apiece, Berryman reveals Henry's trials and sufferings, which in many cases are the reader's as well. Too often, however, the songs are about Berryman.

There is real feeling in *The Dream Songs*. Too much suffering, however, spread not at all thinly over seven thousand lines and interspersed with proportionately more of the same sort of name-dropping and private allusion encountered in the sonnets, becomes oppressive and even boring. There are wonderful moments, notably in the elegies for dead friends—Jarrell, Schwartz, Sylvia Plath. The obsession with suicide that laces many of the poems is lent a special poignance when considered in the light of Berryman's father's, then his own, suicide. Not surprisingly, Henry's father took his life when he was young. Still, readers must be very interested in Berryman as a person to wade through these 385 poems, for Berryman is once again the center of attention, the "star" of his own epic, despite his coy disclaimer that Henry is "not the poet, not me."

In his continuing inability to distance himself sufficiently from his poetry, Berryman places the reader in an awkward position. In *The Personal Heresy: A Controversy* (1939), C. S. Lewis describes the necessity of keeping one's response to a poem separate from one's response to the personality of the poet, a task that Berryman makes unfairly difficult. When readers mix the two, says Lewis, they offend both poet and poem. "Is there, in social life," he asks, "a grosser incivility than that of thinking about the man who addresses us instead of thinking about what he says?" No, says Lewis, "We must go to books for that which books can give us—to be interested, delighted, or amused, to be made merry or to be made wise." As for personalities, living or dead, the response should be some "species of love," be it "veneration, pity," or something in between.

Berryman's personality is hard to love, easier to pity, but what is truly to be pitied is the fact that, had his skills as a poet been a match for his troubled personality, he would without question have been one of the greatest poets of his time.

Richard A. Eichwald

Other major works

LONG FICTION: *Recovery*, 1973.

NONFICTION: *Stephen Crane*, 1950; *The Arts of Reading*, 1960 (with Ralph Ross and Allen Tate); *We Dream of Honour: John Berryman's Letters to His Mother*, 1988.

MISCELLANEOUS: *The Unfortunate Traveller: Or, the Life of Jack Wilton*, 1960 (edited text); *The Freedom of the Poet*, 1976.

Bibliography

Bloom, Harold, ed. *John Berryman: Modern Critical Views.* New York: Chelsea House, 1989. Collects twelve critical essays on Berryman's poetry, representing a variety of approaches. Contains a good index, a chronology, and a bibliography.

Conarroe, Joel. *John Berryman: An Introduction to the Poetry.* Columbia Introductions to Twentieth Century American Poetry. New York: Columbia University Press, 1977. Written after Berryman's death but before his unpublished writings were made available to scholars, this study presents a brief biography followed by insightful explications of representative poems.

Haffenden, John. *John Berryman: A Critical Commentary.* New York: New York University Press, 1980. This rather dense study examines Berryman's major poetry, showing the connections between Berryman's personal and poetic challenges. Although students may find this work difficult, they will be enlightened by the extensive reproductions of Berryman's drafts, notes, and diary entries. Includes a composition chronology and an index.

_____. *The Life of John Berryman.* Boston: Routledge & Kegan Paul, 1982. This long and sometimes difficult volume draws heavily on Berryman's unpublished diaries, letters, and notes to tell the story of the poet's life from his father's suicide to his own. The contrast between Berryman's artistic successes and personal failures is at the center of this unblinking biography.

Halliday, E. M. *John Berryman and the Thirties: A Memoir.* Amherst: University of Massachusetts Press, 1987. A close friend of Berryman, Halliday presents his recollections of his friendship with Berryman from 1933 to 1943. An account of college life in the thirties, glimpses of other writers, and excerpts from Berryman's letters to Halliday make this a touching and fascinating memoir.

Linebarger, J. M. *John Berryman*. New York: Twayne, 1974. After a brief biographical chapter, Linebarger examines Berryman's poetry, dividing it into
four periods. This fine introduction to Berryman's work is perhaps the
best available for the common reader. The volume includes a chronology,
an annotated bibliography, and an index, but contains few quotations from
the poetry.

Mariani, Paul. *Dream Songs: The Life of John Berryman*. New York: William
Morrow, 1990. This highly readable biography conveys at every point Mariani's admiration for Berryman. As he traces Berryman's brilliant and tragic
life, Mariani does not flinch from what was unattractive about the poet.
Instead, he describes with respect Berryman's struggles to overcome his
weaknesses. Includes extensive quotations from letters, essays, and poems,
and numerous photographs.

JOHN BETJEMAN

Born: London, England; August 28, 1906
Died: Trebetherick, Cornwall, England; May 19, 1984

Principal poetry

Mount Zion: Or, In Touch with the Infinite, 1931; *Continual Dew: A Little Book of Bourgeois Verse*, 1937; *Old Lights for New Chancels: Verses Topographical and Amatory*, 1940; *Slick But Not Streamlined*, 1947 (W. H. Auden, editor); *Selected Poems*, 1948 (John Sparrow, editor); *A Few Late Chrysanthemums*, 1954; *Poems in the Porch*, 1954; *Collected Poems*, 1958; *Summoned by Bells*, 1960; *A Ring of Bells*, 1962 (Irene Slade, editor); *High and Low*, 1966; *A Nip in the Air*, 1974; *Ten Late Chrysanthemums*, 1975; *Uncollected Poems*, 1982; *John Betjeman's Collected Poems*, 1985.

Other literary forms

Hand-in-hand with John Betjeman's lifelong commitment to poetry went an equal dedication to the preservation of the best of English architecture, particularly that of the nineteenth century. Throughout his life, he was intent upon opening the eyes of the public to the glories of Victorian architecture, and he and his friends John Piper (the painter) and Osbert Lancaster (the cartoonist) pursued this cause with such dedication and enthusiasm that they have probably done more to influence public taste in this area than anyone since John Ruskin. Such overriding interest in the quality of modern urban life, and, more specifically, its aesthetic excellence or excesses, is to be seen again and again in Betjeman's prose. In 1933, soon after publication of his first volume of verse, he published *Ghastly Good Taste: Or, A Depressing Story of the Rise and Fall of English Architecture.* This work was followed in 1944 by *John Piper*, and then, in the 1950's and early 1960's, a spate of books on landscape and architecture (listed below) as well as various Shell Guides: *First and Last Loves*, essays on architecture (1952); *The English Town in the Last Hundred Years* (1956); *Collins' Guide to English Parish Churches* (1958); *English Churches* (1964, with B. F. L. Clarke). *Betjeman's Cornwall* was published in 1984. He also edited a number of anthologies which illustrate his interests, including *English, Scottish and Welsh Landscape* (1944), a collection of poetry which he edited with Geoffrey Taylor; he also collaborated with Taylor in editing *English Love Poems* (1957). In 1959, *Altar and Pew: Church of England Verses*, edited by Betjeman, was published, and in 1963 *A Wealth of Poetry*, edited with Winifred Hudley, was issued.

Betjeman was also an accomplished and sometimes inspired broadcaster, whether reading his own poems or describing and discussing architecture, and, for the most part, he wrote his own scripts. Unfortunately, none of his broadcasts has been published in book form, although such a book would probably prove to be as popular as his poetry and essays.

Achievements

Betjeman's most notable though least tangible achievement was to make poetry accessible once more to the reading public. Until the publication of his *Collected Poems*, in 1958, he was largely unknown; the publication of this volume by John Murray proved to be something of a literary phenomenon. Compiled and with an introduction by the Earl of Birkenhead, it sold so quickly that it had to be reprinted three times within the month. It has been said that in the history of John Murray's, nothing like it had been known since the publication of George Gordon, Lord Byron's *Childe Harold's Pilgrimage* in 1812, when copies were sold to a clamoring crowd through the windows of the publisher's house on Albermarle Street. The most recent poetic success of unparalleled magnitude was that of Alfred, Lord Tennyson in the mid-nineteenth century. So far-reaching was the effect of the publication of this volume that in 1959, when applicants interviewed for entry into an English School at a modern university were asked to name a modern poet, it is said that they would automatically answer "Betjeman." Prior to this, the most popular answer had been "T. S. Eliot."

It is impossible to explain fully the wide appeal of Betjeman's poetry. At the time it came to the fore, the Movement poets (Philip Larkin, John Wain, Kingsley Amis, and others, to be found in D. J. Enright's *Poets of the 1950's*) were engaged in a philosophical reaction against the neo-Romanticism of the 1940's, typified by the vogue for the work of Edith Sitwell and the Dylan Thomas cult which emerged after that gifted writer's death in America in 1953.

It must have been extremely galling for these poets, engaged in stringent academic opposition to the tyranny of the iambic pentameter and attempting to purge poetry of the lush metaphor and hyperbole of neo-Romanticism, to witness the meteoric rise to fame of a poet such as Betjeman. It is still true that a taste for Betjeman's poetry is regarded with suspicion in some academic and intellectual circles. John Wain, for example, gave voice to a ponderous and unfavorable judgment of Betjeman's verse autobiography *Summoned by Bells* when it was published in 1960; and when Philip Larkin, perhaps the best known of the Movement poets, expressed his own admiration for Betjeman's poetry, he too was greeted with disapprobation. The fact remains, however, that Betjeman's poetry outsells not only all other poetry, but also many novels.

It may be that his poetic contemporaries have regarded Betjeman with suspicion and dislike because of the force of an argument advanced by Robert Graves in his idiosyncratic but fascinating book *The Crowning Privilege* (1955); that is, that poetry is not in itself commercial, so that poetry books which sell do not truly contain poetry. It may also be that the overwhelming success of a poet with an instantly recognizable poetic voice, who lauds and celebrates the mores of a way of life which has virtually vanished in the face of the inexorable march of progress, is not thought to be seemly by more stringent and muscular writers.

Whatever the reasons for Betjeman's success and the scant respect with which his work is sometimes treated by more "serious" poets, there is no doubt that he was extensively honored, not only by the literary establishment but also by the country's ruling elite, by professional and academic bodies, and by an abiding public recognition and popularity.

His *Selected Poems* won the Heinemann Award; he also won the Foyle Poetry Prize twice, the Duff Cooper Prize, and the Queen's Gold Medal for Poetry. He was a member of the Royal Commission on Historical Monuments in England from 1970 until 1976. He was made an Honorary Fellow of Keble College, Oxford, in 1972, and of Magdalen College, Oxford, in 1975. He was also an honorary LL. D. of the University of Aberdeen, an Honorary Litt. D. of the Universities of Oxford, Reading, Birmingham, Exeter, Liverpool, Hull, and of City University, and an Honorary Associate of the Royal Institute of British Architects (ARIBA).

In 1960, he was awarded a CBE, followed by a C. Lit. in 1968; in 1969, he was knighted; and in 1972 he became poet laureate, that is, official court poet, responsible for writing poems for state occasions such as the investiture of the Prince of Wales, and the marriage of the Prince of Wales to the Lady Diana Spencer. As poet laureate, he followed such distinguished practitioners of the art as William Wordsworth, Alfred, Lord Tennyson, and John Masefield.

Betjeman restored the status of poetry to a level where people who would never normally consider opening a book of verse were actually prevailed upon to pay for the privilege of reading his work. When William Wordsworth (with Samuel Taylor Coleridge) published *Lyrical Ballads* in 1798, his expressed intention was to restore the status of the poet to that of "a man speaking to men," as well as to "exalt and transfigure the natural and the common." More than a hundred years later, with no publicity and no stated poetic philosophy, John Betjeman succeeded in both of those aims—perhaps unconsciously, but undeniably.

Biography

John Betjeman was one of those poets who are profoundly affected by their childhood environment. He was born in London in the early years of the twentieth century, into a class-ridden society, where even small differences in income were important in measuring a family's neighborhood status. This would probably have passed unnoticed had Betjeman been a less observant and sensitive child. As it is, although it is obvious from his poetry that none of the finer nuances of middle-class snobbishness escaped his eye, it is unclear whether these small cruelties were profoundly hurtful or whether the objectivity of the artist was already sufficiently developed to protect him. Certainly there is no bitterness in his poetry, so probably the latter explanation is the correct one. He recounts many of the events of his early life in *Summoned by Bells*, transporting the reader back in time to an England reminiscent of the world depicted by Arthur Conan Doyle, Edith Nesbit, and John Galsworthy.

After leaving Oxford without attaining a degree, Betjeman supported himself by teaching, while continuing to write both poetry and topographical essays. In *Summoned by Bells*, he states quite clearly that as soon as he could read and write he knew that he must strive to become a poet. Despite the disappointment that he caused his father by refusing to take his place in the family business, he was always true to that early ambition.

He married in 1933 and had a son and a daughter, although domestic considerations are not of primary importance in his work. His sense of place and his eye for the eccentricities of the English character were far more important to him.

Betjeman was named poet laureate in 1972. Although the post is bestowed as an accolade, it was probably a strain for a craftsman-poet such as Betjeman to have been expected to produce odes and hymns to order. He never found inspiration in the machinations of the higher echelons of humankind, but rather in the idiosyncrasies of its middle ranks. When he entered his seventies and was afflicted by ill health, he was no longer able to write as freely as he once had. Betjeman died in Trebetherick, Cornwall, in 1984. It is to be hoped that his later work, which cannot be judged as anywhere near his best, is not allowed to obscure the very real value and artistic achievement of his most productive middle years.

Analysis

It is somehow appropriate that the first item in the 1958 volume of John Betjeman's *Collected Poems* should be "Death in Leamington," for this poem touches upon many of the themes which preoccupied him. Although he has been sometimes accused of facility, both because of the traditional rhyme and rhythms of his work and because of his tendency to stress the lighthearted and humorous, it soon becomes obvious to the reader that he was as aware of "the skull beneath the skin" as any apparently more serious writer.

"Death in Leamington" deals with the death of an elderly person in the subdued atmosphere of an unfashionable English spa town, at a time when the town is almost as dead as the ostensible subject of the poem. The title is ambiguous, as is much of Betjeman's work. He equates the death of a person, and even of a generation, with the death and decay of their surroundings and traditions, and it is clear that he laments the passing of both.

For a poet who is often referred to as "lighthearted" and "humorous," he is surprisingly often to be found writing on the subject of death. Indeed, in his introduction to Betjeman's *Collected Poems*, the Earl of Birkenhead compares him in this respect with Samuel Johnson. "On a Portrait of a Deaf Man," "Before the Anaesthetic, or A Real Fright," "Exeter," "Inevitable," "N. W. 5 & N. 6," and "Saint Cadoc" are only a few of the other poems in which he touches upon various aspects of man's attitude toward his own mortality.

A particularly striking poem on this theme is "The Heart of Thomas Hardy," which is written with a degree of bathos and black humor. It describes the heart of Thomas Hardy as "a little thumping fig," a flight of poetic fancy which in itself should serve to ensure Betjeman's literary immortality. He further goes on to describe the Mayor of Casterbridge, Jude the Obscure, Tess of the D'Urbervilles and other products of Hardy's imagination coming to life and leaving their graves to confront their creator in the chancel of Stinsford church. The poem is something of a literary joke, but it also illustrates Betjeman's interest in the supernatural.

There are several other ghosts and eerie incidents described in his poetry, notably in "A Lincolnshire Tale," and the "Sir John Piers" poem sequence, the latter being among the finest in Betjeman's canon.

It would be wholly wrong to place too much emphasis on this darker side of Betjeman's work—indeed, many critics deal with it by the simple expedient of ignoring it; thus they feel justified in dismissing Betjeman as a nostalgic, sentimental apologist for a vanished Empire-building middle class. To achieve a balanced view of his work, however, it is necessary to explore all of his primary themes, and it is undeniable that there is a somber thread in the fabric of his work.

Of course it would be equally wrong to ignore the lighter side of his poetry, especially when that is probably what initially attracts the casual reader to Betjeman's writing. The most frequently anthologized of his poems are those which describe his attraction toward large, athletic women—Miss Joan Hunter Dunn (in "A Subaltern's Love-Song"), Pam (in "Pot Pourri from a Surrey Garden"), and Myfanwy (in "Myfanwy" and "Myfanwy at Oxford"). These ideal women and his attitude toward them come together in "The Olympic Girl," where, after eulogizing at some length this perfect and unattainable young woman, he concludes sadly: "Little, alas, to you I mean,/ For I am bald and old and green." This sentiment, in various forms, appears ever more often in Betjeman's work, and strikes a distinctly Prufrockian note. At first glance, T. S. Eliot and Betjeman seem to have little in common; in the early Betjeman, however, it is possible to detect an awareness of Eliot; for example, "Clash Went the Billiard Balls" is very reminiscent of the concluding section of "A Game of Chess" from *The Waste Land* (1922), and Betjeman's personae frequently recall "The Love Song of J. Alfred Prufrock."

Eliot's smoky, desolate urban landscapes are not so far removed from Betjeman's "Slough," or even from his "Middlesex." Nor are Betjeman's delicately observed characters so far removed from Eliot's less personal portraits. The difference is, perhaps, that Eliot's characters are observed, while Betjeman's are experienced. It certainly takes much more intellectual effort to come to terms with Eliot, and perhaps this effort exerts a distancing effect upon the reader, maintaining a welcome emotional detachment. It is much more difficult to maintain detachment from Betjeman's work. He was not a poet much given to analysis and metaphysical themes. Perhaps that is why he is often ignored by critics; they may admit to enjoying his poetry but are unprepared to acknowledge that in writing poetry which is comprehensible, and also of consistently high quality, he has achieved anything worthwhile.

Because Betjeman was often to be heard giving broadcasts and lectures on architecture and aspects of the British countryside which were especially dear to him, he is perhaps most commonly thought of as a "nature," or, more specifically, a "landscape" poet. Yet he was not a nature poet in the Wordsworthian sense. Where he excelled was in his ability to express his delight in a particular area, a particular type of scenery, and convey that delight to the reader. "Ireland with Emily" is an excellent example of this strain in his work; it is a poem which evokes country life in southern Ireland brilliantly, as, in a different mood, does "A Lament for Moira McCavendish." "Matlock Bath," from the collection *High and Low*, is another such poem, describing life in the nonconformist industrial Midlands of England. In other poems he describes the Cornish coast and various parts of London, especially those areas near Highgate, where he spent his childhood, and about which he writes at length in his verse autobiography, *Summoned by Bells*.

It is impossible to discuss the work of John Betjeman fully without reference to his humor, yet a laborious treatment of this topic is the easiest way of rendering the humor itself ineffective and unfunny. Suffice it to say that much of Betjeman's poetry has a considerable element of humor, but that it would be wrong to regard him as merely a funny writer. His humor always has a purpose, and often, as in "A Lincolnshire Tale," he uses humor for special effect, combining it with a degree of the macabre to make the reader chuckle and then shudder.

His best-known and most anthologized poems, such as "Hunter Trials" and "How to Get on in Society," are those which satirize various easily recognizable aspects of English middle-class life. "How to Get on in Society" covers much the same ground as Nancy Mitford does in *Noblesse Oblige* (1956)—that is, the distinction between "U" and "non-U." The speaker in the poem is distinctly "non-U," but with "U" aspirations. Betjeman cleverly picks up all the social and linguistic pointers and strings them together to create a picture of a type of person in a social milieu recognizable to the English reader; yet he does so through only a few simple lines of conversation. Of course the poem is very much of its time; language changes constantly, and such a poem written today would obviously have very different nuances. The same is not true of "Hunter Trials," which applies as much to horse-mad little girls now as it did when it was written.

Betjeman was always interested in social distinctions—"Group Life: Letchworth" is an earlier example of his keen eye for the extreme and the ridiculous. It concludes with a reference to the cult of free love which flourished in some sections of English society, apparently in the wake of D. H. Lawrence. It has been suggested that Betjeman had a very ambivalent attitude toward sex, being able to deal with it effectively in his work only by making it funny. Leaving aside the thought that often the antics of human beings in love are very amusing to the detached observer, it seems unfair to dismiss Betjeman's subtleties so lightly. In "Group Life: Letchworth," he satirizes one aspect of the English attitude toward sexuality. In "Indoor Games near Newbury," he deals with a quite different, pre-sexual love, and in "Beside the Seaside," the agony of adolescent love. Later, in such poems as "Senex" and "Late Flowering Lust," he takes an ironic, sometimes metaphysical look at the immutability of emotions as the flesh ages. He touches the same topic in "Sun and Fun," and it is part of his strength that he maintains his integrity of tone whether writing about a view he admires or a state of affairs which he obviously deplores. This is possibly why some critics seem to disapprove when he strays from the more familiar descriptive and social poetry to write about emotions. Critics are as likely to be alarmed by change as anyone else, but there is no need to think that change is necessarily always for the worse. In Betjeman's case, he merely showed that he could write about most things with skill, insight, and sympathy.

It is difficult to assess the achievement of Betjeman, who had great public success yet remained outside the mainstream of English poetry. Unlike Eliot or Dylan Thomas, Betjeman inspired no school of poets who either imitate or react unfavorably to him. Yet he is widely read and admired, both by the general public (many of whom would never consider reading poetry if it were not for Betjeman) and by other poets. As Kenneth Allott has pointed out in *The Penguin Book of Contemporary Verse* (1962), a poet who won the admiration of W. H. Auden in one poetic generation and of Philip Larkin in another may well rest content. What is certain is that Betjeman's was a strong and individual poetic voice, whose influence, by virtue of his very popularity, has been far-reaching. Reading his work must make readers aware of both the beauties which surround them and the influences which conspire to threaten those beauties. To speak of the morality of art is to venture onto dangerous ground, yet in writing skillfully in a way which encourages readers to view humankind with tolerance and understanding, and the environment with respect, Betjeman must be thought of as a good poet in both senses of the word.

Vivien Stableford

Other major works

NONFICTION: *Ghastly Good Taste: Or, A Depressing Story of the Rise and Fall of English Architecture*, 1933; *John Piper*, 1944; *First and Last Loves*, 1952; *The English Town in the Last Hundred Years*, 1956; *Collins' Guide to English Parish Churches*, 1958; *English Churches*, 1964 (with B. F. L. Clarke); *Betjeman's Cornwall*, 1984.

ANTHOLOGIES: *English, Scottish and Welsh Landscape*, 1944 (edited with Geoffrey Taylor); *English Love Poems*, 1957 (edited with Geoffrey Taylor); *Altar and Pew: Church of England Verses*, 1959; *A Wealth of Poetry*, 1963 (edited with Winifred Hudley).

Bibliography

Davie, Donald. *Thomas Hardy and British Poetry.* London: Routledge & Kegan Paul, 1973. Davie argues that Thomas Hardy—not William Butler Yeats, T. S. Eliot, or Ezra Pound—has had the most far-reaching influence on modern British poetry, and he finds in Betjeman's poetry metrical procedures akin to those of Hardy. This perceptive commentary also marks what is original in Betjeman's works.

Delany, Frank. *Betjeman Country.* London: John Murray, 1983. This remarkable travel book combines biographical commentary on Betjeman with excerpts from the poet's poems and numerous photographs of the places connected with the poems of Betjeman. Includes a primary bibliography.

Harvey, Geoffrey. "John Betjeman: An Odeon Flashes Fire." In *The Romantic Tradition in Modern British Poetry.* New York: St. Martin's Press, 1986. This provocative, informative study rejects the assessment of Betjeman as a minor establishment poet. Harvey views him as a "consistently subversive force in modern verse"—a committed writer mindful of a real audience.

Press, John. *John Betjeman.* London: Longman, 1974. This monograph—an excellent introduction to Betjeman—includes concise sections on his life, his prose works, and his poetry: themes and character, the shorter poems, and the poet's autobiographical poem *Summoned by Bells.* Supplemented by a select bibliography that emphasizes primary works and a three-quarter-page photograph.

Sparrow, John. "The Poetry of John Betjeman." In *Independent Essays.* Westport, Conn.: Greenwood Press, 1977. This expanded version of Sparrow's "Preface" to Betjeman's *Selected Poems* (1948) probes effectively Betjeman's sense of period. Noting Betjeman's "topographical predilection"—his delight in describing a scene and conveying the atmosphere of place—Sparrow locates Betjeman in the tradition of the landscape poet George Crabbe.

Taylor-Martin, Patrick. *John Betjeman: His Life and Work.* London: Allen Lane, 1983. This excellent study of Betjeman is a useful balance of critical commentary and biography. Taylor-Martin views Betjeman as a serious writer, not a light versifier. The text is supplemented by a select bibliography—primary texts, secondary books, and articles—and a list of his recordings. No index.

Tolley, A. J. "The Old Order and the New: Louis MacNeice and John Betjeman." In *The Poetry of the Thirties.* New York: St. Martin's Press, 1975. This useful study examines the poet's collections published in the 1930's, measuring Betjeman against Louis MacNeice and other poets of the 1930's. Tolley's views on the tone of Betjeman's poetry are particularly insightful.

FRANK BIDART

Born: Bakersfield, California; 1939

Principal poetry

Golden State, 1973; *The Book of the Body*, 1977; *The Sacrifice*, 1983; *In the Western Night: Collected Poems, 1965-90*, 1990.

Other literary forms

Frank Bidart is known primarily for his poetry.

Achievements

Deeply engaged in the moral issues of both personal and cultural guilt, Frank Bidart's poetry has won praise for the intensity with which it documents the struggle between the limits imposed by the body and the ideals envisioned by the mind. In 1981, Bidart won the *Paris Review*'s first Bernard F. Conner Prize for his long poem "The War of Vaslav Nijinsky." This extended dramatic monologue highlights Bidart's unique talents: an unsettling insight into the psychology of guilt and anger, a singular style of narrative poetry based on abstract speech with little reliance on traditional poetic devices, and a thematic focus on the suffering occasioned by humankind's ambiguous intermixture of body and spirit.

Biography

Frank Bidart was born in 1939 in Bakersfield, California, where he grew up, in his words, "obsessed with his parents." After he was graduated from the University of California at Riverside, he attended graduate school at Harvard University. He formed a close relationship with poet Robert Lowell while residing in Cambridge, Massachusetts, and soon after began to write poetry with a style and content distinctive from those of his illustrious mentor. Bidart settled in Cambridge and teaches at Wellesley College.

Analysis

Frank Bidart's poetry is decidedly original in style and content. Thematically, his work resembles confessional poetry, since it is obsessed with the family drama along with the attendant guilt and longing for forgiveness. Like Robert Lowell's groundbreaking *Life Studies* (1959), Bidart's poetry abounds with autobiographical revelations of sexual perversion and neurotic family dynamics; like Lowell, Bidart develops personae that dramatically present these topics with an excruciating anguish that often borders on insanity. Unlike Lowell, however, Bidart presents the guilt and suffering of the mind embedded in the raging emotions and chaotic desires of the body with singular directness.

Whereas Lowell's poetic style has a rhetorical eloquence fashioned from the New Critical techniques of irony, fragmentation, and detailed imagery, Bidart's develops directly from an impassioned narrative voice that is abstract rather than particular, flatly prosaic rather than rhythmically colloquial. In Bidart's poetry, the line breaks and the idiosyncratic punctuation function to reproduce the "pauses, emphases, urgencies and languors in the voice." Often the syntax is complex; sometimes sentences stretch over a page or more and are rife with qualifications and contradictions, all signs of an active mind that, though speaking with the eloquence of polite, educated conversation, is in the grip of strong emotion. Bidart's dependence on an articulate, abstract style risks prosaic blandness, but the reward is a remarkably faithful fastening of his distinctive voice to the page.

Bidart's first collection, *Golden State*, begins with the poem "Herbert White," a dramatic monologue prefiguring the thematic focus on insanity and morality in his prizewinning poem "The War of Vaslav Nijinsky," published ten years later in *The Sacrifice*. At first the eponymous narrator of "Herbert White" views his murder and rape of a young child as morally justifiable because the act comes from a unity of body and desire: "When I hit her on the head, it was good." From this point of view, however, life is "without sharpness, richness or line." Only when White splits his awareness from his physical desires does suffering, and hence morality, commence:

> —Hell came when I saw
> > MYSELF . . .
> > > and couldn't stand
> what I see. . . .

Coordinate with White's separation from and feeling of revulsion for the body and natural processes is the advent of Bidart's characteristic stylistic devices. Before the above lines occur, the verse in "Herbert White" is irregular, but when the narrator's split consciousness focuses on the agony of parental rejection, the gnawing guilt of his familial relationships, his sexual perversity, and the suffering occasioned by his body's unbridled instincts, the line breaks become directly reflective of emotional urgency and certain words, such as "MYSELF," are capitalized in order to reproduce the sonic dynamics of impassioned speech. Significantly, the suffering and the guilt cannot be ameliorated by appeal to a higher plane of understanding such as that normally supplied by religion. Devoid of absolutes, the narrator's voice exists only in the domain of his suffering, a voice universalized by the sound, grammar, and vocabulary of the relentless anguish of self-awareness.

The autobiographical poem "Golden State" reveals one of the sources of the emotional distress pervading Bidart's poetry: his father, a millionaire farmer described in the poem as "the unhappiest man/ I have ever known well." The father's unhappiness results not only from his pathetic desire to be a film star, cowboy, or empire builder but also from a "radical disaffection/ from the very possibilities/ of human life." Disconnected from himself and from his family, the father demonstrates to the poet that the search for connections is both initiated and frustrated by the family:

> The exacerbation
> of this seeming *necessity*
> for connection—;
> you and mother taught me
> there's little that's redemptive or useful
> in natural affections. . . .

Bidart is subject to the compelling human need to make something—some meaning, some pattern—out of these natural affections, but he finds little assistance from the conventional means toward establishing a relationship between his life and a larger realm of understanding. In section 4 of "Golden State," Bidart considers and rejects the efficacy of what his education has given him as an aid to understanding the mysterious hold his father wields on his innermost being: "the lies/ of mere, neat poetry"; his readings of Carl Jung that "never get to the bottom/ of what is, or was"; and the very "patterns and paradigms" of his Harvard studies that are rendered effete by his father's sarcasm, "How are all those bastards at Harvard?" Mere objective insight is rejected in section 5, and section 7 demonstrates the inadequacy of psychiatry to effect a reconciliation between the son and his memories of his dead father. Prayer is discovered to be ineffective in section 8. Only by entering into the words of his poem "to become not merely/ a speaker, the 'eye,' but a character" can Bidart represent the actual shape of his inner life. It is precisely in order to represent his inner life that Bidart has developed poetic techniques that eschew the artificiality of traditional prosody, with its dependence on meter, metaphor, image, and irony. Bidart's poetry demands directness, a physical entering of the self into the poem, an embodiment, that reifies the relentless agony and violence of human experience.

The Book of the Body, Bidart's next collection of poetry, presents the poet's sheer disgust at having to enter aesthetically into "the stump-filled material world// things; bodies;/ CRAP." These lines are from the first poem of the book, entitled "The Arc," which sets the collection's pervasive tone of physical laceration (the poem's narrator has lost his arm as a result of a senseless accident) and bodily anxiety ("I'm/ embarrassed to take my shirt off"). An arc could geometrically be part of the unity of a circle, but in this poem an arc is seen as irremediably cut off from wholeness as is the arm of the amputee-narrator; it is an unredeemed segment of time, like a person's life bounded by its birth date and death date between parentheses. Unable to transcend the suffering of his limited physical existence, the narrator can achieve only the equivocal resolution of contemplating "how Paris is still the

city of Louis XVI and/ Robespierre, how blood, amputation, and rubble//
give her dimension, resonance, and grace."

Having explored his obsession with his father in *Golden State*, Bidart now
turns to his mother in the poem "Elegy." References to laceration abound:
the chewing done by his mother's pet dog Belafont, his mother's reply of
"gelding" to the narrator's ambition to become a priest, a love affair that
leads to abortion, the envisioning of death and memory as "a razor-blade
without a handle." Especially interesting is the interconnection made between
being cut off from a satisfying relationship with his mother as well as his
self and discussions of impotent mouths and mutilated breasts. When dreaming of the dog Belafont, the narrator recalls how the dog attempted to kiss
him, but "carefully avoiding the mouth, as/ taught." In the section grotesquely
entitled "Pruning," his mother exclaims, "I'd rather die than let them/ take
off a breast." Mouths that cannot make contact, breasts that are threatened
with excision indicate a lack of connection with the physical world as matter,
"mother."

A morbid rejection of matter and of eating, an act that implicates the self
in matter, forms a large portion of the theme of Bidart's great dramatic monologue from *The Book of the Body*, "Ellen West." Assuming the mask of
the anorexic Ellen West, Bidart dramatizes how acquiring a body that is the
image of the soul necessitates destroying that very body. To Ellen West, food
is inextricably entangled with sex, death, and the material world:

> Even as a child,
> I saw that the "natural" process of aging
>
> is for one's middle to thicken—
> one's skin to blotch;
>
> as happened to my mother.
> And her mother.
> > *I loathed "Nature."*

Only by opposing the body—as, in the poem, did Maria Callas, the great
opera singer, when she drastically trimmed her once-ample body by sixty
pounds, illustrating how her soul "loved eating the flesh from her bones"—
can an ideal approaching great art be realized. Such an art records the un-
ending struggle of the spirit to embody and manifest itself in a medium that
it finds repulsive. Finally, each attempt to reconcile the body and the spirit
heightens a hunger that neither food nor ink, the food of art, can satisfy. At
the end of the poem, Ellen West poisons her body to achieve the ideal self
that the world has sought to poison through food.

Ellen West sacrifices her body for an ideal, but that ideal cannot be directly embodied in art, for art as physical representation partakes of the body,

not the soul. What can be recorded is the struggle itself, the sacrifice—and that is the central theme of Bidart's next book, *The Sacrifice.*

One of the major poems in *The Sacrifice,* "Confessional," extends the thematic conflict of an earlier poem centered on Bidart's mother, "Elegy." In "Confessional," the body, the material world, presents a terrain on which it is impossible for mother and son to find harmony, for in the physical world dwell anger and unredeemable guilt occasioned by Bidart's memory of his childhood predatory wish to supplant both his father and his stepfather in his mother's affections, a situation exacerbated by the mother's excessive emotional dependence on him when he was a child. As an extreme contrast to the condition between the poet and his mother, sections from *The Confessions of Saint Augustine* (c. 397-400) that depict the relationship between Saint Augustine and his mother, Monica, constitute a major portion of the poem. Like Bidart in his childhood, Augustine supplanted his own father to the extent that Monica wished to be buried next to him, not her husband. The unbridgeable gap between Augustine and his mother, on the one hand, and Bidart and his mother, on the other, results from Augustine and Monica's ability within the framework of the Christian mythos to transcend the "tumult of the flesh" and ascend to "the WISDOM that is our SOURCE and GROUND." Entangled in the confusions and desires of the body, Bidart's poetry cannot appeal to a higher level of meaning, however strongly craved: "*Man needs a metaphysics;/ he cannot have one.*" As in the poem "Genesis," a reworking of the first two books of the Bible into Bidart's poetic voice, not only did God rest after the days of creation, but God also "ceased." In the absence of an absolute, no anagogic, no symbolic function of language can mend the chasm between the mutually exclusive pairs: Augustine and his mother with their harmonious heavenly vision, Bidart and his mother with their "unappeasable anger, and remorse."

Also contained in *The Sacrifice* is the remarkable long poem "The War of Vaslav Nijinsky," a dramatic monologue in the persona of Vaslav Nijinsky (1890-1950), a famous dancer who had a formidable talent to turn his body into symbol. Nijinsky is presented as a figure that would—as Friedrich Nietzsche did in his unconditional acceptance of eternal return and thus the cycles of physical existence—say yes to life, were it not for his realization that he is not Nietzsche but the "bride of Christ." The dowry of the bride of Christ is an unrelenting guilt that leads to the rejection of life. There is no relief from this guilt, for "God was silent.// Everything was SILENT." Love, religion, philosophy, art, and mythology cannot assuage Nijinsky's insight that "*All life exists// at the expense of other life*" and that war is a given of life. Only sacrifice serves to atone for the guilt and suffering of the world, and Nijinsky, therefore, according to Bidart, danced "the Nineteenth Century's/ guilt," World War I, on January 19, 1919, in order to redeem, or perhaps destroy, the earth. Like Ellen West, Nijinsky can overcome the body and, by

extension, earthly existence only through annihilation of the body. At the
end of the poem, Nijinsky feels a "need to be as low down as possible" in
his bed at an asylum in Zurich, Switzerland. He has sacrificed his body to
his art.

Bidart's publication of his first three books plus two previously unpublished collections in *In the Western Night: Collected Poems, 1965-90* confronts the reader with an odd ordering of these works: a new collection, *In
the Western Night*, precedes the three previously published books, which are
in reverse chronological order, and another new collection, *The First Hour of
the Night*, ends the entire poetry collection. A possible reason for this arrangement is that *In the Western Night* underscores a theme that has been
muted in the previous works, a theme that revalues those works and resolves
itself in the final collection, *The First Hour of the Night*. In his 1990 review
of *In the Western Night: Collected Poems, 1965-90*, Denis Donoghue noted
that "several of Bidart's most urgent poems are, in some sense that is hard
to describe, mystical." Odd as it may sound, Bidart's earthbound poetry possibly conceals a strong mystical impulse that intuits meaning beneath or beyond physical appearance. Such a mystical theme is strongly suggested in the
first poem of *In the Western Night: Collected Poems, 1965-90*, "To the Dead":

> once we'd been battered by the gorilla
>
> we searched the walls, the intricately carved
> impenetrable panelling
>
> for a button, lever, latch
>
> that unlocks a secret door that
> reveals at last the secret chambers,
>
> CORRIDORS within WALLS,
>
> (the disenthralling, necessary, dreamed structure
> beneath the structure we see,)

After the poem's "we" have been battered by the gorillalike physical life, a
secret chamber hidden behind the veil of material appearance is revealed.
This innermost structure is "disenthralling," liberating from the prison of
the body and the material world.

The working out of the mystical implications of "To the Dead" occurs, as
it should, in the last poem in *In the Western Night: Collected Poems, 1965-90*,
"The First Hour of the Night." Perhaps Bidart's most ambitious poem, it
balances the Western philosophical tradition against the poet's personal feelings of guilt, putting in equilibrium both "*wound* and *balm.*" The occasion
of the poem is the return of the poet to the house of a dead friend, at the
invitation of the friend's son. The son and the poet discover that they share a

sense of unresolved guilt: the son over the death of his father, the poet over the death of a pony that had been his close companion when he was young. Late that night, the poet retires to the guest bedroom and dreams two dreams. In one dream he enters into an etching of *The School of Athens* by the Renaissance painter Raphael, which presents the ancient philosophers unified around the opposing but balanced gestures of Aristotle, representing matter, and Plato, representing spirit. Before entering into this painting in a dream state, the poet describes the panorama from an intellectual, objective point of view that sees a Janus-like unity in the divided philosophical positions of the ancient philosophers. Once embodied in the dream, however, the poet is weighed down with humiliation and guilt and strives unsuccessfully to regain a sense of unity. Philosophers who lived and wrote after the execution of Raphael's painting join the original group, bringing a cacophony of opinions that result in irreparable chaos. Finally, the poet awakes from this dream into "the desolation of/ HISTORY's/ leprosy,—*LEPROSY* of SPIRIT."

The first dream ends in Bidart's customary vision of spirit hopelessly mired in a diseased, repulsive physical state. In the second dream, the poet discovers that he has been carrying the entrails of his pet pony on his back ever since the animal died (when the poet was nine). Entrails not only suggest eating and the processes of the body but also haruspicy, the divination of spirit. For the first time in Bidart's poetry, the mouth, the agent of eating and sexuality, joins with the breast, no longer seen as repulsive as it was in "Elegy" from *The Book of the Body*:

> hungry, SUCKING mouths stretched toward
> swollen, distended udders that I saw must be
>
> painful *unless* sucked—;
>
> . . . RECIPROCITY,—
>   I thought,—
>   *not the chick within*
> *the egg, who by eating its way*
> *out, must DESTROY the egg to become itself* . . .

Destroying in order to become, the way of sacrifice, is abandoned in favor of reciprocity, the interpenetration of matter and spirit. Thus "The First Hour of the Night" ends with a tentative glimmer of transformation possible in the physical world.

Although his later work intimates a conditional transcendence, the bulk of Bidart's poetry envisions the self trapped in history, sunk in the body, devoid of wholeness. Like an animal in a snare, the frustrated spirit experiences only torment, rage, grief, and guilt. The language of his poetry seldom soars, but remains earthbound, flat, prosaic, lexically abstract. Frank Bidart's poetry documents the contemporary moral and psychological state of humankind with such excruciating intensity, however, that it resonates in the depths of every reader.

Kenneth Gibbs

Bibliography
Birkerts, Sven. *The Electric Life: Essays on Modern Poetry.* New York: William Morrow, 1989. In his chapter "Frank Bidart," Birkerts comments on how Bidart's dualistic conception of body and spirit is enlarged to encompass the guilt of Western humankind. Tracing a progression from "Ellen West" to "The War of Vaslav Nijinsky," Birkerts not only addresses the widening of Bidart's themes to include a more general religious point of view but also comments on the interrelation of these themes and Bidart's distinctive style.
Crenshaw, Brad. "The Sin of the Body: Frank Bidart's Human Bondage." *Chicago Review* 33 (Spring, 1983): 57-70. This article contains an insightful discussion of "Ellen West" and clarifies Bidart's construction of an art that presents the ethical paradox of carnality. Bradshaw discusses how Bidart has contracted human ethics within bodily limits, so that customary morality with its exaltation of the spirit becomes severely modified.
Donoghue, Denis. "The Visible and the Invisible." *The New Republic* 202 (May 14, 1990): 40-45. This extensive review of *In the Western Night: Collected Poems, 1965-90* traces Bidart's rather deviatory development toward a quasi-mystical sense of personal experience. Interestingly, Donoghue connects the typography of Bidart's dramatic monologues with his longing to escape the lure of mystical states. Donoghue also demonstrates that Ezra Pound, not Robert Lowell, should be viewed as Bidart's artistic mentor.
Pinsky, Robert. *The Situation of Poetry: Contemporary Poetry and Its Traditions.* Princeton, N.J.: Princeton University Press, 1976. In his overview of poetry of the 1970's, Pinsky gives an early recognition of Bidart's stylistic achievement. He praises Bidart's *Golden State* for taking the risk of rhetorical flatness in order to reproduce a genuine sense of the speaker's voice.
Williamson, Alan. *Introspection and Contemporary Poetry.* Cambridge, Mass.: Harvard University Press, 1984. As part of the chapter "The Future of Personal Poetry," Williamson argues that Bidart is an emotionally moving and artistically significant poet because he speaks from the wholeness of his life. Although employing an abstract poetic style, Bidart, Williamson avers, never becomes vague or dematerialized, but vividly dramatizes the tragic interplay of aggression and guilt.

EARLE BIRNEY

Born: Calgary, Alberta, Canada; May 13, 1904

Principal poetry

David and Other Poems, 1942; *Now Is Time*, 1945; *The Strait of Anian*, 1948; *Trial of a City and Other Verse*, 1952; *Ice Cod Bell or Stone*, 1962; *Near False Creek Mouth*, 1964; *Selected Poems 1940-1966*, 1966; *The Poems of Earle Birney*, 1969; *Pnomes, Jukollages and Other Stunzas*, 1969; *Rag and Bone Shop*, 1971; *What's So Big About Green?*, 1973; *The Bear on the Delhi Road*, 1973; *The Collected Poems of Earle Birney*, 1975; *The Rugged and the Moving Times*, 1976; *Ghost in the Wheels: Selected Poems 1920-1976*, 1977; *Fall by Fury*, 1978; *The Mammoth Corridors*, 1980; *Copernican Fix*, 1985.

Other literary forms

Earle Birney, like many contemporary Canadian poets, both creates and explicates the tradition of his country's writings. To date, he has written or edited twenty-eight volumes, including poetry, fiction, drama, criticism, and anthologies, as well as nearly a hundred short stories, pamphlets, essays, reviews, and articles. The novels *Turvey* (1949), which won the Stephen Leacock medal for humor, and *Down the Long Table* (1955) are well worth reading for an appreciation of Birney's sense of style. Of his critical articles and books, *The Creative Writer* (1966), *The Cow Jumped over the Moon: The Writing and Reading of Poetry* (1972), and *Spreading Time* (1980) are the most notable collections, for they offer invaluable insights into Birney's poetry.

Achievements

Birney's poetry reflects and summarizes the ambiguities, inconsistencies, and changes in direction in Canadian writing during the second half of the twentieth century. His central achievement is simple: he has brought Canadian poetry from traditional conservatism through modernism and, finally, to postmodernism. As a result, his mere presence on the Canadian literary scene has generated everything from respect to contempt. No writer in Canada has stirred as much controversy about the nature, direction, and accomplishment of Canadian poetry; Birney will always be remembered and acknowledged. Literary nationalism had been the catchphrase of Canadian writing, but when it arrived in the form of Earle Birney, Canadians discovered a contentious, outspoken gentleman who shocked the literary establishment.

Biography

Alfred Earle Birney was born on May 13, 1904, in Calgary, Alberta, which was then actually a part of the Northwest Territories. He spent his youth in Calgary, Banff, and Creston, British Columbia, was graduated from Creston High School in 1920, and then worked at a variety of jobs to earn money for university. By 1926, he had been graduated from the University of British Columbia with first-class honors in English literature, and that autumn he entered the University of Toronto as a Leonard Graduate Fellow. During the next year, he concentrated on Old and Middle English, and his studies led to his later imitations of the Anglo-Saxon line in "Anglo-Saxon Street" and "Mappemounde." He was graduated with an M.A. in 1927 and was married the same year.

From 1927 to 1934, he studied at the University of California as well as in Toronto. Two years later, he completed his Ph.D. thesis, "Chaucer's Irony," and received his degree from the University of Toronto. During the years 1936 to 1940, Birney acted as the literary editor of *The Canadian Forum*, writing numerous articles for this journal. When World War II began, Birney served overseas in the Canadian Armed Forces as a personnel officer. He would later use this experience as the basis for his comic war novel *Turvey*. In 1945, at the end of the war, he was appointed professor of English at the University of British Columbia. While at UBC, he was instrumental in establishing the first Department of Creative Writing at a Canadian university. Once the program was set up, he invited American poets such as Charles Olson, Robert Creeley, and Robert Duncan to teach there. To some extent, these writers would greatly affect Birney's view of poetics; in particular, they expounded theories about spacing, breath, and projective verse which led Birney to revise many of his own ideas about these matters. Birney followed their direction, although he did not become a disciple of the Black Mountain movement. By 1963, Birney had become the chairman of the Department of Creative Writing and also editor of *Prism International*. In 1964, Birney left UBC to become writer-in-residence at such institutions across Canada as the universities of Toronto, Waterloo, and Western Ontario. In 1968, as a Canada Council Fellow, he traveled to Australia, New Zealand, and other parts of the world; some of his best poetry deals with these experiences.

Since 1969, Birney has devoted his time primarily to his writing, leaving his career as an educator behind him. In the middle and late 1970's, he concentrated most of his energy on recording the developments in Canadian writing which he witnessed during his lifetime.

Analysis

The most distinguishing characteristic of Earle Birney's poetry is its diversity. Birney cannot be associated with any single place, with any single movement (either political, social, or poetic), or with any single theme—he writes about everything that interests him at the moment it does interest him. The result may be a solitary poem quickly forgotten or an entire book of experiments immediately abandoned after publication. Birney's chameleonlike nature has forced commentators to discuss his work in large, broad generalizations. Yet, Birney's achievement does have a center, and that center rests in his belief that the future is always open and that nothing is ever quite finished or complete or final.

Permanence, for Birney, is an illusion; only death has finality. The recurring images of death, loss, and failure, suggested particularly in the autumnal imagery of his early and middle poetry, are present to emphasize that only one force defeats, or at least temporarily overcomes, death: the creative power inherent in the individual. In conjunction with his firm belief in the inward potential of the individual's creative energy, Birney maintains that art, like anything else, must be the expression of creative change. For these reasons, he will revise, alter, and completely transform an earlier poem to accommodate and reflect the changes he senses in his world.

A volume of Birney's poems might include forms as diverse as pastiche, allegory, Anglo-Saxon forms, narrative and reflective poems, lyrics, limericks, found poems, and concrete or "shapomes" (poems which rely, almost wholly, on their visual, rather than verbal, effect). No single volume amassing all the various forms Birney has used would be satisfactory, for Birney often not only changed and revised poems for later editions but entirely transformed their format and design, as well. A linear poem in one edition may appear in the next as a "shapome." In his *Selected Poems 1940-1966*, Birney added dates after each poem to indicate the impermanence of his own "final" selection. "North of Superior," for example, is followed by the dates 1926-1945. Which is the "real" version? The poem of 1926 (or was this merely the first draft?) or the poem of 1945? Such questions can hardly be answered when the reader thinks of the poem "Mammorial Stunzas for Aimee Simple McFarcin," dated "Toronto 1932-San Francisco 1934," but first printed in 1959, then reprinted in a wholly transformed shape in 1966. The only possible complete and satisfactory edition of Birney's work would include all the versions of the revised and restructured poems, introduced by the following heading: the "final" version of any poem in this edition rests in the invisible creative energy suggested by every visible act of imagination (that is, every altered poem) included here. Such a text, however, still goes against the grain of contemporary publishing; until one is available, Birney will remain more mysterious and elusive than he needs to be or wishes to be.

Analysis of Birney's work inevitably begins with his first major poem, "David," a narrative which records the last day of "youth" in the mountains. Although the poem is entitled "David," it is centrally about Bobby, the narrator. Bobby possesses a naïve and sentimental view of Nature, and David attempts to teach his younger friend the necessity of living in a world where beauty and magnificence have value only when death is recognized as both necessary and inevitable. The lyricism and descriptive detail in the poem move the reader most forcefully at the moments when death and beauty are inextricably entwined in the passages of description.

The climax of the poem is reached when David falls to a ledge far below. Bobby's error has caused the mishap, although David, now crippled, does not press the blame upon his friend. Instead, David asks Bobby to demonstrate that he has grasped the principle of necessary death by pushing him off the ledge so that he will not have to live as an invalid. Bobby finally responds to David's requests. The conclusion of the poem focuses on Bobby's need to reorient and reevaluate his own outlook and attitudes, which he cannot do. For Bobby, Nature is now frightening, horrific, and repugnant. Ironically, David has died for nothing; Bobby's idealism has simply turned to blind pessimism. The poem, however, forcefully depicts man's need to incorporate not only new values but also values which may initially seem incomprehensible and alien. Bobby may fail, but the reader clearly sees that Birney favors David's vision of life, for it allows for both beauty and death without fear.

The initial publication of the poem created a shock, and for years Birney was inundated by letters asking him if he had once pushed a friend off a cliff. The confusion between literature and reality may seem humorous to the more experienced reader, but the fact that such letters were written and sent testifies to the impact of the poem. The same narrative, in later years, however, stirred an even greater debate. Birney suddenly modernized it. He stripped the poem of punctuation and inserted spaces for commas, semicolons, and periods. The argument about the purpose and significance of the changes continues even now: can a traditional poem be "modernized" by simply omitting punctuation? Such a process, for the modern purist, defies any sense of organic form or poetic necessity. For many, Birney's revision was superficial tinkering.

The attacks on the so-called facile alterations of the poem are valid if one accepts the notion that poems of the past must remain in the past, but Birney would not accept that notion. He boldly challenged his detractors to explain their principles, even if they did not have the patience to listen to his reasoning. For Birney, no poem can be imprisoned in the abstraction called "the past": every poem is read in the present; it is experienced in the present, and the sensibility of the present is attuned to verse without punctuation. Neither the sensibility which was at work in the "older" version nor the audience for whom it was intended still exists. The old must be pushed over the cliff to its death; the new must be incorporated.

Birney has not received acceptance on this point, but, whatever a reader's attitude, an understanding of the poet's principles clarifies why Birney so markedly shifts and shifts again, even in experimental forms. In "Anglo-Saxon Street," for example, he creates his best-known satire by using Old English stress and modern "kennings." In "Billboards Build Freedom of Choice," he uses a variation of Olson's projective verse but, at the same time, sports with the ambiguities inherent in the slang of the 1950's and early 1960's. In "There

Are Delicacies," he creates a concrete poem that resembles a timepiece in order to remind a woman that there is only so much time for love. In a book called *What's So Big About Green?*, the poet has the words themselves printed in green ink to accompany his theme in visual form: everything is capable of greenness, freshness, vitality, and rebirth. Birney's constant insistence upon the dynamics of change is not an idle or frivolous gesture; the philosophy gives direction and unity to all he writes.

The philosophy of change, or the all too common lack of it, often leads Birney to lash out with forceful and even vitriolic satires and parodies. Even in these works, Birney's central vision is not lost to anger or outrage. The work "Trial of a City: A Public Hearing into the Proposed Damnation of Vancouver" excellently illustrates the point. The work is a madcap fantasy of the future, the setting a kangaroo court wherein the sentence has already been pronounced, although the case is tried afterward. The powers that be can see no reason for halting the annihilation of the city until a common housewife enters. She stands for the forces of creation and meaning and love. For her, there is neither causality nor inevitable end. Creative response to the moment, her presence insists, allows for life, passion, and continuance. For her, all human "freedom is renewable each moment," but only if the individual exercises his creative energy to embrace and accept.

The theme of "Trial of a City," then, despite its harsh attack on the stultified values of society (represented by the traditionalist, Mr. Legion), is typical of Birney's larger concerns. In form, the work also bears the marks of Birney's experimentalism, including everything from typographical idiosyncrasies in the manner of E. E. Cummings to the use of diction and thought echoing W. H. Auden.

Through the years, Birney has gradually incorporated into his own work all the various developments in poetry since the 1930's and 1940's. His rhetoric based on image has shifted to a rhetoric of voice, and from there to a rhetoric of visual design. At times, the ability to accommodate such disparate poetic modes results in profoundly moving verse dealing with man's place in a hostile world, as in "Mappemounde," and in delightful typographical humor, as in "Appeal to a Lady with a Diaper." Often, however, the all too predictable pursuit of novelty wears thin, and Birney's work becomes tiresome.

The tiresome poems cannot be reread, and therein lies their greatest weakness. On first reading, the timepiece design of the poem "There Are Delicacies" enchants; on the second reading, it bores. The language, the essence of the poetic craft, has been treated too lightly; the reverberations have been too easily lost. One can admire Birney's effort to be consistent, one can sympathize with his healthy and reinvigorating outlook, one can admire the notion that creative acts are always required and always possible, but one cannot always summon the energy to rejoice at poems that seem flat and stale once the novelty has worn off.

In the poems that can be reread, Birney's theme, form, language, typography, and verse form (be they traditional or modern) create fulfilling, enriching experiences. Anyone interested in poetry can read them, for the literary devices enhance the texture of the poems rather than point to themselves as being present and active (thereby inadvertently drawing the reader's eye from the true center of the poem—the content). The most important poems in this category may be loosely called Birney's "travel poems"; they deserve special attention.

Birney is not a regional poet. This point is significant, for the term "travel poem" is used here to encompass all poems wherein Birney's speaker is on the road, in a train, or in a new city, be that city in Canada or Japan. The poems have great force because usually, although not always, the reader, by the end of the poem, knows more than the person who did the traveling. Since the reader can measure both the speaker and what he thinks, as well as the atmosphere and history of the place visited, he is often in a privileged position to judge and evaluate both the ridiculous and the redeeming in human nature. This striking effect in the travel poems is the consequence of Birney's masterful control of both his speaker and his setting. Some of the best of the travel poems are "For George Lamming," "Arrivals," "The Bear on the Delhi Road," "Cartagena de Indias," "El Greco," "November Walk Near False Creek Mouth," and "A Walk in Kyoto." In these and the other travel poems, Birney concentrates on his favorite topic, the moment of needed creative impulse, and the speaker usually discovers his creative force as he reflects upon his experience.

"For George Lamming" best illustrates how Birney concentrates on the moment of change. The free-verse poem, lacking punctuation, suggests fluidity and freedom from beginning to end. It deals with the speaker's sudden insight into an experience he had in Kingston, Jamaica, where, invited to a party, he found himself totally in harmony with all who were there. More than "rum happy," he did not even recognize his joy until he looked in the mirror; then his face "assaulted" him. He was the only white among five or six black couples, and despite the color barrier, the history of black tensions, and the racial prejudice of the ages, these people had allowed him to share "unchallenged" their friendship and intimacy. The speaker will always feel "grateful" for having been allowed, even temporarily, to escape the prison of his own skin and his own prejudices (although he had not recognized them until that moment).

This summary of the poem slips over the numerous subtleties of the "master" and "slave" imagery used throughout (for language itself requires one to "risk words," although they are such "dull/ servants") to make a central point about Birney's artistry at its best: creative insight, for Birney, represents the moment of transcendence of the narrow self. Imagination, in its largest sense, is, for Birney, an act or ability which is not confined to poets or to poetry; it is the act of sympathetic insight and understanding available to all men at all times, provided they transcend themselves. If Birney, at times, insists too loudly, if he presses his experiments too often, if he revises and alters and again alters too persistently—these are merely the signs of his sincerity and consistency. Every altered and modified poem Birney presents can be, and probably should be, read as his unaltering embrace of constant change through individual creative gestures. As such, the poetry of Earle Birney is a testament of one man's unshakable conviction that human growth, development, and perfection are possible.

Ed Jewinski

Other major works

LONG FICTION: *Turvey*, 1949; *Down the Long Table*, 1955.

SHORT FICTION: *Big Bird in the Bush*, 1978.

PLAY: *The Damnation of Vancouver: A Comedy in Seven Episodes*, 1952; *Words on Waves*, 1985 (radio plays).

NONFICTION: *The Creative Writer*, 1966; *The Cow Jumped over the Moon: The Writing and Reading of Poetry*, 1972; *Spreading Time*, 1980; *Essays on Chaucerian Irony*, 1985.

ANTHOLOGIES: *Twentieth Century Canadian Poetry*, 1953; *New Voices*, 1956; *Selected Poems of Malcolm Lowry*, 1962.

Bibliography

Aichinger, Peter. *Earle Birney.* Boston: Twayne, 1979. This introductory study looks at Birney's criticisms of capitalism, modern culture, and militarism. Divided thematically with chapters on biographical background, satire, love and death, myth, nature, poetic technique, and politics, the author concentrates on Birney's poetry over his criticism and prose fiction. The cynicism, raunchiness, and invective in Birney's later work is looked at in a negative light. Contains an annotated bibliography of primary and secondary sources, as well as notes to the text.

Davey, Frank. *Earle Birney.* Toronto: Copp Clark Publishing, 1971. This short study contains two chapters on Birney's poetry: one on the lyrics and the other on the major poems. Special attention is paid to Birney the humanist and to the mythic underpinnings in his work. "David," "The Damnation of Vancouver," "November Walk Near False Creek Mouth," and *The Mammoth Corridors* are given detailed analyses with examples from the poems used extensively. Supplemented by notes and a bibliography.

Fink, Howard, et al. *Perspectives on Earle Birney.* Downsview, Ontario: ECW Press, 1981. A reassessment of Birney by eminent critics and authors, this collection was originally published as a special issue on Earle Birney in

Essays on Canadian Writing 21 (Spring, 1981). Pieces of Birney's poetry are interspersed with observations on his radio drama, Chaucerian scholarship, and political prose.

Lecker, Robert, Jack David, and Ellen Quigley, eds. *Canadian Writers and Their Works*. Poetry series, vol. 2. Downsview, Ontario: ECW Press, 1985. This collection of essays includes an article on Birney by Peter Aichinger, which contains a short introduction to Birney's life, his traditions and worldview, and a critical overview. It looks specifically at the alliterative verse, lyric poetry, experimental verse, and the narrative poems. Includes extensive notes that contain bibliographical references and a select bibliography that lists primary and secondary sources.

Nesbitt, Bruce, ed. *Earle Birney: Critical Views on Canadian Writers*. New York: McGraw-Hill, 1974. This collection of representative critical essays on Birney contains both positive and negative reviews and critical essays on Birney's craft and creativity mixed with a number of his prose pieces. The useful introduction gives an overview and appreciation, while in an epilogue, Birney himself reflects on his career and responds to some of the critical appraisals in the essays.

ELIZABETH BISHOP

Born: Worcester, Massachusetts; February 8, 1911
Died: Boston, Massachusetts; October 6, 1979

Principal poetry

North & South, 1946; *Poems: North & South—A Cold Spring*, 1955; *Questions of Travel*, 1965; *The Complete Poems*, 1969; *Geography III*, 1976; *The Complete Poems, 1927-1979*, 1983.

Other literary forms

In addition to her poetry, Bishop wrote short stories and other prose pieces. She is also known for her translations of Portuguese and Latin American writers. *The Collected Prose*, edited and introduced by Robert Giroux, was published in 1984. It includes "In the Village," an autobiographical revelation of Bishop's youthful vision of, and later adult perspective on, her mother's brief return home from a mental hospital. Like her poetry, Bishop's prose is marked by precise observation and a somewhat withdrawn narrator, although the prose works reveal much more about Bishop's life than the poetry does. Editor Giroux has suggested that this was one reason many of the pieces were unpublished during her lifetime. *The Collected Prose* also includes Bishop's observations of other cultures and provides clues as to why she chose to live in Brazil for so many years.

Achievements

Bishop was often honored for her poetry. Among many awards and prizes, she received the 1956 Pulitzer Prize for Poetry and the 1969 National Book Award for Poetry. Yet, as John Ashbery said, in seconding her presentation as the winner of the *Books Abroad*/Neustadt International Prize for Literature in 1976, she is a "writer's writer." Despite her continuing presence for over thirty years as a major American poet, Bishop never achieved great popular success. Perhaps the delicacy of much of her writing, her restrained style, and her ambiguous questioning and testing of experience made her more difficult and less approachable than poets with showier technique or more explicit philosophies.

For critics, however, and certainly for other poets—those as different as Marianne Moore and Robert Lowell, or Randall Jarrell and Ashbery—hers is a voice of influence and authority. Writing with great assurance and sophistication from the beginning of her career, she achieved in her earliest poetry the quiet, though often playful, tone, probing and examining of reality, the exactness of language, and the lucidity of vision that mark all of her best poetry. Her later poetry is slightly more relaxed than her earlier, the formal patterns often less rigorous; but her concern and her careful eye never waver. Because of the severity of her self-criticism, her collected poems, although relatively few in number, are of a remarkably even quality.

Bishop's place in American poetry, in the company of such other twentieth century poets as Moore, Wallace Stevens, and Richard Wilbur, is among the celebrators and commemorators of the things of this world, in her steady conviction that by bringing the light of poetic intelligence, the mind's eye, on those things, she will enrich her readers' understanding of them and of themselves.

Biography

Elizabeth Bishop is a poet of geography, as the titles of her books testify, and her life itself was mapped out by travels and visits as surely as is her poetry. Eight months after Bishop's birth in Massachusetts, her father died. Four years later, her mother suffered a nervous breakdown and was hospitalized, first outside Boston, and later in her native Canada.

Elizabeth was taken to Nova Scotia, where she spent much of her youth with her grandmother; later, she lived for a time with an aunt in Massachusetts. Although her mother did not die until 1934, Bishop did not see her again after a brief visit home from the hospital in 1916—the subject of "In the Village."

For the rest of her life, Bishop traveled: in Canada, in Europe, in North and South America. She formed friendships with many writers: Robert Lowell, Octavio Paz, and, most influentially, Marianne Moore, who read drafts of many of her poems and offered suggestions. In 1951, Bishop began a trip around South America, but during a stop in Brazil she suffered an allergic reaction to some food she had eaten and became ill. After recovery, she remained in Brazil for almost twenty years. During the last decade of her life, she continued to travel and to spend time in Latin America, but she settled in the United States, teaching frequently at Harvard, until her death in 1979.

In her early poem "The Map," Bishop writes that "More delicate than the historians' are the map-makers' colors." Her best poetry, although only indirectly autobiographical, is built from those mapmakers' colors. Nova Scotian and New England seascapes and Brazilian and Parisian landscapes become the geography of her poetry. At the same time, her own lack of permanent roots and her sense of herself as an observer suggest the lack of social relationships one feels in Bishop's poetry, for it is a poetry of observation, not of interaction, of people as outcasts, exiles, and onlookers, not as social beings. The relationships that count are with the land and sea, with primal elements, with the geography of Bishop's world.

Analysis

In Elizabeth Bishop's poem "Sandpiper," the title bird runs along the shore, ignoring the sea that roars on his left and the beach that "hisses" on his right, disregarding the interrupting sheets of water that wash across his toes, sucking the sand back to sea. His attention is focused. He is watching the sand between his toes; "a student of Blake," he attempts to see the world in each of those grains. The poet is ironic about the bird's obsessions: he is "finical"; in looking at these details he ignores the great sweeps of sea and land on either side of him. For every time the world is clear, there is another when it is a mist. The poet seems to chide the bird in his darting search for "something, something, something," but then in the last two lines of the poem the irony subsides; as Bishop carefully enumerates the varied and beautiful colors of the grains of sand, she joins the bird in his attentiveness. The reward, the something one can hope to find, lies simply in the rich and multivalent beauty of what one sees. It is not the reward of certainty or conviction, but of discovery that comes through focused attention.

The irony in the poem is self-mocking, for the bird is a metaphor for Bishop, its vision like her own, its situation that of many of her poetic personae. "Sandpiper" may call to mind such Robert Frost poems as "Neither Out Far Nor In Deep" or "For Once, Then, Something," with their perplexity about inward and outward vision and man's attempt to fix his sight on something, to create surety out of his surroundings. It may also suggest such other Bishop poems as "Cape Breton," where the birds turn their backs to the mainland, sometimes falling off the cliffs onto rocks below. Bishop does share with Frost his absorption with nature and its ambiguities, the ironic tone, and the tight poetic form that masks the "controlled panic" that the sandpiper-poet feels. Frost, however, is in a darker line of American writers: his emphasis is on the transitoriness of the vision, the shallowness of the sea into which one gazes, the ease with which even the most fleeting vision is erased. For Frost's poet-bird, "The Oven Bird," the nature he observes in midsummer is already ninety percent diminished. Bishop rather prefers the triumph of one's seeing at all. In her well-known poem "The Fish," when the persona finally looks into the eyes of the fish she has caught—eyes, the poet notes, larger, but "shallower" than her own—the fish's eyes return the stare. The persona, herself now caught, rapt, stares and stares until "victory fill[s] up" the boat, and all the world becomes "rainbow, rainbow, rainbow." Like the rainbow of colors that the sandpiper discovers, the poet here discovers beauty; the victory is the triumph of vision.

Like the sandpiper, then, Bishop is an obsessive observer. As a poet, her greatest strength is her pictorial accuracy. Whether her subject is as familiar as a fish, a rooster, or a filling station, or as strange as a Brazilian interior or a moose in the headlights of a bus, she enables the reader to see. The world for the sandpiper is sometimes "minute and vast and clear," and because Bishop observes the details so lucidly, her vision becomes truly vast. She is, like Frost, a synecdochist; for her, the particulars entail the whole. Nature is the matter of Bishop's art; to make her readers see, to enable them to read the world around them is her purpose. In "Seascape," what the poet finds in nature, its potential richness, is already like "a cartoon by Raphael for a tapestry for a Pope." All that Bishop must accomplish, then, as she writes in "The Fish," is simply "the tipping/ of an object toward the light."

Although the world for the sandpiper is sometimes clear, it is also sometimes a mist, and Bishop describes a more clouded vision as well. She translated a poem by Paz, "Objects and Apparitions," that might indicate the fuller matter of her own work; the objects are those details, the grains of sand that reveal the world once they are tipped toward the light. The apparitions occur when one sees the world through the mist and when one turns vision inward, as in the world of dreams. Here, too, the goal is bringing clarity to the vision— and the vision to clarity. As Bishop writes in "The Weed," about drops of dew that fall from a weed onto a dreamer's face, "each drop contained a light,/ a small, illuminated scene."

Objects and apparitions, mist and vision, land and sea, history and geography, travel and home, ascent and fall, dawn and night—these oppositions supply the tension in Bishop's poetry. The tensions are never resolved by giving way; in Bishop's world, one is a reflection of the other, and "reflection" becomes a frequent pun: that of a mirror and that of thought. Similarly, inspection, introspection, and insight suggest her doubled vision. In "Paris, 7 a.m.," looking down into the courtyard of a Paris house, the poet writes, "It is like introspection/ to stare inside," and there is again the double meaning of looking inside the court and inside oneself.

No verbs are more prevalent or important in Bishop's poetry than those of sight: look, watch, see, stare, she admonishes the reader. From "The Imaginary Iceberg," near the beginning of her first book, which compares an iceberg to the soul, both "self-made from elements least visible," and which insists that icebergs "behoove" the soul "to see them so," to "Objects and Apparitions" near the end of her last book, in which the poet suggests that in Joseph Cornell's art "my words became visible," one must first of all see; and the end of all art, plastic and verbal, is to make that which is invisible— too familiar to be noticed, too small to be important, too strange to be comprehended—visible. In "The Man-Moth," the normal human being of the first stanza cannot even see the moon, but after the man-moth comes above ground and climbs a skyscraper, trying to climb out through the moon, which he thinks is a hole in the sky, he falls back and returns to life below ground, riding the subway backward through his memories and dreams. The poet addresses the readers, cautioning them to examine the man-moth's eye, from which a tear falls. If the "you" is not paying attention, the man-moth will swallow his tear and his most valuable possession will be lost, but "if you watch," he will give it up, cool and pure, and the fruit of his vision will be shared.

To see the world afresh, even as briefly as does the man-moth, to gain that bitter tear of knowledge, one must, according to Bishop, change perspectives. In *Questions of Travel*, people hurry to the southern hemisphere "to see the sun the other way around." In "Love Lies Sleeping," the head of one sleeper has fallen over the edge of the bed, so that to his eyes the world is "inverted and distorted." Then the poet reconsiders: "distorted and revealed," for the hope is that now the sleeper sees, although a last line suggests that such sight is no certainty. When one lies down, Bishop writes in "Sleeping Standing Up," the world turns ninety degrees and the new perspective brings "recumbent" thoughts to mind and vision. The equally ambiguous title, however, implies either that thoughts are already available when one is upright or, less positively, that one may remain unattentive while erect. The world is also inverted in "Insomnia," where the moon stares at itself in a mirror. In Bishop's lovely, playful poem "The Gentleman of Shalott," the title character thinks himself only half, his other symmetrical half a reflection, an imagined mirror down his center. His state is precarious, for if the mirror should slip, the symmetry would be destroyed, and yet he finds the uncertainty "exhilarating" and thrives on the sense of "re-adjustment."

The changing of perspectives that permits sight is the theme of Bishop's "Over 2000 Illustrations and a Complete Concordance." The poet is looking at the illustrations in a gazetteer, comparing the engraved and serious pictures in the book with her remembered travels. In the first section of the poem, the poet lists the illustrations, the familiar, even tired Seven Wonders of the World, moving away from the objects pictured to details of the renderings, until finally the "eye drops" away from the real illustrations which spread out and dissolve into a series of reflections on past travels. These too begin with the familiar: with Canada and the sound of goats, through Rome, to Mexico, to Marrakech. Then, finally, she goes to a holy grave, which, rather than reassuring the viewer, frightens her, as an amused Arab looks on. Abruptly, the poet is back in the world of books, but this time her vision is on the Bible, where everything is "connected by 'and' and 'and.'" She opens the book, feeling the gilt of the edges flake off on her fingertips, and then asks, "Why couldn't we have seen/ this old Nativity while we were at it?" The colloquial last words comprise a casual pun, implying physical presence or accidental benefit. The next four lines describe the nativity scene, but while the details are familiar enough, Bishop's language defamiliarizes them. The poet ends with the statement that had she been there she would have "looked and looked our infant sight away"—another pun rich with possibilities. Is it that she would have looked repeatedly, so that the scene would have yielded meaning and she could have left satisfied? Do the lines mean to look away, as if the fire that breaks in the vision is too strong for human sight? The gazetteer into which the poet first looked, that record of human travels, has given way to scripture; physical pictures have given way to reflected visions and reflections, which, like the imaginary iceberg, behoove the soul to see.

Bishop participates in the traditional New England notion that nature is a gazetteer, a geography, a book to be read. In her poem "The Riverman," the speaker gets up in the night—night and dawn, two times of uncertain light, are favorite times in Bishop's poetic world—called by a river spirit, though at first the dolphin-spirit is only "glimpsed." The speaker follows and wades into the river where a door opens. Smoke rises like mist, and another spirit speaks in a language the narrator does not know but understands "like a dog/ although I can't speak it yet." Every night he goes back to the river, to study its language. He needs a "virgin mirror," a fresh way of seeing, but all he finds are spoiled. "Look," he says significantly, "it stands to reason" that everything one needs can be obtained from the river, which draws from the land "the remedy." The image of rivers and seas drawing, sucking the land persists in Bishop's poetry. The unknown that her poems scrutinize draws the known into it. The river sucks the earth "like a child," and the riverman, like the poet, must study the earth and the river to read them and find the remedy of sight.

Not only do the spirits of nature speak, but so too for Bishop does art itself. Her poetry is pictorial not only in the sense of giving vivid descriptions of natural phenomena, but also in its use of artificial objects to reflect on the self-referential aspect of art. Nature is like art, the seascape a "cartoon," but the arts are like one another as well. Bishop is firmly in the *ut pictura poesis* tradition—as is a painting, so a poem—and in the narrower *ekphrastic* tradition: art, like nature, speaks. In "Large Bad Picture," the picture is an uncle's painting, and after five stanzas describing the artist's attempt to be important by drawing everything oversized—miles of cliffs hundreds of feet high, hundreds of birds—the painting, at least in the narrator's mind, becomes audible, and she can hear the birds crying. In the much later "Poem," Bishop looks at another but much smaller painting by the same uncle (a sketch for a larger one? she asks), and this time the painting speaks to her memory. Examining the brushstrokes in a detached and slightly contemptuous manner, she suddenly exclaims, "Heavens, I recognize the place, I know it!" The voice of her mother enters, and then she concludes, "Our visions coincided"; life and memory have merged in this painting as in this poem: "how touching in detail/ —the little that we get for free."

Most explicitly in "The Monument," she addresses someone, asking her auditor to "see the monument." The listener is confused: the assemblage of boxes, turned catty-corner one upon the other, the thin poles hanging out at the top, the wooden background of sea made from board and sky made from other boards: "Why do they make no sound? . . . What is that?" The narrator responds with "It is the monument," but the other is not convinced that it is truly art. The voice of the poet again answers, insisting that the monument be seen as "artifact of wood" which "holds together better than sea or cloud or sand could." Acknowledging the limitations, the crudeness of it, the questions it cannot answer, she continues that it shelters "what is within"—presenting the familiar ambiguity: within the monument or within the viewer? Sculpture or poem, monument or painting, says the poet, all are of wood; that is, all are artifacts made from nature, artifacts that hold together. She concludes, "Watch it closely."

Thus, for Bishop, shifting perspectives to watch the natural landscape (what she quotes Sir Kenneth Clark as calling "tapestried landscape") and the internal landscape of dream and recollection are both the matter and the manner of art, of all arts, which hold the world together while one's attention is focused. The struggle is to see; the victory is in so seeing.

Yet Bishop's poetry is not unequivocally optimistic or affirmative. There are finally more ambiguities than certainties, and—like her double-edged puns—questions, rhetorical and conversational, are at the heart of these poems. Bishop's ambiguity is not that of unresolved layers of meaning in the poetry, but in the unresolvable nature of the world she tests. "Which is which?" she asks about memory and life in "Poem." "What has he done?" the poet asks of a chastised dog in the last poem of *Geography III*. "Can countries pick their colors?" she asks in "The Map." *Questions of Travel* begins with a poem questioning whether this new country, Brazil, will yield "complete comprehension"; it is followed by another poem which asks whether the poet should not have stayed at home: "Must we dream our dreams/ and have them, too?" Bishop poses more questions than she answers. Indeed, at the end of "Faustina," Faustina is poised above the dying woman she has cared for, facing the final questions of the meaning that death gives to life: freedom or nightmare, it begins, but the question becomes "proliferative," and the poet says that "There is no way of telling./ The eyes say only either."

Knowledge, like the sea, like tears, is salty and bitter, and even answering the questions, achieving a measure of knowledge, is no guarantee of permanence. Language, like music, drifts out of hearing. In "View of the Capitol from the Library of Congress," even the music of a brass band "doesn't quite come through." The morning breaks in "Anaphora" with so much music that it seems meant for an "ineffable creature." When he appears, however, he is merely human, a tired victim of his humanity, even at dawn. Yet, even though knowledge for Bishop is bitter, is fleeting, though the world is often inscrutable or inexplicable, hers is finally a poetry of hope. Even "Anaphora" moves from morning to night, though from fatigue to a punning "endless assent."

Bishop's poetry is often controlled by elaborate formal patterns of sight and sound. She makes masterful use of such forms as the sestina and villanelle, avoiding the appearance of mere exercise by the naturalness and wit of the repetitions and the depth of the scene. In "The Burglar of Babylon," she adopts the ballad form to tell the story of a victim of poverty who is destroyed by his society and of those "observers" who watch through binoculars without ever seeing the drama that is unfolding. Her favorite sound devices are alliteration and consonance. In "The Map," for example, the first four lines include "shadowed," "shadows," "shallows," "showing"; "edges" rhymes with "ledges," "water" alliterates with "weeds." The repetition of sounds not only suggests the patterning that the poet finds in the map, but also the slipperiness of sounds in "shadows"/"shallows" indicates the ease with which one vision of reality gives place to another. The fifth line begins with another question: "Does the land lean down to lift the sea," the repeated sound changing to a glide. "Along the fine tan sandy shelf/ is the land tugging at the sea from under?" repeats the patterning of questions and the *sh* and *l* alliteration, but the internal rhyme of "tan" and "sandy," so close that it momentarily disrupts the rhythm and the plosive alliteration of "tan" and "tugging," implies more strain.

Being at the same time a pictorialist, Bishop depends heavily on images. Again in "The Map," Norway is a hare that "runs south in agitation." The peninsulas "take the water between thumb and finger/ like women feeling for the smoothness of yard-goods." The reader is brought up short by the aptness of these images, the familiar invigorated. On the map, Labrador is yellow, "where the moony Eskimo/ has oiled it." In the late poem "In the Waiting Room," a young Elizabeth sits in a dentist's waiting room, reading through a *National Geographic*, looking at pictures of the scenes from around the world. The experience causes the young girl to ask who she is, what is her identity and her similarity, not only with those strange people in the magazine but also with the strangers there in the room with her, and with her Aunt Consuela whose scream she hears from the inner room. Bishop's poetry is like the pictures in that magazine; its images offer another geography, so that readers question again their own identity.

This sense of seeing oneself in others, of doubled vision and reflected identities, leads to another of Bishop's favorite devices, the conceit. In "Wading at Wellfleet," the waves of the sea, glittering and knifelike, are like the wheels of Assyrian chariots with their sharp knives affixed, attacking warriors and waders alike. In "The Imaginary Iceberg," the iceberg is first an actor, then a jewel, and finally the soul, the shifting of elaborated conceits duplicating the ambiguous nature of the iceberg. The roads that lead to the city in "From the Country to the City" are stripes on a harlequin's tights, and the poem a conceit with the city the clown's head and heart, its neon lights beckoning the traveler. Dreams are armored tanks in "Sleeping Standing Up," letting one do "many a dangerous thing," protected. In the late prose piece "12 O'Clock News," each item on a desk becomes something else: the gooseneck lamp, a moon; the typewriter eraser, a unicyclist with bristly hair; the ashtray, a graveyard full of twisted bodies of soldiers.

Formal control, a gently ironic but appreciative tone, a keen eye—these are hallmarks of Bishop's poetry. They reveal as well her limitation as a poet: a deficiency of passion. The poetry is so carefully controlled, the patterns so tight, the reality tested so shifting, and the testing so detached, that intensity of feeling is minimized. Bishop, in "Objects and Apparitions," quotes Edgar Degas, "'One has to commit a painting . . . the way one commits a crime.'" As Richard Wilbur, the writer whom she most resembles, has pointed out, Degas loved grace and energy, strain coupled with beauty. Strain is absent in Bishop's work.

Although there are wonderful character sketches among her poems, the poetry seems curiously underpopulated. "Manuelzinho" is a beautiful portrait of a character whose account books have turned to dream books, an infuriating sort whose numbers, the decimals omitted, run slantwise across the page. "Crusoe in England" describes a man suddenly removed from the place that made him reexamine his existence. These are people, but observers and outsiders, themselves observed. The Unbeliever sleeps alone at the top of a mast, his only companions a cloud and a gull. The Burglar of Babylon flees a society that kills him. Cootchie is dead, as is Arthur in "First Death in Nova Scotia," and Faustina tends the dying. Crusoe is without his Friday, and in "Sestina," although a grandmother jokes with a child, it is silence that one hears, absence that is present. There is little love in Bishop's poetry. It is true that at the end of "Manuelzinho," the narrator confesses that she loves her maddening tenant "all I can,/ I think. Or do I?" It is true that at the end of "Filling Station," the grubby, but "comfy" design of the family-owned station suggests that "Somebody loves us all," but this love is detached and observed, not felt. Even in "Four Poems," the most acutely personal of Bishop's poems and the only ones about romantic love, the subject is lost love, the conversation internal. "Love should be put into action!" screams a hermit at the end of "Chemin de Fer," but his only answer is an echo.

History, writes Bishop in "Objects and Apparitions," is the opposite of art, for history creates ruins, while the artist, out of ruins, out of "minimal, incoherent fragments," simply creates. Bishop's poetry is a collection of objects and apparitions, of scenes viewed and imagined, made for the moment into a coherent whole. The imaginary iceberg in the poem of that name is a part of a scene "a sailor'd give his eyes for," and Bishop asks that surrender of her readers. Her poetry, like the iceberg, behooves the soul to see. Inner and outer realities are in her poetry made visible, made one.

Howard Faulkner

Other major works

SHORT FICTION: "In the Village," in *Questions of Travel*, 1965.
NONFICTION: *The Diary of "Helena Morley,"* 1957 (translation); *Brazil*, 1962.
MISCELLANEOUS: *The Collected Prose*, 1984.

Bibliography

Bloom, Harold. *Elizabeth Bishop: Modern Critical Views*. New York: Chelsea House, 1985. Bloom has gathered fifteen previously published articles on separate poems and on Bishop's poetry as a whole, as well as a new article, "At Home With Loss" by Joanne Feit Diehl, on Bishop's relationship to the American Transcendentalists. "The Armadillo," "Roosters," "In the Waiting Room" are some of the poems treated separately. A chronology and a bibliography complete this useful collection of criticism from the 1970's and early 1980's.

Kalstone, David. *Becoming a Poet: Elizabeth Bishop with Marianne Moore and Robert Lowell*. New York: Farrar, Straus & Giroux, 1989. In a 1977 work, *Five Temperaments*, Kalstone wrote of Bishop and other poets. This book, completed after Kalstone's death, keeps Bishop at the center with many quotations from her correspondence with Marianne Moore (the first long section) and Robert Lowell (the second long section). Includes a preface by Robert Hemenway, an afterword by James Merrill, notes, and an index.

Mullen, Richard. "Elizabeth Bishop's Surrealist Inheritance." *American Literature: A Journal of Literary History, Criticism, and Bibliography* 54 (1982). The liberating inheritance of Surrealist poetry allowed Bishop to "explore the workings of the unconscious and the interplay between conscious perception and dream." After a brief description of Surrealist poetics, Mullen shows how Bishop differs in holding on to the form and reality of the observed object while also expressing its strangeness or dreamlike quality. Mullen uses Bishop's prose poems as examples of dreamscape and the natural world brought together.

Parker, Robert Dale. *The Unbeliever: The Poetry of Elizabeth Bishop*. Urbana: University of Illinois Press, 1988. Parker has the advantage of a longer view of Bishop's writings and criticism. His wide grasp of her life and work leads him to shape her development into three stages: poems of wish and expectation, resignation into poems of place, and finally, as is natural with maturity, poems of retrospection. He focuses on the major poems in each area, with a last chapter on the later poems, some of which, such as "The Moose" had been in her mind for twenty years. Includes particularly fine notes, and an index.

Schwartz, Lloyd, and Sybil P. Estess. *Elizabeth Bishop and Her Art*. Ann Arbor: University of Michigan Press, 1983. This indispensable source gathers critical articles from many admirers, as well as interviews, introductions at poetry readings, explications of specific poems, and a bibliography (1933-1981). Some of Bishop's journal passages demonstrate why she is a preeminent American poet—her realism, common sense, lack of self-pity over losses—as James Merrill calls her "our greatest national treasure."

Stevenson, Anne. *Elizabeth Bishop*. New York: Twayne, 1966. Although outdated, this important first biography places Bishop in her time as a modernist in relation to other twentieth century arts. It emphasizes her technical skills, moral preoccupations, and her acceptance of the terms of contemporary philosophy and science—uncertainty and ambiguity. Supplemented by notes and an index.

Travisano, Thomas. *Elizabeth Bishop: Her Artistic Development*. Charlottesville: University Press of Virginia, 1988. This comprehensive study of Bishop's career traces the evolution of her prose and poetry through three phases. The first, "Prison," uses enclosure as its metaphor; the second, "Travel," breaks through into engagement with people and places; and the third, "History," reconciles her life of loss and displacement to a calm, mature mood of courage and humor. Complemented by a chronology, a bibliography, and an index.

PAUL BLACKBURN

Born: St. Albans, Vermont; November 24, 1926
Died: Cortland, New York; September 13, 1971

Principal poetry

Proensa, 1953 (translation); *The Dissolving Fabric*, 1955; *Brooklyn-Manhattan Transit: A Bouquet for Flatbush*, 1960; *The Nets*, 1961; *Poem of the Cid*, 1966 (translation); *16 Sloppy Haiku and a Lyric for Robert Reardon*, 1966; *Sing-Song*, 1966; *The Reardon Poems*, 1967; *The Cities*, 1967; *In. On. Or About the Premises: Being a Small Book of Poems*, 1968; *Hunk of Skin*, 1968 (translation); *Two New Poems*, 1969; *Three Dreams and an Old Poem*, 1970; *Gin: Four Journal Pieces*, 1970; *The Assassination of President McKinley*, 1970; *The Journals: Blue Mounds Entries*, 1971; *Early Selected Y Mas: Poems 1949-1966*, 1972; *The Journals*, 1975 (Robert Kelly, editor); *Halfway Down the Coast: Poems and Snapshots*, 1975; *Guillem De Poitu: His Eleven Extant Poems*, 1976 (translation); *By Ear*, 1978; *Lorca/Blackburn: Poems of Federico García Lorca Chosen and Translated by Paul Blackburn*, 1979; *Against the Silences*, 1980; *The Selection of Heaven*, 1980; *The Collected Poems of Paul Blackburn*, 1985.

Other literary forms

Paul Blackburn was an ambitious translator, not only of such modern Spanish-language writers as Federico García Lorca, Julio Cortázar, and Octavio Paz, but also of the troubadours, who had some influence on his own verse. Although his work in the Provençal poets was primarily finished by the late 1950's, Blackburn continued to revise his translations for the rest of his life. The substantial manuscript was eventually edited by his friend, the scholar of medieval literature George Economou, and published posthumously as *Proensa: An Anthology of Troubadour Poetry* (1978).

Achievements

Appreciated as a translator, Blackburn limited his reputation as a poet during his lifetime by publishing only a small portion of his poetry and then in very limited editions. His position in literary history can be appreciated through the inevitable comparison with Frank O'Hara. Both poets were born, and graduated from college, in the same years; both were celebrators of the city, primarily New York, in verse that revealed their awareness of centuries of literary history at the same time that they were pursuing some of the more radical modernist innovations in poetic structure and idiom; and both bodies of work reveal warm, generous, witty sensibilities; unfortunately, both poets also died young. Blackburn and O'Hara were, in fact, simultaneously experimenting with the open-form poem, the poem that strives to convey the immediacy of life by presenting the poet's situation, observations, and responses as directly and precisely as possible, according to the chronology of the events themselves as they happened, thus giving the illusion of both inclusiveness and inconclusiveness. The mediating consciousness that shapes and judges experience, that yields a crafted, discursive, linearly logical development of images progressing to a closure that both evolves from and unifies them, is seemingly denied. O'Hara's affinities, however, are with the French: the postsymbolists Pierre Reverdy and Guillaume Apollinaire, and the surrealists; consequently, his "lunch poems" retain a sense of a consciousness willing and directing, a gesture akin to that of the analogical subconscious managing the flow of his "automatic" texts. Blackburn, on the other hand, places the reader almost completely in reality, in the experience itself, perhaps because he is working within the more objectivist American tradition.

Blackburn readily acknowledged that Ezra Pound had the most influence upon his work, along with William Carlos Williams, whom he first encountered through the poetry of Robert Creeley. Charles Olson's essay "Projective Verse" (1950) provided added incentive, as did the poetry of Louis Zukofsky. Blackburn worked in the modernist poetic technique pioneered by Pound and Williams, and E. E. Cummings and T. S. Eliot as well, and defined in 1945 by Joseph Frank in a seminal essay as "spatial form." This technique complements a nondiscursive content by replacing the linear conventions of typographically recorded language, appropriate to discursive content, with a two-dimensional, spatially oriented presentation. The unconventional spacing of words or phrases can establish rhythm by indicating length of pause between verbal elements, and calculated rather than conventional line endings can provide emphasis whenever strategically desirable. Blackburn consistently avails himself of both of these features of spatial form, as did his predecessors. His unique contribution to modernist poetics, however, is to utilize juxtaposition, the primary aspect of spatial form that yields thematic meaning, in the spontaneous, open-form poem of immediate experience to convey definite, if subtle, complex meanings within verse that appears simply to be recording random observations of the ongoing flow of life. The placing of material in different areas on the page according to subject does not merely isolate particular experiences, preserving their phenomenal integrity, but also facilitates a more profound kind of relationship between them. When Blackburn is at his best, he is shrewdly choosing for a given poem inherently related experiences that comment upon one another, yet describing them with complete fidelity to their objective reality and presenting them nonchalantly, extemporaneously, as if they are insignificant coincidences. In this way, Blackburn creates in his poems a living world of joyous activity and sensuous appearance that is nevertheless intrinsically meaningful.

Blackburn was aware, however, that a poem is not merely a written, visual product, but also a spoken, aural event. What made Blackburn the complete poet, the virtuoso, was the other great influence on his poetic career besides

Pound: the troubadours. Music in poetry was for Blackburn at once formal, the orchestration of material for thematic and emotional impact, and aural, the rhythm and sound of the language itself. To be sure, Blackburn, like his contemporaries, sought American speech rhythms and conversational diction, an aesthetic inaugurated by Walt Whitman. Blackburn had a fine ear for colloquialisms and slang, but that ear was also trained by Provençal. Consequently, the play of assonance, consonance, internal rhyme, off-rhyme, and rhythmic nuance inspired by troubadour lyric can be found at times alternating, or even blending, with modern idiom, for atmosphere, emphasis, or wit. Blackburn's range of diction, in fact, enables him to enliven his poetry with irony and humor, formal diction and slang clashing unexpectedly. Despite the minimalist tendencies of many of his contemporaries to strip poetry of all rhetorical beauty, Blackburn found ways to preserve the varied aural richness of language.

The troubadours may also be responsible, along with Blackburn's avowed Mediterranean sensibility, for the one quality of his poetry that is very rare in English verse: the comfortable ease, the relaxed poise, with which he treats the erotic. Cummings was, of course, always aware of the shock that he was creating with his references to sexual love. John Donne and even Robert Herrick are self-conscious by comparison. One would have to go back to Geoffrey Chaucer for a similar natural acceptance of sensuality. Certainly Blackburn's stature as an American poet is enhanced, not diminished, by such a foreign influence as Provençal poetry. A melting-pot culture remains vital by renewing component cultures latent in its native tradition, a program that Pound, as well as Eliot, followed. As Blackburn deliberately takes his place in the tradition of poetry from the Middle Ages on through his work with the troubadours, so he openly acknowledges a similar tradition of modern poetry by occasionally parodying or quoting poets of the immediate past, including Pound, Williams, Eliot, Robert Frost, Walt Whitman, William Butler Yeats, and Gerard Manley Hopkins.

This inclusive view of the modern poetic tradition is indicative of the richness of Blackburn's own poetry: its technical innovations with spatial form, sound and rhythm, and diction; its thematic and emotional range; and its ability to perceive, in the immediate and the personal, the general and the universal. Blackburn's verse is always grounded in private experience, yet it expresses the common concerns of humanity. He is able to structure the immediate without violating it, whereas others of his generation were only able, or simply content, to record. Thus, poetry for him is never therapy through confession, or a notebook of fragments from his reading, or a self-absorbed diary. When one speaks of significant postwar poets, one cannot with any justice mention any one of his contemporaries, no matter how well-respected at the present time, without mentioning Blackburn's name in the same breath.

Biography

Paul Blackburn was the son of the poet Frances Frost. Having been reared in Vermont, New Hampshire, South Carolina, and New York City, he attended New York University and the University of Wisconsin, where he received a B.A. degree in 1950. While at Wisconsin, Blackburn began corresponding with Ezra Pound, whose poetry he admired, and then occasionally visited Pound in St. Elizabeths Hospital, Washington, D.C. At Pound's suggestion, Blackburn began writing to Robert Creeley, who eventually published his poems in the *Black Mountain Review* and put him in touch with Cid Corman, who, in turn, published Blackburn's poems in *Origin* (a quarterly for the creative) and introduced him to Charles Olson, though Blackburn was never to study or teach at Black Mountain College. Pound also encouraged Blackburn's interest in the troubadours that began when he encountered Pound's own quotations and imitations of Provençal verse in *Personae* (1909) and the *Cantos* (1925-1972). In 1953 Blackburn published a small volume of translations through Creeley's Divers Press, the early *Proensa*, that earned him a Fulbright scholarship in 1954 to do research in Provençal poetry at the University of Toulouse in southern France, and he returned as *lecteur américain* the following year. He remained in Europe, principally in Málaga, Spain, and Bañalbufar, Mallorca, with Winifred McCarthy, whom he married in 1954, until 1957, when they returned to New York.

For the next ten years in New York City, in addition to writing and translating, Blackburn worked to establish a sense of community among the poets centered around St. Mark's Church in the Bowery. As well as offering help and encouragement, he organized and tape-recorded weekly poetry readings at the church. His efforts eventually led to the funded Poetry Project at St. Mark's in 1967. He also conducted a "Poet's Hour" on radio station WBAI. In 1963 he was divorced from his first wife and married Sara Golden; that marriage also ended in divorce in 1967, around the time that he was poet-in-residence at the Aspen Writers' Workshop in Colorado. That year also saw the appearance of his most widely circulated collection of poems, *The Cities*, published by Grove Press. Toward the end of 1967, he returned to Europe on a Guggenheim Fellowship, where he met Joan Miller, whom he married in 1968, and with whom he had a son. In September, 1970, he assumed a teaching position at the state college in Cortland, New York, where he died of cancer the following year.

Analysis

Because Paul Blackburn is a poet of immediate observation and spontaneous response, his poetry thrives upon particular places. His work, however, is not rooted in a specific geographical location that is transformed into a frame of mind, as is Frost's New England, or is elevated to a latter-day myth, as is Williams' Paterson. Blackburn's places are the environments in which he happens to be: a town plaza, a boat at sea, a wooded hill, a city street, a subway car, a tavern, a luncheonette, a kitchen, a bedroom. He often generates a poem by immersing himself in his surroundings until man and place are one, the identification stirring in him a particular thought or emotion, a combination of his mood and the suggestion of that particular rush of outside activity. Although his thematic preoccupations and technical goals remain fairly uniform throughout the course of his work, he does tend to prefer certain themes and to express certain emotions through certain techniques when he is living in European cities, and others when he is living in New York. Perhaps because he can see sheep grazing in the town square in Málaga or burros passing through Bañalbufar, when Blackburn is living in Europe he often considers the relationship between man and nature through such concepts as freedom, mutability, eternity, and religiosity; love is portrayed as sentiment. Perhaps because his mind is on the troubadours, living with his hands on their manuscripts to near to Provence, Blackburn's European poetry tends to be meditative and pensive; the sound play more melodious; the language more metaphorical. When he is living in New York, on the other hand, in the densely populated modern city, where concrete substitutes for grass, Blackburn focuses on interpersonal relations, including friendship, complicity, estrangement, and anonymity; love becomes erotic energy. In a city whose traffic rushes and whose subway rumbles and roars, Blackburn's poetry becomes more immediate and involved, conversational and witty; sound is orchestrated for dissonance; metaphor, if resorted to at all, is unexpected, shocking; but the occasional use of symbol is retained.

Blackburn is best read, then, chronologically, according to the place where he is living and writing. The dates given for the poems gathered in *Early Selected Y Mas*, which includes the small, early books of limited circulation, makes such a reading possible for most of the first half of his work. In the poetry written or set in Europe between 1954 and 1958, Blackburn explores man's existence as a creature both fundamentally a part of nature, with its physicality and sensuousness, and separate through his consciousness, will, and ephemerality. In "A Permanence," Blackburn uses the seven-star constellation "the bear" to present nature as an eternal force separate from man: the bear "is there/ even in the day, when we do not see him." Nevertheless, man cannot help responding to nature's perpetually changing life, being natural himself. The lovers in "The Hour," for example, are "hungering" not only for food but also for the first sign of spring after a long winter: they sit "listening to the warm gnawing in their stomach/ the warm wind/ through the blossoms blowing." These lines exemplify the rich grammatical ambiguity made possible by spatial form: the appetites for food and for seasonal renewal are associated not only by repetition of the adjective "warm" but also by the possibility that "wind" as well as "gnawing" can be the object of the preposition "to," modifying "listening." Separation from and unity with nature are confronted simultaneously in "Light." Initially, man and sea are only linguistically related through a simile; day moves inevitably into night, but an effort of the will is required for human action: "My thought drifts like the sea/ No grip between it and my act." By the end of the poem, however, the dark, drifting sea complements and then merges with the poet's gloomy mood. The assertion is metaphoric, but the poet's mind and his perceptual experience have indeed become one: "The sea flashes up in the night/ to touch and darken my sea."

From this contemplation of the relationship between man and nature a religious sense develops, as expressed in "Mestrović and the Trees." For Blackburn, a feeling for the divine is unavoidable: "You never get passed the wood" where "The beginnings of things are shown." Religion for him is a matter of origins, and this poem is Blackburn's own version of the cosmological argument. From man's own existence, which cannot be denied—"Yes we are"—he moves back to origins—"Our mother and father," and by implication, Adam and Eve—to their origin, in nature, through God: "So these trees stand there, our/ image, the god's image." The trees "stand there/ naked" just as man enters the world, his unity with nature now binding him also to the divine. By using the lowercase for God and preceding his name with the definite article, Blackburn indicates that his religion is natural rather than orthodox. Although Blackburn is certain of the existence of the divine, its nature remains an enigma. This mystery, essential to Blackburn's religious experience, is in itself sacred for him and not to be violated by forms and formulas that he considers to be ultimately human fabrications, at best mere approximations of the divine. In "How to Get Through Reality," Blackburn insists upon the separation, epistemological despite a metaphysical complicity, between the temporal and the divine, that is, "Those who work with us . . . who create us from our stone." An impenetrable glass wall separates the two realms, and he celebrates the divine only in the most general of ways, aesthetically: "Our beauty under glass is your reality, unreachable/ sliding our gift to you." The insistence upon the unintelligibility of the divine is portrayed grammatically with a sentence that ends incompletely just at the point God is to be named: "Beauty is the daily renewal in the eyes of." Feeling, the basis of his perception of beauty, provides his only sense of the divine: "One could kick the glass out, no?/ No./ Pass through." Breaking the glass, transcending the temporal, for direct communication with and precise knowledge of the supernatural is impossible; only intimations, illuminations, can pass through the transparency of the glass. A similar warning is sounded in "Suspension," where the poet's vision of the moon is obscured by tree branches: "—Shall I climb up and get it down?/ —No. Leave it alone."

As a consequence, Blackburn's attitude toward orthodox religious forms—language, ceremony, observance—is ambivalent. "Ritual I" presents a religious "Procession," as it moves "with candles" from the church through the various streets of the Spanish town to the chant of "Ave Maria." Because the "'fiesta'" does not "'celebrate,'" but rather "'reenacts'" the "'event,'" *"time emerges."* Blackburn is observing that the religious ritual is "a timeless gesture" because its origin cannot be traced or dated, because it has been perpetuated throughout the course of history, and because it creates anew the event each time it is performed. Through this persistence of religion, this infinite renewal, this timelessness, human time is made possible: the participants too are renewed along with the ritual. Blackburn continues, however, to enlarge the concept of ritual to encompass secular as well as religious life. Midway through the poem a "lady tourist/ . . . joined the procession"; she appeared an "anomaly": "Instead of a rosary, carried/ a white pocketbook." After this secular irregularity in the religious ceremony, Blackburn immediately introduces what appear to be irregularities of subject in a poem describing a sacred ritual: he tells us that he rises everyday "in the dawn light"; he eats "Meat every Thursday/ when the calf/ is killed"; he gets "Mail from the bus at 4:30/ fresh milk at 5." What Blackburn is implying through these juxtapositions is that our everyday lives are composed of rituals that renew life on a daily basis, that make life itself possible. The "german anthropologist," then, "her poor self at the end of the line," is really not at a terminal point; for life, like this yearly ritual, is a perpetual process of renewal, a series of rebirths: "End of a timeless act of the peoples of the earth," hardly an end at all.

After Blackburn's return to New York in 1957, the religious and the secular merge for him to the point where his rituals consist entirely of various activities repeated on a daily basis. Religion becomes the celebration of life, since the divine is immanent in the world itself. In "Ritual IV," for example, Blackburn juxtaposes a description of plants growing in his kitchen with a reenactment of a Saturday morning breakfast with his wife, in order to express the unity of all living things. "You sit here smiling at/ me and the young plants," as the "beams" of sunlight reveal the "dust" that "float[s]" from the plants to them. The poet concludes: "Everything/ grows,/ and rests." Having united the sacred and profane to such a degree, Blackburn occasionally grows impatient with orthodox ceremony. In "Lines, Trees, and Words," walking through a park and overhearing children singing a hymn off-key, a friend observes how they are mutilating "it." Blackburn, however, willfully misunderstands the referent of the pronoun to be the divine and replies, "Don't we all." Any verbal attempt to embody the spiritual will result in such travesty: "Give the child words, give him/ words, he will use them." Characteristically, the poem ends with the preferred indefinite, natural, religious note: "How the trees hang down from the sky." At times, Blackburn will even imply that the more Puritanical strain in orthodox religion might very well obstruct his and others' more spontaneous celebration of the divine through joyous living, as in "Ash Wednesday, 1965."

Most of the poetry that Blackburn wrote between 1958 and 1967 had New York City for its setting and focused more intimately on human psychology: the ways in which people relate to one another, how they react to the world in which they find themselves, and how they regard their own personalities and bodies. In Blackburn's love poems of this period, two symbols, fishing nets and the sea, continually recur, helping him to express his vision of love as unavoidable and overwhelming, as the persistent tide of the sea, and therefore frightening, threatening, as the confining fishing net, at first unnoticed. Love for Blackburn is a force that one can resist only for so long; then one gives in wholeheartedly, though with trepidation. "The Purse Seine" accumulates a number of aquatic images that express this ambivalence: what "gulls" "do that looks so beautiful, is/ hunt"; at once they are "crying freedom, crying carrion"; the eye of the gull, merging with that of his lover, "frightens," for both are the "beautiful killer"; "the net/ is tight," and then "The purse closes" and "we drown/ in sight of/ I love you and you love me." In "Park Poem," the poet reels from "the first shock of leaves their alliance with love"— the complicity of nature in romance. "How to Get Up Off It" is a contemporaneous poem that juxtaposes several random events ultimately related to the persistence of love in nature, and thus in human beings. The poet begins the poem by recalling a mountain climber's words: "'Am I ready for this mountain?'" As "they go up," so does the poet climb love's mountain, sitting with his second wife in front of the Public Library, next to a girl writing a letter to her boyfriend; they are passed by a couple holding hands who wave to them and then witness a mating dance: "The pigeons never seem to tire/ of the game," and neither do people, as the events recorded in the poem demonstrate.

Depending upon his mood, Blackburn can portray love as simply the drive of blind passion that results in a loss of freedom through its satisfaction. In such poems as "Call It the Net," for example, love is a "silken trap . . . the net of lust." In "The Sea and the Shadow," that "damned sea" of sexuality will drive him back to his lover despite his anger at her; the waves become the rhythm of the sexual act: "I will come into your belly and make it a sea rolling against me." At other times, however, sexual love will be a joyous occasion, as in "lower case poem": "of that spring tide i sing/ clutched to one another." At such times, as Blackburn explains in "The Net of Moon," the lovers have achieved a union of the physical and the spiritual, "a just balance be-/ tween the emotion and the motion of the wave on the bay," lust being transformed into love. What Blackburn finds most striking, in the end, is the inevitable nature of both sexuality and love. Upon seeing a pretty girl on the street in "The Tides," the poet exclaims: "Terrible indeed is the house of heaven in the mind." After recalling the act of love, "its flood/ its ebb," the poet can only conclude: "What the man must do/ what the woman must do."

Blackburn accepts, as a natural dimension of human relations, this constant attraction between men and women, which exists as much on the physical as on the emotional level. Rather than trying to resist or repress the erotic impulse, Blackburn celebrates it in a series of erotic poems unique in the language. Never vulgar, tawdry, or exhibitionistic, they involve a drama of emotion as well as of desire, for Blackburn portrays the woman as well as the man being caught in the erotic moment and enjoying it with equal relish. This mutual, if often covert, complicity results in a sense of the erotic as all-pervasive and joyous rather than predatory or compromising. These poems are usually contemporaneous with the events and feelings they describe and involve witty shifts of tone through incongruous diction, ranging from colloquial ("all very chummy") to tabloid cliché ("the hotbed of assignation") to scientific jargon ("hypotenuse," "trajectory"). Two of his best erotic poems appear in *Brooklyn-Manhattan Transit*, for the subway is one of the more likely places to afford the modern troubadour an opportunity to admire the feminine. In "The Once-Over," a pretty blond woman is being appreciated by the poet and the other riders of the car. According to the poet, however, she is deliberately inviting their admiration: she is "standing/ tho there are seats"; "Only a stolid young man . . . does not know he is being assaulted"; "She has us and we her." In "Clickety-Clack," Blackburn is reading out loud a blatantly erotic passage from one of Lawrence Ferlinghetti's poems on the subway car, much to the amusement (and arousal) of a young lady, despite her frown, as the negative prefix split by the line ending from the rest of its root word indicates: she "began to stare dis-/ approvingly and wiggle." "The Slogan" records the provocative stroll of a "wellknit blonde in a blue knit dress" past a group of utility workers, Blackburn describing her walk with terms borrowed from physics. "Hands" portrays a girl entering her room and going to open a window with her boyfriend in pursuit, "bringing/ one thing up, & another down." Even in "The Assassination of President McKinley," the opportunistic proprietor of the drapery shop is not the only one who enjoys "the last rite/ for the assassinated Mr. McKinley."

Blackburn's one long cycle of poems on love, published posthumously as *Against the Silences*, was written between 1963 and 1967, and deals with the dissolution of his second marriage. The cycle moves from uneasy marital contentment ("knowing we love one another/ sometime," "The Second Message"), to the beginning of estrangement ("the thought dissolves & only/ fact remains," "Slippers, Anyone?"), to argument resulting from a misunderstanding of the husband's deepest personal allegiances ("The Value"), to the wife's infidelity ("What Is It, Love?"), and finally to divorce ("Scenario for a Walk-On," in which the poet depicts the separation as the ending of a film). The sequence recalls George Meredith's *Modern Love* (1862), a series of fifty sixteen-line sonnets portraying the psychological dilemmas of an unhappy married couple through dramatic monologue or silent rumination, written the year after Meredith's divorce from his first wife. Because Blackburn's poems focus specifically on the intimate details of his own marriage, automatically recorded in the contemporaneous open-form poem of immediate experience, his cycle has somewhat greater emotional range and depth than Meredith's, which is a more conscious attempt to generalize from personal experience about the condition of romantic love in the modern world, as the title suggests.

In *Against the Silences*, the complexity of the beleaguered husband's feelings is captured in poems that often portray several conflicting emotions at once: confusion, frustration, pain, humiliation, anger, disgust, fear, loneliness. The subtle role that sexual passion assumes in the relationship is also treated. In the early "So Deep We Never Got," the poet wishes his wife to make love to him as a reassurance of her affection: resorting to a favorite symbol, he needs to be with her "chest-deep in the surf/ and those waves coming and coming." In "Monday, Monday," however, the husband uses an offer of sex in an attempt to keep his wife from meeting her lover, but the response remains the same throughout the poem: "away,/ her body pushed me away." In this sequence, Blackburn's idea of love as a net to which one deliberately surrenders oneself attains its most explicit statement: although staying with his wife was always an "act of will" ("The Second Message"), "reasons of choice" are "so obscure" that the process of choice can never ensure happiness: he can only "choose and fear and live it thru" ("Accident"). The result is equally ironic: the possessor of another in love becomes "possessed" by that very love ("The Price").

If Blackburn adds a new genre to English-language verse, or revives one long defunct, through his erotic poems, he contributes to an ongoing tradition with his elegies, which he composed throughout his career. In "The Mint Quality" (1961), the poet attempts to "Sing/ straight as I can" about the death of a vivacious young woman by first giving the details of her automobile accident in France and then presenting her monologue to her friends from the other side of death. The poem becomes ironic when Christiane assures them that *"next time"* she will *"wait til the middle of life/ know what you know/ just to understand."* The poem began with the poet, at middle age, professing his complete incomprehension of the cycle of life and death: "two friends' wives/ are near their term and large./ . . . One/ girl is dead. No choice."

The Reardon Poems is a sequence of seven poems written in memory of Blackburn's friend Robert Reardon: "Bluegrass" presents the unsuccessful operation to save his life; "The Writer" tells of Reardon's vocation—novelist; "The Husband" treats his relationship with his wife and presents her disorientation and loneliness; "16 Sloppy Haiku" are brief glimpses or thoughts of Reardon's last days of life; "The List" consists of Reardon's last rites, as specified by him before his death; and "St. Mark's-in-the-Bouwerie" is an elegy proper on death, its inexplicability amidst life ("When there's nothing anyone can do,/ reality/ comes on fast or slow"). "Seventeen Nights Later at

McSorley's" is the epilogue, employing recorded conversation with great thematic effect; Blackburn is speaking to Reardon's former roommate in the hospital:

> You won't see him again, sez I
> "No?"
> No. You're well again? Mazeltov.
> "No?"
> No.

Perhaps Blackburn's finest elegy is "December Journal: 1968," on the death of his third wife's father, in which practically all of his formal poetic resources come into play. The poem begins with the telephone call informing them of the death; moves through grief and tears to the wake and funeral in a passage in which breakfast and the Eucharist are superimposed; to a meditation on the mystery of life and death, creation and destruction, inspired by an open journal on alchemy lying before the poet; and finally to lovemaking and a renewal of domestic patterns ("'You have to get up and move the car.'/ I existed again, I/ was married to my wife!"). Inspired by his alchemical reading, the poet realizes that life mysteriously renews itself within materials that compose rock; that is, life dwells in and is sustained by essentially inanimate matter, a theme first heard in "How to Get Through Reality." This miracle, and the miracle of the living child in his wife's womb, has by the end of the poem put him at ease.

William Skaff

Other major works

SHORT FICTION: *End of the Game and Other Stories*, 1967 (translation); *Cronopios and Famas*, 1969 (translation); *The Treasure of the Muleteer and Other Spanish Tales*, 1974 (translation).

NONFICTION: "Das Kennerbuch," in *New Mexico Quarterly*, XXIII (Summer, 1953), pp. 215-219; "Writing for the Ear," in *Big Table*, IV (Spring, 1960), pp. 127-132; "The American Duende," in *Kulchur*, VII (Autumn, 1962), pp. 92-95; "The Grinding Down," in *Kulchur*, X (Summer, 1963), pp. 9-18; *Peire Vidal*, 1972 (translation).

ANTHOLOGY: *Proensa: An Anthology of Troubadour Poetry*, 1978.

Bibliography

Charters, Ann, ed. *Dictionary of Literary Biography.* Vol. 16 in *The Beats: Literary Bohemians in Postwar America.* Detroit: Gale Research, 1983. Gives a brief account of Blackburn's life, commenting on how he developed the musical quality in his poetry, considered one of his major strengths. Cites his proficiency in translating Provençal literature, observing that there is an important symbiosis between Blackburn's own poetry and his Provençal translations. Contains critical commentary on *The Dissolving Fabric, In. On. Or About the Premises*, and *The Cities*, among others. Praises the latter for its "diversity and mastery." Includes a useful list of secondary sources.

Malkoff, Karl. *Crowell's Handbook of Contemporary American Poetry*. New York: Thomas Y. Crowell, 1973. The entry on Blackburn lists him not only as a Black Mountain Poet but also as a Projectivist, although like most Projectivists, his poetry is individualistic. Mentions his long sojourns abroad and discusses two of his works, *The Cities* and *The Nets*. Other than some insightful comments about Projectivist poetry—for example, that there is no real distinction between the inner and outer world—there is little noteworthy criticism here.

Marowski, Daniel G., and Roger Matuz, eds. *Contemporary Literary Criticism*. Vol. 43. Detroit: Gale Research, 1987. Lists Blackburn as a noted translator, scholar, and poet, whose poetry combines structural experimentation with colloquial forms. This combination creates a "visual, aural, and psychological reading experience." Gathers together some fine reviews of Blackburn's work, in particular critical commentary of his most widely acclaimed work, *The Journals*. Also notes that since the posthumous publication of *The Collected Poems of Paul Blackburn*, his verse has attracted a wider audience and has undergone critical reevaluation.

Rosenthal, M. L. Review of *The Cities*, by Paul Blackburn. *Poetry* 114 (May, 1969): 129-130. Comments on Blackburn's love of American lingo and his emphasis on the quality of movement, both of which lend his poems qualities of "humor and sensuality." Appreciates Blackburn's focus on the process of the poet's involvement in the poem as a "disciplining subject of the poem, as well as its range in action."

Stephens, Michael. "Common Speech and Complex Forms." *The Nation* 223 (September 4, 1976): 189-190. Reviews *The Cities, The Journals*, and *Halfway Down the Coast*, which he considers a suitable introduction to Blackburn. Notes that the possibility of death that Blackburn explores in *Halfway* becomes the reality of dying in *The Journals*. Commends Blackburn for his ability to appreciate "overheard cadences in common speech," which he says is indicative of Blackburn's love of people.

WILLIAM BLAKE

Born: London, England; November 28, 1757
Died: London, England; August 12, 1827

Principal poetry

Poetical Sketches, 1783; *There Is No Natural Religion*, 1788; *All Religions Are One*, 1788; *Songs of Innocence*, 1789; *The Book of Thel*, 1789; *The Marriage of Heaven and Hell*, 1790; *The French Revolution* (written in 1791, published posthumously); *America: A Prophecy*, 1793; *Visions of the Daughters of Albion*, 1793; *Songs of Innocence and of Experience*, 1794; *Europe: A Prophecy*, 1794; *The [First] Book of Urizen*, 1794; *The Song of Los*, 1795; *The Book of Ahania*, 1795; *The Book of Los*, 1795; *Vala: Or, The Four Zoas* (written 1795-1804, published poshumously; best known as *The Four Zoas*); *Milton: A Poem*, 1804-1808; *Jerusalem: The Emanation of the Giant Albion*, 1804-1820; *The Poems of William Blake*, 1971.

Other literary forms

William Blake's prose includes *An Island in the Moon* (written c. 1784), *To the Public: Prospectus* (1793), *A Descriptive Catalogue* (1809), marginalia, and letters. It is almost a given with Blake scholarship and criticism that the interrelation of poetry and design is vital. David V. Erdman's *The Illuminated Blake* (1975) includes all of Blake's illuminated works, text, and design, with a plate-by-plate commentary.

Achievements

Blake's reputation during his lifetime was not a fraction of what it is today. He worked hard at his trade, that of engraving, but his style was not in fashion, and his commissions were few. His poverty and the laborious process of producing his own illuminated books for sale prevented him from producing more than two hundred copies of his own work in his lifetime. Even the *Songs of Innocence and of Experience*, which he sold sporadically throughout his career, remained virtually unnoticed by his contemporaries. What little reputation he had among his contemporaries was as an artist, ingenious but no doubt mad.

In 1863, Alexander Gilchrist's biography of Blake did much to establish Blake's reputation as an artist and a poet. The Yeats-Ellis edition of Blake (1893) further enhanced his fame, not as a forgotten painter and poet, but as a purveyor of esoteric lore. Accurate transcription of Blake's texts began only in the twentieth century with the work of Geoffrey Keynes. Modern critical work was pioneered by S. Foster Damon in 1924, but it was not until Northrop Frye's *Fearful Symmetry* in 1947 that Blake's work was treated as a comprehensible, symmetrical whole.

A poet-artist who imaginatively remolds his own age and its traditions and then produces poetry, engravings, and paintings within that re-created world is a poet-artist who will attract a wide variety of readers. Blake's profound understanding of the ways in which man deals with the warring contraries within his mind has become a fertile source for modern psychology. Carl Jung referred to Blake as a visionary poet who had achieved contact with the potent wellspring of the unconscious. Blake's devotion to a humanistic apocalypse created through the display of exuberant energies and expanded imaginative perceptions has been an inspiration to two generations of twentieth century writers: first D. H. Lawrence, E. M. Forster, William Butler Yeats, and Aldous Huxley, and later, Norman O. Brown, Allen Ginsberg, Theodore Roszak, Colin Wilson, and John Gardner, among others. If a poet can be judged by the quality and quantity of the attention he receives, Blake has certainly risen in the twentieth century from a vague precursor of Romanticism to one of the six major English Romantic poets.

Biography

William Blake was born in Carnaby Market, London, on November 28, 1757. By the age of four, he was having visions: God put his head through the window to look at him, angels walked among the haymakers, and a tree was starred with angels. The visionary child was spared the rigors of formal schooling and learned to read and write at home. He attended a drawing school for four years and in 1772 began a seven-year apprenticeship to James Basire, engraver. He had already begun three years before to write the lyrics which were later printed in *Poetical Sketches*. It was not as a poet, however, that he would make his living but as an engraver who also could do original designs. The Gothic style of engraving which he learned from Basire was unfortunately somewhat passé. In later years, Blake had to sit back and watch other engravers receive commissions to execute his own designs.

At the age of twenty-two, Blake became a student of the Royal Academy, which meant that he could draw from models, living and antique, and attend lectures and exhibitions for six years. The politics of the day, as well as a spreading evangelical fervor, infused his life as an artist-poet. Blake was part of the 1780 Gordon Riots and was present at the burning of Newgate Prison. He was a vehement supporter of the French Revolution and attended radical gatherings which included William Godwin, Thomas Paine, Mary Wollstonecraft Shelley, and Joseph Priestley. Through John Flaxman, Blake developed an interest in Swedenborgianism. The doctrines of Emanuel Swedenborg seemed both to attract and to repel Blake. *The Marriage of Heaven and Hell* launched an attack on this movement.

In 1782, Blake married Catherine Boucher, whose life apparently became one with his. He tried his hand at running a printshop, but in 1785 it failed. He continued to make a meager living on commissions for designs and engravings, but these were the work of other men. In 1800, he moved to

Felpham near Chichester at the invitation of William Hayley, a minor poet, who attempted for the next three years to guide Blake's life into a financially lucrative mold. Blake returned as impoverished as ever to London in 1803, never to leave it again. In 1804, he was tried for sedition and was acquitted. It is ironic that Blake was not being tried for his pervasive iconoclasm, thoughts expressed in his unpublished work which would have set the eighteenth century on its head, but because a drunk had falsely accused him. In 1809, he had his one and only exhibition of sixteen paintings, an exhibition ignored by everyone except one reviewer, who attacked it viciously.

If the political and religious spirit of this period inspired Blake, it also worked against his prosperity as an engraver. Few in England during the Napoleonic wars could afford the luxury of commissioning the work of an engraver. In the last ten years of his life, Blake attracted the attention of a group of young painters whose admiration doubtless enriched this period of increasing poverty. On August 12, 1827, Blake died singing of the glories he saw in heaven.

Analysis

William Blake's focus is primarily on inner states; the drama of the later books has been called a *psychomachia*, a drama of the divided psyche. Man was once integrated but suffered a Fall when reason sought to dominate the other faculties. The disequilibrium of the psyche, its reduced perception, is the creator of the natural world as it is now known. The notion of "contraries" as defined and developed in *The Marriage of Heaven and Hell* provides a dialectical basis for the regeneration of this psyche. Contraries are to be understood as psychic or mental opposites which exist in a regenerated state, a redeemed paradisiacal state of unlimited energy and unbounded perception. Blake has in his total work depicted the progress to regeneration based on a conflict between contraries. Once contraries are accepted, energy is created, progress is inevitable, and reintegration occurs.

Blake's paradisiacal man differs from fallen man only in that he is aware of his divinity. Paradisiacal man perceives the majesty of the imagination, the passions, the reason, and the senses. The imagination in the redeemed state is called Urthona, and after the Fall, Los. Urthona represents that fourfold, unbounded vision which is the normal attribute of the redeemed man. Such vision is not bound by the particulars it produces through contraction, nor is it bound by the unity it perceives when it expands. Blake, in the imagination's true and saving role as poet, envisions the external world with a fourfold vision. Luvah, the passions or love, is represented after the Fall by Jesus, who puts on the robes of love to preserve some hint of divine love in the fallen world. Urizen, the zoa of reason, is the necessary boundary of energy, the wisdom which supplied form to the energies released by the other contraries. In the fallen world, he is the primary usurper of the dominion of other faculties. Tharmas, the zoa of the senses, has, in his paradisiacal form, unrestrained capacity to expand or contract his senses. In the fallen state, these senses remain but in an enervated condition. Sexuality, the sense of touch shared by two, is a means by which fallen man can regain his paradisiacal stature, but it is unfortunately a suppressed sense. The Blakean Fall which all the personified contraries suffer is a Fall from the divine state to the blind state, to the state where none of their powers are free to express themselves beyond the severe limitations of excessive reason. Each of the contraries has his allotted place in the Fall; each sins either through commission or omission.

Contraries remain a concern of Blake from *The Marriage of Heaven and Hell* to the later prophecies—*The Four Zoas*, 1795-1806, *Milton: A Poem*, and *Jerusalem: The Emanation of the Giant Albion*. The metaphysic of contraries, the theoretical doctrine, is never denied. The opposition of energy to reason, however, dramatized in the Orc cycle, is no longer Blake's "main act" in the later books. From Night IX in *The Four Zoas* onward, Los, who embodies something akin to the Romantic concept of the sympathetic imagination, becomes the agent of regeneration. It is he who can project himself into the existence of his polar opposite, can accept the existence of that contrary in the act of self-annihilation and consequently forgive. Thus, the theory of contraries has not altered; any contrary can assume a selfhood in conflict with dialectic progression itself. Los preserves the dialectic while Orc maintains a hierarchy.

Blake's concern with the earthly states of Innocence and Experience, with a fallen body and its contraries, has been associated with religious apocalypse. Blake's apocalypse involves a progression from Innocence to Experience and an acceptance of the contraries in those states. An acceptance of contraries would lead to the destruction of false perception and disequilibrium and eventually to a complete resurrection of the fallen body. Man would again possess divine proportions through a progressive development of his own nature rather than through obedience to the supposed laws of an external deity. Through the faculty of imagination Blake intuits the divinity of man, the falseness of society, and the falseness of laws based upon societal behavior. He perceives the spiritual essence of man, displaying therefore a spiritual rather than a rational brand of humanism. Blake's assumption that man is a fallen god makes his psychology more than a psychology; and it makes his humanism an apocalyptic humanism. His diagnosis of the divided psyche becomes a revelation, and his therapy, an apocalypse. Blake himself dons the mantle of a prophet.

Able to see God and his angels at the age of four, Blake gave precedence in his life to vision over the natural world. He would continue to see through and not with the eye, and what he saw he would draw in bold outline as ineluctable truth. Ultimately, even the heterodoxy of Swedenborgianism was an encroachment upon the supremacy of his own contact with the spiritual world. Early inspired by the revolutionary spirit of the times, he continued throughout his life to advocate a psychic revolution within each person which would lead to regeneration.

Blake's mission throughout his work is always apocalyptic, although he creates a political terrain in the Lambeth books (*The [First] Book of Urizen*, *The Book of Ahania*, *The Book of Los*, and *The Song of Los*) and a psychological one in his later prophecies (*The Four Zoas*, *Milton*, and *Jerusalem*). His focus moves from a political-societal revolution of apocalyptic proportions to a psychic, perceptual regeneration of each individual person. It is the regenerated person who can perceive both a unity beyond all diversity and a diversity within that unity.

Songs of Innocence and of Experience demonstrates Blake's concern for individual human life, in particular its course from innocence to experience. What are the destructive forces operating early upon man, upon his childhood, which ultimately imprison him and lead to "mind-forged manacles"? In *Songs of Innocence*, a glimpse of energies is uncircumscribed, of what man was and again could be if he rightly freed himself from a limited perception and repressed energies.

The later poems, *The Four Zoas*, *Milton*, and *Jerusalem*, are large-scale epics whose focus is a particularly Romantic one—epistemological and ontological transformation. Los, hero of the imagination, is not a hero who affirms the values of a culture, nor are his strengths and virtues uniformly admired by that culture. Like traditional epics, Blake's epics begin "in medias res" but because the natural world is usually seen unclearly, it is worthless to speak of its beginning, middle, or end. The reader who enters the world of Blake's epics enters a psychic world, becomes a "mental traveller," and in his purest states reaches heights traditionally reserved for deity in the Judeo-Christian tradition and deities in the epics of Homer and Vergil.

Blake's work is not unconnected with the natural world, but he attempts to bracket out all but the irreducible elements of the archetypal, individual human life. Paradoxically, Blake's work is characterized by less structural context than that of any poet of whom one could readily think; yet that work is such a dramatic reaction to the eighteenth century and such a dramatic revelation of the new Romanticism, that it is unrivaled as an intense portrait of both sensibilities. In reaction to John Locke's view that the perceiver is separated from the world because of his incapacity to do more than apprehend the secondary qualities of objects, Blake asserted the supremacy of individual perception. Man perceiving is man imagining, an act which encompasses the totality of an individual's energies and personality. What is perceived is dependent upon the imaginative act. The world can only be construed imaginatively. Man, Blake held, can only apprehend the infinity within him through his imagination. The London of Blake's poem of that name is a pitiable place because man's imagination, his poetic genius, is repressed. London is at every moment available for imaginative transformation; so is every object in the natural world. In this view of imagination, Blake foreshadows Samuel Taylor Coleridge and especially Percy Bysshe Shelley and attacks the rationalism of the eighteenth century. The metaphysics of Francis Bacon, Isaac Newton, and Locke were despicable because they elevated rationality and denied imagination, thus standing in the way of regeneration.

Besides disagreeing with the philosophy and psychology of his own day, Blake criticized traditional religious and aesthetic views. Man's fallen perception created the world, not in seven days, but in what became a moment in time. Jesus was a man of revitalized perceptions, a man fully conscious of his unlimited energies. Jesus was thus a supranatural man, one who had achieved the kind of regeneration that Blake felt it was in every person's power to achieve. In art, Blake applauded the firm outline of Michelangelo and Raphael and despised the indeterminacy of Rubens and Titian. The artist who apprehended with strong imagination drew boldly because the truth was clearly perceived. Socially and politically, Blake, unlike Coleridge and William Wordsworth, remained unreconciled to the *status quo.* Blake's revolutionary zeal, most pronounced in the Lambeth books, remained undiminished, urging him to portray error so that it could be cast out. Only Shelley equals Blake's faith in poetic genius to transform the very nature of man and thus the very nature of the world he perceives.

Songs of Innocence and of Experience shows "the two contrary states of the human soul." The contraries cited in *The Marriage of Heaven and Hell* are "Attraction and Repulsion, Reason and Energy, Love and Hate. . . ." Since, however, these songs are not sung outside either Innocence or Experience but from within those states, the contraries are not fully presented in their ideal forms. The songs are from corrupted states and portray disproportionate contraries. Theoretically, each contrary state acts as a corrective to the other, and contraries in the *Songs of Innocence and of Experience* are suggested either in the text of the poem or in the accompanying design.

The Introduction song to the *Songs of Innocence and of Experience* is a good example not only of Blake's view of the role of Innocence and Experience in regeneration but also of the complexity of these seemingly simple songs. This song manages in its twenty lines to present a transition from absolute sensuous Innocence to a recognition of Experience and finally a transition to a higher state. The first stanza presents an almost complete picture of absolute carefree innocence. The adjective "wild" may imply a condemnation of an aspect of absolute Innocence. Because Blake believed that Experience brings an indispensable consciousness of one's actions so that choice becomes possible, the essential flaw in the state of Innocence is that it does not provide the child with alternatives.

The second stanza of this lyric presents the image of the lamb, a symbol of Christ. The lamb, while creating the image of the innocence of Christ, also exhibits the equally true image of Christ crucified. It is this symbol of Experience which brings tears to the child, and on a psychological level, the child is emerging from a "wild" unconscious realm to a realm of consciousness, of Experience.

The third stanza presents two interesting additions: the pipe is replaced by human song and the child weeps with joy. The pipe had first produced laughter and then tears, but it is the human voice which elicits the oxymoronic reaction of joyful weeping. It is only in the human form that the attributes of the two contrary states of Innocence and Experience can exist harmoniously. "Piping down the valley wild" had brought unconstrained laughter, while the figure of the Christ-lamb had brought a more tearful vision of Experience; yet in stanza three, such contrary reactions exist, unresolved but coexistent, as do the contrary states which foster them.

The fourth stanza alludes to the loss of childhood through the disappearance of the child of the poem and implies that the elemental properties of Innocence remain after the departure of the physical state of childhood. By plucking the hollow reed, Blake, the piper and singer, reveals a move toward creation which is fully realized in the last stanza. From the vision of Experience of stanza two, and the acceptance of the necessary contrary states of Innocence and Experience through their inherent qualities, laughter and tears, presented in stanza three, Blake has reached the higher plateau of conscious selflessness described in stanzas four and five. Through the act of creation, the conscious selfless act, which intends to give joy to every child, the conscious selflessness of Blake's paradisiacal reintegrated state is achieved.

In *The Book of Thel*, Thel, a young girl in Innocence, is fearful of advancing to a state of Experience. Lily, cloud, clay, and worm, symbols of innocence and experience, try to allay her fears. Experience may contain key contraries in extreme form; it may be the wrath of the father and the restraint of morality and the curtailment of vision, but it is a state which provides Thel her only opportunity of advancement, of completion and eventual salvation. Experience is a necessary step to the "peace and raptures holy" described by the Cloud. Thel, however, surveys the traditional misfortune of Experience—mortality. She finds no meaningful comfort in the Lily's belief that from Experience, from death, one flourishes "in eternal vales." Thel laments the consciousness that is hers when she takes a trial step into Experience. She finds morality, which represses sexual energy, unbearable. Thus, in spite of the eventual "peace and raptures holy" which Thel can proceed to from a state of Experience, her first look at that state proves too much for her. She flees Experience and consciousness to the vales of Har, the land of superannuated children, described in the poem *Tiriel*; it is a land of unfulfilled innocents who have refused to graduate into the world of Experience. A *Songs of Innocence* poem, "The Lamb," and a *Songs of Experience* poem,

"The Tiger," depict the nature of perception in those states and the contraries which abide in each state. The poems may be viewed as "contrary poems."

The questions of the child in "The Lamb" are not the reason's questions but imagination's—questions he can answer because he has perceived the identity of himself, the lamb, and God. The equation is formed thus: the lamb is Christ the lamb; the child is Christ as a child; and the lamb and child are therefore joined by their mutual identity with Christ. In Innocence, all life is perceived as one and holy. Since there are two contrary states of the human soul and "The Lamb" is a product of only one, Innocence, it is not possible to conclude that this poem depicts Blake's paradisiacal state. The vines in the design are twisting about the sapling on both sides of the engraving, indicating in traditional symbolism the importance of going beyond childhood into Experience. If the child-speaker can see all life as one, can imaginatively perceive the whole, he cannot perceive the particularity, the diversity, which comprises that unity, which Experience's reason so meticulously numbers and analyzes. Even as the adult speaker of "The Tiger" can see only a fragmented world which his imagination is too weak to unify, so the child-speaker cannot see the fragments that comprise the world.

The spontaneity and carefree abandon of the lamb in Innocence can in Experience no longer be perceived in the form of a lamb. The perceiver in Experience fears the energy of Innocence and therefore shapes it into a form which his reason has deemed frightening—that of a tiger. This form which the tiger of the poem "The Tiger" possesses is symmetrical, its symmetry lying in its perfect relationship with the energy it contains. It is only a "fearful symmetry" to the perceiver in Experience who is riddled with the prejudices of Experience, prejudices regarding what is good and what is evil, what is rational and what is irrational, or wild. The moral hierarchy of Experience— good is good and evil is evil—does not permit the perceiver in Experience to perceive a Keatsian "fineness" in the tiger, a marvelous interrelationship of form and energy.

The reader goes back and forth in this poem from a vision of the energies of the unconscious mind to a perception of the boundaries of those energies. It is the mixture of energy and boundary which the speaker-perceiver finds disturbing. The tiger in the first stanza is seen as a burning figure in the night, perhaps symbolizing the burning vibrant passions repressed in the darkened areas of the mind. The tiger perceived by the speaker can live only in the dark since both reason and moral hierarchy have relegated it to that realm. The tiger is, in its energies, in its fire, too great for the conscious mind to accept; yet, like a recurrent nightmare, the tiger burns brightly and cannot be altogether denied. The tiger cannot be quietly integrated into the personality of the speaker-perceiver without doing severe damage to the structure of self carefully fabricated by reason and moral hierarchy. Rather than transform himself, question himself, the speaker-perceiver questions the tiger's creator. What creator could possibly give form to such uncontrollable energy? How can such energy be satisfactorily bounded? The perceiver in Experience assumes that such energy as the tiger represents can only be denied through repression. It cannot be given necessary form; it must be perceived as having a fearful rather than a fine form. This speaker turns questioner and by his questioning reveals his subservience to analytical reason.

The questioner proceeds under the assumption that no creation can be greater than its creator, that in some way the dangerous, fearful energies of the tiger are amenable to that creator, are somehow part of that creator. Where is such a creator to be found? More specifically, where are those burning energies to be found in the spiritual realm? The questioner is already convinced that the creation of the tiger is a presumptuous act and he therefore concludes that Satan is the great presumer. This tiger is, therefore, in the questioner-perceiver's mind, Satan's work, a hellish creation forged in the fires not of Blake's Hell but of a traditional Hell.

The final questions to be asked are merely rhetorical. The questioner has decided that *his* creator could never have created the tiger. The creator involved here has dared to create the tiger. There exists here a Manichaean split, a desperate attempt to answer the problem of the existence of evil. Part of man has been made by God and that part is good, while Satan has made the evil part of man, the part symbolized by the tiger. The only symbol of energy that the questioner-perceiver is prepared to face is that of the lamb. Yet, while the lamb sufficed in Innocence as representative of certain energies, it is no longer indicative of the growth of energy which is a mature person's in Experience. The tiger of Experience expresses the symbolic balance of energy and reason, fire and form; however, only a perceiver whose energies are brought from Innocence and matured in Experience under the guidance of reason in necessary proportions can perceive that balance. This uncorrupted perceiver can see the child lying down with the tiger, as in "A Little Girl Found." That tiger is the perfect symbol of the balance of contraries and is perceived as such; the tiger of "The Tiger" is also a perfect symbol but improperly perceived.

The *raison d'être* of the incorporation of all contraries as they are perceived in the two contrary states, Innocence and Experience, is provided in *The Marriage of Heaven and Hell*. It fulfills more than a mere metaphysical role. It is the foundation of Blake's prophecy, the basis not of extended system but of vision. *The Marriage of Heaven and Hell* preserves the whole body of contraries by a relentless attack upon all divisive factors. Dualism in all areas is negated and the suppressed half of the fallen body, represented by the suppressed division of contraries, is supported and affirmed in opposition to the deadening voices of the "Angels."

The framework of *The Marriage of Heaven and Hell* is traditional Judeo-Christian religion and morality. Blake completely alters and destroys this traditional structure and replaces it with an equal acceptance of the two contrary states of the human soul and their inherent contraries. Energies which are indigenous to childhood must take their place alongside the necessary contraries of Experience—reason, repulsion, and hate. The traditional moral hierarchy of good over evil allows one state and its contraries to have ascendancy over the other. Blake boldly adopts the standard nomenclature and marries good and evil as true opposites, essential contraries. Both the passive and active traits of man's nature are assumed. Rather than an exclusive emphasis on good, as in the Judeo-Christian ethic, or evil, as in sadism, Blake seeks the reintegration of the unity of man through the opposition of these strategic contraries. Once Blake's doctrine of contraries as presented in *The Marriage of Heaven and Hell* is understood, it becomes clearer what *Songs of Innocence and of Experience* is describing, what the basis of Orc's battle on behalf of energy in the Lambeth books is and in what way Los preserves the contraries in the later books.

The Marriage of Heaven and Hell is a theoretical base for Blake's vision; however, the form of the work is by no means expository. It presents a dialectic of contraries in dialectical form. Blake's dialectic is not a system of reason in the Hegelian sense, not a system leading to an external synthesis and to the creation of new contraries. Blake's dialectic is composed of contraries immanent in the human personality, contraries which do not change but which generate increasing energy.

In the "Argument" section, "keeping the perilous path" refers to primal unity, Blakean primal unity, and means maintaining all contraries. The man in the vale maintains the dialectic between conscious and unconscious mind. In Blake's view, once the "path is planted," once the Fall has occurred, man must journey forward, through Innocence and Experience to reintegration.

In Plate 3, Blake declares the immanence of contraries within the human personality and denies the moral dualism of the Judeo-Christian ethic. These contraries are not illusory; their opposition is real, but one contrary does not subsume or upset another. No hierarchy is imposed. The energies which are traditionally classified as "good" are not superior to the energies traditionally classified as "evil." Neither is the reverse true, since Blake is no disciple of the Marquis de Sade. In Blake's view, the hierarchy of morality is particularly insidious since it prevents man from espousing contraries and achieving the progression resulting from that act.

In Plate 4, Blake indicates that the contraries transcend the dualism of body and soul. It is the Devil who proclaims the body as the only portion of the soul and thus Blake's Devil is his hero, his spokesman. This identification of the soul with the observable, physical body, when combined with Blake's notion of progression based on a dialectic of contraries, implies that although the body is a mere portion of the soul, its most debased portion, it is the only medium available to man by which an amplified body, a spiritual body or soul, can be reached. Contraries existing within the body which are perceived in this fallen world are accepted in pursuit of "ideal" or amplified contraries. In Blake's view, the body and its contraries are sacred.

In Plates 5 and 6, Blake's Devil says that energies are too often repressed. The person who represses his energies in turn suppresses the energies of others. Plate 5 begins the "Proverbs of Hell" section. The proverbs are designed to strengthen the imagination of the reader so that the dynamic of contraries is perceived. Once the reader perceives imaginatively the reality of this dynamic, the dynamic is maintained and energy ensues. Ever-increasing energy leads to ever-expanding perception, and perception, for Blake, ultimately determines ontology. The Proverbs of Hell are pithy "consciousness raisers," each demonstrating the dynamic or dialectic of contraries in both content and form.

Plate 11 continues Blake's assault on the priesthood. In Plates 12 and 13, Blake allies himself with the prophets, Isaiah and Ezekiel—voices of "firm persuasion" and "honest indignation." In Plates 14 and 15, Blake describes the creative process that produced *The Marriage of Heaven and Hell*. He further defines the psychic terrain in Plate 16 by presenting two groups, "Prolific" and "Devourer," that can be seen as personified categories incorporating all dichotomies previously discussed in *The Marriage of Heaven and Hell*; Devil-Evil-Energy-Hell are subsumed by the Prolific, and Angel-Good-Reason-Heaven are subsumed by the Devourer. Plates 17 to 20 contain Blake's "fantastic" satirical drama between an Angel and Blake, as Devil. Limited or bounded perception creates a world and an end for itself that a liberated, diabolical perception can alter in the twinkling of an eye. The Angel perceives such a world of error because he has no sense of the dynamic interplay of contraries, no idea that "Opposition is true Friendship."

Some of the political implications of Blake's doctrines in *The Marriage of Heaven and Hell* are evident in *The French Revolution*. This poem of twenty pages, posthumously published, has no accompanying designs and was written for the radical publisher Joseph Johnson. It is conjectured that by 1791 it was dangerous for an Englishman to express a revolutionary enthusiasm inspired by the French Revolution. Blake's own political radicalism is not in this poem couched in symbolic terms and therefore he may have had second thoughts about printing it and risking imprisonment. Blake chronicles, with ample poetic license, the period in France from June 19 to July 15, when the King's troops were dispersed. Louis XVI and his nobles debate their course of action in the light of the growing revolution outside, and they finally decide to remove the troops surrounding Paris. In Blake's telling, this decision represents a renewed perception on the part of the King and his nobles. The Bastille, a symbol of political repression, consequently falls. In actuality, the Bastille fell before the decision was made to remove the King's troops.

There is more of what will become Blake's completed mythology in *Amer-*

ica: A Prophecy than there is in *The French Revolution*. Besides historical characters such as George Washington, Benjamin Franklin, and Thomas Paine, Blake here introduces Orc and Urizen, personifications of revolutionary energy and reason. In a Preludium or Preface, Vala, the shadowy female who symbolizes North America, is in chains. Her liberation occurs through her sexual relations with the fiery Orc. To Blake, therefore, a successful American revolution is not only political but also sexual. George III is the Angel of Albion (England) who worships Urizen and Urizen's law of the Ten Commandments. These two attempt to saturate America with their own diseases by sending a plague across the Atlantic to America. But the plague is countered by the revolutionary zeal of Orc, who replaces the oppressions of Urizen with genuine political and sexual freedom. All Europe is affected by this revolution, but England, seeking the protection of Urizen, hurries to rebuild the gates of repression, the gates of moral good and evil and a dominant rationality.

Blake's Orc, revolutionary energy, successfully counters Urizen ("your reason") just as the French Revolution countered the Ancient Regime. But the French Revolution lost its revolutionary energy in the tyranny of Napoleonic France. It became obvious to Blake that historical, political solutions—revolutions—could not effect a break in the historical cycle, a break that would be an apocalypse. Thus, in *The Four Zoas*, Orc becomes a destructive force in nature, an opponent of reason totally oblivious to reason's importance on a regenerated scale. Orc becomes as tied to the natural, unregenerated cycle as Vala, the embodiment of the natural process itself.

Although Urizen is easily defeated by Orc in *America*, he remains an important character in Blake's myth. He is at once Nobodaddy, a comical, ridiculous father figure, and the Ancient of Days, depicted with grandeur in the frontispiece to *Europe: A Prophecy*. Urizen represents the urge to structure and systematize, to reduce all to rational terms. In the language of our own day, he recognizes only what can be quantified, and, like a good logical positivist, seeks empirical referents to instill meaning in words.

Europe can be viewed as a continuation of *America* in which revolutionary zeal has been replaced by a repressive conservatism which binds both energies and perceptions. The time is the birth of Jesus, a time of possible regeneration through his example. This possibility is not realized and the world falls into a long sleep, an eighteen-hundred-year sleep of Nature. Los, the poetic genius, naïvely rejoices in a promise of peace while Urizen is attempting to rule outside his own domain; and Los's female counterpart, Enitharmon, is a victim of Urizen's dominion and seeks to bind sexual love with moral law. Urizen solidifies his rule, his brazen book of law which ignores imagination, forgiveness, and the necessity of self-annihilation. Edmund Burke and William Pitt, represented by the characters Palamabron and Rintrah, are also under the dominion of Urizen and Enitharmon. The revolutionary spirit of the youth of England is doomed. Pitt-Rintrah three times attempts to lead England to war, into total devastation. In Blake's view, however, Newton and his system are the real beginning of devastation in England. Newton's blast on the trumpet does not lead to glorious apocalypse but to death-in-life. Enitharmon wakes and calls her perverted children to her—materialism, delusion, hypocrisy, sensualism, and seduction. The poem ends with Orc inspiring the French Revolution, the spirit of which will be challenged by a Urizenic England. Los, the poetic genius, summons his sons to the coming strife, but it is as yet unclear what his precise role will be. That role is defined in *The Four Zoas*, *Milton*, and *Jerusalem*.

In *The [First] Book of Urizen* and *The Book of Los*, Blake does not present a cryptic intermingling of history and myth but rather a first attempt at describing his cosmogony and theogony. *The Book of Los* tells the story of the Fall from Los's point of view and *The [First] Book of Urizen* from Urizen's point of view. Thus, the texts interconnect and gloss each other. The Fall is a fall into creation, one precipitated by Urizen's desire for painless joy, for laws binding everything, for "One King, one God, one Law." Urizen's usurpation of power is clearly an act of the Selfhood, a condition in which the legitimacy and importance of other energies are not recognized.

Los, as imagination, is the epistemological faculty, by which truth or error is perceived. Urizen's revolt on behalf of reason skews perception and plunges Los into the Fall. The world of time and space, the Natural World, is formed by Los, and both Los and Urizen, fallen, are bound to this Natural World. A fall into sexuality follows the fall into materiality. Sexuality is subject to moral constraints. Science is a woven "woof" which is created to hide the void. Orc is born but his youthful exuberance is bound by the perversions of the Net of Religion, a direct product of the perverted dream of Reason. Urizen explores the dens of the material world and observes the shrunken nature of a humanity which has completely forgotten its eternal life.

The Song of Los can be viewed as the mythological framework for *America* and *Europe*. The first part of Los's song, "Africa," recounts history leading up to George III—Guardian Prince of Albion's war against the Americans, as depicted in *America*. What exists here is also a historical counterpart to the mythology presented in *The [First] Book of Urizen* and *The Book of Los*. Dark delusion was given Moses on Sinai, abstract law to Pythagoras, Socrates, and Plato, a wretched gospel to Jesus, and the reprehensible Philosophy of the Five Senses to Newton and Locke. The second section, "Asia," is a continuation of *Europe*; it does not speak of events but of the psychological-physiological consequences of Urizen's reign. King, Priest, and Counsellor can only restrain, dismay, and ruin humanity in the service of Urizen. Orc rages over France, but the earth seems too shrunken, mankind too imprisoned to heed. Again, Orc himself, as revolutionary energy, is a questionable savior, since he is described as a serpent. The energy of the French Revolution had become debased, and although Blake hoped for a renewal of its original energies, he was already too skeptical of revolution to present Orc as a hero.

The Book of Ahania takes its name from Urizen's female counterpart or emanation, who comes into existence when Fuzon, an Orc-like figure, battles Urizen. Urizen immediately calls Ahania sin, hides her, and suffers jealousy. Ahania becomes the "mother of Pestilence," the kind of pestilence that is a result of a sexuality restrained by the moral law. Urizen's mind, totally victimized by a repressive rationality and the resulting morality, breeds monsters. From the blood of one of these monsters, Urizen forms a bow and shoots a rock at Fuzon, killing him. Fuzon is pictured as a revolutionary who has assumed the seat of tyranny previously occupied by Urizen. Urizen nails Fuzon to a tree, an act which imitates the death of Christ, Christ as rebel. Fuzon dies because he has not broken the material cycle and is thus vulnerable to the repressive laws of the material world. In the same fashion, the creators of the French Revolution failed to achieve a significant ontological and epistemological revolution and therefore became ensnared once again in nets of mystery which led to the Reign of Terror. Fuzon and the French Revolutionaries achieve no true revolution and fall victim to the "black rock" which is formed by a mind whose energies are repressed in the name of reason and its countless offshoots.

One of the ways to Blakean regeneration is through sexuality, specifically through a reassimilation of the female emanation and the re-creation of the Edenic androgynous body. In *Visions of the Daughters of Albion*, Oothoon is a female emanation; Theotormon is her male counterpart and a victim of a repressive moral code; Bromion is a spokesman of that code. Sexually, Oothoon represents the Prolific; the Devourer equivalent, the opposing sexual nature, must be created in Experience. Jerusalem, in the poem *Jerusalem*, becomes that female emanation cognizant of the nature of the regenerated, androgynous body, and she has gained that knowledge in Experience.

Oothoon is raped by Bromion, and Theotormon treats her like a harlot because she has been raped. Oothoon's imagination gives her a vision of her intrinsic sexual nature. Her vision is of the body, the sexual body no less, a body that is not distinct from the soul. In her newfound identity, Oothoon tries to bring Theotormon to the same vision, tries to bring him beyond the moral categories; but Theotormon demands a rational proof for all living things. Why, he asks implicitly, should he believe Oothoon is pure when the moral code clearly states that she is not pure? Bromion declares that only what can be perceived by the five senses has merit. Oothoon attacks priests and their restraining moral ethic but finally gives up trying to win Theotormon to her newly liberated vision. Her comprehension of the warped picture of sexuality in Experience as demonstrated by Theotormon and Bromion causes her to conclude that Experience has nothing to offer. Although she is not blinded regarding her own sexual nature, she is unable to reunite with Theo-

tormon, male sexuality, and is denied a vision of sexuality based on energies
of both Innocence and Experience. Thus, sexual relations, androgyny, and
regeneration are denied both Oothoon and Theotormon.

. *The Four Zoas* is an unengraved poem written in two overlapping stages.
The main characters, Luvah, Urizen, Tharmas, and Urthona, are the "zoas"
of the human personality, each representing an inherent, indivisible quality
of the human personality. But these characters are true characters and not
mere allegorical representations. *The Four Zoas* is Blake's account of a split
in the Edenic personality of Man, called Albion, of a Fall into the cycle of
the natural world, and of the labors of Los, the imagination, to reunite and
regenerate the four Zoas. This is both a historical drama inevitably unfolded
in time and space and a psychological drama, one in which time and space
have no validity. As a historical drama, it is possible to make the kinds of
historical connections made in *Europe* or *America*, but this is not a consistent
base from which to read the poem, nor will expectations of a conventional
narrative structure be at all fruitful.

The poem begins when Luvah and Vala rush from the loins and into the
heart and on to the brain, where they replace Urizen's ordering of the body's
life with their own cyclical, generative ordering. This sleeping man, Albion,
who has within him the whole world—the powers to contract and expand—
wakes up in Night VIII of the poem. Albion was asleep because he was in
repose in Beulah, a state of threefold perception between Eden (fourfold
perception) and Generation (twofold perception). To be in Beulah is to be
at rest from the dynamic interplay of contraries of Eden, Blake's paradisiacal
state. The aura of Eden pervades Beulah but the threat of the lower state,
Generation, is always present. A fall into a reduced perception is always
imminent. In *The Four Zoas* that fall occurs. The fall into Generation is a
fall into the natural world; it is Blake's version of the biblical Fall.

In the state of Generation, Urizen declares himself God; the "mundane
shell," the material world, is built, and Jesus appears and is sacrificed so that
regeneration can become possible. Jesus is identified with Luvah, love, with
Orc, revolutionary energy battling Urizen in the Lambeth Books, and with
Albion, Universal Man. Under Jesus' inspiration, Los perceives the errors
of the Fall and begins to build Jerusalem, a spiritual freedom in which regeneration is possible. From Night IX in *The Four Zoas* onward into *Milton* and
Jerusalem, Los, who embodies something akin to the Romantic concept of
sympathetic imagination, becomes the agent of regeneration. It is Los who
can project himself into the existence of his contrary, can accept the existence
of that contrary in the act of "self-annihilation," and can consequently forgive.
Thus, in the later books, the theory of contraries is not altered; any contrary
can assume a selfhood in conflict with dialectical progression itself. Los preserves the dialectic, while Orc maintains a hierarchy—"saviour" and "villain."

The historical John Milton is revived in Blake's *Milton* so that he can experience a personal self-annihilation which leads to the incorporation of his Spectre, Satan. Blake's Milton is a Milton of energy and imagination, a Milton determined to correct his view (expressed in *Paradise Lost*, 1667) that love "hath his seat in Reason." Through self-annihilation, Blake's Milton acknowledges the validity of Reason, his Spectre. Once Milton is united with his Spectre, he can preach effectively to the public. The repression of the reasoning power is peculiar only to the Blakean "heroes," such as Blake's Milton. Outside this Blakean world, in the world of Innocence and Experience, the reasoning power is not repressed but assumes the role of usurper, a faculty of mind which has overridden the powers of all other faculties. Reason as Blake perceived it in the eighteenth century was in complete control. It is this unrepressed, dominant, reasoning power which Milton calls a "Negation." The reasoning power which Blake's Milton finally accepts is reason as Spectre, not as Negation, reason in its Edenic proportions.

An act of self-annihilation also precipitates the union of female emanation and the fallen male principle. Blake's Milton is reconciled with his emanation, Ololon. What Blake's Milton undergoes here becomes a precedent for what Los and other contraries will undergo. In annihilating his Selfhood, the Los-Blake-Devil Selfhood, Blake's Milton shows that reason is a necessary contrary, that man is not ruled by energies alone. The Spectre as reason has been accepted and Blake's Milton attains an expanded perception. His emanation perceives her power fade. In "delighting in his delight," they are again one in sexuality.

Blake's Milton enables the contraries to be saved, enables a dynamic interplay of contraries once again to take place. In contrast, Orc's obdurate maintenance of his own Selfhood and his denial of Urizen's reality in any proportions did not preserve Edenic contraries and could not therefore lead to regeneration. Blake's Milton achieves self-annihilation through forgiveness, itself based upon the imagination. It is Los, the imagination, who perceives the dialectic of contraries and recognizes the message of continued forgiveness. It is Los, the imagination, who is employed by each contrary in recognition of its polar opposite.

In *Jerusalem*, Los and the Spectre of Urthona take center stage. Los addresses his Spectre as "my Pride & Self-righteousness," indicating that the Spectre's presence tends to affirm Los's obdurate Selfhood. Throughout *Jerusalem*, the reader witnesses a "compensatory" relationship between the Spectre and Los, although the Spectre seems to be "watching his time with glowing eyes to leap upon his prey." In Chapter IV, Los ends this continuing struggle with his Spectre by accepting it. Once Los, identified here with Blake, becomes one with his Spectre, he appears to Albion, fallen mankind, in the form of Jesus and preaches forgiveness based on imaginative identification and self-annihilation. Jesus-Los annihilates himself before Albion and thus points to the necessary destruction of the Selfhood. Overwhelmed by this act, imaginatively caught in Jesus-Los's sacrifice, the albatross drops from Albion's neck, and it is the Selfhood. This is the apocalyptic moment when Albion, like the phoenix, descends to the flames and rises anew. Regeneration is intimately connected with self-annihilation, as it was in *Milton*.

Albion's emanation, Jerusalem, is also spiritual freedom. A reassimilation of Jerusalem generates a climate of freedom in which contraries can interact. Jerusalem as an emanation is beyond morality. She represents the whole of life, but a fallen Albion applies "one law" to her. Because of this application of a rigid "one law," a rigid hierarchical ethic, Jerusalem is separated from Albion. A female emanation repressed becomes a tyrant. Blake gives readers a close view of this "proud Virgin-Harlot," whom he calls Vala. The Vala whom Blake presents is corrupt, since she stands for restraint in all areas, especially moral, as opposed to Jerusalem-as-liberty. The Vala figure, advocate of a repressive morality, both tempts and lures, and also upholds the sense of sin. She thus becomes woman-as-tyrant. She is the *femme fatale* who incites desire but never acts. Such a morality turns love into prostitution, the free lover into a prostitute.

Again, Los, the imagination, perceives the validity of Jesus' word to Jerusalem regarding forgiveness, annihilation, and regeneration. Los applies what he has learned, unites with his own Spectre, and sends him forth to preach the methods of regeneration—forgiveness and self-annihilation. Albion regains his Jerusalem; spiritual freedom once again exists; and England itself has apocalyptically become Jerusalem, the city of God.

Joseph Natoli

Other major works

FICTION: *An Island in the Moon*, written c. 1784 (published posthumously); *To the Public: Prospectus*, 1793.

NONFICTION: *A Descriptive Catalogue*, 1809.

ILLUSTRATIONS AND ENGRAVINGS: *The Complaint and the Consolation: Or, Night Thoughts, by Edward Young*, 1797; *Blair's Grave*, 1808; *The Prologue and Characters of Chaucer's Pilgrims*, 1812; *The Pastorals of Virgil*, 1821; *Illustrations of the Book of Job*, 1825; *Illustrations of Dante*, 1827.

Bibliography

Bloom, Harold, ed. *William Blake*. New York: Chelsea House, 1985. Includes thirteen previously published essays or extracts from longer works, with the aim of providing a representative selection of criticism from 1950 to 1980. The essays are of varying difficulty, but no student should miss the contributions of Northrop Frye (overview of Blake's myth), David E. Erdman (Blake and contemporary politics), Robert F. Gleckner (point of view in *Songs of Innocence and of Experience*), W. J. T. Mitchell (Blake's composite art), and Leopold Damrosch, Jr. (Los and apocalypse).

Erdman, David E. *Prophet Against Empire: A Poet's Interpretation of the History of His Own Times.* 1954. 3d ed. Princeton, N.J.: Princeton University Press, 1977. This landmark study reveals how closely Blake's work reflects and comments upon contemporary political and social events. Before Erdman, Blake was often regarded as a mystic and esoteric philosopher who was more interested in a heavenly world than in this one. Erdman shows how deep and passionate was Blake's response to the great events of his day. Indispensable reading for a full understanding of Blake.

Frye, Northrop. *Fearful Symmetry: A Study of William Blake.* Princeton, N.J.: Princeton University Press, 1947. It would be difficult to overestimate the importance of this brilliant and endlessly stimulating book, which reveals perhaps for the first time the full extent of Blake's genius. Frye interprets Blake's myth in terms of archetypal symbolic structures, which he also finds underlying much Western literature and mythology. Almost all later writers have been indebted to Frye, although some contemporary Blake critics are wary of being too captured by his ideas.

Hagstrum, Jean. *William Blake, Poet and Painter: An Introduction to the Illuminated Verse.* Chicago: University of Chicago Press, 1964. In this introductory work, Hagstrum admirably achieves his purpose of providing an overview of Blake's composite art. In part 1, he outlines the artistic tradition in which Blake worked, including Gothic art, the medieval and Renaissance illuminated manuscript, and the emblem books of the seventeenth century. In part 2, Hagstrum examines the relationship between text and design in Blake's works, with full discussions of *Songs of Innocence and of Experience* and Blake's illustrations to the Book of Job. Includes eighty black-and-white plates.

Larrissy, Edward. *William Blake.* Oxford, England: Basil Blackwell, 1985. Blake's criticism has been strongly affected by the revolution in critical theory that has swept through literary studies over the last decade, and this introductory study is useful because it applies these developments to Blake's poems in a way that is intelligible to beginning students. Larrissy emphasizes Blake's political radicalism without ignoring the spiritual aspects of his thought. One drawback to the book is that it undervalues Blake's later works and covers them only briefly.

Lindsay, David W. *Blake: Songs of Innocence and Experience.* London: Macmillan, 1989. A very informative, although brief, introduction that examines a range of critical approaches to *Songs of Innocence and of Experience.* Lindsay's impartial discussions of different interpretations of selected poems will be useful for readers who want a concise survey of the field. The second part of the book gives attention to eight *Songs of Experience* in the context of Blake's other works. Includes a full and up-to-date bibliography.

Percival, Milton O. *William Blake's Circle of Destiny.* 1938. Reprint. New York: Octagon Books, 1977. This introduction to Blake's prophetic books has stood the test of time. Percival demonstrates that Blake's myth was firmly rooted in a traditional body of thought that included Neoplatonism, Kabala, alchemy, Gnosticism, and individual thinkers such as Jakob Böhme, Paracelsus, Emanuel, Swedenborg, and Plotinus. This book should be read as a balance to the works of Harold Bloom, Northrop Frye, and David E. Erdman, who all minimized the esoteric aspects of Blake's thought.

ROBERT BLY

Born: Madison, Minnesota; December 23, 1926

Principal poetry

The Lion's Tail and Eyes: Poems Written out of Laziness and Silence, 1962 (with James Wright and William Duffy); *Silence in the Snowy Fields,* 1962; *The Light Around the Body,* 1967; *The Teeth Mother Naked at Last,* 1970; *Jumping out of Bed,* 1973; *Sleepers Joining Hands,* 1973; *Point Reyes Poems,* 1974; *Old Man Rubbing His Eyes,* 1974; *The Morning Glory,* 1975; *This Body Is Made of Camphor and Gopherwood,* 1977; *This Tree Will Be Here for a Thousand Years,* 1979; *The Man in the Black Coat Turns,* 1981; *Out of the Rolling Ocean, and Other Love Poems,* 1984; *Loving a Woman in Two Worlds,* 1985; *Selected Poems,* 1986.

Other literary forms

Robert Bly has been a prolific critic, translator, and anthologist. His work in these areas complements his poetic accomplishments and has been a significant influence on the internationalization of the literary community in the last third of the twentieth century. His most important works include translations of the poems of Georg Trakl, Juan Ramón Jiménez, Pablo Neruda, Tomas Tranströmer, and Antonio Machado. He has also called attention to the work of other poets through anthologies: *News of the Universe: Poems of Twofold Consciousness* (1980) and *The Winged Life: The Poetic Voice of Henry David Thoreau* (1986).

Bly's writings about the practice of poetry have been published as *Leaping Poetry: An Idea with Poems and Translations* (1975) and *American Poetry: Wildness and Domesticity* (1990). His social criticism has ranged from *A Poetry Reading Against the Vietnam War* (1966, with David Ray) to *Iron John: A Book About Men* (1990), the best-seller that became a primer for the men's movement of the 1990's.

Achievements

Bly is the central poet of his generation. His wide-ranging achievements in poetry, criticism, and translation, as well as his work as editor and itinerant apologist for poetry and various social causes, have made him one of the most conspicuous, ubiquitous, and controversial poets in the United States since the mid-1960's. His significance and influence extend well beyond his own work.

Bly's various accomplishments have been rewarded by a Fulbright Fellowship for translation (1956-1957), the Amy Lowell Traveling Fellowship (1964), two Guggenheim fellowships (1965 and 1972), and a Rockefeller Foundation

Grant (1967). In 1968 *The Light Around the Body*, his most controversial collection of poetry, won the National Book Award.

Biography

Born in the small farming community of Madison, Minnesota, Robert Bly grew up, as he said, a "Lutheran Boy-god." He attended a one-room school in his early years. Upon graduation from high school, he enlisted in the navy, where he first become interested in poetry. After the war, Bly enrolled at St. Olaf's College in Northfield, Minnesota, but after only one year there, he transferred to Harvard University. At Harvard he read "the dominant books" of contemporary American poetry, associated with other young writers (among them John Ashbery, Frank O'Hara, Kenneth Koch, Adrienne Rich, and Donald Hall), worked on *The Harvard Advocate* (which he edited in his senior year), delivered the class poem, and graduated *magna cum laude* in 1950.

Having decided to be a poet, and seeking solitude, Bly moved back to Minnesota; then, in 1951, still "longing for 'the depths,'" he moved to New York City, where he lived alone for several years, reading widely and writing his early poems. In 1953 he moved to Cambridge, Massachusetts, and in 1954 to Iowa City, where he enrolled in the creative writing program at the University of Iowa. His M.A. thesis consisted of a short collection of poems entitled "Steps Toward Poverty and Death" (1956). Bly was married to Carolyn McLean in 1955, and in 1956 they moved to Oslo, Norway, via a Fulbright grant. In Norway, Bly sought out his family roots, read widely, and translated contemporary Norwegian poetry.

In 1957, back in Minnesota, living now on the family farm, Bly continued his work as a translator. In 1958 he founded a magazine, *The Fifties* (which would become *The Sixties*, *The Seventies*, and *The Eighties*), in which he published his translations and early literary criticism. His first book of poetry, "Poems for the Ascension of J. P. Morgan," he did not publish, but in 1962 he published two books: *The Lion's Tail and Eyes: Poems Written out of Laziness and Silence* (written with his friends James Wright and William Duffy), and *Silence in the Snowy Fields*, his first independent book of poetry.

By the mid-1960's Bly was actively engaged in the anti-Vietnam War movement. He and David Ray formed a group called American Writers Against the Vietnam War, and they published an anthology entitled *A Poetry Reading Against the Vietnam War* (1966). Bly attended draft card turn-ins, and he demonstrated at the Pentagon in 1967. When his second book of poems, *The Light Around the Body*—filled with his outspoken poems against the war— won the National Book Award in 1968, Bly donated the prize money to the draft resistance.

During the 1970's, Bly's interests and activities diversified considerably. He studied Sigmund Freud, Carl Jung, Eastern meditation, myths and fairy tales, philosophy, and psychology. He organized conferences on "Great Mother and New Father" culture and consciousness. Bly's poetry, social commentary, and literary criticism during this period reflected his wide-ranging interests. By this point in his career, he said, he believed that he had "gotten about half-way to the great poem."

In 1979 Bly and his wife of more than twenty-five years were divorced. In 1980 he was married to Ruth Ray; they moved to Moose Lake, Minnesota, and lived there for ten years before moving to Minneapolis in 1990.

During the 1980's, Bly continued to work at a rapid pace, writing and publishing widely in several genres, translating, giving readings through-out the United States and overseas, and holding meetings and seminars for groups of women and men. His books during the 1980's document as well as anything the life and activities of this exceedingly visible and yet, finally, ex-tremely private individual.

Analysis

Since Robert Bly has habitually brought his wide-ranging interests in liter-ary history, myth, fairy tales, philosophy, psychology, politics, social con-cerns, and poetry past and present into his own work, his poetry reflects these interests and is enriched by them. Furthermore, because he has been prolific and unsystematic, even at times seemingly self-contradictory, he is extremely difficult to categorize and analyze. Nevertheless, it is possible— indeed necessary—to consider Bly's poetry in terms of the series of various phases it has gone through. These phases, although they are also reflected in Bly's other writings and involvements, are, finally, most evident in his po-etry.

Bly's first published book of poetry, *Silence in the Snowy Fields*, remains the best example to date of his deepest obsession: the notion that a personal, private, almost mystical aura adheres to and inheres with the simplest things in the universe—old boards, for example, or a snowflake fallen into a horse's mane. These things, observed in the silence of contemplation and set down honestly and simply in poems, may, Bly believes, inform human beings anew of some sense of complicity, even communion, they have always had with the world, but have forgotten. Bly's focus has caused his work to be labeled "deep image" poetry. In a 1981 essay, "Recognizing Image as a Form of Intelligence," he explained the term's application to his work: "When a poet creates a true image, he is gaining knowledge; he is bringing up into consciousness a connection that has been largely forgotten." In this sense, these early poems provide the reader with the re-created experience of Bly's own epiphanic moments in the silences of "snowy fields," and they be-come his means of sharing such silences with his readers.

The epigraph to *Silence in the Snowy Fields*, "We are all asleep in the outward man," from the seventeenth century German mystic Jacob Boehme, points up both the structural and the thematic principles upon which Bly builds his book. The three sections of the book suggest a literal and a mental journey. The second, central section, "Awakening," contains twenty-three of the forty-four poems in the book and serves as a structural and thematic transition from "Eleven Poems of Solitude," the first section, to the final section, "Silence on the Roads," which sends both book and reader, via the central "awakening," outward into the world. The solitude and contemplative silence of this first book, then, prepare both poet and reader for the larger world of Bly's work.

The way the world impinges on private life is immediately evident in Bly's next book, *The Light Around the Body.* This is his most famous (or for some, most infamous) book. Like *Silence in the Snowy Fields, The Light Around the Body* shows the strong influence of Boehme (four of the five sections of the book have epigraphs from Boehme), especially in terms of the dichotomy of the inward and the outward person, the "two languages," one might argue, of Bly's first two books. If *Silence in the Snowy Fields* deals primarily with the inward being, clearly the focus of *The Light Around the Body* is on the outward being—here seen specifically in a world at war.

The Light Around the Body was published in the midst of the American obsession with the Vietnam War, and most of the poems in it are concerned with that war, directly or indirectly. The third, central, section of the book (following sections entitled "The Two Worlds" and "The Various Arts of Poverty and Cruelty") is specifically entitled "The Vietnam War." This is the most definitive, the most outspoken and condemnatory group of poems—by Bly or anyone else—on the war in Vietnam. Bly reserves his harshest criticism for American involvement in the war. He does not mince words, and he names names: "Men like [Dean] Rusk are not men:/ They are bombs waiting to be loaded in a darkened hangar" ("Asian Peace Offers Rejected Without Publication").

Perhaps the most famous poem Bly has written is also his most definitive criticism of the Vietnam War. In "Counting Small-Boned Bodies," the speaker of the poem has been charged with keeping the grisly count of war casualties to be reported on the evening news. Shocked by the mounting death tolls, he finds himself trying to imagine ways to minimize these terrifying statistics. The refrain that runs through the poem is, "If we could only make the bodies smaller." The implication is that if the bodies could be made smaller, then people might, through some insane logic, be able to argue the war away. Bly's poems in *The Light Around the Body* ensure that the war will never be forgotten or forgiven.

The last two sections of *The Light Around the Body* ("In Praise of Grief" and "A Body Not Yet Born") move back "inward" from the "outward" world of the war, just as the first two sections of the book had moved "outward" from the "inward" world of *Silence in the Snowy Fields.* Since the war, however, this new inward world can never again ignore or fail to acknowledge the outward world. Therefore, Bly writes "in praise of grief" as a way of getting through, psychologically speaking, both outward and inward conflicts.

The first three poems of the fourth section of the book define a progression back toward a place of rest, calm, peace. In the third poem the body is described as "awakening" again and finding "nourishment" in the death scenes it has witnessed. Such a psychic regeneration, which parallels the inevitable regeneration of nature after a battle, is what is needed to repair the damage the war has done if people are to be restored to full human nature. Thus, in the final section of the book, although the new body is not yet fully born, it is moving toward birth, or rebirth.

Finally, then, although *The Light Around the Body* will no doubt be most often remembered for the overt antiwar poems in it, from the point of view of Bly's developing poetic philosophy it is best seen as a description of the transition from the outer world back into the inner world.

The psychological movement first suggested and then begun in *The Light Around the Body* is followed further inward by Bly's next important book, *Sleepers Joining Hands.* This book contains three distinctly different sections. The first section consists of a series of short lyric poems. Beginning with "Six Winter Privacy Poems," it comes to a climax with a long poem, "The Teeth Mother Naked at Last," Bly's final, psychological response to the war in Vietnam.

The second section of *Sleepers Joining Hands* consists of an essay in which Bly documents many of the philosophical ideas and psychological themes with which he has long been obsessed and which he has addressed (and will continue to address) both in his poetry and in his criticism. Bly here summarizes his thinking in terms of Jungian psychology, father and mother consciousness, the theory of the three brains, and other ideas that he groups together as "mad generalizations." This essay, although it is far from systematic, remains an important summary of the sources of many of Bly's most important poems and ideas.

Thus, although *Sleepers Joining Hands* does not contain Bly's most important poetry, it does discuss much of the theory behind that poetry, and it is an extremely important book. In the central essay, Bly describes in detail the way in which "mother consciousness" has come to replay "father consciousness" during the last several centuries. Four "force fields" make up the Great Mother (or Magna Mater), which, according to Bly, is now "moving again in the psyche." The Teeth Mother, one of these force fields, attempts to destroy psychic life. She has been most evident in the Vietnam War and has caused the "inward" harm that that war has brought to the world. "The Teeth Mother Naked at Last," the climactic poem in the first section of

Sleepers Joining Hands, like the earlier antiwar poems in *The Light Around the Body*, describes the conditions of psychic reality in terms of the presence of the Teeth Mother. It argues that once the Teeth Mother is acknowledged ("naked at last"), she can be dealt with and responded to, and then the outward physical world can be effectively reconnected with the inward psychic or spiritual world.

"Sleepers Joining Hands," the long title poem that constitutes the collection's third section, is an elaborate and challenging poem, a kind of dream journal/journey with overt Jungian trappings. Thematically, it constantly shifts back and forth between dreamed and awakened states. These thematic shifts are evidenced in the structure of the poem. The poem as a whole is a kind of religious quest based in large part on the Prodigal Son story—one of the great paradigms of the journey motif in Western culture. At the end of the poem, bringing to climax so many of his themes, Bly provides *"An Extra Joyful Chorus for Those/ Who Have Read This Far"* in which "all the sleepers in the world join hands."

The next several books in Bly's canon consist of prose poems. Bly believes that when a culture begins to lose sight of specific goals, it moves dangerously close to abstraction, and that such abstraction is reflected in the poetry of the time. Prose poetry, then, often appears as a way of avoiding too much abstraction. Whether this theory holds up historically or not, it certainly can be made to apply in Bly's case, even if only after the fact—the theory having been invented to explain the practice. Certainly, there is ample reason to think that Bly judged that his own work, influenced by the events the world was witnessing, was moving dangerously toward "abstraction," perhaps most conspicuously so in *Sleepers Joining Hands*. For whatever reason, then, Bly turned, in the middle of his career, to the genre of the prose poem. His prose poems of this period are extremely strong work, arguably his strongest poetry.

The two most important collections of prose poems are *The Morning Glory* (which includes as its central section the ten-poem sequence "Point Reyes Poems," published separately the year before, and one of the strongest sequences of poems Bly has written) and *This Body Is Made of Camphor and Gopherwood*. These poems move "deeply into the visible," as the old occult saying Bly quotes as epigraph to *The Morning Glory* demands, and they are poems written "in a low voice to someone he is sure is listening," as Bly suggested they should be in his essay "What the Prose Poem Carries with It" (1977).

The Morning Glory, like *Silence in the Snowy Fields*, contains forty-four poems, suggestive of a new beginning in Bly's career. The poems follow a rather typical pattern. They begin in the most offhand ways, frequently with the speaker alone outdoors, prepared, through his openness to possibilities, for whatever he may find there. These poems are journeys; they move from the known to the unknown. Therefore, what can be learned from them is often difficult to analyze, especially since Bly frequently only suggests what it is or might be. Indeed, often it seems to be something that the body comes to know and only later—if at all—the mind comprehends. In this sense these are poems of preparation, and they frequently imply apocalyptic possibilities.

The Morning Glory ends with several poems that describe transformations. One of the most important of these, "Christmas Eve Service at Midnight at St. Michael's," involves the personal life of the poet, who, six months after his only brother has been killed in an automobile accident, attends a Christmas Eve service with his parents. He and his parents take Communion together and hear the Christian message. Coming so soon after his brother's death, however, this message is "confusing," since the poet knows that "we take our bodies with us when we go." The poem ends in a reverie of transfiguration in which a man (both brother and Christ), with a chest wound, flies out and off over the water like a large bird.

The basic "religious" theme begun in *The Morning Glory* is continued in *This Body Is Made of Camphor and Gopherwood.* Here Bly writes overtly religious "meditations," thus picking up again the aura of the sacred that has been important in his work since the beginning. Indeed, this book immediately reminds the reader of *Silence in the Snowy Fields*, both thematically and in terms of Bly's basic source material.

There are twenty poems in *This Body Is Made of Camphor and Gopherwood*; they are divided into two thematic units. The first ten poems describe, often through dreams, visions, or dream-visions, "what is missing." Not surprisingly, given this theme, Bly frequently uses the metaphor of sleep and awakening. Indeed, the first poem in the book begins, "When I wake." This awakening is both a literal and an imaginative or metaphoric awakening, and it signals at the outset the book's chief concern.

The second section of the book is filled with intensely heightened, almost ecstatic, visionary poems. The crucial transitional poems in *This Body Is Made of Camphor and Gopherwood*—which is itself a crucial transition in Bly's canon—are "Walking to the Next Farm" and "The Origin of the Praise of God." "Walking to the Next Farm" describes the culmination of the transition "this body" has been going through as the poet, his eyes wild, feels "as if a new body were rising" within him. This new body and the energy it contains are further described and defined in the other central poem, "The Origin of the Praise of God." It begins with exactly the same words that several other poems in this book begin with: "My friend, this body." This poem, in the words of Ralph J. Mills, Jr., "a visionary hymn to the body, . . . dramatizes [the] experience of the inner deity" and thus is the paradigm of the entire prose-poem sequence. By the end of the book, this visionary, mystical, yet still fully physical body is finally fully formed and is "ready to sing" both the poems already heard and the poems ahead.

This Tree Will Be Here for a Thousand Years is a second collection of "snowy fields" poems. Bly has said that it should be understood as a companion volume to *Silence in the Snowy Fields* and has indicated that a third group of "snowy fields poems" would be published in the future. In this sense, then, *This Tree Will Be Here for a Thousand Years* is a specific, overt attempt on Bly's part to return to his beginnings. Just as it is a return, however, it is also a new beginning in the middle of his career. Bly is clearly a poet obsessed with a need for constant renewal, and in many ways each of his books, although taking a different direction, also retraces each earlier journey from a different vantage point.

Yet perhaps it is not surprising that, although *This Tree Will Be Here for a Thousand Years* is a new beginning for Bly, it is also a darker beginning, a darker journey than the journey he took in *Silence in the Snowy Fields.* Here the journey envisions its end. This, then, is the book of a man facing his mortality, his death, and walking confidently toward it. As Bly puts it in one of these poems, "there are eternities near." At the same time, there is the inevitable paradox that poems outlive the poet who has written them—and, thus, even poems that speak of death outlive the death of their speaker.

Two later books may be seen as companions to each other: *The Man in the Black Coat Turns* and *Loving a Woman in Two Worlds.* Like *This Tree Will Be Here for a Thousand Years*, these books circle back to Bly's beginnings at the same time that they set out on new journeys. Furthermore, these books are among the most personal and private he has published, and thus they are particularly immediate and revealing.

The Man in the Black Coat Turns is divided into three sections, the central section, as in *The Morning Glory* and *This Body Is Made of Camphor and Gopherwood*, being made up of prose poems. The prose poems here, however, are different from their predecessors in being much more clearly related to Bly's personal experiences; as he says in the first of them, "Many times in poems I have escaped—from myself. . . . Now more and more I long for what I cannot escape from" ("Eleven O'Clock at Night").

More than anything else, the poems in *The Man in the Black Coat Turns* are poems about men. The dominant theme of the book is the father-son relationship. This theme and its association with the book's title is immediately, and doubly, announced at the outset of the book, in the first two poems, "Snowbanks North of the House" and "For My Son, Noah, Ten Years Old," as Bly works the lines of relationship through the generations of his own family: from his father to himself as son, then, as father, through himself to his own son, Noah. The third poem, "The Prodigal Son," places the personal family references into a larger context by relating them to fatherhood and sonship in the New Testament parable. In the final poem in this first section of the book, "Mourning Pablo Neruda," Bly extends the father-son relationship again—this time to include one of his own important poetic "father figures," Pablo Neruda, a poet he has often translated.

The final section of *The Man in the Black Coat Turns* draws all these themes together in "The Grief of Men." This poem is clearly the climactic thesis piece for the whole book. There are, however, a number of important poems grouped together in this last section: "Words Rising," "A Meditation on Philosophy," "My Father's Wedding," "Fifty Males Sitting Together," "Crazy Carlson's Meadow," and "Kneeling Down to Look into a Culvert." In the last of these poems, via the account of a symbolic, ritualized sacrificial death, the poet completes his preparations for another new life.

The poems of *Loving a Woman in Two Worlds* are, for the most part, short—almost half of them contain fewer than eight lines, and eleven of them are only four lines long. Technically speaking, however, this book contains poems in most of the forms and with most of the themes Bly has worked in and with throughout his career. In this sense the collection is rather a tour de force. Many of these poems of *Loving a Woman in Two Worlds* are love poems, and some of them are quite explicitly sexual. The book can be read in terms of the stages of a love relationship. These are poems that focus on the female, on the male and female together, and on the way the man and the woman together share "a third body" beyond themselves, a body they have made "a promise to love."

This book thus charts another version of the "body not yet born" journey with which Bly began his poetry. In the final poem in *Loving a Woman in Two Worlds*, Bly, speaking no doubt to one individual, but to all of his readers as well, writes, "I love you with what in me is unfinished.// . . . with what . . . is still/ changing."

In the 1986 *Selected Poems*, in addition to poems from all of Bly's previous major collections (some of the poems have been revised, in some cases extensively), he has included some early, previously uncollected poems. A brief essay introduces each of the sectional groupings of this book. *Selected Poems*, then, is a compact, convenient collection, and it succinctly represents Robert Bly in the many individual phases of his work.

William V. Davis

Other major works

NONFICTION: *A Poetry Reading Against the Vietnam War*, 1966 (with David Ray); *Leaping Poetry: An Idea with Poems and Translations*, 1975; *Talking All Morning*, 1980; *American Poetry: Wildness and Domesticity*, 1990; *Iron John: A Book About Men*, 1990.

TRANSLATIONS: *Twenty Poems of Georg Trakl*, 1961 (with James Wright); *Forty Poems*, by Juan Ramón Jiménez, 1967; *I Do Best Alone at Night: Poems*, by Gunnar Ekelöf, 1968; *Neruda and Vallejo: Selected Poems*, 1971;

Lorca and Jiménez: Selected Poems, 1973; *Friends, You Drank Some Darkness: Three Swedish Poets, Harry Martinson, Gunnar Ekelöf, and Tomas Tranströmer,* 1975; *Twenty Poems,* by Rolf Jacobsen, 1977; *The Kabir Book: Forty-four of the Ecstatic Poems of Kabir,* 1977; *Truth Barriers: Poems,* by Tomas Tranströmer, 1980; *Selected Poems of Rainer Maria Rilke,* 1981; *Times Alone: Selected Poems of Antonio Machado,* 1983.

ANTHOLOGIES: *News of the Universe: Poems of Twofold Consciousness,* 1980; *The Winged Life: The Poetic Voice of Henry David Thoreau,* 1986.

Bibliography

Davis, William V. *Understanding Robert Bly.* Columbia: University of South Carolina Press, 1988. A book-length study of Bly's poetic career, geared to an understanding of the chronological development and ongoing significance of Bly's life and work through a detailed analysis of individual poems and an in-depth consideration of each of the major books. Includes a primary and secondary bibliography and an index.

Friberg, Ingegard. *Moving Inward: A Study of Robert Bly's Poetry.* Göteborg, Sweden: Acta Universitatis Gothoburgensis, 1977. This first book-length study of Bly is limited, naturally, to his early (pre-1975) career. Friberg gives a somewhat mechanical treatment of images, concepts, and patterns in some of the early poems. Includes a bibliography, but no index.

Jones, Richard, and Kate Daniels, eds. *Of Solitude and Silence: Writings on Robert Bly.* Boston: Beacon Press, 1981. A miscellany of materials on Bly, including essays, memoirs, poems, notes, and documents, as well as new poems and translations by Bly. Includes an extensive primary and secondary bibliography, but no index.

Nelson, Howard. *Robert Bly: An Introduction to the Poetry.* New York: Columbia University Press, 1984. A detailed critical introduction to and analysis of Bly's career through *The Man in the Black Coat Turns,* stressing the way in which his various theories illuminate his poems. Includes a chronology of his life, a primary and secondary bibliography, and an index.

Peseroff, Joyce, ed. *Robert Bly: When Sleepers Awake.* Ann Arbor: University of Michigan Press, 1984. A substantial collection of reviews and essays (including several previously unpublished) on Bly and his work through *The Man in The Black Coat Turns.* Includes an extensive primary and secondary bibliography, but no index.

Sugg, Richard P. *Robert Bly.* Boston: Twayne, 1986. An introductory critical overview of Bly's work and career (stressing a Jungian interpretation), through *The Man in the Black Coat Turns.* (*Loving a Woman in Two Worlds* and *Selected Poems* are mentioned in passing.) Includes a selected bibliography of primary and secondary sources and an index.

LOUISE BOGAN

Born: Livermore Falls, Maine; August 11, 1897
Died: New York, New York; February 4, 1970

Principal poetry

Body of This Death, 1923; *Dark Summer*, 1929; *The Sleeping Fury*, 1937; *Poems and New Poems*, 1941; *Collected Poems 1923-1953*, 1954; *The Golden Journey: Poems for Young People*, 1965 (with William Jay Smith); *The Blue Estuaries: Poems 1923-1968*, 1968, 1977.

Other literary forms

There are two collections of Louise Bogan's criticism, most of it consisting of articles and reviews from her many years with *The New Yorker*: the posthumously published *A Poet's Alphabet* (1970), edited by Robert Phelps and Ruth Limmer, contains all the pieces from *Selected Criticism* (1955) plus other writings previously uncollected. Bogan's brief history of modern American poetry, *Achievement in American Poetry*, appeared in 1950. Her translations include *The Glass Bees* by Ernst Jünger (1960, with Elizabeth Mayer), and three works of Goethe: *Elective Affinities* (1963), *The Sorrows of Young Werther* (1971), and *Novella* (1971); she also edited a translation of *The Journal of Jules Renard* (1964). Ruth Limmer, Bogan's friend and literary executor, also brought out two posthumous collections of personal writings: *What the Woman Lived: Selected Letters of Louise Bogan 1920-1970* (1973) and *Journey Around My Room* (1980), a chronological selection from diaries, letters, and other published and unpublished papers.

Achievements

Bogan devoted her life to poetry in writing, criticism, reviews, lectures, and consulting, and she was recognized with "all the honors that are an honor" for a poet in America. Early in her career she was awarded the John Reed Memorial Prize by *Poetry* magazine; a Guggenheim fellowship followed. In subsequent years she received the Helen Haire Levinson Prize from *Poetry*, the Harriet Monroe Award from the University of Chicago, the Bollingen Prize, and the Senior Creative Arts Award from Brandeis University. Western College for Women and Colby College bestowed honorary degrees. She was elected a Fellow in American Letters of the Library of Congress, a member of the Institute of Arts and Letters, and a member of the American Academy of Arts and Letters.

These honors came in recognition of a substantial body of prose as well as poetry. From 1931 until 1968, Bogan regularly reviewed poetry for *The New Yorker*, contributing notes and reviews on twenty to forty books of poetry every year. Her published criticism helped shape the taste of generations of readers. Less well known but also influential was Bogan's second career as teacher, lecturer, and poet-in-residence. In 1944, she delivered the Hopwood Lecture at the University of Michigan, and for the next twenty-five years she lectured and taught at universities from Connecticut to Arizona and Washington State to Arkansas.

Bogan never cultivated popularity, and, despite the many academic and official honors, popular acclaim for her work has been scant. She received neither the Pulitzer Prize nor the National Book Award. More puzzling has been the neglect by the academic establishment; few scholars have undertaken the thorough examination of her work that has been accorded such contemporaries as Theodore Roethke and Marianne Moore. In the late 1970's, however, stimulated by feminist criticism and an awakening interest in women authors, literary scholars began more extensive studies of Bogan's works.

Biography

About the details of her life Louise Bogan maintained a deliberate and consistent reticence. Yet she also claimed that she had written a searching account of her life; it was all in her poetry, she said, with only the vulgar particulars omitted. The information available about her life substantiates her claim.

The earliest theme to emerge in Bogan's life is the struggle for order amidst chaos and violence. She was born in Livermore Falls, Maine, on August 11, 1897, the second child and only daughter of Mary Helen Shields and Daniel J. Bogan. During the next twelve years the family lived variously in Milton and Manchester, New Hampshire, and in Ballardvale, Massachusetts, before settling, in 1910, in Boston. Life was characterized by extremes of physical and psychological violence between the parents, and between mother and children. While Bogan's father is almost totally absent from her recollections, her mother, a woman of elegance, taste, and ferocious temper, imposed an unpredictable and almost overwhelming presence on the young girl's life. There are startling gaps in memory: an unexplained year in a convent boarding school, two days of blindness at the age of eight. The convent year, the boarding house in Ballardvale, and an art teacher in Boston, however, represented relief from the constant struggle for sanity and order in the chaotic Bogan household. The child Louise relished the soothing atmosphere of order, cleanliness, and competence found in the boarding house, and later the enchantment of Miss Cooper's studio with its precious trinkets and carefully ordered tools. During her teens, Bogan's five years at Boston's Girls' Latin School enlarged her experience of both discipline and disorder; it was here that she received the thorough classical education she treasured so, and here that she encountered firsthand the vigorous New England Protestant bigotry against the Irish. To her classmates, Bogan was a "Mick," and she kept this consciousness of class distinctions throughout her life. The revelation must have amazed the girl steeped in a rich and intricate Catholicism. During this period of childhood and youth, which ended with marriage after one year at Boston University, she began to write.

In 1916, against the strong objections of her mother, Bogan forfeited her scholarship to Radcliffe and married Curt Alexander, a private in the Army. Her overriding motive was escape from a constricting life, but that illusion was very short-lived. Exactly one year after joining her husband in Panama, where she gave birth to a daughter, Maidie, Bogan returned with the child to Boston. Later, she and Alexander attempted to revive the marriage, living first near Portland, Maine, and later in Hoboken, New Jersey; but all they had in common, Bogan recalled, was sex. She began to publish more, establishing a literary life as part of the Greenwich Village artistic milieu, and eventually the two separated. In 1918, Bogan's brother Charles was killed in France, and two years later Curt Alexander died. In 1923 her first collection, *Body of This Death*, came out.

The next twelve years of her life reflected a pattern of increasing professional skill and discipline together with a persistently troubled personal life. From 1925 to 1937 she was married to Raymond Holden. The relationship was stormy, not least because of Holden's infidelities, and marked by a series of moves—to Santa Fe, to Hillsdale, to various addresses in New York City. Material losses took a toll: in 1929 the Holdens' house burned, destroying books, pictures, and manuscripts, and in 1935, while she was separated from Holden, Bogan was evicted from her apartment. In 1937 her mother died. During this period of her life Bogan was hospitalized twice for depression and nervous collapse. She later speculated on the relationship between childhood experience and memory and the many upheavals of her young adult life, locating the beginning of her depression in a visit to the earliest neighborhood the Bogans had lived in after coming to Boston. She continued writing; in 1937, *The Sleeping Fury* appeared.

The period 1937 to 1965 marked a time of maturity, productivity, and fulfillment. In 1937, Bogan moved to the New York apartment that would be her home thenceforth. Three volumes of poetry, as well as two critical works, an anthology, and translations were published. Awards and honors came almost yearly, along with invitations to lecture, read, and consult.

Turmoil and controversy reappeared in her life in 1965, when another depression resulted in hospitalization. The 1960's also saw Bogan's first public political activity, when she took part in the protests against the war in Vietnam. She continued lecturing, reading, and reviewing until, at the age of seventy-two, she resigned from her position as poetry reviewer for *The New Yorker*. Her last collection of poems, *The Blue Estuaries*, appeared in 1968, and she completed the compilation of her reviews that was published as *A Poet's Alphabet*. On February 4, 1970, Louise Bogan died alone in her New York apartment.

Analysis

Louise Bogan's well-known reticence about the details of her personal life extended to her poetry. She said that she had written down her experience in detail, omitting only the rough and vulgar facts. This dichotomy of fact and experience lies at the heart of her poems: they are about experience, not about facts. Four basic thematic concerns emerge in Bogan's work. Many poems center on women or womanhood. This was a theme to which Bogan returned often in her criticism, and her history of modern American poetry is one of the few to acknowledge the contributions of women. A second theme emerges in the many poems that explore the universal human condition of fleshly existence and the disasters and delights of love. Another preoccupation is art, the process of making art, and the artist and his commitment. Finally, the struggle of the mind and spirit for sanity and consolation in the face of insanity, chaos, and meaninglessness inspired the greatest of her poems.

"Women" may be Bogan's most frequently anthologized poem, and it has certainly troubled feminist critics more than any other. The poem is cast as a diatribe by a male speaker who generalizes about women as "they." This catalog of faults outlines the stereotype of "woman" that Bogan herself referred to impatiently in several of her essays. The speaker's harsh tone modulates toward pity for women's habit of using their own benevolence against themselves, but he does not speculate on the causes of the many flaws in women. Neither did Bogan, as evidenced by her letters and criticism: she inherited, without question, the Victorian and Romantic view that applied the dichotomies of emotion and intellect to woman and man, respectively, and then raised those parallel associations to the status of natural law.

In her poems, however, Bogan's perception of stereotypes of gender reflects a more complex vision. "The Romantic," for example, mocks the sentimental ideal of the passionless woman. The romantic had sought to impose his vision of femininity on the young woman and lost both woman and ideal. In both "Women" and "The Romantic" the poet distances herself from the subject. In the first a presumptively male voice discourses, not about any real woman but about the idea of women, while in the second a voice of unspecified gender addresses a man about a woman who has vanished.

Other poems confront more directly the particular heartaches, upheavals, and joys of being a woman, but in these, too, the approach is ordered and the thought kept coherent by various techniques of distancing. In each of the three poems, "The Changed Woman," "Chanson un peu naïve," and "For a Marriage," an anonymous speaker talks about a woman who also remains unspecified and anonymous. "Chanson un peu naïve" expresses an ironic, despairing pity at the destructive results of frequent childbearing and an apparent self-deception that permits its continuance. In "For a Marriage," a dispassionate onlooker reflects on intimacy as a sharing of pain, in this instance the woman's revelation of her pain to be shared by her husband.

"The Changed Woman" is more obscure, referring perhaps to a miscarriage or abortion; the quality of the experience, the dream denied and driven, supersedes factual references. Another treatment of the theme is "The Crossed Apple": here an older person, man or woman, directly addresses a young girl and offers the gift of an apple. The poem invokes the creation myth in Genesis, as the voice suggests that eating the fruit means knowledge as well as sustenance: she will taste more than fruit, blossom, sun, or air.

Such distancing brings order to the chaotic, impulsive, often outrageous realities of women's lives, placing those realities within the bounds of an art that can illuminate and make them meaningful. Those poems in which Bogan uses a woman's voice to articulate a woman's point of view also find means to distance and thus order her subject. "Men Loved Wholly Beyond Wisdom" generalizes about men and women according to familiar stereotypes. For the first five lines women love and therefore demand love excessively, and in the remaining eight lines, the speaker resorts to harsh suppression of her emotions as the solution to the dilemma presented by her feelings and her perceptions of them. "Girl's Song" implies the same problem: the speaker addresses the man who has abandoned her in favor of another woman who, it is implied, will likewise love him in a sacrificial, even destructive way. While this poem expresses resignation rather than the fierce despair of "Men Loved Wholly Beyond Wisdom," the view of women's nature and circumstances is the same: women love excessively, to their sorrow and destruction.

Both of the foregoing poems come from Bogan's early work, and they, like many of the early poems, express the tension between matter and form, instinct and reason, in terms of the relationships between women and men. In three poems published much later in her life she spoke less generally and more directly in the persona of a particular woman with a specific history.

In "The Sorcerer's Daughter" and "Little Lobelia's Song," women speak of their own experience, and both poems spring from recognition of that most fundamental of connections, the relationship between parent and child. The sorcerer's daughter, who can read signs and auguries, finds herself bound to an unfortunate fate. The poem echoes the prophetic pessimism of "Cassandra" without the formal restraint and emotional tension of the earlier poem. "The Sorcerer's Daughter" is no tragedy; from her father the speaker inherits, chiefly, bad luck. In "Little Lobelia's Song" the piteous, helpless, inarticulate voice is an infant addressing its mother. Reflections on Bogan's tumultuous relationship with her own mother are inevitable, although the poem contains no details. The speaker's expression of identity with its mother, and the agony of separation, invite Freudian interpretation. Bogan's own acquaintance with modern psychology emerged from experience as well as theory, and the poem, published not long after her last stay in a mental hospital, is one of a group of three including "Psychiatrist's Song." Seldom did Bogan permit expression of such unalloyed pathos, yet the poem achieves power precisely through its rigid form and the distancing created by the artificial persona; the poet even succeeds with that commonest of clichés, flower as metaphor for child.

"Masked Woman's Song," the third poem of this trilogy, speaks most specifically yet most enigmatically about Bogan's own experience. While the other poems use personae as disguise, the masked woman acknowledges her disguise and thus disarms skepticism. The singer seems to disown her previous sense of the value of artistic and moral order. The poem contains more physical description than most: the man is tall, has a worn face and roped arms. These are matters of fact, not experience, and the poem remains virtually impenetrable. The poet has moved beyond the classical values and virtues to a realm so resistant to description that it defies metaphor, where the familiar images of male and female no longer serve.

As is already evident, Bogan made love in its many varieties a major theme in her poetry. She framed her exposition generally in the Renaissance terms of flesh and spirit, passion and reason. The classical understanding of passion, derived from *passio* (suffering, submission) and related to "passive," regarded the lusts of the flesh not as mere sentiment or feeling but as the fundamental, chaotic, instinctual life of man that provides all force for ongoing life and regeneration, but that also constantly moves to overwhelm and subsume the cognitive being. Thus, the great human enterprise is to balance and harmonize both the instinctual and the mental, the flesh and the spirit.

Bogan's poems express disdain for excess in either direction. In "Several Voices out of a Cloud" the drunks, drug-takers, and perverts receive the laurel, for they have—whatever their flaws—been committed, they have used their creative energy. The pallid, the lifeless, punks, trimmers, and nice people—all of those who denied life in favor of empty form—forgo eternity. The conception, the thesis, and even the terminology are Dantean.

Two poems about men suggest the peculiar dangers of trying to avoid confrontation with passion. In "The Frightened Man" the speaker explains that he feared the rich mouth and so kissed the thin; even this contact proved too much as she waxed while he weakened. His shattered image of the docile woman implies a self-destructive loathing of the real and the fleshly. "Man Alone" explores the subtle complexities of this solipsistic position. The man of the title seems to exist in a hall of mirrors; unable to confront and acknowledge the common humanity and individual otherness of his fellow human beings, he persists in a state of autistic rage. Literally and figuratively he cannot face another person. The man does not suffer an excess but rather a perversion; passion misplaced has devolved into self-absorbed rage and infatuate isolation.

Most of Bogan's poetic statements on the subject of passionate love decry its excesses. She acknowledged and even emphasized the urgency of fleshly desire, but rarely celebrated it for itself. In her poems, giving oneself to overwhelming passion means capitulation, not liberation. Variations on this theme are played in "Women," in "Men Loved Wholly Beyond Wisdom," in "Chanson un peu naïve," and in "Girl's Song." Bogan's clearest critique of excessive love is in "Rhyme," with its echoes of William Shakespeare's sonnet, "The expense of spirit in a waste of shame." In Bogan's poem a lover recollects a former love, addressing the absent one in a tone of wry nostalgia. The speaker articulates the Renaissance perception of excessive love as a form of idolatry, yet also acknowledges the nourishing function that passion can have, for the loved one had been heart's feast to the lover.

"Second Song" and "At a Party" describe the destructiveness of undisciplined love. In "Second Song" the speaker bids farewell to passion, which has garnered mere trinkets and a poisoned spiritual food. The speaker has undergone passion, has suffered it in the classical sense, as a pensioner, and so chooses to become detached from it. Like the speakers in "Rhyme" and "Second Song," the voice in "At a Party" has no specified gender; nor does this persona speak from behind mask or disguise, as do the speakers in many poems about women. When she spoke most directly, Bogan framed her persona as androgynous. This is a Renaissance ideal; one image for the integration of opposing dualities was the figure of the androgyne. "At a Party," however, treats the more cosmic theme of the corruption of nature that can follow from worship of the flesh. The speaker observes a dizzy, drunken revelry that ignorantly mocks the ordered progress of the stars, and then orders flesh to assert primacy over spirit and proclaim the tyranny of the material and the final corruption of value and beauty. Against this projected debacle the speaker then invokes malice and enmity, which may bring salvation. The philosophy and the images recall John Donne and Dante: disorder and perversion affront the natural order of the universe and require stern correctives.

While Bogan's poems on the subject of love consistently treat the hazards and disasters of passion, models of harmonious, productive love exist mainly in the ideal implied by negative examples. The integration of duality, a fruitful union of passion and intellect, is imaged not in the lover, but in the artist.

Bogan expressed more than once her faith in art as a means to sanity and salvation in her troubled personal world, and two of her poems on art specifically explore the great power she attributed to it. "M., Singing" celebrates the capacity of art to articulate the unspeakable. The speaker finds that the melancholy words and subtle music of M.'s song cause the soul's hidden demons to step forth into the light of day. This is healing music, for these corrupt creatures abandon their unseen work of destruction and become subject to rational examination in human space; evil can be neutralized. "Song for a Slight Voice" returns to the theme of possessive love. The discipline of art, the speaker implies, has overcome the exigencies of passion, and the lover's stubborn heart will become an instrument for music, will hear the dance. Art can triumph over witless passion.

In two poems that explore the traditional theme of nature versus art, however, Bogan does not offer a clear-cut statement of superiority for either side. "To an Artist, To Take Heart" is an epigram in which the speaker contrasts the violent ends of Shakespeare's characters Hamlet, Othello, and Coriolanus with the peaceful death of the author who outlived them all. Neither nature nor art wins supremacy, but each finds its fulfillment. The speaker's wry view of the artist as parent to his creations is adumbrated in the title: the work of art does not kill the artist, for the author lives even though his characters die. Verb tenses, however, signify the reverse: "Shakespeare died" in the past, once and for all, whereas "Hamlet, Othello, Coriolanus fall" in the present, as the creation lives after the creator dies.

"Animal, Vegetable, Mineral" is an uncharacteristically long poem of sixty-five lines in rhymed five-line stanzas. It is a meditation on the subject of cross-pollination, which is a work of nature; but it takes as its starting point art objects twice removed from the natural world: a publication of color plates depicting glass models of flowers. Both language and subject matter point to the pervasive theme of cross-pollination, or integration, of nature and art, instinct and mind. Blossoms are Gothic or Baroque, bees are *Empire*. The precise workings of instinct and of natural functions stimulate thought in the human mind, here represented by Charles Darwin, and provide occasion for almost incomprehensible devotion to craft in the work of the Blaschkas, the Czech family of glassblowers who worked for fifty years to produce the botanical models. The speaker remains awed by cross-pollination of science, art, and nature: it is the process itself that is valuable, unfathomable, a loud mystery.

Like "Animal, Vegetable, Mineral," "Roman Fountain" and "Italian Morning"—two poems set in Italy—take visual art as their theme. The first emphasizes the process of making art while the latter focuses on the work of art. Each, too, expresses a quintessential Renaissance theme, the triumph of art over time. In "Roman Fountain" the speaker is a poet sustained and reinvigorated upon seeing water rising and falling in an ornate fountain. The gushing, noisy, ceaselessly moving water fructifies and enlivens the poet's imagination, but it does so because it has been shaped and directed by the carefully wrought fountain created by hands long dead. This perfect union of nature and art elates and inspires the poet. In "Italian Morning," on the other hand, the work of art confronts the speaker with human mortality. Two people awaken in an ornately decorated room, and the calm, silent presence of the painted fruit and flowers conveys a sense of timelessness. In contrast, the speaker's perception of time—placing the hour, naming the year—indicates a paradoxical poverty in human life: time evaporates in the act of being possessed.

These poems suggest a mystical dimension to art that is made even more explicit in two others, "The Alchemist" and "Musician." In the former the alchemist speaker represents the artist who has taken his own self as the base material for transmutation. The alchemist renounces material life and its rewards in search of a wholly spiritual existence and pleasure. Mere breathing will become the vehicle for ecstasy. The connection between breath and transcendent contemplation occurs in mystical traditions of both East and West; in the case of Bogan's alchemist the long search culminates in a vision of reality stripped of illusion, of pure substance without the accident of meaning.

"Musician" portrays process and performance in terms similar to some types of Zen Buddhist aesthetics. Musician and instrument join to produce harmony so effortless and perfect that it seems the instrument has a life of its own. The agent is subsumed in perfect art. Like the figure of the androgyne, the image of the musician with instrument represented to the Renaissance mind the perfect dynamic balance of material and spiritual, matter and form. This ideal of vital integration of opposites pervades Bogan's poems about art, most clearly in the many poems centering on the image of the musician.

Louise Bogan's preoccupation with the achievement of balance, harmony, and fruitfulness through reconciliation of opposites receives its finest expression in the poems that present most explicitly the struggle of the human mind to avert chaos and integrate impulse. Two poems that take a merely clinical look at the issue, "Evening in the Sanitarium" and "Psychiatrist's Song," recall her own experiences with the institutional view of mental illness. These poems are closer to the factual end of the fact-experience continuum, as is "Animal, Vegetable, Mineral," and all three are also very discursive and formally loose by comparison with her other works. For Bogan, it was formal rigor that produced the tension needed to convey intensity of thought and feeling.

Four poems deserve special notice as preeminent expressions of this struggle of the spirit. "Exhortation," "Simple Autumnal," "Kept," and "Henceforth, from the Mind" focus in turn on hate, grief, renunciation, and sublimation as healing powers.

"Exhortation" further elaborates the ideas expressed in "At a Party": the person who is conscious and moral and therefore alive lives in a world of the walking dead—the callous and the ignorant who are impervious to insight or ethics. In material terms, the latter always wins; success and failure rather than good or evil are the terms on which they operate. The speaker in the poem counsels detachment as the only remedy for the thinking, feeling person. The listener is advised to renounce both joy and rage, to leave behind the comforts of love and grief, and to cultivate indifference. This is a harsh doctrine, uncongenial to a vision of man as naturally good or perfectible. It has been called stoic; certainly, it accords with the Catholic philosophy of Bogan's early education, which emphasized the fall of man and a resultant debility of spirit. At the heart of the poem lies a crucial distinction, however: the living dead, preoccupied with trivia and sated with insolence, exist in a state of moribund sterility, passionless and bleak. The speaker's renunciation of passion and rage, grief and joy, does not deny these elements of human life, but rather requires a full realization (in its root meaning) of them. Discipline and detachment, superficially similar to indifference, sustain life in the face of mere repression and ignorance.

"Simple Autumnal," one of Bogan's few sonnets, makes a contrasting assertion: grief denied repudiates both life and death. The speaker compares delayed autumn with delayed grief; time is frozen and so is life. The maturing process seems to come to a standstill in nature as it mirrors the person who refuses grief, so that nature takes on the static character of art and is therefore unnatural. Sorrow could heal, fulfilling life's intent, but feelings remain unreachable. The poem expresses the experience of living death referred to in "Exhortation," but with one difference: in "Simple Autumnal" the speaker comprehends the situation of lifelessness fully, and suffers intensely thereby. The sense of the poem recalls many of Emily Dickinson's works, in particular those such as "Pain Has an Element of Blank" which explore the experience of unreleased pain.

Reminiscent of Dickinson also is the emphasis on renunciation in "Kept." Again, the speaker takes up the theme of movement versus stasis, life against lifelessness. Those who would cling to the past as represented by its artifacts, dolls, and toys, will never be free of it. Nostalgia can trap one in everlasting childishness, for the past must be destroyed in order to be the past. Growth and maturity can occur only in the passage of time. Without the process of growth a reverse process takes place: the person existing in an artificial world diminishes and indeed begins to metamorphosize until only an object remains. As in the two preceding poems, sanity is a function of conscious, heartfelt, and disciplined submission to the natural processes of life and death, growth and decay.

In "Henceforth, from the Mind," Bogan reaches beyond the pain of discipline and renunciation to affirm the final achievement of sublimation. The speaker does not advocate substitution or repression, as the notion of sublimation is often wrongly understood. It is real joy that will spring from the mind, from the tongue—the selfsame exaltation that the younger person ascribes to passion. The form of the poem harmonizes with this theme. The forward motion of the first two stanzas takes momentum from the "henceforth" that begins each and from the emphatic reversal of verb and subject in the two main clauses; the repetition of the rhyming couplets ending each stanza counterbalances this same forward motion. The last two stanzas mirror in their form the perfect transmutation of the material and spiritual that the poem asserts. In a single twelve-line sentence as convoluted as the image of the shell in the first line, syntactical momentum builds until the verb and—finally—the subject appear at the *end* of the sentence, which is also the end of the poem. This reversal of the usual sentence structure is itself a form of echoing: the sea and earth that will henceforth be known from their echoes within memory and imagination sound back to the resonating shell in a grammatical spiral that imitates the convolvulus' physical shape. The shell encloses the ocean, echoing a knowledge of that sea from which it is itself sundered. Sound and motion prevail in the rocking, cradling rhythms of bell and wave, the music of transcendent illumination, echoing through the depths within depths of perfect harmony.

Helen Jaskoski

Other major works

LONG FICTION: *The Glass Bees*, 1960 (translation with Elizabeth Mayer); *Elective Affinities*, 1963 (translation); *The Journal of Jules Renard*, 1964 (translation); *The Sorrows of Young Werther*, 1971 (translation); *Novella*, 1971 (translation).

NONFICTION: *Achievement in American Poetry*, 1950; *Selected Criticism*, 1955; *A Poet's Alphabet*, 1970 (Robert Phelps and Ruth Limmer, editors); *What the Woman Lived: Selected Letters of Louise Bogan 1920-1970*, 1973; *Journey Around My Room*, 1980.

Bibliography

Bowles, Gloria. *Louise Bogan's Aesthetic of Limitation*. Bloomington: Indiana University Press, 1987. Bowles uses a feminist perspective to examine Bogan and her work and asserts that the poet's "limitation" results from her notion of what she could and could not do within the male literary tradition. The author identifies Bogan as a modernist and explores a variety of influences—including William Butler Yeats and the Symbolists—on her poetry.

Collins, Martha. *Critical Essays on Louise Bogan*. Boston: G. K. Hall, 1984. The first collection of scholarly essays on Bogan ever published. The writings of fellow poets, including Ford Madox Ford and W. H. Auden, represent the majority of the thirty-five essays. Topics discussed are varied and range from the tendencies to misunderstand Bogan's work to feminist responses to her poetry. Collins has written an extensive and enlightening introduction.

Frank, Elizabeth. *Louise Bogan: A Portrait*. New York: Alfred A. Knopf, 1985. Although this book is intended for the general reader, it will also satisfy and inform Bogan's scholars. Frank deftly examines the relationship between Bogan's life and work, utilizing a variety of sources including letters, diaries, recollections of people who knew her, and unpublished and uncollected works. The author is imminently qualified for this ambitious—and highly successful—work, as she has studied Bogan for more than ten years.

Limmer, Ruth, ed. *What the Woman Lived: Selected Letters of Louise Bogan 1920-1970*. New York: Harcourt Brace Jovanovich, 1973. This key text offers the most intimate view of Bogan's life and emotions through the use of nearly five hundred of her letters that became available after her death in 1970. Particularly notable are the revelations this book provides about Bogan's feelings toward other poets such as Theodore Roethke. Limmer has edited previous material about Bogan and is the poet's literary executor.

Ridgeway, Jaquelin. *Louise Bogan*. Boston: Twayne, 1984. This ambitious book explores Bogan's childhood experiences that influenced her poetry, the symbols that express her poetic statements, and her use of the formal lyric style long after it had fallen out of favor with her contemporaries. Ridgeway also examines a rarely discussed topic: Bogan's influence on other poets.

EAVAN BOLAND

Born: Dublin, Ireland; September 24, 1944

Principal poetry

23 Poems, 1962; *New Territory*, 1967; *The War Horse*, 1975; *In Her Own Image*, 1980; *Introducing Eavan Boland*, 1981; *Night Feed*, 1982; *The Journey*, 1983; *The Journey and Other Poems*, 1987; *Selected Poems*, 1989.

Other literary forms

Eavan Boland collaborated with Michael MacLiammoir on the critical study *W. B. Yeats and His World* (1971). Boland has contributed essays in journals such as the *American Poetry Review*; she also reviews regularly for the *Irish Times*.

Achievements

Ireland has produced a generation of distinguished poets since 1960, and all of them have been men. Seamus Heaney is the best known of this group of poets to American audiences, but the reputations of Thomas Kinsella, Derek Mahon, Michael Longley, Paul Muldoon, and Tom Paulin continue to grow. Poetry by contemporary Irishwomen is also a significant part of the Irish literary scene. Boland is one of a group of notable women poets including Medbh McGuckian, Eithne Strong, and Eilean Ni Chuilleanain. In an essay published in 1987, "The Woman Poet: Her Dilemma," Boland indicates her particular concern with the special problems of being a woman and a poet. Male stereotypes about the role of women in society continue to be very strong in Ireland and make Irishwomen less confident about their creative abilities. Women must contend as well with another potentially depersonalizing pressure, that of feminist ideology, which urges women toward another sort of conformity. Boland and the other poets mentioned above have managed to overcome both obstacles and develop personal voices.

Biography

Eavan Boland was born on September 24, 1944, in Dublin, Ireland. Her parents were Frederick Boland and Frances Kelly Boland. Her father was a distinguished Irish diplomat who served as Irish ambassador to Great Britain (1950-1956) and to the United States (1956-1964). Her mother was a painter who had studied in Paris in the 1930's. Boland's interest in painting as a subject for poetry can be traced to her mother's encouragement. Because of her father's diplomatic career, Boland was educated in Dublin, London, and New York. From 1962 to 1966, she attended Trinity College, Dublin; begin-

ning in 1967, she taught at Trinity College for a year. In 1968, she received
the Macauley Fellowship for poetry.

In the 1980's, Boland reviewed regularly for the arts section of the *Irish
Times.* In 1987, she held a visiting fellowship at Bowdoin College. She married Kevin Casey, the novelist, with whom she had two children, Sarah, born
in 1975, and Eavan, born in 1978.

Boland began writing poetry in Dublin in the early 1960's. She recalls this
early period: " . . . scribbling poems in boarding school, reading Yeats after
lights out, revelling in the poetry on the course. . . . Dublin was a coherent
space then, a small circumference in which to . . . become a poet. . . . The
last European city. The last literary smallholding." After her marriage, Boland left academe and moved out of Dublin and into the suburbs to become
"wife, mother and housewife." *In Her Own Image* and *Night Feed* focus on
Boland's domestic life in the suburbs and especially on her sense of womanhood.

Analysis

Hearth and history provide a context for the poetry of Eavan Boland. She
is inspired by both the domestic and the cultural. Her subjects are the alienating suburban places which encourage one to forget one's cultural roots, her
children with their typically Irish names, demystified horses in Dublin streets
that can still evoke the old glories from time to time, and the old Irish stories themselves, which may at times be vivid and evocative and at times
mere nostalgia. Boland's distinctly female perspective is achieved in several
poems about painting which note the dominance of male painters in the history of art from the Renaissance to the Impressionists, painters such as Jan
van Eyck, Edgar Degas, Jean Auguste Dominique Ingres, and Auguste Renoir. Women were painted by these artists in traditional domestic or agrarian
postures. Boland perceives woman as far less sanitized and submissive. Her
collection *In Her Own Image* introduces such shocking and taboo subjects as
anorexia, mastectomy, masturbation, and menstruation.

Two of Boland's most recent volumes, *In Her Own Image* and *Night Feed*,
deal exclusively with the subject of woman. *Night Feed* for the most part
treats suburban woman and chronicles the daily routine of a Dublin housewife in a quite positive way. The book has poems about babies' diapers,
about washing machines, about feeding babies. The cover has an idyllic drawing of a mother feeding a child. The other volume, however, *In Her Own
Image*, published two years before *Night Feed*, seems written by a different
person. Its candid and detailed treatment of taboo subjects contrasts sharply
with the idyllic world of *Night Feed.* Boland's ability to present both worlds
testifies to her poetic maturity.

The need for connection is a major theme in Boland's poetry. Aware of
traditional connections in Irish and classical myths, she longs for an earlier

period when such ties came instinctively. Her sense of loss with respect to these traditional connections extends beyond mythology to Irish history as well, even to Irish history in this century. Modern-day Dubliners have been cut off from the sustaining power of myth and history. Their lives, therefore, seem empty and superficial. Surrounded with the shards of a lost culture they cannot piece together these shards into a coherent system.

The alienation of the modern urban Irish from their cultural roots is the subject of Boland's poem "The New Pastoral." She considers alienation from a woman's perspective. Aware of the myths which have traditionally sustained males, Boland desires equivalent myths for females. She longs for a "new pastoral" which will celebrate women's ideals, but she finds none. She encounters many domestic "signs," but they do not "signify" for her. She has a vague sense of once having participated in a coherent ritual, of having "danced once/ on a frieze." Now, however, she has no access to the myth. Men seem to have easier access to their cultural roots than women do. The legends of the cavemen contain flint, fire, and wheel, which allowed man "to read his world." Later in history, men had pastoral poems to define and celebrate their place in the world. A woman has no similar defining and consoling rituals and possesses no equivalent cultural signs. She seems a "displaced person/ in a pastoral chaos," unable to create a "new pastoral." Surrounded with domestic signs, "lamb's knuckle," "the washer," "a stink/ of nappies," "the greasy/ bacon flitch," she still has no access to myth. Hints of connection do not provide a unified myth. "I feel/ there was a past,/ there was a pastoral/ and these/ chance sights—/ what are they all/ but late amnesias/ of a rite/ I danced once/ on a frieze?" The final image of the dancer on the frieze echoes both John Keats's Grecian urn and William Butler Yeats's dancers and golden bird. The contemporary poet, however, has lost contact. Paradoxically, the poem constitutes the "new pastoral" which it claims is beyond its reach. The final allusion to the dancer on the frieze transforms the mundane objects of domestic life into something more significant, something sacred.

Boland seems in conflict over whether women should simply conform to male stereotypes for women or should resist these pressures to lead "lesser lives," to attend to "hearth not history." Many poems in *Night Feed* accept this "lesser" destiny, poems such as "Night Feed," "Hymn," and "In the Garden." The several poems in this volume which deal with paintings, "Domestic Interior," "Fruit on a Straight-Sided Tray," "Degas's Laundresses," "Woman Posing (After Ingres)," "On Renoir's 'The Grape-Pickers,'" all deal with paintings by male painters which portray women in traditional domestic or rural roles. The women in these paintings appear content with their "lesser lives." Poems such as "It's a Woman's World" seem less accepting, however, more in the spirit of *In Her Own Image*, which vigorously rejects basing one's identity on male stereotypes. "It's a Woman's World" complements "The New Pastoral" in its desire for a balance between hearth and history.

> as far as history goes
> we were never
> on the scene of the crime. . . .
> And still no page
> scores the low music
> of our outrage.

Women have had no important roles in history, Boland asserts. They produce "low music," rather than heroic music. Nevertheless, women can have an intuitive connection with their own "starry mystery," their own cosmic identity. The women in those paintings apparently pursuing their "lesser lives," may have a sense of "greater lives." The male world (including male artists) must be kept in the dark about this, must keep believing that nothing mythic is being experienced.

> That woman there,
> craned to the starry mystery
> is merely getting a breath
> of evening air,
> while this one here—
> her mouth
> a burning plume—
> she's no fire-eater,
> just my frosty neighbour
> coming home.

The "woman's world" and the "starry mysteries" are presented far less romantically in Boland's volume *In Her Own Image*. The poems in this volume refuse to conform to male stereotypes of woman as happy domestic partner. They explore male/female conflicts in the deepest and most intimate psychic places. The title *In Her Own Image* indicates the volume's concern with the problem of "identity." Boland wishes to be an individual, free to determine her own life, but other forces seek to control her, to make her conform to female stereotypes. A woman should be perfect, unchanging, youthful, pure, in short, should be ideal. Male-dominated society does not wish women to explore their own deepest desires. Women transform these social messages into the voice of their own consciences, or, in Sigmund Freud's terms, their own superegos: "Thou shalt not get fat!" "Thou shalt not get old!" "Thou shalt not get curious."

These naysaying inner voices dominate the first three poems of *In Her Own Image*: "Tirade for the Mimic Muse," "In Her Own Image," and "In His Own Image." The "mimic muse" in the first poem urges the speaker to "make up," to conceal aging with cosmetics. The illustration for this poem shows a chunky and unkempt woman gazing into a mirror and seeing a perfect version of herself, thin, unwrinkled, physically fit. The phrase "her own image" in the second poem refers to another idealization, the "image" of perfection which the speaker carries around inside herself. She finally frees herself of this psychic burden by planting it outside in the garden. The illustration shows a naked woman bending over a small coffin. The third poem, "In His Own Image," considers the pressures of a husband's expectations on a wife's sense of self. The speaker in this third poem does not try to reshape her features with makeup. She is battered into a new shape by a drunken husband. No illustration appears with this poem.

The speaker's "tirade" in "Tirade for the Mimic Muse" begins at once and establishes the intensely hostile tone of much of *In Her Own Image*: "I've caught you out. You slut. You fat trout." She despises the impulse in herself to conform to a stereotype, to disguise the physical signs of time passing: "the lizarding of eyelids," "the whiskering of nipples," "the slow betrayals of our bedroom mirrors." In the final section of the poem, the authentic self has suppressed those conforming impulses: "I, who mazed my way to womanhood/ Through all your halls of mirrors, making faces." Now the mirror's glass is cracked. The speaker promises a true vision of the world, but the vision will not be idyllic: "I will show you true reflections, terrors." Terrors preoccupy Boland for much of this book.

"In Her Own Image" and "In His Own Image" deal with different aspects of the "perfect woman." The first poem has a much less hostile tone than does "Tirade for the Mimic Muse." The speaker seems less threatened by the self-image from which she wishes to distance herself. Images of gold and amethyst and jasmine run through the poem. Despite the less hostile tone, Boland regards this "image" as a burdensome idealization which must be purged for psychic health: "She is not myself/ anymore." The speaker plants this "image" in the garden outside: "I will bed her,/ She will bloom there," safely removed from consciousness. The poem "In His Own Image" is full of anxiety. The speaker cannot find her center, her identity. Potential signs of identity lie all around her, but she cannot interpret them. "Celery feathers, . . . / bacon flitch, . . . / kettle's paunch, . . . / these were all I had to go on, . . . / meagre proofs of myself." A drunken husband responds to his wife's identity crisis by pounding her into his own desired "shape."

> He splits my lip with his fist,
> shadows my eye with a blow,
> knuckles my neck to its proper angle.
> What a perfectionist!
> His are a sculptor's hands:
> they summon
> form from the void,
> they bring

me to myself again.
I am a new woman.

How different are these two methods of coping with psychic conflict. In "In Her Own Image," the speaker plants her old self lovingly in the garden. In "In His Own Image," the drunken husband reshapes his wife's features with violent hands. The wife in the second poem says that she is now a "new woman." If one reads this volume as a single poem, as Boland evidently intends that one should (all the illustrations have the same person as their subject), one understands that the desperate tone of other poems in the book derives from the suffering of this reshaped "new woman," victim of male exploitation.

The next four poems of *In Her Own Image* deal with very private subjects familiar to women but not often treated in published poems: anorexia, mastectomy, masturbation, and menstruation. Both poems and Constance Hart's drawings are startlingly frank. The poet wants readers to experience "woman" in a more complete way, to realize the dark side of being female. The poems further illustrate Boland's sense of alienation from cultural myths or myths of identity. She desires connections, but she knows that she is unlikely to have them. She is therefore left with images which signify chaos rather than coherence, absence rather than presence, emptiness rather than fullness.

Two of the four poems, "Anorexia" and "Mastectomy," read like field reports from the battle of the sexes. The other two poems, "Solitary" and "Menses," have a female perspective but are also full of conflict. In the illustrations for "Anorexia," a very determined, extremely thin, naked woman, arms folded, looks disapprovingly at a fat woman lolling on a couch. An anorexic woman continues to believe that she is fat, despite the fact that she is a virtual skeleton. Boland introduces a religious level in the first three lines: "Flesh is heretic./ My body is a witch./ I am burning it." The conviction that her body is a witch runs through the whole poem. Here, in an extreme form, is the traditional Roman Catholic view that soul and body are separate. The body must be punished because, since the Fall, it has been the dwelling place of the devil. The soul must suppress the body in order for the soul to be saved. This tradition provides the anorexic with a religious reason for starving herself. In this poem, she revels in the opportunity to "torch" her body: "Now the bitch is burning." A presence even more disturbing than the witch is introduced in the second half of the poem, a ghostly male presence whom the anorexic speaker desires to please. To please this unnamed male presence, the speaker must become thin, so thin that she can somehow return to the womb imagined here paradoxically as male: "I will slip/ back into him again/ as if I had never been away." This return to the male womb will atone for the sin of being born a woman, with "hips and breasts/ and lips and heat/ and sweat and fat and greed."

In "Mastectomy," male-female conflict predominates. Male surgeons, envious of a woman's breasts (an effective transformation of the male-centered Freudian paradigm), cut off a breast and carry it away with them. The shocking drawing shows one gowned male surgeon passing the breast on a serving dish to another gowned male surgeon. The woman who has experienced this physical and psychological violation cries despairingly "I flatten to their looting." The sympathetic words of the surgeon before the operation belie the sinister act of removing the breast. It can now become part of male fantasy, as a symbol of primal nourishment and primal home: "So they have taken off/ what slaked them first,/ what they have hated since:/ blue-veined/ white-domed/ home/ of wonder/ and the wetness/ of their dreams."

The next two poems, "Solitary" and "Menses," deal with equally private aspects of a woman's life, autoeroticism and menstruation. "Solitary" has a celebratory attitude toward self-arousal. The drawing shows a relaxed naked female figure lying on her stomach. Religious imagery is used in this poem as it is in "Anorexia," but here the body is worshiped rather than feared. The only negative aspect of "Solitary" is its solitude. The female speaker is unconnected with another person. Solitary pleasures are intense but less so than the pleasures of intercourse. The reader is taken on a journey from arousal to orgasm to postorgasmic tranquillity. The religious language at first seems gratuitous but then perfectly appropriate. The speaker affirms the holiness of her body: "An oratory of dark,/ a chapel of unreason." She has a few moments of panic as the old words of warning flash into her mind: "You could die for this./ The gods could make you blind." These warnings do not deter her, however, from this sacred rite:

> how my cry
> blasphemes
> light and dark,
> screams
> land from sea,
> makes word flesh
> that now makes me
> animal.

During this period of arousal and climax, her "flesh summers," but then it returns again to winter: "I winter/ into sleep." "Menses" deals with the private act of menstruation. A cosmic female voice addresses the speaker as menstruation begins, attempting to focus her attention solely on the natural powers working in her body. The speaker resists this effort. She feels simultaneously "sick of it" and drawn to this process. She struggles to retain her freedom. "Only my mind is free," she says. Her body is taken over by tidal forces. "I am bloated with her waters./ I am barren with her blood." At the end of the poem, the speaker seems more accepting of this natural cycle. She reflects on two other cycles which she has experienced, childbirtn and intercourse. All three cycles, she begins to see, make her a new person: "I am bright and original."

The final three poems of *In Her Own Image*, "Witching," "Exhibitionist," and "Making-up," return to the theme that "Myths/ are made by men" (from "Making-up"). Much of a woman's life is spent reacting to male stereotypes. In "Witching," Boland further explores the idea of woman-as-witch, which was introduced in "Anorexia." Historically, women accused by men of being witches were doomed. The charges were usually either trumped-up or trivial. Boland's witch fantasizes about turning the table on her male persecutors and burning them first: "I will/ reserve/ their arson,/ make/ a pyre/ of my haunch . . . the stench/ of my crotch"—it is a grim but fitting fate for these male witch-burners. Another male stereotype, woman-as-stripper, is treated in the poem "Exhibitionist." This poem has the last accompanying drawing, a vulnerable young woman pulling her dress up over her head and naked to those watching her, perhaps as Boland feels naked toward those who have read through this volume. The male observers in "Exhibitionist" have in mind only gratifying their lusts. The speaker detests this exploitation and hopes to have a deeper impact on these leering males, hopes to touch them spiritually with her shining flesh: "my dark plan:/ Into the gutter/ of their lusts/ I burn/ the shine/ of my flesh." The final poem, "Making-up," returns to the theme of "Tirade for the Mimic Muse," that women must alter their appearances to please men, but that men have no such demands placed upon them. The poem rehearses a litany of transformations of the speaker's "naked face." "Myths/ are made by men," this poem asserts. The goddesses men imagine can never be completely captured by that "naked face." A woman's natural appearance inevitably has flaws; it is not perfect like that of a goddess. Women are encouraged by men to disguise these flaws to make themselves look perfect. From these "rouge pots," a goddess comes forth, at least in men's eyes. Women should really know better.

> Mine are the rouge pots,
> the hot pinks, . . .
> out of which
> I dawn.

Eavan Boland is determined to make poetry out of her domestic life. *In Her Own Image* and *Night Feed* indicate that she has turned to the very ordinary subjects of hearth, rather than to the larger subjects of history, which she explored in her earlier volumes *New Territory* and *The War Horse*. In "The Woman Poet: Her Dilemma," Boland admits to uncertainty about this new orientation. She is encouraged especially, however, by the example of French and Dutch genre painters, whose work she calls "unglamorous, workaday, authentic," possessing both ordinariness and vision: "The hare in its muslin bag, the crusty loaf, the women fixed between menial tasks and hu-

man dreams." In her own equally ordinary domestic life, she believes that
she has found a personal voice.

Boland's next major collection, *The Journey and Other Poems*, explores
more fully the poetic implications of this uncertainty. *In Her Own Image* and
Night Feed offer opposed accounts of Boland's concerns as a woman and
a writer, the former vehemently critical and openly outraged at sexual in-
justices, the latter more generously idyllic and positive about the domestic
side of her femininity. In *The Journey and Other Poems*, Boland incorporates this ambivalence into the fabric of her poems, channeling the tension
between her contrary aspects into an antithetical lyric energy; each piece,
that is, derives its form and force from a doubleness in the poet's mind, an
impulse to be at once critical and affirmative. Instead of lamenting her inner
confusions and contradictions, however, Boland builds a new sense of the
lyric poem and engages with renewed vigor the vexed questions of gender,
tradition, and myth that characterize her work.

The collection is divided into three sections, forming a triptych. In traditional religious painting, a triptych is composed of three canvases, side by
side, the outer two either elaborating upon or supporting visually the central
portion, which usually contains the main subject of the work. In *The Journey and Other Poems*, the first and third sections comment upon, refocus,
and expand the thematically dense matter of the central section, which contains "The Journey"—one of Boland's finest lyric achievements—and its
"Envoi." Furthermore, Boland uses the structure of the triptych to underscore the ambivalence she feels. In the first section, the reader encounters
memorial and idyll; in the third section, one finds the opposite, a vehement
critique of inherited sexual mores and the patriarchal "tradition." Only in
the central portion of the volume, "The Journey," does Boland take on both
aspects at once and attempt, not to reconcile one to the other, but to reani-
mate and re-energize what she calls a dying, diminished poetic language.

The volume opens with a nostalgic tribute to the poet's mother, "I Remember." Boland recalls her mother's studio, and her almost irrepressible
need, as a child exploring that room, "to touch, to handle, to dismantle it,/
the mystery." Boland longs for the mystery of innocence and the childlike
wonder of a lost time—before the harsh realities of Irish economics and
suburban alienation had taken root—when the world seemed balanced, "composed" and beautiful; but in the poem that world is veiled and hidden from
her, like the otherworldly elegance of her mother's "French Empire chairs"
over which opaque cotton sheets have been draped. Similarly, in "The Oral
Tradition," when Boland overhears two women exchanging gossip—figures
who, emblematically, "were standing in shadow"—she longs for "a musical
sub-text," an "oral song" which seems only to express itself in "fragments
and innuendoes," which nevertheless resonate with "a sense/ suddenly of
truth." Boland wants to discover the archetypal "truth" buried under opaque

surfaces, and, as she says in "Suburban Woman: A Detail," to find traces of the lost "goddess" within her instinctive, feminine memory. She expresses her need to be "healed into myth" through poetry and to recover the deeply ingrained, basic "patterns" of her womanhood.

The third section, on the other hand, works negatively, upsetting traditional myths of the archetypal feminine. In "Listen. This Is the Noise of Myth," Boland starts to recount a "story" of "a man and woman," setting the stage for a traditional version of domestic order, but she becomes self-conscious and critical, calling her own methods into question, making her characters—especially the woman—into "fugitives" from their traditional roles. Boland proposes to "set truth to rights," defiantly dismantling the old stories. She laments that even she must put "the same mirrors on the old magic" and return to the "old romances." Despite the sweet lure of story-telling, Boland wants to remake her own role as an author, and though she finds herself repeatedly thwarted by the "consolations of the craft," she struggles on.

Several poems in the third section echo Boland's other work. "Tirade for the Lyric Muse" recalls her "Tirade for the Mimic Muse," but here the subject is plastic surgery. The speaker addresses a sister "in the crime," an epithet which suggests a fellow poet, but one who, for Boland, has betrayed herself and her implicit commitment to "truth" by having the ordinary "surface" of her face altered to conform to a false notion of "skin deep" beauty. The true "music" of poetry, for Boland, cannot be captured by outward conformity to the "cruel" standards of a male world. Poems such as "Fond Memory" and "An Irish Childhood in England: 1951" respond to lyrics such as "I Remember" in the first section, rejecting nostalgia and finding in Boland's own indelible Irishness a sense of exile and insecurity. To be an English-speaking Irish native is to be a perpetual outcast. Irishness, for Boland, represents her own inability to settle upon a given set of values or a certain appearance of "truth"; her nationality, paradoxically, undermines easy acceptance of the safe "myths" she craves.

If the first section works to rediscover the force of myth, and the last section to dismantle the false safety net of traditional roles, the central portion—"The Journey"—springs directly from a double impulse. "The Journey" is a dream-vision, a description of a mental journey to the underworld undertaken in the poet's dreams. Many medieval poets, including Geoffrey Chaucer, wrote dream-visions. Like these poets, Boland depicts herself falling asleep over an open book of classical poetry. This connection to tradition, both medieval and ancient, is important to the poem, which describes a poetics, an account of how poems are or ought to be written. Boland searches for a new, vital form of writing. She begins by stating angrily that "there has never . . . been a poem to an antibiotic. . . ." She questions what is the proper subject for poetry, introducing antibiotics as something about which no one would bother to write. She espouses the ordinary and the domestic rather than the ethereal of the "unblemished" as a basis for poetry. In order to heal us, and to repair our diminished relationship to "the language," poetry must look with renewed energy to the particulars of everyday life.

In her dream, Boland descends with Sappho—the greatest ancient female poet, whom she has been reading—to the land of the dead, where she meets the ghosts of mothers and housewives, women in whose experiences Boland has been trying to discover her mythical roots. Boland pleads with her mentor to let her "be their witnesses," but she is told that what she has seen is "beyond speech." She awakens, only to find "nothing was changed," despite her vision of "truth," and she weeps. This poetic "misery," taken up in the poem's "Envoi," comes from disappointment at being incapable of resuscitating the lost myths of womanhood, the anxiety of trying to bless "the ordinary" or to sanctify "the common" without the comfort of a traditionally sanctioned muse. Boland's work, to revive the feminine in poetry, results in a difficult mixture of discovery, desire, dissatisfaction, and rage. "The Journey" is a complex poem, and one of Boland's best works. It expresses both a naïve, dreamy faith in the power of myth and "truth" and a severe self-consciousness that calls the elements of her feminine identity into question. The ability to dwell poetically upon such a problematic doubleness in a single poem truly indicates Boland's literary accomplishment.

Kevin McNeilly
Arthur E. McGuinness

Other major work
NONFICTION: *W. B. Yeats and His World*, 1971 (with Michael MacLiammoir).

Bibliography
Boland, Eavan. "The Serinette Principle: The Lyric in Contemporary Poetry." *Parnassus* 15, no. 2 (1989): 7-25. Boland writes obliquely about her own poetic practice in relation to her American contemporaries. The lyric poem, she argues, should achieve the "serinette" principle, a complex idea which is emblematized by the eighteenth century hand-organs used to teach caged birds to sing; that is, the lyric must, however tenuously, liberate the reader's limited perception from the narrow confines of time. The new lyric, epitomized for Boland by the work of Jorie Graham and Robert Hass, recognizes the time-honored impulse of song but has "reshaped [its] contents." Boland looks to such work for plasticity, experiment, and expansiveness.
Johnston, Dillon. *Irish Poetry After Joyce*. Notre Dame, Ind.: University of Notre Dame Press, 1985. Johnston uncovers a "broader and more com-

prehensive Irish identity" in part by discussing the feminine side of the poems of Medbh McGuckian, Eilean Ni Chuilleanain, and Boland. He argues, briefly, that Boland's *Night Feed* concentrates on the domestic woman, and that she looks with jaded wit at the local homebody, following in the footsteps of Patrick Kavanaugh.

McElroy, James. "The Contemporary Fe/Male Poet: A Preliminary Reading." In *New Irish Writing*, edited by James Brophy and Eamon Grennan. Boston: Twayne, 1989. McElroy examines the same trio of writers as Johnston with considerably more depth. In particular, he defends Boland against critical charges of "stridency" and overstatement, arguing that her recurrent confrontations with the Irish domestic woman constitute a crucial part of her poetics of recovery and renewal, and that her willful reiterations of "female miseries" form a powerful catalog of matters that must be treated emphatically if Irish poetry is to recover its potency.

McGuiness, Arthur E. "Hearth and History: Poetry by Contemporary Irish Women." In *Cultural Contexts and Literary Idioms in Contemporary Irish Literature*, edited by Michael Kenneally. Totowa, N.J.: Barnes & Noble Books, 1988. McGuiness redresses an imbalance in the critical treatment of Irish women poets, contrasting McGuckian, Boland, and Eithne Strong. He examines the theme of "hearth and history," troublesome issues of domesticity and culture. He finds in Boland's work a "distinctively feminine perspective" on taboo subjects such as masturbation and anorexia. Boland dwells on present-day alienation from mythical connectedness and longs for the instinctive spiritual balance of an earlier period in Irish history.

Reizbaum, Marilyn. "An Interview with Eavan Boland." *Contemporary Literature* 30, no. 4 (1989): 470-479. Boland discusses women's poetry, feminism, Ireland, Yeats, tradition, and the muse. Her comments are accessible to all readers and useful for understanding her poetry.

PHILIP BOOTH

Born: Hanover, New Hampshire; October 8, 1925

Principal poetry

Letter from a Distant Land, 1957; *The Islanders*, 1961; *Weathers and Edges*, 1966; *Margins: A Sequence of New and Selected Poems*, 1970; *Available Light*, 1976; *Before Sleep*, 1980; *Relations: Selected Poems, 1950-1985*, 1986; *Selves: New Poems*, 1990.

Other literary forms

Philip Booth's poetry forms the basis of his literary reputation. He has given readings of his works on both radio and television, and he has edited several volumes of poetry.

Achievements

The finely crafted poetry of Philip Booth has a strong, clear connection with his ancestral home of Castine, Maine, a colonial coastal village of fewer than seven hundred year-round residents. Through his poetry, Booth has carefully captured this place; he is at home with its blustery winters, its tides and charts, its starkness, its dry humor, its sparse, homely conversation, and its flora, fauna, and animals. Yet, like Emily Dickinson, through an intimate closeness with one place, the poet speaks of our humanity and becomes universal.

Booth's poems move from engaging openings to clear, satisfying conclusions and are meticulously placed in each volume, moving toward a final resolution of their themes. Booth husbands his language, but his poems hold a richness of meaning and look with curiosity and wonder at the miracle of human life. The poet, whose works have been translated into French, Portuguese, Finnish, Dutch, and Italian, and have been lauded by fellow poet Maxine Kumin as having a "wonderfully consistent tone," is recognized as one of the best of late twentieth century writers. His first collection of poems, *Letter from a Distant Land*, won the 1957 Lamont Prize of the Academy of American Poets. Additional honors include Guggenheim and Rockefeller fellowships, grants from the National Institute of Arts and Letters and from the National Endowment for the Arts, and awards from *Poetry*, *Saturday Review*, *The Virginia Quarterly Review*, and *Poetry Northwest*. In 1983, Booth was elected a fellow of the Academy of American Poets. His 1986 collection *Relations* earned for him the Maurice English Poetry Award.

Biography

As his poetry suggests, Philip Booth is a New Englander, a man of Down

East sensibilities and humor. Born in 1925 in Hanover, New Hampshire, to a Dartmouth English professor and his wife, and having grown up both in New Hampshire and in Maine, he settled in the white-clapboard, black-shuttered, 130-year-old house in Castine which has belonged to his family for five generations. Thomas Jefferson appointed Booth's maternal great-great-grandfather to serve as customs collector in Castine two hundred years ago, and the Greek revival house on Main Street where the poet would reside has belonged to his mother's family for nearly a century.

Booth received his undergraduate degree at Dartmouth College in New Hampshire; there, as a freshman in a noncredit seminar during the summer of 1943, he met Robert Frost, who acted as an occasional grandfather for Booth's three daughters during the early years of his marriage (in 1946, to Margaret Tillman). Booth was graduated from Dartmouth in 1947, taught at Bowdoin College in Maine in 1949, and then dropped out of teaching for a while. He hoped to be a novelist and, to pay the bills for the next four years, worked in both Vermont and New Hampshire at jobs that included a stint in Dartmouth's admissions office, work as a traveling ski-book salesman, and some time in a carpentry shop. After deciding that he was not a good storyteller but rather a good wordsmith, Booth turned his attention to writing poetry. He earned his master's degree at Syracuse University, and for the next twenty-five years he served as senior poet in the creative writing program there. During these years he edited several volumes of *Syracuse Poems*.

Since the early 1950's, Booth has published poetry in many leading literary magazines and journals, including *Harper's*, *The Kenyon Review*, *The New Yorker*, and *Saturday Review*.

Analysis

Philip Booth's list of accomplishments is impressive, and his reputation is international, but he is, most of all, a humanist speaking to an individual audience, one person at a time. Although he is widely identified as a regional poet who writes of life in a harsh, cold northern climate, Booth's subjects cover the whole range of human experience. The powerful forces of nature and human relations with them, play prominently in his work, but his poems also speak of other human concerns: love, sex, marriage, children, aging, poverty, death, and the mysteries of existence. In his earliest collection, *Letter from a Distant Land*, his poetic patterns are fairly traditional; however, as one moves to his later poems, one finds less attention to form and sometimes an abandonment of rhyme and stanza. In all Booth's works, one senses the struggle of form and matter; his themes are of human loneliness and vulnerability set against the impersonal forces of nature. This struggle is never fully reconciled, but the poet examines the need for the coexistence of humankind and the natural world.

In the sonnet "Good Friday, 1954," which appears in *Letter from a Distant*

Land, the number of lines and the rhyme scheme follow the traditional pattern, but the poet uses slant rhyme, with "lodged" and "judged" ending the sixth and eighth lines. The poem's final line reveals Booth's closeness to the New England school headed by Robert Frost and its belief in the moral function of poetry: "To spike a rumor sacrifice a man." "The Wilding," another early poem, issues a springtime call to love; Booth plays on the sexual suggestiveness of jack-in-the-pulpits and maidenhair fern. E. E. Cummings' playfulness is echoed in "a sweet fern questionmark/ whorls green as green is today,/ and ferns ask no answer a swallow/ can't fly." The youthful joy and exuberance of this poem fill the reader with hope and expectation. Another early poem, "First Lesson," instructs a daughter about trusting the father who is cradling her head in the "cup" of his hand as he gently urges her to learn to swim. Just as the swimmer learns to trust the sea, a person can learn to survive by remembering experiences that, like the sea, "will hold you." "Chart 1203" captures the essence of sailing's allure and challenge in saying of the sailor, "He knows the chart is not the sea." The Atlantic coast is threatening, Booth says, only for the sailor who is not familiar with its eccentricities and relies on charts and maps alone to guide him. The sailor must have "local knowledge of shoal/ or ledge." The poem celebrates the thrill of meeting a challenge and surviving through a combination of good luck and skill.

The volume's title poem, "Letter from a Distant Land," combines slant rhyme and true rhyme. The poem, a lengthy meditation about the area around Henry David Thoreau's Walden Pond and the changes it has undergone since the nineteenth century, is written in terza rima, with long sentences and a doubly alternating rhyme scheme. The rhyme and meter are, nevertheless, so subtle, with approximate combinations such as "desk" and "risk," that the reader hardly notices them. In this way the poem does have the flavor of a letter written from a distant land to a friend, with themes of the connectedness of writer and reader, the natural world and human values.

In *Weathers and Edges,* New England voices speak with terse language and dry humor. The arrangement of the poems moves from works such as "Heart of Darkness," which deals with large human concerns, to personal poems of private experience such as "Cleaning Out the Garage," and then outward again to a series of sea poems set on the Maine coast. The reader of "Heart of Darkness" is struck by the short lines arranged as a column on the page: the poem itself is presented as "some sort of base/ to start out from." The stanza arrangement in "Cleaning Out the Garage" is less lean. Filling out the page, its four stanzas move from nine to ten to eleven and finally to twelve lines, ironically accumulating lines as the garage is cleaned out and its contents diminished, and ending with an almost Frostian moral: the speaker has learned, after discarding all the "useless stuff" stored since his boyhood, "how to let go what won't do." "Report from the Scene," an immediate description of the effects of severe local thunderstorms on boats moored in a Maine harbor, is arranged in eleven two-line stanzas; in it, the forces of nature seem nearly overwhelming, but two people "with reflex love" reach for each other and face the storm. The individuals watching the violent storm are an image of human vulnerability in the face of natural forces, but as the two reach out toward each other, they and the storm are able to co-exist.

Relations includes selections from all Booth's previous collections, as well as thirty-one new poems. The later works use terse Down East language, slanted syllables, and simple Anglo-Saxon diction, omitting rhyme and meter. The fragmentation of short lines and stanzas gives these poems a conversational quality. Woven into these works is the theme of human isolation but also of love and connectedness with the world, for the poet often looks to nature for answers and for the reassurance of order. The title poem, "Relations," explores relationships not only of people to one another over space and time but also among lines in a poem, of words to other words, and of the limits the poet imposes on them. These poems do not offer certainties for the reader, but rather uncertainties, as the poet struggles to find his way through questions such as "Where did I come from?" and "Where am I going?" Booth speaks of this searching as a "coming to terms" with experience, and of human relationships as giving meaning to life.

Originally published in *Margins*, "Supposition with Qualification" questions the eternal mystery of being. The speaker discusses a man who "if he could say it" certainly meant to do so, but who is never clear about what "it" means. Instead, the man intended to say "how it felt when he let himself/ feel." It is, however, difficult for him to let himself feel anything without allowing his mind to get in the way. The poem includes several question words: "what," "how," "when." Even with the need to know suggested by these words, the man does not want to intellectualize but to feel, to "give himself up," although the qualification itself, "if he could say it," suggests his inability to do so, as well as the human need to question and articulate experience.

"The Man on the Wharf," which is arranged in direct two-line stanzas, describes a man, drunk with Jim Beam whiskey, who has lost his woman. He watches another man shuck clams; although he does not know why he watches, one senses in him a questioning about his life and his loss: he "swallows no answer/ but questions in bourbon this seeming harbor." "Seeming harbor" questions what is real and what is imagined, while the man turns to perhaps the most fundamental source for answers in the poem's concluding lines: "The sea is all he can ask."

"The Stranding" journeys inward, as the first-person speaker puts his eyes to the eyes of his own skull to look through both pairs of eyes into his own head, only to find a "stranding," a sense of being left alone in a helpless position, of being separated from his essential self. The speaker, though, can hardly see himself, and, when he considers calling to his inner self by name, he realizes that the inner self whom he can barely see is listening to porpoises, not to the self on the outside calling to him. Perhaps in answer to the universal question "Who am I?" the speaker finds isolation. In simple, carefully sharpened language arranged in stanzas of three short lines each, the poem successfully creates the effect of the speaker explaining to an individual listener what happened as he searched for himself.

Reminding one of David Waggoner's "Return to the Swamp," "The Question Poem" also deals with eternals. What does the wind mean? What "sudden discipline" determines the course of birds' migrations? Do the seabirds fish for answers, too? No answers are offered, but, like any human being, the speaker finds it impossible to imagine a world in which he himself is absent. He does seem to find some hint of a response to his questions in the mysteries of the sea and its creatures as they move in their carefully ordered, delicately balanced relationships to one another.

Several works in *Available Light* try to come to terms with harsh winters, the freeze of a late spring, the poet's Puritan need to take inventory constantly, and the nearly mystical experience of a dream. "Entry," a terse, honed poem that is skinny on the page, describes bitter cold weather that has lasted for four days, drifted snow coming in large flakes, and a "small sun." The poet's words "quicken," or give life to, the silence and allow an entry for him, suggesting Booth's fascination with the life-giving power of words. "Adding It Up" uses what light is available as the speaker's mind begins to open up before dawn, while he lies in bed tallying his life and its concerns. As his mind opens and he meticulously counts, his body prepares for the first humorously ordinary job of the day: "cleaning up after/ an old-maid Basset in heat." With humor the speaker looks at himself and inventories his Puritan characteristics: being sorry, worrying, counting.

Set against such straightforwardness, "Dreamscape" has a visionary quality in its carefully shaped free verse. In contrast to "Supposition with Qualification," in which the speaker struggles with wanting to give himself up to experience, the speaker in "Dreamscape" lets the dream experience take control of the poem. The opening stanza describes the familiar road to town as the speaker has "always" known it: the steep hill, the filled-in old British canal, the spruce trees, the five houses. The certainty of "always," however, is denied by the vision of the road in the dream. In the second stanza, beginning with the word "but," the poet presents the road in his dream, with the left side now cleared into pasture in which "miniature bison" are kneeling. Avoiding the questioning of experience found in some of Booth's earlier works, he neither can nor wants to explain this dreamscape. The organic process of the poem takes on a life of its own, offering a sharing of the dream's experience and suggesting the chance that this dream experience opens up a wholly new perspective.

"How to See Deer" comments directly on the subtler theme of an earlier poem, "Shag." "Shag" first describes the poet's observations of seven cormorants (shags), follows with ruminations about what ornithologists say regarding their strange flights, and concludes as the poet continues to observe and to row "as if/ on vacation from knowledge." Here Booth has tried to let the experience speak for itself, and to avoid explaining it or generalizing from it. "How to See Deer" makes a similar point, but much more overtly, in contrast to Booth's usual practice: by advising, if one purposely sets out to see deer—or, by extension, to experience anything—that the deer will not be seen. Serendipity is a factor; however, taking "your good time," trusting "your quick nature," learning to listen and to observe, to "see/ what you see," will permit one to experience joy. Perceptions and experiences cannot be forced; if, however, one is alert and receptive, one is able to participate in life.

Like Booth's earlier works, *Before Sleep* is divided into parts, but they are concurrent rather than consecutive, with tightly woven interaction. These pieces are separated into poems and "Night Notes": the forty-three poems appear on numbered pages indicated in the table of contents; the eighteen "Night Notes," offering commentaries on the poems to which they are juxtaposed, appear between listed poem titles and are not given page numbers. The collection's title, reminiscent of the famous Frost poem "Stopping by Woods on a Snowy Evening," brings to mind the long sleep of death. The poems themselves, however, offer meditations on how to live life. There are no formal stanzaic patterns here; rhyme and even approximate rhyme are absent. Figurative language is also sparse; Booth uses mostly simple words and gives particular attention to the word "nothing," which exists by itself, contradicting the view—held by Booth in his early years—that nothing exists in isolation.

The opening poem, "Not to Tell Lies," describes a man who wishes to strip life down to the barest essentials. Initially, the lines are short, but they quickly become longer, only to shorten again to the single word "lies." This arrangement is striking, for it suggests a wedge used to force the truth into a limited space, without anything extraneous. The poet is coming to terms with his age, having reached his sixth decade and returned to live year-round in the ancestral Maine home. Items in his upstairs room, "which corners late sun," include a schooner model, the portrait of a daughter, a rock brought from Amchitka by the speaker's doctor, an ancestor's photograph, and books by Henry David Thoreau and Herman Melville—men who also made outward and inward journeys. As in earlier poems, Booth uses sea metaphors—for example, his bed has been "moored . . . perpendicular to the North wall,/ whenever he rests his head is compassed barely west/ of Polaris"—but all the poem's other words catalog what he has gathered and sorted through "in order not/ to tell/ lies. Following this poem, and integral to its meaning, is a "night note" introducing the idea of "nothing." The room just described is nothing, Booth says, when separated from the life he lives within it; the person, the poet, is more "vital" than the room, and his "virtue" is "not/ in my own life to live/ as if nothing/ were more important."

As the collection progresses, one senses the nothingness of death but also the meaning and sometimes the meaninglessness of life. "The House in the Trees," the collection's final entry, pictures a continuous moving toward life, affirming the possibility of continuing to build for the future, although, like the house "in the process/ of being built," the poet's life and art may not reach complete fulfillment before his death. In this process, in the sense of "constantly being arrived at," life and art are affirmed.

The title poem of *Relations* is a poem of affirmation; the speaker does not deny life's uncertainties, but wonders at the miracle of each moment, amazed at the movement of the spheres,

> . . . by how
>   to each other
>   we're held, we keep
>
>   from spinning out
>   by how to each other
>   we hold.

The staggered placement of the poem's lines suggests how each line relates to those that follow and precede it. "From broken dreams," says the poem, "we wake to every day's/ brave history." That all persons do this, that history involves experience, and perhaps as well that opening oneself to each day's experience is "brave" indicate the commonality of persons, their dependence on one another. As the poem progresses, the speaker becomes more personal, naming his village's zip code, 04421, and a specific woman. Janet, the town's postmaster, is "spun into light" by the planets' movements, as all people are. Moving from the specific person in Castine to the inclusive "we" once more, Booth combines thanksgivings for his peninsular village and, by extension, for life.

Booth alludes to the theme of *Selves* in *Vermont Academy Life* (Fall/Winter 1979/1980): "I read because . . . my many selves . . . need to experience other lives." In *Selves*, once again, he presents beautifully moving, tightly made, sometimes humorous poems that employ a minimum of figurative language. The volume's prologue, from Wallace Stevens' *Esthétique du Mal* (1945), introduces the theme of the many selves within each human being. Participation in these poems allows the reader to become part of the creative process and, in turn, to begin to discover his or her own many selves. The poems combine philosophical speculation about universal mysteries with ordinary, mundane topics such as losing a glove, splitting wood with a wedge

and an ax, and spreading manure. While commenting on each person's inability to feel another's feelings completely, and while expressing concern for
the future given past and present ecological disasters, these poems give thanks
for life, music, sex, food, and relationships, for awareness, consciousness,
and wonder. Traditional rhyming and restrictive forms are eschewed in favor
of the comfortable patterns of common speech, so that these works are very
accessible.

The epigraph poem "Reaching In," with parallels from physics and probability theory, expresses deep concern with and respect for how each reader
experiences the poem. Booth asks his readers to "weigh each word before
you believe me"; there is an implied reward for the reader who follows this
directive. The first "reaching" in the poem is that of the physicist who reaches
in to measure momentum. The second use of the word is literal: the poet
reaches through the dark at night on his way to the bathroom, and like the
physicist's changing of the photon's position, the poet's "feet displace the
shape of the dark." The third "reaching" is internal but also cosmic: "Reaching in, I trembled the landscape." The unusual transitive use of "trembled"
continues the opening image. The word "you" in stanza 3 begins in reference to a particular person but subsequently moves to the individual reader
and beyond. This poem suggests how to experience the poems that follow.

Some of the poems in part 1 are eloquent pictures of rural poverty. With
simple, direct language "Poor" describes the impossibility of planning ahead
when one has very little. Moose Coombs has never been able to afford the
time to seek out seasoned wood for heating the kitchen stove. Instead he has
brought home green wood, which burns too intensely and coats the chimney
with creosote; the result is a sudden fire that destroys his wife and his house.
There are no metaphors here, but the ordinary language brings the event
home and shows its pointless tragedy.

In "Civilities," with humor, fondness, and appreciation, the poet turns
to his grandmother's knowledge of "right words, and which/ to use when."
Without ever using the four-letter word for excrement, Booth makes it humorously present. His portraits of Mr. Bowden delivering and of Mrs. Hooke
paying for "spring dressing" are painted with tender humor and fond respect, as the poet, years later, prepares the same perennial garden they tended
with "lovely dark clouds of cowdung."

Further poems in this volume speak of the isolation of aging, of survival,
and of the hopefulness of life. "Fallback" poignantly describes an elderly
couple imprisoned in a home for the aged. Concrete, direct language brings
home the predicament of the old couple, who have been together for sixty-
two years. They are now perfunctorily tended by a young nurse who "looks
like a grebe" and who cannot and probably does not care to know the elderly woman's tender memories of love and caring: how her husband in years
past spread out his jacket for picnics and how they "made love/ in the sweet-

fern high on an island." The husband's mind is now gone, and the wife's body is impossibly frail, but the memories are sturdy and real.

"Provisions," in reaction to a book on survival tactics left on an airplane, speaks against the directions it offers about what to take when one is fleeing a nuclear disaster and agrees only with the advice "Leave objects behind" (especially, Booth says, the survival book itself). His advice, instead, is to take poems, Thoreau, the memory of a tune by Bach, and sustaining memories. As the old woman in "Fallback" finds, it is the experiences of life that will sustain one.

The final piece in the collection, "Presence," is a poem of wonder. In simple, two-line stanzas, the poet speaks of the singular mystery "that we are here, here at all." The very title suggests an almost worshipful attitude toward life, that there is a being, a presence, a hint of a supernatural influence felt nearby. "Presence" offers the opportunity for joy in life, brief as it is, and an affirmation of being.

While all Booth's poetry explores the struggle and isolation of human existence, his ultimate response to both is positive. He embraces the old but important observation of John Donne that we are all, with our fears, affirmations, sorrow, and happiness, joined in the large human family. We are part of one another, and we share in the sorrows, mysteries, and joys of life. Booth's poems, with their universal themes and simple language, enlarge and expand that life.

Linda K. Martinez

Bibliography

Booth, Philip. Interview by Rachel Berghash. *The American Poetry Review* 18 (May/June, 1989): 37-39. This interview was conducted in Maine for radio station WBAI in New York City and was aired in two parts in August, 1986. The poet discusses his sense of place and roots in Castine, offering some biographical information. He also talks about his views on survival, his philosophy of poetry, and his largest collection, *Relations*.

_____. Interview by Stephen Dunn. *New England Review and Bread Loaf Quarterly* 9 (Winter, 1986): 134-158. Dunn is one of the four former students to whom Booth dedicated *Selves* and from whom the poet says he is still learning. This interview, conducted in the Booth ancestral home, offers good insight into the poems of Booth's seventh volume, *Relations*.

Naughton, Jim. "From Ache in the Arch to 'Edge.'" *The Post Standard*, April 12, 1983, sec. D. Naughton presents some biographical information of the poet as a teenager and as the senior poet in the Syracuse Creative Writing Program. This article is based on an interview with the poet and includes comments from Booth on how he writes poetry.

Rotella, Guy L. *Three Contemporary Poets of New England: William Mer-*

edith, Philip Booth, and Peter Davison. Boston: Twayne, 1983. Rotella places Booth in a New England regional context alongside Meredith and Davison, providing biographical information along with analysis of the poetry. Includes an index and a bibliography.

WILLIAM LISLE BOWLES

Born: Kings Sutton, England; September 24, 1762
Died: Salisbury, England; April 7, 1850

Principal poetry

Fourteen Sonnets, 1789, 1794, 1796, 1798; *Verses to John Howard*, 1789; *The Grave of Howard*, 1790; *Verses on the Benevolent Institution of the Philanthropic Society, for Protecting and Educating the Children of Vagrants and Criminals*, 1790; *A Poetical Address to the Right Honourable Edmund Burke*, 1791; *Elegy Written at the Hot-Wells, Bristol*, 1791; *Monody, Written at Matlock*, 1791; *Elegiac Stanzas, Written During Sickness at Bath*, 1796; *Hope: An Allegorical Sketch*, 1796; *St. Michael's Mount*, 1798; *Coombe Ellen*, 1798; *Song of the Battle of the Nile*, 1799; *Poems*, 1801; *The Sorrows of Switzerland*, 1801; *The Picture*, 1803; *The Spirit of Discovery: Or, The Conquest of the Ocean*, 1804; *Bowden Hill*, 1806; *The Little Villager's Verse Book*, 1806, 1837 (children's literature); *Poems*, 1809; *The Missionary*, 1813; *The Grave of the Last Saxon*, 1822; *Ellen Gray*, 1823; *Days Departed*, 1828; *St. John in Patmos*, 1832; *Scenes and Shadows*, 1835.

Other literary forms

Although best known as a poet, William Lisle Bowles also published an edition of Alexander Pope, pamphlets of literary criticism regarding Pope (in a famous controversy with Lord Byron and others), sermons, antiquarian works, and an autobiographical fragment. A number of his letters are also extant (see Garland Greever's edition of them), but he is more memorably preserved in the recollections of others, as Thomas Moore and Samuel Taylor Coleridge fondly described and preserved his eccentricities.

Achievements

Few people today regard Bowles as a major poet, and some would speak contemptuously of him, for all his enormous output. Sharply contrasting with a modern sophisticated dismissal of his work, however, was the immediate and forceful influence that Bowles exerted upon the first generation of British Romantic poets, including William Wordsworth, Robert Southey, Charles Lamb, and above all Samuel Taylor Coleridge. For them he was the herald of a new sensibility, almost a Vergil to follow beyond the desiccated landscape of neoclassical detachment into a richer vale of fresh response and honest moralizing. Having been educated in part by the poets he inspired, modern readers find it hard to appreciate Bowles's originality. Largely because he was transitional to better poets than himself, Bowles now appears to be of historical interest only. He is frequently omitted from modern anthologies altogether and appears in some literary histories only as a footnote to Coleridge.

Biography

William Lisle Bowles was born on September 24, 1762, at Kings Sutton, Northamptonshire (his father's vicarage), the son and grandson of clergymen and the eldest of seven children. At seven he moved with his parents to Uphill, Somerset; on the journey southward young Bowles saw the Severn Valley and derived from it a lifelong association of poetry with picturesque scenery.

From 1775 to 1781 Bowles was educated at Winchester School under Dr. Joseph Warton, who had written an essay critical of Alexander Pope and was a pre-Romantic advocate of descriptive poetry. Warton's feeling for nature, dislike of neoclassical rules, and knowledge of Vergil impressed Bowles (see his "Monody on the Death of Dr. Warton," 1819), who thereafter followed and enlarged upon Warton's precepts. In 1781 Bowles went on to Trinity College, Oxford, where his master, Thomas Warton, Joseph's brother, further reinforced Bowles's dislike of neoclassicism and preference for lyric poetry, the ode and sonnet in particular. Bowles wrote "On Leaving Winchester School," his first important poem, retrospectively in 1782.

His record at Oxford was that of an unusually able student. In 1782, for example, Bowles won a scholarship that sustained him for the next five years. In 1783 his "Calpe Obsessa" (on the Siege of Gibraltar) was the Latin prize poem. Three years later, however, in 1786, Bowles's father died, leaving the family in difficult financial straits. Though Bowles received his B.A. degree the next year, his engagement to a niece of Sir Samuel Romilly appeared imprudent to her parents and was summarily broken off. In his disappointment, Bowles elected to travel through northern England, Scotland, Belgium, Germany, and Switzerland. While thus relieved, he composed a series of sonnets; published in 1789 at Bath as *Fourteen Sonnets*, they quickly made him famous.

Wordsworth, on vacation from Cambridge, read Bowles's sonnets that Christmas in London, as he was walking the streets with his brother John, and (as Mary Moorman has it in her biography of Wordsworth), "their graceful melancholy, dwelling on the memories of beloved places, at once made a strong appeal." Bowles's influence on Wordsworth is traceable in the latter's work from *Descriptive Sketches* (1793) to "Lines Composed a Few Miles Above Tintern Abbey" (1798). The first edition of Bowles's sonnets that Wordsworth read, however, was a rarity, for only one hundred copies were published. There soon followed a second edition (also 1789) containing twenty-one sonnets, which Coleridge read—he was then a seventeen-year-old schoolboy at Christ's Hospital—and transcribed endlessly for his literary friends. As J. Shawcross has remarked, "in Bowles's sonnets Coleridge found the first genuinely unconventional treatment of Nature, the first genuine stimulus to an understanding of her 'perpetual revelation'" (*Biographia Literaria*, 1817). One of those to whom Coleridge sent Bowles's sonnets was Robert

Southey, who soon shared his enthusiasm for them. "Buy Bowles poems, and study them well," he advised a friend in 1794. "They will teach you to write better, and give you infinite pleasure." Bowles was a major influence on Coleridge and his circle from 1789 to 1797, and these years were also the Wiltshire parson's most prolific.

The *Fourteen Sonnets* proved to be a remarkable success. Following the first and second editions of 1789, there was a third in 1794 containing twenty-seven sonnets and thirteen other poems. The fourth edition of 1796 was little changed, but the fifth (1796; two new poems) and sixth (1798; thirty sonnets and sixteen other poems, including *Hope*) both contained additions and plates. Less significant, except as evidence of Bowles's continuing popularity, were editions seven (1800), eight (1801), nine (1805), and ten (1809). Coleridge followed the earlier editions as they appeared and even wrote Bowles (whom he visited in September, 1797) to comment on his various omissions and emendations.

Coleridge acknowledged his own profound indebtedness to Bowles in a sonnet of December, 1794, "To the Rev. W. L. Bowles," which was printed in the *Morning Chronicle*, a London newspaper, on the day after Christmas, together with a note from Coleridge praising Bowles's sonnets XIII ("At a Convent"), XIX, and XXV as "compositions of, perhaps, unrivalled merit." In *Poems on Various Subjects* (1796), Coleridge reprinted his Bowles sonnet in a revised form. That same year he also published *A Sheet of Sonnets*, twenty-eight in all, designed to be bound up with Bowles's own, which Coleridge praised effusively in his Preface. By 1802, however, Coleridge was no longer satisfied with Bowles, who had "indeed the *sensibility* of a poet," but "not the *Passion* of a great Poet" (*Collected Letters*, 1956-1959).

Having met with considerable success, Bowles published much during these years. Among the poems added to later editions of his sonnets, for example, were humanitarian verses on John Howard, slavery, and the American Indian. His *Verses on the Benevolent Institution of the Philanthropic Society* (1790) furnished the epigraph to Southey's "Botany Bay Eclogues" (written in 1794). Bowles's *Elegy Written at the Hot-Wells, Bristol* was translated into French by Madame de Staël, who also admired his sonnets and *The Spirit of Discovery*. Both *Elegy Written at the Hot-Wells, Bristol* and *Monody, Written at Matlock* continued the strain of poetic melancholy that Bowles inherited from Thomas Gray and then applied to Romantic settings. He also wrote elegiac tributes to fellow clergymen during these years, as well as melancholy reflections occasioned by his own serious illness in December, 1795, from which the allegorical poem called *Hope* resulted. Writing to John Thewall in November, 1796 (the poem had actually appeared a few weeks before the year of its imprint), Coleridge found *Hope* to be a poem "without plan or meaning, but the component parts are divine." In addition to Bowles's own sickness, there had been that of Harriet Wake, his fiancée, who died a year following their engagement, in 1793. In 1797, Bowles married Magdeline Wake, his dead fiancée's younger sister.

Though his influence on Coleridge's circle was now waning (Coleridge's visit that year had been disillusioning), Bowles came before the public as an established author, producing a series of longer poems: *Hope* in 1796; *Coombe Ellen* and *St. Michael's Mount* in 1798; *Song of the Battle of the Nile* in 1799; the seventh edition of his *Sonnets* (including *Hope* and a preface), in 1800; *The Sorrows of Switzerland* in 1801; *The Picture* in 1803; and *The Spirit of Discovery* in 1804. It was a remarkably prolific sequence of now-forgotten poems.

In 1804 Bowles was appointed vicar at Bremhill, Wiltshire, where he continued to live for most of his remaining years. He was also appointed prebendary of Salisbury Cathedral and spent some time there every year. Bowles's sonnets continued to be popular, and he published yet another long poem in an eighteenth century mode (*Bowden Hill*) but quickly gained a new and more controversial reputation with his ten-volume edition of Pope and his essay on Pope's "Poetical Character" in 1806. His views on Pope were criticized in the *Edinburgh Review* of January, 1808, and Lord Byron (influenced by the review) satirized Bowles in the anonymous first edition of *English Bards, and Scotch Reviewers* (1809), though John Cam Hobhouse wrote the actual lines on Bowles. In the acknowledged second edition (1809) Byron substituted lines of his own on Bowles, castigating him for opposing Pope, ridiculing his long poems ("Stick to thy sonnets, man!—at least they sell"), and jibing erroneously at an episode from *The Spirit of Discovery*, a poem which Byron had not seen at first hand, as he admitted to Bowles three years later. Relations after 1812 were cordial, and Bowles even proposed that Byron add some lines (he did not) to Bowles's forthcoming long poem *The Missionary*. This latest effort, though it had four editions, was dismissed by George Daniel in *The Modern Dunciad* (1814): "While Bowles exists," he asked, "can satire want a dunce?" Similarly, John Hamilton Reynolds characterized Bowles as a gabbling goose in *The Champion* of April 7, 1816, and Bowles's outraged reply of May 12 did nothing to improve his reputation. That same year Coleridge visited Bowles at Bremhill and had the temerity to "correct" his poems, for which he was hardly forgiven. The public, it seemed, had tired of Bowles and his evangelistic inanities.

Nevertheless, it was Coleridge who paid Bowles the tribute that immortalized him in literary history. In Chapter 1 of *Biographia Literaria*, Coleridge specifically recalled his first acquaintance with Bowles's sonnets in 1789 and how, with almost equal delight, he later read three or four more publications by the same author, inlcuding *Monody, Written at Matlock* and *Hope*. Bowles and Cowper were, for Coleridge, "the first who combined natural thoughts with natural diction; the first who reconciled the heart with the head." Coleridge also stated that Bowles's works "were of great advantage in the formation and establishment of my taste and critical opinions." Thus was the Wiltshire poet defended against his critics. Though later ones have often found Coleridge's enthusiasm for Bowles inexplicable, his words are clear enough. Perhaps some of Coleridge's generosity toward Bowles reflected the assistance that Bowles had given him (through Byron) toward the publication of *Sibylline Leaves* (1817).

After 1817, Bowles was closely associated with Thomas Moore, of Sloperton Cottage (a three-hour walk from Bremhill), who has left a fine record of Bowles's eccentricities. In February, 1818, for example, Moore and his wife spent three or four days with Bowles at Bremhill and observed: "What an odd fellow it is! and how narrowly, by being a *genius*, he has escaped being set down for a *fool!*" But, Moore went on, "he is an excellent creature notwithstanding." That September, Moore praised Bowles in his diary as a delightful "mixture of talent and simplicity," then repeated his earlier opinion about Bowles's poetry almost word for word. That October, as well, Bowles seemed to Moore "the most delightful of all existing parsons or poets," for all his genius and blundering alike. There are brief glimpses in Moore also of Louisa Stuart Costello (1799-1877), the artist and poet whom Bowles had taken as his protégée. She is best known in literary history for *Songs of a Stranger* (1825), which was dedicated to Bowles. Her *Specimens of the Early Poetry of France* (1835) was dedicated to Moore.

The controversy over Pope began in earnest in 1819, when Thomas Campbell's *Specimens of the English Poets* appeared, championing Pope. Bowles immediately replied with a pamphlet essay on "The Invariable Principles of Poetry" (1819) addressed specifically to Campbell, whose remarks on Pope had been excerpted by the *Morning Chronicle* as an answer to Bowles. Bowles's pamphlet, originally intended as a public letter to Moore, was supposedly dictated by its author to a waiter in the bar of the White Hart pub, Salisbury. In all, Bowles wrote six pamphlets pertaining to the Pope controversy, two of them in response to letters from Byron. J. J. Van Rennes has listed twenty-nine publications generated by the controversy as a whole.

In the thirty years remaining to him, Bowles published six more volumes of poetry, including *The Grave of the Last Saxon, Ellen Gray, Days Departed, St. John in Patmos, Scenes and Shadows* (with an autobiographical fragment), and, for children, *The Little Villager's Verse Book*; none, except perhaps the last, had enduring merit. His more important medium in his later years was prose, and his most characteristic product the sermon. However welcome they may have been as guidance, Bowles's sermons seem not to have had more than local impact. Bowles remained productive until 1844, when the death of his wife crushed him. In January, 1845, he resigned his vicarate at Bremhill and retired to Salisbury, where he endured five years of senile helplessness until his death on April 7, 1850.

Analysis

William Lisle Bowles was, with Thomas Warton and Charlotte Smith, among those who in the latter eighteenth century sought to revive the sonnet form. His own sonnets are particularly noteworthy for their responsiveness to landscape. Their diction was influential, though less original than one might think, as some investigation of late eighteenth century descriptive poetry and the picturesque travel effusions of William Gilpin (1724-1804) confirm. If Bowles borrowed from other writers, however, greater writers borrowed from him. Thus, "To the River Wensbeck" is echoed by Samuel Taylor Coleridge in "Kubla Khan" and "Dejection: An Ode" (line 96). Similarly, Bowles's sonnet "To the River Itchin" influenced Coleridge's "To the River Otter," and his poem "On Leaving Winchester School" probably inspired two similar poems, "Sonnet: On Quitting School for College" and "Absence. Farewell Ode on Quitting School for Jesus College, Cambridge," by the better poet. Though ostensibly dated 1788, Coleridge's "Sonnet: To the Autumnal Moon" is almost surely an imitation of Bowles, just as Coleridge's "Anthem for the Children of Christ's Hospital" is an adaptation of Bowles's "Verses on the Philanthropic Society." Coleridge's sonnet "Pain" should also be compared with Bowles's sonnet XI, "At Ostend," to which it is indebted. Coleridge was not only indebted to Bowles for imagery, phrases, and subjects, but for attitudes as well. Thus, Bowles's early poems are topographical and melancholic, with time his major theme. He then moved toward more outgoing, humanitarian utterances and eventually to public manifestos full of noble sentiments but of no other lasting interest.

In Bowles's later sonnets, written after 1789 (when John Milton's influence on him became more evident), the diction is less stilted and of some historical importance. Sonnets XXIII to XXVII, for example, probably influenced William Wordsworth's "Tintern Abbey," which specifically echoes XXVII ("On Revisiting Oxford"). Sonnets XX and XXII anticipate the imagery of Percy Bysshe Shelley. Bowles was among the first of the minor descriptive poets to abandon much of eighteenth century diction in favor of a fresher, more experiential imagery, even if his own was weak, occasionally trite, moralistic, and too often encumbered by personification. Granting that Bowles failed to achieve poetry of lasting distinction himself, his own work still pointed toward the heights that Wordsworth and Coleridge achieved. While Wordsworth's pronouncements in his Preface to *Lyrical Ballads* (the edition of 1800) do not always reflect his own poetic practices, they are surprisingly like a pro-and-con discussion of Bowles.

Unfortunately, Bowles failed to develop as a poet beyond the promise of his later sonnets. His longer and more pretentious poems attracted readers in their day, but now seem disappointingly flat. Among the best of them is *Monody, Written at Matlock*, which was a favorite with Coleridge. In it, an eighteenth century mind saturated with the melancholy of Thomas Gray confronts the Romantic landscape of the peak. Though a monody is normally a lament or dirge, often about another poet's death, it is hard to see what Bowles had to be so gloomy about, as there seems to be little connection between the landscape and his reflections, which are the expected ones of a poet revisiting a scene of his youth. There is, however, no better poem to compare with Wordsworth's "Tintern Abbey" to help one see both the conventionality and the originality of Wordsworth's masterpiece.

A second longer poem of interest is *The Picture*, which (like Wordsworth's "Elegiac Stanzas,") is based on a painting owned by Sir George Beaumont—in this case, a landscape by Peter Paul Rubens. Compared with Bowles's sonnets, *The Picture* already seems heavy-handed and regressive. It is still an interesting attempt at landscape aesthetics, however, and gathers within a single poem many of Bowles's characteristic pieties. Finally, there are good things in both *Coombe Ellen* and *St. Michael's Mount*, though the poems are overlong, easily outrunning their inspiration. Even at this early date, Bowles had begun to display his characteristic faults of insipidity, loquaciousness, and unoriginality.

Bowles's longest poem (in five books) is *The Spirit of Discovery*, which, beginning with Noah, moves from the Egyptians, the Phoenicians, the Babylonians, and the Greeks to the discoveries of Columbus and Captain Cook. An appended prose analysis sufficiently describes the poem, which is a curious mixture of heroic aspiration and credulity. While several of the Romantic poets, including Southey and Rogers, were attracted to Columbus and the age of exploration, only Coleridge (who preceded all of them) created major poetry on the theme, with *The Rime of the Ancient Mariner* (1798). Bowles's *The Spirit of Discovery*, for all its length and notes, is a pretentious failure, as were his works that followed. The only other work requiring mention is *The Missionary*, a long poem in eight cantos about Spaniards and Indians in South America; showing the influence of Wordsworth, Robert Southey, and Sir Walter Scott, it involved some new techniques and was popular for a time.

Dennis R. Dean

Other major works

PLAY: *The Ark: A Dramatic Oratorio*, 1824.

NONFICTION: Pamphlets on the Pope controversy, 1819-1826; *Illustrations of Those Stipendous Monuments of Celtic Antiquity Avebury and Silbury, and Their Mysterious Origin Traced*, 1827; *Hermes Baritannicus*, 1828; *The Parochial History of Bremhill*, 1828; *The Life of Thomas Ken, D.D.*, 1830; *Annals and Antiquities of Lacock Abbey*, 1835; sermons and pamphlets on religious controversies (various dates, to 1838); *A Wiltshire Parson and His Friends: The Correspondence of William Lisle Bowles*, 1926 (Garland Greever, editor).

Bibliography

Little, Geoffrey, and Elizabeth Hall. "Coleridge's 'To the Rev. W. L. Bowles': Another Version?" *The Review of English Studies: A Quarterly Journal of English Literature and the English Language* 32 (May, 1981): 193-196. This fine assessment of Bowles's poetry offers an illuminating overview of Bowles's poetic development.

Modiano, Raimonda. "Coleridge and Wordsworth: The Ethics of Gift Exchange and Literary Ownership." *The Wordsworth Circle* 20 (Spring, 1989): 113-120. In this comprehensive essay, Modiano provides informative coverage of English literature from 1800 to 1899 and examines the views of Coleridge, Wordsworth, and Bowles.

Rennes, Jacob Johan van. *Bowles, Byron, and the Pope-Controversy.* Amsterdam: H. J. Paris, 1927. Bowles, who is referred to here as a "sonneteer of no mean deserts," edited a volume of Alexander Pope's works. In his edition, Bowles criticized Pope, which prompted George Gordon, Lord Byron to leap to his defense. This volume chronicles the correspondence that surrounded this controversy and provides useful background of Bowles and his contemporaries.

Vinson, James, ed. *Great Writers of the English Language.* 3 vols. New York, St. Martin's Press, 1979. The entry on Bowles, by Tony Bareham, calls him a second-rank poet, without much individuality. Nevertheless, he acknowledges that Bowles was carefully competent with an eye for details, and notes the popularity of *Fourteen Sonnets*, which restored dignity to a verse form that had been "neglected for the last two generations."

Wu, Duncan. "Wordsworth's Readings of Bowles." *Notes and Queries* 36 (June, 1989): 166-167. A perceptive and thorough reading of Bowles's poetry makes this essay worth consulting. Central to an appreciation and understanding of Bowles's imagination.

ANNE BRADSTREET

Born: Northampton, England; 1612(?)
Died: Andover, Massachusetts; September 16, 1672

Principal poetry

The Tenth Muse Lately Sprung Up in America, 1650; *Several Poems Compiled with Great Variety of Wit and Learning,* 1678.

Other literary forms

Anne Bradstreet's published collections in 1650 and 1678 consist entirely of poetry, and her reputation rests on her poems. She left in manuscript the prose "Meditations Divine and Morall" (short, pithy proverbs) and a brief autobiography written especially for her children.

Achievements

Bradstreet and Edward Taylor are the two foremost Colonial American poets. They form a classic study in contrasts: she was emotional, he cerebral; she secular, he spiritual; she feminine, he masculine; she stylistically straightforward, he complex; she generically varied, he generically limited; she well known by her contemporaries, he little known until the twentieth century. These are, of course, only generalizations; however, they suggest a special problem that Bradstreet criticism has overcome only in the past few decades: the inability to divorce her work from biographical, historical, and personal elements.

One of Bradstreet's distinctive poetic strengths is her generic variety. She wrote epics ("The Four Monarchies" and the "Quaternions"), dialogues ("A Dialogue Between Old England and New," among others), love lyrics, public elegies (on Sir Philip Sidney, Guillaume de Salluste Du Bartas, and her parents, for example), private elegies (on her grandchildren and daughter-in-law), a long meditative poem ("Contemplations"), and religious verse. Few other Puritan poets successfully tackled so many genres.

Although Bradstreet's contemporaries admired her early imitative poetry ("The Four Monarchies," the "Quaternions," and the elegies on Sidney, Du Bartas, and Queen Elizabeth I), her later personal poetry is what endures (and endears). Poems included in *The Tenth Muse Lately Sprung Up in America* fall within an essentially Renaissance tradition, while those in *Several Poems Compiled with Great Variety of Wit and Learning* initiate a distinctive tradition of *American* literature. Bradstreet's love poems to her husband are admired for their wit, intricate construction, emotional force, and frank admission of the physical side of marriage: as she says in "To my Dear and Loving Husband," "If ever two were one, then surely we./ If ever man were lov'd by wife, then thee." Bradstreet's personal elegies on her grandchildren skillfully dramatize the Puritans' unremitting battle between worldliness (grieving for the dead) and unworldliness (rejoicing in their salvation). But her masterpiece is probably her long meditative poem "Contemplations," praised for its maturity, complexity, and lyricism. Her love poems, personal elegies, and "Contemplations" reveal the human side of Puritanism from a woman's vantage point.

Biography

Through her poetic voices, Anne Bradstreet assumes a clear (but complex) presence, yet factual data about her are surprisingly scant. Joseph McElrath, editor of *The Complete Works of Anne Bradstreet* (1981), shows that even her birth date is uncertain. She was probably born in 1612 in Northampton, England, but may have been born as late as 1613, one of Thomas Dudley and Dorothy Yorke's six children.

In 1619 the family moved to Sempringham, where Dudley became steward to the Earl of Lincoln. Both Thomas Dudley and his employer allowed the prospective poet an unusually good education for a woman. Scholars even speculate that she had access to the Earl's library. There she may have read staples of humanism: William Shakespeare, Sir Philip Sidney, Sir Walter Raleigh, Du Bartas, and Cervantes. In 1621, Simon Bradstreet joined the Earl's household to assist Dudley; but in 1624, the Dudleys moved to Boston, England, and Simon Bradstreet left to work for the Countess of Warwick.

When the poet was about sixteen, as she records in her autobiographical prose, "the Lord layd his hand sore upon me & smott mee with the small pox." After her recovery in 1628, she and Simon Bradstreet married, and two years later, the Dudley and Bradstreet families left for America aboard the *Arbella*.

For Anne Bradstreet, the transition was not entirely smooth, and her prose autobiography speaks of "a new World and new manners at which my heart rose, But after I was convinced it was the way of God, I submitted to it & joined to the chh., at Boston." After brief spells in Salem, Boston, Cambridge, and Ipswich, the Bradstreets moved to North Andover, Massachusetts, where Anne Bradstreet reared eight children, wrote, and shared her husband's life as he rose from judge to governor of the colony. Although the poet was susceptible to many illnesses and was childless for several years, her supremely happy marriage compensated for, and helped her to overcome, these "trials."

As the governor's wife, Bradstreet enjoyed a socio-economic status conducive to writing. In the mid-1640's, Bradstreet had completed the poems which appeared in her first collection. Bradstreet herself did not supervise their printing; John Woodbridge, her brother-in-law, probably carried the manuscript to London, where it was published in 1650. Bradstreet expresses mixed feelings about its publication, largely because of the printing errors. The poem "The Author to Her Book" mildly chides "friends, less wise than true" who exposed the work "to publick view." Poems in the collection are mainly public in tone and content, while those in her second collection (published posthumously in 1678) are mainly private and personal.

Bradstreet was a known, respected, and loved poet in both the Old and New Worlds. Her death in 1672 called forth elegies and eulogies. These lines from the Preface to _The Tenth Muse Lately Sprung Up in America_, probably written by Woodbridge, best convey Bradstreet's qualities: "It is the Work of a Woman, honoured, and esteemed where she lives, for her gracious demeanour, her eminent parts, her pious conversation, her courteous disposition, [and] her exact diligence in her place."

Analysis

Anne Bradstreet wrote poetry from the 1640's to her death in 1672. Naturally, her work developed and deepened over this thirty-year period. The critic Kenneth Requa's distinction between her public and private poetic voices (in "Anne Bradstreet's Poetic Voices," _Early American Literature_, XII, 1977) is a useful way to assess her poetic development. Her public voice, which dominates the early poetry, is eulogistic, imitative, self-conscious, and less controlled in metaphor and structure. Most of the poems in _The Tenth Muse Lately Sprung Up in America_ illustrate these traits. Her private voice—more evident in _Several Poems Compiled with Great Variety of Wit and Learning_—is often elegiac, original, self-confident, and better controlled in metaphor and structure. Any attempt to divide Bradstreet's work into phases has its dangers. Here, however, it is convenient to consider representative elegies from three roughly chronological stages: "poetic" involvement, conventional involvement, and personal involvement.

Almost all the verse in her first collection conveys Bradstreet's public, poetic involvement. Specifically, in secular poems such as the "Quaternions," "The Four Monarchies," and the elegies on famous Elizabethans, Bradstreet as professional poet or bard dominates and controls. "In Honour of Du Bartas" (1641) contains the typical Renaissance characteristics of public content, imitative style, classical allusions, and secular eulogy. The poem's content could hardly be more public, since it dutifully details the accomplishments of Bradstreet's mentor Du Bartas—his learning, valor, wit, and literary skill. Although Bradstreet contrasts her meager poetic powers with Du Bartas' unlimited powers, her involvement is not personal; rather, it eventually points a favorite moral for Renaissance poets. No matter how bad the writer, the dead person (in this case a poet, too) will "live" in the poem's lines. The "Quaternions"—a quartet of long poems on the four elements, the four humors, the four ages of man, and the four seasons—and the interminable rhymed history "The Four Monarchies" are similarly public in content.

An extension of public content and bardic involvement is imitative style. For example, "In Honour of Du Bartas" contains conventional images like the simile comparing Bradstreet's muse to a child, the hyperbole declaring that Du Bartas' fame will last "while starres do stand," and the oxymoron in "senslesse Sences." Although Bradstreet's early imitative style is skillful, it hinders her from expressing the unique voice of her later work. Furthermore, tradition compels her to scatter her public poems with classical allusions. In the three elegies on Du Bartas, Sidney, and Queen Elizabeth I, these allusions are a conventional part of the Renaissance pastoral elegy, and in the "Quaternions" they imitate the medieval/Renaissance debates.

Finally, these lengthy early poems may contain secular eulogy, also a characteristic of the pastoral elegy, and hyperbole, common in the debate form. The opening lines of "In Honour of Du Bartas," for example, state that Du Bartas is "matchlesse knowne" among contemporary poets. In such a richly literary age, Bradstreet obviously uses hyperbole and eulogy to emphasize Du Bartas' greatness for her.

The second phase—conventional involvement—includes religious poems within a public or orthodox context. In many ways this is a transitional voice, for some poems recall the imitativeness and bardic self-consciousness of the first phase, while others anticipate the domestic content and individual voice of the third phase. A few poems (such as "David's Lamentations for Saul" and "Of the vanity of all worldly creatures") are from *The Tenth Muse Lately Sprung Up in America*; more are from her second collection (the elegies on Thomas and Dorothy Dudley and "The Flesh and the Spirit," for example). In this poetry, Bradstreet moves closer to mainstream Puritan verse. The elegies on her parents are conventionally formal and fit the pattern of the New England funeral elegy, whose hallmark was public praise of the dead one's life and virtues to overcome personal grief. "The Flesh and the Spirit," "As weary pilgrim now at rest," and "Of the vanity of all worldly creatures" treat the theme of worldliness versus unworldliness generally and impersonally to reach orthodox conclusions.

Bradstreet's elegy on her father, "To the memory of my dear and ever honoured Father Thomas Dudley," begins with an apparently personal touch: Bradstreet's claim to write from filial duty, not custom. Even so, as she reminds her readers, this filial duty allows her to praise her father's virtues fully and publicly, not partially and privately. In later elegies, Bradstreet does not explain so defensively why she follows certain conventions; indeed, she frequently modifies or ignores them. In this early elegy, however, these conventions constrain Bradstreet's own voice so that she writes forced lines such as these: "In manners pleasant and severe/ The Good him lov'd, the bad did fear,/ And when his time with years was spent/ If some rejoyc'd, more did lament." Lacking are the emotional force, personal involvement, and dramatic struggle between flesh and spirit found in the later poems.

Another characteristic apparent in the second phase is Bradstreet's use of fairly standard poetic structure. "The Flesh and the Spirit," for example, is in dialogue/debate form, while "As weary pilgrim, now at rest" and "Of the vanity of all worldly creatures"—both meditations—examine the battle between body and soul to attain the eternal peace that only Christ's love will bring. "David's Lamentations for Saul" is a versified retelling of the scriptural story. Bradstreet's epitaphs on her mother and father, as already stated, follow the form of the Puritan elegy.

Standard, often biblical, imagery is another distinct aspect of the second phase. While this imagery is to some extent present in the earlier and later phases, it is particularly evident in the middle stage. In the first stage, Bradstreet's images are traditionally Renaissance, and in the third stage, they are biblical but infused with emotive and personal force. The elegy on Thomas Dudley illustrates the traditionally biblical images found in phase two: Dudley has a "Mansion" prepared above; and, like a ripe shock of wheat, he is mown by the sickle Death and is then stored safely. The other orthodox poems also use biblical images almost exclusively.

Appropriately, in these poems, Bradstreet generally excludes the personal voice. Only "As weary pilgrim, now at rest," the theme of which is the heaven-bound soul housed within the "Corrupt Carcasse," succeeds in combining the general and individual situations. Universality and individuality form the special strength of Bradstreet's masterpiece, "Contemplations." This thirty-three verse meditative poem fits best into the second stage because of its spiritual content. Given the poem's importance, however, it must be discussed separately. Bradstreet skillfully evokes a dramatic scene—she walks at dusk in the countryside—then uses it to explore the relationships among man, God, and nature.

In stanzas one to seven, the poet acknowledges nature's potency and majesty by looking first at an oak tree and then at the sun. If they are glorious, she muses, how much more glorious must their creator be? Stanzas eight to twenty recall man's creation and fall, extending from Adam and Eve to Cain and Abel and finally to Bradstreet's own day. The answer to man's misery, however, is not nature worship. Instead, man must acknowledge that God made him alone for immortality. In stanzas twenty-one to twenty-eight, the poet considers the amoral delight of nature—the elm, the river, the fish, and the nightingale—incapable of the tortures of free will. Stanzas twenty-nine to thirty-three show that beyond the natural cycle, only man ("This lump of wretchedness, of sin and sorrow," as the poet states) can be resurrected within the divine cycle.

"Contemplations" contains some of Bradstreet's most original and inspired poetry within the three-part structure of the seventeenth century meditation. These parts correspond to the mental faculties of memory, understanding, and will. In the first part, the person creates or recalls a scene; in the second part, he analyzes its spiritual significance; and last, he responds emotionally *and* intellectually by prayer and devotion. Clearly, these are the three basic structural elements of "Contemplations." Although Bradstreet ultimately returns to orthodoxy, this poem is no mere religious exercise; it is "the most finished and musical of her religious poems."

The third phase of Bradstreet's poetry includes love lyrics, elegies on grand-children and a daughter-in-law, and other works inspired by private matters (the burning of Bradstreet's house, the publication of her first collection, the poet's eight children). Yet, unlike the poems of the previous stage, which are overwhelmingly spiritual, the poems of the third phase are primarily secular. If they deal with religious matters—as the elegies do, for example—it is within a personal context. One critic calls Bradstreet "the worldly Puritan," and these late poems show the material face of Puritanism. Bradstreet's personal involvement affects structure, tone, rhythm, and metaphor. "In memory of my dear grand-child Elizabeth Bradstreet" illustrates many of these changes.

Because she was more comfortable writing of private matters in a private voice, Bradstreet's poetic structure arises naturally from content and context. The elegy on Elizabeth, for instance, divides into two seven-line stanzas (it is a variation of the sonnet form). In stanza one, the poet says farewell to her grandchild and questions why she should be sad since little Elizabeth is in Heaven. In stanza two, Bradstreet explains that nature's products perish only when they are ripe; therefore, if a newly blown "bud" perishes, it must be God's doing. The structure aptly complements the poet's grief, disbelief, and final resignation. Both stanzas effortlessly follow the rhyme scheme ababccc. Bradstreet's love poems are also constructed in an intricate but uncontrived way. Both poems entitled "Another [Letter to her Husband]" show careful attention to structure. The first poem of this title personifies the sun and follows the sun's daily course; the second ties together three images and puns suggesting marital harmony (*dear/deer*, *heart/hart*, and *hind/hind*).

A marked difference in the poetry of the third phase is its tone. Instead of sounding self-conscious, bookish, derivative, over-ambitious, or staunchly orthodox, Bradstreet's later poetry is poised, personal, original, modest, and unwilling to accept orthodoxy without question. Another tonal change is subtlety, which the elegy on Elizabeth illustrates well. Throughout the poem Bradstreet hovers between the worldly response of grief and the unworldly one of acceptance. This uneasy balance, finally resolved when Bradstreet accepts God's will, makes the elegy especially poignant. The poet's other late elegies on her grandchildren Anne and Simon and her daughter-in-law Mercy are also poignant. The secular love poetry that Bradstreet wrote to her husband—often while he was away on business—conveys playfulness, longing, and, above all, boundless love. The tone of Bradstreet's late poetry tends to be more varied and complex than the tone of her early poetry, the only notable exception being "Contemplations," placed in phase two.

Bradstreet's rhythm reflects her increased poetic self-confidence. Gone are the strained lines and rhythms characteristic of the "Quaternions" and "The

Four Monarchies"; instead, the opening lines of Bradstreet's elegy on Elizabeth show how private subject matter lends itself to natural, personal expression: "Farewel dear babe, my hearts too much content,/ Farewel sweet babe, the pleasure of mine eye,/ Farewel fair flower that for a space was lent,/ Then ta'en away unto Eternity." The delicate antithesis in lines one to three and the repetition of "Farewel" add emotional force to the content and emphasize Bradstreet's difficulty in accepting Elizabeth's death. The other late elegies are rhythmically varied and use antithesis to underscore life's ever-present duality: flesh/spirit, worldliness/unworldliness. For example, within the elegy on three-year-old Anne, Bradstreet conveys her problem in coming to terms with yet another grandchild's death when she uses this forced, monosyllabic rhythm, "More fool then I to look on that was lent./ As if mine own, when thus impermanent." The love poetry is also written with special attention to rhythmic variety.

The poet's metaphoric language in the later works is free of bookishness and imitativeness. She does not resort to classical allusions or literary images but chooses familiar, often domestic or biblical, metaphors. In the elegy on Elizabeth, the entire second stanza comprises a series of images drawn from nature. Bradstreet heightens her grandchild's death by saying how unnatural it is compared to the natural cycle of trees, fruit, corn, and grass. The love poetry draws on nature images too—the sun, fish, deer, and rivers, for instance. In her late personal poetry, Bradstreet also feels comfortable using some extended images. "The Author to Her Book," for example, extends the metaphor of Bradstreet's relationship as author/mother to her book/child, while "In reference to her Children, 23 June 1659" humorously compares Bradstreet and her children to a mother hen and her chicks. These images are original in the sense that they arise in an unaffected, apparently spontaneous, way. They are not original in the sense of being innovative.

The elegies on Du Bartas, Thomas Dudley, and Elizabeth Bradstreet are representative of stages in Bradstreet's poetic career. Her poetry has always been known, but now, more than ever, critics agree on her importance as one of the two foremost Colonial poets. Until recently, scholarship focused on biographical and historical concerns. Modern criticism, on the other hand, concentrates on structure, style, theme, and text. This move toward aesthetic analysis has deepened scholarly appreciation of Bradstreet's talent. In addition, the rise of women's studies ensures her place as a significant female voice in American poetry. She has stood the test of time as "a writer of unquestionably major stature."

K. Z. Derounian

Other major works

MISCELLANEOUS: *The Complete Works of Anne Bradstreet*, 1981 (Joseph R. McElrath and Allan P. Robb, editors).

Bibliography

Cowell, Pattie, and Ann Stanford, eds. *Critical Essays on Anne Bradstreet.* Boston: G. K. Hall, 1983. An excellent collection of essays by a variety of Bradstreet scholars. Part 1 includes criticism from the Colonial period to the twentieth century. The essays cover issues as diverse as Bradstreet's role in the American female literary tradition, the role of religion in the poet's life and work, and her inventive use of language.

Martin, Wendy. *An American Triptych: Anne Bradstreet, Emily Dickinson, Adrienne Rich.* Chapel Hill: University of North Carolina Press, 1984. Examines how the American experience has been transformed in the works of three American women poets. The section on Bradstreet focuses on the relationship between the poet's commitment to the religious values of her culture and her desire to create an alternative vision in her art.

Piercy, Josephine K. *Anne Bradstreet.* New York: Twayne, 1965. This 145-page work attempts to remedy Bradstreet's critical neglect by arguing that her poetry is important not only as a historical phenomenon but also as a real contribution to American literature. Analyzes the effects of Bradstreet's spiritual growth and struggle with orthodoxy in her poetry and prose and outlines the poet's development as a writer from imitative apprenticeship to maturity. Contains extensive notes and a bibliography.

Rich, Adrienne. "Anne Bradstreet and Her Poetry." Foreword to *The Works of Anne Bradstreet.* Cambridge, Mass.: The Belknap Press of Harvard University Press, 1967. Feminist poet Adrienne Rich's thirteen-page foreword to the collected works of Bradstreet provides an excellent overview of Bradstreet's life and work. Rich particularly stresses personal, historical, and literary influences on Bradstreet's development as a writer and views Bradstreet as a feminist breaker of silence and a transforming force in the literary world of her time.

Stanford, Ann. *Anne Bradstreet: The Worldly Puritan.* New York: Burt Franklin, 1974. Written as an introduction to the works of Bradstreet. Discusses the body of the author's poetry in the light of the prevailing literary forms and examines how Bradstreet fashioned these forms into a personal voice for argument between the world she knew and the greater world she envisioned. Contains extensive notes, a bibliography, and appendices.

Tyler, Moses C. *A History of American Literature During the Colonial Period.* New York: G. P. Putnam's Sons, 1897. Although the work is dated, Tyler remains one of the best historians and critics of American literature of the colonial period. Tyler is one of the earliest critics to give full recognition to Bradstreet's writing.

White, Elizabeth Wade. *Anne Bradstreet: The Tenth Muse.* New York: Oxford University Press, 1971. Although Bradstreet's writing became the object of increasing interest and discussion in the twentieth century, White maintains that her life and historical background have been neglected.

Calls Bradstreet the first resident poet of English-speaking North America and the first significant British poet. In this first full-length biography of Anne Bradstreet, White uses Bradstreet's writings to find a key to unlock her complex personality. Contains numerous illustrations, an appendix, and a bibliography.

EDWARD KAMAU BRATHWAITE

Born: Bridgetown, Barbados; May 11, 1930

Principal poetry

Rights of Passage, 1967; *Masks,* 1968; *Islands,* 1969; *The Arrivants: A New World Trilogy,* 1973 (includes *Rights of Passage, Masks,* and *Islands*); *Other Exiles,* 1975; *Days and Nights,* 1975; *Black & Blues,* 1976; *Mother Poem,* 1977; *Word Making Man: A Poem for Nicólas Guillèn,* 1979; *Sun Poem,* 1982; *Third World Poems,* 1983; *X/Self,* 1987.

Other literary forms

Edward Kamau Brathwaite has published scores of books, articles, and reviews as a historian and literary critic. Among his historical studies are *The Development of Creole Society in Jamaica, 1770-1820* (1971), one chapter of which was expanded and published as *Folk Culture of Slaves in Jamaica* (1970); *Contradictory Omens* (1974); *Caribbean Man in Space and Time* (1974); and *History of the Voice* (1984). His historical studies have delineated the historical pressures that have shaped present-day Caribbean life. He is particularly interested in the transmission of African culture to the New World, the " 'little' tradition of the ex-slave," and its promise to serve as a "basis for creative reconstruction" in postemancipation, postcolonial Creole society. His literary criticism has sought out the presence of African traditions in Caribbean literature and has helped to develop a vigorous, indigenous school of West Indian criticism. Brathwaite's work as poet, critic, and historian has made available to a wide audience the rich cultural heritage of Caribbean people.

Achievements

Brathwaite is one of the most popular and critically acclaimed writers to emerge in the West Indies during the remarkable period in the region's history and literature following World War II. He epitomizes the intensified ethnic and national awareness of his generation of writers—which includes Derek Walcott, Wilson Harris, Michael Anthony, Martin Carter, Samuel Selvon, John Hearne, and Austin Clarke, to name several of the more prominent—whose writing seeks to correct the destructive effects of colonialism on West Indian sensibility. Brathwaite's aim, as he has described it, is to "transcend and heal" the fragmented culture of his dispossessed people through his poetry, reexamining the whole history of the black diaspora in a search for cultural wholeness in contemporary Caribbean life.

Brathwaite offers his poetry as a corrective to the twin problems of the West Indian: dispossession of history and of language. The West Indian writer labors in a culture whose history has been distorted by prejudice and malice, the modern version of which is the commonplace notion, after James Anthony Froude and V. S. Naipaul, that nothing was created or achieved in the West Indies. The Afro-Caribbean's history is the record of being uprooted, displaced, enslaved, dominated, and finally abandoned. Brathwaite's reclamation of racial pride centers on rectifying the significance of the Middle Passage not as the destroyer but as the transmitter of culture.

The second problem that the writer confronts, that of language, is an aspect of cultural dispossession. The diversity of Creole languages, hybrids of many African and European tongues, reinforces the insularity of the individual and devalues the expressively rich languages that the people use in their nonofficial, personal, most intimate lives. Brathwaite's poems in Bajun dialect extend the folk traditions of Claude McKay and Louise Bennett and ground his work in the lives of the people for and about whom he writes.

The problem of language, however, is not a matter of choosing the Creole over the metropolitan language. It is a deeply political and spiritual problem, since, as Brathwaite writes, it was with language that the slave was "most successfully imprisoned by the master, and through his (mis-)use of it that he most effectively rebelled." With nearly all other means of attaining personal liberty denied, the slave's last, irrevocable instrument of resistance and rebellion was language. For Brathwaite, a West Indian writer, Caliban in William Shakespeare's *The Tempest* (1611), written at the beginning of England's experiment in empire, is the archetype of the slave who turns his borrowed language against his master. To turn his instrument of rebellion into one of creation is Brathwaite's task. Accordingly, in his poem "Caliban" (*The Arrivants*), Brathwaite's persona begins by celebrating the morning of December 2, 1956, the start of the Cuban Revolution, which remains a symbol of self-determination in the region. In the second section of the poem, Brathwaite adapts Shakespeare's " 'Ban Ban Caliban,'/ Has a new master" cursechant to the hold of a slave ship, articulating a spirit of resistance which turns in the final section to an assertion of endurance. At the end of the poem, the slaves' nightly limbo on deck becomes the religious ceremony— the seed of African culture carried to the New World—of the assembled tribes, who are able to raise their ancestral gods and be for the moment a whole people. What he achieves in "Caliban" Brathwaite achieves in his poetry at large: he uses his languages, both Creole and metropolitan English, to define the selfhood of the group in positive terms, contrary to the negations of the colonizers. "Within the folk tradition," Brathwaite writes, "language was (and is) a creative act in itself; the word was held to contain a secret power." His term "nation language" (defined in *History of the Voice*) for the language of the people brought to the Caribbean, as opposed to the official language of the colonial power, has profoundly influenced the theory and criticism of African-American literature. Brathwaite continues in *Mother Poem* and *Sun Poem* to explore the resources of both his native Bajun dialect and contemporary standard English. In his poetry, the power of the word is to conjure, to evoke, to punish, to celebrate, to mourn, to love. He uses language boldly as one who seeks its deepest power: to reveal and heal the wounds of history.

Biography

Lawson Edward Kamau Brathwaite was born in Bridgetown, Barbados, on May 11, 1930, the son of Hilton Brathwaite and Beryl Gill Brathwaite. He enrolled at Harrison College in Barbados, but won the Barbados Scholarship in 1949, enabling him the next year to read history at Pembroke College, University of Cambridge, England. He received an honors degree in 1953 and the Certificate of Education in 1955.

His earliest published poems appeared in the literary journal *Bim*, beginning in 1950. The poems of that decade, some of which are collected in *Other Exiles* and, in revised form, in *The Arrivants*, portray an estranged world fallen from grace; a world that can be redeemed through poetic vision—a creative faith that sustains the more complex fashionings of his later work. Brathwaite shared with other West Indian writers of his generation a strong sense of the impossibility of a creative life in the Caribbean, and the equal impossibility of maintaining identity in exile in England or North America. That crisis of the present he understood as a product of his island's cultural heritage fragmented among its several sources: European, African, Amerindian, and Asian.

His reading of history at Cambridge heightened both his sense of the European culture which had been the dominant official culture of the West Indies and his need to understand the African culture that had come with the slaves on the Middle Passage. His search led him to Africa, where from 1955 to 1962 he served as an education officer in Kwame Nkrumah's Ghana. His career in Ghana (and in Togoland in 1956-1957 as United Nations Plebiscite Officer) provided the historical and local images that became *Masks*, the pivotal book of *The Arrivants*. In Ghana, he established a children's theater and wrote several plays for children (*Four Plays for Primary Schools*, 1961, and *Odale's Choice*, 1962). He married Doris Welcome in 1960; and he has a son, Michael Kwesi Brathwaite.

Brathwaite returned to the West Indies after an exile of twelve years to assume a post as Resident Tutor at the University of the West Indies in St. Lucia (1962-1963) and to produce programs for the Windward Islands Broadcasting Service. His return to the Caribbean supplied the "centre" that his poetry had lacked:

> I had, at that moment of return, completed the triangular trade of my historical origins. West Africa had given me a sense of place, of belonging; and that place . . . was the West Indies. My absence and travels, at the same time, had given me a sense of movement and restlessness—rootlessness. It was, I recognized, particularly the condition of the Negro of the West Indies and the New World.

The exploration of that sense of belonging and rootlessness in personal and historic terms is the motive for Brathwaite's subsequent work in poetry, history, and literary criticism. He began in 1963 as lecturer in history at the University of the West Indies at Kingston, Jamaica, where he is now professor of social and cultural history. He earned his Ph.D. at the University of Sussex in England (1965-1968). His dissertation became *The Development of Creole Society in Jamaica, 1770-1820*, a study of the assimilation of cultures by various groups within the colonial hierarchy.

His poetry continues to explore the cultural heritage of the West Indies in historical and personal terms. *The Arrivants*, begun upon his return to the West Indies in 1972, represents a turning away from the introspection of his early poems toward a larger historical perspective on the Caribbean, as well as the beginnings of a personal solution to the problems of exile and cultural fragmentation.

Analysis

Edward Kamau Brathwaite's early poetry in *Bim*, collected later in *Other Exiles*, with its themes of anxiety and alienation, changed under the search for racial and cultural identity while in exile. Brathwaite became surer of his European heritage while he was a student in England and recovered the remnants of his African heritage while working in Ghana. Those two great cultures, in conflict in the New World for the last four centuries, are the forces that shape Brathwaite's personal and racial history and the poetics through which he renders his quest for wholeness.

He is equally indebted to the Euro-American literary tradition through the work of T. S. Eliot and to the Afro-West Indian tradition through the work of Aimé Césaire. Brathwaite draws upon Eliot's musical form in *Four Quartets* (1943) for his own use of musical forms developed in stages of the black diaspora—work song, shanto, shango hymn, spiritual, blues, jazz, calypso, ska, and reggae—for his poetic rendering of historic and lyric moments. He also draws his aesthetic for rendering modern industrial and mercantile society in the United States and the Caribbean from Eliot's *The Waste Land* (1922). From Césaire's *Cahier d'un retour au pays natal* (1968; *Notebook of the Return to My Native Land*), Brathwaite derives the epic and dialectical structure of his trilogy as well as the surrealistic heightening of language that propels the movement from the reality of the Caribbean as wasteland to the vision of the Caribbean as promised land.

That movement can be discerned in the three books of *The Arrivants* through the poet's reconstruction of racial history and his tracing of his personal history. *Rights of Passage*, the first book of the trilogy, contains the restless isolation of his early life in Barbados that sends him into exile in England and Africa, as well as a recollection of the first phase of the black diaspora, the advent of the slave trade and the Middle Passage. The original dispersal of tribes from Ethiopia to West Africa, as well as his own search for his African origins, is the subject of *Masks.* In *Islands*, racial and personal history merge in the exile's return to the West Indies. The fruits of that return will become manifest in his planned second trilogy.

Readers of *The Arrivants* who focus on its historical dimension figure Brathwaite as the epic poet of the black diaspora, while those who focus on the autobiography make him the hero of the poem. Taking both approaches as valid, with the binocular vision that the poem requires, one can see that the central figure of the rootless, alienated West Indian in exile and in search of home is the only possible kind of hero for a West Indian epic. That questing poet's voice is, however, often transformed into the voice of a precolonial African being fired upon by a white slaver; the Rastafarian Brother Man; Uncle Tom; a *houngan* invoking Legba; or some other historic or mythic figure. Brathwaite's use of personae, or masks, derives equally from the traditions of Greek drama (dramatic monologue) and African religious practice (chant or invocation). One communal soul speaks in a multiplicity of guises, and the poet thereby re-creates not only his own quest as victim and hero, but also the larger racial consciousness in which he participates. The poet's many masks enable him to reconstruct his own life and the brutal history that created "new soil, new souls, new ancestors" out of the ashes of the past.

Combining racial history and personal quest in *The Arrivants*, Brathwaite has fashioned a contemporary West Indian myth. It is not the myth of history petrified into "progress," but that of a people's endurance through cycles of brutal oppression. Across centuries, across the ocean, and across the three books of this poem, images, characters, and events overlay one another to defy the myth of progress, leading in the poem only to heaven swaying in the reinforced girders of New York, and to the God of capitalism floating in a soundless, airtight glass bubble of an office, a prisoner of his own creation. For the "gods" who tread the earth below, myth is cyclical, and it attaches them to the earth through the "souls" of their feet in repetitions of exodus and arrival.

The trilogy begins with one tribe's ancient crossing of the Sahara desert, their wagons and camels left where they had fallen, and their arrival at a place where "cool/ dew falls/ in the evening." They build villages, but the cattle towns breed flies and flies breed plague, and another journey begins, for across the "dried out gut" of the riverbed, a mirage shimmers where

> trees are
> cool, there
> leaves are
> green, there
> burns the dream
> of a fountain,
> garden of odours,
> soft alleyways.

This is the repeated pattern of their history: exodus across desert, savannah, ocean; in caravan, ship or jet plane; visitations of plague, pestilence, famine, slavery, poverty, ignorance, volcanos, flood. The promised land is always elsewhere, across the parched riverbed ("Prelude") or in the bountiful fields of England, not in Barbados ("The Cracked Mother").

The connections between history and biography and the difficult process of destroying the colonial heritage in favor of a more creative mode of life are evident in the six poems that comprise the "Limbo" section of *Islands*. In "The Cracked Mother," the first poem of "Limbo," the dissociation of the West Indian's sensibility—regarding his attitudes toward self, race, and country—threatens to paralyze the poet's dialectical movement toward a sustaining vision. The poet's rejection of his native land in favor of England is an acceptance of the colonial's position of inferiority. That attitude is instilled in young West Indians, such historians as Walter Rodney, Frantz Fanon, and Brathwaite have argued, by the system of colonial education that taught an alien and alienating value system. The debilitating effects of such an education are the subject of "The Cracked Mother." The three nuns who take the child from his mother to school appear as "black specks . . . / Santa Marias with black silk sails." The metaphor equates the nuns' coming with that of Columbus and anticipates the violence that followed, especially in the image of the nuns' habits as the sails of death ships. With her child gone, the mother speaks in the second part of the poem as a broken ("cracked") woman reduced to muttering children's word-games which serve as the vehicle for her pain:

> See?
> She saw
> the sea . . .
> I saw
> you take
> my children . . .
> You gave your
> beads, you
> took
> my children . . .
> Christ on the Cross
> your cruel laws teach
> only to divide us
> and we are lost.

History provides the useful equation of nuns' habits with sails and the nuns' rosary with the beads that Columbus gave to the inhabitants of his "discovered" lands, but it is Brathwaite's own biography that turns metaphor into revelation in the last two parts of the poem, showing how ruinous the colonial mentality is, even to the point of rejecting the earth under one's feet (another "cracked mother") because it is not England.

Brathwaite's corrective begins in "Shepherd," the second poem of the "Limbo" section. Having recalled the damage of his early education and having felt again some of the old abhorrence of the colonial for himself, the poet returns to the African drumbeats of *Masks* to chant a service of possession or reconnection with the gods of his ancestors. The poet then addresses his peers in proverbs, as would an elder to his tribe:

> But you do not understand.
> For there is an absence of truth
> like a good tooth drawn from the tight skull
> like the wave's tune gone from the ship's hull
> there is sand
> but no desert where water can learn of its loveliness.

The people have gifts for the gods but do not give them, yet the gods are everywhere and waiting. Moving in *Islands* toward the regeneration promised in *Masks*, Brathwaite continues with "Caliban" to explore the potential for liberty inherent in the Cuban Revolution, then moves at the moment of triumph back into the slave ship and the limbo that contained the seeds of African religion and identity.

The "Limbo" section ends with the beautiful poem "Islands," which proposes the alternatives that are always present in every moment of Caribbean history: "So looking through a map/ of the islands, you see/ . . . the sun's/ slums: if you hate/ us. Jewels,/ if there is delight/ in your eyes." The same dichotomy of vision has surrounded every event and personage in the poem, all infolded upon the crucial event of the Middle Passage: Did it destroy a people or create one? Brathwaite's account of the voyage in "New World A-Comin" promises "new worlds, new waters, new/ harbours" on the one hand, and on the other, "the flesh and the flies, the whips and the fixed/ fear of pain in this chained and welcoming port."

The gods have crossed with the slaves to new soil, and the poet has returned to the origin of his race to discover his communal selfhood in African rite, which requires participation by all to welcome the god who will visit one of them. *The Arrivants* is a long historical and autobiographical poem, and it is also a rite of passage for the poet-priest who invites the god to ride him. Brathwaite's incantatory poems in *Masks* are his learning of the priest's ways, which restores his spirit in *Islands.* The refrain *"Attibon Legba/ Ouvri bayi pou'moi"* (Negus) is the Voodoo *houngon's* prayer to the gatekeeper god Legba to open the door to the other gods. The prayer is answered in the final poem *"Jou'vert"* ("I Open"), where Legba promises

> hearts
> no longer bound
> to black and bitter
> ashes in the ground

> now waking
> making
> making with their
> rhythms some-
> thing torn
> and new.

In *Mother Poem*, the first book of Brathwaite's planned second trilogy, the central figure is not the restless poet but the mother he has left and returned to, the source of his life. The types of motherhood established in "The Cracked Mother" (*The Arrivants*) are reiterated here as the poet's human mother and his motherland, Barbados. Both "mothers" are established in the first poem, "Alpha," the origin. Barbados is the mother-island of porous limestone (thus absorbing all influence of weather and history), cut by ancient watercourses that have dried up in sterility. Her dead streams can be revived only by the transfigured human mother who "rains upon the island with her loud voices/ with her grey hairs/ with her green love." The transfiguration that occurs in the last lines of the book must wait, however, for the woman to endure the dream-killing, soul-killing life of the island that is dominated by "the man who possesses us all," the merchant, the modern agent of bondage ("name-tracks").

The mother is his victim, no matter whether she "sits and calls on jesus name" waiting for her husband to come home from work with lungs covered with jute from the sugar sacks, or whether she goes out after his death to sell calico cloth, half-soled shoes, and biscuits, or persuades her daughter to sell herself to the man who is waiting: "It int hard, leh me tell you/ jess sad/ so come darlin chile/ leh me tell he you ready you steady you go" ("Woo/ Dove").

She gets no help from her men, who are crippled, destroyed, frightened, or sick from their lives of bondage to the merchant. One man goes to Montreal to work for nine years and sends back nothing ("Woo/ Dove") and another goes to work for life in the local plantation, brings nothing home, and loses three fingers in the cane-grinder ("Milkweed"). Nor does she receive comfort from her children, "wearing dark glasses/ hearing aids/ leaning on wine" ("Tear or pear shape"), who were educated by Chalkstick the teacher, a satirical composite of the colonial educator whose job is to see that his pupils "don't clap their hands, shake their heads, tap their feet" or "push bones through each others' congolese nostrils" ("Lix"). Nor does her help come from her sisters ("Dais" and "Nights"), or from her Christianity ("Sam Lord").

Rather, the restoration of her powers as life-giver begins in the guttural, elemental, incantatory uttering of "Nametracks," where, as a slave-mother beaten by her owner, she reminds herself and her huddled children in dark monosyllables like the word-game of "The Cracked Mother" that they will endure while "e di go/ e go di/ e go dead," that despite all his power, he "nevver maim what me." Her eyes rise from the plot of land she has bought with her meager earnings, the land that has sustained her and her children, to the whole island and a vision of revolutionary solidarity with her people: "de merchants got de money/ but de people got de men" ("Peace Fire"). With full realization that her child will be born to the life of "broken islands/ broken homes" ("Mid/Life"), in "Driftwood," the human mother still chooses to suffer the "pour of her flesh into their mould of bone." The poem ends with the mother re-created in clay by the potter who can work again, in stone by the sculptor whose skill has returned, and in her words gathered by the poet as rain gathering in the dry pools flows once more past the ruins of the slave and colonial world, refreshing and renewing the ancient life of the island.

Brathwaite's second volume on Bajun life moves from *Mother Poem*'s focus on the female characters (and character) of the island to the male principle of the tropical sun and of the various sons of Barbados. The pun of sun/son is derived from a number of historical and mythological associations, including that of Christianity (Brathwaite renames himself Adam as the boy-hero of the poem, and spells the pronoun "his" as "ihs" or Iesu Hominum Salvator) and various African traditions. The sun, for instance, contains "megalleons of light," the invented word associating it with the Egyptian god Ra's sun-ship, the galleons of European explorers, and the enormous nuclear energy that eclipses or perhaps anticipates the holocaust that Western man has in his power. The complexity of the sun/son as controlling metaphor, as it evokes various ethnic and historical images, extends through time and geographic space the significance of the narrative, even as it complements and completes the female principle of *Mother Poem.*

The mythologies evoked in the poem contribute to the meaning of the life of the son Adam, as he begins to understand the West Indian male's sunlike course of ascent, dominance, and descent, played out through the rituals of boyhood games and identity-seeking, adolescence, adult sexual experience, marriage and paternity, and finally death. In an early encounter, Adam wrestles the bully Batto underwater in a life-or-death rite of passage that initiates him into the comradeship of his peers, but which, Brathwaite suggests, fails (as the other games that "had little meaning" fail) to prepare him for the struggles of adult manhood ("Son"). The types of fathers portrayed ("Clips") fall into roles available from Christian, bourgeois, and Rastafarian cultures that are equally dead-ended. These fathers are unable to pass on to their sons any mode of fulfilling identity or action, even as in his soliloquy the father laments his own diminishment, his being displaced as the head of his family by his own son.

The central incidents of Adam's life introduce him to the cares and costs of adulthood. On his Sunday School trip to the Atlantic coast he enters the adult world, in part by hearing the story of Bussa's slave rebellion, a story of the painful price one pays for asserting his personhood ("Noom"). He conducts his courtship of Esse ("Return of the Sun") with a blithe but growing awareness of the consequences of one's sexual life in determining social and political roles ("Fleches"). The death of Adam's grandfather ("Indigone"), the final event in the poem, reveals to him the cyclical nature of manhood in which he begins to locate himself: "and i looked up to see my father's eye: wheeling/ towards his father/ now as i his sun moved upward to his eye." The cultural determinants of dispossession and lack of identity that so condition the natural progress and decline of masculine life are transcended in the poem's ultimate vision of a world capable of beginning anew. The final section ("*Son*") returns to the cosmic, creative domain of the poem's invocation ("Red Rising"), but with a clarified focus on creation and growth as the first principles of the natural and hence human world. The image of emerging coral returns the reader to the genesis of the island at the beginning of *Mother Poem* ("Rock Seed"), completing the cycle of the poems with the "coming up coming up coming up" of his "thrilldren" to people a world renewed.

Robert Bensen

Other major works

PLAYS: *Four Plays for Primary Schools*, 1961; *Odale's Choice*, 1962.

NONFICTION: *Folk Culture of Slaves in Jamaica*, 1970; *The Development of Creole Society in Jamaica, 1770-1820*, 1971; *Contradictory Omens: Cultural Diversity and Integration in the Caribbean*, 1974; *Caribbean Man in Space and Time*, 1974; *Our Ancestral Heritage: A Bibliography of the Roots of Culture in the English-Speaking Caribbean*, 1976; *Wars of Respect: Nanny, Sam Sharpe, and the Struggle for People's Liberation*, 1977; *The Colonial Encounter: Language*, 1984; *History of the Voice: The Development of Nation Language in Anglophone Caribbean Poetry*, 1984.

Bibliography

Brown, Lloyd W. *West Indian Poetry*. 2d ed. London: Heinemann, 1978. In his chapter on Brathwaite, Brown describes the "cyclical vision" of *The Arrivants* as Brathwaite's "discovering and imitating the cycles of history" in his art. Brown's placement of the poem's West Indian archetypes within this cyclical structure is often tenuous, but his exploration of the political and cultural milieu of those types is very useful.

McWatt, Mark A. "Edward Kamau Brathwaite." In *Fifty Caribbean Writers*, edited by Daryl Cumber Dance. New York: Greenwood Press, 1986. While this study traces the shift of the West Indies from "wasteland" to "promised land" in Brathwaite's poetry, it more importantly recounts the critical debate over the relative merits of the poetry of Brathwaite and Derek A. Walcott in relation to West Indian society.

Povey, John. "The Search for Identity in Edward Brathwaite's *The Arrivants.*" *World Literature Written in English* 27 (1987): 275-289. Povey details both the historical causes of the lack of a coherent regional identity and Brathwaite's exploration of European and African elements that have shaped the region. Povey studies autobiographical aspects of *The Arrivants*, in particular the reversal of the route of the slave trade that Brathwaite's own career has made.

Rohlehr, Gordon. " 'Megalleons of Light': Edward Brathwaite's *Sun Poem.*" *Jamaica Journal* 16 (1983): 81-87. Rohlehr draws together *Mother Poem* and *Sun Poem* in reading their parallel movements, passages, and themes. Those peoms revive the redemptive view of history taken in *The Arrivants*. Rohlehr expertly delineates the patterns of imagery and their thematic relations, particularly in the poem's depiction of the West Indian's distorted self-image and cultural dispossession.

—————. *Pathfinder: Black Awakening in "The Arrivants" of Edward Kamau Brathwaite.* Tunapuna, Trinidad: Gordon Rohlehr, 1981. This lengthy work is an indispensable companion to *The Arrivants*. Rohlehr's commentary is compendious and meticulous. It clarifies what the poem's language and syntax leave obscure to a non-West-Indian reader, and identifies the poem's references unfailingly, including the many musical references that are essential to Brathwaite's technique. Lack of an index, however, hampers efforts to locate specific topics.

Thomas, Sue. "Sexual Politics in Edward Brathwaite's *Mother Poem* and *Sun Poem.*" *Kunapipi* 9 (1987): 33-43. In her seminal feminist reading, Thomas analyzes the sexual politics inherent in the poet's portrayal of, and commentary on, racial and sexual stereotypes. She finds Brathwaite's ideology to be patriarchal, with the liberated husband supplanting the colonizer in a continuing subordination of the West Indian woman.

NICHOLAS BRETON

Born: London(?), England; c. 1545
Died: London, England; c. 1626

Principal poetry

A Smale Handfull of Fragrant Flowers, 1575; *The Workes of a Yonge Wyt Trust Up with a Fardell of Pretie Fancies,* 1577; *A Floorish upon Fancie,* 1577; *The Toyes of an Idle Head,* 1582; *A Handfull of Holesome Hearbes,* 1584; *Brittons Bowre of Delights,* 1591; *Pilgrimage to Paradise,* 1592; *The Phoenix Nest,* 1593; *A Solemne Passion of the Soules Love,* 1595; *The Arbor of Amorous Devices,* 1597; *England's Helicon,* 1600; *Pasquils Mad-Cappe, Throwne at the Corruptions of These Times,* 1600; *Pasquils Fooles-Cappe,* 1600; *Pasquils Passe and Passeth Not,* 1600; *Pasquils Mistresse: Or, The Worthie and Unworthie Woman,* 1600; *Melancholike Humours,* 1600; *The Soules Heavenly Exercise,* 1601; *The Ravisht Soule, and the Blessed Weeper,* 1601; *No Whippinge nor Trippinge, but a Kinde Friendly Snippinge,* 1601; *The Longing of a Blessed Heart: Or, Breton's Longing,* 1601; *The Soules Harmony,* 1602; *The Mothers Blessing,* 1602; *Olde Mad-Cappes New Gally-mawfrey,* 1602; *A True Description of Unthankfulnesse,* 1602; *The Passionate Shepheard,* 1604; *The Soules Immortal Crowne,* 1605; *Honest Counsaile,* 1605; *The Honour of Valour,* 1605; *The Uncasing of Machiavels Instructions,* 1613; *I Would, and Would Not,* 1614; *The Hate of Treason,* 1616; *The Countess of Pembroke's Passion,* 1853; *Poems by Nicholas Breton,* 1952 (Jean Robertson, editor).

Other literary forms

After 1600, Nicholas Breton's attention turned to prose essays, dialogues, and fiction, including proverb collections and character sketches. *Auspicante Jehova: Maries Exercise* (1597) and *Divine Considerations of the Soule* (1608) are devotional treatises; such works as *Wits Private Wealth* (1607) and *Crossing of Proverbs* (1616) collect proverbs and other practical advice; *Wits Trenchmour: Or, A Conference Between a Scholler and Angler* (1597) and *The Figure of Foure* (1597) discourse upon daily life, including angling and other country pleasures. Breton's dialogues of youth and age, country and city, traveler and stay-at-home include *A Dialogue Full of Pithe and Pleasure* (1603), *The Wil of Wit, Wits Will or Wils Wit* (1597), *An Olde Mans Lesson and a Young Mans Love* (1605). The vogue for traveler's tales appears not only in the dialogues but also in prose tales such as *Wonders Worth the Hearing* (1602) and *A Mad World, My Masters* (1603), while contemporary events are addressed in *A Murmurer* (1607), on the occasion of the Gunpowder Plot. Breton's romantic fiction, *The Strange Fortune of Two Excellent Princes* (1600) and *Grimellos Fortunes* (1604) frequently contains lyrics within the narrative, including the frequently anthologized "I would thou wert not fair, or I were wise." Always highly popular in London's booming pamphlet market, Breton was particularly successful with the epistolary *A Poste with a Packet of Mad Letters*, a much-reprinted series begun around 1603. His modern reputation as a prose writer depends chiefly on his contributions to the prose character, as in his *Characters upon Essaies, Morall and Divine* (1615), *The Good and the Badde* (1616), and especially *Fantasticks* (1626), containing characterizations of love, money, the seasons, the holidays, the times of day, and the months of the year. Many of the afore-mentioned titles (those without dates) may be found in Alexander B. Grosart's informative volumes on *The Works of Nicholas Breton*, (1879, 1966). Breton's prose works were immensely successful best-sellers, a fact often cited to account for the extreme rarity of copies today.

Achievements
One of the first English authors to earn a living entirely by writing, Breton spent fifty years producing literary works which encompass the height of the Renaissance and the beginning of the Jacobean period. A transitional figure, he provides a link between two related but highly contradictory sensibilities. Working in the major poetic categories of moral allegory in the style of Edmund Spenser, of lyric and pastoral in the Arcadian mode, of devotional meditation akin to that of Robert Southwell, and of popular verse satire, Breton bridges the gap between traditional and progressive, literary and colloquial, in a controlled and assured presentation which appears almost classical in its decorum. He treats the major topics of human and divine love, moral virtue, holiness, and spiritual experience, honor and humility, court and country, the real versus the ideal social world, and the emotions of exultation and melancholy, integration and alienation. His settings in the Arcadian bowers of Renaissance pastoral prefigure Marvellian gardens, while his perception of the freshness and vigor of rural life, coupled with the depth and complexity of urban experience, helps to form the modern apprehension of the change in cultural values characteristic of early commercial capitalism. His conception of contemporary psychology of humors and the melancholy stance connects classical and medieval typology to the "humourous" characters of Ben Jonson and the seventeenth century dramatists, embodying the tension between traditional humanism and the new commercial ethic.

Always a popular writer with a keen sense of self-presentation and audience awareness, Breton's Renaissance poetic looks forward to Metaphysical paradox. With careful prosody, simple diction, clear thought, and accessible imagery, he writes a consistently craftsmanlike verse which, as C. S. Lewis has noted in his definitive *English Literature in the Sixteenth Century* (1944), escapes the confines of the drab, undergoing gradual "aurification" into the golden. As one of the first such poets, and one with so long and distinguished a record of successful publication, Nicholas Breton helped establish the poetics of the high Renaissance. Perhaps because of a lingering bias against the "popular" writer, or perhaps simply because of the extreme rarity of his surviving books, Breton has not always been accorded the attention he merits in literary histories and anthologies, an omission which still waits to be remedied.

Biography

The Breton, or Britton, family traced its roots to the company of William the Conqueror and held ancestral lands in Lincolnshire and in Layer-Breton, Essex, where Sir John LeBretoune was a knight banneret at the time of Edward I. Nicholas Breton's father, William, sought his living in London trade, establishing a respectable fortune speculating in church properties which had been confiscated during the Reformation. By the time of Nicholas' birth around 1545, the family comprised prosperous members of London's mercantile class, holding its "capitall mansion house," according to William Breton's will, in Redcrosse Street, maintaining its country seats as well.

Following their father's death, the Breton sons' financial situation underwent a significant change, one which dictated the need to pursue professional careers. The marriage of the young men's mother, Elizabeth Bacon Breton (through whom the family was remotely connected with Sir Francis Bacon's family), to the poet George Gascoigne drained William Breton's substantial legacy away from his sons in a series of complicated legal maneuvers. Nevertheless, Nicholas Breton's youth seems to have been comfortable and even advantageous, being, as he was, a part of the cultured middle class which so enjoyed the widening horizons of the English Renaissance. Although he seems to have been destined for one of the professions, Breton spent only a short while at Oriel College and never attained an academic degree. Nevertheless, he was familiar with classical and contemporary authors (Ovid, Francisco Petrarch, Dante, Torquato Tasso, Lodovico Ariosto, and Pastor Fido became his literary models) and with the courtly arts, which were to play a prominent role in his career as a poet in search of a patron. Although not much is known about his domestic life other than that he frequently adopted the literary pose of paterfamilias, it is known that he married Ann Sutton around 1592, and the births of four of their children and the deaths of two appear in the parish register of St. Giles, Cripplegate. For the apocryphal tradition that Ann was an "unquiet wife," little evidence can be found.

Of greater relevance to his literary career was Breton's close association with the Sidney circle, in the aura of which most of his lyric and divine poems were written. Mary Sidney, Countess of Pembroke, appears as the ideal lady, a paragon of wisdom; the record of Breton's largely unsuccessful pursuit of her favor appears in various of his tales.

Although his early canon is still uncertain, Breton's literary career seems to have begun around 1575; this rather late date suggests that his poems had been circulating in manuscript form some time before. In any case, *A Floorish upon Fancie* was published in 1577. In 1589, Breton was mentioned in George Puttenham's *Arte of English Poesy* (reprinted in 1970), and he had the dubious fortune to be mocked by Thomas Nashe in 1591. The 1590's saw the publication of his first mature works, lyric and devotional poems in the Arcadian or Spenserian manner. His first aesthetically successful poem, the *Pilgrimage to Paradise*, a moral allegory in the Spenserian style with lyrics in the pastoral mode of Arcadianism, signals his break with the older tradition of Gascoigne. Many of Breton's lyrics, some still unidentified, appeared in the popular anthologies of the period. That his reputation as a lyric poet was firmly established is evidenced by the publication of *Brittons Bowre of Delights* by Richard Jones in 1591, which capitalized on the poet's name even though only about half the verses in the volume are Breton's, including his rather pedestrian elegy on the death of Sir Philip Sidney, "Amoris Lachrimae." *The Arbor of Amorous Devices* contains what is possibly Breton's best-known lyric, "Phillida and Coridon," played as a morning song by three musicians in country garb for Queen Elizabeth's entertainment at Elvetham, Hampshire, in 1591.

At the end of the century, Breton's attention turned to meditative devotional poetry with an intensity that his appreciative nineteenth century editor, Alexander B. Grosart, attributes to a conversion experience. The devotional series, from *A Solemne Passion of the Soules Love* to *The Soules Harmony*, presents a search for repentance, absolution, and spiritual union with the transcendent in the Christian Platonist and progressive English Protestant tradition. Breton's religious thought, while intensely personal and meditative, is always staunchly orthodox and accessible, avoiding the religious syncretism and esoteric influences characteristic of some of his contemporaries; it is staunchly conservative in its condemnation of what was popularly conceived of as atheism, represented as Machiavellianism or Epicureanism.

Throughout this period at the turn of the century, Breton adopted with increasing regularity the mask of the melancholy poet. This mask was a product of the contemporary psychology of humors and very conventional in the pastoral lyric; easy to see in this stance, however, is the growing alienation of the artist, divorced from both courtly influence and the common life, and always uncertain of status, conscious of the division between the pamphleteer's market and the calling of the New Poet whose advent had been perceived by Spenser. In his immensely popular *Pasquil* series, entertaining and edifying verse satires in the colloquial vein, Breton plays upon the melancholy aspect of the satirist. After the death of Elizabeth in 1603, his energies turned away from divine poetry to conventional moralizing in the popular mode, especially in the role of a crusty old paternal type, and ultimately away from verse to prose, particularly in the form of the dialogue and the character. It is as a prose writer that he is primarily thought of in seventeenth century studies. No one is sure of the circumstances or even the date of his death which, as is perhaps fitting for one who lived so entirely by his pen, is usually assumed to be 1626, the year his last printed work *Fantasticks*, was published.

Analysis

Nicholas Breton's earliest published works introduce the theme of love and its loss, a concern which perhaps dominates all of his verse. In the role of a self-deprecating journeyman poet trying his wings in "small handfuls" of flowers or herbs, sentiments "trussed up," "floorishes," or "toyes," Breton addresses courtly—that is, fanciful—love in a landscape peppered with gardens, dream visions, and the familiar courtly personifications of desire versus disdain. Fancy, the spirit of courtly love, keeps a school and a fort manned with allegorical figures and rustic types, where the young poet-lover receives an education in the ways of the court and courtliness. Banished into rural obscurity, he must struggle for reinstatement, a trial by which he learns to distrust "fansy fonde," affected courtliness, and infatuation, and to practice the important Bretonian virtue of patience—the long suffering of undeserved slights in an atmosphere of pervasive, although vague, dissatisfaction, at the close of which he abruptly rejects all and turns his thoughts to eschatology. Although slight in themselves, and hopelessly old-fashioned in the style of Gascoigne and the older generation, these early works do establish the persona of the speaker, the themes of love and the ethical-religious life, and the pastoral mode for the mature works to come.

Of these, surely the best-known are Breton's many lyrics, published in the popular verse anthologies. These lyrics are in the Petrarchan vein and the pastoral mode; to them Breton owes his reputation as a poet of "sweetness and purity," of a great sensitivity for nature and rural life. The earliest lyrics in *Brittons Bowre of Delights*, although conventional in imagery and plodding in meter, still possess a simple, musical appeal, whether celebrating ideal courtly love or complaining against love and fortune. One of Breton's favorite devices is foretelling doomsday in a series of unlikely perfections never found in the world, such as when "Words shall be deeds, and men shall be divine." In these poems and those in *The Phoenix Nest*, Breton introduces his pastoral lady, Phyllis, or Phillida, and the "silly shepherd" poet, whose vulnerable expressiveness permits the restorative working of the idyll, as well as his familiar setting of the garden with its herbal and rustic lore, such as in "A Strange Description of a Rare Garden-plot," where all the herbs are "weeds of wo," allegorical flowers. The well-known "Phillida and Coridon," or "In the merry moneth of May," shows the naïve pastoral ideal in its dialogue, which begins in courtly coquetry ("He would loue, and she would not") but quickly moves into a pastoral world of frankness and good nature, and thus to lovers' oaths, "with kisses sweet concluded." The poem ends with a pastoral apotheosis in which Phillida becomes "Lady of the May," the queen of love, and that emotion, so long "abused" and "deluded" by courtly affection, is set right. This ideal world is darkened in "A sweete Pastorall," or "Good Muse rock me asleepe," by loss of love, the wreck of the shepherd's flock, and the silencing of the birds. In *The Arbor of Amorous Devices* the lady has become even more ideal, perhaps in keeping with the growing influence of Mary Sidney, more wise and "rich" in accomplishments, and more associated with virtue (Phillis) as opposed to the erotic Venus, whose Amor she blinds in "A Pastoral" ("On a hill there grows a flower").

Ultimately human love is rejected in favor of the divine. In Sonnet 3 of *The Passionate Shepheard*, Breton celebrates the advent of "wise" over foolish love and castigates "Lust the excremente of love." For the shepherd Bonerto, ideal love becomes the means of restoring faith and reason to a world darkened by age, death, and care; he says to his Aglaia, "I hate the world, but for they [thy] love." In this late collection of perhaps earlier verses, the shepherd and his lady live in the country of Minerva, or wisdom. In simple Marvellian couplets, they celebrate the pastoral ideal, free from dissimulation and conflict, which is the blight of the urban world. Breton's pastoral lyric attempts to re-create the Elizabethan Arcadia in a context which looks forward to Augustan gardens.

Among all of Breton's lyrics, perhaps the single most perfect is "A Sweet Lullabie," a simple, expressive treatment of the Bretonian topics of faithlessness and patience in an abandoned woman's song to her child, "Thy fathers shame, thy mothers griefe." Although it is crying, the infant is mercifully unaware of life's more sorrowful realities and the difficulties ensured by its uncertain legitimacy. The "Poor soule that thinkes no creature harme" is an eloquent contrast to an unfeeling world. As the baby is comforted by the song, the mother begins to hope that the child's charms can restore innocence and rightness to the world, securing the grace of both God and its "father false." The poem ends with the mother's wish that upon her death the child may vindicate her reputation, "Tell how by love she purchast blame," and appeal to its father's "gentle heart"—for although "His sugred words that me betrayde," he is yet of a "noble mind." This leads to a reversed ending in which the child laughs while the mother weeps, asking that it be shielded from the world's cruel inconstancy, "thy fathers qualitie."

Turning from the lyric to more serious moral allegory in the Spenserian mode, Breton's *Pilgrimage to Paradise* recounts a dream vision in which the poet-pilgrim journeys from the "vain conceits" of courtliness to heavenly delights. Passing through the wilderness of the world with its assorted mythical temptations and metamorphosized creatures, he confronts the seven-headed monster of vice, the familiar medieval specter of the deadly sins, which he overcomes with angelic assistance, after avoiding the twin pitfalls of melancholy on one hand and overweening ambition on the other. Joining medieval personification to heroic epic, Breton illustrates the virtue of patience—here, informed moral choice—by setting ethical extremes, wealth and wisdom, gold and grace, against one another. To cross a turbulent sea, the pilgrim joins forces with a stoic fisherman, who has fled the court for a life of stalwart independence, thus uniting the active and the contemplative. The two negotiate a number of nautical perils to enter the city of the world, leading to a favorite Bretonian portrayal of a variety of human types—courtiers, merchants, churchmen, and foolish lovers—creating the city as a center of discontent, "outwarde wealth so ful of inwarde wo." Next, they encounter a more positive image of Renaissance culture, the university, and then the idealized court of Elizabeth, the "princely Queen," followed immediately by its dark mirror-image, a bloody battlefield, one of the small Brueghelesque landscapes which constitute an interesting aspect of Breton's vision. Ultimately they arrive at the church "Not built of lime or stone," a royal garden, a vision of the eternal bucolic in which is neither weed nor worm. The second part of the Pilgrimage, the "Countesse of Pembrokes love," presents the Countess as "true loves saint," the Phoenix of an earthly paradise addressing divine love in a soliloquy overheard by the poet. Rejecting all worldly pleasures and comparing herself to Mary Magdalen, she longs to be united with Christ, the true Phoenix.

This early Breton poem shows his Christian Platonist view of *caritas*, divine love, the basis of Breton's poetry in the many "passions" that followed. An undated but probably contemporary poem, addressed to Mary Sidney and, possibly for that reason, sometimes ascribed to her, is *The Countess of Pembroke's Passion*—"passion" being a Bretonian term for an extended meditation delineating the speaker's religious emotions. Repenting his early "fruitless labours and ruthless love," the poet meditates upon Christ's passion, especially the example it gives of patience. Compared to later meditative poetry in the Metaphysical tradition, Breton's poem might seem conventional, but it does contain an unaffected, calm piety, a simple conversational style, plain diction and imagery, as well as a dynamic emotional tone cast in simple yet flowing sestinas rhyming ababcc.

Breton's devotional poetry connects earlier religious polemic with later meditative poetry by developing the themes of the moral allegory in an interior and contemplative vein, attempting—in the style of Southwell, but without his extravagance—to cast religious experience in lyrical imagery. *A Solemne Passion of the Soules Love*, perhaps the most consistently satisfying of these attempts, celebrates the creative relationship between divine love and the human world. Standard biblical images join the more Petrarchan Phoenix and sun to create a sense of the contradiction between human weakness and divine perfection—lowly pebble and "azurde ski"—to be resolved through meditation. This exploration of spiritual transcendence, from despondency to ecstasy, appears most plainly in a two-part divine poem, *The Ravisht Soule, and the Blessed Weeper*, which first explores the experience of spiritual enlightenment (ravishment), and then offers the example of Mary Magdalen, whose lament and consolation at Christ's tomb is overheard in the poet's dream vision. *The Longing of a Blessed Heart*, an extended definition of divine-Platonic love, illustrates the relationship between the divine and the human and the transformation of the natural world by love. The poem's definition distinguishes *caritas* from other kinds of love in a discursive, conversational style anticipating the mood of seventeenth century meditative poetry: "Some thinke it [love] is a babe of Beautie's getting,/ Nurst up by Nature, and Time's onely breeding;/ A pretty work to set the wits a wheeting."

In his successful *Pasquil* series, Breton extends the quality of love or charity to the social world in an attempt to correct the vices of an increasingly complex order, applying an essentially medieval form to the matter of emerging seventeenth century policy. Prefiguring Jonsonian comedy of humors, Breton's satirist is a humorist suffering from extreme feelings motivated by anger or sorrow to which he gives vent in impassioned speech. In *Pasquils Mad-Cappe, Throwne at the Corruptions of These Times*, the satirist inveighs against the abuse of wealth and power, the ascendance of illusion over reality, folly above reason, conditions motivated by "Pride, power, and pence." His multitude of wealthy rascals is set against the good poor man "free from Fancie's vanities," who goes begging among the rich asses and dunces. "It is money makes or mars the man," Pasquil says, offering instead a pastoral ideal where "Pride shall goe down, and virtue shall encrease." *Pasquils Fooles-Cappe* addresses those too obtuse to heed the first jeremiad in order to bring about a more "honest kindness," without swaggerers, spendthrifts, lazy wives, wandering husbands, absent-minded professors, or unscrupulous satirists. In the later installments of the *Pasquil* series, the conditions of melancholy and ambivalence render all human choice valueless. In *I Would, and Would Not*, the poet first claims and then rejects the entire gamut of human enterprise, resolving finally to preserve his own identity as a "religious servant" of common sense and a corrector of folly. It is not difficult to see in these complaints the dissatisfaction connected with the poet's uncertain status, the dangers of dwelling continually in the "fancy," concerns which appear in "An Epigraph upon Poet Spencer" in the *Melancholike Humours*, where the Spenserian characters lament that their creator has been forgotten.

In a lighter, more familiar vein, are the sententious proverbs and aphorisms so popular among London's common readers, sentiments for wall samplers such as the Polonius-like patter of *Honest Counsaile*: "Nor pull up Hearbes, and cherish Weedes,/ Nor tittle-tattle, more than needs," or the maternal pithiness of *The Mothers Blessing*, or a twist on the familiar in a Machiavellian father's ruthless counsel in *The Uncasing of Machiavels Instructions*, properly rejected by his pious son. In *Pasquils Mistresse* the satirist debates the opposing characters of the worthy woman, whose Platonic intellect is her glory, and her unworthy opposite, the victim of feeling and folly.

Especially after the accession of James, Breton's moral verse occupies a considerably less lofty plane. *The Soules Immortal Crowne*, a heroic encomium of the seven moral virtues dedicated to the King, is remarkable chiefly for the extent to which "vertue," a variation of Renaissance *virtú* implying will and strength, displaces patience. Other verses dwell upon gratitude and its polar opposite, ingratitude, the most virulent extreme of which Breton saw in the Gunpowder Plot of 1607. The end of *The Hate of Treason*, written for that occasion, glorifies the Jacobean court, castigating the mad aspirations of the "rebellious beastly Rablement," as *The Honour of Valour* glorifies the marital virtues of Lord Mountjoy by contrasting his stalwart traditionalism with the "drosse" of the present court in a vision of the eternal heroic rising above the "Dunghill" of contemporary policy. Although a far cry from the vision of the earlier divine poetry, these heroic ventures show Breton's concern with the ability of the human to transcend its limitations.

Whereas Breton's lyrics and moral allegory had early undergone the Elizabethan transformation from drab to golden, his later divine poetry and verse satire connect that change to the emerging seventeenth century consciousness. Always decorous in tone and diction yet iconoclastic in its perception of audience and of the self, Breton's Renaissance verse, set squarely in the mainstream of the moral and intellectual currents of his time, looks forward to the Metaphysical and the neoclassical alike.

Janet Polansky

Other major works

FICTION: *The Strange Fortune of Two Excellent Princes*, 1600; *Grimellos Fortunes*, 1604.

NONFICTION: *The Figure of Foure*, 1597; *Auspicante Jehova: Maries Exercise*, 1597; *Wits Trenchmour: Or, A Conference Between a Scholler and Angler*, 1597; *The Wil of Wit, Wits Will or Wils Wit*, 1597; *Wonders Worth the Hearing*, 1602; *A Mad World, My Masters*, 1603; *A Dialogue Full of Pithe and Pleasure*, 1603; *A Poste with a Packet of Mad Letters*, 1603; *An Olde Mans Lesson and a Young Mans Love*, 1605; *Wits Private Wealth*, 1607; *A Murmurer*, 1607; *Divine Considerations of the Soule*, 1608; *Crossing of Proverbs*, 1616; *The Court and Country*, 1618.

MISCELLANEOUS: *Characters upon Essaies, Morall and Divine*, 1615; *The Good and the Badde*, 1616; *Fantasticks*, 1626; *The Works of Nicholas Breton*, 1879, 1966 (2 volumes; Alexander B. Grosart, editor).

Bibliography

Bullen, Arthur Henry. *Elizabethans*. New York: E. P. Dutton, 1924. Bullen sketches the life and work of ten English authors of the Elizabethan period.

He repeats the sketchy details known about Breton's life, then shows how the prolific author fits into his historic context. Interesting reading for all students.

Garnett, Richard, and Edmund Grosse. *English Literature: An Illustrated Record.* 2d ed. 2 vols. New York: Macmillan, 1935. Garnett and Grosse include a substantial essay on Breton and place him in context of the English literary history. This is an older study, but a valuable one. Suitable for all levels.

Kunitz, Stanley, and Howard Haycraft, eds. *British Authors Before 1800: A Biographical Dictionary.* New York: Wilson, 1952. Provides a short biographical entry that seems to be based on the information provided in Sir Sidney Lee's article. Points out that Breton's literary influences come from the medieval period and not from his English Renaissance contemporaries. Breton was thought to have been a little too prolific. His only work of any distinction is his pastoral poems.

Lee, Sidney, Sir. "Nicholas Breton." In *The Dictionary of National Biography*, edited by Sir Leslie Stephen and Sir Sidney Lee. Vol. 2. Reprint. London: Oxford University Press, 1921-1922. This essay is the most interesting and detailed article about the life of Breton. Lee describes why Breton's birth and death dates are in doubt and insinuates that the poet had an affair with his patroness, Mary Sidney, the Countess of Pembroke. Provides a detailed primary biography along with the whereabouts of Breton's few remaining first editions.

Tannenbaum, Samuel Aaron, and Dorothy R. Tannenbaum. *Nicholas Breton: A Concise Bibliography.* New York: S. A. Tannenbaum, 1947. Breton has been almost completely ignored by scholars over the last three centuries. The Tannenbaums have published one of the only sources of any kind available on this Elizabethan poet. It is immensely valuable for the serious Breton student.

ROBERT BRIDGES

Born: Walmer, England; October 23, 1844
Died: Boar's Hill, England; April 21, 1930

Principal poetry

Poems, 1873; *The Growth of Love*, in 24 Sonnets, 1876, 1890; *Poems, Second Series*, 1879; *Poems, Third Series*, 1880; *Prometheus, the Firegiver*, 1884 (verse masque); *Nero Part I*, 1885 (verse drama); *Eros and Psyche*, 1885; *The Feast of Bacchus*, 1889 (verse drama); *Palicio*, 1890 (verse drama); *The Return of Ulysses*, 1890 (verse drama); *The Christian Captives*, 1890 (verse drama); *Achilles in Scyros*, 1890 (verse drama); *Shorter Poems, Books I-IV*, 1890; *The Humours of the Court*, 1893 (verse drama); *Shorter Poems, Book V*, 1893; *Nero Part II*, 1894 (verse drama); *Poetical Works of Robert Bridges*, 1898-1905 (six volumes); *Demeter*, 1905 (verse masque); *Poems Written in MCMXIII*, 1914; *October and Other Poems*, 1920; *The Testament of Beauty*, 1927-1929, 1930; *Poems*, 1931 (M. M. Bridges, editor).

Other literary forms

Although Robert Bridges wrote poetry extensively, he was also a prolific scholar. His monograph on *Milton's Prosody* (1893, 1901) is a model of research. His *Collected Essays, Papers, Etc.* have been published in thirty parts by Oxford University Press (1927-1936). Bridges is probably most known in modern times for his correspondence with Gerard Manley Hopkins (1844-1889). Hopkins' letters to Bridges have been published (Oxford University Press, 1935, 1955), but Bridges destroyed his letters to Hopkins. The *Correspondence of Robert Bridges and Henry Bradley, (1900-1923)*, has been published (1940), as well as his *Three Friends: Memoirs of Dolben, Dixon, and Henry Bradley* (1932). Bridges also wrote a few poems in Latin.

Achievements

Bridges was Poet Laureate of England from 1913 until his death in 1930. In the last years of his life, he was generally thought to be the leading lyric poet of his time. His restrained, classical style was opposed to the extremes of Ezra Pound and T. S. Eliot and the rising tide of modernism in literature. Since his death, Bridges has fallen into obscurity. His six volumes of collected poems and plays are seldom read even by specialists. Even if Bridges is not rehabilitated as a poet, however, he will be remembered as a significant scholar and editor. Bridges saved the poems of his friend Gerard Manley Hopkins from obscurity by editing them in 1918, giving the world one of the major precursors of modernism. Bridges' studies of language and metrics were pioneering work and he was one of the first to carry out real literary research in the modern sense. Finally, he is an important innovator in poetic form, whose discoveries place him on a par with acknowledged revolutionaries such as T. S. Eliot, Ezra Pound, Gerard Manley Hopkins, and Walt Whitman as a creator of new forms of expression in poetic language.

Biography

Robert Seymour Bridges explicitly requested that no biography or biographical study should ever be made of him. He destroyed many of his personal papers and his heirs have respected his wishes. Although there is no formal biography, the outlines of his life are well-known. Robert Bridges was the next-to-last child in a family of nine, born to comfortable landed gentry. Bridges went to Eton in 1854, where he showed an inclination toward the "Oxford Movement." He matriculated at Corpus Christi College, Oxford University, in 1863, where he was athletic and popular as an undergraduate. He rowed stroke in the Corpus Christi boat in 1867, but took only a gentleman's second class degree in *literae humaniores*, the study of classical languages and the literature and philosophy of ancient Greece and Rome. At Oxford he became a close friend of the brilliant but somewhat eccentric Gerard Manley Hopkins, who became one of the most important modernist poets in English. Bridges and Hopkins carried on an extensive correspondence after their undergraduate days; although Bridges destroyed his letters to Hopkins, Hopkins' letters to Bridges have been published and provide a fascinating glimpse into the poetic workshop of these two talented men and their complicated personal relationship. Although Bridges was independently wealthy, he entered medical studies after he had completed the work for his B.A. degree at Oxford and earned his degree in medicine in 1874. He practiced for some time in various hospitals in London, sometimes under grueling conditions. In 1877 he was appointed assistant physician in the Hospital for Sick Children, Great Ormond Street. In 1881 he suffered a severe illness, apparently pneumonia with complications, and retired from his medical career at the age of thirty-seven.

In 1882 Bridges moved to Manor House, Yattendon, Berkshire. Two years later he married Monica Waterhouse, the daughter of a famous architect. There, too, he and Harry Ellis Wooldridge produced *The Yattendon Hymnal* (1895-1899). In 1907, he moved to his final residence, Chilswell House, at Boar's Hill near Oxford. After his first collection of *Poems* in 1873, Bridges had been publishing lyric poetry and closet dramas steadily. His fame as a poet and man of letters increased over the decades until he was appointed Poet Laureate of England to succeed Alfred Austin in 1913. That year, together with Henry Bradley, Logan Pearsall Smith, and Walter Raleigh, he founded the society for Pure English. In his final years Bridges was an enormously influential figure in the literary world, editing the poems of his long-since dead friend, Gerard Manley Hopkins, in 1918, and composing his long philosophical poem *The Testament of Beauty* (1927-1929, 1930). He was decorated with the Order of Merit in 1929 and received honorary degrees from Oxford, St. Andrews University, Harvard, and the University of Michigan. He died at Chilswell, April 21, 1930.

Analysis

In the first half of the twentieth century, a literary revolution occurred. Ezra Pound, T. S. Eliot, and their associates overpowered the previous genteel Victorian style of polite verse. To the advocates of this modernist revolution, the lyric poems of Robert Bridges seemed to represent everything corrupt in art: Bridges was traditional, a craftsman, controlled, impersonal, polished, moral, and optimistic. Although he had served as poet laureate from 1913 until 1930 and was a very influential and respected writer for the last forty years of his life, the use of modernism obliterated his fame within a few years after his death, so that he is virtually unknown by readers today. This fall from favor is not justified, and probably Bridges will one day be restored to his rightful position as a counterweight to T. S. Eliot in the 1920's, a worthy opponent of the new wave.

Bridges wrote only a few insignificant poems as a schoolboy. His serious inspiration came rather late, so that the poems collected in his first book, *Poems* appear to have been written mainly in the preceding year. The 1873 collection is uneven, sometimes unsophisticated, and Bridges later tried to buy and destroy all the copies printed. He rewrote, added some poems, and deleted others entirely for his second series (1879) and his third series (1880). The *Shorter Poems* in four books published in 1890 grew out of the earlier volumes and established him as one of the leading poets of his time.

The 1880 *Poems, Third Series*, contains the justly famous "London Snow." This poem, written in rhymed iambic pentameter, describes London under an unusually heavy snowfall. Characteristically, Bridges describes the scene with detachment and great attention to detail. He tries to be accurate and not to inject an "unreal" sentiment into the scene. He tries to avoid the "pathetic fallacy," or the projection of imagined feelings onto Nature. "When men were all asleep the snow came flying,/ In large white flakes falling on the city brown." There is nothing supernatural in Bridges' scene, nor is there any extravagant emotion. The snow falls until the city is buried under a seven-inch, bright-white coating. The citizens of London awake early because of the unaccustomed light reflected from the whiteness. The city is strangely hushed as business has come to a halt. Schoolboys taste the pure snow and throw snowballs. The trees are decked with snowy robes. Only a few carts struggle through the nearly deserted streets and the sun gleams on the dome of St. Paul's Cathedral. Then, "sombre men, past tale of number" go forth to battle against the snow, trampling dark paths as they clear the streets and break the charm of the scene.

This moving poem in the plain style contrasts with the dark life in the city and the momentary ability of nature to create a miraculous transformation in the very heart of man's urban environment. It suggests the momentary, but muted, spark of recognition of the city workers that there is some power of Nature above human control. Bridges never resorts to any word or image in his text which is not plausible, easily understood, and "realistic." Comparing his description of London to T. S. Eliot's urban scenes, the reader easily sees a contrast between the modernist vision and the calm, controlled, delicate feelings of the more traditional work of Bridges.

Another highly praised poem in the 1880 *Poems* is "On a Dead Child." Bridges was for some years a terribly overworked young doctor in an urban hospital. He once calculated that he had less than two minutes to spend with each of his patients a day. There is no doubt that he saw much of death. Under the circumstances, it would be easy to become callous, to shut out feelings altogether. On the other hand, no topic is more likely to lead the artist into sentimentality than the death of a young child. Bridges' poem delicately employs understatement. The speaker is probably a physician whose very young patient has just died. The poem is written in seven stanzas each of four lines rhyming abba. The length of the lines varies, probably following in a muted way the practice of "sprung rhythm" which Hopkins and Bridges developed in some of their lyrics. In the first three stanzas, the speaker notes how beautiful the dead child is, how disappointed the hopes of its parents must be. Then as the speaker performs his last services to the corpse, it seems that the infant hand clasps and holds his fingers momentarily. He thinks then about the universality of death hanging over all people; "Little at best can all our hopes avail us/ To life this sorrow, or cheer us, when in the dark,/ Unwilling, alone we embark." Bridges typically recognizes the hardness of the human lot, born to pain and death. He states plainly and directly man's condition, then faces it without whining or screaming, but with optimistic courage. In the death of a child he sees the death of all mankind. There is no use pretending that death is not fearful; still, the manful course is to face fate with whatever assistance reason can offer.

The poem which best exemplifies Bridges's mind and art is "Low Barometer." Written in seven stanzas, each of four lines rhyming abab, the poem imitates the long measure of the hymnal or the four-stress ballad line. Romantic poets frequently wrote poems about storms; typically they would imagine themselves standing on a mountain peak in the middle of lightning and rain, calling for their spirits to match the wild frenzy of nature. Bridges' poem attacks such Romantic evocations. He does not want emotional storms; he prefers reason, control, understatement. A low reading on the barometer signals a coming storm, and the first stanza describes such an impending gale. On such a night, when the storm beats against the house, supernatural fears arise in man, terrors of "god or ghost." When man imagines weird presences, his "Reason kens he herits in/ A haunted house." Reason becomes aware of the feeling of guilt and fear normally suppressed in everyday life. This "Pollution and remorse of time" awakened by the storm is aroused in the depths of the mind, like some monster which with "sightless footsteps" mounts the stair and bursts open the door. Some men try to control such horrible feelings by religion, but the monstrous images roam the earth until Nature itself at dawn withdraws the storm and thrusts "the baleful phantoms underground" once more. Nature restores calm and order in the end.

Many poets celebrate raw emotion: love, fear, or anger at its highest pitch. Bridges did not value emotion for its own sake. He felt that feeling should be restrained by reason, although reason itself knows that it is not sufficient to meet man's ultimate crises, such as death. A wise man seeks control and balance; only the ignorant gives himself over to uncontrolled emotion. Bridges wrote a sonnet sequence, *The Growth of Love*, first published in 1876 with twenty-four sonnets, but extensively revised in later versions. This work is modeled on the sonnet sequence of William Shakespeare, although the individual poems are written more in the style of John Milton. The traditional erotic sonnet sequence takes the form of the utterances of a lover; some of the poems in the sequence are addressed to the beloved lady praising her beauty, some are poems of seduction, and some are laments at her "cruelty." Frequently the sonnet sequence has an overall plot, involving a rival for the lady's affection, who receives the lover's scorn. Other poems address a faithless beloved, in which the lover is caught in a love-hate relationship with his lady. Usually the sequence traces the progress of a love affair as the lover approaches the lady, woos her, wins her, rejoices in his victory, but sees her affections cool as another lover intrudes into his domain.

Bridges constructs *The Growth of Love* in the tradition of such a sequence, but typically he "tones down" the violence of emotion in each of the traditional postures. The reader expects the lover to be hot and passionate, but Bridges' speaker is calm and analytical as he examines his relationship. As a picture of human love, these poems are disconcertingly cool. It is frequently the case that erotic poetry is a vehicle for a religious or philosophical idea. For example, the biblical Song of Solomon appears to be spoken by a lover to his beloved, but an analogical reading of the text reveals that the song is about the love of man and God. Probably Bridges intended his erotic sonnet sequence to have a similar analogical meaning. If one understands the beloved to be, not a woman, but the ideal moral perfection in life, the overall detachment in the work is understandable. The broad argument of *The Growth of Love* is reflected in Bridges' later long philosophical poem *The Testament of Beauty*.

The *Poetical Works* of Robert Bridges were published between 1898 and 1905 in six volumes. More than four of these volumes are composed of poetical dramas and masques. Obviously, Bridges spent much effort in writing dramatic poetry. Equally obviously, these plays are quite unsuitable for the stage, lacking action and sharp characterization. All of the plays except *Nero Part I* were intended to be performed, but only the masques *Prometheus, the Firegiver* and *Demeter* and the play *The Humours of the Court* (1893) were actually produced—and these in amateur renditions only. It is difficult to see why Bridges expended so much energy in this kind of writing. In contrast, Robert Browning began his literary career with a series of more or less failed plays, but went on to develop his dramatic monologues as a new and powerful form of poetry; one can see Browning building on his early failures. No such clear line of development, however, is discernible in Bridges. Most of his plays were written in the decade of the 1880's, and when his influential collected *Poems* of 1890 appeared, his lyric poems were seen not to represent a logical progression from the dramatic works with which he had been occupied.

His best plays are historical: *Nero Part I* and *Nero Part II*. While this study of the decline of the Roman emperor Nero into madness and violence is a reasonable topic for a play, it is one unsuited to Bridges' talents. When the author of such work writes the speeches of a mad character, he must assume the mask and speak with a certain amount of sympathy for the eccentric point of view of a madman. In Bridges' best poetry, however, unlike Browning in his dramatic poems, he never plays the devil's advocate; and it is precisely this that is required for a satisfactory dramatic treatment of Nero, one of those figures who, like the fearful men in the storm in "Low Barometer," are swept up by the "unbodied presences" and "horrors of unhoused crime." Bridges never puts himself *inside* such figures; he always stands outside them, describing them, judging them, evaluating them. While this is the strength of his poetry, it makes it nearly impossible for him to bring to life a character who is vicious or insane.

Bridges wrote four masques based on classical mythology; his model was probably Milton's *Comus* (1634). Albert Guérard in *Robert Bridges: A Study of Traditionalism in Poetry* (1942) maintains that Bridges' earliest and most impressive masque, *Prometheus, the Firegiver*, "symbolizes the substitution of the God of Love of the New Testament for the Angry God of the Old Testament; or, more generally, of modern Christianity for all less 'human' religions." Many readers, however, will agree with Bridges' friend and best critic, Gerard Manley Hopkins, who warned him that he should not try to write about the Greek gods in any case, because they were frigid and remote from modern experience.

In his last years, Bridges wrote a long philosophical poem, *The Testament of Beauty*. The poem falls into four books: *Introduction, Selfhood, Breed, Ethick*. The overall problem is to fit modern science into a meaningful framework: the relationship of Darwinian theories of evolution to the moral purpose behind death and suffering. *The Testament of Beauty* seems to move digressively and its argument is not entirely clear. The *Introduction* discusses at length the ramifications of evolution. The second book, *Selfhood*, studies egotism, self-preservation, and selfishness in their manifestations in the lowest forms of life up to their presence in man's highest artistic accomplishments and his darkest violence. The book discusses the carnage of World War I. Can all evolution be moving toward such pointless destruction? The third book, *Breed*, treats sexual instinct. It traces the growth of love from elementary sex to spiritual love. The fourth book, *Ethick*, explores the role of "reason" in conduct. As one would expect from Bridges' other works, "reason" is the key, the difference between humane, ethical behavior and mere brutality. Reason balances the instincts and the impulses of the human organism, molding evolutionary pressures into moral refinement.

Bridges' study of the metrical form of Milton's poetry is one of the earliest examples of truly scientific observation applied to literary problems. *Milton's Prosody* was first published in 1893 and later republished in expanded form with the inclusion of a paper by his associate William Johnson Stone, "Classical Metres in English Verse," in 1901. Poetry differs from prose, Bridges contends, in that poetry maintains some controlled repetition or patterning in the language which is not found in normal, everyday speech. For Bridges, there were four types of meter in English verse: (1) accentual syllabic, (2) accentual, (3) syllabic, and (4) quantitative. Each controls a different element of language so as to create a repetitive pattern. Accent involves the relative loudness with which a syllable is pronounced. Some poems, such as traditional ballads, seem to follow a pattern only in the number of loudly pronounced syllables in each line, no matter how many unstressed syllables occur. This is purely accentual verse. Other poems seem to have the same number of syllables in corresponding lines, but varying numbers of accents. This is syllabic verse. Classical poetry in Latin and Greek appeared to have been regulated by long and short vowel sounds, and it was traditionally thought that patterns of long and short syllables could be made up into "feet," or metrical units, based on the vowel quantity of each syllable. In Milton's *Paradise Lost* (1667), however, Bridges discerned an accentual-syllabic system which forms its patterns of repetition based on both the number of syllables in each line and the position of the more loudly pronounced syllables.

What is unusual about Bridges' study is his method of basing his generalizations on close scientific observation. Critics of his work might argue that when he deals with Milton's language, there is room for much misunderstanding. Is he talking about the production of sound by the human voice apparatus or is he talking about the code of written speech, so many marks on a page? Is he perhaps talking about the way the human mind apprehends sound? Apparently he is governed by thinking of language as the production of sound. He says that language has *stress*, unwittingly referring perhaps to the stress felt when one pronounces a syllable more loudly than another by exercising the diaphragm muscles. So long as one grants that he is talking about the production of sound, his study seems well-argued.

Milton's Prosody is subtitled "An Examination of the Rules of Blank Verse in Milton's later poems with an account of the versification of 'Samson Agonistes' and general notes." Typically the blank verse line has three characteristics: (1) it has ten syllables, (2) it has five stresses, (3) it is rising; the stresses are on the even-positioned syllables. Bridges first establishes that these characteristics occur in *Paradise Lost* and then examines cases which seem to deviate from the norm, trying for a generalization that can account for all exceptions, much as a law of physics is deemed "true" when it explains all occurrences. In separate chapters he examines exceptions to the number of syllables being ten, the number of stresses being five, and the position of stresses being rising. These discussions are too detailed for summary here, but they should be examined by any serious student of English metrics. When Bridges turns to Milton's later poems, *Paradise Regained* and *Samson Agonistes* (both 1671), he finds that there is a much less rigid patterning, and he tries to account for the wider variations found in these poems.

The final section of Bridges' 1901 volume is taken up with William Johnson Stone's "Classical Metres in English Verse: A history and criticism of the attempts hitherto made, together with a scheme for the determination of the quantity of English Syllables, based on their actual phonetic condition." This essay is particularly important because it is the basis for Bridges' actual experiments in writing English poetry in the quantitative measures of Latin and Greek. Stone's study, however, contains many doubtful statements about the nature of classical languages. He believed that there was no difference between the classical long/short vowel quantity and modern spoken English vowels, and this assumption is improbable. Nevertheless, Stone proposes a method for determining the quantity of English vowels and for establishing in modern English a meter comparable to his understanding of Latin and Greek meters. Stone's death caused Bridges to feel obliged to justify or demonstrate Stone's theory in practice, and so Bridges attempted the metrical experiments published in his collected poems. Bridges also made a number of translations from classical languages into English in which he tried to preserve in English the metrical quantitative structure of the original language. Some of these translations are of extremely high artistic quality, such as the translation of Homer's *Iliad*, Book XXIV.

From about 1890 to 1930 Bridges was considered one of England's leading lyric poets. His fame was eclipsed at his death, although it will probably be revived somewhat when disinterested historical study is possible. He will almost certainly become established as an important, if minor, poet, part of the background against which the great modernists rebelled. His most important contribution to literature has not as yet been fully recognized: he was a pioneering scholar and experimentalist in metrics, and his greatest achievement was not (as he thought) his dramatic poems, nor his long philosophical verse, but his experiments in quantitative meters.

Todd K. Bender

Other major works

PLAYS: *Prometheus, the Firegiver*, 1884 (verse masque); *Nero Part I*, 1885 (verse drama); *The Feast of Bacchus*, 1889 (verse drama); *Palicio*, 1890 (verse drama); *The Return of Ulysses*, 1890 (verse drama); *The Christian Captives*, 1890 (verse drama); *Achilles in Scyros*, 1890 (verse drama); *The Humours of the Court*, 1893 (verse drama); *Nero Part II*, 1894 (verse drama); *Demeter*, 1905 (verse masque).

NONFICTION: *Milton's Prosody*, 1893, 1901; *John Keats*, 1895; *The Necessity of Poetry*, 1918; *Collected Essays, Papers, Etc.*, 1927-1936; *Correspondence of Robert Bridges and Henry Bradley, 1900-1923*, 1940; *Three Friends: Memoirs of Dolben, Dixon, and Henry Bradley*, 1932.

Bibliography

Guérard, Albert, Jr. *Robert Bridges: A Study of Traditionalism in Poetry.* Cambridge, Mass.: Harvard University Press, 1942. This standard work on Bridges includes a comprehensive study of the lyric, dramatic, and philosophical poems. Guérard contends that Bridges is misunderstood if regarded only as a poet of happy emotions and that he is intensely serious and his view of life is far from completely rosy. The dramatic poems and plays form the bulk of Bridges' work, and their study has been neglected. This book, heavily influenced by the critic Yvor Winters, defends Bridges' traditionalism. Includes a conspectus of Bridges' sources and analogues.

Ritz, Jean-Georges. *Robert Bridges and Gerard Hopkins, 1863-1889: A Literary Friendship.* London: Oxford University Press, 1960. Bridges and the late Victorian poet Gerard Manley Hopkins were close friends from the days of their college years at Oxford. Ritz discusses Bridges' academic interests and friendships and analyzes in detail his correspondence with Hopkins. (Only Hopkins' letters to Bridges have survived.) Particularly valuable is the presentation of each poet's discussion of the verse of the other. Hopkins endeavored to give Bridges' poems more drama and a personal touch. Ritz is especially informative on the way in which Bridges' poetry reflects his character.

Smith, Nowell Charles. *Notes on "The Testament of Beauty."* London: Oxford University Press, 1931. A standard guidebook to Bridges' most famous poem. Smith begins with a brief discussion of its theme. The poem attempts to present the place of man in the universe, principally using Charles Darwin's theory of evolution as a background. It thus aims to be a modern equivalent of Lucretius' *On the Nature of Things*, summing up science and philosophy poetically. The bulk of the book consists of detailed notes on the poem. The author explains unusual words, paraphrases Bridges' meaning, and points out references to other poets such as John Milton and William Wordsworth.

Sparrow, John. *Robert Bridges*. London: Longmans, Green, 1962. Sparrow centers his study on Bridges' doctrine that poetry should express beauty, understood as a form of goodness. Bridges had the ability to portray vividly scenes from nature, a principal source of his poetic inspiration. His diction is carefully calibrated to evoke the moods he wishes to convey. He was particularly adept at using difficult meter as an instrument of emotional presentation. Although Sparrow devotes some attention to Bridges' failures, he rates him among the foremost English poets as he was unsurpassed in the creation of beautiful poems.

Stanford, Donald E. *In the Classic Mode: The Achievement of Robert Bridges*. Newark: University of Delaware Press, 1978. This book offers a detailed analysis of Bridges' experiments in meter: accentuated verse, quantitative meter, and neo-Miltonic syllabics. The work aims to give a full portrait of Bridges' literary corpus and includes the most detailed discussions of his plays in the secondary literature. Bridges' criticism also comes in for attention, particularly his study of John Keats. The discussion of George Santayana's influence on *The Testament of Beauty* is excellent.

Thompson, Edward. *Robert Bridges, 1844-1930*. London: Oxford University Press, 1944. The author, a friend of the poet, devotes much attention to the shorter poems such as "London Snow." He notes Bridges' extreme sensitivity to physical suffering and shows how this fact is reflected in his poems. Thompson includes a number of amusing anecdotes, many of which depict efforts by Bridges' acquaintances to bait him about his distaste for modern poetry. His dislike of Robert Browning was particularly strong. Thompson gives a good discussion of Bridges' World War I anthology, *The Spirit of Man*.

EMILY BRONTË

Born: Thornton, Yorkshire, England; July 30, 1818
Died: Haworth, Yorkshire, England; December 19, 1848

Principal poetry

Poems by Currer, Ellis, and Acton Bell, 1846 (with Charlotte Brontë and Anne Brontë); *The Complete Poems of Emily Jane Brontë*, 1941 (C. W. Hatfield, editor); *Gondal's Queen: A Novel in Verse by Emily Jane Brontë*, 1955 (Fannie E. Ratchford, editor).

Other literary forms

Although Emily Brontë published only one novel, *Wuthering Heights*, it is this work for which she is best known. When the novel was published in 1847, it won some praise for its originality and power, but in general, reviewers found its violence disturbing and its dominant character, Heathcliff, excessively brutal. *Wuthering Heights* did not offer the charm and optimism that many readers wanted to find in a work of fiction. As is often the case with original work, it took time for the world to appreciate it fully; today, however, *Wuthering Heights* is given a prominent place among the significant novels of the nineteenth century, and is often discussed for its elaborate narrative structure, its intricate patterns of imagery, and its powerful themes of the soul's anguish and longing.

By the time Brontë began *Wuthering Heights*, she had long been using her imagination to create stories full of passionate intrigue and romance. First, as a young child she participated in a series of family games called Young Men's Plays, tales of military and political adventures primarily directed and recorded by the older children, her sister Charlotte and her brother Branwell. After Charlotte left for school in 1831, Emily and her younger sister Anne began their own creation, a long saga of an island they called Gondal, placed in the north Pacific yet very much resembling their own Yorkshire environment. They peopled this island-world with strong, passionate characters. Unfortunately, nothing remains of their prose chronicle of Gondal. Two journal fragments and two of the birthday notes that she and Anne were in the habit of exchanging make mention of this land. These notes also offer some insight into the everyday world of the Brontë household and are of great interest for this reason. The only other extant prose, besides a few unrevealing letters, is a group of five essays which she wrote in French as homework assignments while a student in Brussels. This material has since been translated by Lorine White Nagel and published under the title *Five Essays Written in French* (1948). Some similarities can be seen between the destructive and powerful descriptions of nature and human character discussed in these essays and the world of Brontë's poetry and fiction.

Achievements

Brontë did not at first desire public recognition for her poetry. In fact, when her sister Charlotte accidentally discovered a notebook of her poems, it took time for Emily to accept this discovery, even though Charlotte found the poems impressive and uncommon. More time was required for Charlotte to persuade this very private poet to join with her and Anne in a small publishing venture. Once persuaded, Emily did contribute twenty-one of her poems to the slim, privately printed volume entitled *Poems by Currer, Ellis, and Acton Bell*. To disguise her sex, each sister chose a pseudonym corresponding to the first letter of her name. This disguise also protected Emily's privacy, which she very much desired to keep; she resented Charlotte's later unintentional disclosure of Ellis Bell's true identity. This disclosure occurred after the three sisters had all published novels under the name of Bell, arousing considerable curiosity in the literary world. Unfortunately, their collection of poems sold only two copies. Later, after Emily's death, Charlotte, convinced of her sister's talent, tried to keep her poetic reputation alive by including eighteen previously unpublished poems in a second edition of *Wuthering Heights* and Anne's first novel, *Agnes Grey* (1847); however, despite her efforts, it was not until this century that Emily Brontë's poems received any serious critical attention.

Interest in the poetry began as biographers sought to piece together the life of the Brontë family. It increased when the fantasy land of Gondal was discovered. Attempts were made to reconstruct the story from the poems, for it became clear that Emily had written many of her poems as part of that world of passion and guilt. Further attention was given to the poetry as *Wuthering Heights* gained in recognition, although readers were inclined to interpret the poems merely as an apprenticeship to a more masterful novel. Only since the midpoint of this century has criticism begun to focus on the poems for their own sake.

Because of the seeming quietness of Brontë's life and because she was never part of a literary circle beyond that of her own home, there is a temptation to see her as an example of the isolated genius, sculpturing her forms in an instinctive style. On the contrary, Brontë was a skillful poet working within the traditions of her Romantic predecessors, handling standard poetic forms with subtle and effective variations. Although the dramatic extremes she found in the works of Sir Walter Scott and George Gordon, Lord Byron led her at times to employ conventional phrases and touches of melodrama, at her best she was able to embody in controlled verse an intensity of genuine feeling which sprang from a love of nature and a worship of the imagination. In her poems of the night winds and the whirling snowstorms of the moors, she distinguishes herself as a poet of nature's starkly vital powers. In her poems of the imagination, she places herself in the visionary company of William Wordsworth and William Blake. Throughout her poetry she expresses the desire of the soul to transcend the mortal limitations of time and space in order to merge with a larger presence, the source of all energy and life. She was an artist faithful to her visions, whose poems attest the strength of the individual soul.

Biography

Emily Jane Brontë was the fifth of six children, five girls and a boy, born to an Anglican clergyman of Irish descent, Patrick Brontë, and his Cornish wife, Maria Branwell. When Emily was two years old, the family moved to Haworth, where her father had accepted a permanent curacy. Haworth, a place now often associated with the Brontë name, is a village on the moors of West Riding, Yorkshire in the north of England. In Emily's day, this rural spot was quite removed from the changing events of city life. The parsonage itself is an isolated building of gray stone near an old cemetery with its slanting worn tombstones. In this somber-looking house, in this quiet village, Emily spent most of her life.

The people filling this world were few in number. As parson's children, Emily and her brother and sisters were not encouraged to associate with the village children, who were regarded as lower in social status. Their father seems to have valued his privacy, often keeping to himself, even dining alone, although there is no reason to doubt his affection for his children. As a result of these social limitations, the children provided their own entertainment, which often consisted of acting out imaginative games and later writing them down. Their education was in part provided by their aunt, Elizabeth Branwell, who came to care for them after their mother died in September, 1821, shortly after their arrival in Haworth. Tutors in art and music were occasionally hired for the children, and at least two libraries were available to them: their father's, and that of the Keighley Mechanics' Institute.

Emily left Haworth few times in her life. When she did, it was usually to continue her education or to gain employment. At the age of six, she and three of her sisters—Maria, Elizabeth, and Charlotte—were sent to the Clergyman Daughters' School at Cowan Bridge. Their stay was brief, for when the two older sisters, Maria and Elizabeth, were stricken with tuberculosis, from which they later died, their father had all his daughters sent home. Several years later, in 1835, Emily attended school for a few months at Roe Head with Charlotte. Their plan was to prepare themselves better for one of the few occupations open to them, that of governess. While at Roe Head, Emily became extremely distressed with her situation. In later years, after her death, Charlotte indicated that she believed the cause to have been intense homesickness. Shortly after this rather unsuccessful venture from home, Emily did leave again, this time to take a position as a teacher at a large school near Halifax called Law Hill; but again her stay was brief. She returned home, obviously unhappy with her life as a teacher. One last trip from Haworth was taken in 1842, when she accompanied Charlotte to Brussels to attend Madame Héger's school. The sisters wanted to increase their knowledge of German and French in order to become better qualified to open their own school, a project which was to remain only in the dreaming and planning stages. While in Brussels it again became clear that Emily was not comfortable in an environment strange to her, and when the sisters returned home in November, 1842, for their aunt's funeral, Emily remained, seemingly content to do so. Thereafter, she stayed at the parsonage, helping with the household chores. Her family accepted this choice and considered her contribution to the running of the household a valuable one. In September, 1848, Emily caught a cold while attending her brother's funeral. It developed into an inflammation of the lungs from which she never recovered. Her death was perhaps hastened by her refusal to seek medical attention until the very end.

Much consideration has been given to Brontë's inability to adjust to life away from Haworth. Emphasis has been placed on her love of the moors, which was so intense that she could not long be away from the heather and open fields. It is true that her work indicates an abiding—at times compelling—love for their somber beauty; however, some attention should also be given to the fact that all of these journeys from home required adjusting to a structured world, one perhaps hostile to the private world of her imagination. It is clear that the powers of the imagination played a dominant role in Brontë's emotional life from her childhood on. Apparently, at home in the parsonage, she found an environment which suited the needs of her imagination and its creative powers.

Analysis

When interpreting Emily Brontë's poetry, one must first confront the Gondal problem: What is the significance of that exotic world of emotional drama that so occupied her imagination? Some readers argue that this imaginary world of rebellion and punishment, death and lost love, permeated all her work; others maintain that her finer poems were composed outside its dramatic, at times melodramatic, influences. Brontë's own division of the poems into two notebooks, one entitled "Gondal Poems," the other left untitled, would suggest a clear separation; yet a subjective lyrical voice can be heard in many of the Gondal poems, and echoes of the Gondal drama can be heard in non-Gondal material. Since the original prose saga has been lost, perhaps no completely satisfactory solution can be found; nevertheless, a thematic approach to Brontë's poetry does provide a unifying interpretation.

Many of her Gondal characters are isolated figures who yearn for a time of love or freedom now lost. In the non-Gondal poems, the same voice of longing can be heard: the speakers of such poems as "The Philosopher" and "To Imagination" desire a time of union and harmony, or, as in "O Thy Bright Eyes Must Answer Now," a time of freedom from the restraints of reason and earthly cares. The Gondal characters, with their exotic-sounding names (such as Augusta Geraldine Almeda and Julius Brenzaida), are not beings separate and distinct from the poet herself; they are masks through which Brontë speaks. Therefore, although Brontë often uses the dramatic forms of direct address, inquiry, and dialogue, none of her poems can be adequately analyzed as if it were a dramatic monologue prefiguring the work of Robert Browning. She does not attempt to delineate a character through the subtleties of his speech in a particular time and place. The desperate situations in which she places her dramatic figures merely provide appropriate circumstances in which to express the emotional and at times mystical experiences of her own private world. Continually, her poems emphasize the creative power of the individual spirit as it struggles to define itself in relation to the "Invisible," the unseen source of all existence. This struggle in all its intensity is the predominant theme of her poetry, whether it is set in a Gondal prison or on a Yorkshire moor.

Intensity is one of Brontë's distinguishing characteristics. Her poetry gives the impression of having been cut as close to the center of feeling as possible. The portrayal of such passionate intensity can easily lead to excessive exclamations in which meaning is scattered, if not lost; in Brontë's case, however, her skillful handling of form provides the needed restraint. She achieves this control over her subject through such structuring devices as simple metrical patterns (she was especially fond of tetrameter and trimeter), strong monosyllabic rhymes, parallel phrasing, repetition of key words, and appropriately placed pauses. Her use of these devices allows her to shape the intensity into ordered movements appropriate to the subject, whether it be a mournful one or one of joyous celebration.

One of the best examples of Brontë's use of these structuring techniques to control feeling can be found in her best-known love poem, "Rosina Alcona to Julius Brenzaida," one of her Gondal poems often anthologized under the title "Remembrance." Rosina Alcona is addressing her lover Julius, now dead for fifteen years. She asks to be forgiven for going on with her own life after losing him. The anguish which the speaker feels is captured in the wave-like rhythms established in the first stanza through the use of pauses and parallel phrasing: "Cold in the earth, and the deep snow piled above thee!/ Far, far removed, cold in the dreary grave!" Monosyllabic rhyme and the repetition of significant words also aid in embodying the emotional quality of a yearning that is held in check.

Brontë often achieves control through repetition of a key word, one that is repeated but with varying connotations. In the beginning lines of the poem, the word "cold" presents two aspects of the literal circumstances: the lover lies cold in the grave, and the coldness of winter is upon the land. As the poem progresses, "cold" evolves in meaning to encompass the life of the speaker as well. Without her lover, the warmth and light of her life are gone.

He was both the sun and stars, and without him the heavens are now dark. Her life through the fifteen years following Julius' death has been winter, continually as barren as the snow-covered land, and to endure such barrenness she herself has had to become "cold." She has had to "check the tears of useless passion" and to chill the "burning wish" to follow him to the grave. Moreover, losing him to death has taught her one of the "cold" realities of life: "existence can be cherished" even after all love and joy are gone from one's own life.

This expanded definition of the word "cold" is underscored by Brontë's use of antithesis, another technique typical of her style. In stanza three, Brontë juxtaposes the image of the lover lying cold and still in his grave and the wild movements of the weather which will ultimately lead to the warmth of spring. In the final stanza, she returns to the same pair of opposites: stillness and movement. The speaker refuses to indulge too much in "Memory's rapturous pain," her wild feelings of love and sorrow, for fear that she could not then face the "empty world again," the still frozen world of her own life. With this last description of the "empty world," Brontë returns to the image of coldness with which she began, and the tolling, elegiac poem is brought to rest, although with the phrase "rapturous pain" she points to the restless, unreconciled feelings of the speaker. These conflicting desires between the longing to remember lost love and the need to forget point in turn to the paradoxical nature of the whole poem: the speaker tells of the necessity of forgetting her lover, and yet the poem itself attests to her loving memory of him.

In the non-Gondal poem "The Philosopher" there is a description of "warring gods" within the "little frame" of the speaker's physical self. This image could easily serve as a metaphor for much of Brontë's poetry: within the confines of poetic structure she attempts to hold conflicting forces and their related images. "Oh Thy Bright Eyes Must Answer Now" is a significant poem in the Brontë canon, for it clearly sets forth the dimensions of these conflicts. The first half of the poem presents the conflict between imagination and reason, between spiritual needs and earthly cares. The speaker turns to the "bright eyes" of the "radiant angel" of her vision, to summon it to speak and defend her choice to worship its power, rejecting the demands of Reason, who in "forms of gloom" with a "scornful brow" judges and mocks her "overthrow." By the world's standards, she has been overthrown, for she has failed to achieve wealth and glory. She has shunned the "common path" and chosen the "strange road."

The second half of the poem examines the inner conflict regarding her relationship to the overseeing "radiant angel" of this strange road. In stanza five, she addresses this angel as "Thee, ever present, phantom thing—/ My slave, my comrade, and my King!" The speaker controls the influence, good or ill, of this angel. Consequently, he is her slave, and yet he is a comrade, an equal who is always with her, bringing her "intimate delight," and finally—

seeming to contradict completely these two roles of slave and comrade—he is her King, directing and dictating. In these lines Brontë is expressing the conflicting desires within the soul itself: a desire to remain free without being isolated, and a desire to maintain individual identity while simultaneously merging with a larger and more powerful being.

The last stanza of this poem points to the troublesome question underlying the complicated life of Brontë's visions: Is she wrong to choose a faith that allows her own soul to grant her prayers? In a very real way, her own imagination has conjured up the angel who will defeat Reason. It is characteristic of Brontë to place such emphasis on individual power and will. Although this emphasis prefigures the work of later writers in which the self creates its own reality and its own gods, the unorthodox road that Brontë chose to follow did not lead her to this extreme conclusion. The last two lines of "Oh Thy Bright Eyes Must Answer Now" return to her "God of Visions": he must "plead" for her. Her power was expressed in her choice to worship him, and now he must come to defend her. Throughout Brontë's work there remains an emphasis on an outside power which could and would exist whether she herself existed or not. One of the last written and most famous of her poems, "No Coward Soul Is Mine," is a ringing affirmation of her faith in her choice of visions. Her soul stands sure in its relationship to the "Being and Breath" that "can never be destroyed." When suns and universes are gone, it will still remain.

Many of Brontë's poems describing nature also concern this prevailing spirit, and occasionally they seem to present a pantheistic vision; however, although the natural world clearly had the power to stir and inspire her, nature and her God of Visions are not synonymous. Primarily, Brontë uses nature to parallel a state of mind or soul, as she does in "Remembrance," where the cold snow-covered hills objectify the restrained feelings of the speaker. Often the open moors and the movement of the winds are used to embody the wild, free feelings of the human soul. In "Aye, There It Is! It Wakes To-night," Brontë uses the powerful and violent images of the storm to describe a person being transformed into pure spirit as her soul awakens to knowledge of some supreme spiritual power. Like lightning, her "feeling's fires flash," her gaze is "kindled," a "glorious wind" sweeps all memory of this mortal world from her mind, and she becomes "the essence of the Tempest's roaring." The last stanza concludes that this visionary experience prefigures the life of the soul after death, when, free from the prison of the body, it shall rise: "The dungeon mingle with the mould—/ The captive with the skies." In these last two lines, Brontë plays upon a rather conventional simile of the body as prisonhouse of the soul to create an original effect. First, she unexpectedly and suddenly introduces the word "mould" to represent the process of the body's decay and the dust to which it returns, and second, she compares the action of the soul after death to this process of decay: the body will "mingle" with the earth; the soul with the skies. There is in this last line a sense of triumphant release, effectively represented in the long vowel sound of "skies" which sharply contrasts with the earlier mournful sounds of "cold" and "mould." Throughout the poem, Brontë has again controlled an intensely emotional subject through antithesis, simple monosyllabic rhymes, and terse metrical patterns.

Perhaps the most famous of Brontë's poems depicting this visionary experience is the lengthy fragment of the Gondal poem "Julian M. to A. G. Rochelle," which Brontë published under the title "The Prisoner." The fragment consists of lines 13-44 and lines 65-92 of the original with four new lines added at the end to provide an appropriate conclusion. This slightly revised excerpt, although beginning with the voice of Julian telling of his decision to wander rather casually through the family dungeons, primarily concerns the mystical experiences of one of the prisoners. When she speaks, she displays a spirit undefeated by her imprisonment. Her body is able to endure the chains, for her soul is open to a nightly "messenger" who offers her the hope of "eternal liberty." Her response to this messenger occurs in a series of stages. First, she experiences a mingling of pain and pleasure as visions rise before her. Then she loses all awareness of her earthly self; the world and the body are forgotten. She then is able to experience an "unuttered harmony." Her outward senses and conscious mind have become numb in order that the "inward essence" can be released. In the final stage, this inward essence—in one burst of energy, as if leaping—attempts to merge with the "Invisible," the "Unseen," which she also describes as a "home" and a "harbour." At this point, because she cannot completely escape the body and still live, she suddenly and painfully returns to a knowledge of her earthly self and its prison, the literal prison in which she finds herself and the prison of her own body. Only after death can she finally and permanently join with the "Unseen," and so she looks forward to Death as heralding the complete and lasting union with the source of these nightly divine visions.

Brontë's decision to excerpt these particular stanzas from one of her Gondal poems, and the fact that once excerpted they still function as a unified whole, again suggest that Gondal merely provided the stage and the costumes for a drama that was actually taking place in Brontë's own self. In fact, in this case the poem benefits from the cutting of the frame stanzas which are full of conventional descriptions of stone dungeons and Lord Julian's somewhat expected romantic response to the fair prisoner. Obviously, Brontë's interest and poetic talent lay in examining and capturing the visionary experience.

As the fame of the Brontë family increased, Emily Brontë herself became a figure of legend. She was described as a passionate genius of almost mythic proportions, possessing supreme will and strength. This interpretation was encouraged very early by Charlotte, whose respect for her sister increased greatly during the last months of her life: in Charlotte's eyes, her seemingly unobtrusive sister had become a solitary being, towering above others, heroically hastening to her death. So long has this view been presented that it is now inextricably woven with Emily Brontë's name and image. She herself left so few biographical clues that perhaps the actual woman must always be seen from a distance; however, in her work there is indeed evidence of a poet of original, imaginative power, who, having chosen her God of Visions, was able to give poetic expression to the essential emotions of the human soul.

Diane D'Amico

Other major works
NOVEL: *Wuthering Heights*, 1847.
NONFICTION: *Five Essays Written in French*, 1948 (Lorine White Nagel, translator); *The Brontë Letters*, 1954 (Muriel Spark, editor).

Bibliography
Chitham, Edward, and Tom Winnifrith. *Brontë Facts and Brontë Problems.* Basingstoke, England: Macmillan, 1983. Contains four essays on the poetry of Emily Brontë, one of which questions the Ratchford thesis. Others look at the influence of Percy Bysshe Shelley, other sources of inspiration, and the development of vision. Includes an index.
Duthie, Enid L. *The Brontës and Nature.* Basingstoke, England: Macmillan, 1986. Duthie admires the terseness and Blakean quality of the poetry but is more concerned in placing it in a wider context in its response to nature. Supplemented by a select bibliography and an index.
Gerin, Winnifred. *Emily Brontë.* New York: Oxford University Press, 1971. This biography remains one of the most useful in considering Emily Brontë as a poet, since it systematically integrates poetry with biography, quoting crucial poems fully. Contains appendices, a full bibliography, and an index.
Homans, Margaret. *Women Writers and Poetic Identity: Dorothy Wordsworth, Emily Brontë, and Emily Dickinson.* Princeton, N.J.: Princeton University Press, 1980. Three major nineteenth century writers are compared in terms of difficulty in being poetesses. Includes an index.
Pykett, Lynn. *Emily Brontë.* Basingstoke, England: Macmillan, 1989. One of the Women Writers series, it offers in two chapters a rereading of her poetry in terms of its issue with Romanticism as well as with Victorian stereotyping. Complemented by a bibliography and an index.
Ratchford, Fanny E. *Gondal's Queen.* Austin: University of Texas Press, 1955. In this classic study, Ratchford reconstructs the Gondal saga, placing the Gondal poetry at the appropriate places in the saga. A brilliant piece of literary reconstruction. Contains appendices and indexes.

RUPERT BROOKE

Born: Rugby, England; August 3, 1887
Died: Aboard a hospital ship on the Aegean Sea; April 23, 1915

Principal poetry

Poems, 1911; *1914 and Other Poems*, 1915; *Collected Poems*, 1915; *Complete Poems*, 1932; *The Poetical Works of Rupert Brooke*, 1946 (Geoffrey Keynes, editor).

Other literary forms

Rupert Brooke's lasting work is to be found exclusively in his poetry, but his work in several other literary forms at least deserves mention. Brooke was attracted to the theater, and two of his works, one as a critic and one as an artist, reflect this interest. *John Webster and the Elizabethan Drama* (1916) was written as his fellowship dissertation and later published; although much criticized for its lack of scholarly decorum, it reveals a lively style and an author fascinated with the remarkable developments in Elizabethan theater. His only play, a one-act tragedy entitled *Lithuania* (1935), can be read with some satisfaction despite its bizarre plot and uncertain tone. As always with Brooke, his skill with language helps to camouflage his errors and excesses. As a journalist, Brooke mixed with strong effect the lyricism of a poet with the enthusiastic observations of an excited traveler, most prominently in a series of articles which described his tour of the United States, Canada, and the South Seas, written for the *Westminster Gazette*. In these delightful pieces he adeptly and wittily penetrates such subjects as the American personality, a baseball game at Harvard, the grandeur of the Rocky Mountains, and others. These display British wonder, sometimes dismay, at the "new world," but always stop short of tasteless condescension. Finally, Brooke was a masterful and enthusiastic correspondent; one finds in his letters enchanting representations of matters both personal and universal as he comments on a variety of subjects.

Achievements

Any attempt to measure the achievement of Brooke, poet, must also account for the impact of Brooke as a dashing public figure in life, and as a hero and martyr in death. This is not to devalue the richness of his best verse, for his canon is mostly sound, and the tragedy of his early death is amplified by the tragedy of artistic potential cut short. Still, if ever a poet has been linked with an era, his physical presence and intellectual attributes defining the sentiments of a nation and its people, then that poet is Rupert Brooke. Any evaluation of his work is at once confused and enriched by the clamor that surrounded his life, art, and death. His life as student, citizen, and soldier reflects values prized by the British as they entered the twentieth century and endured World War I. His art is complex, but not in a metaphysical way. Rather, its mystery can be ascribed to the tension produced when the convictions of a traditionalist in matters of form and structure are linked with the passionate voice of an exuberant Romantic. Brooke's preference for sonneteering is well-known. His topics and themes are more often quaint and predictable than unique and shocking (an effect he often desired to achieve). The poetry is classically graceful and romantically intense, always ultimately sustained by a gift for language. Finally, however, Brooke's death during World War I, the sometimes crude publicity which surrounded it and his memory, and the subsequent legendary status accorded him, ensured for all time that critics would find it difficult to separate his life from his art, in an attempt to assess his legacy.

Biography

Rupert Chawner Brooke was born in Rugby, England, on August 3, 1887. His father, William Parker Brooke, was a Rugby schoolmaster, an undistinguished but competent classical scholar, a person perhaps most noticeable for his very *lack* of noticeable traits. Rupert's mother, Mary Ruth Cotterill, dominated the family and is often described as an organizer—energetic, efficient, strict, even domineering. One of Rupert's brothers, Dick, died after a short illness in 1907; another, Alfred, was killed in World War I three months after Rupert's death. Several commentators have made much of the death of a child who would have been Rupert's older sister, implying that somehow Rupert was always affected by the notion of being a disappointing replacement for an adored and much-lamented daughter.

Rupert realized many benefits from, but at the same time was assuredly strained by, his family's association with the British educational system. Although not unhealthy, neither was he robust, and he was heartily encouraged to develop his intellectual skills first and foremost. As a youth he exhibited a tendency to role-play, most often typified by world-weariness and grandiloquent language. His more engaging qualities included an active mind, interest if not excellence in some sports, and (to understate) a pleasing appearance which later became a significant part of his legend.

His life at Rugby was notable for the variety of his academic, social, and even athletic, interests, and for his ability to develop close friendships with interesting people, a trait that stayed with Brooke always. Many of his friends were remarkable and passionately loyal to him; even mere acquaintances could not deny intense curiosity about him. As a poet, his early works show a young man enchanted with words and full of the impulse to parody the masters. He was more enthusiastic than polished, becoming increasingly so with each English poet whose secrets he discovered, digested, and imitated. Brooke adored writing contests and seemed to delight in shocking the sensibilities of his friends and family.

As a student at King's College, Cambridge, Rupert continued these activities, but now for the first time found real independence from his family in a stimulating and glamorous setting. In addition to his reading and writing, he now discovered the delights of political debate, the mysteries of such disciplines as psychology, and the pleasures of acting. He excitedly joined political discussions, joined the Cambridge Fabian Society, and worked diligently on its behalf. As an actor he exhibited no real talent, in spite of his ability to deliver poetic lines with great enthusiasm and a physical presence which, according to many, was spectacular. His career at Cambridge, undistinguished academically, was nevertheless solid. He cultivated still more fascinating friends, showed a preference for "modern" works, and matured as a poet. At the same time he confessed a weary tolerance for life, an attitude that his many activities would seem to contradict.

After his formal education and before World War I, Brooke found both peace and adventure. He spent some time reading and writing in a charming setting, Grantchester, and reveled in his surroundings and leisure, a welcome relief from his school years. For excitement, Brooke embarked in 1913 to explore America and the South Seas, an excursion financed by the *Westminster Gazette*; the newspaper had commissioned him to send back impressions of his tour. He must have enjoyed himself; the pace was hectic and he was greeted enthusiastically and with respect by his various hosts. His articles, often supremely "British" and critical of a general lack of culture in the Americas, are nevertheless important and enjoyable, suggesting increasing powers of observation and description.

His return to Britain was personally triumphant and satisfying. Brooke had confessed homesickness during his travels, but was little prepared for his outright joy at once again reaching British soil. His friends greeted him exuberantly and a series of social and artistic activities kept him busy. His future, as artist, as critic, even perhaps as politician, seemed assured.

His dreams were to be stalled, shattered, and canceled by World War I. It is a curious measure of the impact of Brooke's work and personality that he, with limited exposure to battle, eventually dying of blood poisoning, should ultimately be accorded the lavish praise of his countrymen, who saw him as the spokesman for a generation of heroes. With many of his friends, he had expressed early disgust for the very notion of war, but changed attitudes quickly, voicing the desire to find high adventure while ridding the world of the Prussian menace. He joined the Artists' Rifles, sought a commission, and eventually landed a post as a sublieutenant in the Royal Naval Division. His only significant action was to march with a brigade in relief of Antwerp, a time during which he witnessed the realities of war. The column, however, retreated quickly after a few days of occupying trenches.

Later, his division received its orders for the Aegean, and Gallipoli. En route, Brooke contracted dysentery; his condition weakened, he would fail and seem to rally from time to time; he lingered, and finally died, April 23, 1915, at the age of twenty-seven, aboard a French hospital ship, in the company of a school friend. He was buried the same day on the nearby island of Skyros, where a memorial was later raised in his honor.

Brooke's memory, however, lived on, sometimes in ways which were flattering and meaningful, other times in ways which were distorted and tasteless. The poet who wrote with conviction about fair England and the soldier's duty and privilege to serve, was mourned and eulogized by many, not the least of whom was Winston Churchill, who had recognized the value of Brooke's verse. Beyond his work, there were other matters, more difficult to pinpoint, but significant nevertheless, which contributed to his fame. His background, education, and even his dashing good looks (he was called the "fair-haired Apollo," to his embarrassment) represented what was best about "the Empire," and much of the British approach to this war was intimately involved, of course, with "the Empire" and all it implied. It is too bad, in a way, that this fine poet and remarkable person has had to bear these burdens, for the excessive publicity obscures what is best about his work and life. Paul Fussell has rightly called World War I an "ironic" war; by that he means that the gestures and ideals of the participants appear almost ludicrous in the context of the brutal efficiency of the new century. There is much that is ironic about World War I's most famous poet, too, for today Brooke is often admired, often condemned; but in both cases, usually for the wrong reasons.

Analysis

The best approaches to understanding and appreciating the poetry of Rupert Brooke are to reveal the themes of place and sentiment which dominate his works, and to recognize the fascinating way in which he blends structural integrity and fluency which appears spontaneous, passionate, bordering on the experimental.

Perhaps the work which most reveals these traits is "The Old Vicarage, Grantchester." Written in Berlin in 1912, this unusual poem, sometimes flippantly comic and other times grossly nostalgic, shows Brooke's tendency to idealize the past, or the "other place," wherever and whenever he was not. Written in octosyllabic couplets, it can be praised for the clarity and tension of its best lines; it can also be condemned for the immature slackness of its worst. A homesick traveler, Brooke sits at a café table in Berlin, conscious of the activity, much of it repulsive, about him. He begins with a graceful recounting of the natural splendor of Grantchester and its environs, but these pleasant thoughts are rudely interrupted by the guttural sound of the German language spoken around him—"*Du lieber Gott!*"—which sets up an immediate and abrupt passage in which the "here" and "there" are effectively juxtaposed.

The sudden introduction of a phrase, in Greek, which means "if only I were," is a nice touch (linking Classical and British civilization), followed by repetition of his desire, to be "in Grantchester, in Grantchester." There is a long catalog of reasons why one would wish to be "in Grantchester," detailing not only the natural splendor of the place, but also much more. Among the many pleasures, the most notable are the educational tradition (especially a reverence for classics), familiar and comfortable personalities, and the respect for truth and decorous behavior which may be found there.

It is true that this poem is extended far too long and becomes tediously redundant; it is just as true that some of the lines cause the reader to cringe, often because Brooke seems not to have considered the veracity of his assertions ("And men and women with straight eyes,/ Lithe children lovelier than a dream"), at other times because his slickness is *only* cute ("Ah God! to see the branches stir/ Across the moon at Grantchester!"). Still, one finds "The Old Vicarage, Grantchester" to be solid, mostly complete, if slightly flawed. First, Brooke manages to describe Grantchester fully, with sufficient detail to make the reader understand why the poet is moved to such excess and to sympathize with him. This is not only a celebration of pastoral elegance, but also a characterization of the people of Grantchester verging on a statement of values tending toward thematic richness. The vocabulary of fiction employed here is no accident, as the poem has many qualities of the introductory chapters of a novel, complete with protagonist and dramatic action. Second, there is an irony in some of the passages which establishes a tone distinctly superior to juvenile "romanticizing."

In short, "The Old Vicarage, Grantchester" represents the best and worst of Brooke; not surprisingly, it is the kind of poem that leads to conflicting and confusing evaluations of his work. Those who praise him for his sensitive descriptions of his homeland, those who see in the poem evidence of wit and sparkling phrasing, and those who cringe at his excessive sentimentality will all find here numerous examples to support their contentions.

Whereas "The Old Vicarage, Grantchester" is vintage Brooke, he is best known for his sonnets, particularly those he wrote during 1914, shortly before his death, which glamorized the fate of martyred soldiers. Brooke evidently found great satisfaction in the sonnet form, and obviously the long relationship was liberating rather than inhibiting, for he showed thematic and structural flexibility while remaining true to the principles of sonneteering. In addition to his evocation of place, Brooke treated in his sonnets such diverse subjects as death, memory, time, psychic phenomena, growing up, lust, and, of course, the pain and pleasure of idealized love as found in the grand traditions of the sonnet. He wrote in the Petrarchan manner, complete with the requisite imagery of the distant and taunting enamorata; he mastered the English form and the difficult closing couplet of the Shakespearean sonnet; and he exhibited the logical strength and confidence so apparent in the Miltonic brand. When bored, he tried variations, such as introducing a sonnet with the couplet (as in "Sonnet Reversed"); his experiments are never disruptive, but suggestive of the strength of the form, and anticipatory of later twentieth century inventions (E. E. Cummings, for example, might be mentioned here).

The five "1914" sonnets reflect Brooke's facility in the sonnet form, while at the same time incorporating sentiments which touched his countrymen profoundly. All deal with the transcending reward which awaits those who make the supreme sacrifice for home and country during The Great War. Again, depending on one's perspective, the sonnets are either inspiring and gallant calls-to-arms for a generation of martyrs, or naïve and morbid musings which typify the tragic waste of the conflict. The first, "Peace," alludes, ironically, to the new life evident in those whose existence had turned stale, who now benefit from clarity of purpose. Those who must die lose little except "body" and "breath," and are glad to escape their environment. The second sonnet in this sequence, "Safety," can be linked with "Peace," in that those who are sacrificed are referred to as "we." Again the comforting thought recurs that a soldier's death (what might be called a "good death") is to be embraced, not feared, for it presumes the existence of a condition beyond suffering and fear, beyond time, even.

The next two sonnets of 1914, "The Dead" (I) and "The Dead" (II), refer to the martyrs in the third person, but the philosophy remains much the same. In the first, the poet calls for public recognition of an honorable departure from life: "Blow out, you bugles, over the rich Dead!/ There's none of these so lonely and poor of old,/ But, dying, has made us rarer gifts than gold." Ancestral dignity is the rationale for these extreme sentiments; "holiness," "honor," and "nobleness" are evoked as those who pour out "the red sweet wine of youth" are finally able to realize their true "heritage." In the second sonnet of this pair, the celebration is of a pastoral bent, not only in the description of those youths who exist so intimately with the natural world (" . . . Dawn was theirs,/ And the sunset, and the colours of the earth."), but also in the elegiac sestet, where the world of the dead is little-changed in its excellence.

In "The Soldier," Brooke writes in the first person. Perhaps it is this immediacy ("If I should die, think only this of me") which made the sonnet so touching for his countrymen. More likely it is the sentiments expressed which captured the tragedy of a proud nation losing its best young men in war, and somehow finding solace in the loss. Some might even call the poem overbearing, chauvinistic. In the opening lines, the poet asserts that mourning should be brief, for wherever he may lie, that spot becomes "for ever England," where the "rich earth" is more enriched by "a dust whom England bore, shaped, made aware." In the sestet, lest the reader think that only the physical is to be exalted, Brooke suggests that the English soul, "this heart," or "pulse in the eternal mind" will inhabit the universe, much to our advantage.

Brooke's poetry, then, is by turns admirable and condemnable. Yet another way to account for this baffling but intriguing trait is to place his work in relationship to what is called "The Georgian Revolt." Brooke's role in this curious, little-understood era was a significant one: first, he was a close friend of Edward Marsh, whose Georgian anthologies set the tone for the period and who was eventually chosen to write Brooke's official biography; second, Brooke contributed to the anthologies and worked diligently to publicize the "Georgian" productions; third, the nature of Brooke's public and artistic reputation is as debatable as the confused reputation of "Georgian" poetry.

What "Georgian" has come to mean, of course, is the overly romantic, intellectually slack, structurally contrived efforts of a few "waspish" poets who refused to accept the birth of the twentieth century. The original plan of Marsh, Brooke, and others had been to provide a forum through which a new, energetic brand of modern poetry could transcend the stifling dominance of what was being called "Edwardian" poetry. The early volumes of Georgian work reveal this kind of energy, at least in comparison to later volumes after the war, when many of the best contributors had either died (Brooke and Isaac Rosenberg, among others), lost interest (Robert Graves, Siegfried Sassoon), or gone their own ways (Ezra Pound, D. H. Lawrence). Unfortunately, the later examples of Georgian poetry are frequently used by critics to describe the whole movement; for poets and critics of the late 1920's and 1930's, who demanded rock-hard language and precise imagery, there was nothing to do but to attack the Georgians with a vengeance.

Anyone who wishes to be objective in his evaluation of Brooke's short poetic career must acknowledge Brooke's weaknesses as well as his strengths. There is the untempered voice of boyish spontaneity, the popularizer of mindless and almost laughable patriotic sentimentalism, the friendly versifier of late Georgian poetry which did little but describe nature redundantly. This Rupert Brooke penned such lines as "There was a damned successful Poet; There was a Woman like the Sun./ And they were dead. They did not know it." ("Dead Men's Love"); he probably deserves ridicule for having done so. On the other hand, fortunately, there is also the exuberant *and* mature voice of a craftsman, the defender of the noble sentiments of a nation in crisis, and the innovative artist who sought freshness and vitality even as he worked within traditional forms. This Brooke deserves acclaim.

Robert Edward Graalman, Jr.

Other major works

PLAY: *Lithuania*, 1935.

NONFICTION: *John Webster and the Elizabethan Drama*, 1916; *Letters from America*, 1916; *The Prose of Rupert Brooke*, 1956; *The Letters of Rupert Brooke*, 1968.

Bibliography

Brooke, Rupert, Walter de la Mare, and Maurice Browne. *Rupert Brooke.* Port Washington, N.Y.: Kennikat Press, 1968. The eulogistic lecture by de la Mare given in 1919, four years after Brooke's death, helped perpetuate the image of Brooke as a wit, closer in spirit to the young John Donne than to George Gordon, Lord Byron, and Percy Bysshe Shelley; Browne's recollections, first published in 1927, reinforce that view.

Delaney, Paul. *The Neo-Pagans: Rupert Brooke and the Ordeal of Youth.* New York: Free Press, 1987. In 1911, Virginia Woolf half-derisively gave Brooke and his carefree circle the label "neo-pagans." In this balanced appraisal, Delaney focuses on the flaws in the group's philosophies that undermined their optimism about the future, causing conflicts and fragmenting their relationships. Contains notes and references, a bibliography, and an index.

Hassall, Christopher. *Rupert Brooke: A Biography.* New York: Harcourt, Brace & World, 1964. This elaborate, if flawed, account of Brooke's life remains the most authoritative and comprehensive. Although it attempts to find the man behind the myth, it suffers from Hassall's refusal to publish material he considered to be too private. Contains a discussion of the critical reception given to the only collection of Brooke's poems published in his lifetime, and a detailed index.

Lehmann, John. *The Strange Destiny of Rupert Brooke.* New York: Holt, Rinehart and Winston, 1981. In this highly praised combination of biography and literary criticism, Lehmann explores Brooke's psychological history and explains why Brooke's friends expressed conflicting judgments about his character and abilities. Contains an index and a brief biography.

Pearsall, Robert Brainard. *Rupert Brooke: The Man and the Poet.* Amsterdam: Rodopi, 1974. Pearsall's biography, less complete than Christopher Hassall's account, derives in large part from the King's College (Cambridge) collections of Brooke's papers and from Brooke's published letters. Pearsall is fairly objective, giving a sympathetic and insightful reading of Brooke's better prose and poetry but criticizing especially distasteful and sentimental material. For a discussion of Brooke's relations to others, Paul Delaney's *The Neo-Pagans* is more thorough. A bibliography supplements the text.

Rogers, Timothy. *Rupert Brooke: A Reappraisal and Selection from His Writings, Some Hitherto Unpublished.* London: Routledge & Kegan Paul, 1971. Rogers says that Brooke has often been judged unfairly; the poetry has created the myth, and the myth has obscured the best in Brooke's work. Along with his collection of representative prose and verse, Rogers provides critical commentary, arguing persuasively that the charge of dullness frequently leveled at Brooke is unwarranted. A bibliography concludes this slight volume.

GWENDOLYN BROOKS

Born: Topeka, Kansas; June 7, 1917

Principal poetry

A Street in Bronzeville, 1945; *Annie Allen*, 1949; *The Bean Eaters*, 1960; *Selected Poems*, 1963; *In the Mecca*, 1968; *Riot*, 1969; *Family Pictures*, 1970; *Aloneness*, 1971; *Beckonings*, 1975; *Primer for Blacks*, 1980; *To Disembark*, 1981; *The Near-Johannesburg Boy*, 1986; *Blacks*, 1987; *Gottschalk and the Grand Tarantelle*, 1988.

Other literary forms

In addition to the poetry on which her literary reputation rests, Gwendolyn Brooks has published a novel, *Maud Martha* (1953); a book of autobiographical prose, *Report from Part One* (1972); and volumes of children's verse. An episodic novel, *Maud Martha* makes some use of autobiographical materials and shares many of the major concerns of Brooks's poetry, particularly concerning the attempts of the person to maintain integrity in the face of crushing environmental pressures. *Report from Part One* recounts the personal, political, and aesthetic influences which culminated in Brooks's movement to a black nationalist stance in the late 1960's. Since that time she has written introductions to, and edited anthologies of, the works of younger black writers. These introductions frequently provide insight into her own work. Several recordings of Brooks reading her own work are available.

Achievements

Working comfortably in relation to diverse poetic traditions, Brooks has been widely honored. Early in her career, she received numerous mainstream literary awards, including the Pulitzer Prize for Poetry in 1950 for *Annie Allen*. She has served as Poet Laureate of Illinois since 1969 and has received more than fifty honorary doctorates. Equally significant, numerous writers associated with the Black Arts Movement recognize her as an inspirational figure linking the older and younger generations of black poets. Brooks's ability to appeal both to poetic establishments and to a sizable popular audience, especially among young blacks, stems from her pluralistic voice which echoes a wide range of precursors while remaining unmistakably black. Her exploration of America in general and Chicago in particular links her with Walt Whitman and Carl Sandburg. Her exploration of the interior landscape of humanity in general and women in particular places her in the tradition of Emily Dickinson and Edna St. Vincent Millay. At once the technical heir of Langston Hughes in her use of the rhythms of black street life and of Robert Frost in her exploration of traditional forms such as the sonnet, Brooks nevertheless maintains her integrity of vision and voice.

This integrity assumes special significance in the context of African-American writing of the 1950's and 1960's. A period of "universalism" in black literature, the 1950's brought prominence to such poets as Brooks, LeRoi Jones, and Robert Hayden, all of whom provided clear evidence that African-American poets matched the technical and intellectual range of their white counterparts. During this period of intellectual and aesthetic integration, Brooks never abandoned her social and racial heritage to strive for the transcendent (and deracinated) universalism associated by some African-American critics with T. S. Eliot. Responding to William Carlos Williams' call in *Paterson* (1946-1951) to "make a start out of particulars and make them general," Brooks demonstrates unambiguously that an African-American writer need not be limited in relevance by concentrating on the black experience.

The 1960's, conversely, encouraged separatism and militancy in African-American writing. Even while accepting the Black Arts Movement's call for a poetry designed to speak directly to the political condition of the black community, Brooks continued to insist on precision of form and language. While Jones changed his name to Amiri Baraka and radically altered his poetic voice, Brooks accommodated her new insights to her previously established style. An exemplar of integrity and flexibility, she both challenges and learns from younger black poets such as Haki R. Madhubuti (Don L. Lee), Sonia Sanchez, Carolyn Rodgers, and Etheridge Knight. Like Hughes, she addresses the black community without condescension or pretense. Like Frost, she writes technically stunning "universal" poetry combining clear surfaces and elusive depths.

A recipient of more than fifty honorary doctorates, Brooks was appointed to the Presidential Commission on the National Agenda for the Eighties; she was the first black woman elected to the National Institute of Arts and Letters. She was named Consultant in Poetry to the Library of Congress for 1985-1986.

Biography

Gwendolyn Brooks's poetry bears the strong impress of Chicago, particularly of the predominantly black South Side where she has lived most of her life. Although she was born in Topeka, Kansas, Brooks was taken to Chicago before she was a year old. In many ways she has devoted her career to the physical, spiritual, and, more recently, political exploration of her native city.

Brooks's life and writings are frequently separated into two phases, with her experience at the 1967 Black Writers' Conference at Fisk University in Nashville serving as a symbolic transition. Prior to the Conference, Brooks was known primarily as the first black Pulitzer Prize winner in poetry. Although not politically unaware, she held to a somewhat cautious attitude. The vitality she encountered at the Conference crystallized her sense of the insufficiency of universalist attitudes and generated close personal and artistic friendships with younger black poets such as Madhubuti, Walter Bradford, and Knight. Severing her ties with the mainstream publishing firm of Harper and Row, which had published her first five books, Brooks transferred her work and prestige to the black-owned and operated Broadside Press of Detroit, Third World Press of Chicago, and Black Position Press, also of Chicago. Her commitment to black publishing houses remains unwavering despite distribution problems which render her later work largely invisible to the American reading public.

Educated in the Chicago school system and at Wilson Junior College, Brooks learned her craft under Inez Cunningham Stark (Boulton), a white woman who taught poetry at the South Side Community Art Center in the late 1930's and 1940's. Brooks's mother, who had been a teacher in Topeka, had encouraged her literary interests from an early age. Her father, a janitor, provided her with ineffaceable images of the spiritual strength and dignity of "common" people. Brooks married Henry Blakely in 1939 and her family concerns continued to play a central role in shaping her career. The eleven-year hiatus between the publication of *Annie Allen* and *The Bean Eaters* resulted at least in part from her concentration on rearing her two children, born in 1940 and 1951. Her numerous poems on family relationships reflect both the rewards and the tensions of her own experiences. Her children grown, Brooks concentrated on teaching, supervising poetry workshops, and speaking publicly. These activities brought her into contact with a wide range of younger black poets, preparing her for her experience at Fisk. As Poet Laureate of Illinois, a position she has held since 1969, she continues to encourage the development of younger poets through personal contact and formal competitions.

The division between the two phases of Brooks's life should not be overstated. She evinced a strong interest in the Civil Rights Movement during the 1950's and early 1960's; her concern with family continued in the 1980's. Above all, Brooks continues to live with and write of and for the Chicagoans whose failures and triumphs she sees as deeply personal, universally resonant, and specifically black.

Analysis

The image of Gwendolyn Brooks as a readily accessible poet is at once accurate and deceptive. Capable of capturing the experiences and rhythms of black street life, she frequently presents translucent surfaces which give way suddenly to reveal ambiguous depths. Equally capable of manipulating traditional poetic forms such as the sonnet, rhyme royal, and heroic couplet, she employs them to mirror the uncertainties of characters or personae who embrace conventional attitudes to defend themselves against internal and external chaos. Whatever form she chooses, Brooks consistently focuses on the struggle of people to find and express love, usually associated with the family, in the midst of a hostile environment. In constructing their defenses and seeking love, these persons typically experience a disfiguring pain. Brooks devotes much of her energy to defining and responding to the elusive forces, variously psychological and social, which inflict this pain. Increasingly in her later poetry, Brooks traces the pain to political sources and expands her concept of the family to encompass all black people. Even while speaking of the social situation of blacks in a voice crafted primarily for blacks, however, Brooks maintains the complex awareness of the multiple perspectives relevant to any given experience. Her ultimate concern is to encourage every individual, black or white, to "Conduct your blooming in the noise and whip of the whirlwind" ("The Second Sermon on the Warpland").

A deep concern with the everyday circumstances of black people living within the whirlwind characterizes many of Brooks's most popular poems. From the early "Of De Witt Williams on His Way to Lincoln Cemetery" and "A Song in the Front Yard," through the later "The Life of Lincoln West" and "Sammy Chester Leaves 'Godspell' and Visits UPWARD BOUND on a Lake Forest Lawn, Bringing West Afrika," she focuses on characters whose experiences merge the idiosyncratic and the typical. She frequently draws on black musical forms to underscore the communal resonance of a character's outwardly undistinguished life. By tying the refrain of "Swing Low Sweet Chariot" to the repeated phrase "Plain black boy," Brooks transforms De Witt Williams into an Everyman figure. Brooks describes his personal search for love in the pool rooms and dance halls, but stresses the representative quality of his experience by starting and ending the poem with the musical allusion.

"We Real Cool," perhaps Brooks's single best-known poem, subjects a similarly representative experience to an intricate technical and thematic scrutiny, at once loving and critical. The poem is only twenty-four words long, including eight repetitions of the word "we." It is suggestive that the subtitle of "We Real Cool" specifies the presence of only seven pool players at the "Golden Shovel." The eighth "we" suggests that poet and reader share, on some level, the desperation of the group-voice that Brooks transmits. The final sentence, "We/ die soon," restates the *carpe diem* motif in the vernacular of Chicago's South Side.

On one level, "We Real Cool" appears simply to catalog the experiences of a group of dropouts content to "sing sin" in all available forms. A surprising ambiguity enters into the poem, however, revolving around the question of how to accent the word "we" which ends every line except the last one, providing the beat for the poem's jazz rhythm. Brooks has said that she intended that the "we" *not* be accented. Read in this way, the poem takes on a slightly distant and ironic tone, emphasizing the artificiality of the group identity which involves the characters in activities offering early death as the only release from pain. Conversely, the poem can be read with a strong accent on each "we," affirming the group identity. Although the experience still ends with early death, the pool players metamorphose into defiant heroes determined to resist the alienating environment. Their confrontation with experience is felt, if not articulated, as existentially pure. Pool players, poet, and reader cannot be *sure* which stress is valid.

Brooks crafts the poem, however, to hint at an underlying coherence in the defiance. The intricate internal rhyme scheme echoes the sound of nearly every word. Not only do the first seven lines end with "we," but the penultimate words of each line in each stanza also rhyme (cool/school, late/straight, sin/gin, June/soon). In addition, the alliterated consonant of the last line of each stanza is repeated in the first line of the next stanza (Left/lurk, Strike/sin, gin/June) and the first words of each line in the middle two stanzas are connected through consonance (Lurk/strike, Sing/thin). The one exception to this suggestive texture of sound is the word "Die" which introduces both a new vowel and a new consonant into the final line, breaking the rhythm and subjecting the performance to ironic revaluation. Ultimately, the power of the poem derives from the tension between the celebratory and the ironic perspectives on the lives of the plain black boys struggling for a sense of connection.

A similar struggle informs many of Brooks's poems in more traditional forms, including 'The Mother," a powerful exploration of the impact of an abortion on the woman who has chosen to have it. Brooks states that the mother "decides that *she*, rather than her world, will kill her children." Within the poem itself, however, the motivations remain unclear. Although the poem's position in Brooks's first book, *A Street in Bronzeville*, suggests that the persona is black, the poem neither supports nor denies a racial identification. Along with the standard English syntax and diction, this suggests that "The Mother," like poems such as "The Egg Boiler," "Callie Ford," and "A Light and Diplomatic Bird," was designed to speak directly of an emotional, rather than a social, experience, and to be as accessible to whites as to blacks. Recreating the anguished perspective of a persona unsure whether she is victim or victimizer, Brooks directs her readers' attention to the complex emotions of her potential Everywoman.

"The Mother" centers on the persona's alternating desire to take and to evade responsibility for the abortion. Resorting to ambiguous grammatical structures, the persona repeatedly qualifies her acceptance with "if" clauses ("If I sinned," "If I stole your births"). She refers to the lives of the children as matters of fate ("Your luck") and backs away from admitting that a death has taken place by claiming that the children "were never made." Her use of the second person pronoun to refer to herself in the first stanza reveals her desire to distance herself from her present pain. This attempt, however, fails. The opening line undercuts the evasion with the reality of memory: "Abortions will not let you forget." At the start of the second stanza, the pressure of memory forces the persona to shift to the more honest first person pronoun. A sequence of spondees referring to the children ("damp small pulps," "dim killed children," "dim dears") interrupts the lightly stressed anapestic-iambic meter which dominates the first stanza. The concrete images of "scurrying off ghosts" and "devouring" children with loving gazes gain power when contrasted with the dimness of the mother's life and perceptions. Similarly, the first stanza's end-stopped couplets, reflecting the persona's simplistic attempt to recapture an irrevocably lost mother-child relationship through an act of imagination, give way to the intricate enjambment and complex rhyme scheme of the second stanza, which highlight the mother's inability to find rest.

The rhyme scheme—and Brooks can rival both Robert Frost and W. B. Yeats in her ability to employ various types of rhyme for thematic impact—underscores her struggle to come to terms with her action. The rhymes in the first stanza insist on her self-doubt, contrasting images of tenderness and physical substance with those of brutality and insubstantiality (forget/get, hair/air, beat/sweet). The internal rhyme of "never," repeated four times, and "remember," "workers," and "singers," further stresses the element of loss. In the second stanza, Brooks provides no rhymes for the end words "children" in line 11 and "deliberate" in line 21. This device draws attention to the persona's failure to answer the crucial questions of whether her children did in fact exist and of whether her own actions were in fact deliberate (and perhaps criminal). The last seven lines of the stanza end with hard "d" sounds as the persona struggles to forge her conflicting thoughts into a unified perspective. If Brooks offers coherence, though, it is emotional rather than intellectual. Fittingly, the "d" rhymes and off-rhymes focus on physical and emotional pain (dead/instead/made/afraid/said/died/cried). Brooks provides no easy answer to the anguished question: "How is the truth to be told?" The persona's concluding cry of "I loved you/ All" rings with desperation. It is futile but it is not a lie. To call "The Mother" an antiabortion poem distorts its impact. Clearly portraying the devastating effects of the persona's action, it by no means condemns her or lacks sympathy. Like many of Brooks's characters, the mother is a person whose desire to love far outstrips her ability to cope with her circumstances and serves primarily to heighten her sensitivity to pain.

Perhaps the most significant change in Brooks's poetry involves her analysis of the origins of this pervasive pain. Rather than attributing the suffering to some unavoidable psychological condition, Brooks's later poetry indicts social institutions for their role in its perpetuation. The poems in her first two volumes frequently portray characters incapable of articulating the origins of their pain. Although the absence of any father in "The Mother" suggests sociological forces leading to the abortion, such analysis amounts to little more than speculation. The only certainty is that the mother, the persona of the sonnet sequence "The Children of the Poor," and the speaker in the brilliant sonnet "My Dreams, My Works Must Wait Till After Hell" share the fear that their pain will render them insensitive to love. The final poem of *Annie Allen*, "Men of Careful Turns," intimates that the defenders of a society which refuses to admit its full humanity bear responsibility for reducing the powerless to "grotesque toys." Despite this implicit accusation, however, Brooks perceives no "magic" capable of remedying the situation. She concludes the volume on a note of irresolution typical of her early period: "We are lost, must/ Wizard a track through our own screaming weed." The track, at this stage, remains spiritual rather than political.

Although the early volumes include occasional poems concerning articulate political participants such as "Negro Hero," her later work frequently centers on specific black political spokespersons such as Malcolm X, Paul Robeson, John Killens, and Don L. Lee. Since the early 1960's, a growing anger informs poems as diverse as the ironic "The Chicago *Defender* Sends a Man to Little Rock," the near-baroque "The Lovers of the Poor," the imagistically intricate "Riders to the Blood-Red Wrath," and the satiric "Riot." This anger originates in Brooks's perception that the social structures of white society value material possessions and abstract ideas of prestige more highly than individual human beings. The anger culminates in Brooks's brilliant narrative poem "In the Mecca," concerning the death of a young girl in a Chicago housing project, and in her three "Sermons on the Warpland."

The "Warpland" poems mark Brooks's departure from the traditions of Euro-American poetry and thought represented by T. S. Eliot's *The Waste Land* (1922). The sequence typifies her post-1967 poetry, in which she abandons traditional stanzaic forms, applying her technical expertise to a relatively colloquial free verse. This technical shift parallels her rejection of the philosophical premises of Euro-American culture. Brooks refuses to accept the inevitability of cultural decay, arguing that the "waste" of Eliot's vision exists primarily because of our "warped" perceptions. Seeing white society as the embodiment of these distortions, Brooks embraces her blackness as a potential counterbalancing force. The first "Sermon on the Warpland" opens with Ron Karenga's black nationalist credo: "The fact that we are black is our ultimate reality." Clearly, in Brooks's view, blackness is not simply a physical fact; it is primarily a metaphor for the possibility of love. As her poem "Two Dedications" indicates, Brooks sees the Euro-American tradition represented by the Chicago Picasso as inhumanly cold, mingling guilt and innocence, meaningfulness and meaninglessness, almost randomly. This contrasts sharply with her inspirational image of the Wall of Heroes on the South Side. To Brooks, true art assumes meaning from the people who interact with it. The Wall helps to redefine black reality, rendering the "dispossessions beakless." Rather than contemplating the site of destruction, the politically aware black art which Brooks embraces should inspire the black community to face its pain with renewed determination to remove its sources. The final "Sermon on the Warpland" concludes with the image of a black phoenix rising from the ashes of the Chicago riot. No longer content to accept the unresolved suffering of "The Mother," Brooks forges a black nationalist politics and poetics of love.

Although her political vision influences every aspect of her work, Brooks maintains a strong sense of enduring individual pain and is aware that nationalism offers no simple panacea. "The Blackstone Rangers," a poem concerning one of the most powerful Chicago street gangs, rejects as simplistic the argument, occasionally advanced by writers associated with the Black Arts Movement, that no important distinction exists between the personal and the political experience. Specifically, Brooks doubts the corollary that politically desirable activity will inevitably increase the person's ability to love. Dividing "The Blackstone Rangers" into three segments—"As Seen by Disciplines," "The Leaders," and "Gang Girls: A Rangerette"—Brooks stresses the tension between perspectives. After rejecting the sociological-penal perspective of part one, she remains suspended between the uncomprehending affirmation of the Rangers as a kind of government-in-exile in part two, and the recognition of the individual person's continuing pain in part three.

Brooks undercuts the description of the Rangers as "sores in the city/ that do not want to heal" ("As Seen by Disciplines") through the use of off-rhyme and a jazz rhythm reminiscent of "We Real Cool." The disciplines, both academic and corrective, fail to perceive any coherence in the Rangers' experience. Correct in their assumption that the Rangers do not want to "heal" themselves, the disciplines fail to perceive the gang's strong desire to "heal" the sick society. Brooks suggests an essential coherence in the Rangers' experience through the sound texture of part one. Several of the sound patterns echoing through the brief stanza point to a shared response to pain (there/ thirty/ready, raw/sore/corner). Similarly, the accent cluster on "Black, raw, ready" draws attention to the pain and potential power of the Rangers. The descriptive voice of the disciplines, however, provides only relatively weak end rhymes (are/corner, ready/city), testifying to the inability of the distanced, presumably white, observers to comprehend the experiences they describe. The shifting, distinctively black, jazz rhythm further emphasizes the distance between the voices of observers and participants. Significantly, the voice of the disciplines finds no rhyme at all for its denial of the Rangers' desire to "heal."

This denial contrasts sharply with the tempered affirmation of the voice in part two which emphasizes the leaders' desire to "cancel, cure and curry." Again, internal rhymes and sound echoes suffuse the section. In the first stanza, the voice generates thematically significant rhymes, connecting Ranger leader "*Bop*" (whose name draws attention to the jazz rhythm which is even more intricate, though less obvious, in this section than in part one) and the militant black leader "*Rap*" Brown, both nationalists whose "country is a Nation on no *map.*" "Bop" and "Rap," of course, do not rhyme perfectly, attesting to Brooks's awareness of the gang leader's limitations. Her image of the leaders as "Bungled trophies" further reinforces her ambivalence. The only full rhyme in the final two stanzas of the section is the repeated "night." The leaders, canceling the racist association of darkness with evil, "translate" the image of blackness into a "monstrous pearl or grace." The section affirms the Blackstone Rangers' struggle; it does not pretend to comprehend fully the emotional texture of their lives.

Certain that the leaders possess the power to cancel the disfiguring images of the disciplines, Brooks remains unsure of their ability to create an alternate environment where love can blossom. Mary Ann, the "Gang Girl" of part three, shares much of the individual pain of the characters in Brooks's early poetry despite her involvement with the Rangers. "A rose in a whiskey glass," she continues to live with the knowledge that her "laboring lover" risks the same sudden death as the pool players of "We Real Cool." Forced to suppress a part of her awareness—she knows not to ask where her lover got the diamond he gives her—she remains emotionally removed even while making love. In place of a fully realized love, she accepts "the props and niceties of non-loneliness." The final line of the poem emphasizes the ambiguity of both Mary Ann's situation and Brooks's perspective. Recommending acceptance of "the rhymes of Leaning," the line responds to the previous stanza's question concerning whether love will have a "gleaning." The full rhyme paradoxically suggests acceptance of off-rhyme, of love consummated leaning against an alley wall, without expectation of safety or resolution. Given the political tension created by the juxtaposition of the disciplines and the leaders, the "Gang Girl" can hope to find no sanctuary beyond the reach of the whirlwind. Her desperate love, the more moving for its precariousness, provides the only near-adequate response to the pain that Brooks continues to see as the primary fact of life.

Craig Werner

Other major works

LONG FICTION: *Maud Martha*, 1953.

NONFICTION: *Report from Part One*, 1972; *Young Poet's Primer*, 1980.

CHILDREN'S LITERATURE: *Bronzeville Boys and Girls*, 1956; *The Tiger Who Wore White Gloves*, 1974; *Very Young Poets*, 1983.

ANTHOLOGY: *Jump Bad: A New Chicago Anthology, 1971.*

MISCELLANEOUS: *The World of Gwendolyn Brooks*, 1971.

Bibliography

Baker, Houston A., Jr. *The Journey Back: Issues in Black Literature and Criticism.* Chicago: University of Chicago Press, 1980. The value of Baker's treatment of Brooks (accessible through the index) is his examination of the shift in her thinking and her art generated by her experience at the Fisk University Writers' Conference in 1967. Baker sets her in the context of the larger movement toward a "Black Aesthetic."

Kent, George E. *A Life of Gwendolyn Brooks.* Lexington: University Press of Kentucky, 1990. This biography, actually completed in 1982 just before Kent's death, is based on interviews with Brooks and her friends and family. Integrates discussions of the poetry with a chronicle of her life. Especially valuable is an extensive recounting of the events and speeches at the 1967 Fisk conference, which changed the direction of her poetry. D. L. Melhem's afterword provides an update to 1988.

Melhem, D. L. *Gwendolyn Brooks: Poetry and the Heroic Voice.* Lexington: University Press of Kentucky, 1987. Beginning with a biographical chapter, Melhem employs a generally laudatory tone as he subsequently looks closely at the earlier poetry collections (through *Aloneness*). He surveys the later works within a single chapter, and also examines *Maud Martha* and *Bronzeville Boys and Girls.* Melhem's treatment gives attention to both structures and themes. Includes notes and an index, as well as a bibliography of her works (organized by publisher, in order to show the commitment she made to small black-run presses after the late 1960's).

Miller, R. Baxter, ed. *Black American Poets Between Worlds, 1940-1960.* Tennessee Studies in Literature 30. Knoxville: University of Tennessee Press, 1986. To this collection Harry B. Shaw contributes "Perceptions of Men in the Early Works of Gwendolyn Brooks," which looks at *A Street in Bronzeville, Annie Allen, Maud Martha,* and *The Bean Eaters* for their largely positive depictions of urban African-American men. "Define . . . the Whirlwind: Gwendolyn Brooks' Epic Sign for a Generation," by R. Baxter Miller, focuses on Brooks's epic achievement "In the Mecca." Each of these essays has notes, and the book is indexed.

Mootry, Maria K., and Gary Smith, eds. *A Life Distilled: Gwendolyn Brooks, Her Poetry and Fiction.* Urbana: University of Illinois Press, 1987. An introductory overview by Mootry is followed by a look at Brooks's sense of place ("The World of Satin-Legs, Mrs. Sallie, and the Blackstone Rangers" by Kenny J. Williams), her aesthetic (essays by George E. Kent, Norris B. Clark, and R. Baxter Miller), and the militancy that emerged in her "second period" (by William H. Hansel). The middle section comprises essays on individual collections, while the book's final two essays examine *Maud Martha.* Features notes, and a selected bibliography that not only lists Brooks's works but also surveys critical sources in great detail, including book reviews and dissertations. No index is provided.

Shaw, Harry B. *Gwendolyn Brooks.* Boston: Twayne, 1980. A largely thematic overview of Brooks's works through the mid-1970's, with chapters entitled "Death," "The Fall from Glory," "The Labyrinth," and "Survival." There is a biographical chronology and a chapter detailing the principal events of her life. "Black Microcosm" assesses her achievement in rendering the African-American experience in her poetry. The bibliography is annotated, and the book also provides notes and an index.

STERLING BROWN

Born: Washington, D.C.; May 1, 1901
Died: Takoma Park, Maryland; January 13, 1989

Principal poetry

Southern Road, 1932; *The Last Ride of Wild Bill and Eleven Narrative Poems*, 1975; *The Collected Poems of Sterling A. Brown*, 1980.

Other literary forms

Sterling Brown produced several studies of African-American literature: *Outline for the Study of the Poetry of American Negroes* (1931), *The Negro in American Fiction* (1937), and *Negro Poetry and Drama* (1937). With Arthur P. Davis and Ulysses Lee, he edited *The Negro Caravan* (1941). Brown also published numerous scholarly pieces in leading journals on subjects relating to African-American culture and literature.

Achievements

Sterling Brown is considered an important transitional figure between the Harlem Renaissance era and the period immediately following the Depression. Brown's fame is based not only on his poetry but also on his achievements as a critic, folklorist, scholar, and university teacher. As an acknowledged authority on African-American culture, Brown served on many committees and boards and participated in numerous scholarly and research activities. Among these were the Carnegie Myrdal Study, the American Folklore Society, the Institute of Jazz Studies, the editorial board of *The Crisis*, the Federal Writers' Project, and the Committee on Negro Studies of the American Council of Learned Societies.

Brown's poems and critical essays have been anthologized widely, and he was a memorable reader of his own poetry, especially on such recordings as *The Anthology of Negro Poets* (Folkways) and *A Hand's on the Gate*. He cowrote an article with Rayford Logan on the American Negro for *Encyclopaedia Britannica*. Brown was a Guggenheim Fellow (1937-1938) and a Julius Rosenwald Fellow (1942). He was an eminent faculty member at Howard University in Washington, D.C., from 1929 to 1969.

Biography

Born into an educated, middle-class African-American family, Sterling Allen Brown was the last of six children and the only son of Adelaide Allen Brown and the Reverend Sterling Nelson Brown. His father had taught in the School of Religion at Howard University since 1892, and the year Brown was born, his father also became the pastor of Lincoln Temple Congregational Church. The person who encouraged Brown's literary career and admiration for the cultural heritage of African-Americans, however, was his mother, who had been born and reared in Tennessee and graduated from Fisk University. Brown also grew up listening to tales of his father's childhood in Tennessee, as well as to accounts of his father's friendships with noted leaders such as Frederick Douglass, Blanche K. Bruce, and Booker T. Washington.

Brown attended public schools in Washington, D.C., and was graduated from the well-known Dunbar High School, noted for its distinguished teachers and alumni; among the latter were many of the nation's outstanding black professionals. Brown's teachers at Dunbar included literary artists such as Angelina Weld Grimke and Jessie Redmon Fauset. Moreover, Brown grew up on the campus of Howard University, where there were many outstanding African-American scholars, such as historian Kelly Miller and critic and philosopher Alain Locke.

Brown received his A.B. in 1922 from Williams College (Phi Beta Kappa) and his M.A. in 1923 from Harvard University. Although he pursued further graduate study in English at Harvard, he never worked toward a doctorate degree; however, Howard University, the University of Massachusetts, Northwestern University, Williams College, Boston University, Brown University, Lewis and Clark College, Lincoln University (Pennsylvania), and the University of Pennsylvania eventually granted him honorary doctorates. In September, 1927, he was married to Daisy Turnbull, who shared with him an enthusiasm for people, a sense of humor, and a rejection of pretentious behavior; she was also one of her husband's sharpest critics. She inspired Brown's poems "Long Track Blues" and "Against that Day." Daisy Turnbull Brown died in 1979. The Browns had one adopted child, John L. Dennis.

In 1927, "When de Saints Go Ma'ching Home" won first prize in an *Opportunity* writing contest. From 1926 to 1929, several of the poems that Brown later published in *Southern Road* were printed in *Crisis, Opportunity, Contempo*, and *Ebony and Topaz*. His early work is often identified with the outpouring of black writers during the New Negro Movement, for he shared with those artists (Claude McKay, Countee Cullen, Jean Toomer, and Langston Hughes) a deep concern for a franker self-revelation and a respect for the folk traditions of his people; however, Brown's writings did not reflect the alien-and-exile theme so popular with the writers of the Renaissance.

Brown's teaching career took him to Virginia Seminary and College, Lincoln University (Missouri), and Fisk University. He began teaching at Howard University in 1929 and remained there until his retirement in 1969. He was also a visiting professor at Atlanta University, New York University, Vassar College, the University of Minnesota, the New School, and the University of Illinois (Chicago Circle). Several years after coming to Howard University, Brown became an editor with the Works Progress Administration's Federal Writers Project. Along with a small editorial staff, he coordinated the Federal Writers Project studies by and about blacks. Beginning in 1932,

Brown supervised an extensive collection of narratives by former slaves and initiated special projects such as *The Negro in Virginia* (1940), which became the model for other studies. His most enduring contribution to the project was an essay, "The Negro in Washington," which was published in the guidebook *Washington: City and Capital* (1937).

Brown's first fifteen years at Howard were most productive. During this period (1929-1945), he contributed poetry as well as reviews and essays on the American theater, folk expressions, oral history, social customs, music, and athletics to *The New Republic*, *The Journal of Negro Education*, *Phylon*, *Crisis*, *Opportunity*, and other journals. His most outstanding essay, "Negro Characters As Seen by White Authors," which appeared in *The Journal of Negro Education* in 1933, brought attention to the widespread misrepresentation of black characters and life in American literature. Only after Brown's retirement from Howard in 1969 did he begin reading his poems regularly there. This long neglect has been attributed to certain conservative faculty members' reluctance to appreciate a fellow professor whose interests were in blues and jazz. Brown was widely known as a raconteur. Throughout his career as a writer, he challenged fellow African-American writers to choose their subject matter without regard to external pressures and to avoid the error of "timidity." He was a mentor who influenced the black poetry movement of the 1960's and 1970's, and poets such as Margaret Walker, Gwendolyn Brooks, Langston Hughes, and Arna Bontemps, along with critics such as Addison Gayle and Houston Baker, learned from him.

In the five years before his retirement, Brown began to exhibit stress caused by what he perceived to be years of critical and professional neglect as well as unachieved goals. Inclined toward periods of deep depression, he was occasionally hospitalized in his later years. He died in Takoma Park, Maryland, on January 13, 1989.

Analysis

The poetry of Sterling Brown is imbued with the folk spirit and culture of African-Americans. For Brown there was no wide abyss between his poetry and the spirit inherent in slave poetry; indeed, his works evidence a continuity of racial spirit from the slave experience to the African-American present and reflect his deep understanding of the multitudinous aspects of the African-American personality and soul.

The setting for Brown's poetry is primarily the South, through which he traveled to listen to the folktales, songs, wisdom, sorrows, and frustrations of his people, and where the blues and ballads were nurtured. Brown respected traditional folk forms and employed them in the construction of his own poems; thus he may be called "the poet of the soul of his people."

Brown's first published collection of poems, *Southern Road*, was critically acclaimed by his peers and colleagues James Weldon Johnson and Alain

Locke, because of its rendering of the living speech of the African-American, its use of the raw material of folk poetry, and its poetic portrayal of African-American folk life and thought. Later critics such as Arthur P. Davis, Jean Wagner, and Houston Baker have continued to praise his poetry for its creative and vital use of folk motifs. Some of the characters in Brown's poetry, such as Ma Rainey, Big Boy Davis, and Mrs. Bibby, are based on real people. Other characters, such as Maumee Ruth, Sporting Beasley, and Sam Smiley seem real because of Brown's dramatic and narrative talent. He is also highly skilled in the use of poetic techniques such as the refrain, alliteration, and onomatopoeia, and he employs several stanzaic forms with facility. Brown's extraordinary gift for re-creating the nuances of folk speech and idiom adds vitality and authenticity to his verse.

Brown is successful in drawing upon rich folk expressions to vitalize the speech of his characters through the cadences of Southern speech. Though his poems cannot simply be called "dialect poetry," Brown does imitate Southern African-American speech, using variant spellings and apostrophes to mark dropped consonants. He uses grunts and onomatopoeiac sounds to give a natural rhythm to the speech of his characters. These techniques are readily seen in a poem that dramatizes the poignant story of a "po los boy" on a chain gang. This poem follows the traditional folk form of the work song to convey the convict's personal tragedy.

Brown's work may be classed as protest poetry influenced by poets such as Carl Sandburg and Robert Frost; he is able to draw upon the entire canon of English and American poetry as well as African-American folk material. Thus he is fluent in the use of the sonnet form, stanzaic forms, free-verse forms, and ballad and blues forms.

In *Southern Road*, several themes express the essence of the Southern African-American's folk spirit and culture. Recurring themes and subjects in Brown's poetry include endurance, tragedy, and survival. The theme of endurance is best illustrated in one of his most anthologized poems, "Strong Men," which tells the story of the unjust treatment of black men and women from the slave ship, to the tenant farm, and finally to the black ghetto. The refrain of "Strong Men" uses rhythmic beats, relentlessly repeating an affirmation of the black people's ability and determination to keep pressing onward, toward freedom and justice. The central image comes from a line of a Carl Sandburg poem, "The strong men keep comin on." In "Strong Men," Brown praises the indomitable spirit of African-Americans in the face of racist exploitation. With its assertive tone, the rhythm of this poem suggests a martial song.

Some of the endurance poems express a stoic, fatalistic acceptance of the tragic fate of the African-American, as can be seen in "Old Man Buzzard," "Memphis Blues," and "Riverbank Blues." Another important aspect of the endurance theme as portrayed by Brown is the poetic characters' courage when they are confronted with tragedy and injustice. In the poem "Strange Legacies," the speaker gives thanks to the legendary Jack Johnson and John Henry for their demonstration of courage.

Brown's poems reflect his understanding of the often tragic destinies of African-Americans in the United States. No poet before Brown had created such a comprehensive poetic dramatization of the lives of black men and women in America. Brown depicts black men and women as alone and power-less, struggling nevertheless to confront an environment that is hostile and unjust. In this tragic environment, African-American struggles against the schemes of racist whites are seen in "The Last Ride of Wild Bill," pub-lished in 1975 as the title poem of a collection. A black man falls victim to the hysteria of a lynch mob in "Frankie and Johnnie," a poem that takes up a familiar folktale and twists it to reflect a personal tragedy that occurs as a result of an interracial relationship. Brown emphasizes that in this story the only tragic victim is the black man. The retarded white girl, Frankie, reports her sexual experience with the black man, Johnnie, to her father and suc-ceeds in getting her black lover killed; she laughs uproariously during the lynching. "Southern Cop" narrates the mindless killing of a black man who is the victim of the panic of a rookie police officer.

Yet Brown's poems show black people not only as victims of whites but also as victims of the whole environment that surrounds them, including nat-ural forces of flood and fire as well as social evils such as poverty and igno-rance. Rural blacks' vulnerability to natural disasters is revealed in "Old King Cotton," "New St. Louis Blues," and "Foreclosure." In these poems, if a tornado does not come, the Mississippi River rises and takes the peas-ant's arable land and his few animals, and even traitorously kills his children by night. These poems portray despairing people who are capable only of futile questions in the face of an implacable and pitiless nature. The central character of "Low Down" is sunk in poverty and loneliness. His wife has left and his son is in prison; he is convinced that bad luck is his fate and that in the workings of life someone has loaded the dice against him. In "Johnny Thomas," the title character is the victim of poverty, abuse by his parents and society, and ignorance. (He attempts to enroll in a one-room school, but the teacher throws him out.) Johnny ends up on a chain gang, where he is killed. The poem that most strongly expresses African-American despair of the entire race is "Southern Road," a convict song marked by a rhythmic, staccato beat and by a blues line punctuated by the convict's groan-ing over his accursed fate:

> My ole man died—hunh—
> Cussin' me;
> Old lady rocks, bebby,
> huh misery.

The African-American's ability to survive in a hostile world by mustering humor, religious faith, and the expectation of a utopian afterlife is portrayed in poems depicting the comical adventures of Slim Greer and in one of Brown's popular poems, "Sister Lou." The series of Slim Greer poems, "Slim Greer," "Slim Lands a Job," "Slim in Atlanta," and "Slim in Hell," reveal Brown's knowledge of the life of the ordinary black people and his ability to laugh at the weaknesses and foolishness of blacks and whites alike. With their rich exaggerations, these poems fall into the tall tale tradition of folk stories. They show Slim in Arkansas passing for white although he is quite dark, or Slim in Atlanta laughing in a "telefoam booth" because of a law that keeps blacks from laughing in the open. In "Slim Lands a Job," the poet mocks the ridiculous demands that Southern employers make on their black employees. Slim applies for a job in a restaurant. The owner is complaining about the laziness of his black employees when a black waiter enters the room carrying a tray on his head, trays in each hand, silver in his mouth, and soup plates in his vest, while simultaneously pulling a red wagon filled with other paraphernalia. When the owner points to this waiter as one who is lazy, Slim makes a quick exit. In "Slim in Hell," Slim discovers that Hell and the South are very much alike; when he reports this discovery to Saint Peter, the saint reprimands him, asking where he thought Hell was if not the South.

In "Sister Lou," one of his well-known poems, Brown depicts the simple religious faith that keeps some blacks going. After recounting all the sorrows in Sister Lou's life, the poem pictures Heaven as a place where Sister Lou will have a chance to allow others to carry her packages, to speak personally to God without fear, to rest, and most of all to take her time. In "Cabaret," however, Brown shows the everyday reality that belies the promises God made to his people: the black folk huddle, mute and forlorn, in Mississippi, unable to understand why the Good Lord treats them this way. Moreover, in poems such as "Maumee Ruth," religion is seen as an opium that feeds people's illusions. Maumee Ruth lies on her deathbed, ignorant of the depraved life led by her son and daughter in the city, and needing the religious lies preached to her in order to attain a peaceful death.

Sterling Brown's poems embrace themes of suffering, oppression, and tragedy yet always celebrate the vision and beauty of African-American people and culture. One such deeply moving piece is "Remembering Nat Turner," a poem in which the speaker visits the scene of Turner's slave rebellion, only to hear an elderly white woman's garbled recollections of the event; moreover, the marker intended to call attention to Turner's heroic exploits, a rotting signpost, has been used by black tenants for kindling. A stoic fatalism can be seen in the poem "Memphis Blues," which nevertheless praises the ability of African-Americans to survive in a hostile environment because of their courage and willingness to start over when all seems lost: "Guess we'll give it one more try." In the words of Sterling Brown, "The strong men keep a-comin' on/ Gittin' stronger. . . . "

Betty Taylor-Thompson

Other major works

NONFICTION: *Outline for the Study of the Poetry of American Negroes*, 1931; *The Negro in American Fiction*, 1937; *Negro Poetry and Drama*, 1937; *The Negro Caravan*, 1941 (edited, with Arthur P. Davis and Ulysses Lee).

Bibliography

Davis, Arthur P. "Sterling Brown." In *From the Dark Tower: Afro-American Writers, 1900-1960*. Washington, D.C.: Howard University Press, 1982. A comprehensive study by the dean of African-American critics, who knew Brown personally and taught with him at Howard on African-American writers during the New Negro Renaissance and through the 1950's. The essays on individual writers are supplemented by ample introductory material, and there is also an extensive bibliography, listed by author.

Ekate, Genevieve. "Sterling Brown: A Living Legend." *New Directions: The Howard University Magazine* 1 (Winter, 1974): 5-11. A tribute to the life and works of Sterling Brown in a magazine published by the university where he taught for forty years. This article analyzes Brown's literary influence on younger poets and assesses his importance in the African-American literary canon.

Gabbin, Joanne V. "Sterling Brown." In *Dictionary of Literary Biography*, vol. 50, edited by Trudier Harris and Thadious Davis. Detroit: Gale Research, 1987. An evaluative reference study of the life and literary achievements of Brown, with a list of all of his writings and bibliography of secondary sources.

Redding, Saunders. *To Make a Poet Black*. Chapel Hill: University of North Carolina Press, 1939. This pioneering study gives an effective overview of the intellectual and literary influences and processes involved in the development of African-American poets. Although it includes only a few pages on Brown himself, it is essential background reading in African-American poetics.

Wagner, Jean. "Sterling Brown." In *Black Poets of the United States, from Paul Laurence Dunbar to Langston Hughes*. Urbana: University of Illinois Press, 1973. A comprehensive and insightful study of the poetry of Brown, covering the subjects, themes, and nuances of his poetry. Wagner's writing on Brown is warm and appreciative.

ELIZABETH BARRETT BROWNING

Born: Durham, England; March 6, 1806
Died: Florence, Italy; June 29, 1861

Principal poetry

The Battle of Marathon, 1820; *An Essay on Mind, with Other Poems*, 1826; *The Seraphim and Other Poems*, 1838; *Poems, by Elizabeth Barrett Barrett*, 1844; *Poems*, 1850 (including *Sonnets from the Portuguese*); *Casa Guidi Windows*, 1851; *Aurora Leigh*, 1856; *Poems Before Congress*, 1860; *Last Poems*, 1862.

Other literary forms

Elizabeth Barrett Browning was an accomplished Greek scholar, and from her translations she learned a great deal of her own prosody. In 1833, she published a weak translation of Aeschylus' *Prometheus Bound* (date undetermined). In 1850, she included in her collected poems an entirely new and substantially improved version of the same play. "The Daughters of Pandarus," a selection from the *Odyssey* (c. 800 B.C.), was translated for Anna Jameson's *Memoirs and Essays Illustrative of Art, Literature, and Social Morals* in 1846. She modernized selections from *The Canterbury Tales* (1387-1400) for R. H. Horne's edition of Geoffrey Chaucer in 1841. She submitted occasional translations to periodicals, such as three hymns of Gregory Nazianzen which appeared in the *Athenaeum*, January 8, 1842. Mrs. Browning also published a modest amount of prose criticism. Four articles on Greek Christian poets appeared anonymously in the *Athenaeum* during 1842. For the same journal, she published five articles (all in 1842) reviewing an anthology of English verse entitled *The Book of the Poets* (1842). Later in the same year, she reviewed a new edition of William Wordsworth. In 1843, she reviewed R. H. Horne's *Orion: An Epic Poem in Three Books* (1843) for the *Athenaeum*, and then she gave up literary criticism in order to devote more time to her poetry.

Achievements

Mrs. Browning's principal biographer, Gardner Taplin, believes that "It is the quality of her life even more than her artistic achievements which will live" (*The Life of Elizabeth Barrett Browning*, 1957). The reasons for this fact, he believes, are to be found "in her fulfillment as [a woman], in her courageous and impassioned protests against injustice to individuals and subject peoples, and in her broad, generous, idealistic, Christian point of view." Literary critics since her time have insisted upon thinking of Mrs. Browning as a great woman poet, or as the Sappho of the age, or as the first woman to write a sustained sequence of sonnets. Her husband thought of her simply as having written the finest sonnets since William Shakespeare. The headnote to "Seraphim" indicates specifically that she invited comparison with Aeschylus. "A Drama of Exile" is a continuation of the Adamic drama just beyond the events described by John Milton and clearly invites comparison with him. Her sonnets can be compared with those of Petrarch, Shakespeare, Milton, and William Wordsworth. Whether she meets the measure of these models is problematical in some cases, doubtful in others. Still, her aim is consistently high and her achievement is historically substantial. She gave a strong voice to the democratic revolution of the nineteenth century; she was a vigorous antagonist of those she thought were the enemies of children, of the world's dispossessed, and of popular government.

Biography

In 1861, Elizabeth Barrett Browning died in her husband's arms in a rented apartment (unfurnished for the sake of economy). She had been born in one of the twenty marbled bedrooms of her father's estate, Coxhoe Hall. Mr. Barrett, her father, had inherited a substantial fortune and the promise of remunerative properties from his family in Jamaica. When Elizabeth was three years old, the family moved to a still larger home, Hope End, in Herefordshire. This was to be her home until the abolition of slavery brought about sharp retrenchments in the Barrett family's affairs in 1832. After three years at Sidmouth, on the channel coasts, the family moved to London. Elizabeth was twenty-nine. Her family's congregational Protestantism and its strong support for the Reform Bill of 1832 had already helped to establish the intellectual landmarks of her poetry—Christian idealism and a sharp social conscience. In London, as her weak lungs became a source of chronic anxiety, the dark and reclusive habits which were to lend a fearful realism to Elizabeth Barrett's ideals became fixed in her mode of life.

Such anxiety found its consolations in a meditative piety which produced an increasingly intense inwardness in the poet. This fact partly explains why her poems are so commonly reflective, and so rarely narrative or dramatic. Eventually, she even gave up attending chapel services. In 1837, her lungs were racked by a persistent cough. In 1838, she left London for Torquay, hoping the sea air would afford her some relief. When her brother Edward ("Bro") had concluded his visit there and planned to return to London, Elizabeth pleaded with him to stay. He did so, but in the summer of 1840, as he was boating with friends, a sudden squall capsized the boat; and Bro was drowned. Elizabeth, who had been using laudanum fairly steadily since arriving in Torquay, almost lost her mind from guilt and distress. Macabre visions came to her and prompted in her a sharply balanced ambivalence between a wish to live and a wish to die.

Elizabeth returned to the family home at 50 Wimpole Street in London, more nervous and withdrawn than ever. She rarely descended the stairs, and in the darkened room came to depend ever more heavily on the morphine, "my amreeta, my elixir," which dulled her physical and spiritual pains. She called her room a "hermitage," a "convent," a "prison." The heavy curtains were always drawn. After her marriage, the images of her poems became less abstract and more concrete as she came to participate afresh in the parade of life's affairs. For readers of her poetry, the Casa Guidi windows of later years seem dramatically open as the colorful banners and the sounds of singing pass by.

In January of 1845, Robert Browning, then an obscure poet, wrote to thank Elizabeth for praising him in a poem she had recently published. She replied to the letter but was not anxious to meet him. She had already declined twice to receive calls from the venerable Wordsworth, whom she had met earlier. She did receive Browning several months later, however, and their famous courtship began. Both parties claimed that they had never been in love before, yet Elizabeth did have a history of strong attachments to men. When she had lived at Hope End, her informal tutor in Greek, H. S. Boyd, had become so confidential with her that quarrels with his wife resulted over the time spent with Elizabeth. At Sidmouth, she had formed a friendship with George Hunter, a minister, whose wife was allegedly mad. Years later, during Browning's courtship, Hunter even followed him once to Elizabeth's room, where an unseemly encounter took place. Browning, on the other hand, characteristically formed strong attachments to women—the Flowers sisters, Fanny Haworth, Julia Wedgwood. Still, for these two idealists, love was something quite particular, not a vague sentiment, and their claim seems authentic enough.

The principal obstacle to their courtship was Elizabeth's father. Strong-willed, pietistic, politically liberal, Edward Moulton Barrett saw Robert Browning as a footloose adventurer with a barely supportable claim to being a sometime-poet. Browning had no reliable means of support, and Mr. Barrett was certain that if the two were married Browning would merely live off Elizabeth's ample but not boundless fortune.

On September 12, 1846, while her family was away, Elizabeth, nearly fainting with fear, made her way to Saint Marylebone Parish Church. Robert met her there, and they were married. It was the first time he had seen her away from Wimpole Street. She returned home for one week and then slipped out of the house to begin the long journey to Italy with her husband. She never saw her father again. He wrote her a cruelly condemnatory letter, disinherited her, and sent her books out of the house to be stored (the bills to go to Elizabeth). She was forty years old, a poet widely respected in England and America.

The Brownings' most enduring home in Italy was at Florence in the Casa Guidi, a fifteenth century palace located very near the palace of the Grand Duke of Tuscany. Although Mrs. Browning's health was a constant concern to them, it is nevertheless clear that in Italy she recovered something of the vitality of her youth. She lived quietly with her husband, but enjoyed occasional walks to the bridges of the Arno and trips to the local churches, which were filled with incomparable treasures of art. She entertained guests more readily than she had in London and was able to accept the praise which great figures of the world brought to her doorstep in recognition of her growing fame.

In 1846, Cardinal Giovanni Masoni-Ferretti was elected Pope Pius IX. He immediately freed thousands of political prisoners, provoking the anger of the Austrian government. Disturbances broke out in Florence. The Grand Duke granted the people of Tuscany a constitution. The ecstatic populace of Florence marched to the Ducal Palace—right beneath the Casa Guidi windows. Later, however, when it appeared that Austria would intervene, the Pope refused to sanction a war between two Catholic countries, and the hopes of Italian nationalists were curtailed. Riots broke out; the liberals saw their near goals slipping away—and, in 1851, Elizabeth published *Casa Guidi Windows*, a reflection on these events.

Elizabeth's health was in fact sufficiently improved that on March 9, 1849, she was able to deliver a child—her only one—without the expected complications. Indeed, she became exhilarated and active just after the birth of her son, seeming much stronger than when she first married.

During the last ten years of her life, Mrs. Browning traveled extensively between Venice, Paris, and England. She found England, however, a somewhat alien place, more unyielding in manner than the Continent. When she was in London, she wrote seeking a reconciliation with her father, asking him at least to see her child. In reply, she received two packets containing the letters she had written home in the years since her marriage—all unread.

At the close of 1856, back in Italy, Mrs. Browning published a "novel in verse," *Aurora Leigh*. Critics gave the book a somewhat ungenerous reception, but the public bought out issue after issue. It was a genuine best-seller. She was by now a true celebrity.

One volume of poems remained to her. In many ways it was her most controversial. *Poems Before Congress* is hardly a book, more nearly a pamphlet of poems. In it she praises Louis Napoleon, who had raised the fears of England again—Napoleon *redivivus*. English friends alleged that Mrs. Browning was politically unsophisticated for supporting the French. Mrs. Browning replied, however, that this Napoleon would pry Italy loose from Austrian fingers; thus, her refrain is the same—Italian nationalism. The freedom of her adopted land would not be abandoned just because it caused fears at home. In the same spirit with which she had opposed slavery when abolition meant the loss of her family's fortune, she now opposed colonialist friends. Some in her own day said that Mrs. Browning was politically naïve; but no one has ever denied the magnanimity of her love for humankind.

As the Italian national movement gained strength, Giuseppe Mazzini, Giuseppe Garibaldi, and the Conte di Cavour all unified great territorial patches of the peninsula; but Mrs. Browning's strength waned. She could no longer keep up with her husband's vitality. She languished under the long struggle with her weak lungs. On a June night in 1861, protesting the fuss made over her, she lay down to sleep. Later she roused and, struggling to cough, relaxed into death.

Analysis

Elizabeth Barrett Browning did not think it a kindness when critics praised her as a "woman poet." She would think it much closer to essentials if she were praised instead as a Christian poet. An evangelical of an old Victorian strain, she prized learning, cultivated Greek as the language of the Christian revelation, studied the work of the church fathers, and brought a fine intellectual vigor to the manifestly Christian ethos which shapes her work.

Like her husband, Mrs. Browning suffered somewhat at the close of the nineteenth century from the uncritical applause of readers who praised the religious thought in her work merely as religious thought. A century after her death—and again like her husband—Mrs. Browning began to enjoy the approbation of more vigorous critics who called attention to an element of intellectual toughness in her work which earlier critics had ignored. Now it is widely agreed that her poetry constitutes a coherent working out of evangelical principles into a set of conclusions which bear on the most pressing issues of modern times: the progress of liberal democracy, the role of militant nationalism, the ambivalences of the "woman question," and the task of the poet in a world without decisive voices.

In each case, the resolution she works toward is a further realization of the evangelical principle of the priesthood of persons. In many evangelical thinkers, a contradiction appears at this point: the antinomian doctrine of the depravity of man seems to contravene the doctrine of the high efficacy of individual thought; evangelicalism has, therefore, often encouraged a strong anti-intellectual bias among its followers. Since redemption is a matter of divine grace extended to childlike faith, there is no great need for secular learning. Mrs. Browning, however, worked out a reconciliation of the dilemma: fallen men can govern themselves well by a system of checks and balances which allows the many (because it is in their interest to do so) to restrain the venality of the powerful few. This reconciliation of the evangelical paradox allowed Mrs. Browning not only to affirm the great egalitarian movements of her day, but also to believe that in them history was making "progress" on an enormous, though not continuous, scale. As a result, the poet is able to maintain a rather rigorous evangelicalism which is progressive, yet is not so facile and glibly optimistic as her early readers sometimes supposed. If it is her evangelicalism which endeared her to her own age, it is her wry, even grim sense of the role which personal failures must play in any realistic expectation of progress which has interested more recent critics.

The evolution of the ideas discussed above can be traced from Mrs. Browning's first serious volume, *The Seraphim and Other Poems*, to her *Last Poems*. The title poem of the first volume is an attempt to transform the story of Jesus' crucifixion into a classical tragedy. She had just finished translating Aeschylus' *Prometheus Bound* and was determined to make of Christ a hero equal in tragic significance to Prometheus. Two angels descend from heaven, attending the death of Christ. The entire perspective given to the reader is through the eyes of these two angels. The poem fails because readers never see its tragic hero; they only hear from afar three among Christ's last sayings. Thus, Jesus never appears in the poem as a dramatic figure. It is possible, of course, that Mrs. Browning was reluctant to bring Christ on stage and put fictitious words in his mouth. It seems hopeless, then, to expect that the hero will evoke the tragic empathies which Prometheus does; thus, her poem is not a genuinely tragic drama.

In her second major volume, *Poems, by Elizabeth Barrett Barrett*, Mrs. Browning makes two important advances. The first is that her leading poem, "A Drama of Exile," is no longer a mere account of events. Rather, there is more invention and conflict than in earlier poems: outside the garden, surrounded by a sinister-seeming nature, Eve meets Lucifer for the first time since her fall. On this occasion she rejects him. Then, in a mystical vision, Adam and Eve see and hear the omnipotent Christ rebuking the taunting spirits of fallen nature and the pride of the triumphant Lucifer. Eve now forgives Lucifer and Christ forgives Eve. Here, the poet ventures a dramatic representation of her views with a series of invented situations which constitute a small episode in her effort to build a poetically Christian mythology.

The second advance of this volume over her previous one is technical. It is at this point in her career that Mrs. Browning begins to experiment with the sonnet. The volume contains twenty-eight sonnets on various subjects. All are Italian in form (divided between an octet and a sestet), and in all cases the first eight lines rhyme abba abba. In the last six lines, however, Mrs. Browning uses two different patterns. Some of the poems end with a cdcdcd pattern. Others end cdecde. The profit to the poet is that her attempts with the sonnet force on her a verbal economy which is more rigorous than that in her earlier volumes. Petrarch, for example, brought this Italian form to its pitch of perfection, allowing himself the five rhyme values of abcd and e (two rhyme values fewer than William Shakespeare uses); Mrs. Browning occasionally restricts herself to four rhyme values in a single sonnet—abcd. This practice imposes upon her vocabulary even stricter limits than those imposed by either the Petrarchan or the Shakespearean form. Furthermore, the sonnets—some about grief, tears, and work, with two about George Sand—force her to be less diffuse. They force her to find the concrete image which will quickly communicate a complex feeling, rather than simply talking the feeling out as she does earlier: "Experience, like a pale musician, holds a dulcimer of patience in his hand. . . ." Her religious sentiments also are forced into sharper images: "pale-cheeked martyrs smiling to a sword."

It is also in *Poems, by Elizabeth Barrett Barrett* that she includes the romance "Lady Geraldine's Courtship," which was to have significant repercussions for her. It is in this poem that she praises Robert Browning—eliciting his first letter to her—and it is here that she first attempts a theme which will not be fully realized until *Aurora Leigh*: that romance is plausible but handicapped in an unromantic (that is, an industrial, mercantile) age.

The last poem in the volume of 1844, though brief, is an important one in the poet's canon. "The Dead Pan" consists of thirty-nine stanzas, each containing six lines of iambic tetrameters (which do occasionally fall into an unheroic jog-trot), together with a seventh line of four syllables acting as a refrain. The poem produces just the image necessary to give Mrs. Browning's religious thought the freshness, clarity, and invention necessary if she is to avoid mere clichés of faith in the search for an authenticating power in her poems. The subject of the poem is the ancient claim made by Plutarch (in *De Oraculorum Defectu*) that at the very hour of Christ's crucifixion a supernatural cry went out across the sea, "Great Pan is dead," and that from that moment the pagan oracles lost their vision and power. In the poem, Mrs. Browning utters a long roll call of the pagan deities, and names them to witness that the prophetic power of an old world, mythopoeic and visionary, personified in the spirits of place—of forest, stream, and grotto—has been subsumed by a Christianity which is the new crown triumphant to a faded, classical past.

The poem is also a challenge to the skepticism and materialism of the poet's own age. The Christian religion has subsumed the ancient gifts of mystery and vision and has sanctified them by a revelation which marks them as being true, and by an ethic which adds to them the imperative to love. For Mrs. Browning, the oracular voice of the modern world is heard in poetry. Some nineteenth century thinkers believed that, with the death of the mythopoeic consciousness, men had entered an age of rational secularism from which there could be no historical return. Matthew Arnold was such a thinker. For him, the loss of mythopoeic sensibility implied the loss of tragic sensibility. Against this sort of plaintive skepticism Mrs. Browning raised her protest. The Christian narrative constitutes the mythos of modern times, and the oracular voice of poetry constantly reinvigorates this mythology. The creativity and the virtuoso invention of Christian poets proves the vitality of the myths from which they draw, to which they add their stories and songs. Pan is dead, but the spirit—now illuminated by science—is as quick as ever.

Mrs. Browning's next collection appeared six years later, after her famous elopement to Italy. *Poems* is marked by the distinction of containing *Sonnets from the Portuguese*, which prior to this time had been available only in a small private edition. These forty-four sonnets had been completed in 1847. They are technically more sure-handed than the earlier ones. The same Italian octet is here abba, abba, but Mrs. Browning has decided unequivocally on a sestet which rhymes cdcdcd. The e rhyme has disappeared. She limits herself to four rhyme values in each sonnet. The effect is a tight, organically unified sequence of sonnets. This impression of technical unity is enhanced by the single-minded theme of the poems: "this very love which is my boast." The poet has nevertheless avoided sameness in the sonnets by avoiding clichés and by writing from her own varied experience of love. For her, love had been exhilarating and risky during the days of her engagement; it had cruelly forced on her the determination to defy her father; it had sorrowfully jux- taposed her frailty to Robert's vigor; it had pitted her will to live against her expectation of an early death. These experiences provide the images which keep her poems from being merely conventional and confessional. Through- out them all there is a grim sense of herself which tries to avoid melodramatic self-deprecation on the one hand, while expressing an honest sense of her own limits on the other. This ironic view of herself gives the poems an underlying psychological realism which holds their Romanticism in check: "What can I give thee back, O liberal/ and princely giver" (Sonnet VIII); "Accuse me not, beseech thee, that I wear/ Too calm and sad a face" (Sonnet XV); "Unlike are we, unlike, O princely heart" (Sonnet III).

In 1851, Mrs. Browning published her sustained political poem, *Casa Guidi Windows*. By this time she had found a clear political expression for her evangelical ethic, "Manhood's right divine . . . to elect and legislate." The poem is written in iambic pentameter, which is well suited to protracted discourse. To avoid a too-liberal capitulation to prosaic looseness, however, the poet uses a generalized rhyme scheme: ababbcdcdefefef, through verse paragraphs of various lengths. The interlocking triple rhymes serve as a restraint on the rhetoric of the poem, but it is not a heavy-handed check. The incidents in the poem are few; thus, the burden of success is thrown upon its ideas.

During 1847, the Brownings were living in apartments in the Guidi Palace overlooking the Piazza del Gran Duca, a public square in Florence. From her windows Mrs. Browning was witness to a number of enthusiastic demonstra- tions of popular support for an Italian nationalism aimed at severing Italy's dependence upon the Austrian hierarchy—a dependence forced upon the country in the post-Napoleonic European settlement engineered by Metter- nich. This nationalism culminated in a revolt which failed in 1848. From her windows, Mrs. Browning saw the joyful crowds agitating for national auton- omy. Part I of her poem celebrates their libertarian hopes, "*O bella libertà*." The Florence of Dante, Petrarch and Boccaccio is a political prisoner; its poets and artists are suppressed. Still, it is not merely for the sake of its heroic past that Italy deserves to be free. "We do not serve the dead—the past is past. God lives and lifts his glorious mornings up/ Before the eyes of men awake at last. . . ." It is God who has made men free. Piety is on the side of liberty. The first part of the poem is a rhetorical appeal to the Grand Duke of Florence, and especially to Pope Pius IX, to side with the people in this great controversy. The poet's evangelical suspicion of Church authority is laid aside in the hope that "authority" will do justice against Austria.

Part II of *Casa Guidi Windows* was written in 1851 after the failure of the revolution. Mrs. Browning had seen th somber faces of the defeated loitering in the square. The leaders, she believed, had failed the people. The Duke had taken "the patriot's oath," but "Why swear at all," she asks, "thou false Duke Leopold." The Pope has also vacillated: "Priests, priests—there's no such name," she protests. Her evangelical instinct was true; the Pope has failed; "All Christians! Levi's (priestly) tribe is dispossest." Her grim disappointments at the failure of Italian nationalism in Part II are balanced against the exalted hopes of Part I and are resolved into a more subdued hopefulness for the future: "We will trust God. The blank interstices/ Men take for ruins, He will build into/ With pillared marbles. . . ." Popular sovereignty will win out.

Mrs. Browning's longest poem, *Aurora Leigh*, appeared at Christmas, 1856. It is a narrative poem fulfilling her earlier wish to set a romance in an unromantic age. The ironies of such a circumstance are resolved for her when it becomes manifest to the protagonists that love is not only a "romantic" experience, but also a universal ethic. It therefore disarms the meanness of spirit, the poverty of values which the poet associated with the growing skepticism of a scientific and industrial age. The poem consists of nine books of approximately (but by no means uniformly) twelve hundred lines each, all in unrhymed iambic pentameter—blank verse. The poet had by then discovered from her own experience, as so many poets have, the suitability of blank verse for high eloquence upon serious subjects. Although this poem has a more detailed narrative framework than most of Mrs. Browning's poems, it still is characterized by long reflective passages in which she devotes intense thought to the important ideas that arise from the narrative events. From the beginning, critics have observed that her characters are not persuasive, the incidents seem improbable, and the diction is uniformly stilted. The themes discussed, however, are confronted with a directness and boldness almost unequaled among Victorian poets.

Aurora Leigh is born in Italy of an English father and an Italian mother. Orphaned early, she travels to England to be reared by her father's sister. She becomes a retiring, moderately successful poet. Her cousin Romney, who has inherited the Leigh title and fortune, is a deeply compassionate Christian socialist with a strongly activist disposition. Aurora and Romney are drawn to each other, yet they so little understand each other that there is constant friction between them. This concatenation of events and characters allows

Mrs. Browning to bring together all of the ideas she most cares about and to work them out in a single crowning achievement. The state-of-England question (the poor and the privileged), the Germanic North and the Latin South (England and Italy), the condition of women, the role of the artist in a socially conscious world, the nature of progress, nationalism, and the impact of science are among the issues finally woven into the poem. After years of circling about each other, proposed marriages to third parties, and the exhaustion of Romney's fortune on an ungrateful community of the poor, Aurora and Romney recognize that their ambivalence toward each other is actually a rigorous—that is, a not very sentimental—form of love.

The issues of the poem are resolved in the most comprehensive working out of these problems which Mrs. Browning ever undertook. Romney acknowledges that his social activism has been too doctrinaire, too manipulative; it has ignored the practical realities of human experiences. Aurora acknowledges that the ferocity of her independence has masked a deep need for intimacy. Each finds that love—as both an ethic and a sentiment—gives complexity and vitality both to the social question (Romney's problem) and to individual identity (Aurora's problem). The poet believes that this kind of love is grounded in an eternal Divine and is therefore the key to resolving the antinomies in an age of conflict—nationalists against empires, poor against rich, men against women, faith against doubt.

According to Lionel Trilling, "Behind the [nineteenth century] struggle of romanticism and rationalism lies . . . the diminution of the power of Christianity" (*Matthew Arnold*, 1939). Mrs. Browning was keenly interested in this issue, and her poetry, when viewed as an organic whole, is a substantial and single-minded effort to infuse fresh force into Christian thought by a poetic quickening of the Christian mythos, as many of her poetic fictions show. For example, in "A Drama of Exile," Christ appears to Adam and Eve in a vision, "in the midst of the Zodiac"; he rebukes the Earth Spirits who have been taunting the people for their sins. "This regent and sublime Humanity," he tells the spirits "Though fallen, exceeds you . . . by their liberty to fall."

The poet's effort to take the ancient images of Christendom and elaborate them by sheer poetic invention into a revivified myth gives her work its unity; but it also imposes upon her poems certain inherent limitations. She never quite comes to grips with the possibility that if Pan is truly dead, then her own vision lacks oracular authenticity. In "The Seraph and the Poet," however, she presses her case that the modern visionary is the poet:

> Sing, seraph with the glory
> heaven is high;
> Sing, poet with the sorrow! earth is low: The universe's inward
>   voice cry "Amen" to either song for joy and woe:
> Sing, seraph—poet,—sing on equally!

By imputing death to Pan, Mrs. Browning has imputed death to other mythologies than her own. All mythologies, however, share a common epistemology, a common access to the morning-time sense of the world and to the tragic conception of human experience. Mrs. Browning severs these ties which her mythology shares with the other great visionary images of the universe. This separation imposes upon her conception of faith a somewhat sectarian and doctrinaire limit. It means that her themes tend to be stated as issues (nationalism, poverty) rather than ideas. In her poems, there is no rigorous testing of her own first principles. Still, she is one of the great libertarians of her age, and all the disinherited of the world—children, women, slaves, poets—and all who love freedom will find in her work a brave and unequivocal voice.

L. Robert Stevens

Other major works

NONFICTION: *The Letters of Elizabeth Barrett Browning*, 1897; *The Letters of Robert Browning and Elizabeth Barrett Barrett*, 1899; *Diary by E. B. B.: The Unpublished Diary of Elizabeth Barrett Browning*, 1831-1832, 1969 (Philip Kelly and Ronald Hudson, editors).

MISCELLANEOUS: *Prometheus Bound, Translated from the Greek of Aeschylus: And Miscellaneous Poems*, 1833.

Bibliography

Dally, Peter. *Elizabeth Barrett Browning: A Psychological Portrait.* London: Macmillan, 1989. In a confident and matter-of-fact tone, Dally traces Browning's feelings about her fate, family, marriage, and literary life. Beginning with her childhood regret that the family fortune grew from the slave trade, Dally records her emotional life through childhood, courtship, marriage, and life in Italy. Contains notes, a select bibliography, and an index.

Forster, Margaret. *Elizabeth Barrett Browning: A Biography.* London: Chatto & Windus, 1988. This full-length biography of Browning expands our understanding of her childhood years through hundreds of letters uncovered since the standard works of Dorothy Hewlett (1952) and Gardner Taplin (1957). Forster uses feminist critics in her interpretation of the long poem *Aurora Leigh*, which is now considered a major work. An essential chronological study. Supplemented by thirty-three illustrations, a chronology, notes, a bibliography, and an index.

Hewlett, Dorothy. *Elizabeth Barrett Browning: A Life.* New York: Alfred A. Knopf, 1952. Intending to return Browning to the high esteem given to her in her lifetime and by Robert Browning, Hewlett adds historical and political background to her detailed study of family letters and memorabilia. Includes interesting anecdotes, poem drafts, a playbill from early family theatricals, ten illustrations, references, and an index.

Leighton, Angela. *Elizabeth Barrett Browning.* Brighton, England: Harvester Press, 1986. Part of a series entitled Key Women Writers, this valuable study uses feminist theory to revisit the most frequently anthologized poems of Browning and to explore the less well-known works. Topics include the influence of family, the male literary tradition, her sexual isolation, and political opinions. Complemented by notes, a bibliography, and an index.

Mermin, Dorothy. *Elizabeth Barrett Browning: The Origins of a New Poetry.* Chicago: University of Chicago Press, 1989. Part of a series entitled Women in Culture and Society, this essential study brings Browning out of the sentimental arena and reveals her as a poet who negotiated her way through fierce gender and class barriers. Eight chapters arranged chronologically focus on her emotional and artistic development. Contains notes, a bibliography, and an index.

Stephenson, Glennis. *Elizabeth Barrett Browning and the Poetry of Love.* Ann Arbor: University of Michigan Research Institute, 1989. The linguistic and thematic problems of a woman poet writing about love in a male-dominated poetic tradition forced Browning to invent a feminine rhetoric. Women wrote about love from within a conventional mask. In this study, Barrett Browning is shown to have rejected the mask and dramatized new possibilities in her early ballads as well as in her sonnets and longer poetic works. Includes notes, a bibliography, and an index.

Taplin, Gardner. *The Life of Elizabeth Barrett Browning.* London: John Murray, 1957. Until Margaret Forster's 1988 biography, Taplin's was the standard work on Browning. It filled a major gap in Victorian studies with a comprehensive study of letters and other sources. It is still useful. Twenty chapters give a chronological picture of the poet's early family life of wealth and comfort, her decision to elope and live in Italy, and her literary success. Contains notes, a bibliography, an index, and ten plates.

ROBERT BROWNING

Born: Camberwell, London, England; May 7, 1812
Died: Venice, Italy; December 12, 1889

Principal poetry

Pauline, 1833; *Paracelsus*, 1835; *Sordello*, 1840; *Bells and Pomegranates*, 1841-1846 (published in eight parts and containing the following works of poetry: *Dramatic Lyrics*, 1842; and *Dramatic Romances and Lyrics*, 1845); *Christmas Eve and Easter Day*, 1850; *Men and Women*, 1855 (2 volumes); *Dramatis Personae*, 1864; *The Ring and the Book*, 1868-1869 (4 volumes); *Balaustion's Adventure*, 1871; *Prince Hohenstiel-Schwangau: Saviour of Society*, 1871; *Fifine at the Fair*, 1872; *Red Cotton Nightcap Country: Or, Turf and Towers*, 1873; *Aristophanes' Apology*, 1875; *The Inn Album*, 1875; *Pacchiarotto and How He Worked in Distemper*, 1876; *The Agamemnon of Aeschylus*, 1877 (drama translation in verse); *La Saisiaz, and The Two Poets of Croisac*, 1878; *Dramatic Idyls*, 1879-1880 (in two parts); *Jocoseria*, 1883; *Ferishtah's Fancies*, 1884; *Parleyings with Certain People of Importance in Their Day*, 1887; *Poetical works*, 1888-1894 (17 volumes); *Asolando*, 1889; *Robert: The Poems*, 1981 (2 volumes).

Other literary forms

Robert Browning wrote letters copiously. Published volumes of his correspondence include *Letters of Robert Browning and Elizabeth Barrett Browning, 1845-1846* (1926, Robert B. Browning, editor, 2 volumes), as well as volumes of correspondence between Browning and Alfred Domett, Isa Blagden, and George Barrett. Baylor University holds extensive manuscript and document collections concerning Browning from which *Intimate Glimpses from Browning's Letter File: Selected from Letters in the Baylor University Browning Collection* was published in 1934. An additional collection of about four hundred *New Letters of Robert Browning* has also been published (1950, W. C. DeVane and Kenneth L. Knickerbocker, editors).

For a short time, Browning also attempted to write plays. Unfortunately, the impracticality of performing his particular dramas on stage doomed them to failure. The majority of these works can be found in the *Bells and Pomegranates* series, published between 1841 and 1846.

Achievements

Browning is, with Alfred, Lord Tennyson, one of the two leading Victorian poets. Although Browning did not invent the dramatic monologue, he expanded its possibilities for serious psychological and philosophical expression, and he will always be considered a master of the dramatic poem. Browning's best poetry appears in three volumes: *Men and Women, Dramatis Personae*, and *The Ring and the Book*. Browning typically writes as if the poem

were an utterance of a dramatic character, either a creation of his own imagination or his re-creation of some historical personage. He speaks through a
mask, or dramatic persona, so that his poems must be read as little plays, or
as scenes or fragments of larger dramas. The dramatic mask allowed him to
create in his audience a conflict between sympathy and judgment: As the
reader often judges the dramatic speaker to be evil, he nevertheless sympa-
thizes with his predicament. The dramatic monologue allows the author to
explore the thoughts and feelings of deviant psychology to an extent seldom
practiced before. On the other hand, when the author always speaks through
a character, taking on the limitations and prejudices of a dramatic figure, he
conceals his own feelings and ideas from his reader. His critics charge that
he evaded the writer's most important duty by failing to pass judgment on
his characters, and by presenting murders, villains, and whores without a
word of moral reprobation. He is accused of valuing passion for its own
sake, failing to construct his own framework of values that would allow the
reader to evaluate and judge the ethical position of his characters. Nevertheless, Browning deserves to be read as a serious innovator in poetic form; his
conception of dramatic character influenced modern fiction as well as poetry.

Biography
   Robert Browning was born in a London suburb, Camberwell, on May 7,
1812. His family could be characterized as comfortably middle-class, politically
liberal, and dissenting in religion. His father, a prosperous employee of the
Bank of England, had collected a large private library. The family was dominated to some extent by the powerful personality of Browning's mother, the
former Sarah Anna Wiedemann from Dundee, who was deeply committed
to the Congregational religion. At a time when Oxford and Cambridge were
religious institutions, admitting only Anglican students, Browning attended
the newly instituted University of London for a short time in 1828, but he did
not complete a coherent course of study. Browning was largely self-taught
and, like many autodidacts, he had difficulty appreciating how deeply learned
he was and judging what his more conventionally educated audience would
be likely to know. His poetry bristles with allusions and historical references
that require a specialist's explanation.
   As a boy, Browning showed remarkable enthusiasm for the work of Percy
Bysshe Shelley. Such an admiration is particularly surprising in the light of
their divergent beliefs. Shelley was antireligious, especially in his youth, and
was in fact expelled from his university for publishing a pamphlet on the
necessity of atheism, while Browning's mother was firmly committed to a
fundamentalist and emotional Christian belief. In any event, throughout his
life, Browning depicted churchmen in an unfavorable light in his poems—a
tendency that is perhaps understandable in a follower of Shelley, but one that
suggests considerable tension between the mother and her son over religious

matters. Shelley glorified the romantic rebel, as in his depiction of Prometheus, for example; Browning's father, on the other hand, was employed by the Bank of England, and the family comfort depended on the stability and success of that existing order. Shelley's extremely liberal ideas about politics and personal relationships must have been difficult to fit harmoniously into the boy's comfortable, religious, suburban home life.

In 1852, when Browning was forty years old, a collection of letters supposed to have been written by Shelley was published, and Browning was engaged to write the "Preface." The letters were discovered later to be spurious and the volume was withdrawn from publication, but Browning's "Preface" remains one of his most important explanations of his artistic theory. In the "Preface," Browning makes his famous distinction between "objective" and "subjective" writers, which can be imagined as the difference between the mirror and the lamp. An objective poet reflects or mirrors the outer world, making it clearer and easier to understand by writing about what takes place outside himself. The subjective poet, however, is like a lamp projecting from his inner flame a light by which the reader sees everything in a new way. Although the words "subjective" and "objective" seem to get hopelessly tangled as the argument proceeds, it appears that Browning views his dramatic characters as lamps, shedding their light on the world, allowing the reader to imagine the inner flame that produces such rays of fancy and imagination, shaping and distorting whatever they fall upon.

At the age of twenty, Browning published *Pauline*, which was to be the first step in a massive work projected to be the utterances of a series of characters distinct from the author himself. The work is in the tradition of Romantic confessional writing. John Stuart Mill wrote an unpublished review of *Pauline*, which eventually came to Browning's attention, in which he accused the poet of having a more intense and morbid self-consciousness than he had ever before seen in a sane man. These cutting words are particularly ironic coming from the author of Mill's *Autobiography* (1873), a totally self-conscious production. Nevertheless, Browning was stung by the criticism and in the future tried to hide his own identity, his personal self, ever more cleverly behind the mask of dramatic speakers. *Pauline* was followed by *Paracelsus* and *Sordello*. These three works all treat the predicament of an artist or seer at odds with his environment and his historical age. The phenomenon of alienation, estrangement from one's own culture and time, is one of Browning's repeated topics, as is the role of the artist and the artist's relationship to society at large. Betty B. Miller in *Robert Browning: A Portrait* (1953) argues that there is a close identification between Browning and the central characters in these three works, so that Paracelsus is Browning, his garden at Wurzburg is identical to Browning's garden at the family home in Camberwell, and so on.

For about ten years, from 1837 to 1847, Browning devoted much of his energy to writing stage plays. These must be considered practical failures, although *Strafford* (1837) ran for five performances on the professional stage with the famous tragedian William Charles Macready in the hero's role. Browning had difficulty in treating external action, which is necessary in a staged performance, and turned instead to internal conflicts which were invisible to his audience. Although the plays simply did not work on stage, they were the workshop for the great dramatic monologues in *Men and Women* and *Dramatis Personae*.

In 1845-1846 Browning courted the semi-invalid poet Elizabeth Barrett. They were married on September 12, 1846, and fled immediately to Italy. The popular imagination has clothed this romance in a gauze of sentimentality, so that Browning appears as a knight in shining armor rescuing his maiden from her ogre of a father. Even a cursory reading of the Browning-Barrett letters suggests that the romance was rather more complicated and contradictory. Miller's *Robert Browning: A Portrait* suggests that Browning had a need to be dominated by a woman. His mother supplied that role until her death in 1840, and then he found her surrogate in Elizabeth Barrett, who was a considerably more famous writer than he was at the time. Miller points to places where Elizabeth simply took the controlling hand in their relationship and points to the nine-year period of silence between *Men and Women* and *Dramatis Personae* as the consequence of Elizabeth's domination of Browning until her death, June 29, 1861. The truth is probably not so sinister as Miller thinks, nor so blissful as depicted in modern popular plays such as *Robert and Elizabeth*. There appear to have been areas of gross disagreement between Elizabeth and Robert that would have been difficult to reconcile in day-to-day life. For example, Elizabeth, like Browning's mother, believed in the spiritual world, while Browning distrusted those who made supernatural claims.

The publication of *The Ring and the Book*, along with the earlier *Men and Women* and *Dramatis Personae*, established Browning as one of the major writers of the nineteenth century. *The Ring and the Book* tells, from a number of sharply differing points of view, the story of a scandalous murder case. It resembles the plan of Browning's earliest work, *Pauline*, in that it represents the speech of "Brown, Smith, Jones, and Robinson," who are characters quite distinct from the author. It was a project of which Elizabeth had disapproved in her lifetime. Browning's later works became more and more cryptic and complex as he further pushed his ideas of dramatized poetry, but his fame grew rapidly, spurred by the formation of the Browning Society in London in 1881. Following his death in Venice, December 12, 1889, his body was moved to England and interred in Westminster Abbey.

Analysis

"Porphyria's Lover," published along with "Johanes Agricola" under the caption "Madhouse Cells" in *Dramatic Lyrics*, exemplifies Robert Browning's use of the dramatic monologue. Written in sixty lines of iambic quatrameter (rhymed ababb), the poem is spoken entirely by a dramatic character, much like the soliloquies in William Shakespeare's plays. Typically, the monologue can occur only at a moment of inaction, enabling the character to pause from whatever he has been doing and reflect for a moment. What he proceeds to say implies a larger framework of surrounding circumstances: the dramatic situation. Understanding the dramatic situation within a monologue necessitates reader participation in order to discover the circumstances that are only implied in the poem.

By looking closely at the text of "Porphyria's Lover," the reader learns that the speaker is a man who has just strangled his lover, Porphyria. The dead woman's head rests on his shoulder as he speaks, and he looks with approval upon the murder he has committed. The speaker relates the events of the dark, stormy evening: Alone in a cottage, he waited for his beloved Porphyria to enter. Evidently, her absence had been the result of her attendance at a "gay feast," one of the "vainer ties" which Porphyria presumably cultivated. Left alone, the speaker had become obsessed by the need for Porphyria's presence, and, when she finally entered the cottage, her lover could only think, "mine, mine, fair, perfectly pure and good." Strangling her in her own hair, he has propped her dead head on his shoulder, and so he sits as he speaks his monologue. Exultant that he has done the perfect thing, he ends his speech with the words, "And yet God has not said a word."

The dramatic monologue is always spoken by a dramatic character, creating a condition called limited narration. Everything that the reader hears is limited to what the speaker sees, thinks, and chooses to tell. Frequently, limited narration can be "unreliable," so that the reader has reason to believe that the speaker is mistaken or lying. In "Porphyria's Lover" the problem of unreliable narration occurs when the speaker says that the perfect thing to do in his situation was to strangle his beloved.

Some critics point to a poem such as this and assert that Browning's form of writing is vicious, that he evades his duty as a moral teacher by not passing judgment on his characters' actions. In reply, many scholars argue that Browning has indeed provided sufficient guidance for the reader to form a normative judgment, thus overriding the limited and defective judgment of the murderer. The careful reader of this poem will find much evidence to indict the speaker as a madman and criminal. His very mention of God in the closing line reveals an expectation of punishment. Such an expectation could only result from a subconscious admission of guilt. Thus, even the murderer in a deranged way has brought a moral judgment upon himself. Browning has developed a situation that produces a conflict in the reader between sympathy for the character and judgment of him. The beauty rather than the fault of this poem is Browning's mastery at creating such a conflict and involving the reader in its solution.

"My Last Duchess," another poem published in *Dramatic Lyrics*, exhibits many of the features discussed with reference to "Porphyria's Lover," while showing a considerable advance in artistic power and seriousness. Browning's dramatic poems fall into three categories: soliloquies, in which the persona speaks alone or *solus* on stage; monologues, in which a single speaker on stage addresses a defined dramatic audience, who must be imagined present; and epistles, monologues constructed as if they were letters written from one character to another. "My Last Duchess" is a monologue, having a speaking persona and a clearly defined dramatic audience. The dramatic situation of this poem is derived from history. The subtitle of the poem is "Ferrara," and it is likely that the persona is Browning's dramatization of Alfonso II, the fifth Duke of Ferrara. Alfonso II married Lucrezia de' Medici, daughter of Cosimo I de' Medici, Duke of Florence. The de' Medici family were newly arrived upstarts in comparison with the more ancient house of Ferrara. The Duchess of Alfonso II, Lucrezia de' Medici, died at the age of seventeen in 1561, it being said that she was poisoned. Three years later Alfonso contracted to marry Barbara, niece of the Count of Tyrol.

The dramatic situation of "My Last Duchess" probably involves Duke Alfonso II imagined as addressing an envoy from the Count of Tyrol in order to negotiate the details of his wedding with Barbara. One of the main objectives of the Duke's speech is to "soften up" his adversary in the negotiations so as to extract from him the maximum dowry and to exact the most dutiful compliance with his wishes by his future wife and in-laws. The reader must imagine the Duke walking with his guest in the Duke's art gallery while an entertainment is going on for the other guests in the lower hall of his castle. The Duke pauses before a painting covered by a curtain, asks his guest to sit, and opens the curtain to display a striking portrait of his previous wife, who is dead. While the envoy contemplates the picture of the dead former wife, the Duke explains that he was not completely happy with his last mate. She did not appreciate the value of his "nine hundred years old name" and so the Duke "gave commands" and her annoying smiles stopped completely. She stands in the portrait as if alive, and he invites the envoy to gaze on her. Then the Duke suggests that they join the party below, mentioning in passing that he is sure that the Count will give him any dowry that he desires. As they descend the stairs, the Duke points out a statue of the pagan god Neptune taming a sea horse, which recapitulates the struggle of the Duke with the envoy. The envoy has no chance of winning a contest of will with the Duke, just as the sea horse must submit to the god of the sea. The power is all in the Duke's hands.

"The Bishop Orders His Tomb at St. Praxed's Church" appeared in *Dramatic Romances*. Subtitled "Rome, 15—," it appears to refer to a real place, the church of St. Praxed near Rome, but unlike "My Last Duchess" it does not seem to refer to a particular person or historical event. One must construct a general idea of a worldly bishop in Italy in the sixteenth century on his deathbed speaking these lines. The dying man has his "nephews" or illegitimate sons, including his favorite, Anselm, at his bedside to communicate his last wishes to them. From the details of his speech, the reader learns that the sons' mother, the Bishop's mistress, was a beautiful woman, and that the Bishop had a rival for power called old Gandolf, who is buried in St. Praxed's Church. The Bishop orders his sons to build him a tomb in the church that will put Gandolf's to shame by its richness. Such a tomb will be costly to build, but the dying bishop makes a shocking revelation to the boys: There was once a fire in the church from which the Bishop saved an enormous semiprecious stone, a lump of lapis lazuli, which he hid. He now tells the boys where to find the buried treasure, provided they will put it on his funeral statue as a decoration.

The depiction of the Bishop's character is a study in hypocrisy. One expects a churchman to be humble and honest, to deny his physical desires, to abstain from sex and the gratification of worldly lusts. As his mind wanders and he nears death, this bishop appears to be just the opposite. Rather than living celibate, he has fathered these sons who stand around him and he has loved their voluptuous mother. Rather than showing generosity to his enemies, even at the moment of death he is filled with petty jealousy of old Gandolf. He has stolen the church's jewel from the conflagration. He even confuses Christianity and paganism as he describes the frieze he wants on his tomb as a mixture of erotic pagan elements and Christian scenes. Next to the depiction of the virgin martyr St. Praxed, he wants a Bacchic orgy with "one Pan ready to twitch the Nymph's last garment off."

Works such as "The Bishop Orders His Tomb at St. Praxed's Church" were influential on the novel and the short story as well as on modern poetry, for they expanded the notion of character in fiction. Character is sometimes defined as what man habitually chooses to do. A character is said to be a liar if he usually lies. Another is a brave man if he usually refuses to run from danger. Browning writes many poems about churchmen, perhaps because their ethical character is so sharply defined. The minute one sees a character dressed as a bishop, one expects that this man will habitually act in a certain way, that his actions will be loving, self-sacrificing, humble, Christian, and that he will not put his faith in the material world, but concern himself with heavenly goals. Browning puts such a character in a moment of unusual stress in which his expected role crumbles, and one sees through his public face to an inner set of unexpected feelings. At any other time in his life, the Bishop of St. Praxed's, dressed in his robes and healthy and strong, would never have revealed that he was subject to lust, greed, pride, and all the un-Christian characteristics he reveals to his sons on his deathbed. Browning has found a moment when the Bishop's public face cracks and his inner personality is revealed. The poem explores the conflict between the public role and the private personality of a man.

In addition to "The Bishop Orders His Tomb at St. Praxed's Church," Browning wrote a number of other poems about religious hypocrites, including "Bishop Blougram's Apology," published in *Men and Women*. The dramatic situation is a nineteenth century dinner party given by Blougram for a young newspaperman, who is an unbeliever. Blougram talks at length to the younger man and, perhaps a bit intoxicated by his own importance or an unusual amount of wine, confesses some things that he would not normally say in public because they do not fit the expected role of a bishop. The newspaperman Gigadibs despises Blougram because, while the Bishop is intelligent enough to know that miracles and the historically untrue parts of the Bible are mere superstition, he nevertheless publicly professes to believe in them. He must therefore be a hypocrite. Apparently Gigadibs has also accused the Bishop of profiting from his profession of belief and so achieving a comfortable and powerful position in life. Perhaps the poem refers to the Roman Catholic Cardinal Wiseman and Cardinal John Henry Newman, whose *Apologia pro Vita Sua* (1864) may be reflected in the title of Browning's poem.

Blougram's reply to Gigadibs' charges is important for an understanding of Browning's idea of characterization in fiction. At line 375 and following, Blougram suggests that Gigadibs thinks that a few intelligent people will always look at Blougram and "know me whether I believe in the last winking virgin, as I vow, and am a fool, or disbelieve in her and am a knave." Even so, Blougram maintains that these intelligent people will be those most fascinated with him because he maintains an impossibly contradictory balance:

> You see lads walk the street . . . what's to note in that? You see one lad o'erstride a chimney-stack; him you must watch—he's sure to fall, yet stands! Our interest's on the dangerous edge of things. The honest thief, the tender murderer, the superstitious atheist . . . we watch while these in equilibrium keep the giddy line midway: one step aside, they're classed and done with. I, then, keep the line. . . .

Browning's characters are people caught in impossible contradictions, frequently between their expected or usual pattern of behavior and some contrary inner impulse. The situations named by Blougram as fascinating are explored in Browning's poetry: the tender murderer is Porphyria's lover, for example. As in nearly all of Browning's dramatic poems, "Bishop Blougram's Apology" leaves the reader struggling to find a normative judgment. Is Blougram a hypocritical exploiter of religion for his own worldly benefit and therefore subject to scorn, or is he something else? Even though the concluding lines of the poem are spoken as if in the voice of Browning himself, it is still difficult to say whether one should approve of Blougram or despise him. In that impossible "equilibrium" the reader is fascinated.

Browning took the dramatic situation of the poem "Andrea del Sarto"

mainly from Giorgio Vasari's *Lives of the Painters* (1550, 1568) which includes
a discussion of the painter Andrea del Sarto, called the "faultless painter"
because of the technical perfection of his art. Andrea married a widow,
Lucrezia del Fede, in 1512 and was subsequently summoned from Florence,
Italy, to work at the court of Francis I of France at Fontainebleau. According
to Vasari's story, Francis I gave Andrea money to purchase art works in
Florence, but he misappropriated the funds and had to live in hiding because
he allowed himself to be dominated by the artful and wicked Lucrezia. A self-
portrait of Andrea and Lucrezia hung in the Pitti Palace at Florence while
the Brownings were residents in Italy. Mrs. Browning's cousin, John Kenyon,
asked Browning to send him a photograph of the painting and, so the story
goes, Browning composed and sent him this poem instead.

The poem illustrates the idea of the "magnificent failure," one of Browning's
most important concepts. In order to understand the "magnificent failure"
the reader must be aware of thinking current in the 1850's concerning the
relation of art to society. For example, John Ruskin in *The Stones of Venice*
(1851-1853) makes a distinction between slave art and free art. Slave art, such
as an Egyptian pyramid, sets up a simple design so that any slave can execute
it perfectly. Free art, such as a Gothic cathedral, engages the creative impulses
of every worker so that it is never completed and is marked by the luxuriant
variety of every worker's creation. A perfect, finished, polished work of art
signifies that the artist set his design too low, did not strive to reach beyond
the limits of his power. Perfect art is the sign of moral degeneration. Andrea's
painting is slave's work because it is perfect.

In the poem, Andrea del Sarto is speaking to his dramatic audience, and
his wife Lucrezia, who is impatient with him, wishes to go out in the evening
to join her "cousin," or lover, who is whistling for her in the street. In the
opening lines, the reader learns that Lucrezia is not kind to the painter and
that he must bribe her to stay with him a few minutes. Andrea is unhappy,
thinking how his art is not of the highest order despite all its perfection. He
never fails to make a perfect drawing because he never sets his design beyond
his ability, "but a man's reach should exceed his grasp, or what's a heaven
for?" He considers a painting by Raphael and shows how the drawing of an
arm in it is poor, but when he corrects the draftmanship, he loses all of the
"play, the insight and the stretch" of the imperfect original. He laments his
lost productive times when he worked in France and regrets that he must now
live in exile. He pathetically asks Lucrezia to be his companion so that he
can work more and give her more money. At the conclusion of the poem,
Lucrezia's "cousin" whistles for her again while Andrea, who is a faultless
painter, envies the glory of less perfect artists.

Andrea paints designs that never challenge his ability and completes perfectly all his undertakings. Ironically, this perfection in art signifies his moral
degeneration, for he is a slave to the beautiful but ignorant and unfeeling

Lucrezia and to the profit motive, so that he must paint trivial works to earn gold, which Lucrezia simply gives to her "cousin" lover. Artists such as Raphael fail in their work because they set their sights so high that they can never finish or complete their designs perfectly. Although they fail, their works are magnificent. Andrea's perfect works are merely slavish.

In the middle of the nineteenth century, there was a revival of interest in knightly romances and the so-called "matter of Britain," the ancient stories concerning King Arthur's court, evident in Tennyson's *Idylls of the King* (1859) and many other poems of the period. Frequently, the failed quest of the courtly romance was a vehicle for the idea of magnificent failure. Arthur had tried to establish a court of perfect chivalry, but he had failed in the attempt. Nevertheless, his failure was more noble than a practical compromise would have been. Each of his knights must fail in some important way, suffer humiliation and death, even as Christ did, so that the nobility of their endeavor may show forth. Browning's "Childe Roland to the Dark Tower Came" is in this tradition of the courtly failed quest and the magnificent failure.

The subtitle of the poem refers to Shakespeare's *King Lear* (1606), specifically a song by the character Edgar in Act III, Scene 4. Lear on the heath encounters Edgar disguised as a madman. Lear calls him a philosopher and takes him with his company. At the conclusion of the scene, Edgar pronounces some riddling or nonsense lines, including "Child Rowland to the dark tower came." These are apparently garbled snatches of traditional ballads. "Childe" means any untested knight, and Browning's poem constructs a nightmare quest for his untried knight, Childe Roland, who tells of his weird adventure. The poem is best considered a journey into the mind, a psychological rather than a physical quest. Childe Roland tells of his perilous journey across a wasted land in which a cripple advises him to turn into an "ominous tract" where the Dark Tower hides. As soon as he leaves the road, it vanishes. Everything in the enchanted land is sick, wounded, and in torment. Childe Roland thinks of his companions who have failed before him. He crosses a river and stumbles unaware on the "round squat turret." He imagines he sees all his dead companions ranged along the hillside overlooking the arena, yet "dauntless" he sets his horn to his lips and blows the cry, "Childe Roland to the Dark Tower Came."

Like many of Browning's poems, this work seems laden with ambiguity. There are at least three possibilities: the tower is not the true object of a knight's quest and thus Childe Roland is lost when he takes the advice of the cripple to leave the highroad, and he is punished for deviating from his proper goal; or, the tower is the true quest, but Childe Roland's discovery is that it is worthless and ugly when he finds it (therefore, his life is wasted); or, the tower is the quest and is in itself meaningless, but the dedication of Roland creates success out of failure—although the tower is "squat" and ugly, he has played his proper role and even in the face of overwhelming forces, he blows defiance, dauntless to the last.

"Childe Roland to the Dark Tower Came" invites comparison with the surrealist nightmares of Franz Kafka, and Browning's use of a wasteland as a symbol for man's alienation and his evocation of a failed courtly quest foreshadow T. S. Eliot's *The Waste Land* (1922). "Childe Roland to the Dark Tower Came" is one of Browning's most interesting works and it foreshadows developments in the modernist revolution some fifty years after its publication.

The Ring and the Book is Browning's most important poem. Written in blank verse, rhymed iambic pentameter, it appeared in four volumes between November, 1868, and February, 1869. In 1860, Browning came across in Florence a collection of old documents and letters telling the story of the murder trial of Guido Franceschini, who was executed in Rome in 1698. Browning called this volume *The Old Yellow Book*; it has been translated into English by Charles W. Hodell and was published in 1911. From the lawyers' arguments and other documents emerges a particularly sordid case of "divorce Italian style." In 1693, Count Guido Franceschini, an impoverished nobleman forty years old, from the north of Italy, married a thirteen-year-old commoner, Francesca Pompilia, in Rome. She was the daughter of Pietro and Violante Comparini. Pietro had opposed the marriage, knowing that the Count was not as wealthy as he seemed. His wife, however, was attracted by the possibility of a nobleman for a son-in-law and contrived to have the marriage take place. The Comparini family gave all their possessions as dowry to Count Guido, expecting to live in comfort on his estate. The Count, angry to find that the Comparini family was less wealthy than he imagined, harassed them until they were forced to flee from his house. They sued for the return of Pompilia's dowry on grounds that she was not their natural daughter, but a common prostitute's child whom they had adopted. Count Guido increased his cruelty to his child bride, even though she sought help from the local bishop and governor. Pompilia fled from Count Guido's castle with the dashing young priest Caponsacchi in 1697 but Count Guido apprehended the couple near Rome on April 28, 1697. They were charged with adultery; Caponsacchi was banished, and Pompilia was confined to a nunnery from which she was released on bond to bear her child, a son, at the house of the Comparini on December 18, 1697, almost exactly nine months after her flight from Guido's castle with Caponsacchi. Her son Gaetano stood to inherit the Count's name and estate. Two weeks later, Count Guido broke into the Comparini house and murdered Pietro and Violante, and left Pompilia mortally wounded. Pompilia lived four more days, long enough to accuse Count Guido of the assault. He and his companions were arrested fleeing toward his estate. The bulk of *The Old Yellow Book* presents the legal arguments in this dark case. The murders were admitted, but Count Guido claimed that he was justified as an injured husband to defend his honor. When he was found guilty, he appealed to the Pope, who refused to intervene. Count Guido was beheaded February 22, 1698, in Rome, while his accomplices were hanged. Finally, a convent brought suit to claim the estates forfeited by Pompilia's allegedly adulterous action, but a court ruled that she was innocent and gave all property to her son Gaetano.

Browning converted the material of *The Old Yellow Book* into one of the first relativistic narrative masterpieces. Some authors tell their readers what to think about their characters; others make their readers think for themselves. Browning is one of the latter, presenting his readers with questions rather than giving them answers. In twelve books, Browning tells and retells the story of Pompilia, Count Guido, and the priest Caponsacchi, through their eyes and through the eyes of their lawyers, the eyes of the Pope considering Guido's appeal, and the eyes of three factions of the vulgar population of Rome. Naturally, when Guido explains his action, he not only argues in defense of what he did, but also actually believes that he is right. In his own mind, he is blameless. Likewise, when the reader sees through the limitations and prejudices of Pompilia or of Caponsacchi, the point of view dictates what is right and what is wrong. Many readers coming to Browning's text try to penetrate the tangle of conflicting judgments and opinions presented in these twelve books, and try to say that Browning's sympathy lies with Pompilia or that the Pope speaks for the author. Yet, if there is a single, clear-cut normative judgment, why did Browning feel compelled to write the contradictory monologues that argue against it? More likely, Browning intentionally created a powerful experimental literary form, rather like the limited narration novels of Henry James. Browning's text provides a complicated stimulus, but each reader constructs in his mind his own evaluation of the relative guilt or justification of Count Guido, Pompilia, Caponsacchi, the Pope, and the Comparini family.

Stories are sometimes said to fall into two classes. There are stories such as mediocre mystery tales that cannot bear a second reading. Once the audience has heard the tale to its end, they know "who done it." All questions are solved, so that a second reading would be unnecessary and boring. On the other hand, there is a second kind of story that is so constructed that each reading only deepens the questions in the readers' minds. Every reader is drawn back to the text over and over and the third or fourth reading has as much interest as the first. In *The Ring and the Book* Browning converted a gruesome but mediocre mystery tale into a work of this second type which poses troubling questions about right and wrong, judging and pardoning. Every character evokes some spark of sympathy when allowed to speak for himself or herself. Every character seems subject to guilt when seen through hostile eyes.

The Ring and the Book illustrates Browning's concern with the infinite moment, the instant when a character can act decisively to break out of his characteristic pattern of expected behavior and do the unforeseen. The priest

Caponsacchi's flight with the Count's child-bride is an example of the dizzy equilibrium between expected social behavior and contradictory impulse. The reader asks, "How could he do it and still be a priest of God, forsaking his vows of celibacy and all his ordinary rules of conduct?" The reader can imagine what it is to be a priest and what it is to be a lover, but how can there exist such a contradictory character as a lover/priest? The same question can be posed for Pompilia, the childlike innocent yet renegade wife, who is the final winner of them all eventually when her son inherits the estate. The reader has seen many times in literature the childlike, innocent woman, and equally often has encountered the sexual sharpster, but how can these contradictory roles be balanced in a single character?

Boyd Litzinger in *Time's Revenges: Browning's Reputation as a Thinker 1889-1962* (1964) reviews the critical reception of Browning's work during the decade after his death and finds that his immense popularity was based on three chief beliefs among his readers: Browning was a defender of Christianity, although his specific beliefs were subject to considerable doubt; he was admired for an optimistic world view and his works were thought to urge man to higher and higher efforts to improve his condition; and he was considered to be a serious philosopher and man of ideas. This analysis seems seriously misguided. Browning's religious teachings are contradictory at best. His frequent comic and hostile portraits of churchmen are hard to reconcile with conventional Christian belief. His alleged optimism does not account for the gray sadness of Andrea del Sarto's world, nor the bloody trial of Count Guido, nor even the dauntless but perhaps meaningless call of Childe Roland's horn in the face of the Dark Tower. As a "philosopher," Browning seems to have a taste more for questions than for answers, and although he expands certain ideas such as the conflict of social role versus private personality, or the concept of magnificent failure, he does not develop a coherent system comparable to the philosophic poetry of John Milton.

From the perspective of the present, Browning claims a place of first importance as a protomodernist, a writer who anticipated some of the major developments in art and literature occurring at the beginning of the twentieth century. His use of the dramatic monologue anticipated and to a degree influenced the limited and unreliable narration of such masterpieces of modernism as Joseph Conrad's *Heart of Darkness* (1902) and Ford Madox Ford's *The Good Soldier* (1915). His conception of relativistic and fragmented worlds in which a character is not at home anticipated the vision of T. S. Eliot's *The Waste Land*. His sense of character defined by the conflict between social roles and internal impulses held in a sometimes unstable equilibrium was confirmed by modern psychology. Browning is most interesting when seen not as a Victorian sage but as a forerunner of modernism.

Todd K. Bender

Other major works

PLAYS: *Strafford*, 1837; *Pippa Passes*, 1841; *King Victor and King Charles*, 1842; *The Return of the Druses*, 1843; *A Blot in the 'Scutcheon*, 1843; *Colombe's Birthday*, 1844; *Luria*, 1846; *A Soul's Tragedy*, 1846 (the seven preceding titles were published in the *Bells and Pomegranates* series, 1841-1846).

NONFICTION: *Letters of Robert Browning and Elizabeth Barrett Browning, 1845-1846*, 1926 (Robert B. Browning, editor); *Intimate Glimpses from Browning's Letter File: Selected from Letters in the Baylor University Browning Collection*, 1934; *Browning's Essay on Chatterton*, 1948 (Donald A. Smalley, editor); *New Letters of Robert Browning*, 1950 (W. C. DeVane and Kenneth L. Knickerbocker, editors); *The Letters of Robert Browning and Elizabeth Barrett Browning 1845-1846*, 1969 (Elvan Kintner, editor).

MISCELLANEOUS: *The Works of Robert Browning*, 1912 (F. C. Kenyon, editor, 10 volumes); *The Complete Works of Robert Browning*, 1969-

Bibliography

Armstrong, Isobel. *Robert Browning*. Athens: Ohio University Press, 1975. This fairly simple book provides the best general introduction to the poet, his life, his cultural context, and his work. Armstrong identifies the outstanding features of the major poems and presents sound basic readings. Supplemented by a full index and a helpful bibliography.

Chesterton, G. K. *Robert Browning*. New York: Macmillan, 1903. Although somewhat dated, this medium-length book is full of perceptive insights and is one of the best overviews of the poet. Chesterton opens up the major monologues by relating them to one another and showing how they contribute to the evolution of Browning's thought. The index is helpful for cross-referencing.

Crowell, Norman B. *A Reader's Guide to Robert Browning*. Albuquerque: University of New Mexico Press, 1972. An extremely useful volume for those interested in sampling critical approaches to Browning's major dramatic monologues. Crowell summarizes the stands taken by various previous readers, raising questions and suggesting openings for further interpretations. Can also be used as a guide to basic research, but it does not cover the longer works.

DeVane, W. C. *A Browning Handbook*. Rev. ed. New York: Appleton-Century-Crofts, 1955. For two generations of literary students, this was the first reference on Browning, and it has not been superseded. Contains entries for the major phases of Browning's life and for all of his writing. Although easy to use if the student has specific topics to pursue, the focus is old-fashioned, concentrating on a biographical and a literary-historical background. Includes a thorough index.

Irvine, William, and Park Honan. *The Book, the Ring, and the Poet: A Biography of Robert Browning*. New York: McGraw-Hill, 1974. The standard academic biography of the poet, this study is thorough, meticulous, detailed, fully documented, and illustrated. Although rather heavy for beginning students, it collects more biographical information than any other source. Complemented by an index and a select bibliography.

Jack, Ian. *Browning's Major Poetry.* Oxford, England: Clarendon Press, 1973. One of the leading scholars of Victorian literature presents detailed analyses of Browning's primary works. Contains definitive, substantial accounts, deep and rewarding, but sophisticated. The critical apparatus is complete, with a solid index and a bibliography.

WILLIAM CULLEN BRYANT

Born: Cummington, Massachusetts; November 3, 1794
Died: New York, New York; June 12, 1878

Principal poetry

Poems, 1821, 1832, 1834, 1836, 1839; *The Fountain and Other Poems*, 1842; *The White-Footed Deer and Other Poems*, 1844; *Poems*, 1854; *Thirty Poems*, 1864; *Hymns*, 1864, 1869; *The Iliad of Homer*, 1870 (translation); *Poems*, 1871, 1875; *The Odyssey of Homer*, 1871-1872 (translation); *The Poetical Works of William Cullen Bryant*, 1876; *The Flood of Years*, 1878.

Other literary forms

William Cullen Bryant wrote a substantial body of prose: tales, editorials, reviews, letters, appreciations, sketches or impressions, and critical essays. In 1850, he published *Letters of a Traveller: Or, Notes of Things Seen in Europe and America*; in 1859, *Letters of a Traveller, Second Series*: and in 1869, *Letters from the East*. He reviewed the careers of a number of his contemporaries in such pieces as *A Discourse on the Life and Genius of James Fenimore Cooper* (1852) and *A Discourse on the Life and Genius of Washington Irving* (1860). In 1851, he published his *Reminiscences of the Evening Post*, and in 1873, a collection of *Orations and Addresses*. His *Lectures on Poetry*, delivered to the Athenaeum Society in 1826, was published in 1884.

Achievements

Bryant's central achievement as a man of letters was his contribution to the developing sense of a national identity. Although Bryant's verse is often indistinguishable from the eighteenth and nineteenth century English verse of his models, he begins to draw lines of contrast, first, by his choice of subject matter—prairies, violets, gentians, Indian legends—and, second, by developing a characteristic poetic voice which can be seen in retrospect to be the early stage of the development of a nationally distinctive poetry.

Bryant's participation in the formative stages of American poetry was a natural corollary to the second of his two major achievements, his career as a journalist. As the editor and part-owner of the *Evening Post* for almost fifty years, he championed liberal social and political causes which were as much a part of the newly emerging national identity as was his poetry. His vigorous support of freedom of the press, of abolition, of the Republican Party, and of John Frémont and Abraham Lincoln, are among his most notable achievements as a journalist.

Although minor in comparison with his two major achievements, Bryant's lectures on poetic theory to the Athenaeum Society in 1826 shed light on his own poetry and on some of the cultural assumptions of his period. Bryant's emphasis on "moral uplift and spiritual refinement" as the aim of poetry is balanced by his interest in native speech and natural imagery as resources to be tapped by the poet.

Biography

William Cullen Bryant was born on November 3, 1794, in Cummington, Massachusetts, to Dr. Peter and Sarah Snell Bryant. The poet enjoyed a close family life and, from an early age, benefited from the positive influences of both parents, as well as from those of his maternal grandfather, Ebenezer Snell. The latter's Calvinist influence, though muted, is evident in the language of the poetry and in the recurrent image of an angry God threatening retribution for man's sins. His mother's gentler religious influence bore directly on his precocity as a reader in general, and of the Bible in particular, at the age of four. Bryant was later to remember those conducting the religious services of his very early childhood experiences as "often poets in their extemporaneous prayers."

A counter, and as time passed more prevailing, influence was that of his liberal physician father, Dr. Peter Bryant, who encouraged the poet in his early experiments with satires, lampoons, and pastorals. Under that encouraging tutelage, Bryant published his first poem of substance, "The Embargo," in 1808, at the age of thirteen; three years later he set about translating the third book of the *Aeneid*. In 1817, Dr. Bryant took copies of several of his son's poems to his friend Willard Phillips, one of the editors of the *North American Review*. "Thanatopsis" and one other poem were published immediately in the journal's September issue. "Inscription for the Entrance to a Wood" and "To a Waterfowl" appeared subsequently.

Meanwhile, Bryant had been preparing himself for a legal career and was admitted to the bar in 1815. He began practicing law in 1816 in Great Barrington, Massachusetts. In 1825, he assumed editorship of the *New York Review*, and in 1829 he began his fifty-year career as a major journalist when he became part-owner and editor-in-chief of the New York *Evening Post*. From that position he was to champion freedom of speech, abolition, the right of workmen to strike, Frémont, the Republican Party, and Lincoln and the Union cause. When he died in 1878, the *Evening Post* continued his policies under the leadership of his son-in-law, Parke Godwin.

Although Bryant was to continue writing poetry throughout his life, most of it, and particularly those poems on which his reputation rests, was written by the early 1830's. By the middle of the century, though he was still an active and vigorous journalist, he had become something of an institution to writers such as Nathaniel Hawthorne, Herman Melville, and Oliver Wendell Holmes. Ralph Waldo Emerson included Bryant among the imagined faculty of his ideal college, because, as he noted in his Journal, "Bryant has learned where to hang his titles, namely by tying his mind to autumn woods, winter mornings, rain, brooks, mountains, evening winds, and wood-birds. . . . [He is] American."

Bryant married Frances Fairchild in 1821. They had two daughters, Fanny and Julia, who inherited the sizable estate left at his death on June 12, 1878, which resulted from a fall and head injury on May 29.

Analysis

William Cullen Bryant wrote his poetry over a fifty-year span, but the apex of his career came in the early 1830's, very close to an exact midpoint between William Wordsworth's 1800 Preface to the *Lyrical Ballads* (1798) and Walt Whitman's *Leaves of Grass* (1855). In retrospect, Bryant's poetry, especially his blank verse, can be seen in terms of a development moving from Wordsworth's theories and examples to the American model of Whitman's free verse, celebrating the self and the newly emerging national identity. At its best, Bryant's verse reflects the evolutionary dynamics of a national poetry in the making; at its worst, it is stale repetition of eighteenth century nature poetry, cast in static imitation of Wordsworthian models.

"Thanatopsis," one of Bryant's earliest successes and his most enduring one, survives as a poem rather than as an artifact because its rhythmic and syntactic fluidity has kept it readable for well over a century and a half. Blank verse has always offered the poet writing in English the best medium, short of free verse, for such fluidity, and that fact, along with the survival of the Romantic ideal of a natural or colloquial language, goes a long way toward explaining the poem's survival. Since, however, it is obvious that not all of Bryant's blank verse has been so successful, "Thanatopsis" invites a more detailed examination. The basis of its rhythmic character lies primarily in the relationship between the blank verse structure and the sentence structure. Since few of the lines are end-stopped, the syntactic rhythm is stronger than the theoretical rhythm of blank verse—that is, of five-stress, iambic lines. An examination of the great variety of sentence length relative to line length and of the accentual stress pattern of both will provide some illustrative detail for this aspect of the poem's character.

There are three thematic sections in the poem, the second beginning at line thirty-one, with "Yet not to thine . . . ," the third at line seventy-three, with "So live. . . ." The opening independent clause of section one, ending with a semicolon in line three, has all the rhetorical quality of a sentence. It and the opening sentence of section two are two-and-a-half lines long. The third section has only one sentence, running through the final nine lines of the poem. Two other very long sentences are those beginning at line eight, running over eight lines, and at line sixty-six, running over six. The two shortest sentences are at lines twenty-nine and sixty, respectively. The first of these, beginning with "The oak/ Shall send his roots abroad," has twelve syllables, two more than the blank verse line. The latter has only nine syllables, one short of the prescribed ten. Even this shortest sentence, however, occupies parts of two lines, thus contributing to rather than diminishing the dominance of the syntactic over the verse structure. That dominance prevails in large part simply because of the variety of sentence lengths, which constitute a variety of rhetorical subunits within the thematic and blank verse structures of the poem. The relationship between these syntactical subunits and the blank verse can be best illustrated by simple scansion of representative passages.

The poem begins with a two-and-a-half line independent clause: "To him who in the love of Nature holds/ Communion with her visible forms, she speaks/ A various language. . . ." If, for the sake of illustration, one ignores the sentence-sense of this phrase, the first two lines scan perfectly as iambic pentameter. The artificiality of the resulting illustration is so apparent, however, as to prompt a quick second scansion of the clause as a whole, which shifts the emphasis from line units to grammatical units—to, in this case, an introductory prepositional phrase, a relative clause, and a main clause. In that second scansion, "who," as the first word of the relative clause, is stressed, immediately throwing off the iambic regularity of the first reading. "In" loses its stress, becoming the first syllable of an anapest, "in the love." A second anapest occurs in line two in "visible forms." The most dramatic alteration of the blank verse line comes at the end of the grammatical unit in line three, where the rhythm shifts momentarily from rising to falling, to the dactyl of "various," and the trochee of "language." The opening lines of section two, lines thirty-one through thirty-three, maintain a greater iambic regularity than does the first clause, although at the end of the sentence, "couch," the first word of line thirty-three, is stressed and is followed by the anapest "more magnificent." In the closing nine-line sentence of the poem, the syntactic counterpoint to the blank verse rhythm is of a more subtle kind. The opening anapests of line seventy-four, "The innumerable," *if* one sounds the schwa in the middle of the word, is followed immediately by the initial stress of "caravan." The rhythm of the prepositional phrase "in the silent halls," of line seventy-six, prevails over the artificiality of a strict iambic reading which calls for a stress on "in." Anapests occur in each of the final four lines. Line seventy-eight has an initial stress on "Scourged," and the final line has the interesting juxtaposition of stresses in "About him," that is probably best described as a spondee.

The language of "Thanatopsis," particularly the dominance of syntactical over blank verse rhythm, is very close to what might be called the vernacular mode. Except for its diction, the "still voice" of the poem approximates, almost as closely as does Whitman's free verse, the voice of American colloquial speech. A dramatic illustration of that characteristic can be made by reading "Thanatopsis" side by side with almost any poem of Henry Wadsworth Longfellow's. Adjustments must be made from the late twentieth century perspective to accommodate Bryant's diction and imagery to that sense of his achievement, but in "Thanatopsis" those adjustments can be made rather easily. Except for the second-person pronouns, "thee," "thou," and "thine," there is very little diction that dates the poem.

If Bryant's rhythm and diction point forward in time to the emerging American voice, his imagery and his overt moral didacticism provide the ballast which holds him most securely to his own time. The general and abstract plane of much of his imagery clearly reflects eighteenth century influence. In some instances, it clogs the otherwise fluid syntax, effectively cutting off any prospects of vitality for the twentieth century sensibility. One of his better poems, "A Forest Hymn," suffers in this way because of the density of images such as "stilly twilight," "mossy boughs," "venerable columns," "verdant roof," and "winding aisles." Although the imagery of "Thanatopsis" is typical in this respect—that is, its imagery is more general and abstract than particular and concrete—it does not impede the syntactic flow of the poem. This is due, in part, to the fact that the subject of the poem, the meditation on death, calls for and sustains general imagery as much as any subject can. The "innumerable caravan" of the dead and the "silent halls of death" have no concrete, experiential counterparts. The "gay" and "the solemn brood of care," on the other hand, do, and they contribute to that eighteenth century ballast which counteracts Bryant's forward motion. Those counter melodies of the static and the dynamic, of the past and of the present progressive, are nowhere more evident than in the closing lines of the first section of the poem, which juxtapose the stock images of the "insensible rock" and the "sluggish clod" with the concrete imagery of one of the most memorable lines in American poetry: "The oak/ Shall send his roots abroad and pierce thy mould."

The blank verse and the theme of "Thanatopsis" together make the general imagery less obtrusive than it is in many of Bryant's poems. The same can be said of his overt moral didacticism, which is better sustained in this blank verse meditation on death than it is in poems such as "The Yellow Violet," "To the Fringed Gentian," and "To a Waterfowl," where the fragile lyricism is overburdened for twentieth century sensibility by the didactic uses to which he puts the flowers and the birds. Other blank verse poems which hold up well in much the same way as does "Thanatopsis" are "A Forest Hymn" and "The Prairies," although the eighteenth century stock imagery somewhat impedes the syntactic and rhythmic flow of the former. "The Prairies," on the other hand, is remarkable for the fluid sweep of its opening thirty-four lines of impressionistic description, motivated by Bryant's first visit to Illinois in 1832. The marvelously vibrant sense of life in these lines provides an excellent example of the major counterpoint in Bryant's poetry to the stoic resignation evinced in the earlier meditation on death. The terms of that early poem are broader than those of what might be called a mortality theme; the counterpoint in Bryant is really between the two larger themes of mutability and plenitude. His prevailing preoccupation is not so much with mortality as with change, and that somber theme is countered by his affirmative sense of a natural plenitude that guarantees a continuing replenishment of all that passes.

Bryant's affirmative resolution of his brooding preoccupation with the mutability of all things puts him in the early mainstream of the emerging national literature. He would continue to be read for his place in literary history, for the fuller understanding of the development of that national literature to which he contributes, even if his verse were wholly uncongenial to the contemporary reader. His celebration of the American landscape and his affirmation of a progressive spirit became overtly central themes for Ralph Waldo Emerson, Henry David Thoreau, and Whitman. Bryant's best poetry prefigures the American Renaissance in both content and form, theme and style, and thus he continues to be read and to be readable as one of America's literary pioneers.

Lloyd N. Dendinger

Other major works

NONFICTION: *Letters of a Traveller: Or, Notes of Things Seen in Europe and America*, 1850; *Reminiscences of the Evening Post*, 1851; *A Discourse on the Life and Genius of James Fenimore Cooper*, 1852; *Letters of a Traveller, Second Series*, 1859; *A Discourse on the Life and Genius of Washington Irving*, 1860; *Letters from the East*, 1869; *Lectures on Poetry*, 1884.

MISCELLANEOUS: *Orations and Addresses*, 1873.

Bibliography

Brenner, Rica. "William Cullen Bryant." In *Twelve American Poets Before 1900*. New York: Harcourt, Brace & World, 1933. Reprint. Freeport, N.Y. Books for Libraries Press, 1968. An older, but still useful, appreciative essay on Bryant and his writing. Surveys his style and themes from his earliest to his latest poetry and considers the impact of his turn from law to journalism. Bryant's translations of the *Iliad* and the *Odyssey* are described as a fitting culmination of his work.

Ferguson, Robert A. *Law and Letters in American Culture*. Cambridge, Mass.: Harvard University Press, 1984. Bryant is examined as a major contributor to American culture as a lawyer-writer. He is shown in his writing through a crisis to break away from the law to become America's first national poet. Chapter 7 focuses on the "creative context" of Bryant's poetic career. Includes notes and an index.

Justice, James H. "The Fireside Poets: Hearthside Values and the Language of Care." In *Nineteenth-Century American Poetry*, edited by A. Robert

Lee. New York: Barnes & Noble Books, 1985. Asserting that the "Fireside Poets" established poetry as an American treasure, Justice presents Bryant as one of the firmest to show how personal values could be merged with public service. His conversion from older verse styles to newer, Romantic ones is the focus of the discussion of his work. Complemented by notes and an index.

McLean, Albert F. *William Cullen Bryant.* Rev. ed. Boston: Twayne, 1989. The first four chapters survey Bryant's life, examine his poems of nature, analyze "Thanatopsis" in detail, and classify several poems of "progress." The last three chapters evaluate Bryant's prose and translations, explicate his poetic theory and style, and review his reputation. Supplemented by a chronology, notes, a select bibliography, and an index.

Peckham, Harry Houston. *Gotham Yankee: A Biography of William Cullen Bryant.* New York: Vantage Press, 1950. Reprinted by Folcroft Library Editions, 1970. Correcting misrepresentations of Bryant, Peckham describes him as a poet with an interesting personality and an interesting career as a journalist and poet. In eleven chapters, Bryant's life is narrated from its beginnings, when he was a delicate child, through his legal work of drudgery, to his last years of eloquence. Contains illustrations, notes, a bibliography, a chronology, and an index.

Ringe, Donald A. *The Pictorial Mode: Space and Time in the Art of Bryant, Irving, and Cooper.* Lexington: University Press of Kentucky, 1971. Bryant is given priority among writers who shared a pictorial aesthetic. Representation of space in Bryant's poetry is analyzed as a view of expansive nature, with precision of detail in the play of light and shadow. Time is examined as a force of contrast and continuity. Includes notes and an index.

CHARLES BUKOWSKI

Born: Andernach, Germany; August 16, 1920

Principal poetry

Flower, Fist and Bestial Wail, 1959; *Poems and Drawings*, 1962; *Longshot Poems for Broke Players*, 1962; *Run with the Hunted*, 1962; *It Catches My Heart in Its Hand*, 1963; *Crucifix in a Deathhand*, 1965; *Cold Dogs in the Courtyard*, 1965; *The Genius of the Crowd*, 1966; *The Curtains Are Waving*, 1967; *At Terror Street and Agony Way*, 1968; *Poems Written Before Jumping out of an 8 Story Window*, 1968; *A Bukowski Sampler*, 1969; *The Days Run Away Like Wild Horses over the Hills*, 1969; *Fire Station*, 1970; *Mockingbird Wish Me Luck*, 1972; *Me and Your Sometimes Love Poems*, 1972; *While the Music Played*, 1973; *Burning in Water, Drowning in Flame*, 1974; *Africa, Paris, Greece*, 1975; *Scarlet*, 1976; *Maybe Tomorrow*, 1977; *Love Is a Dog from Hell*, 1977; *We'll Take Them*, 1978; *Legs, Hips and Behind*, 1978; *Play the Piano Drunk Like a Percussion Instrument Until the Fingers Bleed a Bit*, 1979; *Dangling in the Tournefortia*, 1981; *War All the Time: Poems 1981-1984*, 1984; *The Roominghouse Madrigals: Early Selected Poems, 1946-1966*, 1988.

Other literary forms

In addition to poetry, Charles Bukowski has published both stories and novels and first achieved recognition with *Notes of a Dirty Old Man* (1969). This volume brought him to the attention of many who were previously unfamiliar with his work. In conjunction with his first novel, *Post Office* (1971) and a volume entitled *Erections, Ejaculations, Exhibitions and General Tales of Ordinary Madness* (1972), about half of which was reissued in *Life and Death in the Charity Ward* (1973), *Notes of a Dirty Old Man* established his reputation as a no-holds-barred commentator, full of rage, yet capable of surrealistic farce. In addition to subsequent novels which include *Factotum* (1975), *Women* (1978), *Ham on Rye* (1982), and *Hollywood* (1989), there is *South of No North* (1973), which reprints both *Confessions of a Man Insane Enough to Live with Beasts* (1965) and *All the Assholes of the World and Mine* (1966); a picture narrative of his trip abroad, *Shakespeare Never Did This* (1979); a screenplay, *Barfly* (1981); and assorted illustrations. His sketches underscore his farcical tone, especially in *You Kissed Lilly* (1978), a satire of the comics in which his Thurberesque style complements his prose.

Achievements

Few people familiar with Bukowski's work are indifferent to it. While he has neither won nor curried favor among academic or mainstream poets, he has attained an international reputation and has been widely translated. From the first, he has sought to create a "living poetry of clarity" which defies the proprieties and "cages" established by academics and editors. He has been compared with Henry Miller, Jack London, Louis-Ferdinand Céline, Antonin Artaud, François Villon, and Arthur Rimbaud and has had an acknowledged influence on Tom Waits, his musical heir.

He has carried the Beat manifesto to its logical conclusion without compromising his vision or pandering to the idolatrous public. By incorporating the vantage point of the underclass, he has artistically wrought the unfashionable voices of the streets, the factories, the racetracks, and other less seemly social enclaves. He fuses the rawness of life with a personal sensitivity; he conveys the horrors as well as the pathos of poverty, blue collar jobs, hangovers, and jailyards. He has never been a media personality, as the Beats were. Once it became financially feasible, he began refusing all invitations for readings to guard his private self, convinced that it was readings which had killed Dylan Thomas. This reticence, with his exclusive reliance on small publishers, makes his international reputation all the more impressive.

Perhaps his most significant achievement is his successful forging of a new American poetics which is characterized by its accessibility and its spontaneous narrative voice. Unlike T. S. Eliot's "vertical poetry," Bukowski's is a "horizontal poetry" which photographs the jagged surfaces of society and forces the reader to peer into the baser regions of human existence, to see mankind for what it is. His unique blend of powerful, physical imagery and sardonic wit allows the reader to grasp and yet transcend the essential absurdity of existence.

Biography

One cannot come to terms with the poetry of Henry Charles Bukowski, Jr., without acknowledging the fact that his is an extremely personal and autobiographical poetry; the terror and agony are not merely "felt-life" but life as Bukowski has known it. His survival is a thing of wonder. As Gerald Locklin notes, he "has not only survived problems that would kill most men, he's survived with enough voice and talent left to write about it." He is a practicing alcoholic whose life revolves around the racetrack, women, and writing.

Born to a German mother and an American serviceman father on August 16, 1920, in Andernach, Germany, Bukowski came to the United States in 1922 with his family. They settled in Los Angeles, later the milieu for much of Bukowski's work. His father, a milkman, was a harsh and often violent man who struggled with his own powerlessness by wielding a razor strap. The resultant hostility and animosity, evident in many of his poems, coupled with a blood disease which left his face badly pockmarked, predisposed Bukowski to a life on the fringes of society.

At about the age of sixteen, partly to escape and partly because of a desire to become a writer, Bukowski began to haunt the public library, seeking literary models. His own self-directed reading was far more important in shaping his literary credo than the two years he spent at Los Angeles City College. He was drawn to the works of Louis-Ferdinand Céline, John Fante, Fyodor Dostoevski, Ivan Turgenev, and the early Ernest Hemingway; in later years, he was attracted by Franz Kafka and Albert Camus. Just as the creative writing class in which he had enrolled seemed fraudulent and banal, however, so too did the voices of many of the "masters."

Bukowski's career as a writer had a rather fitful start. After receiving hundreds of rejections, "Aftermath of a Lengthy Rejection Slip" was accepted by *Story* in 1944 and *Portfolio* published "20 Tanks from Kasseldown." These publications were followed by ten years of virtual silence during which only four pieces were published. Toward the end of this literary hiatus, two important changes occurred. He began working sporadically at the Post Office, where he stayed fourteen years (until 1970, when John Martin of Black Sparrow Press convinced him to quit). This job provided the first steady source of income Bukowski had known. More important, however, was the shock of landing in the charity ward in 1955 near death from a bleeding ulcer. After receiving eleven pints of blood, he emerged "900 years older," promptly disregarded the warnings to quit drinking, and began publishing poetry in various little magazines. It was his appearance in *Outsider* and his friendship with editors Jon and Gypsy Lou Webb, who dubbed him "outsider of the year" in 1962, that launched his career. With their assistance, he began to develop an important reputation among editors and readers of the little magazines, ultimately establishing a friendship with John and Barbara Martin, who have published the bulk of his work.

The barrage of women in his work reveals Bukowski's penchant for womanizing; he seems to fall from one affair to another, yet his work reveals several significant pairings. Toward the beginning of his ten-year silence, he met Jane, "the first person who brought me any love" and began a relationship which was to continue until she finally died of alcoholism. While their relationship, as *Factotum* demonstrates, was interrupted by intervening affairs, his cross-country meandering, and his two-and-a-half-year marriage to Barbara Fry, a Texas millionairess who edited *Harlequin*, it was a durable bond which inspired countless sensitive poems. Following Jane's death, Bukowski became involved with Frances, who bore his only child, Marina. Much later, both Linda King and Linda Lee Beighle were to play central roles in his life. The works dedicated to these women constitute a tribute of sorts and demonstrate that while his personal life has often been tempestuous, he has the capacity and need for love. This is important to bear in mind to avoid misreading his oeuvre by exaggerating his sexism.

Analysis

Living on the periphery of society, Charles Bukowski has forged a brutally honest poetic voice. The futility and senselessness of most human endeavor conjoined with the desperation and essential solitude of the individual are constants reinforcing his "slavic nihilism." The trick, he suggests, is "carrying on when everything seems so terrible there is no use to go on. . . . You face the wall and just work it out. . . . Facing it right with yourself, alone." It is this kind of courage and stoicism which informs Bukowski's canon. He is not a poet's poet, nor a people's poet, but a personal poet using his craft to ensure his own survival.

Bukowski's "tough guy" image is less posturing than self-protective. One senses that he is an idealist soured by the ravages of time, wearied by political betrayals and rather appalled by the vacuity of the American left and contemporary American writers who seem to be playing it safe and producing pallid prose and senselessly arcane poetry. Interestingly, in his best poems, the tough guy persona falls away and one discovers a sensitive poet who has chosen to adopt a savage bravado. Clearly, he knows the reality of the seamy side of life; his poetry teems with grotesque and sordid imagery; but unlike those who would write in order to reform, Bukowski is content to capture the pathos and rawness of the streets.

His first four chapbooks properly acclimate the reader to Bukowski's dual vision—his rawness and his compassion. They also reveal the risks inherent in this kind of personal, reportorial poetry. At his best, he blends seemingly incongruous elements to plunge the reader into a surreal landscape. At his worst, he succumbs to self-pity, mired in his own mundane reality.

Flower, Fist and Bestial Wail is the most consistently crafted of the four books and includes one of his best-known poems, "The Twins," which transforms his lingering animosity toward his father into a transcendent statement of shared humanity and mortality. The poem is replete with antithetical images: "We looked exactly alike, we could have been twins. . . . he had his bulbs on the screen ready for planting while I was laying with a whore from 3rd street." His own ambivalence is suggested by the scarecrow image he presents as he realizes "I can't keep him alive no matter how much we hated each other." So, he stands, "waiting also to die." Read in conjunction with "All-Yellow Flowers," "The Twins" establishes one of the dominant motifs in Bukowski's work—the transient nature of life and the exaggerated import which human beings attach to ephemera.

These poems have the cadence of impending catastrophe. Beginning with "10 Lions and the End of the World," Bukowski moves from the mundane to the apocalyptic without missing a beat; he forges a vantage point which is both ironic and sentimental as he ponders the cost of the pell-mell pace of modern life.

In Bukowski's world almost anything is possible. Although the potential for violence is ever present, it defies logic. His is the spirit of farce. He is constantly challenging the contours of reality. He employs a farcical dialectic to conjoin the bizarre and the mundane; he uses brutal undercutting, as in "Love Is a Piece of Paper Torn to Bits," in which a ship out of control and a wife being "serviced" by another are divested of significance while a worrisome cat is promoted to center stage. By focusing on the cat and the "dishes with flowers and vines painted on them," he effectively understates his angst. Similarly, in "I Cannot Stand Tears," a guard kills a wounded goose because "the bird was crying and I cannot stand tears."

Also evident in this first volume is Bukowski's justification for callous machismo as a defense against "the lie of love"; he establishes his argument by infusing his poems with countless oxymorons which rearrange the signposts of reality. In "Soiree," a bottle becomes a "dwarf waiting to scratch out my prayers," and in "His Wife, The Painter," a bus becomes "insanity sprung from a waving line"; he speaks of the sunlight as a lie and markets smelling of "shoes and naked boys clothed." "Soiree" also announces the impossibility of sustaining a relationship; "Did I Ever Tell You" captures the tragicomic element of love. The inescapable conclusion from this panoply is that love is futile, duplicitous, or, at best, based on mutual concessions. This explains the frequent crassness in Bukowski's work, which was already evident in "No Charge."

Longshot Poems for Broke Players contains several poems which do justice to the existentialism and craftsmanship which Bukowski demonstrated in his first volume. "The State of World Affairs From a 3rd Floor Window," for example, melds an essentially voyeuristic point of view with reflections on a nuclear-infested world. Its tone is mellow and its counterpoint suggests the possibility of survival. Survival, it seems, is a matter of perspective, a point forcefully echoed in "The Tragedy of the Leaves," which embodies Bukowski's belief that what is needed is "a good comedian, ancient style, a jester with jokes upon absurd pain; pain as absurd because it exists." It concludes with an empathetic identification with his landlady "because the world had failed us both."

The surrealism of "What a Man I Was," which lampoons the legendary status of various Western heroes, is accelerated and refined in "The Best Way to Get Famous Is to Run Away," which revolves around the proverbial desire to live underground, away from the masses and the absurdity of explaining "why." Inherent in this piece, as well as in "Conversations in a Cheap Room" and "Poems for Personnel Managers," is the unattainability of resonance, the inability to comprehend the suffering of others: "Age was a crime . . . Pity picked up the marbles and . . . Hatred picked up the cash." A blend of the sensitive and ironic, an easy movement through cliché and culture dignifies these pieces. The result is a litany of sorts dedicated to those who have fallen through the cracks of the dream, unveiling a world of fraudulent promises which routinely casts aside those who do not conform to the dictates of propriety.

Run with the Hunted, the most uneven of Bukowski's early works, is more freewheeling than *Poems and Drawings*; it displays flashes of insight in "Old Man, Dead in a Room" and reaches innovative heights in "Vegas." Bukowski interweaves the abstract and the concrete to capture the impossibility of communication and the essential insanity of social and artistic convention. The majority of the poems, however, seem self-indulgent and pointlessly crass.

Having gained recognition from the early chapbooks, Bukowski assumed a surer direction. *It Catches My Heart in Its Hand* culls some of the best from the early chapbooks and adds many new pieces. In this work, Bukowski mocks his own former self-pity and transforms it into a literary device with which to document the passage of time, as in "Old Poet" and "The Race." The danger of sanctifying art receives a lighter handling in "The Talkers," which is both a critique of "art for art's sake" and a renunciation of those who would hide behind abstraction and pretense.

Artistic distance is even more evident in *Crucifix in a Deathhand*, which centers around reawakened memories, senses deadened by the workaday world, and actual confrontations with death. In "Sunflower" and "Fuzz," for example, Bukowski mutes his personal voice to universalize his own anguish; he often seems, as in "Grass," to be observing himself. The workaday world, the province of "little men with luck and a headstart" emerges as deadening in "Machinegun Towers & Timeclocks" and "Something for the Touts, the Nuns, the Grocery Clerks and You. . . ." Bukowski is equally contemptuous of the bovine mentality of the masses and the group-think of the counter-culture. In "This," he elevates himself above any prescriptions and becomes his own measuring rod. His is the stance of the loner, seeking pleasures where he finds them and deferring to no one. Survival, he suggests, demands egotism; otherwise, one can only await the fiery cleansing of the bomb contemplated in "A Report Upon the Consumption of Myself."

Bukowski's disdain for all that is average becomes more overt in a single-poem chapbook, *The Genius of the Crowd* (1966), a jeremiad cautioning the poet to avoid the profane influence of the culture. More boldly than any previous poem, it unmasks Bukowski's contempt for the masses and asserts that "There is enough treachery, hatred, violence, absurdity in the average human being to supply any given army on any given day." This is reinforced by the suggestion that most preaching is duplicitous, a game of mirrors.

A very different impression is gleaned from *Cold Dogs in the Courtyard*, over which Bukowski was given editorial control. In a prefatory note, he explains that he chose those poems he felt had been unduly neglected. What emerges is a collection keynoted by an almost tender melancholia. "Imbecile Night," for example, establishes a delicate balance with which he endures the dreary cadence of darkness. Informing these poems is a sense of awe as he notes the consonance of nature's marvels and human invention, especially apparent in "It's Nothing to Laugh About." Compounding this is the poignant juxtaposition of the substantial and the ephemeral, as in "Existence," a poem built around the Post Office and the exaggerated importance attached to "dead letters." Like the roof in "2 Outside as Bones Break in My Kitchen," the letters maintain but fail to nurture the human spirit.

In "Layovers," the memories of lost love and the dreams of renewal serve as a reprieve from Bukowski's encounters with death. Serving a similar function are encounters with the unexpected, as in "Experience," and anarchistic protests such as the one depicted in "What Seems to Be the Trouble, Gentlemen?" These poems work, in part, because they lack the self-congratulatory tone of *The Genius of the Crowd* and the self-indulgence of *The Curtains Are Waving* (1967). *The Curtains Are Waving* again reveals the limits of Bukowski's style; in an attempt to come to terms with his angst, he is left decrying his fate.

By the time *At Terror Street and Agony Way* appeared, Bukowski had apparently regained artistic control; the volume substitutes self-mockery for self-pity. While he continues to probe the plight of those caught under the technocratic juggernaut, he does so more emblematically and with greater levity. In "Red and Gold Paint," he conceives of luck and art as miracles against the cunning caprices of bosses, wars, and the weather. It is only playing against the odds, he repeatedly suggests, which ensures survival. Those who relinquish the good fight or never begin, he implies in "Reunion," may ingratiate themselves, but they never really live.

This volume is more thematically unified by the primacy of terror and agony in Bukowski's perspective. The lost innocence of "As I Lay Dying," the gratuitousness of "Beerbottle," and the resultant agony of blinding dreams in "K.O." quietly undergird the wanton destruction of "Sunday Before Noon" and the defeated dreams of "7th Race." Similarly, "I Wanted to Overthrow the Government" records Bukowski's suspicion of revolutionary schemes: "The weakness was not Government but Man, one at a time . . . men were never as strong as their ideas and . . . ideas were governments turned into men."

Bukowski's next volume, *Poems Written Before Jumping out of an 8 Story Window*, constitutes a reversal. Absent are the literary allusions, the calm and urbanity of *At Terror Street and Agony Way*. The old shrillness is back as Bukowski dons the "beast" persona and vents his spleen, abandoning all finesse. Rapine, murder, and Gothic elements dominate; an alcoholic fog blurs his vision. Even the best piece, "The Hairy Hairy Fist, and Love Will Die," despite its relentless "beat" and its examination of the individual turned back on himself, deafened by silence, is reduced in magnitude.

The publication of *A Bukowski Sampler* in 1969 signaled a change. In a little less than eighty pages, Doug Blazek assembled some of the best of Bukowski's work. His selection, a fairly representative one allowing the neophyte a full taste of Bukowski, also includes an editor's introduction, a letter from Bukowski, and several tributes from admirers of his work. Published about six months after *Notes of a Dirty Old Man*, the volume was directed at the growing Bukowski audience and the burgeoning counterculture.

While *The Days Run Away Like Wild Horses over the Hills* again culls poems from the early chapbooks, the majority of the pieces are new and fresh. Since the book is dedicated to Jane, it is not surprising to find death as the leitmotiv. What is surprising is the almost sensual tone. In several poems to Jane, one can feel both the depth of Bukowski's love and the anguish which her death occasioned. While there are the obligatory accounts of womanizing, these pale before his elegies to Jane and his references to Frances and Marina. His attitude is encapsulated in "Birth," where the male dominion is muted by "small female things and jewels."

Allusions are multiplied without pretension; in "Ants Crawl My Drunken Arms," he criticizes the banality of popular culture which prefers Willie Mays to Bach and the killing realities which essentially devoured Arthur Rimbaud, Ezra Pound, and Hart Crane. In "The Sharks" and "The Great One," the artist emerges as victim, and in "The Seminar" and "On a Grant" the pretense and incestuousness of the literary establishment are mocked through both the form and the content of the poems.

In *Mockingbird Wish Me Luck*, his next collection, Bukowski probes the culturally sanctioned disparities and skewed priorities which produce "shipping clerks who have read the Harvard Classics" and allow the powerful "a 15 percent take on the dream." "Hogs in the Sky" suggests that survival is a miracle, and yet, no more than a proper rehearsal for death "as old age arrives on schedule." The paraplegic who continues to play the longshots in "The World's Greatest Loser" is merely an extreme illustration of the fact that "nobody had any luck." Hence, the aspiring writer becomes a random assassin in "The Garbageman" and an ace crapshooter in "Moyamensing Prison."

Much of the humor in these poems is self-deprecatory, as in "The Last Days of the Suicide Kid," but subtler ironies emerge as well: the cost of success in "Making it" and the very real risk of becoming a noted writer in "The Poet's Muse." Bukowski recognizes that often the skid row bums have more brains, more wit, and sometimes more satisfaction than those who have "won." Again it is a question of perspective—something which is a rare commodity in America, he notes in "Earthquake."

The second part of this volume is teeming with primordial images and energies. Monkey feet, lions, and mockingbirds stalk and taunt the poet and reader while the mass media relentlessly promote diversions and distractions. The gullibility of the masses, not a new theme, is used to establish Bukowski's own superiority and contempt for platitudes. Recording his experiences with the draft board in "WW2," he compares himself to the draftees, concluding: "I was not as young as they." Not as young, perhaps, because he, like

Robinson Jeffers, whom he eulogizes in "He Wrote in Lonely Blood," has solitary instincts and an understanding of what is essential. Yet, in both "The Hunt" and "The Shoelace," he realizes that it is the little things which tip the scale and "sometimes create unemployed drunks . . . trying to grab for grunion."

The final section of *Mockingbird Wish Me Luck* is unified by the risks of love. Love, a tenuous miracle, endures for Bukowski only with Marina, who is the subject of several poems. "The Shower" suggests that others, like Linda King, will eventually pass out of his life despite the depth of their mutual feelings. At the other extreme are the large number of women who are sought because they are, by definition, "one-week stands." The only alternative to the ebb and flow is represented by the "old fashioned whore" and the "American matador" who opt out of conscriptive relationships.

These conversational poems are often riddled by the banter and banality which characterize the bulk of daily interactions, yet Bukowski insists on the need for style—"a fresh way to approach a dull or dangerous thing." Herein lies the key to Bukowski's poetic credo—he does not seek new themes, but, rather, reworks the old from a new angle of vision. This approach is especially germane to *Burning in Water, Drowning in Flame*, which reprints many poems that had gone out of print and redirects his probing of such phenomena as love's impermanence. *Burning in Water, Drowning in Flame* constitutes a fitting conclusion to the third stage of Bukowski's career. Including sections of poems from *It Catches My Heart in Its Hand*, *Crucifix in a Deathhand*, and *At Terror Street and Agony Way* (to which *The Curtains Are Waving* has been added), it is a testimony to his growing reputation, and, having been published by one of the more prestigious small presses, accomplishes the aim of *A Bukowski Sampler* with considerable finesse.

In addition to making selections from earlier volumes, this one includes a section of new poems. These are not gentle poems. Beginning with "Now," which compares writing poetry with lancing boils, Bukowski moves to "Zoo," which questions whether, in fact, humans have evolved significantly. "The Way" represents a brutal culmination, resembling the cascading cadence of Allen Ginsberg's "Howl" while managing not to fall away or to lose its sardonic tone.

The reportorial style which informs these poems is wryly explained in "Deathbed Blues" and panned in "My Friend, Andre," and while it is not always effective, at its best it gives testimony to the moral dignity which is attainable despite the depravity which threatens to consume the human spirit. "Death of an Idiot," which calls to mind "Conversations with a Lady Sipping a Straight Shot" in *The Days Run Away Like Wild Horses over the Hills*, displays compassion and achieves its impact by understatement.

Bukowski's later poetry is more persistently autobiographical and more finely honed than his earlier work. Many of the poems, especially in *Love Is a Dog from Hell*, have fictional analogues in *Women*. A tendency already apparent in "Hell Hath no Fury . . ." in *Burning in Water, Drowning in Flame*, becomes more evident here; the poems often seem merely to have been transplanted into (or from) the novel. Similarly, several of the poems in *Dangling in the Tournefortia* correspond to *Shakespeare Never Did This*, and others clearly reveal the influence of Bukowski's move to San Pedro—a move which has not tempered his perspective.

Love Is a Dog from Hell, like the chapbook *Scarlet* which it incorporates, has loves and lusts as its primary focus. The proper context for viewing these poems is suggested by Bukowski's comment that "love is ridiculous because it can't last and sex is ridiculous because it doesn't last long enough." It is the tragicomedy which impels him. Refusing to defer to feminist sensibilities, he relates one sexual adventure after another, capturing both the eternal search and the predictable defeats which await everyone in "Another Bed."

Women are portrayed in a variety of stances; sometimes merely objects, they are at other times capable of turning the male into an object, as the black widow spider in "The Escape" and the teeth mother in "A Killer" are inclined to do. The women range from aspiring artists and reformers to whores, and the latter have the edge "because they lie about nothing." While some may take offense at the sexism in these pieces, it seems to cut both ways; the men are no less demeaned than the women. This is still the world of the streets where proprieties and pretense fall away. In poems such as "One for Old Snaggle-tooth," dedicated to Frances, Bukowski's sensitivity is economically and precisely conveyed.

The second section is concerned with the tragedies and inhumanities which transform artists into madmen or panderers. "What They Want" reads like a top ten list of artistic casualties. The artist emerges as vulnerable and damned in "There Once Was a Woman Who Put Her Head in an Oven," which calls to mind Sylvia Plath. Yet, in "The Crunch," Bukowski suggests that the artist is able to utilize the isolation and failure which drive others over the edge. Both survival and creativity seem to demand solitude, as long as it is not irreversible.

Primarily a reissue of several chapbooks, *Play the Piano Drunk Like a Percussion Instrument Until the Fingers Begin to Bleed a Bit* lacks the thematic unity of the preceding volume, but it does demonstrate Bukowski's continuing iconoclasm and his ability to revive old themes. The title deadpans the conception of the typewriter as a musical instrument, a theme first introduced in "Chopin Bukowski" in *Love Is a Dog from Hell*.

Beginning with "Tough Company," which turns poems into gunslingers waiting to receive their due, Bukowski unleashes his acerbic wit against ersatz holiday gaiety, feigned idealism, parental protocol, the notion of a limited nuclear war, and the pretense of civilization, which is compared to fool's gold in "Through the Streets of Anywhere." While there is a sense of absurdity and subterfuge rampaging through these poems, there is also a sense of durability and substance. Again the losers at the racetrack bars, in the bowels of the slaughterhouses, and in the sterile rooming houses are pummeled but maintain their dignity, accepting their exclusion and their inability to affect their fates: "We are finally tricked and slapped to death like lovers' vows, bargained out of any gain." They await the arrival of the urban renewal cranes in "2347 Duane," and while they occasionally master the bravado of Bogart, as in "Maybe Tomorrow," more often they simply await death, as in "The Proud Thin Dying." If one is careful, "Horse and Fist" implies, one may yet survive despite the open-endedness of the game. In the meantime, it is best to "play the piano drunk like a percussion instrument until the fingers begin to bleed a bit."

There is an interesting movement in *Dangling in the Tournefortia*, Bukowski's collection. Several of the early poems are retrospective, establishing a counterpoint against which to view his current status—something which is overt in poems such as "Guava Tree." It seems that he is suspicious of his newly won success, recognizing that he "can fail in many more ways now," as he says in "Fear and Madness," knowing that there are more "suckerfish" who will insist upon intruding and fretting about the state of his soul. Yet, "Notes Upon a Hot Streak" reveals the pleasure he takes in the "lovable comedy" which "they are letting me win for this moment."

While success has not tempered his perspective, it has tempered his rage; even his references to his father's brutality are softened, and while death continues to loom, it no longer threatens to overwhelm him or his poetry. The more balanced tone is reinforced by his use of the tournefortia, a tropical tree with delicate flowers and a fleshy fruit, as a metaphor for the interplay of love and lust, being and nothingness. Again the tempestuous love affairs are paraded, sometimes callously but often with a quick parry, as in "The Descent of the Species" and "Snap Snap." In "The Lady in Red," he explores the compensatory function served by heroes such as Dillinger during the Depression; in "Fight On" and "Blue Collar Solitude," the needed respite offered by a good street brawl and/or several drinks; and in "Nothing," seeing a supervisor besotted somehow eases the pain and agony of the job.

As one of the most prolific and well-known of the underground poets, Bukowski has pinned his success on the authenticity of his voice. Even a casual encounter with his work reveals the lack of pretense and the refusal to kowtow to the critics. He has refused to be beaten; as he suggests in *The Last Generation* (1982), a single-poem broadside, it may be harder to be a genius with the proliferation of publishers and writers, but it is worth the attempt. There are too many unsung characters of the "unholy parade" and too many poems which demand to be written.

His bawdiness no less than his free-form style constitutes a manifesto of sorts. American poetry has long been cautious and unduly arcane, thereby excluding a large part of the potential poetry audience and a wide range of subjects and sentiments. Booze, hard loving, and horse racing, while not generally seen as poetic subjects, dominate Bukowski's oeuvre. His crassness, which weakens some of his pieces, has in his best work been complemented by a sensitive understanding of the fringes of society. Beneath the veneer, one senses a man who is unaccustomed to and rather afraid of love; a man who simultaneously disdains and applauds the masses because of his own ambivalent self-concept.

C. Lynn Munro

Other major works

LONG FICTION: *Post Office*, 1971; *Factotum*, 1975; *Women*, 1978; *Ham on Rye*, 1982; *You Get So Alone at Times That It Just Makes Sense*, 1986; *Hollywood*, 1989.

SHORT FICTION: *Notes of a Dirty Old Man*, 1969; *Erections, Ejaculations, Exhibitions and General Tales of Ordinary Madness*, 1972; *Life and Death in the Charity Ward*, 1973; *South of No North*, 1973; *The Most Beautiful Woman in Town and Other Stories*, 1983; *The Day It Snowed in L.A.*, 1986.

PLAY: *Barfly*, 1981.

NONFICTION: *Shakespeare Never Did This*, 1979.

Bibliography

Cain, Jimmie. "Bukowski's Imagist Roots." *West Georgia College Review* 19 (May, 1987): 10-17. Cain draws a parallel between Bukowski's poetry and the work of William Carlos Williams, America's premier Imagist poet. Cain claims that Bukowski's rough-and-tumble poetry shows palpable Imagist influences. For advanced students.

Cherkovski, Neeli. *Hank: The Life of Charles Bukowski*. New York: Random House, 1991. This is the first full-length biography of Charles Bukowski. It is written by a fellow poet who published a magazine with him in the late 1960's. Contains excerpts from Bukowski's poems and letters. For all students.

Graalman, Bob. "Charles Bukowski." In *American Poets Since World War II: Part 1, A-K*, edited by Donald J. Greiner. Vol. 5 of *Dictionary of Literary Biography*. Detroit: Gale Research, 1980. Describes Bukowski as "a member of the modern confessional school" and analyzes his consistent technique: "the straightforward, gemlike image." It is Bukowski's persona, Graalman argues, that is memorable, more than particular Bukowski poems. Includes a brief resource list.

McDonough, Tom. "Down and (Far) Out." *American Film* 13 (November, 1987): 26-30. McDonough discusses how Bukowski's real-life alcoholism was portrayed in the 1987 biographical film *Barfly*. In the film, the drunken Bukowski was played by actor Mickey Rourke, while Faye Dunaway played his drinking companion. Gives an interesting popular insight to Bukowski's life.

Wakoski, Diane. "Charles Bukowski." In *Contemporary Poets*, edited by James Vinson and D. L. Kirkpatrick. 4th ed. New York: St. Martin's Press, 1985. Wakoski traces Bukowski's rising popularity but laments the fact that though "Americans . . . honor truth," and Bukowski's poems are distinguished by their unselfpitying truthfulness, he has not received much serious criticism. Includes a list of his publications up to 1984.

BASIL BUNTING

Born: Scotswood-on-Tyne, England; March 1, 1900
Died: Hexham, England; April 17, 1985

Principal poetry

Redimiculum Matellarum, 1930; *Poems 1950*, 1950; *First Book of Odes*, 1965; *Loquitur*, 1965; *The Spoils: A Poem*, 1965; *Briggflatts*, 1966; *Two Poems*, 1967; *What the Chairman Told Tom*, 1967; *Collected Poems*, 1968, 1978, 1985; *Descant on Rawley's Madrigal* (*Conversations with Jonathan Williams*), 1968.

Other literary forms

Basil Bunting wrote little aside from poetry. Although he claimed that he had no use for literary criticism, he did write a small amount of critical prose. With Ezra Pound, Bunting edited the *Active Anthology* (1933), which contained a number of his poems. He contributed prose to *Agenda* and *Poetry*. In an article entitled "English Poetry Today" (*Poetry*, February, 1932), Bunting descants on the poetry of the time. His remarks reveal much about his own poetic practice. The poet also elaborates upon his attitudes in an interview entitled "Eighty of the Best . . . " (*Paideuma*, Spring, 1980).

Achievements

Bunting, in his own self-deprecating estimation, was a "minor poet, not conspicuously dishonest." His poetic career, like his life, was quixotic. He began in the tradition of the 1920's, following the lead of Pound and Louis Zukofsky, but his work did not appear in print until a limited edition of 1930 was published in Milan. His adherence to the school of Pound and the relative obscurity of his work kept him from being read by a British audience who had turned to the new men of the 1930's such as W. H. Auden, Louis MacNeice, and Stephen Spender. A collection of his poems published twenty years later in Texas (the poet himself was residing in Persia) did little to widen his audience. It was not until the 1960's, especially with the publication of *Briggflatts*, that Bunting was rediscovered.

Bunting was quick to acknowledge the influence of Pound and Zukofsky. He was a close friend of Pound, who dedicated *Guide to Kulchur* (1938) jointly to Bunting and Zukofsky. Bunting's early poems exhibit the brittle precision, vigor, and social commentary of Pound's *Cantos* (1925-1972). In these early poems one also finds, ingeniously rendered in modern idiom, showpiece passages of Horace, Lucretius, Niccolò Machiavelli, the Persian poet Firdusi, Rūdakī of Samarkand, and others (Bunting was a master of languages). Such "translations" are actually free resurrections in English of the poetry of another language. Again after the manner of Pound, Bunting skillfully captures the character of the speaker in Browningesque dramatic monologues. T S. Eliot's influence looms large in Bunting's use of literary allusion and his expression of the bleaker side of existence. Bunting frequently echoed Eliot's style, but with satiric intent. He believed Eliot's later poetry to be dishonest in its support of reactionary social and literary institutions. Nevertheless, he owed much to Eliot both in his use of allusion and in the creation of mood.

Bunting's place in letters is secured through his handling of rhythm, rhyme, meter, assonance, consonance, alliteration—in short, the sounds of poetry. He claimed Edmund Spenser as an influence. His emphasis was on everything that a poem gains by being spoken aloud. In his early Latin translations he experimented with meters difficult to employ in a stressed language such as English. Later poems exhibit a free play of heavy stresses filled with spondees, trochees, and dactyls, against no identifiable iambic background. Rather, stress corresponds to the meaning of the words. Some critics have doubted the existence of recognizable rhythms in Bunting's mature poetry, but the presence of so many stressed syllables creates its own kind of meter. The poet himself has suggested that his dominant meter is the four-beat line of Old English oral poetry. In his most accomplished poem, *Briggflatts*, rough monosyllables force precise speech; the reader finds that he must articulate each consonant, exaggerating frequent stresses. The effect is not the contortions of Gerard Manley Hopkins' sprung rhythm, but rather the ictus of a pagan drum beat—without the monotony of Rudyard Kipling's meter. Against his line of strong stress the poet plays a counterpoint of assonance, consonance, internal rhyme, and alliteration. This play of sounds does much to achieve a music which, according to Bunting, is the being of poetry.

Bunting's poetic career blossomed late, with the publication of *Briggflatts*, an autobiographical poem in which he triumphantly reclaims the speech of his native Northumbria. The influence of William Wordsworth is clear in this poem, and one feels that more than any other modern poet Bunting was able to achieve the Romantic ideal of using the language of ordinary men. With flinty precision, this language of real men is forged into masculine, heavily stressed lines which resonate sounds and themes from one to another. This is Bunting's major poetic accomplishment.

Biography

Basil Bunting was born in Scotswood-on-Tyne, Northumberland, on March 1, 1900. He was reared and educated a Quaker and speaks fondly of the Briggflatts Meeting House, constructed by the Friends in 1675 and still in use today. When he was eighteen, Bunting refused the draft and was imprisoned in Wormwood Scrubs Prison for a year. Glimpses of the harsh prison conditions can be found in the poem "Villon" (1925). After release, he studied at the London School of Economics. At about the same time, he began to write Imagist poetry. This early work contains, in the manner of Pound, dramatic monologues and vignettes from other poets, but the influence of Eliot, whom he met in the mid-1920's, also makes itself known. Bunting left for Paris in 1923, beginning an odyssey which kept him out of England for much of the next fifty years. From Paris he joined Pound in Rapallo, where the two became close friends. There he met and married Marian Culver, an American. The marriage lasted until 1935 and produced three children.

In the late 1920's Bunting was for a short time music critic of *The Outlook* in London. He returned to Italy where he lived until 1933. In Rapallo, Bunting and Pound edited the *Active Anthology*, which contained a number of Bunting's earliest poems. These are the most Poundian of Bunting's work. In the 1930's he lived in the United States, and from 1937 to 1939 he earned a living as captain of a private yacht which sailed the Mediterranean and crossed to the United States. The rise of Adolf Hitler overcame his pacifism and in 1939 he returned to England to join the Royal Air Force. Bunting spent most of the war in Iran, where his facility with languages was put to good use in Intelligence. After the war he stayed in Iran as Persian correspondent for *The Times*. In 1948 he married an Iranian, Sima Alladadian. Many of his Middle Eastern experiences are captured in *The Spoils*, a poem written in 1951 but not published until 1965. In 1951 he returned to England. In the mid-1960's, the Pound critic Hugh Kenner was instrumental in bringing Bunting to the University of California at Santa Barbara, where he taught until he accepted a position at the University of Durham, England. He subsequently retired to Black Fells Village, Northumberland, England. Bunting died in Hexham, England, in 1985.

Analysis

Until the publication of *Briggflatts*, Basil Bunting's poetry was largely ignored, both because it had been published obscurely and because it was viewed as highly derivative—mere Poundian pastiche. In retrospect, the poems of the 1920's and 1930's show to what extent this estimation is unjustified. It is impossible to deny that—on the road to developing his own voice—Bunting wrote poems that were strongly influenced by Eliot's manner and, more particularly, Pound's. Even in his earliest work, however, Bunting can be identified by the sound of his lines, especially by the cadence of stresses which alliteration reinforces and to which assonance and internal rhyme frequently add counterpoint. This attention to sound is very characteristic of his work. In his own estimation, while music is not all there is to a poem, it is the one essential ingredient. In the *Collected Poems* he classified his short lyrics as "Odes" and his longer poems as "Sonatas." (More than one critic, of course, has denied any but a metaphorical connection between music and poetry.) By "music," Bunting seems to be making a claim for a special interplay between the sound and meaning of words in a poem; his use of the word "ode" seems to be an appeal to poetry's source in the chants and dances of the Greek chorus. While Bunting did not appropriate the strophe and antistrophe format in the manner of Pindar, his heavily stressed meter resembles those complex rhythms best expressed in dance. In fact, Bunting claimed that, aside from its use in poetry, meter is perhaps best expressed through physical movement. Bunting's heavily stressed lines can be best appreciated in a comparison with the oral chants which accompany primitive dance.

Perhaps the best way to approach Bunting is by way of the loose verse translations he calls "Overdrafts." Here Bunting follows Pound's lead, attempting to revive in the idiom of modern English the spirit of a foreign poem. As David Gordon has shown (*Paideuma*, Spring, 1980), Bunting was able, in a 1931 translation from Horace, to create an English accentual syllabic version of *ionic a minore* meter. In this and other similar performances the poet extends the range of English metrics and prepares himself for the heavily stressed line which distinguishes his poetry. Not only is the meter of the original poem revitalized, but also the words of the poem are rendered in a modern idiom which sometimes defies the sense and historical/cultural setting of the original. Thus, the lady in the Horatian passage is deprived of "gin." She has mislaid her "workbox." Her lover is a "middle-weight pug" who wears "track-shorts." In the notes to the *Collected Poems*, the poet indicates that such "mistranslation" is intentional.

The "overdrafts" record something of the poet's interests over the years. In 1927 he translated a passage of Lucretius, and in 1931 two by Horace. In 1932, he rendered a few lines of Louis Zukofsky into Latin. He translated Catullus into English in 1933, the Persian poet Firdusi in 1935, Rūdakī of Samarkand in 1948, Manuchehri in 1949, and Sa'dī in 1949. Perhaps the most striking translation is a passage from Machiavelli entitled "How Duke Valentine Contrived" (1933). This short narrative of Italian intrigue is presented in delightfully colloquial English. Duke Valentine, the reader is told admiringly, was a "first rate humbug" who fools his enemies with "rotten promises." When the Duke decides to "put an end" to his enemies, one of them is seen "blubbering" over his fate. Such unobtrusive use of colloquialism revitalizes the story for modern readers.

From the earliest odes, Bunting's style is characterized by its concentration. While these short poems owe much to Pound, they sometimes lack the clarity of visual impression native to Imagist poetry. Nevertheless, they frequently capture an emotion with sleight of hand, as when they speak of the "pangs of old rapture," the "angriness of love," and the "savour of our sadness," and they frequently exhibit tactile and auditory images not easily achieved in poetry. For Bunting, waves of the sea consist not only in their visual impression, but also in their sound, "crying a strange name." A rain storm is seen in a "mudmirrored mackintosh," but its dampness is also "wiped and smeared" in tactile experience. Grass is "silent," a lake "slinks," children are "scabby." Visual images are never really separate from sound and touch. Thus, the mosaic of the Imagist poem is felt as "stone shouldering stone." Many of the odes might be classified as love poetry, but their view of human emotion and sexuality is as stark as their rough meter suggests.

Bunting's longer poems, his "Sonatas," exhibit the same concentration as his "Odes." Some readers have objected that their "musical" qualities require too much of mind and memory for even the most avid reader. "Villon" has been accused of obscurity, lacking both a central persona and a metrical norm through which a reader might trace musical variations. In the early poetry the use of voices rather than a persona shows the influence of Eliot rather than that of Pound. Bunting's is a poetry of mood and allusion. "Villon," a meditation on life and death, salutes a kindred spirit who lives after death only in the tracings of poetry. In the poem, the poet's own experiences in prison are incorporated in an appreciation of Villon's loneliness and suffering. Bunting's close identification with Villon the man arises from his own experiences in prison. Like Villon, Bunting saw himself as a powerless outsider commenting on the characters who people social institutions. The poem is a fit beginning for a poetic career which casts a dour eye on human life.

The wit of Bunting's social commentary is reminiscent of that of George Bernard Shaw, though it contains more of the spirit of George Orwell (in prose) and of Charles Chaplin (in motion pictures). In "Chomei at Toyama" (1932) the reader is given a delightful picture of human society, painted by a man who chooses to live poor and alone rather than be the editor of "the Imperial Anthology." Bunting enjoys making fun of the petty official (see Ode 23 "The Passport Officer") and the artist who sells himself to the party line. Especially biting is the portrait of the playwright (in "Aus Dem Zweiten Reich," 1931) who is known for having written more plays than William Shakespeare. This caricature of a man is able to speak about plays, politics, and poetry without saying anything at all. For Bunting, poetry requires honesty. He gives no quarter to the humbug, cheat, cheapjack, and boaster.

Bunting saw in Eliot's lighter verse and in his conversion to institutional Christianity a wandering from the honesty which true poetry requires. More important, he disliked what he considered Eliot's lack of economy. He preferred William Butler Yeats's greater concentration but denounced what he considered to be Yeats's own posturing. Bunting criticized the word "horseman" in Yeats's epitaph as a pandering to social elitism as well as an improper violation of the meter of the line. Much of Bunting's career can be seen as an effort to escape a natural inclination to write in the manner of Eliot. "Attis: Or Something Missing" (1931) is a satirical pastiche capturing Eliot's technique in ways that Bunting could never expunge from his own poetry. For Bunting, what seems to be "missing" from Eliot's work is the inner fortitude to denounce imposture in a corrupt social establishment of which Eliot so much wanted to be a part. Here the sharp meter and concentrated images which Bunting learned from Pound do much to hide Eliot's influence. In "The Well of Lycopolis" (1935) Bunting presents a wasteland more dour than Eliot's. It is Dante's *Inferno* transposed to the ordinary world, an *Inferno* without metaphysical extension, with neither *Purgatorio* nor *Paradiso*. Against the relief of Bunting's poetry, Eliot's Romanticism becomes glaringly obvious.

The lengthy sonata entitled *The Spoils* is frequently read as a transition to the poetry of *Briggflatts*. In its own right *The Spoils* is a poem of great beauty, capturing the essence of Middle Eastern life and culture. In this poem Bunting follows his former practice of including his own experiences—gathered during and after the war—with the literature and history which created the spirit of the region. The images of the poem are, in fact, "the spoils" which the poet brings back in his native tongue. Bunting's feeling for the interconnectedness of poetry and dance shows in allusions to the biblical Song of Songs, which arose, so scholars conjecture, as a play or chant probably enacted at the wedding service. It is in *The Spoils* that the distinctively Anglo-Saxon meter (characteristic of *Briggflatts*) begins to predominate. By easing the line and allowing more unstressed syllables back into his verse, the poet is able to capture the rhythms of an ancient chant. In such lines the effect is heightened by the use of pure English monosyllables. The result is not a predictable iamb, but instead a line of three and four heavy stresses thrown in sharp relief.

Bunting conquers the heavily stressed line in *Briggflatts*, a poem which returns to claim the poet's birthright in the language of Northumberland and the beat of Anglo-Saxon poetry. This autobiographical poem no longer merely incorporates Bunting's experience. *Briggflatts* is a return to roots, not only to the language and countryside of Northumbria, but also to the Romantic project of expressing the poet in the poetry. Here Bunting's professed debt to Wordsworth, a "Northerner," becomes apparent in the sweetly recounted spots of childhood memory, in the employment of the language of the common man, and in the identification with place by which a man can measure the unfolding of his life. *Briggflatts* records the poetic life of Bunting. Pound is there, and Eliot too. Their voices are now muted, however, against Bunting's own clear Northumbrian song. The poem is composed of simple English monosyllables which are artfully placed together with precision and condensation. To use the poet's own image, the pebbles are arranged in a mosaic. Most important is the seeming artlessness of the whole; gone are the set pieces and the satiric pastiche. In their place is the compact music of Domenico Scarlatti, with "never a boast or a see-here."

Wm. Dennis Horn

Other major work

ANTHOLOGY: *Active Anthology*, 1933 (with Ezra Pound).

Bibliography

Agenda 8 (Autumn, 1966). The entire issue is devoted to Bunting's poetry and includes essays by established critics and poets. Kenneth Cox discusses Bunting's economy of language and willingness to take risks with unexpected word choice. Robert Creeley notes Bunting's deep English roots and his ear for the English language. Sir Herbert Read comments on Bunting's insistence on music in poetry, and Charles Tomlinson explores the roots of that music in the work of Ezra Pound and William Carlos Williams and examines the musical structure of *Briggflatts*.

Agenda 19 (Spring, 1978). Another special issue on Bunting and his poetry. Peter Dale sets out to attack Bunting's analogy of poetry with music and tries to find meaning instead, while Roland John discusses why the critics have neglected Bunting's work. Peter Makin wonders to what degree the sound of a poem can communicate emotion, and Anthony Suter wonders also whether Bunting neglects meaning in his pursuit of sound. Also examines Bunting's creative process in an interview with Peter Quartermain.

Paideuma 9 (Spring, 1980). This issue gathers essays on, and tributes to, Bunting. In the analysis of "Villon," Peter Dale considers three ways of using musical form in poetry, David Gordon charts the use of rhythm and idiom in Bunting's career, and Hugh Kenner pays tribute to Bunting's distinctive reading voice. One of the best and most enjoyable is Carroll Terrell's "Basil Bunting in Action," which is a mixture of criticism, memoir, biography, and documentary.

Quartermain, Peter. *Basil Bunting: Poet of the North*. Durham, N.C.: Basil Bunting Poetry Archive, 1990. This twenty-four-page pamphlet is the text of a lecture delivered on Bunting's poetry. The talk was given in The Mountjoy Lecture series.

Terrell, Carroll F. *Basil Bunting: Man and Poet*. Orono, Maine: National Poetry Foundation, 1981. This introduction to Bunting's poetry contains an introduction by the editor as well as an annotated bibliography of critical works. The first three essays are biographical and are followed by essays on Bunting's "Sonatas" and the odes. A five-essay section on *Briggflatts* is followed by sections on his criticism and translations. Supplemented by a primary bibliography and an index.

Weatherhead, Andrew Kingsley. *The British Dissonance: Essays on Ten Contemporary Poets*. Columbia: University of Missouri Press, 1983. Weatherhead discusses Bunting's poetry in an essay alongside those of other British poets such as Ted Hughes, Anselm Hollo, Charles Tomlinson and Matthew Mead. Supplemented by an index and a bibliography of works by the poets.

ROBERT BURNS

Born: Alloway, Ayrshire, Scotland; January 25, 1759
Died: Dumfries, Scotland; July 21, 1796

Principal poetry

Poems, Chiefly in the Scottish Dialect, 1786 (Kilmarnock edition), 1787 (Edinburgh edition), 1793 (2 volumes).

Other literary forms

As a pure poet, Robert Burns had neither the time nor the desire for other literary forms. For *The Scots Musical Museum*, edited by James Johnson between 1787 and 1803, he wrote "Notes on Scottish Song," wherein he tried to collect all of the information he could about the poetic tradition of his native land. He suggested possibilities for authorship, identified the poems' native regions and the occasions of their composition, cited fragments and verses of traditional songs, and set forth critical comments and engaging anecdotes.

Following the publication and success of the 1786 edition of his *Poems*, Burns set off on a series of trips that carried him over much of Scotland. Narratives of two of those journeys, *Journal of a Tour in the Highlands Made in 1787* and *Journal of the Border Tour*, eventually found their way into print in 1834.

Achievements

Burns's most significant poetry was written in what may loosely be termed *Scots*—the northern dialect of English spoken regularly by Scottish peasants and informally by Scottish gentry. When the poet attempted to write in standard eighteenth century British English, he came forth as a different person: stiff, conventional, and genteel, seemingly trying too hard to find his place within the poetic tradition of his day. No matter what the dialect, however, literary historians have termed Burns a "pre-Romantic," a poet who anticipated William Wordsworth, gave new life to the English lyric, relied heavily upon literary forms and legends peculiar to the Scottish folk culture, and (certainly the most Wordsworthian quality of them all) wrote in the actual language of the common people. Few realize, however, that the pre-Romantic label is based primarily on Burns's songs, while the bulk of his poetry was written in the forms favored by the majority of eighteenth century poets. He also wrote satire, verse epistles to friends and fellow poets, and even a variation on the mock-epic narrative ("Tam O'Shanter"). An argument could easily be advanced that Burns ranks as a first-rate practitioner of those forms.

Nevertheless, as a writer of satire, epistle, and mock-heroic, Burns does not belong entirely to the neoclassical mainstream which followed John

Dryden, Alexander Pope, and Oliver Goldsmith. With his dialect and intricate stanza forms, his poems evinced a heartiness and exuberance, and even a certain "roughness." Burns had little use for Horace, Homer, and the other models for English neoclassicism; instead, he turned to a clearer tradition that had been established during the so-called golden age of Scottish poetry by the major Scottish Chaucerians: Robert Henryson (1430-1506), William Dunbar (1465-1530), and Gavin Douglas (1474-1522). Following the efforts of Allan Ramsay (1686-1758) and Robert Fergusson (1750-1774)—earlier Scottish poets who had collected the ancient poems and had written new ones based on the older models—Burns committed himself to the bards and songs of his native land. He refined the work of his eighteenth century predecessors, but he was also perceptive enough to learn from them and to retain characteristic subjects, forms, stanza patterns, and language.

No matter how academic, the discussion of Burns's poetry seems never to circumvent his songs. Almost to a line, those short pieces have gained wider fame and prompted more discussion than have his longer poems. Burns wrote more than three hundred songs on every subject imaginable within the context of late eighteenth century Scotland. Within the confines of those songs, Burns gave himself almost totally to the emotions of the moment; he reached out, touched the essence of rural Scotland, and brought it lyrically to life. He gave his readers the excitement and the genuineness of love, work, friendship, patriotism, and even inebriation (a point that has been greatly overemphasized). He portrayed universal character types, national heroes as well as lowly tavern revelers, and he took delight in sketching the grand parades of humanity as they passed before his vivid and lyrical imagination. Thus, Burns's poetic achievement was really very simple. He assumed the mantle of Scotland's national poet at a time when the country was struggling to preserve its cultural identity. Yet, if Burns spoke for Scotland, he stood also for all English-speaking people, who, as they prepared to undergo the political and technological traumas of the nineteenth century, needed frequent reminders of their national, political, and artistic heritage.

Biography

Robert Burns was born on January 25, 1759, in Alloway, some three miles south of the seaport town of Ayr. He was the first son of William Burnes (the original spelling of the family name that the poet eventually altered) and Agnes Broun. The father belonged to a lowly class of Scots agricultural society: he was a *cotter*, one who occupied a cottage on a farm in exchange for labor. As such, he engaged in a constant struggle to keep himself, his illiterate wife, and their seven children fed and clothed. In 1766, the elder Burnes leased seventy acres near Ayr and committed his family to farming. High rents and poor soil, however, only increased the size of the family debt. Young Robert studied at a small village school, where, for three years, he read English literature, wrote essays, and learned mathematics. After the practicalities of elementary education had been mastered, further learning came only as time would permit. The local schoolmaster, John Murdock, managed to teach the boy some French, and in 1775, the sixteen-year-old Burns journeyed across the Doon River to Kirkoswald, where he studied the rudiments of surveying. At home, the senior Burnes assumed responsibility for the balance of his son's education: geography, history, devotional and theological literature, and more mathematics. Although chores related to the family farm assumed a high priority, young Burns managed to find time for the Bible, Presbyterian theology, and any books he could beg or borrow from friends and neighbors.

In 1777, William Burnes moved his family some twelve miles to the northwest, to Lochlie Farm, between Tarbolton and Mauchline. There, eighteen-year-old Robert emerged as a sociable, sensitive, and handsome young man. He debated in the Tarbolton Bachelors' Club, a group of serious albeit boisterous young men; he joined the Freemasons; he discovered women. In 1781, he attempted to embark upon a business career in the flax-dressing industry at Irvine, on the coast. The venture proved to be a failure, and for the most part Burns rooted himself to the family farm in central Ayrshire, where he remained until the publication of the Kilmarnock edition of his *Poems* in 1786. William Burnes died in 1784, leaving his family heavily in debt. Robert and his brother Gilbert remained on the farm, however, and the poet's early verse indicates the degree to which he involved himself in the activities, associations, and gossip of the local people.

Burns had begun to write poetry around 1773, when he was fourteen. The poems tended, primarily, to be song lyrics in the Scots vernacular, although (probably as a result of Murdock's influence) he tried his hand at some moral and sentimental pieces in standard English. The manuscripts of those poems reveal considerable roughness. Burns needed models, and not until he came upon the work of two Scots poets, Robert Fergusson and Allan Ramsay, did he learn how to write nonlyric poetry in the Scots vernacular that would appeal to the hearts and minds of his countrymen. Three years prior to the publication of the Kilmarnock edition, he put together a commonplace book (several versions of which have been published), containing both his poems and remarks concerning his poetic development. Thus, the period 1785-1786 marked Burns's most significant literary output. It also proved to be the time when he would have to pay dearly for liaisons with various young women of the area. In May, 1785, his first daughter was born to Elizabeth Paton, a former servant; in all, he fathered nine illegitimate children, four by his future wife, Jean Armour (those were two sets of twins). He accepted responsibility for rearing and supporting all of them. Another affair with a servant girl, Mary Campbell—the "Highland Mary" of the song—ended tragically when the girl died giving birth to another Burns child.

Despite these domestic problems, the Kilmarnock edition of poems was published, bringing Burns success and some money. More important, the volume took him out of Ayrshire and into Edinburgh, where he gained the praise of the critic Henry Mackenzie (1745-1831) and the publisher William Creech (1745-1815), and where he arranged for publication and subscriptions for a new edition of his poems. From November, 1786, to mid-1788, Burns lived in Edinburgh, seeking to establish himself in its social and intellectual atmosphere. Although his congenial personality and intellectual curiosity appealed to the upper levels of Edinburgh society, they were not enough to erase the stigma of low social birth. The upper classes ultimately rejected him. Thus, the young poet drifted to the late-hour social clubs frequented by printers, booksellers, clerks, and schoolmasters. Through it all, he pondered about how to earn a living, since neither poetry nor social contacts enabled him to meet his financial obligations. Four separate tours throughout Scotland and the editorship of James Johnson's *The Scots Musical Museum* yielded no relief from financial pressures.

In March, 1788, Burns rented a tract of land for farming in Ellisland, Dumfriesshire, after which he finally married Jean Armour. He then began a struggle to support his family, a contest that was not eased even upon his securing an appointment (September, 1789) as tax collector and moving to Dumfries. His literary activities were limited to collecting and writing songs, in addition to the composition of some nonlyric pieces of moderate quality. Although "Tam O'Shanter" belongs to this period, Burns misused his talents by trying to emulate the early eighteenth century poets—composing moral epistles, general verse satires, political ballads, serious elegies, and prologues for theatrical pieces.

Burns died on July 21, 1796, the result of a heart condition that had existed since his youth. The details of his life have been much overstated, particularly the gossip about his drinking and his excessive sexual appetite. For serious students of his poetry, Burns's autobiography can be found within the sound and the sense of his writing.

Analysis

To an extraordinary degree, Robert Burns is *the* poet of Scotland, a Scotland that—despite its union with England—remained for him and his readers a totally independent cultural, intellectual, social, and political entity. Undoubtedly, Burns will always be identified exclusively with Scotland, with its peculiar life and manners communicated to the outside world through its distinctive dialect and fierce national pride. He justly deserves that identification, for he not only wrote about Scottish life and manners, but he also sought his inspiration from Scotland—from his own Ayrshire neighborhood, from its land and its people.

Scotland virtually drips from the lines of Burns's poetry. The scenes of the jocular "Jolly Beggars" have their source in Poosie Nansie's inn at Mauchline, while the poet and Tam O'Shanter meet the witches and the warlocks at midnight on the very real, local, and familiar Alloway Kirk. Indeed, reality obscures even the boldest attempts at erudite romanticism. Burns alludes to actual persons, to friends and acquaintances whom he knew and loved and to whom he dedicated his songs. When he tried his hand at satire, he focused upon local citizens, identifying specific personages or settling for allusions that his eighteenth century Scottish readers would easily recognize. In "The Cotter's Saturday Night"—which features a clear portrait of his own father—the poet reflects his deep attachment to and sincere pride in the village of Alloway and the rural environment of Ayrshire. He viewed the simple scenes in "The Cotter's Saturday Night" as the real essence of Scotland's heritage. Burns began with a sincere love and respect for his neighbors, and he sustained that attitude throughout his life and his work. Without the commitment to Scotland, he never would have conquered the hearts of its native readers nor risen to become the acknowledged national poet of the land north of the Tweed.

Burns's poetry gained almost immediate success among all classes of the Scottish population. He knew of what he wrote, and he grasped almost immediately the living tradition of Scottish poetry, assimilating the qualities of that tradition into his own verse forms and distinct subject matter. For example, the stanzaic forms in such poems as "To a Mouse" (and its companions) had been in existence for more than three hundred years. Burns early had become familiar with the Scottish Chaucerians (John Major, James I of Scotland, Robert Henryson, William Dunbar, Gavin Douglas, Sir David Lindsay) and the folk poets closer to his own day (Allan Ramsay, James Macpherson, Robert Fergusson); he took the best from their forms and content and made them his own. Thus, he probably could not be termed an "original" poet, although he had to work hard to set the tone and style to his readers' tastes. His countrymen embraced his poetry because they found the cadence, the music, and the dialect to be those of their own hearts and minds. The vigor and the deep love may have been peculiar to Burns, but the remaining qualities had existed longer than anyone could determine.

Still, writing in the relatively remote confines of Scotland at the end of the eighteenth century, Burns was not totally alien to the neoclassical norm of British letters. If Alexander Pope or Henry Fielding or Tobias Smollett could focus upon reality and write satires to expose the frailties of mankind, so could Burns be both realistic and satiric. In his most forceful poems—such as "Holy Willie's Prayer," "The Holy Fair," "Address to the Unco Guid"—he set out to expose the religious hypocrites of his day, but at the same time to portray, clearly and truthfully, both the beautiful and the ugly qualities of Scottish life and character. Burns's poetry may not always be even in quality or consistent in force, but it certainly always conveys an air of truthfulness.

If Burns's poetry reverberates with the remoteness of rural Scotland, it is because he found the perfect poetic environment for the universal themes of his works. In 1803, William Wordsworth stood beside his grave and contemplated "How Verse may build a princely throne/ On humble truth." The throne was carved out of Burns's understanding of the most significant theme of his time— the democratic spirit (which helps to explain Wordsworth's tribute). Throughout, the Scottish bard salutes the worth of pure man, the man viewed outside the context of station or wealth. Certainly, Burns was sensitive to the principles and causes that spawned the revolutions in America and in France; in fact, closer to home, the Jacobite rebellion sparked by the landing of the Young Pretender from France had occurred only nine years before the poet's birth. By nature, he was a political liberal, and his poems take advantage of every opportunity for man or beast to cry for freedom. Again, it was Wordsworth who identified Burns as a poet of the literary revolution—Romanticism—that later rushed through the open gates and into the nineteenth century.

Few will question that, ultimately, Burns's strength as a poet is to be found in the lyrical quality of his songs. That quality simply stood far above his other virtues—his ability to observe and to penetrate until he discovered the essence of a particular subject, his skill in description and satire, and his striving to achieve personal and intellectual independence. In his songs, he developed the ability to record, with the utmost ease, the emotions of the common people of whom he wrote. Burns's reliance on native Scottish tradition was both a limitation and a strength. For example, although he genuinely enjoyed the poetry of James Thomson (1700-1748), the Edinburgh University graduate who ventured to London and successfully challenged the artificiality of English poetry, Burns could not possibly have written a Scottish sequel to *The Seasons* (1726-1730). Instead, he focused upon the simple Scottish farmer, upon the man hard at work and enjoying social relationships, not upon the prevalent eighteenth century themes of solitude and retirement. In Burns, then, the reader sees strong native feeling and spontaneous expression, the source of which was inherited, not learned.

Another quality of Burns's poetry that merits attention is his versatility, the range of human emotions that exists throughout his verse. He could function as a satirist, and he could sound the most ardent notes of patriotism. His humor was neither vulgar nor harsh, but quiet, with considerable control—as in "Address to the Deil," "To a Mouse," and "To a Mountain Daisy." As a lover, as one who obviously loved to love and be loved, he wrote lyrical pieces that could capture the essence of human passion. The lyric forms allowed for the fullest expression of his versatility, most of which came about during the last ten years of his relatively short life.

From 1787 until his death in the summer of 1796, Burns committed himself to steady literary activity. He became associated with James Johnson, an uneducated engraver and enthusiastic collector and publisher of Scottish songs. From 1787 to 1804, Johnson gathered those songs into a five-volume

Scots Musical Museum, and Burns served as his principal editor. Then the poet became associated with George Thomson, whose *Select Collection of Scottish Airs* reached six volumes between 1793 and 1811. Burns's temperament seemed suited to such a combination of scholarly activity and poetic productivity, but he never accepted money for his contributions. The writing, rewriting, and transformation of some three hundred old songs and ballads would serve as his most singular gift to his nation. In reworking those antiquated songs and popular ballads, he returned to Scotland, albeit in somewhat modified form, a large portion of its culture that had for so long remained in obscurity. Thus, an old drinking song emerged as "Auld Lang Syne," while a disreputable ballad became "John Anderson My Jo." Finally, the Johnson and Thomson collections became outlets for certain of his more famous original songs: "For A' That and A' That," "Scots, Wha Hae wi' Wallace Bled," as well as such love lyrics as "Highland Mary" and "Thou Lingering Star." Because of his love of and gift for the traditional Scots folk songs and ballads, Burns wrote and sang for Scotland. He became the voice and the symbol of the people and captured the national sentiment.

It would be a mistake, however, to assume that all is happily rustic, nationalistic, or patriotic with Burns. On the contrary, he has a decidedly melancholy or mournful strain. A look at such poems as "A Bard's Epitaph" and the "Epistle to a Young Friend" demonstrates that the intellect and the passion of the poet were far from being comfortably adjusted. A conflict raged within the mind and heart of Burns as the sensibilities of an exceedingly gifted soul vied with the sordid lot that was his by birth and social position (or the lack of it). Despite the appearance and even the actuality of productivity during his last five years, the final stage of Burns's career reflects, in the soberest of terms, the degradation of genius. Nevertheless, his muse remained alive and alert, as his passions seethed within him until they found outlets in rhyme. Burns controlled his passion so that, particularly in his songs, there is abundant evidence of sense and beauty. To his credit, he remained aware of the conflict within him and drew strength from the clash of experiences, of habits, and of emotions which, somehow, he managed to regulate and harmonize. Few will argue that certain of the songs ("Mary Morison," "My Nanie O," and "Of A' the Airts the Wind Can Blow") hang heavy with serious and extremely pathetic and passionate strains. Since such heaviness had its origin in the Scottish tradition, Burns could effectively hide his own melancholy behind the Lugar or the banks of Bonnie Doon.

Such conclusions invariably lead to the question of a religious or moral element in Burns's poetry. Assuredly, the more religious among Burns scholars have difficulty with such poems as "The Holy Fair," "Holy Willie" and the satiric pieces in which the poet ridiculed religious and ecclesiastical ideals and personages. No doubt Burns's own moral conduct was far from perfect, but the careful reader of his poetry realizes immediately that Burns never ridiculed religion; rather, he heaped scorn only upon those religious institutions that appeared ridiculous and lacked the insight to recognize obvious weaknesses. Indeed, the poet often seems to be looking for virtue and morality, seeking to replace the sordid scenes of his own world with the piety of another time and place. He sought a world beyond and above the grotesqueness of his own debauchery, a world dominated by order, love, truth, and joy. That is about the best he could have done for himself. Even had Burns been the epitome of sobriety, morality, and social and religious conformity, religious expression would probably not have been high on his list of poetic priorities. He inherited the poetic legacy of Scotland—a national treasure found outside the limits of the Kirk, a vault not of hymns and psalm paraphrases, but of songs and ballads. Such were the constituent parts of Burns's poetic morality.

Burns's language and poetic methods seem to distract only the impatient among his readers. To begin with, he believed that the vernacular ought never to be seen as low or harsh, or even as prostituted English. Rather, Burns came to know and to understand the Scots dialect and to manipulate it for his own poetic purpose. At the outset, he claimed to have turned his back upon formal bodies of knowledge, upon books, and to have taken full advantage of what he termed "Nature's fire" as the only learning necessary for his art. Nature may have provided the attraction toward the Scots dialect, but Burns himself knew exactly what to do with it. Close attention to his letters and to the details of his life will yield the steps of his self-education. He read Thomas Salmon's *Geographical and Historical Grammar* (1749) and a *New System of Modern Geography, History, and Modern Grammar* (1770), by William Guthrie (1708-1770), both of which provided descriptions and examples of Scotland's traditions and language, although nothing of poetic contexts. Then he turned to Jethro Tull (1680-1740), the Hungerford farmer and inventor, who wrote several volumes on the general subject of "horse-hoeing husbandry" (1731-1739), and to the Reverend Adam Dickson of Edinburgh, who wrote *A Treatise on Agriculture* (1762, 1765, 1769) and the two-volume *The Husbandry of the Ancients* (1788). Thus, Burns was well versed in the specifics of rural Scotland by the time he discovered his most helpful source, the poetry of Robert Fergusson, who had managed successfully to capture the dialect of enlightened Edinburgh. Burns had his models, and he simply shifted the sounds and the scenes from Scotland's capital to rural Ayrshire.

To simplify matters even further, Burns himself had actually stood behind the plow. Little wonder, then, that the Kilmarnock edition of the *Poems* succeeded on the basis of such pieces as "The Twa Dogs," "The Holy Fair," "Address to the Deil," "Halloween," "The Cotter's Saturday Night," "To a Mouse," and "To a Mountain-Daisy." Burns had effectively described Scottish life as Scots themselves (as well as those south of the Tweed) had come to know it. More important, the poems in that initial collection displayed to the world the poet's full intellectual range of wit and sentiment, although his readers received nothing that had not already been a part of their long tradition. Essentially, the Edinburgh edition of the following year gave the world more of the same, and Burns's readers discovered that the poet's move from Ayrshire to Edinburgh had not changed his sources or his purpose. The new poems—among them "Death and Dr. Hornbook," "The Brigs of Ayr," "Address to the Unco Guid," "John Barleycorn," and "Green Grow the Rushes"—still held to the pictures of Scottish life and to the vernacular, still held to the influence of Robert Fergusson's *Scots Poems* (1773).

By the time Burns had done some substantive work on James Johnson's *The Scots Musical Museum*, however, his art had assumed a new dimension, the writing and revision of the Scots song. The poet became a singer, providing his own accompaniment by the simple means of humming to himself as he wrote, and trying (as he explained) to catch the inspiration and the enthusiasm so strongly characterized in the traditional poetry. He set out to master the tune, then to compose for that particular strain. In other words, he demanded that for the song, musical expression must dictate the poetic theme. Nevertheless, Burns was the first to admit his weakness as a musician, making no claims even to musical taste. For him, as a poet, music was instinctive, supplied by nature to complement his art. Thus, he felt unable to deal with the technical aspects of music as a formal discipline. What he *could* do, however, was to react quickly to what he termed "many little melodies" and to give new and fresh poetic and musical expression to something like "Scots Wha Hae," one of the oldest of Scottish airs. Through the songs, Burns clearly preserved tradition, while, at the same time, he maintained his originality. This tradition was the genuine expression of the people who, from generation to generation, echoed the essence of their very existence; Burns gave it sufficient clarity and strength to carry it forward into the next century and beyond. The effect of those more than three hundred songs was, simply, to cede Burns the title of Scotland's national poet—a title that he earned because of his poetic rather than his political voice.

Perhaps the one poem that demonstrates Burns's ability as a serious and deliberate craftsman, a true poet, is "Tam O' Shanter" (1790, 1791). More than anything else, that piece of 224 lines transports its creator away from the "Heaven-taught plowman" image, from the label of the boy genius whose poetry is nothing more than one large manifestation of the spontaneous overflow of his native enthusiasm. Burns wrote "Tam O' Shanter" for a volume on Scottish antiquity and based it on a witch story told about Alloway Kirk, an old ruin near the poet's house in Ayr. Yet, he turned that tale into a mock-heroic rendering of folk material that comes close, in genre and in poetic quality, to Geoffrey Chaucer's "The Nun's Priest's Tale." Burns specifically set out to construct his most sustained and most artistic production; in his own words, he remained aware of the "spice of roguish waggery" within the poem, but he also took considerable pains to ensure that the force of his poetic genius and "finishing polish" would not go unrecognized. Burns's manipulation of his dipsomaniacal hero and his misadventures constitutes a masterful blending of the serious and the comic. The moralists of his day objected vehemently to the ribald elements of the poem. Early in the next century, William Wordsworth, whose strongest drink was probably water, attacked the attackers of "Tam O' Shanter" (as well as those who objected to all of Burns's poetry on moral grounds) by labeling them impenetrable dunces and narrow-minded puritans. Wordsworth saw the poem as a delightful picture of the rustic adventurer's convivial exaltation; if the poem lacked clear moral purpose, maintained England's laureate, it at least provided the clearest possible moral effect.

The final issue raised by Burns's poetry is his place in literary history—an issue that has always prompted spirited debate. There is no doubt that Burns shares common impulses with Wordsworth and the Romantic movement, particularly in his preoccupation with folklore and the language of the people, yet neither is there any evidence of Burns's fundamental dissatisfaction with the dominant critical criteria and principal literary assumptions of eighteenth century England. The readers of his songs will be hard put to discover lush scenery or majestic mountains, or even the sea—although all were in easy reach of his eye and his mind. If he expressed no poetic interest in such aspects of nature close at hand, however, he turned even less in the direction of the distant and the exotic. Instead, he looked long and hard at the farmer, the mouse, the louse, and he contemplated each; the mountains, the nightingale, the skylark he also saw, but chose to leave them to the next generation of poets. In other words, Burns did not seek new directions for his poetry; instead, he took full advantage of what existed and of what had come before. He grasped literary imitation firmly and gave that form the most significance and prominence it had enjoyed since the late Restoration and the Augustan age. Burns wrote satire and he wrote songs, but he invented neither. Rather, he served as an exploiter of tradition; he gathered inherited motifs, rhetorical conventions, and familiar language and produced art. The reader of the present century should see no less or expect no more from Burns's poetical character.

Samuel J. Rogal

Other major works

NONFICTION: *Journal of a Tour in the Highlands Made in 1787*, 1834 (Allan Cunningham, editor); *Journal of the Border Tour*, 1834 (Allan Cunningham, editor); *The Letters of Robert Burns*, 1931 (John De Lancey Ferguson, editor, 2 volumes).

Bibliography

Bentman, Raymond. *Robert Burns*. Boston: Twayne, 1987. This complete introduction to the life and works of Robert Burns describes Burns's background, analyzes his poetry and songs, then places him in the context of late eighteenth century literature. Includes an annotated secondary bibliography and is suitable for high school students and college undergraduates.

Daiches, David. *Robert Burns and His World*. New York: Viking Press, 1971. A well-illustrated book that combines Burns's biography with snippets of his writing. Daiches explains how Scottish society profoundly influenced Burns's work. A lively book that is suitable for all students.

Fitzhugh, Robert T. *Robert Burns, the Man and Poet: A Round, Unvarnished Account*. Boston: Houghton Mifflin, 1970. Fitzhugh mixes poetry with anecdote in this biography of Burns. He has even attached an appendix with Burns's health record, gleaned from his correspondence. The author analyzes Burns's poetic writing separately from his songs, for he asserts that Burns did not consider his songs to be poetry.

Jack, R. D. S., and Andrew Noble, eds. *The Art of Robert Burns*. London: Vision Press, 1982. The nine essays contained in this book place Burns in a wide social and literary context, outside his native Scotland. They seek to show Burns as a complex writer, and not merely a "cosy representative of Scottish virtues." Suitable for intermediate and advanced students.

Snyder, Franklyn Bliss. *The Life of Robert Burns*. 1932. Reprint. Hamden, Conn.: Shoestring Press, 1968. The best biography of Burns, although some of the writing seems dated. Snyder recounts Burns's life in a sentimental way that reduces the poet to a Scottish stereotype. Yet it is a factual account accessible to all levels of students.

SAMUEL BUTLER

Born: Strensham, England; February 8, 1612
Died: London, England; September 25, 1680

Principal poetry
Hudibras, Parts I-III, 1663, 1664, 1678.

Other literary forms
Samuel Butler wrote essays and prose Characters in addition to verse. His best-known essay is *The Case of King Charles I Truly Stated*, which argues that the execution of Charles I was unjustified. Butler's essay was published in Robert Thyer's *The Genuine Remains in Verse and Prose of Samuel Butler* (1759) and it displays his excellent understanding of English law—an understanding that plays an important role in *Hudibras*—and his ability to pick apart a point of view, a trait manifested in his carefully reasoned satire.

Of greater literary significance are his Characters, which were probably composed during 1667 to 1669, nearly two hundred of which have been uncovered since Butler's death. The most complete edition of the Characters is that of Charles W. Daves. As with *Hudibras*, Butler took a popular literary form of the seventeenth century and modified it to suit his satiric purposes. His Characters feature politicians, judges, lovers, and zealots, and in each sketch, he demonstrates his abhorrence of immoderation, his contempt for hypocrisy, his disgust with irrational thought, and his willingness to expose fraud and ostentation wherever they might be found. Although some of the Characters were intended for publication, others were probably intended to serve as raw material which Butler could mine for his poetry.

Achievements
Butler's greatest achievement was to embody in a single work the failures, hypocrisy, and foolishness of an age. *Hudibras* captures the dark spirit of seventeenth century England, and the wit which made his contemporaries regard Butler as a great comic satirist also reveals the flaws in their philosophies. In Butler's stingingly accurate portrait of his time lies much of his literary strength and weakness. If one reads and understands *Hudibras*, one learns to understand the culture of Oliver Cromwell's England and of Restoration England. Butler's misanthropic point of view illuminates his society; even though he was a Loyalist, and the surface thrust of *Hudibras* is an attack on Cromwellian Puritans, Butler spares no one from his sharp insights. *Hudibras* is necessarily specific, and Butler's allusions to events and people were readily recognized in his time. Such particularity has made Butler's satire dependent on his readers' understanding of the 1600's. Thus, what made Butler's contemporaries laugh and wince may puzzle modern readers.

Hudibras brought Butler fame; he became known as "Hudibras Butler" or simply as "Hudibras." Such verse is still called Hudibrastic, and its imitations are called Hudibrastic satires. The poem stands out not only as one of the great achievements in satire but also as a work that inspired multitudes of imitations and helped to shape the forms of satire after its time. Its influence stretched from the seventeenth century to America after the Revolution. Indeed, the poem's assault on cultural elitism appealed to antimonarchists and egalitarians, in spite of Butler's evident Loyalist views. Butler expanded the bounds of satire, writing in verse when contemporary literary theorists said satire was best suited to prose. Critics still argue over whether *Hudibras* is satire, burlesque, heroic satire, satirical burlesque, or something else entirely. Butler showed that satire could, like *Don Quixote de la Mancha* (1605, 1615), mock a literary genre, expose the foibles of a class of people, and provide insights into the intellectual controversies of an era. Butler influenced the satirists who followed him, although few produced works which could match *Hudibras* for wit, insight, and bitterness.

Biography

Two distinct portraits of Samuel Butler have developed since his death—one traditional and the other historical. Most sketches of Butler's life rely on the traditional version, based primarily on the accounts of John Aubrey, who knew him, and Anthony à Wood, a contemporary of Butler who admitted that he was uncertain of his facts. One reason why most short biographies rely on the traditional accounts is that the historical ones have been uncertain and contradictory. Evidence in the form of letters, notes, and public documents has been hard to come by, and new evidence sometimes contradicts the old. Only since the mid-twentieth century has historical evidence begun to supplant the traditional version of Butler's life.

Both versions agree on the major aspects of Butler's youth. He was born in Strensham, England, on February 8, 1612, and was baptized on February 14. His father, also named Samuel, was a farmer who rented property from the local gentry and had a home and lands in Barbourne. The elder Butler was evidently learned and maintained a large and diverse library that he left to his eight children when he died. Samuel was then only fourteen years of age.

Butler probably attended King's School in Worcester, north of Strensham. Tradition claims that he also attended college—perhaps Oxford, although records show no evidence of his having continued his formal education after leaving King's School. He probably became a secretary for various gentlemen and gentlewomen. Through these people, he became acquainted with some of the leading minds of his day, possibly including John Seldon, a legal historian who knew Ben Jonson, Thomas Hobbes, and others. Butler had ample opportunity to observe the pretentiousness of England's social and intellectual elite, and he may have learned about England's laws and theology from such people as Seldon.

In 1642, King Charles I raised his standard at Nottingham. In 1649, he was executed. Tradition has it that during these tumultuous years, Butler served as a clerk to Sir Samuel Luke, a member of Parliament from Bedfordshire, and that Luke served as the model for the character Hudibras. Other models have been suggested by historians, yet Butler probably used several Puritans as inspiration for Hudibras. He might have begun *Hudibras* before 1649, and it might have been his response to having to survive by serving parliamentarians while harboring loyalist sentiments.

Some accounts indicate that fragments of *Hudibras* were copied and circulated before the Restoration. Butler had already written essays defending the monarchy and was almost certainly working on *Hudibras* when Oliver Cromwell died in 1658. Charles II entered London in 1660, at which time works by Loyalists became popular. When *Hudibras*, Part I, was published in late 1662 (it was postdated 1663), it caught the fancy of the public and of the King; Charles II was said to quote from the poem from memory. Butler probably made enough money from the sale of *Hudibras*, Part I, and later *Hudibras*, Part II, to live well.

Butler apparently invested his money unwisely; or, perhaps he spent it too rapidly. Some accounts assert that Charles II gave Butler three hundred pounds as a royal grant. Other accounts maintain that Charles II gave Butler a one hundred pound annuity. Others assert that both were given; still others mention neither. What seems likely is that Charles II was dilatory in fulfilling any promises he made to Butler. By 1673, Butler had become secretary to the Duke of Buckingham. Not until 1677, apparently, did Charles II provide Butler with any monetary support. In 1678, *Hudibras*, Part III, was published, in part to provide Butler with income beyond that which came from his secretarial work.

Tradition holds that Butler was unjustly neglected by an ungrateful king who failed to fulfill promises made to the poet. History indicates that Charles II was freer with his promises than with his money. Butler's own sharp misanthropic wit may have cost him royal and noble help; he seems to have found fault with everyone he knew—a practice that might have alienated potential patrons. Regardless of what he was promised and what he actually received, he lived in a poor part of London and died on September 25, 1680, in genuinely miserable poverty. He was buried in the graveyard of St. Paul's, in Covent Garden. A bust of him resides in the Poets' Corner of Westminster Abbey.

Analysis

Samuel Butler's stature as a poet is founded on one work: *Hudibras*. In it, he demonstrates considerable skill in prosody; yet many critics are uncertain about the work's status as poetry, describing it as doggerel. One of Butler's objectives in *Hudibras* is the debasement of heroic verse; thus, although he is undoubtedly a poet, his verse is not what is commonly thought of as poetry. This contradiction is one of many inherent in Butler's great work. He displays a broad knowledge of literature and philosophy—a knowledge which is the product of an inquisitive and thoughtful mind—yet he presents his knowledge only to portray it as foolish. Although *Hudibras* became famous as a political satire and remains best known for its portrayal of seventeenth century English politics, two of its three parts are devoted to social satire.

Hudibras is written in rhyming tetrameter couplets, a verse form that in Butler's day was associated with heroic poetry. Philosophically a rationalist, Butler objected to poetry which defied probability by describing magic, fairies, enchanted castles, flying horses, and other fantastic places, creatures, and events. Thus, he took a verse form that would be familiar to his audience and subverted it by using it to describe false heroes and sordid events, and by employing strange rhymes and odd plays on words. *Hudibras* abounds with such irreverent rhymes as: "And Pulpit, Drum Ecclesiastik,/ Was beat with fist, instead of a stick," from Part I; and from Part II,

> Quoth *Hudibras*, You lie so ope,
> That I, without a *Telescope*,
> Can find your Tricks out, and descry
> Where you tell truth, and where you lie

Throughout his poem, Butler's verse is exuberantly barbaric; the rhymes are wildly original, and the wordplay is rapid and clever. Instead of romantic language, Butler creates witty wordplay, thus trivializing heroic verse.

Much of Butler's brilliance as a poet is manifested in his mutilation of language. By deliberately using his couplets to present doggerel, he subverts the ideas he wishes to attack with his diction. Analytically gifted and capable of perceiving truth in the folly of others, he insists on expressing his rationalist understanding of truth by exposing the particulars of folly. His analytical character and rationalist point of view make him seem more part of the modern era than of the English Renaissance that nurtured him. His models were works such as Edmund Spenser's *The Faerie Queene* (1590-1596) and Miguel de Cervantes' *Don Quixote*, but he could not empathize with *The Faerie Queene* as he could with *Don Quixote*. Thus, he mocks Spenser's epic work and its kin with satire more harsh than that found in Cervantes' satirical romance. Butler's verse mocks not only ideas but also the very modes in which they are expressed.

Butler includes careful allusions to *The Faerie Queene*, the masterwork of English Renaissance heroic verse, to emphasize his implicit intent to satirize the Arcadian romances of his sixteenth century predecessors. Each canto of *Hudibras* begins with an "Argument," as does each canto of *The Faerie*

Queene. More important, the name *Hudibras* is taken from Spenser's poem: "He that made loue vnto the eldest Dame,/ Was hight Sir *Huddibras*, an hardy man;/ Yet not so good of deedes, as great of name." Butler takes this character who was "not so good of deedes" and places him in Puritan England. This act, coupled with his perverse versification, makes *Hudibras* satirical in its most fundamental elements: language and character.

The first part of *Hudibras* is organized by the elements of an epic quest. Like Cervantes' *Don Quixote*, *Hudibras* features a knight-errant who misperceives his world. Hudibras, the character, seems much like Don Quixote; he seeks to right wrongs, is afflicted by low characters whose natures he misapprehends, and is accompanied by a sort of squire. Even his fatness seems, in context, to be in deliberate contrast to Quixote's thinness. Yet, for all the seeming borrowing from *Don Quixote*, Hudibras is significantly different from his predecessor, just as Butler's misanthropic view of life is different from that of Cervantes. Given the misery inflicted on Cervantes, one might expect him to have a cold view of the world, but *Don Quixote* is a gentle satire and readers can sympathize with its unfortunate protagonist. Hudibras is an inherently unsympathetic character; he is boorish, greedy, cowardly, and self-righteous. Don Quixote seeks giants; Hudibras seeks nonconformity with Puritanical notions of virtue. One tries to combat the masters of evil; the other bullies only those who appear weak. In addition, Don Quixote's companion, Sancho Panza, is a slow but good-natured man, while Hudibras' companion, Ralph, is an angry man who despises Hudibras and rivals his master in greed, deceit, and foolishness. Butler's treatment of his characters is cold, dispassionate, and often harsh; Cervantes' compassion is a notable feature of his work.

Whatever the origins of Butler's misanthropy, his even-handed scorn makes *Hudibras* curiously egalitarian. Butler, a royalist, leaves no character unscathed, and no idea is introduced for purposes other thán to expose its emptiness. Hudibras, the Puritan, is an obvious target of Butler's antipathy, but Ralph is a religious Independent and receives the same treatment from Butler, who describes Ralph's manner of learning as one "that costs no pains/ Of Study, Industry, or Brains." Their antagonists are often cruel and usually equally self-righteous, no matter what their political leanings.

The plot of *Hudibras* follows a traditional pattern of romance. A knight-errant, spurned by a woman, seeks to lose his sense of loss in questing. While on his quest, he encounters dangers and assorted exotic characters. Eventually, he wins the attentions of a woman. In the case of questing Hudibras, his first adventure involves an encounter with bearbaiters and a fiddler with a wooden leg. Hudibras sees a village audience dancing merrily to the fiddler Crowdero's music and watching the bear. As a good Puritan magistrate, he is offended by the frivolity of the dancers and the immorality of the bearbaiters. Further, he recognizes the public merrymaking as a threat to public order and thus to the government. As a good logician, Hudibras deduces that such a threat represents a Roman Catholic plot to overthrow the Protestant government; the merrymakers are conspirators and Crowdero is their leader. Hudibras seeks to arrest the fiddler and a fight ensues. In the melee, the knight-errant falls from his mount onto the bear, angering the animal. It escapes its keeper and scatters the mob. Victorious, Hudibras and Ralph place Crowdero in the village stocks. Trulla, a physically powerful woman, leads the villagers in a counterattack. After much confusion, Hudibras and Ralph are defeated and replace Crowdero in the stocks. The first part of the poem ends with the Puritan and the Independent debating both the blame for their failure and the relative importance of logic and inspiration.

No great imagination is required for one to understand how the tale of the follies of a Puritan would have appealed to King Charles II and the Royalists. Some of Butler's contemporaries read specific political figures into the roles of the villagers, yet Butler's satire is too general to support such identifications. Ideas are the targets of his satirical wit; thus, Hudibras' reasoning is more representative of Butler's satire than are the comic characters that people his narrative. Hudibras, the Puritan, sees a Popish plot where none could possibly be; he is so consumed by theory and prejudice that he does not understand reality. This notion is the heart of Butler's satire. In the crazy behavior of Hudibras in Part I, Butler expresses his contempt for the way the Puritans interpreted reality. If his satire is taken as a portrait of ideas, then Butler finds the ideas of the Puritans to be empty, hypocritical, and warped.

In Parts II and III, Butler's satire shifts from the political to the social. In this shift, Butler anticipates the thematic thrust of Restoration comedy, which focused on society and on the relationship between men and women. Hudibras is released from the stocks through the intercession of the Widow, who helps Hudibras on the basis of his promise to take a whipping as punishment for his misbehavior. Hudibras plans for Ralph to take his whipping for him and plots to marry the Widow, who is rich. Ralph also wants the Widow for himself. Much of the narrative focuses on the efforts of Hudibras to evade a whipping and to woo the Widow. In the process, Butler reveals the ethical depravity not only of Hudibras but of the other characters as well, and he exposes the emptiness of the love conventions of the epic romance. Even the intended victim of Hudibras and Ralph, the Widow, is no innocent. She does not mind someone marrying her for her money if he is open about it. Her objections to Hudibras and Ralph are based on their subterfuges: the lies about the whipping, the pretense of love, and the general duplicity. The decreased contemporary popularity of Parts II and III, in comparison to Part I, was probably a tribute to the accuracy of Butler's satire rather than a reflection of any loss of inspiration. While Part I exposed the falseness of the preceding generation, Parts II and III illustrated the hypocrisies of its intended readership; Butler's audience was asked to see its own falseness, thus anticipating Alexander Pope's *The Dunciad* (1728-1743), Jonathan Swift's satires, and the more gentle comedies of William Wycherley, William Congreve, and Richard Sheridan.

Hudibras is distinguished by its verse, which spawned a school of imitations called Hudibrastic. It is also distinguished by its wit and vigor, which make for a lively narrative. Its satire is unusually sophisticated and wideranging, attacking a poetic genre, a style of verse, and the politics, theology, and manners of Butler's society.

Kirk H. Beetz

Other major works
MISCELLANEOUS: *The Genuine Remains in Verse and Prose of Samuel Butler*, 1759 (Robert Thyer, editor); *Characters, Observations, and Reflexions from the Notebooks*, 1908 (A. R. Waller, editor); *Samuel Butler, 1612-1680: Characters*, 1970 (Charles W. Daves, editor).

Bibliography
Furbank, P. N. *Samuel Butler: 1835-1902.* Cambridge, England: Cambridge University Press, 1948. Aims mostly to discredit the attack made by Malcolm Muggeridge in 1936 on Butler and Butler's admirers. Argues that, like Oscar Wilde, Butler had a quarrel with society, but Butler's self-protectiveness prevented him from achieving greatness. A brief bibliography precedes the text.

Henderson, Philip. *Samuel Butler: The Incarnate Bachelor.* Bloomington: Indiana University Press, 1954. One of the best biographies of Butler, and the first to deal with Butler's private life. Focuses on Butler's personality rather than his work. Readable and illuminating. Argues against such mistaken prevailing views that Butler hated his father. Contains a detailed chronology.

Holt, Lee. *Samuel Butler.* Rev. ed. Boston: Twayne, 1989. In his critical evaluation, Holt summarizes and quotes extensively from a wide range of Butler's work, much of it no longer available. Extends the reader's knowledge of Butler's varied accomplishments. Includes biographical information, a chronology, notes, references, a lengthy selected bibliography, and an index with brief annotations.

Jeffers, Thomas L. *Samuel Butler Revalued.* University Park: Pennsylvania State University Press, 1981. An appreciation rather than a panegyric, this critical study focuses on *The Way of All Flesh* because it was composed during the period when Butler thought most creatively about evolution, his religion, and his family. Contains lengthy notes, a selected bibliography, and an index.

Stillman, Clara. *Samuel Butler: A Mid-Victorian Modern.* New York: Viking

Press, 1932. The most thoughtful, comprehensive, and useful general discussion of Butler. Stillman saw him primarily as a philosopher and as an exponent of ideas around which his twentieth century heirs revolve. Contains an index and a bibliography, many of whose entries are now inaccessible.

Turner, Frank Miller. *Between Science and Religion: The Reaction to Scientific Naturalism in Late Victorian England.* New Haven, Conn.: Yale University Press, 1974. Examines Butler and five other representative Victorians because they made the common discovery that neither Christian orthodoxy nor the new scientific naturalism could satisfy their spiritual needs. Contains useful bibliographic essays on each subject and an index.

GEORGE GORDON, LORD BYRON

Born: London, England; January 22, 1788
Died: Missolonghi, Greece; April 19, 1824

Principal poetry

Fugitive Pieces, 1806; *Poems on Various Occasions,* 1807; *Hours of Idleness,* 1807; *Poems Original and Translated,* 1808; *English Bards and Scotch Reviewers,* 1809; *Hints from Horace,* 1811; *Childe Harold's Pilgrimage,* Cantos I-IV, 1812-1818, 1819 (the four cantos published together); *The Curse of Minerva,* 1812; *Waltz: An Apostrophic Hymn,* 1813; *The Giaour,* 1813; *The Bride of Abydos,* 1813; *The Corsair,* 1814; *Ode to Napoleon Buonaparte,* 1814; *Lara,* 1814; *Hebrew Melodies Ancient and Modern,* 1815; *The Siege of Corinth,* 1816; *Parisina,* 1816; *Poems,* 1816; *The Prisoner of Chillon, and Other Poems,* 1816; *Monody on the Death of the Right Honourable R. B. Sheridan,* 1816; *The Lament of Tasso,* 1817; *Manfred,* 1817 (verse drama); *Beppo: A Venetian Story,* 1818; *Mazeppa,* 1819; *Don Juan,* Cantos I-XVI, 1819-1824, 1826 (the sixteen cantos published together); *Marino Faliero, Doge of Venice,* 1821 (verse drama); *The Prophecy of Dante,* 1821; *Sardanapalus,* 1821 (verse drama); *The Two Foscari,* 1821 (verse drama); *Cain:A Mystery,* 1821 (verse drama); *The Vision of Judgment,* 1822; *Heaven and Earth,* 1822 (verse drama); *The Age of Bronze,* 1823; *The Island,* 1823; *Werner,* 1823 (verse drama); *The Deformed Transformed,* 1824 (unfinished verse drama); *The Complete Poetical Works of Byron,* 1980-1986 (5 volumes).

Other literary forms

It should be noted that the titles of Byron's principal poetic works include dramatic as well as lyrical and narrative works. Lord Byron wrote eight plays in all, most of which focused on either speculative or historical subjects and were never intended for the stage. He designated them "mental theatre," or closet drama modeled after classical principles, and clearly regarded the plays as among his most important productions. Complementing Byron's extraordinarily prolific and diverse career as a poet is his versatility as a writer of epistolary prose. During his lifetime Byron composed more than 2,900 letters, which have been scrupulously edited by Leslie A. Marchand and published between 1973 and 1982 in twelve volumes under the title *Byron's Letters and Journals.* The sheer immensity of this correspondence is matched only by the unlimited range and immediacy of Byron's voice as he speaks without reserve on a variety of topics. In addition to these private documents, along with John Keats's letters the most revealing correspondence of the British Romantic poets, Byron also published the combative *Letter to [John Murray] on the Rev. W. L. Bowles' Strictures on the Life and Writings of Pope* (1821) and, in the first number of Leigh Hunt's *The Liberal* (1822), "A Letter to the Editor of 'My Grandmother's Review.'" *The Parliamentary*

Speeches of Lord Byron, comprising three addresses he made while a member of the House of Lords, was issued in 1824, well after he had grown disillusioned with what he called "Parliamentary mummeries."

Achievements

If poets can be judged by the intellectual and cultural myths which they inspire, then Byron must be deemed the most broadly influential of the Romantic writers. Through his creation of a brooding and defiant persona known as the "Byronic Hero"—according to Peter L. Thorslev, Jr., a composite blend of the attributes of Cain, Ahasuerus, Satan, Prometheus, Rousseau's Child of Nature, the Man of Feeling, the Gloomy Egoist, the Gothic Villain, and the Noble Outlaw—Byron exerted a profound impact on the entire nineteenth century and its conception of the archetypal Romantic sensibility. The essential trait that came to be associated with "Byronism" is what Bertrand Russell, in his *History of Western Philosophy* (1945), identifies as "Titanic cosmic self-assertion." Signifying less a specific stance than a generalized attitude, the phrase denotes a proud, often despairing, rebellion against any institutional or moral system that threatens to rob the self of its autonomy, centrality, and independence. Something of the extent to which this outlook captured the imagination of the age can be gauged from a brief list of artists and thinkers whose works reflect Byron's influence: in Germany, Johann Wolfgang von Goethe, Heinrich Heine, Ludwig van Beethoven, and Friedrich Nietzsche; in France, Honoré de Balzac, Stendhal, Hector Berlioz, and Eugène Delacroix; in Russia, Aleksandr Pushkin and Fyodor Dostoevski; and in America, Herman Melville. Even Matthew Arnold, that most Wordsworthian of Victorian critics, admitted in his 1850 poem "Memorial Verses" that the collective English soul "Had *felt* him like the thunder's roll." Thirty-one years later, Arnold's view had not changed: "The power of Byron's personality," he wrote, approvingly quoting A. C. Swinburne, "lies in . . . '*the excellence of sincerity and strength.*'"

What fascinated nineteenth century audiences about Byron was not simply the larger-than-life character of the man transmuted into art, but also the flinty integrity of his mind that penetrated all deception and constantly tested the limits of skepticism. In this respect Byron seems peculiarly modern. Although often considered a Romantic paradox because of various antitheses in his nature (he led the Romantic revolution toward "expression" in poetry, for example, but was thoroughly Augustan in his literary ideals and a lifelong admirer of Alexander Pope), he rarely succumbs to the temptation of believing his own fictions and always examines his experience with obsessive self-honesty. In conversations with his friend and confidante Lady Blessington, Byron thus confessed to being "so changeable . . . such a strange *mélange* of good and evil, that it would be difficult to describe me," but he goes on to say: "There are but two sentiments to which I am constant—a strong love of liberty, and a detestation of cant." These last qualities undoubtedly explain why the vein of satire was so congenial to him as a poet. In both the barbed heroic couplets of *English Bards and Scotch Reviewers*, the scathing burlesque that launched his career, and the seriocomic use of ottava rima in *Don Juan*, the epic satire which he never lived to complete, Byron sought to expose the smug complacencies and absurd pretensions of his time and, if possible, to restore to it the ability to see itself objectively. The dark *Weltschmerz* of poems such as *Childe Harold's Pilgrimage* may attest his personal despair over whether that goal could ever be accomplished, but in all his variegated moods he writes with energetic conviction born of "sincerity and strength." Byron's seminal achievement, therefore, may be his capacity for embodying the strivings of a deeply restless age, for articulating those longings and doing what all great poets do—namely, to return the imagination to the world.

Biography

George Gordon, the sixth Lord Byron, was born with a clubbed right foot, a deformity that caused him considerable suffering throughout his life and did much to shape his later character. He was descended from two aristocratic and colorful families: his father, who died when Byron was three years old, was Captain John ("Mad Jack") Byron, a rake and fortune hunter who traced his ancestry back to the time of William the Conqueror; his mother, Catherine Gordon of Gight, was the irascible and outspoken heiress who liked to boast of her lineal connection to James I of Scotland. After her husband squandered the Gordon inheritance, Mrs. Byron moved to Aberdeen, where she reared her son under straitened financial circumstances and the Calvinistic creed of Scottish Presbyterianism. With the death of his great-uncle in 1798, the ten-year-old Byron became a titled English peer and took up residence at the patrimonial estate of Newstead Abbey in Nottingham. During this period the precocious young lord fell in love with two cousins named Mary Duff and Margaret Parker, was initiated into premature sexual dalliance by a nurse, and began his zealous regimen of swimming, boxing, fencing, and horsemanship to compensate for his physical lameness.

While at Harrow (1801-1805) and subsequently at Cambridge (1805-1807), Byron started to develop some of the strong attachments and habits that remained with him into adulthood. Though he little relished formal schooling, he periodically immersed himself in reading, became infatuated with Mary Chaworth, and cultivated lasting friendships with his half sister Augusta Leigh as well as with John Cam Hobhouse, Scrope Davies, Francis Hodgson, and others. He also incurred sizable debts for his extravagant revelries at Newstead during college vacations, and, simultaneously, he was entering the arena of literary authorship. His first few volumes of juvenilia, *Fugitive Pieces* and *Poems on Various Occasions*, were privately printed and circulated; *Hours of Idleness*, however, his ensuing venture into the public domain, prompted caustic notice by Henry Brougham, which in turn fueled the retaliatory satire of *English Bards and Scotch Reviewers.* Shortly thereafter, tiring of his life of routine dissipation, Byron prepared to leave England.

The next seven years were momentous ones in Byron's life. Before committing himself to what he thought might eventually be a Parliamentary career, he determined to broaden his education by visiting other lands and peoples. Accordingly, in 1809 he embarked with Hobhouse on an exhilarating tour through Portugal, Spain, Malta, Albania, Greece, and Asia Minor. The vivid scenes and experiences of this two-year excursion provided Byron with the materials for Cantos I-II of his autobiographical travelogue *Childe Harold's Pilgrimage* and his several Eastern tales in verse. Eight months after his return to England in 1811, *Childe Harold's Pilgrimage* was published and Byron became an overnight celebrity: "I awoke one morning," wrote the nobleman-poet, "and found myself famous." Because Byron was readily identified with the melancholic, jaded, and quasierotic hero of his poem, he was besieged by ladies of fashion and lionized by the beau monde of Regency London. Foremost among those giddily vying for the attentions of the handsome and aristocratic young author was Lady Caroline Lamb, a flamboyant, decidedly eccentric woman who to her delight discovered Byron to be "mad—bad—and dangerous to know." Perhaps as much to escape such frenzied pursuit as for any other reason, Byron in early 1815 married Annabella Milbanke, a demure and somewhat priggish "bluestocking" whom Byron dubbed "my Princess of Parallelograms." The ill-fated marriage dissolved a year later, after the birth of a daughter Augusta Ada, when Lady Byron learned of her husband's incestuous relations with his half sister. Socially ostracized by all but his close friends and beset by creditors, Byron left England on April 25, 1816, never to return.

The legendary final phase of Byron's career, which saw his full maturation as a poet, was crowded with events that ensured his lasting renown. Journeying through France to Switzerland, he spent his first summer in exile near Geneva, where he met two other expatriates, Percy Bysshe Shelley and Mary Shelley, with whom he enjoyed many evenings of intellectual conversation. While there, Byron also completed Canto III of *Childe Harold's Pilgrimage,* began *Manfred,* and tried unsuccessfully to stay uninvolved with Mary Shelley's persistent stepsister Claire Clairmont, who, in January, 1817, bore him a daughter, Allegra. By the spring of that year Byron had established himself in Venice, "the greenest isle" of his imagination, where he diverted himself with numerous affairs while periodically exploring the antiquities of Florence and Rome.

The atmosphere of Italy did much to stimulate his literary creativity in new directions. By the end of 1817 he finished *Childe Harold's Pilgrimage* IV, an elegiac canto signaling Byron's decisive break with the past, and, influenced by John Hookham Frere's *Whistlecraft,* a mock-heroic satirical poem in the flexible form of ottava rima, he completed the experimental *Beppo*, which looks forward to the narrative style of *Don Juan*. The period from 1818 to 1822 brought additional changes. Wearying of his promiscuous debaucheries on the Grand Canal in Venice, Byron met the Countess Teresa Guiccioli of Ravenna, then nineteen years old, and soon became her devoted *cavalier servente*. This attachment, in turn, drew him into the revolutionary Carbonari struggle against Austrian rule in Northern Italy, an interest reflected in his political dramas (*Marino Faliero, The Two Foscari*, and *Sardanapalus*). With the defeat of the Carbonari movement in 1821, Byron followed the Gambas, Teresa's family, to Pisa, where he again joined the Shelley circle, which now included Edward John Trelawny and Thomas Medwin, and composed his devastating satire *The Vision of Judgment*. News of Shelley's drowning in July, 1822, however, stunned and sobered Byron. Shortly thereafter, he left for Genoa with Countess Guiccioli, but found his thoughts increasingly preoccupied with the Greek War of Independence. The final chapter of his life, always dominated by the trait that Lady Blessington called "mobility," forms a fitting memorial to Byron's restless spirit. Elected a member of the London Greek Committee, a Philhellene organization, the poet felt obligated to translate his political convictions into action. Despite skepticism concerning various Greek leaders' loyalty to the cause and despite a presentiment of his own imminent death, Byron set forth to do what he could. Sailing for Missolonghi in late December, 1823, he devoted his personal fortune and energy to forming a united front against the Turks. Four months later he died of a fever; to this day he is hailed as a national hero by the Greek people.

Analysis

The history of Lord Byron's poetic development intersects at every stage with the saga of his life; yet it is only one of many paradoxes that he valued the writing of poetry primarily for the opportunity it afforded him to escape what he termed "my own wretched identity." More than anything else, poetry for Byron was a means both of sublimation and, ultimately, of self-realization. In his letters he thus suggests the former function when he speaks of poetry as "the lava of the imagination whose eruption prevents an earthquake," the volcanic metaphor signifying the cathartic release that the process of writing afforded him. The precise way in which it fulfilled the second function, however, is less obvious. Through the dynamics of self-projection, of investing much of his own multifaceted character in his personae, Byron strives to transcend the narrow limits of "personality" and achieve a more comprehensive perspective on himself and his experience. The essential goal of this artistic quest, which constitutes a progressive ontology, is delineated in Canto III of *Childe Harold's Pilgrimage*: "'Tis to create, and in creating live/ A being more intense." To trace Byron's growth as a poet, therefore, is to witness him reaching beyond subjectivism and attempting to realize that intensity of being that comes about through the continuous act of self-creation. Any account of Byron's achievement must begin with the poems collected in *Hours of Idleness* and the early satires. In the Preface to the 1807 miscellany, his highly self-conscious debut as a poet, the nineteen-year-old Byron calls attention to himself by posing as an unlikely author (one "accustomed, in my younger days, to rove a careless mountaineer on the Highlands of Scotland"), by minimizing the merits of his literary endeavor ("to divert the dull moments of indisposition, or the monotony of a vacant hour, urged me 'to this sin'"), and by passing preemptive judgment on his work ("little can be expected from so unpromising a muse"). Such ingenuous posturing is clearly meant to invite, under the guise of dismissing, public recognition and acclaim. Despite the transparency of the subterfuge, the poems comprising *Hours of Idleness* form a revealing self-portrait in which Byron, while paraphrasing past idioms in poetry and exploiting eighteenth century literary conventions, obliquely seeks to discover a mythologized pattern for his emerging sense of himself. The one theme sounded repeatedly is what Robert F. Gleckner designates "the ruins of paradise," or the fall from youthful innocence. As he explores the experience of spiritual loss and shattered illusions, Byron can be seen moving toward this latter belief that "the great object of life is Sensation— to feel that we exist—even though in pain."

Admittedly imitative in style, often to the point of mannerism, *Hours of Idleness* revolves around several episodes of separation and disenchantment that, for the speaker, spell the end of an idealized, prelapsarian past. The short poem "Remembrance," composed in 1806 but not published until 1832, epitomizes both the tone and outlook of the volume as a whole:

> My days of happiness are few:
> Chill'd by misfortune's wintry blast,
> My dawn of life is overcast,
> Love, Hope, and Joy, alike adieu!—
> Would I could add Remembrance too!

Although the lines verge on doggerel, the same mood of melancholic nostalgia informs such other generally more successful poems as "On Leaving Newstead Abbey," "The First Kiss of Love," "On a Distant View of the Village and School of Harrow on the Hill," and "Lachin y Gair." In all of these works Byron cannot disown the power of memory because, though denounced as a curse, it alone provides glimpses of what in "Childish Recollections" he refers to as "the progress of my youthful dream," the foundation for his concept of self. This tension gives rise in other lyrics to a plangent wish to escape the "dark'ning shades" of maturity, regaining the uncompromised or "freeborn soul." Knowing the fatuity of the desire, however, the poet resorts at last to a kind of protective cynicism. In "To Romance," for example, abandoning what he derides as the "motley court" of "Affectation" and "sickly

Sensibility," he admits that "'tis hard to quit the dreams,/ Which haunt the unsuspicious soul" but abjures the past as illusory and refuses any longer to be the dupe of his romantic fancy. Embittered by his early discovery, as Byron was later to write in *Childe Harold's Pilgrimage* III, that "life's enchanted cup but sparkles near the brim," the poet in *Hours of Idleness* fluctuates between moments of elegiac regret and tenacious hope, the ambivalent response itself prefiguring the skeptical idealist of the major poems to follow.

The Popean satires, which were composed shortly after the 1807 collection, disclose Byron's reaction to his disillusionment and punctured faith. In *English Bards and Scotch Reviewers, Hints from Horace,* and *The Curse of Minerva*— all written during the next four years—Byron lashes out at various individuals whom he regarded as typifying the literary and moral shortcomings of his age. The motto of "these degenerate days," he announces in *English Bards and Scotch Reviewers,* is "Care not for feeling," and so in arraigning nearly all his contemporaries except Samuel Rogers and Thomas Campbell he poses as the hardened realist determined to expose error on every hand: "But now, so callous grown, so changed since youth,/ I've learned to think, and sternly speak the truth." In the diatribe Byron often vents his anger indiscriminately, but the acrimony of his attack stems from a keen sense of embarrassment and outrage at the reception accorded *Hours of Idleness* by such critics as Henry Brougham in the *Edinburgh Review.* Thus, before indicating all those "afflicted," as his Preface charges, "with the present prevalent and distressing *rabies* for rhyming," Byron debunks himself as well:

> I, too, can scrawl, and once upon a time
> I poured along the town a flood of rhyme,
> A school-boy freak, unworthy praise or blame;
> I printed—older children do the same.
> 'Tis pleasant, sure, to see one's name in print;
> A Book's a Book, altho' there's nothing in't.

The same irreverent or inconoclastic spirit pervades *Hints from Horace,* a mocking jab at contemporary literary practice from the vantage point of Horace's *Ars Poetica* (13-8 B.C., *The Art of Poetry*), and *The Curse of Minerva,* a Swiftian condemnation of Lord Elgin for his despoiling Greek sculpture. In these strident satires Byron alters his earlier poetic stance through two mechanisms: by adopting the voice of savage indignation and by spurning the accepted standards of his age. The detachment that he tries to win through both devices is another step toward his large aesthetic goal of self-realization.

A crucial phase in that ongoing process involves the composition, spanning the period from 1809 to 1817, of *Childe Harold's Pilgrimage* and, to a lesser extent, of the exotic Oriental tales that include *The Giaour, The Bride of Abydos, The Corsair,* and *Lara.* These verse narratives are significant because in them two sides of Byron's complexity as an artist are counterbalanced—the usually antithetical modes that Keats, in his letters, conceptualizes as the "egotistical sublime" and "the camelion [sic] Poet." Though Keats associated the first quality with William Wordsworth, the element of the "egotistical sublime" in Byron reveals itself in the highly developed reflexivity of his semiautobiographical poems and in his tendency to concentrate on his own immediate thoughts and emotions. At the same time, however, there emerges an equal but opposite impulse that reflects Byron's essentially centrifugal rather than centripetal habit of mind. This is his characteristic propensity for employing a gamut of masks or personae through which he endeavors to escape the restrictive confines of self-consciousness, especially as molded by memory, and to achieve the intensity of being that comes with self-transcendence. Together, these intertwined modalities—the "egotistical" and the "chameleonic"—make up the unique "strength" of Byron's imagination.

Readers of the time were nevertheless inclined to recognize only the former tendency in his works and so to find him guilty of facile exhibitionism. Certainly when Byronism was rampant no one impersonated Byron better than Byron himself; yet, if one allows for this susceptibility, the earnestness with which the poet responded to his detractors is instructive. Echoing the well-known protest lodged in his 1820 "Reply to Blackwood's *Edinburgh Magazine,*" he expostulated a year later to Thomas Moore that "a man's poetry is a distinct faculty, or soul, and has no more to do with the every-day individual than the Inspiration with the Pythoness when removed from her tripod." Similarly, in the privacy of his journal for 1813, while writing the very poems that incurred the charge, he remarks: "To withdraw *myself* from *myself* (oh that cursed selfishness!) has ever been my sole, my entire, my sincere motive in scribbling at all; and publishing is also the continuance of the same object, by the action it affords to the mind, which else recoils upon itself." The vehemence of these statements should not be allowed to obscure Byron's clear point regarding the psychology of composition. The vicarious world of poetry, as he views it, makes possible a release from the concentricity of the mind that otherwise, to borrow two of his favorite images in *Childe Harold's Pilgrimage*, would sting itself to death like the scorpion ringed by fire or consume its scabbard like a rusting sword.

Byron first expands upon this aesthetic in *Childe Harold's Pilgrimage* III-IV, but some attention to the earlier cantos is prerequisite to understanding the later two. When he began the travelogue in 1809 while touring Europe and the Levant, Byron conceived of a work in Spenserian stanza form which would depict, in the eighteenth century tradition of topographical or "loco-descriptive" poetry, his vivid impressions of the scenes and peoples he visited, intermixed with meditative reflections. "For the sake of giving some connection to the piece," which otherwise, according to the Preface, "makes no pretension to regularity," Byron introduces the "fictitious character" of

Harold, who serves as the nominal hero-protagonist, although this syntactical function is about all that can be claimed for him. Out of "the fulness [sic] of satiety," it is true, Harold "resolve[s]" to leave England behind, having run through "Sin's long labyrinth"; yet in his wandering pilgrimage through Spain, Portugal, Albania, and Greece he remains a curiously static, one-dimensional figure and is little more than a partial projection of Byron's darker moods (for example, misanthropy, remorse, cynicism, and forced stoicism). As such, he adumbrates the explicit theme of Cantos I-II: that is, "Consciousness awaking to her woes." Neither Harold nor Byron, however, has yet learned "what he might be, or he ought," and it is somehow fitting that Canto II should close in a Greece stripped of its ancient grandeur and heroes.

Throughout this half of the poem, Byron's protagonist bears a marked resemblance to the poet himself, but it is well not to overlook the punning assertion made in the 1812 Preface that Harold is "the child of imagination." Shortly before the publication of Cantos I-II, in a letter to Robert Charles Dallas, Byron reinforces the distinction between himself and his central character: "If in parts I may be thought to have drawn from myself, believe me it is but in parts, and I shall not own even to that . . . I would not be such a fellow as I have made my hero for all the world." The disclaimer has not won wide acceptance, largely because in the holograph copy of the poem Byron initially christened his protagonist "Childe Burun"; yet the first two cantos themselves substantiate the dissociation which Byron's comment to Dallas emphasizes. On the one hand, they dramatize the alienated figure of Harold, who, like the tortured hero of *Lara*, is portrayed as "a stranger in this breathing world,/ An erring spirit from another hurled;/ A thing of dark imaginings"; on the other hand, they are mediated by a separate narrrator who, distanced from the foreground objectively recognizes that "the blight of life" that overtakes men like Harold is "the demon Thought," or the canker of self-consciousness. In actuality, *both* entities are Byron, and through the dichotomy he seeks to plumb his own contradictory nature.

By the time that Byron came to write Canto III, however, life had paradoxically imitated art: exiled from England by public vilification for his alleged cruelty toward his wife, the poet became that which before he had only imaged. This turn of events contributed to a new coalescence or ironic similarity between the author and his persona. Byron still does not identify himself completely with his titular hero, but he is now able to assimilate Harold as an exponent of himself without capitulating to the kind of Haroldian *Angst* that suffuses Cantos I-II. He seems to register this altered orientation in the following lines: "Yet am I changed; though still enough the same/ In strength to bear what time can not abate,/ And feed on bitter fruits without accusing Fate." Implicit in the passage, with its allusion to John Milton's *Paradise Lost* (1667), is an undertone of confidence that even despair can be transformed into a source of stimulation and proof of his endurance. Byron now is speaking *in propria persona*. No longer rhapsodizing as in Canto I "a youth,/ Who ne in virtue's ways did take delight," he is instead dealing with himself as a social and moral pariah—"the wandering outlaw of his own dark mind." The full assurance that he can avoid entrapment from within remains to be found, but the seeds of spiritual recovery are before him.

The groundwork is laid at the start of Canto III when, after the framing device of an apostrophe to his daughter, Byron declares his artistic manifesto for the work: "'Tis to create, and in creating live/ A being more intense, that we endow/ With form our fancy, gaining as we give/ The life we image, even as I do now." Reflecting Shelley's influence on Byron in 1816, the passage continues and reveals that the poet now views his quotidian identity as "Nothing," as a hollow fiction, while the project of art discloses to him an ideal "other" or truer self which he will appropriate through the act of creating. The poem itself, in short, becomes the vehicle for self-discovery. Thus, although Harold continues to be much the same character as he was in Cantos I-II, what has changed greatly is Byron's positioning of himself as artist *vis-à-vis* the poem. He no longer depends on his protagonist as a surrogate or alter ego; even though the disease of self-consciousness has not been expunged, his faith has been restored in the imagination's ability to locate new horizons of meaning in an otherwise entropic world.

Both the third and fourth cantos of *Childe Harold's Pilgrimage* contain clear evidence of his shift in outlook. The two major scenes visited in Canto III are Waterloo and the Swiss Alps, locales which by their historical associations stand symbolically opposed. In the former, Byron finds only the tragic vanity of life and the futility of worldly ambition; in the latter, he surveys the benign sublimity and undisturbed repose of nature. Initially, it would seem that he is elevating one sphere above the other, idealizing the serenity of "throned Eternity" in contrast to the agitation of "earth-born jars." He is, to some extent, but in a unique manner. Rather than treating these landscapes as discrete alternatives, Byron exploits them as provisional constructs for raising questions and defining some of his own misgivings about the human condition. Thus, if at Waterloo he rejects the "wretched interchange of wrong for wrong" within society, in the Alps he sees nothing "to loathe in nature, save to be/ A link reluctant in a fleshly chain."

In much the same way, he responds ambivalently to the fallen figureheads of each domain—Napoleon Bonaparte and Jean Jacques Rousseau—whom he envisions as variants of himself. Both the Napoleon who was "conqueror and captive of the earth" and the "inspired" Rousseau whose oracles "set the world in flame" were men of unbounded energy, yet each was responsible for the shambles of the French Revolution and each was subverted by "a fever at the core,/ Fatal to him who bears, to all who ever bore." Byron recognizes their failure as potentially his own as well: "And *there* hath been thy bane," he proclaims. The stanza's rhetoric reverberates with his affinity for these individuals and suggests that Byron, as Jerome J. McGann observes in *Fiery Dust* (1968), is coming to the realization that "to 'know oneself' one must submit to immediate and partial acts of perception." Within *Childe Harold's Pilgrimage* III, therefore, the poet moves further toward the understanding that to be human means to be a pilgrim, but a pilgrim ever in the process of redefining himself and the world that he inherits.

Canto IV continues the archetypal pattern of the journey, in this case one extending from Venice to Rome, but broadens at the end to reveal a significantly matured Byron arriving at the genuine goal or embodiment of his questing spirit. Centered around the elegiac motif or *sic transit gloria mundi*, the last canto weighs the respective claims of both art and nature to permanence as Byron tries to decipher the enigma of man's existence. "The moral of all human tales," he postulates, is the inevitability of ruin and unfulfilled hopes, such that "History, with all her volumes vast,/ Hath but *one* page." This stark lesson occasionally moves the poet to invective, as when he declares that "Our life is a false nature—'tis not in/ The harmony of things." Nevertheless, in the poetry of Torquato Tasso, the sculpture of Venice, and the Colosseum in Rome, he discerns a grandeur and genius which transcend the melancholy attrition of time. That discovery, in turn, rekindles conviction as to the vitality of his own essential self, a realization heightened when Byron finds that he has outgrown the fictive prop of Harold:

> But where is he, the Pilgrim of my song,
> The being who upheld it through the past?
> . . . .
> He is no more—these breathings are his last;
> His wanderings done, his visions ebbing fast,
> And he himself as nothing. . . .

In the poem's concluding apostrophe to the sea near Albano, conceived as a "glorious mirror" and thalassic "image of Eternity," Byron achieves the true goal toward which he has been tending all along. Awesome in its untrammeled energy, the ocean becomes the symbol of the creating self that the poet has reclaimed. "My Pilgrim's shrine is won," writes Byron, for "I am not now/ That which I have been." With that declaration, Byron enters upon the last great phase of his poetic career.

The monumental epic *Don Juan* forms the inspired climax to Byron's evolution as an artist, but to understand how this is so requires brief attention to a disturbing undercurrent in *Childe Harold's Pilgrimage*. Despite the general movement toward self-apprehension in that work, there yet occur moments when the inadequacy of language to articulate "all I seek,/ Bear, know, feel" subverts the poet's faith in his enterprise. Thus, although in Canto III he would willingly believe that "there may be/ Words which are things," he has not found them; nor is he able to disguise from himself the knowledge that language is part of the disintegrated syntax of a fallen world. Along the same lines, after pondering in Canto IV the disappointed ideals of such poets as Dante and Petrarch, he ruefully admits that "what we have of feeling most intense/ Outstrips our faint expression." The intransigence of language, its inherent circularity as an instrument of meditation, was for Byron tied to the kind of Metaphysical despair dramatized in *Manfred* and *Cain*, and by way of overcoming those quandaries he adopts in *Don Juan* a more radically versatile poetics.

The chief difference between *Childe Harold's Pilgrimage* and his later "epic of negation," as Brian Wilke describes *Don Juan* in *Romantic Poets and Epic Tradition* (1965), lies in Byron's refusal any longer to be controlled by "the stubborn heart." After opening with the farce of Juan's sexual initiation, before which he pauses to berate Plato as a charlatan, Byron makes his new outlook resoundingly clear:

> No more—no more—Oh! never more, my heart,
> Canst thou be my sole world, my universe!
> . . . .
> The illusion's gone for ever, and thou art
> Insensible, I trust, but none the worse,
> And in thy stead I've got a good deal of judgment,
> Though heaven knows how it ever found a lodgement.

Cognizant of the fictiveness of all experience, he plans to make his rambling medley of a poem mirror the manifold delusions and deceptions that man allows to impose upon his right of thought. In the face of such knowledge "Imagination droops her pinion," turning "what was once romantic to burlesque"—lines aptly capturing the shift from his stance in *Childe Harold's Pilgrimage*. In composing his "versified Aurora Borealis," however, Byron obviously sensed a creative exhilaration linked to his complete separation of himself from his hero. His letters written during the work's early stages reveal an exuberant confidence in the undertaking which, as he told Thomas Moore, was "meant to be a little quitely facetious upon every thing." Thus, addressing his old friend Douglas Kinnaird in 1819, he expressed a typically high-spirited opinion of his achievement: "As to 'Don Juan'—confess—confess—you dog—and be candid—that it is the sublime of *that there* sort of writing—it may be bawdy . . . but it is not *life*, is it not *the thing*?—Could any man have written it—who has not lived in the world?"

Byron's governing purpose in *Don Juan* is to "show things really as they are,/ Not as they ought to be." Toward that end he does not forbear lampooning all the assorted follies and philistine pretenses of "that microcosm on stilts,/ Yclept the Great World," for he sees its attachment to illusion as the root cause of men's inability to recognize or accept the truth about themselves. Byron's attack is all the more effective because he exempts neither himself as poet nor the function of language from his skeptical scrutiny. Overturning all conventional notions of structure and voice in poetry, he is intent upon making his "nondescript and ever-varying rhyme" demystify itself at every turn. Both serious and cynical, he consequently avers that compared to the epic myths of Vergil and Homer "this story's actually true," then later reminds his audience that his work "is only fiction,/ And that I sing of neither mine nor me." Nearly every stanza of *Don Juan* unmasks itself in similar fashion through the whimsical freedom of Byron's style. Fearless of incongruities in a world permeated by fraud, the poem's narrator defends his fluid cynicism in the name of verisimilitude (his aim is to "show things existent") while simultaneously debunking traditional concepts of authorial integrity: "If people contradict themselves, can I/ Help contradicting them, and everybody,/ Even my veracious self?" True "sincerity" in these terms is equated with inconsistency, paradox, and radical doubt, an outlook anticipated as early as 1813 when Byron, with uncanny self-knowledge and prescience, remarked in his journal that "if I am sincere with myself (but I fear one lies more to one's self than to any one else), every page should confute, refute, and utterly abjure its predecessor." By constantly deflating the artifices on which his own poem is built, Byron seeks to generate a self-critical model for exposing the larger abuses of his society.

Don Juan is, as William Hazlitt was quick to note in *The Spirit of the Age* (1825), a "poem written about itself," but foremost among the vices it satirizes are the contemporary prevalence of cant and the moral blindness or hypocrisy which it fosters. Both traits are first encountered in the character of Donna Inez, Juan's mother, in Canto I. A prodigy of memory whose brain is filled with "serious sayings darken'd to sublimity," she is walking homily—"Morality's prim personification"—who sees to it that her son is taught from only the most carefully expurgated classics. Unable to find anything to censure or amend in her own conduct, Donna Inez nevertheless carries on a clandestine affair with Don Alfonso, the husband of her close friend Julia, and later writes in fulsome praise of Catherine the Great's "maternal" attentions to Juan. Such self-deceiving and myopic piety moves Byron to wish for "a *forty-parson power* to chant/ Thy praise, Hypocrisy," the vice that he regards as endemic to his age and culture at all levels.

On a larger scale, he dramatizes the disastrous consequences of cant and its ability to obscure human realities in the Siege of Ismail episode beginning in Canto VII. Here his target is in part the gazettes and their debased glorification of war, particularly as they promote "the lust of notoriety" within modern civilization. Spurred on by the hope of being immortalized in the newspapers or war dispatches, a polyglot collection of soldiers join with the Russians in devastating the Turkish fortress. Before recounting scene after scene of the mindless butchery, in which thirty thousand are slain on both sides, Byron reflects on whether "a man's name in a *bulletin*/ May make up for a *bullet in* his body." The final irony is that the gazettes, preoccupied with trivial gossip of the beau monde at home, generally garble the names of the dead and thoroughly distort the facts of the campaign. Determined to unriddle "Glory's dream," Byron shows that it is founded on nothing more than an abject appetite for fame and conquest. His greatest ire is reserved for someone such as the Russian leader Aleksandr Suwarrow, who, in a dispatch to Catherine after the slaughter, can glibly write, " 'Glory to *God* and to the Empress!' (*Powers/ Eternal! such names mingled!*) 'Ismail's our's.' " The same purblind insensitivity, he charges, makes it possible for Wordsworth to speak of carnage as " 'God's daughter.' " In all these instances, Byron shows how language is a ready instrument for the perversion of thought and action.

His own aesthetic in *Don Juan* thus bases itself on an unswerving respect for truth, "the grand desideratum" in a society glutted with cant and equivocation. Early in the poem he comments that his is "the age of oddities let loose," such that "You'd best begin with truth, and when you've lost your/ Labour, there's a sure market for imposture." The lines also echo his mocking Dedication of the work to Robert Southey, who succeeded Henry James Pye as poet laureate in 1813, and his arraignment there of the other so-called Lake Poets. Having disowned the radical politics of their youth, they are depicted as comprising a "nest of tuneful persons" who now warble sycophantic praise for the Tory regime of King George III. Their apostasy in Byron's eyes is all the more reprehensible because they have, in effect, become the hirelings of the "intellectual eunuch Castlereagh," a master of oratorical "trash of phrase/ Ineffably—legitimately vile." To counteract this mounting Tower of Babel in his age, Byron persistently explodes the enchantment of words and their tendency to falsify reality. There is, accordingly, an underlying method to his chameleonic *mobilité* and digressiveness in the poem, for he demonstrates that only by doubting the language-based constructs, which man imposes upon experience, can he, like the poet himself, avoid the pitfall of "universal egotism." Viewed in this light, the whole of *Don Juan* becomes an open-ended experiment in linguistic improvisation, a poem that demythologizes the very act by which it comes into being.

Because Byron's mock-epic attempts to encompass no less than "life's infinite variety," any synopsis of its innumerable subjects and themes is doomed to failure. From the opening line in which the narrator declaims "I want a hero" and then seems arbitrarily to settle on "our ancient friend Don Juan," it is evident that the ensuing comedy will follow few established conventions or patterns. This impression is reinforced later in Canto XIV, when Byron points out his technique in composing *Don Juan*: "I write what's uppermost, without delay." The stated casualness in approach, however, belies the artistic integrity of the satire. Jerome J. McGann, in *Don Juan in Context* (1976), convincingly shows that the poem is "both a critique and an apotheosis of High Romanticism," primarily because it implicitly denies that any imaginative system can be an end unto itself while also endeavoring to reinsert the poetic imagination back into the context of a fallen world. If there is one crux around which the entire mosaic turns, it is that of the fundamental opposition between nature and civilization. After Juan's idyllic love affair with Haidée, "Nature's bride," is destroyed by her jealous father in Canto IV, Byron suggests that the Fall is man's permanent condition; he conducts his hero into slavery at Constantinople in Canto V, into the bloodbath of the Siege of Ismail in Cantos VII-VIII, into the lustful tyranny of the Russian Empress in Cantos IX-X, and finally into the fashionable corruptions of English society in Cantos XI-XVII. Not all, however, is moral cannibalism. By the introduction of such unspoiled figures as Haidée at the start and Aurora Raby at the end, Byron ascribes a certain redemptive value to natural innocence that offsets, even if it does not quite counterbalance, the ruling vices of society. *Don Juan* thus immerses itself in all the unflattering details of "life's infinite variety," but always with the purpose of embodying the human realities with which the artist must deal. Byron distills the complexity of the matter in a few words: "I write the world."

In this century as in his own, Byron has often been criticized as a poet for his many supposed failures—for not projecting a coherent metaphysic, for not developing a consistent attitude to life, for not resisting the Siren call of egotism, for not paying sufficient attention to style, and for not, in short, being more like Wordsworth, Samuel Taylor Coleridge, Keats, and Shelley. Because he did not adopt the vatic stance of his contemporaries or espouse their belief in organicism, he has been labeled the leading exemplar of Negative Romanticism. Common to such estimates, however, is a reluctance to recognize or concede Byron's uniqueness as a poet. Although he did not share with others of his time an exalted conception of the imagination as being equivalent, in Keats's metaphor, to "Adam's dream," he was able ultimately to do what the other four poets generally could not—namely, to accept the mixed quality of human experience. Through his ironic detachment and comic vision he permanently enlarged the domain of poetry and made it meaningful in a fresh way. This he accomplished through his skeptical idealism and his acceptance of his own paradoxes as a man and poet. "I am quicksilver," he wrote to a friend in 1810, "and say nothing positively." Therein lies perhaps the essence of his "sincerity" and "strength," traits that continue to make him an enduring cultural force.

Robert Lance Snyder

Other major works

NONFICTION: *Letter to [John Murray] on the Rev. W. L. Bowles' Strictures on the Life and Writings of Pope*, 1821; "A Letter to the Editor of 'My Grandmother's Review,'" 1822; *The Blues: A Literary Eclogue*, 1823; *The Parlia-*

mentary Speeches of Lord Byron, 1824; *Byron's Letters and Journals*, 1973-1982 (12 volumes; Leslie A. Marchand, editor).

Bibliography

Blackstone, Bernard. *Byron: A Survey.* London: Longman, 1975. Blackstone is something of a maverick among scholars, and his approach to Byron is unusual. Blackstone possesses a strong awareness of the significance of Byron's places, and his readings are full of provocative insights into the deepest levels of significance in the poems. Sometimes, he makes Byron sound more like William Blake than Byron, but open-minded readers will find this book stimulating and rewarding.

Bloom, Harold, ed. *George Gordon: Lord Byron.* New York: Chelsea House, 1986. A collection of nine critical essays. Bloom's overview of Byron's major poems, G. Wilson Knight's seminal essay on the conflict in Byron between "history and tragic insight," Northrop Frye's emphasis on the interconnections of Byron's poetry and his life, and George M. Ridenour's essay on Byron's poems of 1816 are all suitable for beginning students. The other essays are more suitable for those with some prior knowledge of Byron and Byron's criticism.

Graham, Peter W. *Don Juan and Regency England.* Charlottesville: University Press of Virginia, 1990. Six self-contained but interrelated essays that explore Byron's comic masterpiece in the context of various aspects of the culture of Regency England. Graham argues that in *Don Juan*, Byron continually advocated a cosmopolitan point of view, satirizing traditional English insularity. Readers should have some familiarity with *Don Juan* before tackling this volume, but Graham writes jargon-free prose and each essay is highly illuminating.

Manning, Peter J. *Byron and His Fictions.* Detroit: Wayne State University Press, 1978. Emphasis is on the psychoanalytic perspectives of Byron. Manning detects recurrent psychological themes in Byron's poetry, particularly an oedipal conflict, and he uses this insight to shed light on recurring plot patterns and the experiences of Byron's heroes. Manning's approach is not as narrow as this might suggest. He skillfully integrates psychoanalytic concepts with other, more traditional approaches, and the result is a very rewarding and illuminating study.

Marchand, Leslie A. *Byron: A Portrait.* Chicago: University of Chicago Press, 1970. The best biography for the general reader. It is based on Marchand's definitive three-volume biography published in 1957, but includes research done in the 1960's. Marchand's portrait of Byron is balanced and free of bias. Includes fifty-six illustrations, genealogical tables, and two maps showing Byron's travels from 1809 to 1811, and Byron's Greece.

McGann, Jerome J. *Fiery Dust: Byron's Poetic Development.* Chicago: University of Chicago Press, 1968. One of the most important modern studies of Byron. McGann examines the continuity of Byron's poetic development and the "phenomenon of Byronic self-expression": how Byron used the materials of his own life to create a Byronic personality in his work. The longest section is on *Childe Harold's Pilgrimage*, partly because it reveals so much about Byron's life and thoughts at that time. Also discusses *The Giaour, The Prisoner of Chillon, Cain*, and other tales and plays.

Rutherford, Andrew. *Byron: A Critical Study.* Edinburgh, Scotland: Oliver & Boyd, 1961. An excellent introduction to Byron's poetry, suitable for the general reader. More than half the book is devoted to the later satires, which Rutherford regards as Byron's best work. He places a low value on the earlier phase of Byron's work, including *Childe Harold's Pilgrimage* and the tales, a view which has been challenged by a number of later critics, including Jerome J. McGann, above.

CAEDMON

Born: Northumbria, England; early seventh century
Died: Whitby Abbey, Northumbria, England; c. 680

Principal poetry
"Hymn," c. 670.

Other literary forms
The "Hymn" is the only work that has been definitely attributed to Caedmon.

Achievements
The history of Caedmon, the first voice in English poetry, is passed down through the cleric and historian Bede who, in his *Ecclesiastical History of the English People* (731), tells the story of the humble layman to whom the gift of poetry was given one night in a dream. Bede lists many works composed by Caedmon; the only piece which can be identified with any certainty, however, is the nine-line "Hymn" fragment in praise of God the Creator.

Brief though it is, this poem defines and directs the course of English poetry, combining for the first time the meters of Nordic heroic poetry with the subject matter of the Scriptures, Christianizing the literary tradition and speaking for a culture. That the "Hymn" was held in great esteem is evidenced by the fact that versions of it exist in seventeen manuscripts ranging from the early eighth to the later fifteenth century; Caedmon's "Hymn" is the only piece of early poetry to have been preserved in this manner. Caedmon is a figure of shadow and legend, with a single biographical source and no written records; his hymn is a rich and appropriate beginning for the English poetic tradition.

Biography
The single source for the life of Caedmon, Bede's *Ecclesiastical History*, was completed in 731. Written in Latin and later translated into Old English, Bede's history describes the Abbey of Whitby in Northumbria, founded by St. Hilda and ruled by her from 658 until 680. Twin communities, one for men and one for women, flourished under the direction of the Abbess. To this abbey came the layman Caedmon, not to test a religious vocation but to seek employment in caring for the monastery animals. Caedmon was not young when he came to Whitby, Bede comments, but no mention is made of his earlier life. Humble and unassuming, Caedmon had his quarters with the farm animals and lived almost unnoticed by the other monastery residents.

Because of his extreme shyness, the story continues, Caedmon was never able to take his turn at the recitation and singing when, as was the custom, the harp was passed around after the communal evening meal. In order to avoid embarrassment, Caedmon would always find some excuse to leave the gathering and tend the animals, knowing that he would not be able to sing and entertain the others should the harp be passed to him. Bede's account, it should be remarked, is an invaluable description of this culture; the secular (not religious) music, the gathering to drink beer together, the shared responsibility for entertainment—all these facets of early English life are clarified in the *Ecclesiastical History*.

One evening, having left the gathering, Caedmon was sleeping when he had a dream. "Someone" came to him and commanded, "Caedmon, sing me something." When Caedmon protested, the visitant repeated the direction, asking that Caedmon sing of "the beginning of created things." Still in his dream, Caedmon obeyed the vision, breaking into song of the "first-shaping." The vision vanished.

When he awakened, unsure of what had happened, Caedmon found that he was able to recall the entire song. Still led by divine urgings, he went to the Abbess, sang the "Hymn" for her, and explained the occurrence of the night before. St. Hilda, realizing that the powers of God were involved, encouraged Caedmon, exhorting him to devote his life to composing music for the glory and praise of God.

Thereafter Caedmon became a monk, spending his days composing music. His gift stayed with him always, although he never learned to read or write. Others in the monastery would read the Scripture aloud; Caedmon would then make a metrical paraphrase of what he had heard. Because the gift of inspiration was to serve God's glory, Bede explains, Caedmon was able to compose only religious verse. Bede lists many of Caedmon's compositions, all of them biblical; poems of similar subject matter appeared in a 1655 Junius Manuscript by François Dujon. Dujon believed that the four scriptural poems were originals from Caedmon; modern scholarship, however, rejects any such claim. It may be that other members of the monastery imitated Caedmon's gift, or, more likely, that later writers were moved to continue the tradition. The remarkable care taken to preserve the hymn suggests that it was widely regarded as the first piece of English alliterative poetry.

According to Bede, Caedmon died in the monastery at Whitby after receiving the Eucharist and falling into a peaceful slumber. Given his story, it would be surprising if Bede were to record any other sort of death, for he clearly intends to shape the Caedmon narrative to an argument for the religious inspiration of poetry.

Analysis

Although Bede's *Ecclesiastical History* details the composition of Caedmon's "Hymn," it does not reproduce it, giving instead a prose paraphrase. Bede, himself a fine stylist, remarks quite accurately that his Latin prose cannot reproduce a vernacular hymn; poetry, he points out, does not translate well. In most of the early manuscripts of the *Ecclesiastical History*, however, the poem itself is included, often as a marginal gloss but occasionally in the body of the manuscript itself. There are seventeen of these manuscripts, both in Caedmon's own Northumbrian and in West Saxon, with the majority in the latter. The nine lines of the "Hymn" are given here in a modern English translation:

Now let us herald	heaven-kingdom's guardian,
Maker of might	and his mind-thoughts,
The work of the wonder-Father	When he of wonders, each one
Eternal Lord	established in the beginning.
He first shaped	for the sons of men
Heaven as a roof	the holy Creator;
And then the middle-earth	for mankind, the Protector,
Eternal Lord,	afterwards made
For men, this firmament,	Our Father almighty.

The "Hymn" is a kind of early English psalm; it sings the praises of God, invites the hearers to join in, details the specifics of creation, and moves to a realization that all life has been created not only for God's glory but also for the "sons of man," those who revere and love God. Although Caedmon had been instructed to sing of the "making of things," he chooses—or is inspired to choose—lyric rather than narrative, praise rather than instruction.

It is not surprising to the contemporary reader that Caedmon would sing a song in praise of God in response to a dream vision, but it is significant in the history of English poetry that formal Christianity had been introduced in England less than a century before. The Romans who had occupied the island had been Christians, but without formal practice of the religion, Christianity had nearly died out, preserved only in small pockets. Not until Pope Gregory sent St. Augustine to the island in 597 did a formal mission begin; by Caedmon's time, England had reverted to Christianity, and the great monastic tradition which was to stimulate learning was beginning to flower.

Critical debate flourishes over the nature of Caedmon's inspiration. Was he inspired to "remember" songs and rhythms he had already heard? Was he moved to sing a hymn whose words he may not even have understood? Was he simply an instrument for God's power? Was he indeed a deliberate composer? It is of course tempting to align Caedmon with both the biblical tradition of the unknowing prophet who speaks the words God puts in his mouth and the classical "seer" who sees and describes but does not always understand. Bede clearly identifies Caedmon as the one selected by God not only for divine glory but also to begin a tradition; because Bede was writing almost fifty years after Caedmon lived, he had an interesting perspective. Whatever one's theories of critical inspiration, the Caedmon "Hymn" holds irresistible appeal for the scholar who finds the Christian tradition and metrical artistry in such a rich blend.

Caedmon's words describe God as king and father, powerful and provident, clearly reflecting the concept of king as the one responsible for his people's welfare and who, in return for praise and veneration, will reward his subjects with care for their needs. The creation references suggest a sort of giant meadhall, with heaven as a roof; the sons of men are all enclosed, safe from enemies, and singing their gratitude. This same anthropomorphism runs throughout most early English poetry; God is like his people in the most literal sense. At the same time, there is a strong suggestion of transcendence or otherness. Twice God is described as eternal and the focus of the poem is clearly on the marvels and wonders of this incomprehensible but splendid "Glory-Father." The poem is charged with energy; there is something peculiarly English about the emphasis on God's actions, deeds: God establishes, shapes, makes—words suggesting concrete and deliberate actions. The deeds, however, are more than mere activities; they are "mind-thoughts," concepts put into reality by the creativity of God. The creative outburst of the poet hymns the creative energy of the first Shaper. The poet, both as an inspired mystic and as a worker dependent on the lord of the monastery for sustenance, shines through these lines.

This first voice in English poetry, therefore, is essentially religious in its themes. Like the voice in the Psalms, the speaker views the array of creation and claims it "for the sons of men," echoing the Genesis story as well. It is not surprising that the scriptural stories which appear in early poetry are elemental tales of creation, providence, and power; they are also, however, dramatic narratives which eventually were incorporated into the saints' legends and traditions. Although Bede explains that all of Caedmon's poetry was religious and rooted in Scripture, the nine-line fragment which begins the tradition is an especially appropriate inauguration.

The Caedmon "Hymn" has far greater significance for the student of literature as the first example of the poetic form which would influence English poetry through the fifteenth century, recurring from time to time in later writers even into the twentieth. The four-stress, alliterative line, here less precise and sophisticated than in *Beowulf* and in much later works of writers such as William Langland and the Pearl-Poet, gives to English poetry a grace and strength which bring the ancient Nordic heroic literature into the developing English language.

Essentially, the poetry works in this way: Each line has four stresses, two on each side of the pause or caesura. Unstressed syllables are not significant and may occur in any quantity or, occasionally, not at all. Of the four stresses, two or more will alliterate with one another, the stress directly after the pause serving as the "rhyme-giver" or alliterative key. Vowels assonate with other vowels. The first four lines of Caedmon's hymn, then, move as follows, with stresses underlined:

Nu sculon herigan   heofonrices weard
Metodes meahte   and his modgepanc,
Weorc wuldorfaeder,   swa he wundra gehwaes,
Ece drihten,   or onstealde.

The pace is majestic, deliberate; the unstressed syllables, falling as they do in two's and three's, give an almost chantlike tone to the poetry. The alliteration serves the singer, who would be using a small harp like instrument for accompaniment, and unifies the poem, setting up expectations and satisfying them in more than one way. Although the poem does not formally play with rhyme, it does make use of several sound devices; some later verse in this tradition uses internal and occasionally external rhyme as well. The alliterative rhythms, however, give the poem its most definitive structure.

The poem also shows the first use of kennings, rich figures of speech which make tiny metaphors, usually hyphenated, for common terms. Here the kennings are relatively simple; later, in *Beowulf*, for example, they become more graphic. The more complex the notion, the more apt the kennings are: heaven, for example, becomes "heaven-kingdom"; God is "wonder-Father"; earth becomes "middle-yard." God's creative word-become-act is "mind-thought," the most complex of the kennings.

In his *Anglo-Saxon Poetry* (1980), Jeff Opland terms Bede's story of Caedmon "a source of unparalleled importance in any attempt to reconstruct the history of oral poetry in Anglo-Saxon times." The claim is not extravagant. Caedmon's fragment reaches back into the heroic tradition for meter and form, blends it with Christian myths for inspiration and story, and originates English poetry as it is now known. Histories of English literature rightly devote major sections to such great figures as Geoffrey Chaucer, William Shakespeare, and John Milton. Nearly eight hundred years before Chaucer burst into joyous couplets, Caedmon, the precursor, burst into praise.

Katherine Hanley

Bibliography

Fry, Donald K. "Caedmon as a Formulaic Poet." In *Oral Literature: Seven Essays*, edited by Joseph J. Duggan. New York: Barnes & Noble Books, 1975. Drawing on Bede's *Ecclesiastical History*, Fry presents Caedmon's "Hymn" as an oral composition and Caedmon as the founder of "Old English Christian vernacular poetry." Fry accomplishes this by examining the Latin and Old English versions of the "Hymn" to determine the genesis of diction.

_____. "The Memory of Caedmon." In *Oral Traditional Literature: A Festschrift for Albert Bates Lord*, edited by John Miles Foley. Columbus, Ohio: Slavica, 1981. Fry proposes that Caedmon's *Hymn* was written on a formulaic basis. He defines "formulaic" as the "typical traditionally expressed" and states that this type of poetry is easy to memorize and, therefore, is more easily disseminated to the nonliterate public.

Greenfield, Stanley B., and Daniel G. Calder. *A New Critical History of Old English Literature.* New York: New York University Press, 1986. Although only devoting thirteen pages of text to Caedmon, this book provides excellent insight into Caedmon's *Hymn* and problems that have confronted scholars for centuries. Useful for a broad overview of Old English literature.

Hieatt, Constance B. "Caedmon in Context: Transforming the Formula." *Journal of English and Germanic Philology* 84 (October, 1985): 485-497. Supplies evidence that Caedmon's *Hymn* may draw not only from traditional pagan themes as background for its Christian base but also from inherited oral tradition, therefore echoing the established "type-scene."

O'Keeffe, Katherine O'Brien. "Orality and the Developing Text of Caedmon's 'Hymn.'" *Speculum: A Journal of Medieval Studies* 62 (January, 1987): 1-20. Approaches Caedmon's *Hymn* from an oral and literate background and from the consequential reception as opposed to a more traditional study of the composition. Stresses the gradual shift from the oral tradition to the written one and analyzes the ramifications of this shift.